Lecture Notes in Computer Science 12307

More information about this series at http://www.springer.com/series/7412

Yuxin Peng · Qingshan Liu ·
Huchuan Lu · Zhenan Sun ·
Chenglin Liu · Xilin Chen ·
Hongbin Zha · Jian Yang (Eds.)

Pattern Recognition and Computer Vision

Third Chinese Conference, PRCV 2020
Nanjing, China, October 16–18, 2020
Proceedings, Part III

Springer

Editors
Yuxin Peng
Peking University
Beijing, China

Huchuan Lu
Dalian University of Technology
Dalian, China

Chenglin Liu
Chinese Academy of Sciences
Beijing, China

Hongbin Zha
Peking University
Beijing, China

Qingshan Liu
Nanjing University of Information Science
and Technology
Nanjing, China

Zhenan Sun
Chinese Academy of Sciences
Beijing, China

Xilin Chen
Institute of Computing Technology
Chinese Academy of Sciences
Beijing, China

Jian Yang
Nanjing University of Science
and Technology
Nanjing, China

ISSN 0302-9743   ISSN 1611-3349 (electronic)
Lecture Notes in Computer Science
ISBN 978-3-030-60635-0   ISBN 978-3-030-60636-7 (eBook)
https://doi.org/10.1007/978-3-030-60636-7

LNCS Sublibrary: SL6 – Image Processing, Computer Vision, Pattern Recognition, and Graphics

This Springer imprint is published by the registered company Springer Nature Switzerland AG
The registered company address is: Gewerbestrasse 11, 6330 Cham, Switzerland

Preface

Welcome to the proceedings of the Third Chinese Conference on Pattern Recognition and Computer Vision (PRCV 2020) held in Nanjing, China.

PRCV is the merger of Chinese Conference on Pattern Recognition (CCPR) and Chinese Conference on Computer Vision (CCCV), which are both the most influential Chinese conferences on pattern recognition and computer vision, respectively. Pattern recognition and computer vision are closely interrelated and the two communities are largely overlapping. The goal of merging CCPR and CCCV into PRCV is to further boost the impact of the Chinese community in these two core areas of artificial intelligence and further improve the quality of academic communication. Accordingly, PRCV is co-sponsored by four major academic societies of China: the Chinese Association for Artificial Intelligence (CAAI), the China Computer Federation (CCF), the Chinese Association of Automation (CAA), and the China Society of Image and Graphics (CSIG).

PRCV aims at providing an interactive communication platform for researchers from academia and industry. It promotes not only academic exchange, but also communication between academia and industry. In order to keep at the frontier of academic trends and share the latest research achievements, innovative ideas, and scientific methods in the fields of pattern recognition and computer vision, international and local leading experts and professors are invited to deliver keynote speeches, introducing the latest advances in theories and methods in the fields of pattern recognition and computer vision.

PRCV 2020 was hosted by Nanjing University of Science and Technology and was co-hosted by Nanjing University of Information Science and Technology, Southeast University, and JiangSu Association of Artificial Intelligence. We received 402 full submissions. Each submission was reviewed by at least three reviewers selected from the Program Committee and other qualified researchers. Based on the reviewers' reports, 158 papers were finally accepted for presentation at the conference, including 30 orals, 60 spotlights, and 68 posters. The acceptance rate is 39%. The proceedings of PRCV 2020 are published by Springer.

We are grateful to the keynote speakers, Prof. Nanning Zheng from Xi'an Jiaotong University, China, Prof. Jean Ponce from PSL University, France, Prof. Mubarak Shah from University of Central Florida, USA, and Prof. Dacheng Tao from The University of Sydney, Australia.

We give sincere thanks to the authors of all submitted papers, the Program Committee members and the reviewers, and the Organizing Committee. Without their contributions, this conference would not be a success. Special thanks also go to all of the sponsors and the organizers of the special forums; their support made the conference a success. We are also grateful to Springer for publishing the proceedings and especially to Ms. Celine (Lanlan) Chang of Springer Asia for her efforts in coordinating the publication.

We hope you find the proceedings enjoyable and fruitful.

September 2020

Yuxin Peng
Qingshan Liu
Huchuan Lu
Zhenan Sun
Chenglin Liu
Xilin Chen
Hongbin Zha
Jian Yang

Organization

Steering Committee Chair

Tieniu Tan — Institute of Automation, Chinese Academy of Sciences, China

Steering Committee

Xilin Chen — Institute of Computing Technology, Chinese Academy of Sciences, China
Chenglin Liu — Institute of Automation, Chinese Academy of Sciences, China
Yong Rui — Lenovo, China
Hongbin Zha — Peking University, China
Nanning Zheng — Xi'an Jiaotong University, China
Jie Zhou — Tsinghua University, China

Steering Committee Secretariat

Liang Wang — Institute of Automation, Chinese Academy of Sciences, China

General Chairs

Chenglin Liu — Institute of Automation, Chinese Academy of Sciences, China
Xilin Chen — Institute of Computing Technology, Chinese Academy of Sciences, China
Hongbin Zha — Peking University, China
Jian Yang — Nanjing University of Science and Technology, China

Program Chairs

Yuxin Peng — Peking University, China
Qingshan Liu — Nanjing University of Information Science and Technology, China
Huchuan Lu — Dalian University of Technology, China
Zhenan Sun — Institute of Automation, Chinese Academy of Sciences, China

Organizing Chairs

Xin Geng	Southeast University, China
Jianfeng Lu	Nanjing University of Science and Technology, China
Liang Xiao	Nanjing University of Science and Technology, China
Jinshan Pan	Nanjing University of Science and Technology, China

Publicity Chairs

Zhaoxiang Zhang	Institute of Automation, Chinese Academy of Sciences, China
Jiaying Liu	Peking University, China
Wankou Yang	Southeast University, China
Lianfa Bai	Nanjing University of Science and Technology, China

International Liaison Chairs

Jingyi Yu	ShanghaiTech University, China
Shiguang Shan	Institute of Computing Technology, Chinese Academy of Sciences, China

Local Coordination Chairs

Wei Fang	JiangSu Association of Artificial Intelligence, China
Jinhui Tang	Nanjing University of Science and Technology, China

Publication Chairs

Risheng Liu	Dalian University of Technology, China
Zhen Cui	Nanjing University of Science and Technology, China

Tutorial Chairs

Gang Pan	Zhejiang University, China
Xiaotong Yuan	Nanjing University of Information Science and Technology, China

Workshop Chairs

Xiang Bai	Huazhong University of Science and Technology, China
Shanshan Zhang	Nanjing University of Science and Technology, China

Special Issue Chairs

Jiwen Lu   Tsinghua University, China
Weishi Zheng   Sun Yat-sen University, China

Sponsorship Chairs

Lianwen Jin   South China University of Technology, China
Jinfeng Yang   Civil Aviation University of China, China
Ming-Ming Cheng   Nankai University, China
Chen Gong   Nanjing University of Science and Technology, China

Demo Chairs

Zechao Li   Nanjing University of Science and Technology, China
Jun Li   Nanjing University of Science and Technology, China

Competition Chairs

Wangmeng Zuo   Harbin Institute of Technology, China
Jin Xie   Nanjing University of Science and Technology, China
Wei Jia   Hefei University of Technology, China

PhD Forum Chairs

Tianzhu Zhang   University of Science and Technology of China, China
Guangcan Liu   Nanjing University of Information Science
                            and Technology, China

Web Chair

Zhichao Lian   Nanjing University of Science and Technology, China

Finance Chair

Jianjun Qian   Nanjing University of Science and Technology, China

Registration Chairs

Guangyu Li   Nanjing University of Science and Technology, China
Weili Guo   Nanjing University of Science and Technology, China

Area Chairs

Zhen Cui   Nanjing University of Science and Technology, China
Yuming Fang   Jiangxi University of Finance and Economics, China

Chen Gong	Nanjing University of Science and Technology, China
Yahong Han	Tianjin University, China
Ran He	Institute of Automation, Chinese Academy of Sciences, China
Qinghua Hu	Tianjin University, China
Hua Huang	Beijing Institute of Technology, China
Na Lei	Dalian University of Technology, China
Haojie Li	Dalian University of Technology, China
Zhichao Lian	Nanjing University of Science and Technology, China
Liang Lin	Sun Yat-Sen University, China
Zhouchen Lin	Peking University, China
Jian Lu	Shenzhen University, China
Liqiang Nie	Shandong University, China
Wanli Ouyang	The University of Sydney, China
Jinshan Pan	Nanjing University of Science and Technology, China
Xi Peng	Sichuan University, China
Nong Sang	Huazhong University of Science and Technology, China
Hanli Wang	Tongji University, China
Hanzi Wang	Xiamen University, China
Jingdong Wang	Microsoft, China
Nannan Wang	Xidian University, China
Ruiping Wang	Institute of Computing Technology, Chinese Academy of Sciences, China
Jianxin Wu	Nanjing University, China
Jinjian Wu	Xidian University, China
Lifang Wu	Beijing University of Technology, China
Gui-Song Xia	Wuhan University, China
Yong Xia	Northwestern Polytechnical University, China
Jin Xie	Nanjing University of Science and Technology, China
Jufeng Yang	Nankai University, China
Wankou Yang	Southeast University, China
Yang Yang	University of Electronic Science and Technology of China, China
Xiaotong Yuan	Nanjing University of Information Science and Technology, China
Huaxiang Zhang	Shandong Normal University, China
Lijun Zhang	Nanjing University, China
Shanshan Zhang	Nanjing University of Science and Technology, China
Wangmeng Zuo	Harbin Institute of Technology, China

Contents – Part III

Machine Learning

Machine Learning

Federated Generative Adversarial Learning

Chenyou Fan[1]([⊠]) and Ping Liu[2]

[1] Shenzhen Institute of Artificial Intelligence and Robotics for Society (AIRS),
Shenzhen, China
fanchenyou@gmail.com
[2] Institute of High Performance Computing (IHPC), A*STAR, Singapore, Singapore
pino.pingliu@gmail.com

Abstract. This work studies training generative adversarial networks under the federated learning setting. Generative adversarial networks (GANs) have achieved advancement in various real-world applications, such as image editing, style transfer, scene generations, etc. However, like other deep learning models, GANs are also suffering from data limitation problems in real cases. To boost the performance of GANs in target tasks, collecting images as many as possible from different sources becomes not only important but also essential. For example, to build a robust and accurate bio-metric verification system, huge amounts of images might be collected from surveillance cameras, and/or uploaded from cellphones by users accepting agreements. In an ideal case, utilize all those data uploaded from public and private devices for model training is straightforward. Unfortunately, in the real scenarios, this is hard due to a few reasons. At first, some data face the serious concern of leakage, and therefore it is prohibitive to upload them to a third-party server for model training; at second, the images collected by different kinds of devices, probably have distinctive biases due to various factors, *e.g.*, collector preferences, geo-location differences, which is also known as "domain shift". To handle those problems, we propose a novel generative learning scheme utilizing a federated learning framework. Following the configuration of federated learning, we conduct model training and aggregation on one center and a group of clients. Specifically, our method learns the distributed generative models in clients, while the models trained in each client are fused into one unified and versatile model in the center. To the best of our knowledge, this is the first work on touching GAN training under a federated learning setting. We perform extensive experiments to compare different federation strategies, and empirically examine the effectiveness of federation under different levels of parallelism and data skewness.

Keywords: Federated learning · Generative Adversarial Network · Non-IID data

© Springer Nature Switzerland AG 2020
Y. Peng et al. (Eds.): PRCV 2020, LNCS 12307, pp. 3–15, 2020.
https://doi.org/10.1007/978-3-030-60636-7_1

1   Introduction

Traditional machine learning methods require to gather training data into a central database and perform centralized training. However, as there are more and more edge devices such as smartphones, wearable devices, sensors, and cameras connecting to the World Wide Web, the data for training a model might be spread on various equipment. Due to privacy concerns, it might not be possible to upload all the data needed to a central node through public communications. How to safely access data on these heterogeneous devices to effectively train models has become an open research problem. To this end, federated learning has become a rapidly developing topic in the research community [17,22,36], as it provides a new way of learning models over a collection of highly distributed devices while still preserving data privacy and communication efficiency. Federated learning has witnessed many successful applications in distributed use cases such as smartphone keyboard input prediction [7], health monitoring [24,32], IoT [35], and blockchain [14].

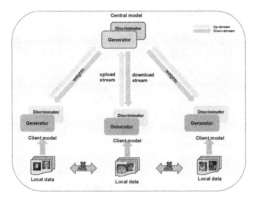

Fig. 1. The task of generative learning under federated learning scheme. To preserve data privacy, remote devices exchange only model weights with a central server periodically to learn a global model. No data exchange would happen during any stage of communications.

Although federated learning has been applied successfully on discriminative model learning, how to apply it to generative learning is still under exploration. Generative Adversarial Network (GAN) [6] is one typical type of generative models which aims to gain generative capabilities based on game theory and deep learning techniques. Under the traditional machine learning framework, GANs have achieved huge successes in various applications such as realistic images/videos generation [6,13,28,31], face editing [8,10], domain adaptation [20,21], and style transferring [30]. Though many efforts [19,22,36] have been made in boosting the performance of classification tasks with federated learning, there is little work of assessing whether existing federated learning framework works on generative learning or not. In real scenarios, we observe that data for generative learning are distributed among various equipment, *e.g.*, hand-written digits and signatures are stored in thousands of millions of mobile devices, facial images are stored in edge devices and IoT participants, etc. And therefore, it becomes urgent and necessary to understand whether the federated learning scheme is suitable for learning GANs.

In this paper, we propose a novel method of using a federated learning framework in GAN training; other than that, we discuss four strategies of synchronizing the local models and central model in the proposed method. We quantitatively evaluate the effectiveness of each strategy. Furthermore, we extensively study the GAN training quality under different data distribution scenarios and examine whether federated GAN training is robust to non-IID data distribution. In summary, our contributions include:

- We formulate the federated generative adversarial learning outline with algorithm details, which is the first work in this direction to the best of our knowledge.
- We propose and compare four synchronization strategies for unifying local Generators and Discriminators to central models.
- We extensively study the training quality with different data distributions of different datasets under our framework.

2   Related Work

Federated learning has become a rapidly developing topic in the research community [17,22,36], as it provides a new way of learning models over a collection of highly distributed devices while still preserving data privacy and communication efficiency. Federated learning has witnessed many successful applications in distributed use cases such as smartphone keyboard input prediction [7], health monitoring [24,32], IoT [35], and blockchain [14].

Model averaging has been widely used in distributed machine learning [5,33,34]. In distributed settings, each client minimizes a shared learning target (in most cases, a loss function) on their local data, while the server aggregates clients' models by computing a uniform or bootstrap average of local model weights to produce the global model. McMahan *et al.* [22] extended this learning strategy to the federated learning setting, in which data could be non-IID, and communications between clients and servers could be constrained. They proposed the FedAvg method to fuse local client models into a central model, and demonstrated its robustness of applying on deep learning models such as Convolutional Neural Networks (CNNs) and Recurrent Neural Networks (RNNs) with IID and moderately non-IID data. Zhao *et al.* [36] discussed that FedAvg might suffer from weight divergence on highly skewed data, and several other works made attempts to propose robust federated learning in such cases [18,27]. Recent work [19] also discussed how to further improve the safety of communications during federated training using Additively Homomorphic Encryption [1].

Generative Adversarial Network (GAN) [6] aims to learn generative models based on game theory and deep learning techniques. Since its origin, GANs have witnessed huge successes in applications like generating realistic images [2,6,13] and videos [28] in computer vision areas. Conditional GAN (cGAN) [23] is a natural extension of GAN which aims to generate images with given labels or attributes, such as human genders [26], image categories [12] and image styles [13].

To our best knowledge, the only similar work is from a technical report [3] which conceptually mentioned the possibility of using federated learning ideas in generative tasks. However, no further details were provided in this article. Besides, a seemingly related work [9] studied a type of adversarial attack under a collaborative learning environment. Their main purpose is to demonstrate that, by manipulating local training data, attackers could generate adversary training samples that harm the learning objective of a normal user. This is entirely different to the federated learning setting that no unsafe local data exchange should happen during client-client or client-server communications.

3   Approach

We consider distributed GAN training on one center and a group of clients with the common communication-efficient federated learning framework [16,22]. Commonly, each client device possesses its local data with (usually) biased data distribution. E.g., personal devices are mostly used to take portraits, while surveillance cameras are often used to monitor street views. **We aim to train a unified central GAN model with the combined generative capacities of each client model.** Yet we prohibit transferring any client data to the center as the communications between clients are costly and unsafe. In the following sections, we will (1) investigate four types of synchronization strategies that arise naturally for federated GAN training, (2) briefly introduce the conditional GAN models' objective functions and architectures, and (3) summarize our proposed algorithm.

3.1   Synchronization Strategies

FedAvg [22] is a widely used federated learning framework that fuses client models to a central model by averaging the model weights. With FedAvg, the central model should be synchronized back (*downloaded*) to clients periodically for training on local data, and after certain iterations, the clients *upload* their local models to the central server for fusing into a new global model.

In our study, however, training federated GANs is more complicated, as two parameter sets for generator (G) and discriminator (D) have to be communicated between the center and clients. This communication mechanism does not exist in a non-federated learning setting, while it is essential in a federated learning setting. How to guarantee an effective and efficient synchronization across the clients and the server becomes an open question. We propose four types of synchronization strategies during communications. **Sync D&G** synchronizes both

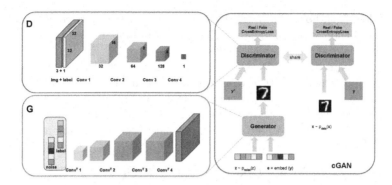

Fig. 2. Architecture of a Conditional GAN with Generator G and Discriminator D. For G, the sampled noise vector $\mathbf{z} \sim \mathcal{N}(0,1)$ and a class label embedding vector $\mathbf{e}$ are fed into a deep neural network to generate a new image. For D, an image together with its label-spanned mask are fed into a deep neural network to predict whether the input image is real or fake.

the central model of D and G to each client. **Sync G** synchronizes central G model to each client. **Sync D** synchronizes central D model to each client. **Sync None** synchronizes neither G nor D from the center to clients. Please see Fig. 1 for the illustration of the overall process. These approaches still maintain the independence of each client during local training stage, while enable information propagation across clients during synchronization between server and clients' models.

3.2 Conditional GAN (cGAN) Model

In our paper, one important mission is to analyze how data distribution affects GAN training in a federated setting. Therefore, we will study conditional GANs (cGANs) [23], which can manipulate the class distribution of generated images, e.g., generate "horse" images given the horse label. We will simulate different class distributions in clients' training data. Then we will evaluate the training status of cGANs and analyze the robustness against skewed data distributions.

$$\min_{G} \max_{D} V(D,G) = \mathbb{E}_{\mathbf{x} \sim p_{data}}[\log D(\mathbf{x}|\mathbf{y})] + \mathbb{E}_{\mathbf{z} \sim p_z}[\log(1 - D(G(\mathbf{z}|\mathbf{y})|\mathbf{y}))]. \quad (1)$$

In a cGAN, the discriminator (D) and generator (G) play the minimax game with the objective function shown in Eq. 1. Intuitively, D learns to criticize the fidelity of given images while G learns to generate fake images with given labels as realistic as possible. In Fig. 2, we demonstrate the typical architecture of D and G with Convolutional Neural Network structures. G takes a noise vector $\mathbf{z}$ and an additional label $\mathbf{y}$ to conditionally generate an image with a given label. For hand-written digit generation, the given labels indicate the digits from 0 to 9 to be generated. For the task of natural image generation, the provided labels indicate the image classes, e.g., on CIFAR-10, the classes are plane, car, bird, cat, deer, dog, frog, horse, ship, truck. D takes an image and its conditional label to predict whether it is real or fake. The conditional label is expanded to image size and attached along image channels.

Our implementations of D and G networks follow DCGAN's [26] designs: D consists of four convolutional layers with BatchNorm [11] and LeakyReLU [29]; G consists of four transposed convolutional layers with BatchNorm and LeakyReLU, followed by a tanh function to map features into normalized pixel values between -1 and 1. We alternatively update D by ascending its stochastic gradient

$$\nabla_{\theta_D} \frac{1}{m} \sum_{i=1}^{m} [\log D(\mathbf{x}_i|\mathbf{y}_i) + \log(1 - D(G(\mathbf{z}_i|\mathbf{y}'_i)|\mathbf{y}'_i))] \tag{2}$$

and update G by descending its stochastic gradient

$$\nabla_{\theta_G} \frac{1}{m} \sum_{i=1}^{m} \log(1 - D(G(\mathbf{z}_i|\mathbf{y}'_i)|\mathbf{y}'_i)) \tag{3}$$

in which $\mathbf{x}$ is a sampled batch of m real images with true labels $\mathbf{y}$, $\mathbf{z}$ and $\mathbf{y}'$ are m sampled noise vectors and labels. Intuitively, D is distinguishing real images from fake images conditioned on the given labels, while G is attempting to fool D by producing as realistic images as possible given designated labels.

3.3   Algorithm Outline

We summarize our algorithm of *federated GAN learning* as follows. At each communication round, a subset of clients is randomly selected. Each client in the subset trains an updated model of GAN with Eq. (2) and (3) based on their local data. After an epoch of training, the updated parameters of G and D are sent to the server via network communications. The server aggregates client models by weight averaging (or other model fusion techniques) to construct an improved central model. Finally, according to the chosen synchronization strategy mentioned in Sect. 3.1, each client pulls back the global model to reconstruct their local model. Each client then performs the next round of local model training. The above steps are repeated until convergence or some stopping criteria are met. The details of the algorithm are shown in Algorithm 1.

We implemented our algorithm and cGANs in PyTorch [25]. The network parameters are updated by Adam solver [15] with batch size 64 and a fixed learning rate of 0.0002. For each experimental setting, we train cGANs for at least 60 epochs with the federating step (communication between the center and clients) happening at the end of every epoch. We will release our source code for boosting further research.

4   Experiments

We demonstrate the federated GAN training results on the MNIST and CIFAR-10 benchmark datasets. We first visualize samples of generated images for qualitative evaluation. Then we introduce the metrics to quantitatively evaluate GAN

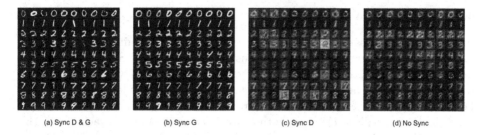

(a) Sync D & G	(b) Sync G	(c) Sync D	(d) No Sync

Fig. 3. Samples of generated hand-written digits with different synchronization strategies. From (a) to (d), we (a) synchronize both central D and G model to each client, (b) synchronize only G model to each client while their individual D model is retained, (c) synchronize only D model to each client while their G model is retained, (d) synchronize neither central D or G to any client.

Algorithm 1. Federated Generative Learning algorithm.

Input: A global GAN model with parameters (w_0^D, w_0^G) for Discriminator (D) and Generator (G) on central server S; local GAN models with parameters $\{(w_1^D, w_1^G), \ldots, (w_n^D, w_n^G)\}$ on n clients $C = \{C_1, \ldots, C_n\}$; local private data $D = \{D_1, \ldots, D_n\}$; Sync_FLAG indicates whether to synchronize central G and/or D back to clients.

Output: Fully trained global GAN model (w_0^D, w_0^G).

1 **for** communication round $t = 1, 2, \ldots, T$ **do**
2   Select K random clients from all clients C
3   **for** each client $k = 1, 2, \ldots, K$ **in parallel do**
4   Update discriminator w_k^D of client k
5   • sample a batch of m real images **x** with true labels **y**
6   • sample a batch of m noise vectors **z** and labels **y**′ from D_k
7   • update w_k^D by *ascending* stochastic gradient in Eq (2)
8
9   Update generator w_k^G of client k
10   • sample a batch of m noise vectors **z** and labels **y**′
11   • update w_k^G by *descending* stochastic gradient in Eq (3)
12   Update central model by averaging client weights
13          $w_0^D \leftarrow \frac{1}{K} \sum_{k=1}^{K} w_k^D$
14          $w_0^G \leftarrow \frac{1}{K} \sum_{k=1}^{K} w_k^G$
15   **if** *Sync_D&G* or *Sync_D* **then**
16   **for** each client c in C **in parallel do**
17            $w_c^D \leftarrow w_0^D$
18   **if** *Sync_D&G* or *Sync_G* **then**
19   **for** each client c in C **in parallel do**
20            $w_c^G \leftarrow w_0^G$
21 **return** (w_0^D, w_0^G)

---

training results. After that, we conduct experiments to evaluate the performance of different synchronization strategies proposed in Sect. 3.1. By simulating IID and various non-IID data distributions, we further investigate the efficiency of model training with different data skewness levels. This enables us to probe the robustness of GAN training under federated learning framework.

4.1   Visualization

In Fig. 3, we show samples of digits generated by GANs trained with different synchronization strategies, which are illustrated in Sect. 3.1. Specifically, in the federating step, a sampled collection of clients upload their Gs and Ds to the center. The center fuses their weights to form central model G and D with FedAvg or any other federated learning framework. As a quick reminder, strategy (a) Sync D & G will synchronize both central D and G model to each client, (b) Sync G will synchronize central G model back to each client, (c) Sync D will synchronize central D model to each client, (d) synchronize neither central D or G to any client. Obviously, strategy (a) and (b) are visually better than (c) and (d), while (a) and (b) are comparable in image qualities. In Fig. 4, we show samples of images generated for CIFAR-10 classes with strategy Sync D & G and Sync G. We again found that these two strategies are comparable in visual quality. Curiously, the overall image quality is not as great as the generated digits in Fig. 3. This is because of less training samples in CIFAR-10, and more complex patterns in natural images. However, how to improve GAN training with more data or with more capable neural network architecture is out of the scope of this paper. We will focus on how federated learning settings affect GAN training in the rest of the paper.

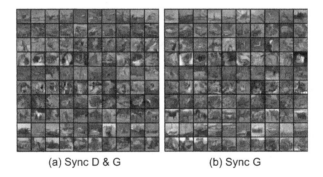

(a) Sync D & G   (b) Sync G

Fig. 4. Generated images of CIFAR-10 classes - from top to bottom - plane, car, bird, cat, deer, dog, frog, horse, ship, truck. We show results of Sync D&G and Sync G strategy.

4.2   Metrics

We use two metrics for measuring the performance of cGANs on the image generation task. **1. Classification score (Score)** measures the "reality" of a generator by using a pre-trained strong classifier f_o to classify generated images. In practice, we trained classifiers on MNIST and CIFAR-10, which yield a 99.6% and 90% accuracy on testing sets, respectively. We utilize the classifier as an oracle and apply it to generated samples to provide pseudo ground truth labels. Then we compare the pseudo ground truth labels with the conditional labels which are used to generate those images. The consensus between ground truth labels and conditional labels are taken as classification scores. Intuitively, the more realistic and fidelity the generated images are, the **higher** scores they will get. **2. Earth Mover's Distance (EMD).** Also known as Wasserstein distance [2], it measures the distance between the distribution of real data P_r and generated data P_g. In practice, EMD is approximated by comparing average softmax scores of drawn samples from real data against the generated data such that

$$EMD((\mathbf{x}_r, \mathbf{y}_r), (\mathbf{x}_g, \mathbf{y}_g)) = \frac{1}{N} \sum_{i=1}^{N} f_o(\mathbf{x}_r^i)[y_r^i] - \frac{1}{N} \sum_{i=1}^{N} f_o(\mathbf{x}_g^i)[y_g^i] \qquad (4)$$

in which $(\mathbf{x}_r, \mathbf{y}_r)$ are real data samples, $(\mathbf{x}_g, \mathbf{y}_g)$ are generated data samples, f_o is the oracle classifier mentioned above. EMD measures a relative distance between real data and fake data. Obviously, a better generator should have a **lower** EMD by producing realistic images closer to real images.

4.3   Result of Different Training Strategies on IID Data

In an ideal case, data across the federated clients are independent and identically distributed (IID). We assume the IID condition and assume there are two federated clients. In Fig. 5(a), we show the training results of all four synchronize strategies in two worker cases on the MNIST dataset. Congruent with visual intuitions from Fig. 3, Sync D&G (purple line), and Sync G (green line) are much better than Sync D (blue line) and Sync None (red line). The Scores and EMDs for the former two strategies are around 0.99 and 0.05. Scores for the latter two are about or lower than 0.8, while EMDs are above 0.4.

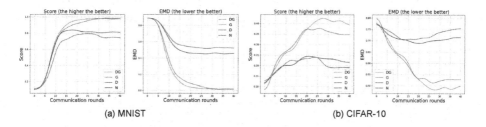

(a) MNIST   (b) CIFAR-10

Fig. 5. Illustrations of training qualities influenced by different synchronization strategies. We show the Scores (the higher the better) and EMDs (the lower the better) on MNIST and CIFAR-10 datasets.

In Fig. 5(b), we show training results on CIFAR-10 dataset and observe a similar trend: Sync D&G significantly outperforms other methods. Sync G comes the second but is still much better than Sync D and Sync None. A question arises naturally: why is Sync D performing worse than Sync G? Our explanation is that by synchronizing central D across clients, the discriminative capacity of each client model grows rapidly. Unless we also synchronize G (as Sync D&G does), the capacity of D exceeds G and thus rejects more samples of generated images. This harms and even stops the learning of G. Similar observation has also been reported by [2, 4] in which they found the generator stops training if discriminator reaches optimum too early. Sync D & G or Sync G would avoid this pitfall. In another aspect, by synchronizing G instead of both G and D, the communication costs could be reduced by about half in both upload and download streams. The trade-off between reducing communication costs and increasing training qualities should be considered case-by-case. **For real-world applications when communication costs are essentially high, such as edge devices, we recommend to synchronize G to reduce costs while sacrifice some generative capacity. Otherwise, we recommend to synchronize both D and G.** In the following experiments, we will synchronize both D and G at default unless otherwise stated.

4.4   Result of Training GAN on Different Numbers of Clients with IID Data

In this section, we investigate federated GAN training with IID data on different numbers of clients. We build the training set of each client by randomly choosing 50% of the total training samples with replacement to simulate IID data. We conduct three sets of experiments with $k = 2, 4, 6$ federated clients. We also compare federated learning with a baseline method (k=1) by training GAN on a single client with the same amount of training data, simulating the situation that each client trains on its own data without federation. We show the results in Table 1 on both MNIST and CIFAR-10 dataset.

Table 1. Results of different numbers of federated workers on IID training data. The "Optimal Rounds" column indicates how many communication rounds are needed for central models to reach optimal. Best preforming numbers are highlighted for each column.

Workers Num k	MNIST			CIFAR-10		
	Optimal rounds	Score	EMD	Optimal rounds	Score	EMD
k = 1 (Local)	35	0.975	0.023	40	0.40	0.51
k = 2 (Fed)	25	0.990	0.004	25	0.428	0.475
k = 4 (Fed)	25	**0.993**	**0.002**	30	0.432	0.471
k = 6 (Fed)	30	**0.994**	**0.002**	35	**0.456**	**0.457**

First, training GANs on federated clients (Fed) always outperforms training on a single worker (Local) with the same amount of local data. Moreover, we found that with increase in number of clients $k = 2, 4, 6$, the metrics are slightly improving in terms of both Score and EMD on both MNIST (score: 0.99 v.s. 0.993 v.s. 0.994) and CIFAR-10 datasets (scores: 0.428 v.s. 0.432 v.s. 0.456). The higher evaluation score indicates that GAN training benefits from more federated workers, given IID training samples over clients. However, we also observed that training with more numbers of workers leads to slower convergence, as a trade-off for performance. On CIFAR-10, it took 25 communication rounds for central models to reach optimal when $k = 2$, while it took 35 rounds when $k = 6$.

4.5   Result of Training GAN with Non-IID Data

Recent research [18, 36] observed that common federated learning methods such as FedAvg are not robust to non-IID data. In this section, we will verify the performance of GAN training with non-IID data of different data skewness levels. Let us suppose a dataset has N classes, and there are k clients. To simulate non-IID data across clients, we sort the data first by class. For each class, we randomly choose one client to allocate a fraction $p > 0.5$ of the total training samples of that class, and then randomly allocate fraction $1 - p$ of samples to other clients. This mimics a realistic scenario that data distribution is skewed across the clients, and the skewness is adjustable by p. A larger p indicates a higher degree of data skewness. We examine the training quality under different data skewness levels with different numbers of clients.

Table 2. Results of training cGANs with non-IID data with data skewness level $p = 0.7$ and $p = 0.9$. We only show the results of CIFAR-10 due to page limits.

Workers Num k	CIFAR p = 0.7			CIFAR p = 0.9		
	Optimal rounds	Score	EMD	Optimal rounds	Score	EMD
k = 2 (Fed)	30	0.40	0.50	30	**0.37**	**0.52**
k = 4 (Fed)	35	**0.44**	**0.45**	40	0.35	0.57
k = 6 (Fed)	40	0.42	0.48	30	0.31	0.58

In Table 2, we demonstrate the experiment results on CIFAR-10 with $k = 2, 4, 6$ and $p = 0.7, 0.9$. Results for different k are shown in different rows, and $p = 0.7$ and $p = 0.9$ are shown in separate columns. Obviously, the overall performance of $p = 0.7$ is better than $p = 0.9$, as the overall Score of $p = 0.7$ is above 0.40 while Score of $p = 0.9$ is less than 0.37. This indicates that the more skewed of the data distribution, the less effective federated training of GANs. We also found that a larger number k of federated clients is more affected by skewed data distribution. For example, in Table 1 IID case, as well as in Table 2 (p=0.7), $k = 6$ outperforms $k = 2$ for both cases (IID and moderately non-IID). In contrast, in Table 2 (p=0.9), we found that $k = 6$ performs worse than $k = 2$ in Score (0.30 v.s. 0.35, higher the better) and EMD (0.60 v.s. 0.55, lower the better) with highly non-IID(p=0.9) data. This accuracy drop can be explained by the weight divergence theory proposed by [36] such that more clients lead to faster divergence of model weights with non-IID training data. We would like to encourage researchers to tackle the problem of federated learning of GANs with non-IID data in future.

5 Conclusion

We presented a comprehensive study of training GAN with different federation strategies, and found that synchronizing both discriminator and generator across the clients yield the best results in two different tasks. We also observed empirical results that federate learning is generally robust to the number of clients with IID and moderately non-IID training data. However, for highly skewed data distribution, the existing federated learning scheme such as *FedAvg* is performing anomaly due to weight divergence. Future work could further improve GAN training by studying more effective and robust model fusion methods, especially for highly skewed data distribution.

References

1. Acar, A., Aksu, H., Uluagac, A.S., Conti, M.: A survey on homomorphic encryption schemes: theory and implementation. ACM Comput. Surv. (CSUR) **51**, 1–35 (2018)
2. Arjovsky, M., Chintala, S., Bottou, L.: Wasserstein GAN. In: ICML (2017)
3. Augenstein, S.: Federated learning, diff privacy, and generative models (2019). https://inst.eecs.berkeley.edu/~cs294-163/fa19/slides/federated-learning-in-practice.pdf. Accessed 15 Mar 2020
4. Bang, D., Shim, H.: Improved training of generative adversarial networks using representative features. In: ICML (2018)
5. Chen, J., Pan, X., Monga, R., Bengio, S., Jozefowicz, R.: Revisiting distributed synchronous SGD. arXiv preprint arXiv:1604.00981 (2016)
6. Goodfellow, I., et al.: Generative adversarial nets. In: NeurIPS (2014)
7. Hard, A., et al.: Federated learning for mobile keyboard prediction. arXiv preprint arXiv:1811.03604 (2018)
8. He, Z., Zuo, W., Kan, M., Shan, S., Chen, X.: AttGAN: facial attribute editing by only changing what you want. IEEE Trans. Image Process. **28**, 5464–5478 (2019)
9. Hitaj, B., Ateniese, G., Perez-Cruz, F.: Deep models under the GAN: information leakage from collaborative deep learning. In: ACM CCS (2017)
10. Hu, B., Zheng, Z., Liu, P., Yang, W., Ren, M.: Unsupervised eyeglasses removal in the wild. IEEE Trans. Cybern. (2020)
11. Ioffe, S., Szegedy, C.: Batch normalization: accelerating deep network training by reducing internal covariate shift. In: ICML (2015)
12. Isola, P., Zhu, J.Y., Zhou, T., Efros, A.A.: Image-to-image translation with conditional adversarial networks. In: CVPR (2017)
13. Karras, T., Laine, S., Aila, T.: A style-based generator architecture for generative adversarial networks. In: CVPR (2019)

14. Kim, H., Park, J., Bennis, M., Kim, S.L.: Blockchained on-device federated learning. IEEE Commun. Lett. **24**, 1279–1283 (2019)
15. Kingma, D.P., Ba, J.: Adam: a method for stochastic optimization. In: ICLR (2015)
16. Konečný, J., McMahan, H.B., Yu, F.X., Richtárik, P., Suresh, A.T., Bacon, D.: Federated learning: Strategies for improving communication efficiency. In: NIPS Workshop on Private Multi-Party Machine Learning (2016)
17. Li, T., Sahu, A.K., Talwalkar, A., Smith, V.: Federated learning: challenges, methods, and future directions. arXiv preprint arXiv:1908.07873 (2019)
18. Li, X., Huang, K., Yang, W., Wang, S., Zhang, Z.: On the convergence of FedAvg on non-IID data. In: ICLR (2019)
19. Liu, Y., Chen, T., Yang, Q.: Secure federated transfer learning. arXiv preprint arXiv:1812.03337 (2018)
20. Luo, Y., Liu, P., Guan, T., Yu, J., Yang, Y.: Significance-aware information bottleneck for domain adaptive semantic segmentation. In: ICCV (2019)
21. Luo, Y., Liu, P., Guan, T., Yu, J., Yang, Y.: Adversarial style mining for one-shot unsupervised domain adaptation. arXiv preprint arXiv:2004.06042 (2020)
22. McMahan, H.B., Moore, E., Ramage, D., Hampson, S., et al.: Communication-efficient learning of deep networks from decentralized data. In: AISTATS (2017)
23. Mirza, M., Osindero, S.: Conditional generative adversarial nets. arXiv preprint arXiv:1411.1784 (2014)
24. Pantelopoulos, A., Bourbakis, N.G.: A survey on wearable sensor-based systems for health monitoring and prognosis. IEEE Trans. Syst. Man Cybern. **40**, 1–12 (2009)
25. Paszke, A., et al.: Automatic differentiation in pytorch (2017)
26. Radford, A., Metz, L., Chintala, S.: Unsupervised representation learning with deep convolutional generative adversarial networks. arXiv preprint arXiv:1511.06434 (2015)
27. Sattler, F., Wiedemann, S., Müller, K.R., Samek, W.: Robust and communication-efficient federated learning from non-IID data. IEEE Trans. Neural Netw. Learn. Syst. (2019)
28. Vondrick, C., Pirsiavash, H., Torralba, A.: Generating videos with scene dynamics. In: NeurIPS (2016)
29. Xu, B., Wang, N., Chen, T., Li, M.: Empirical evaluation of rectified activations in convolutional network. arXiv preprint arXiv:1505.00853 (2015)
30. Yang, Z., Hu, Z., Dyer, C., Xing, E.P., Berg-Kirkpatrick, T.: Unsupervised text style transfer using language models as discriminators. In: NeurIPS (2018)
31. Yang, Z., Dong, J., Liu, P., Yang, Y., Yan, S.: Very long natural scenery image prediction by outpainting. In: ICCV (2019)
32. Zhang, H., Li, J., Kara, K., Alistarh, D., Liu, J., Zhang, C.: ZipML: training linear models with end-to-end low precision, and a little bit of deep learning. In: ICML (2017)
33. Zhang, S., Choromanska, A.E., LeCun, Y.: Deep learning with elastic averaging SGD. In: NeurIPS (2015)
34. Zhang, Y., Duchi, J.C., Wainwright, M.J.: Communication-efficient algorithms for statistical optimization. In: JMLR (2013)
35. Zhao, Y., Zhao, J., Jiang, L., Tan, R., Niyato, D.: Mobile edge computing, blockchain and reputation-based crowdsourcing IoT federated learning: a secure, decentralized and privacy-preserving system. arXiv preprint arXiv:1906.10893 (2019)
36. Zhao, Y., Li, M., Lai, L., Suda, N., Civin, D., Chandra, V.: Federated learning with non-IID data. arXiv preprint arXiv:1806.00582 (2018)

Learning Diverse Features
with Part-Level Resolution
for Person Re-identification

Ben Xie[1], Xiaofu Wu[1(✉)], Suofei Zhang[1], Shiliang Zhao[1], and Ming Li[2]

[1] Nanjing University of Posts and Telecommunications, Nanjing 210003, China
{1018010631,zhangsuofei,1018010632}@njupt.edu.cn, xfuwu@ieee.org
[2] Alibaba Group, Hangzhou 311121, China
sebastian.lm@alibaba-inc.com

Abstract. Learning diverse features is key to the success of person re-identification. Various part-based methods have been extensively proposed for learning local representations, which, however, are still inferior to the best-performing methods for person re-identification. This paper proposes to construct a strong lightweight network architecture, termed PLR-OSNet, based on the idea of Part-Level feature Resolution over the Omni-Scale Network (OSNet) for achieving feature diversity. The proposed PLR-OSNet has two branches, one branch for global feature representation and the other branch for local feature representation. The local branch employs a uniform partition strategy for part-level feature resolution but produces only a single identity-prediction loss, which is in sharp contrast to the existing part-based methods. Empirical evidence demonstrates that the proposed PLR-OSNet achieves state-of-the-art performance on popular person Re-ID datasets, including Market1501, DukeMTMC-reID and CUHK03, despite its small model size.

Keywords: Person re-identification · Person matching · Feature diversity · Deep learning

1 Introduction

In recent years, person re-identification (Re-ID) has attracted increasing interest due to its fundamental role in emerging computer vision applications such as video surveillance, human identity validation, and authentication, and human-robot interaction [2,3,6,11,28,32]. The objective of person Re-ID is to match any query image with the images of the same person taken by the same or different cameras at different angles, time or location.

Person Re-ID was often formulated as a metric-learning problem (or a feature-embedding problem) [4,19], where the distance between intra-class samples is required to be less than the distance between inter-class ones by at least

---

The first author is student.

© Springer Nature Switzerland AG 2020
Y. Peng et al. (Eds.): PRCV 2020, LNCS 12307, pp. 16–28, 2020.
https://doi.org/10.1007/978-3-030-60636-7_2

a margin. Unfortunately, a direct implementation of this idea requires to group samples in a pairwise manner, which is known to be computationally intensive. Alternatively, a classification task is employed to find the feature-embedding solution due to its advantage on the implementation complexity. Currently, various state-of-the-art methods [3,6,9,10] for person Re-ID have evolved from a single metric-learning problem or a single discriminative classification problem to a multi-task problem, where both the discriminative loss and the triplet loss are employed [20]. As each sample image is only labeled with the person ID, an end-to-end training approach usually has difficulty to learn diverse and rich features without elaborate design of the underlying neural network and further use of some regularization techniques.

In the past years, various part-based approaches [1,22,29] and dropout-based approaches [7] have been proposed in order to learn rich features from the ID-labeled dataset. Differing from conventional pose-based Re-ID approaches [15, 19], part-based approaches usually locate a number of body parts firstly, and force each part meeting an individual ID-prediction loss in getting discriminative part-level feature representations [5,21,24]. Dropout-based approaches, however, intend to discover rich features from enlarging the dataset with various dropout-based data-augmentation methods, such as cutout [8] and random erasing [34], or from dropping the intermediate features from feature-extracting networks, such as Batch BropBlock [6].

The performance of part-based methods relies heavily on the employed partition mechanism. Semantic partitions may offer stable cues to good alignment but are prone to noisy pose detections, as it requires that human body parts should be accurately identified and located. The uniform horizontal partition was widely employed in [21,22], which, however, provides limited performance improvement.

This motivates the work in this paper, where we propose a novel two-branch lightweight architecture for discovering rich features in person Re-ID. In particular, we employ the idea of part-level feature resolution in developing a strong two-branch baseline for person Re-ID. Compared to the popular part-based method of PCB [22], our method differs mainly in two aspects. One is the use of global branch for facilitating the extraction of a global feature, and the other is the use of a single ID-prediction loss for part-level feature resolution. We briefly summarize the main contribution of this paper as follows:

1. Based on the omni-scale network (OSNet) baseline [35], we propose a lightweight two-branch network architecture (PLR-OSNet) for person Re-ID. Its global branch adopts a global-max-pooling layer while its local branch employs a part-level feature resolution scheme for producing only a single ID-prediction loss, which is in sharp contrast to existing part-based methods. The proposed architecture is shown to be effective for achieving feature diversity.

2. Despite its small model size, the proposed PLR-OSNet is very efficient as depicted in Fig. 1 for achieving the state-of-the-art results [2,3,6,9,14, 16,22,23,30] on the three popular person Re-ID datasets, Marktet1501,

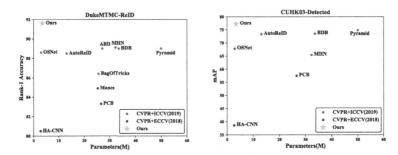

Fig. 1. The performance of different baselines on the DukeMTMC-reID and CUHK03-Detected datasets. We compare the proposed method with other baselines published in CVPR, ECCV and ICCV (2018/2019).

DukeMTMC-reID and CUHK03. It achieves the rank-1 accuracy of 91.6% for DukeMTMC-reID and 84.6% for CUHK03-Labeled without using re-ranking.[1]

2   Related Work

We review the relevant work about embedded feature learning, discriminative feature learning and part-based feature learning. Besides of various problems for person Re-ID, we are particularly interested in achieving feature diversity throughout this section.

2.1   Embedded Feature Learning

Person Re-ID can be formulated as a feature-embedding problem, which looks for a function mapping the high-dimensional pedestrian images into a low-dimensional feature space. This feature-embedding formulation requires the mapping function to ensure that given any anchor image, any positive image from the same person should has a lower distance to the anchor in the feature space compared to any negative image from a different person. This is known to be the objective of the triplet loss in training.

For an efficient feature-embedding learning, the batch hard triplet loss [18] was proposed to mine the hardest positive and the hardest negative samples for each pedestrian image in a batch. However, it is sensitive to outlier samples and may discard useful information due to its hard selective approach. To deal with these problems, Ristani et al. proposed the batch-soft triplet loss [18], which introduce a weighting factor for each pair distance. One hyper-parameter that exists in all of the triplet loss variations is the margin. To eliminate the manual parameter of the margin, the softplus function $\ln(1 + \exp(\cdot))$ instead of $[\cdot]_+ = \max(0, \cdot)$ in the triplet loss function was introduced in [10], which is known to be soft-margin triplet loss.

---

[1] Source codes are available at https://github.com/AI-NERC-NUPT/PLR-OSNet.

2.2   Discriminative Feature Learning

A feature-embedding approach requires to group the pedestrian images into pairs for training, which is not efficient in general. Discriminative feature learning is more efficient by training a classification task, where each person is regarded as a single class. As each pedestrian image in a training dataset is only labeled by a single person ID, a fundamental problem in the field of person Re-ID is how to learn diverse features from the ID-labeled dataset.

To get diverse features from an end-to-end training approach, multi-branch network architectures have been widely employed [6,22], where a shared-net is often followed by multiple subnetwork branches. To achieve feature diversity, distinct mechanisms should be imposed among different branches, such as attention [2,3], feature dropping [6,26], and overlapped activation penalty [28].

2.3   Part-Based Feature Learning

Part-based feature learning with hand-crafted algorithms had been pursued for a long time for the purpose of person retrieval before the era of deep-learning. In [22], the Part-based Convolutional Baseline (PCB) network was proposed, which employs uniform partition on the conv-layer for learning part-level features. Essentially, it employed a 6-branch network by dividing the whole body into 6 horizontal stripes in the feature space and each part feature vector was used to produce an independent ID-prediction loss. The idea of PCB was very welcome and widely adopted for developing stronger methods in the recent years for person Re-ID [16,24,30].

The part-level feature learning has an intuitive advantage for extracting diverse features from the ID-labeled pedestrian images. However, the pristine division strategy usually suffers from misalignment between corresponding parts due to large variations in poses, viewpoints and scales. In particular, the use of multiple ID-prediction loss (an independent ID loss for each part) may fail to capture the semantic part-level features since a pedestrian image may simply contain the semantically different parts at a uniformly-divided pedestrian part. This may partially explain the limited performance advantage of various PCB-based algorithms, compared to the state-of-the-art methods [2,26].

3   PLR-OSNet

3.1   Part-Level Feature Resolution

For PCB with n-part resolution, it produces n part-level feature vectors by dividing the whole body into n horizontal stripes in the feature space. As shown in Fig. 2, the input image goes forward through the stacked convolutional layers from the backbone network to form a 3-D tensor T. PCB employs a conventional average pooling layer to spatially down-sample T into n pieces of column vectors $\mathbf{g}_1, \mathbf{g}_2, \cdots, \mathbf{g}_n$, followed by n classifiers in order to produce n ID-predication loss. Note that the classifier is implemented by a fully-connected (FC) layer

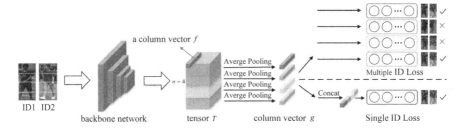

Fig. 2. Single ID loss vs. multiple ID loss with part-level feature resolution. The input image goes through backbone network to obtain a 3-D tensor, which is vertically split into $n = 4$ part-level features, and then averages each part-level tensor into a vector. These n part-level vectors are used to drive n independent ID losses in PCB, or simply concatenated for driving a single ID loss in training. The use of multiple ID loss in training may lead to false prediction of the person ID with some part-level features.

and a softmax function. Hence, when the batch of input labeled samples are $\{(x_i, y_i), i = 1, \cdots, N_s\}$, PCB employs the multiple ID-prediction loss as

$$L_{m-id} = \sum_{p=1}^{n} L_{id}^p, \tag{1}$$

$$L_{id}^p = -\frac{1}{N_s} \sum_{i=1}^{N_s} \log\left(\frac{\exp((\mathbf{W}_p^{y_i})^T \mathbf{g}_p^i + b_{y_i})}{\sum_j \exp((\mathbf{W}_p^j)^T \mathbf{g}_p^j + b_j)}\right). \tag{2}$$

where $\mathbf{W}_p^j$, $\mathbf{W}_p^{y_i}$ are the j-th and y_i-th column of the weight matrix $\mathbf{W}_p$ (the p-th classifier designated for $\mathbf{g}_p$), respectively.

By forcing each part-level feature vector to meet an independent ID-prediction loss, one may obtain useful part-level features for discriminating different persons. However, many part-level feature vectors may simply fail to catch any discriminative information for different persons, as shown in Fig. 2. Therefore, the use of PCB is practically limited for getting discriminative part-level information.

In order to learn discriminative features with part-level resolution, we propose to concatenate n part-level feature vectors into a single column vector $\mathbf{g} = [\mathbf{g}_1^T, \mathbf{g}_2^T, \cdots, \mathbf{g}_n^T]^T$, which is further used to produce the ID-prediction loss

$$L_{s-id} = -\frac{1}{N_s} \sum_{i=1}^{N_s} \log\left(\frac{\exp((\mathbf{W}^{y_i})^T \mathbf{g}^i + b_{y_i})}{\sum_j \exp((\mathbf{W}^j)^T \mathbf{g}^j + b_j)}\right). \tag{3}$$

Here, $\mathbf{W}^j$, $\mathbf{W}^{y_i}$ are the j-th and y_i-th column of the weight matrix $\mathbf{W}$ (the single classifier for $\mathbf{g}$), respectively. As the vector $\mathbf{g}$ contains the full information about the input image, the use of a single ID-prediction loss could drive $\mathbf{g}$ to learn sufficient discriminative information.

The proposed approach is somewhat similar to OSNet, where the tensor T is followed by a global average pooling (GAP) for getting a global descriptor

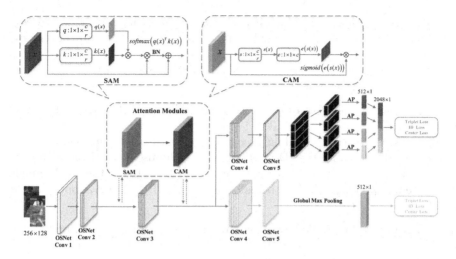

Fig. 3. The overall network architecture of PLR-OSNet. During testing, the feature embedding concatenated from both global branch and local branch is used for the final matching distance computation.

$\bar{\mathbf{g}} = \frac{1}{n} \sum_{p=1}^{n} \mathbf{g}_p$. Instead of using the GAP in OSNet, the proposed part-level resolution approach uses average pooling in each part to retrieve part-level feature vectors and the final descriptor $\mathbf{g}$ is of rich local information, which might be simply filtered with the GAP $\bar{\mathbf{g}}$ in OSNet.

3.2 Proposed Network Architecture

We employ an 2-branch neural network architecture, by modifying the recently-proposed OSNet baseline. Figure 3 shows the overall network architecture, which includes a backbone network, a global branch (orange colored arrows), and a local branch (blue colored arrows).

Attention Modules: Compared to the OSNet, attention modules are explicitly employed in Fig. 3, where both spatial attention module (SAM) and channel attention module (CAM) are used in the shared-net.

For SAM, we employ the version of [3], which was designed to capture and aggregate those semantically related pixels in the spatial domain. To further reduce the computational complexity, we use a 1×1 convolution that forms a functions $q(x)$ (or $k(x)$) to reduce the number of channels c to c/r of the input x.

For CAM, the squeeze-and-excitation mechanism [12] is employed with slight modifications detailed in Fig. 3. Compared to the channel attention module in [3], it does not require to compute the channel affinity matrix and therefore can be implemented more efficiently.

Shared-Net: The recently-proposed OSNet is employed as the backbone network for feature extraction. OSNet uses a lightweight network architecture for omni-scale feature learning, which is achieved by employing the factorised convolutional layer, the omni-scale residual block and the unified aggregation gate. The shared-net consists of the first 3 conv layers and 2 transition layers from OSNet. As shown in Fig. 3, we insert SAM + CAM modules in both conv-2 and conv-3 layers for the shared-net.

Global Branch with Global-Max-Pooling: The global branch consists of the conv4 and conv5 layers, a Global-Max-Pooling (GMP) layer to produce a 512-dimensional vector, providing a compact global feature representation for both the triplet loss and the ID-prediction loss. The use of GMP is mainly for achieving the feature diversity between the global branch and the local branch, where average pooling is known to be popular in PCB [22] and adopted in the local branch.

Local Branch with Part-Level Feature Resolution: The local branch has the similar layer structure but with the average pooling (AP) in replace of GMP. To achieve feature diversify, a uniform partition strategy is employed for part-level feature resolution, and four 512-dimensional features are then concatenated for producing just one ID-prediction loss. The use of a single ID-prediction loss is unique in this paper, while PCB and its variations employed a multiple ID-prediction loss with an independent ID-prediction loss for each part.

3.3   Loss Functions

The feature vectors from the global and local branches are concatenated as the final descriptor for the person Re-ID task. The loss function at either the global branch or the local branch is the sum of a single ID loss (softmax loss), a soft margin triplet loss [10] and a center loss [25], namely,

$$L_{total} = L_{s-id} + \gamma_t L_{triplet} + \gamma_c L_{center}, \tag{4}$$

where γ_t, γ_c are weighting factors.

4   Experiments

4.1   Datasets

The Market1501 dataset [31] has 1,501 identities collected by six cameras and a total of 32,668 pedestrian images. Following [31]. The dataset is split into a training set with 12,936 images of 751 identities and a testing set of 3,368 query images and 15,913 gallery images of 750 identities.

The DukeMTMC-reID dataset [17] contains 1,404 identities captured by more than 2 cameras and a total of 36,411 images. The training subset contains 702 identities with 16,522 images and the testing subset has other 702 identities.

The CUHK03 dataset [13] contains labeled 14,096 images and detected 14,097 images of a total of 1,467 identities captured by two camera views. With splitting just like in [31], a non-overlapping 767 identities are for training and 700

Table 1. Comparison of our proposed method with state-of-the-art methods for the three person Re-ID datasets.

Method	Market1501		DukeMTMC		CUHK03-Labeled		CUHK03-Detected	
	mAP	rank-1	mAP	rank-1	mAP	rank-1	mAP	rank-1
HA-CNN [14] (CVPR'18)	75.7	91.2	63.8	80.5	41.0	44.4	38.6	41.7
PCB [22] (ECCV'18)	81.6	93.8	69.2	83.3	–	–	57.5	63.7
Mancs [23] (ECCV'18)	82.3	93.1	71.8	84.9	63.9	69.0	60.5	65.5
MGN [24] (ACM MM'18)	86.9	95.7	78.40	88.7	67.4	68.0	66.0	68.0
Local CNN[27] (ACM MM'18)	87.4	**95.9**	66.04	82.23	–	–	–	–
IAN [11] (CVPR'19)	83.1	94.4	73.4	87.1	–	–	–	–
CAMA [28] (CVPR'19)	84.5	94.7	72.9	85.8	–	–	–	–
MHN [2] (CVPR'19)	85.0	95.1	77.2	89.1	72.4	77.2	65.4	71.7
Pyramid [30] (CVPR'19)	88.2	95.7	79.0	89.0	76.9	78.9	74.8	78.9
BagOfTricks [9] (CVPRW'19)	85.9	94.5	76.4	86.4	–	–	–	–
ABD [3] (ICCV'19)	88.28	95.6	78.59	89.0	–	–	–	–
BDB [6] (ICCV'19)	86.7	95.3	76.0	89.0	76.7	79.4	73.5	76.4
SONA [26] (ICCV'19)	88.67	95.68	78.05	89.25	79.23	81.85	76.35	79.10
Auto-ReID [16] (ICCV'19)	85.1	94.5	75.1	88.5	73.0	77.9	69.3	73.3
OSNet [35] (ICCV'19)	84.9	94.8	73.5	88.6	–	–	67.8	72.3
PLR-OSNet	**88.9**	95.6	**81.2**	**91.6**	**80.5**	**84.6**	**77.2**	**80.4**

identities for testing. The labeled dataset contains 7,368 training images, 5,328 gallery, and 1,400 query images for testing, while the detected dataset contains 7,365 images for training, 5,332 gallery, and 1,400 query images for testing.

4.2   Implementation Details

Our network is trained using a single Nvidia Tesla P100 GPU with a batch size of 64. Each identity contains 4 instance images in a batch, so there are 16 identities per batch. The backbone OSNet is initialized from the ImageNet pre-trained model. The total number of epoches is set to 120 [150], namely, 120 for both Market-1501 and DukeMTMC-reID, and 150 for CUHK03, respectively. We use the Adam optimizer with the base learning rate initialized to 3.5e-5. With a linear warm-up strategy in first 20 [40] epochs, the learning rate increases to 3.5e-4. Then, the learning rate is decayed to 3.5e-5 after 60 [100] epochs, and further decayed to 3.5e-6 after 90 [130] epochs.

For training, the input images are re-sized to 256×128 and then augmented by random horizontal flip, random erasing, and normalization. The testing images are re-sized to 256 × 128 with normalization.

4.3   Comparison with State-of-the-Art Methods

We compare our work with state-of-the-art methods, in particular emphasis on the recent remarkable works (CVPR'19 and ICCV'19) on person Re-ID, over the popular benchmark datasets Market-1501, DukeMTMC-ReID and CUHK03. All reported results are obtained without any re-ranking [33] or multi-query fusion

Query Global Part-1 Part-2 Part-3 Part-4

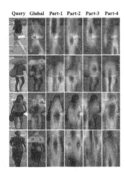

Fig. 4. Left: Visualization of class activation maps (CAMs) for the global branch and the local branch. The proposed architecture allow the model to learn diverse features (marked in orange). Right: Three Re-ID examples of PLR-OSNet and OSNet on DukeMTMC-reID. Left: query image. Upper-Right: top-10 results of PLR-OSNet. Low-Right: top-10 results of OSNet. Images in red boxes are negative results. PLR-OSNet boosts the retrieval performance.

[31] techniques. The comparison results are listed in Table 1. From Table 1, one can observe that our proposed method performs competitively among various state-of-the-art methods, including PCB [22], IAN [11], CAMA [28], MHN [2], Pyramid [30], BagOfTricks [9], ABD-Net [3], BDB [6], SONA [26], Auto-ReID [16], OSNet [35], et al.

As shown, *our PLR-OSNet has achieved the best mAP performance among various state-of-the-art methods for all the three datasets.* For DukeMTMC-reID, PLR-OSNet obtained 91.6% Rank-1 accuracy and 81.2% mAP, which significantly outperforms all existing methods. For CUHK03, PLR-OSNet even outperforms SONA in both mAP and Rank-1 accuracy, which might be the best performing algorithm for CUHK03.

Besides of its strong competition in both Rank-1 and mAP performance, PLR-OSNet has a lightweight network architecture inherited from OSNet. It only has only 3.4M parameters while the recently-available Robust-ReID has 6.4M parameters.

4.4   Visualization

Visualization of Feature Diversity Between Two Branches: In Fig. 4 (Left), we show the visualization of class activation maps (CAMs) for the global feature vector and 4 local part-level feature vectors. Note that the local branch produces 4 part-level feature vectors, corresponding to part-1, part-2, part-3 and part-4. As shown, these part-level features have some degree of diversity compared to the global features. This means that the proposed PLR-OSNet architecture allows the model to learn diverse features, which is key to the high performance of person Re-ID.

Re-ID Visual Retrieving Results: We compare PLR-OSNet with OSNet more directly from visual retrieving results. Three retrieved examples are shown in Fig. 4(Right). One can see that OSNet fails to retrieve several correct images among the top-10 results. Taking the second query as an example, PLR-OSNet is able to find correct images of the same identity in the top 10 results whilst OSNet gets 5 incorrect ones.

Table 2. The use of global features on the final performance

Global features	Market1501		DukeMTMC		CUHK03-Labeled		CUHK03-Detected	
	mAP	rank-1	mAP	rank-1	mAP	rank-1	mAP	rank-1
No	86.9	94.6	79.8	90.2	77.5	81.2	73.4	77.6
Yes	**88.9**	**95.6**	**81.2**	**91.6**	**80.5**	**84.6**	**77.2**	**80.4**

Table 3. Single ID Loss vs. Multiple ID Loss

Method	Market1501		DukeMTMC		CUHK03-Labeled		CUHK03-Detected	
	mAP	rank-1	mAP	rank-1	mAP	rank-1	mAP	rank-1
Multiple ID loss	85.6	94.4	77.0	89.4	79.4	83.1	74.7	78.4
Single ID loss	**88.9**	**95.6**	**81.2**	**91.6**	**80.5**	**84.6**	**77.2**	**80.4**

Table 4. The use of attention modules on the final performance

Attention modules	Market1501		DukeMTMC		CUHK03-Labeled		CUHK03-Detected	
	mAP	rank-1	mAP	rank-1	mAP	rank-1	mAP	rank-1
No	88.4	95.0	81.0	90.8	79.5	82.4	76.8	79.4
Yes	**88.9**	**95.6**	**81.2**	**91.6**	**80.5**	**84.6**	**77.2**	**80.4**

4.5   Ablation Studies

Benefit of Global Features: PCB employed a uniform partition strategy for producing part-level features, which did not consider any possibility of the use of global features. The proposed PLR-OSNet, however, introduces a global branch, which uses *global-max-pooling* for extracting global features as shown in Fig. 3. With the use of global features, PLR-OSNet performs significantly better as depicted in Table 2 for all the three datasets. For CUHK03-Label, PLR-OSNet achieves the Rank-1 accuracy of 84.6% with the global features, without which it simply can obtain 81.2% Rank-1 accuracy. This suggests that the global branch and the local branch reinforce each other, both contributing to the final performance.

Single ID Loss vs. Multiple ID Loss: PLR-OSNet uses only single ID loss for multiple part-level features, which is sharply contrast to PCB and its variants, where each part-level feature vector is employed to drive an ID loss so that the number of ID loss is equal to the number of separated parts. The use of ID loss for each part-level feature can force it to learn the feature at each specified part with the ID-labeled dataset. The drawback, however, is that some part-level features may fail to produce any reliable ID prediction. By concatenating multiple part-level feature vector into a single feature vector, a single ID prediction is much more reliable.

With the use of multiple feature concatenation followed by a single ID loss, PLR-OSNet performs significantly better as shown in Table 3 for all the three datasets. For Market1501, PLR-OSNet obtains 88.9% mAP, which surpasses its counterpart (with multiple ID loss) about 3.3%.

Benefit of Attention Modules: The attention modules have been widely employed in various state-of-the-art methods for person Re-ID. Therefore, we also insert these popular attention modules in the shared net as shown in Fig. 3. Experiments results are shown in Table 4 for all the three datasets. Clearly, it achieves consistently improved performance for all three datasets.

5   Conclusion

In this paper, we propose a new OSNet structure with part-level feature resolution for person Re-ID. With a two-branch network architecture, the proposed PLR-OSNet concatenates various uniformly-partitioned part-level feature vectors to a long vector for producing a single ID prediction loss, which is proved to be more efficient than the existing part-based methods. Extensive experiments show that PLR-OSNet achieves state-of-the-art performance on popular person Re-ID datasets, including Market1501, DukeMTMC-reID and CUHK03. In the mean time, its model size is significantly smaller than various state-of-the-art methods, thanking to the lightweight architecture of OSNet.

References

1. Bai, X., Yang, M., Huang, T., Dou, Z., Yu, R., Xu, Y.: Deep-person: learning discriminative deep features for person re-identification. Pattern Recogn. **98**, 107036 (2020)
2. Chen, B., Deng, W., Hu, J.: Mixed high-order attention network for person re-identification. In: Proceedings of the IEEE International Conference on Computer Vision, pp. 371–381 (2019)
3. Chen, T., et al.: ABD-Net: attentive but diverse person re-identification. In: Proceedings of the IEEE International Conference on Computer Vision, pp. 8351–8361 (2019)
4. Chen, W., Chen, X., Zhang, J., Huang, K.: Beyond triplet loss: a deep quadruplet network for person re-identification. In: Proceedings of the IEEE Conference on Computer Vision and Pattern Recognition, pp. 403–412 (2017)
5. Cheng, D., Gong, Y., Zhou, S., Wang, J., Zheng, N.: Person re-identification by multi-channel parts-based CNN with improved triplet loss function. In: Proceedings of the IEEE Conference on Computer Vision and Pattern Recognition, pp. 1335–1344 (2016)

6. Dai, Z., Chen, M., Gu, X., Zhu, S., Tan, P.: Batch dropblock network for person re-identification and beyond. In: Proceedings of the IEEE International Conference on Computer Vision, pp. 3691–3701 (2019)
7. Dai, Z., Chen, M., Zhu, S., Tan, P.: Batch feature erasing for person re-identification and beyond. arXiv preprint arXiv:1811.07130 (2018)
8. DeVries, T., Taylor, G.W.: Improved regularization of convolutional neural networks with cutout. arXiv preprint arXiv:1708.04552 (2017)
9. He, T., Zhang, Z., Zhang, H., Zhang, Z., Xie, J., Li, M.: Bag of tricks for image classification with convolutional neural networks. In: Proceedings of the IEEE Conference on Computer Vision and Pattern Recognition, pp. 558–567 (2019)
10. Hermans, A., Beyer, L., Leibe, B.: In defense of the triplet loss for person re-identification. arXiv preprint arXiv:1703.07737 (2017)
11. Hou, R., Ma, B., Chang, H., Gu, X., Shan, S., Chen, X.: Interaction-and-aggregation network for person re-identification. In: Proceedings of the IEEE Conference on Computer Vision and Pattern Recognition, pp. 9317–9326 (2019)
12. Hu, J., Shen, L., Sun, G.: Squeeze-and-excitation networks. In: Proceedings of the IEEE Conference on Computer Vision and Pattern Recognition, pp. 7132–7141 (2018)
13. Li, W., Zhao, R., Xiao, T., Wang, X.: DeepReID: deep filter pairing neural network for person re-identification. In: Proceedings of the IEEE Conference on Computer Vision and Pattern Recognition, pp. 152–159 (2014)
14. Li, W., Zhu, X., Gong, S.: Harmonious attention network for person re-identification. In: Proceedings of the IEEE Conference on Computer Vision and Pattern Recognition, pp. 2285–2294 (2018)
15. Qian, X., et al.: Pose-normalized image generation for person re-identification. In: Proceedings of the European Conference on Computer Vision, pp. 650–667 (2018)
16. Quan, R., Dong, X., Wu, Y., Zhu, L., Yang, Y.: Auto-ReID: searching for a part-aware convnet for person re-identification. In: Proceedings of the IEEE International Conference on Computer Vision, pp. 3750–3759 (2019)
17. Ristani, E., Solera, F., Zou, R., Cucchiara, R., Tomasi, C.: Performance measures and a data set for multi-target, multi-camera tracking. In: Hua, G., Jégou, H. (eds.) ECCV 2016. LNCS, vol. 9914, pp. 17–35. Springer, Cham (2016). https://doi.org/10.1007/978-3-319-48881-3_2
18. Ristani, E., Tomasi, C.: Features for multi-target multi-camera tracking and re-identification. In: Proceedings of the IEEE International Conference on Computer Vision, pp. 6036–6046 (2018)
19. Su, C., Li, J., Zhang, S., Xing, J., Gao, W., Tian, Q.: Pose-driven deep convolutional model for person re-identification. In: Proceedings of the IEEE International Conference on Computer Vision, pp. 3960–3969 (2017)
20. Su, C., Zhang, S., Xing, J., Gao, W., Tian, Q.: Deep attributes driven multi-camera person re-identification. In: Leibe, B., Matas, J., Sebe, N., Welling, M. (eds.) ECCV 2016. LNCS, vol. 9906, pp. 475–491. Springer, Cham (2016). https://doi.org/10.1007/978-3-319-46475-6_30
21. Suh, Y., Wang, J., Tang, S., Mei, T., Mu Lee, K.: Part-aligned bilinear representations for person re-identification. In: Proceedings of the European Conference on Computer Vision, pp. 402–419 (2018)
22. Sun, Y., Zheng, L., Yang, Y., Tian, Q., Wang, S.: Beyond part models: person retrieval with refined part pooling (and a strong convolutional baseline). In: Proceedings of the European Conference on Computer Vision, pp. 480–496 (2018)

23. Wang, C., Zhang, Q., Huang, C., Liu, W., Wang, X.: Mancs: a multi-task attentional network with curriculum sampling for person re-identification. In: Proceedings of the European Conference on Computer Vision, pp. 365–381 (2018)
24. Wang, G., Yuan, Y., Chen, X., Li, J., Zhou, X.: Learning discriminative features with multiple granularities for person re-identification. In: Proceedings of the 26th ACM International Conference on Multimedia, pp. 274–282 (2018)
25. Wen, Y., Zhang, K., Li, Z., Qiao, Yu.: A discriminative feature learning approach for deep face recognition. In: Leibe, B., Matas, J., Sebe, N., Welling, M. (eds.) ECCV 2016. LNCS, vol. 9911, pp. 499–515. Springer, Cham (2016). https://doi.org/10.1007/978-3-319-46478-7_31
26. Xia, B.N., Gong, Y., Zhang, Y., Poellabauer, C.: Second-order non-local attention networks for person re-identification. In: Proceedings of the IEEE International Conference on Computer Vision, pp. 3760–3769 (2019)
27. Yang, J., Shen, X., Tian, X., Li, H., Huang, J., Hua, X.S.: Local convolutional neural networks for person re-identification. In: Proceedings of the 26th ACM International Conference on Multimedia, pp. 1074–1082 (2018)
28. Yang, W., Huang, H., Zhang, Z., Chen, X., Huang, K., Zhang, S.: Towards rich feature discovery with class activation maps augmentation for person re-identification. In: Proceedings of the IEEE Conference on Computer Vision and Pattern Recognition, pp. 1389–1398 (2019)
29. Zhao, L., Li, X., Zhuang, Y., Wang, J.: Deeply-learned part-aligned representations for person re-identification. In: Proceedings of the IEEE International Conference on Computer Vision, pp. 3219–3228 (2017)
30. Zheng, F., et al.: Pyramidal person re-identification via multi-loss dynamic training. In: Proceedings of the IEEE Conference on Computer Vision and Pattern Recognition, pp. 8514–8522 (2019)
31. Zheng, L., Shen, L., Tian, L., Wang, S., Wang, J., Tian, Q.: Scalable person re-identification: a benchmark. In: Proceedings of the IEEE International Conference on Computer Vision, pp. 1116–1124 (2015)
32. Zheng, L., Yang, Y., Hauptmann, A.G.: Person re-identification: past, present and future. arXiv preprint arXiv:1610.02984 (2016)
33. Zhong, Z., Zheng, L., Cao, D., Li, S.: Re-ranking person re-identification with k-reciprocal encoding. In: Proceedings of the IEEE Conference on Computer Vision and Pattern Recognition, pp. 1318–1327 (2017)
34. Zhong, Z., Zheng, L., Kang, G., Li, S., Yang, Y.: Random erasing data augmentation. arXiv preprint arXiv:1708.04896 (2017)
35. Zhou, K., Yang, Y., Cavallaro, A., Xiang, T.: Omni-scale feature learning for person re-identification. In: Proceedings of the IEEE International Conference on Computer Vision, pp. 3702–3712 (2019)

Open Set Domain Adaptation with Entropy Minimization

Xiaofu Wu$^{(\boxtimes)}$, Lei Cheng, and Suofei Zhang

Nanjing University of Posts and Telecommunications, Nanjing, China
{xfuwu,zhangsuofei}@njupt.edu.cn, chanleimi@163.com

Abstract. Unsupervised domain adaptation has achieved great progress in the past few years. Nevertheless, most existing methods work in the so-called closed-set scenario, assuming that the classes depicted by the target samples are exactly the same as those of the source domain. In this paper, we tackle the more challenging scenario of open set domain adaptation with a novel end-to-end training approach, where the samples of unknown class can be present in the target domain. Our method employs entropy minimization for performing unsupervised domain adaptation, where unknown samples are aggressively used in training by forcing the classifier to output the probability of 0.5 on the unknown class. Experimental evidence demonstrates that our approach significantly outperforms the state-of-the-art in open set domain adaptation.

1 Introduction

In the past years, domain adaptation has incurred increasing interest since the massive labelling of a large-scale dataset is often costly [12–14,18,21,21]. With domain adaptation, a new target task often resorts to finding a similar task, where the fully-labeled dataset (source domain) is available.

Most domain adaptation methods assumed that both the source domain and the target domain share the class of their samples, which, however, is often not realistic in many practical scenarios, where unknown samples could appear in the target domain. The concept of open set domain adaptation is thus introduced in [4], which clearly differs with that of the traditional scenario of closed-set domain adaptation.

The goal of open set domain adaptation is to classify unknown target samples as unknown and to classify known target samples into correct known categories. In [4], the authors considered to employ some unknown source samples for learning to separate unknown target samples from known target samples and an assign-and-transform-iteratively (ATI) process is formulated for transferring from source domain to target domain. A more challenging open set domain adaptation was introduced in [17], which does not require any unknown source samples. With adversarial learning [10], the classifier in [17] was trained to force the soft-max layer to output the probability of τ (typically, $\tau = 0.5$) on the unknown class. With this manner, the proposed classifier attempts to make a boundary between unknown and known samples.

© Springer Nature Switzerland AG 2020
Y. Peng et al. (Eds.): PRCV 2020, LNCS 12307, pp. 29–41, 2020.
https://doi.org/10.1007/978-3-030-60636-7_3

In this paper, we consider the open set scenario in [17], where the accessibility to the unknown samples in the source domain is totally prohibited. For this challenging scenario, we make several contributions:

1. We propose an end-to-end training framework with entropy minimization (OSDA-EM) to solve the difficult problem of unsupervised open set domain adaptation. It can be efficiently implemented by the standard stochastic gradient decent without use of adversarial learning.
2. We propose to employ a special neural network architecture, which consists of a normalized feature map and a simple one-layer classifier with weight normalization.
3. We demonstrate the effectiveness of our approach on both Office-31 and the cross-dataset benchmark of [19] for visual object recognition. It outperforms the state-of-the-art in open set domain adaptation and source code is available at https://github.com/AI-NERC-NUPT/OSDA-EM.

2   Background and Related Work

2.1   Closed-Set Domain Adaptation

Consider the problem of classifying an image x in a K-classes problem. For unsupervised domain adaptation, we are given a source domain $\mathcal{D}_s = \{(x_i^s; y_i^s)\}_{i=1}^{n_s}$ of n_s labeled examples and a target domain $\mathcal{D}_t = \{x_j^t\}_{j=1}^{n_t}$ of n_t unlabeled examples. The source domain and target domain are sampled from joint distributions $P(x^s; y^s)$ and $Q(x^t; y^t)$ $(P \neq Q)$, respectively.

For a closed-set scenario, it is assumed that both the source and target domains completely share the class of their samples. Let $\mathcal{Y}_s$ and $\mathcal{Y}_t$ denote the label sets of $\mathcal{D}_s$ and $\mathcal{D}_t$, respectively. This means that $\mathcal{Y}_s = \mathcal{Y}_t$.

For this scenario, the problem is to exploit a bunch of labeled images in $\mathcal{D}_s$ for training a deep neural-network (DNN) based classifier $y = f_\theta(x)$ (θ represents all parameters of the DNN) that, during inference, provides probabilities of a given test image $x \in \mathcal{D}_t$ belonging to each of the K classes as

$$f_\theta(x) = [\mathbb{P}(\mathrm{cls}(x) = 1), \cdots, \mathbb{P}(\mathrm{cls}(x) = K)]. \tag{1}$$

For unsupervised domain adaptation, the goal is to design the classifier $y = f_\theta(x)$ such that the target risk $\epsilon_t(f) = \mathbb{E}_{(x^t; y^t) \sim Q}[f_\theta(x^t) \neq y^t]$ can be minimized. Since the target risk $\epsilon_t(f)$ cannot be computed in the scenario of unsupervised domain adaptation, the domain adaptation theory [2,3] suggests to bound the target risk with the sum of the cross-domain discrepancy $D(P; Q)$ [2] and the source risk $\epsilon_s(f) = \mathbb{E}_{(x^s; y^s) \sim P}[f_\theta(x^s) \neq y^s]$.

Instead of explicitly minimizing the cross-domain discrepancy, a broad class of domain adaptation methods employ entropy minimization as a proxy for mitigating the harmful effects of domain shift. The entropy minimization is performed on the target domain, which may take explicit forms [9] or implicit forms [7,20]. In what follows, we shall revisit the basic domain adaptation method with entropy minimization.

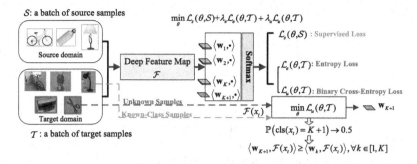

Fig. 1. OSDA-EM employs an end-to-end training approach with entropy minimization. The employed neural network consists of a deep feature map and a simple classifier with normalized weight templates. The weight template designated to the unknown class is aggressively trained by forcing the classifier to output the probability of 0.5 on the unknown class for any input target sample.

With supervised learning on the source domain, the classifier is trained to minimize the standard cross-entropy loss over a batch of source samples $\mathcal{S}$ (with batch-wise training),

$$\mathcal{L}_s(\theta, \mathcal{S}) = \frac{1}{|\mathcal{S}|} \sum_{(x,y) \in \mathcal{S}} \ell(y, f_\theta(x)) \tag{2}$$

with $\ell(y, \hat{y}) = <y, \hat{y}> = -\sum_{j=1}^{K} y_j \log \hat{y}_j$ and $|\mathcal{S}|$ denotes the cardinality of the set $\mathcal{S}$.

To adapt to the unlabeled target domain, the entropy loss over a batch of target samples $\mathcal{T}$

$$\mathcal{L}_e(\theta, \mathcal{T}) = -\frac{1}{|\mathcal{T}|} \sum_{x_t \in \mathcal{T}} <f_\theta(x_t), \log f_\theta(x_t)> \tag{3}$$

is minimized as an efficient regularization technique for implementing transfer learning. Therefore, the standard domain adaptation method with entropy-minimization-only (EMO) seeks to solve the following problem

$$\min_\theta \left[\mathcal{L}_s(\theta, \mathcal{S}) + \lambda_e \mathcal{L}_e(\theta, \mathcal{T}) \right], \lambda_e > 0. \tag{4}$$

Unfortunately, as a necessary but not sufficient condition for minimization of the target risk $\epsilon_t(f)$ [16], this simple regularization technique may result into some trivial solutions.

With each unlabeled image $x_t \in \mathcal{T}$ as input, we can perform the inference over the network f_θ to obtain the softmax predictions $f_\theta(x_t)$ (1). Then, we can compute the predicted category distribution in $\mathcal{T}$ as

$$\hat{\mathbf{q}} = \frac{1}{||\mathbf{z}||_1} \mathbf{z} = \frac{1}{|\mathcal{T}|} \mathbf{z}, \tag{5}$$

where

$$\mathbf{z} = \sum_{x_t \in \mathcal{T}} f_\theta(x_t) = \left[\sum_{x_t \in \mathcal{T}} \mathbb{P}(\mathrm{cls}(x_t) = 1), \cdots, \sum_{x_t \in \mathcal{T}} \mathbb{P}(\mathrm{cls}(x_t) = K) \right] \tag{6}$$

and $||\mathbf{z}||_1 = \sum_{k=1}^K |z_k| = |\mathcal{T}|$.

To avoid trivial solutions of the EMO method, we propose to maximize the predicted category diversity for any training target batch $\mathcal{T}$ in [22]. The entropy of the predicted category distribution $\hat{\mathbf{q}} = [\hat{q}_1, \hat{q}_2, \cdots, \hat{q}_K]$ (5) is employed for measuring the diversity of individual categories among a batch of target samples. For implementation purpose, it is more convenient to minimize its negative form, namely,

$$\mathcal{L}_d(\theta, \mathcal{T}) = -H(\hat{\mathbf{q}}) = \sum_{k=1}^K \hat{q}_k \log \hat{q}_k. \tag{7}$$

The proposed end-to-end training approach in [22] for closed-set scenarios can be formulated as

$$\min_\theta \left[\mathcal{L}_s(\theta, \mathcal{S}) + \lambda_e \mathcal{L}_e(\theta, \mathcal{T}) + \lambda_d \mathcal{L}_d(\theta, \mathcal{T}) \right], \tag{8}$$

where $\lambda_e > 0, \lambda_d > 0$ are two positive weight factors.

Experiments in [22] show that the use of category-diversity loss (7) can push the entropy minimization away from trivial solutions. MEDM outperforms state-of-the-art methods on several popular closed-set domain adaptation datasets with the setting of $\lambda_e = 1, \lambda_d = 0.5$. Since MEDM performs stable when λ_d varies in $(0, 1]$ [22]. In what follows, $\lambda_e = 1, \lambda_d = 0.5$ is always assumed.

2.2   Open Set Domain Adaptation

For more realistic open set scenarios, there exists samples in the target domain, where their classes are not included in the source label space of $\mathcal{Y}_s$. Therefore, we have to include an unknown class $K + 1$ for the target label set, namely, $\mathcal{Y}_t = \mathcal{Y}_s \cup \{K + 1\} = \{1, \cdots, K, K + 1\}$.

With open set domain adaptation, the problem is to exploit the labeled images of K classes in $\mathcal{D}_s$ for training a statistical classifier $y = f_\theta(x)$ such that the target risk $\epsilon_t(f) = \mathbb{E}_{(x^t; y^t) \sim Q}[f_\theta(x^t) \neq y^t]$ could be minimized. During inference, it can provide probabilities for a given test image $x_t \in \mathcal{D}_t$ to belong to each of the $K + 1$ classes as

$$f_\theta(x) = [\mathbb{P}(\mathrm{cls}(x) = 1), \cdots, \mathbb{P}(\mathrm{cls}(x) = K + 1)]. \tag{9}$$

Compared to the closed-set scenario, the problem is that there are insufficient or even no labeled samples in the source domain for telling us what is the difference between unknown and known samples. This means that whenever the source risk $\epsilon_s(f) = \mathbb{E}_{(x^s; y^s) \sim P}[f_\theta(x^s) \neq y^s]$ is minimized, the resultant classifier f_θ has a probability of zero for deciding if any sample x_t is from the unknown class, namely, $\mathbb{P}(\mathrm{cls}(x_t) = K + 1) = 0$.

3   Towards Entropy Minimization for Open Set Scenarios

In this section, we propose a novel open set domain adaptation approach with entropy minimization (OSDA-EM). The key idea is shown in Fig. 1.

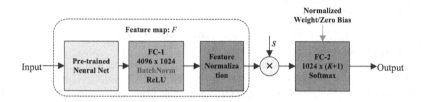

Fig. 2. Neural Network Architecture

3.1   Neural Network Structure

For the proposed OSDA-EM, we employ a special neural network architecture shown in Fig. 2. It has a pre-trained neural net (for example, AlexNet or VGGNet), followed by two fully-connected layers, FC-1 of size 4096×1024 and FC-2 of size $1024 \times (K + 1)$. Batch-normalization, ReLU activation are only employed at the FC-1 layer. The last label prediction layer of a pre-trained network is omitted and features are extracted from the second to last layer. We also employ feature normalization and scale multiplication between the FC-1 and FC-2 layers.

Essentially, the employed neural network ($f_\theta = \mathcal{C} \circ \mathcal{F}$) consists of a feature map $\mathcal{F}$ and a final classifier $\mathcal{C}$ (FC-2), where the feature map $\mathcal{F} : \mathbb{R}^{H \times W \times 3} \to \mathbb{R}^D$ consists of a pre-trained net and FC-1 layer in Fig. 2 ($D = 1024$). For any input sample x, its D-dimensional feature is

$$\mathbf{u} = \mathcal{F}(x) \tag{10}$$

where $\|\mathbf{u}\|_2 = 1$ is enforced by using an L2-normalization layer. Then, the scale layer scales the input unit vector to a fixed radius given by the parameter s

$$\mathbf{u} \to s \cdot \mathbf{u}. \tag{11}$$

The final classifier $\mathcal{C}$ consists of a fully-connected layer (FC-2) and a softmax layer. Let the weight matrix of this fully connected layer be denoted as W, which is of size $D \times (K + 1)$ for discriminating $K + 1$ classes. Let $\mathbf{w}_k$, $\mathbf{w}_y$ be the k-th and y-th column of W, respectively. With zero biases and normalized weights $\|\mathbf{w}_k\| = 1$, the standard softmax loss can be computed as

$$\mathcal{L}_s(x, y) = -\log\left(\frac{\exp(s\langle \mathbf{u}, \mathbf{w}_y \rangle)}{\sum_k \exp(s\langle \mathbf{u}, \mathbf{w}_k \rangle)}\right). \tag{12}$$

For any labeled training sample $(x, y) \in \mathcal{D}_s$, the final classifier's weight templates $\{\mathbf{w}_k\}_{k=1}^K$ should meet the following requirement

$$\langle \mathbf{w}_y, \mathcal{F}(x) \rangle > \langle \mathbf{w}_k, \mathcal{F}(x) \rangle, \forall k \neq y \tag{13}$$

when the training process converges.

3.2   An End-to-End Training Approach for Open Set Domain Adaptation

For open set domain adaptation, we are interested in the labeling prediction for the target dataset $\mathcal{D}_t$. For each $x_t \in \mathcal{D}_t$, let us define

$$d_{tk} = \|\mathcal{F}(x_t) - \mathbf{w}_k\|_2^2 = 2\left(1 - \langle \mathbf{w}_k, \mathcal{F}(x_t) \rangle\right). \tag{14}$$

since $\|\mathcal{F}(x_t)\|_2 = 1$ and $\|\mathbf{w}_k\|_2 = 1$ with the use of architecture shown in Fig. 2.

In [4], an assign-and-transform-iteratively (ATI) adaptation method was proposed for open set scenarios, which was formulated as the iteration process of solving the assignment problem and estimating the mapping from the source domain to the target domain.

As shown in [4], ATI starts with a pre-trained neural network for feature embedding ($\mathbf{u}_t = \mathcal{F}(x_t)$ for any $x_t \in \mathcal{D}_t$). This neural network is pre-trained with the fully-labeled source dataset, and the weight template $\mathbf{w}_k$ after training can be seen as the representative (or the mean feature) of all samples in the source domain labeled by class k. Hence, d_{tk} in (14) represents the distance between the target sample x_t and the mean feature of class k in the source domain just as in [4].

Essentially, the determination of the weight template $\mathbf{w}_{K+1}$ is to make a boundary between known and unknown samples. Our proposed end-to-end approach starts with a usual initialization of $\mathbf{w}_{K+1}$. After the training of labeled source dataset $\mathcal{D}_s$, $\{\mathbf{w}_k\}_{k=1}^K$ could be well determined while $\mathbf{w}_{K+1}$ keeps as the initialized vector (with normally-distributed components).

Let $(x_t, y_t) \in \mathcal{D}_t$ be any input target sample and assume that $y_t \neq K + 1$. With entropy minimization, one can expect that

$$\langle \mathbf{w}_{y_t}, \mathcal{F}(x_t) \rangle \geq \langle \mathbf{w}_{K+1}, \mathcal{F}(x_t) \rangle \tag{15}$$

holds with high probability since x_t is strongly correlated with the source samples labeled with y_t.

Let $\hat{\tau} \triangleq \mathbb{P}(\mathrm{cls}(x_t) = K + 1)$ be the softmax output for the unknown class whenever x_t is inferred over the network θ and $\mathbf{p}_{\hat{\tau}} \triangleq (\hat{\tau}, 1 - \hat{\tau})$ be the corresponding binary distribution. Let $\mathbf{p}_\tau = (\tau, 1 - \tau)$ denote a binary distribution parameterized by $0 < \tau < 1$. In order to force $\mathbb{P}(\mathrm{cls}(x_t) = K + 1) \to \tau$, we can employ the Kullback Leibler (KL) distance between $\mathbf{p}_\tau$ and $\mathbf{p}_{\hat{\tau}}$ as

$$d_{KL}\left(\mathbf{p}_\tau \| \mathbf{p}_{\hat{\tau}}\right) = \tau \log \frac{\tau}{\hat{\tau}} + (1 - \tau) \log \frac{1 - \tau}{1 - \hat{\tau}} = -\tau \log \hat{\tau} - (1 - \tau) \log(1 - \hat{\tau}) + \nu(\tau),$$

where $\nu(\tau) = \tau \log \tau + (1 - \tau) \log(1 - \tau)$ is a constant for a fixed τ. This is exactly what a binary cross entropy loss

$$\mathcal{L}_u(\theta, x_t) = -(1 - \tau)(1 - \log(\mathbb{P}(\text{cls}(x_t) = K + 1))) - \tau \log(\mathbb{P}(\text{cls}(x_t) = K + 1)) \qquad (16)$$

introduced in [17] wants to do.

By setting $\tau = 0.5$, we have that

$$\mathbb{P}(\text{cls}(x_t) = K + 1) \geq \mathbb{P}(\text{cls}(x_t) = k), \forall k \in [1, K] \qquad (17)$$

if the training process converges. Hence, the minimization of $\mathcal{L}_u(\theta, x_t)$ over the network θ means that

$$\langle \mathbf{w}_{K+1}, \mathcal{F}(x_t) \rangle \geq \langle \mathbf{w}_k, \mathcal{F}(x_t) \rangle, \forall k \in [1, K]. \qquad (18)$$

Now, it is reasonable to propose an end-to-end training approach for open-set domain adaptation by

$$\min_\theta \mathcal{L}_s(\theta, \mathcal{S}) + \lambda_e \mathcal{L}_e(\theta, \mathcal{T}) + \lambda_u \mathcal{L}_u(\theta, \mathcal{T}), \qquad (19)$$

where $\lambda_u \geq 0$ is a constant parameter and

$$\mathcal{L}_u(\theta, \mathcal{T}) = \frac{1}{|\mathcal{T}|} \sum_{x_t \in \mathcal{T}} \mathcal{L}_u(\theta, x_t)$$

denotes the mean form of a binary cross entropy loss (16) for any target batch $\mathcal{T}$.

The justification of the use of (19) is shown in Fig. 1 and can be further stated as follows:

– Whenever $y_t = K + 1$, the update of θ towards the minimization of $\mathcal{L}_u(\theta, x_t)$ aims to push $\mathbf{w}_{K+1}$ towards a correct classification of the unknown target samples.
– When $y_t \neq K + 1$, we notice that (15) may still holds with high probability due to the coexistence of supervised loss $\mathcal{L}_s(\theta, \mathcal{S})$ in (19). Hence, the update of θ towards the minimization of $\mathcal{L}_u(\theta, x_t)$, together with the minimization of $\mathcal{L}_s(\theta, \mathcal{S})$, contributes much less than the case of $y_t = K + 1$, as two objectives should be compromised.

3.3   Avoiding Trivial Solutions

Avoiding One-Class Solution with Diversity Maximization. The use of entropy-minimization-only may produce trivial solutions, where all target samples may be recognized as a single class. For any input batch $\mathcal{T}$, such a trivial solution often has small category-diversity for the estimated category distribution $\hat{\mathbf{q}}$ defined in (5).

For open-set scenarios, we, however, employ the following form of the category-diversity loss

$$\mathcal{L}_d(\theta, \mathcal{T}) = \sum_{k=1}^{K} \frac{\hat{q}_k}{\sum_{j=1}^{K} \hat{q}_j} \log \frac{\hat{q}_k}{\sum_{j=1}^{K} \hat{q}_j}. \tag{20}$$

where the unknown class ($K + 1$-th class) is not included. This is due to our stringent assumption that no any unknown samples are available in the source domain.

With the inclusion of (20), (19) can now be formulated as

$$\min_{\theta} \left[\mathcal{L}_s(\theta, \mathcal{S}) + \sum_{v \in \{e,d,u\}} \lambda_v \mathcal{L}_v(\theta, \mathcal{T}) \right], \lambda_v > 0. \tag{21}$$

Avoiding All-Unknown-Class Solution with Binary Diversity Loss. In many cases, the above method (21) does work. However, when the number of unknown samples dominate in the target domain, the formulation (21) may still result into a trivial solution, where all target samples could be recognized as unknown class. Hence, we propose a binary diversity loss for avoiding such a trivial solution.

For a batch of input target samples $\mathcal{T}$, let $\hat{q}_{K+1}$ be the proportion of target samples in $\mathcal{T}$ inferred as the unknown class

$$\hat{q}_{K+1} = \frac{1}{|\mathcal{T}|} \sum_{x_t \in \mathcal{T}} \mathbb{P}(\text{cls}(x_t) = K + 1). \tag{22}$$

Clearly, we have that

$$1 - \hat{q}_{K+1} = \frac{1}{|\mathcal{T}|} \sum_{x_t \in \mathcal{T}} \sum_{k=1}^{K} \mathbb{P}(\text{cls}(x_t) = k). \tag{23}$$

Then, we define the negative entropy loss of the binary distribution ($\hat{q}_{K+1}, 1 - \hat{q}_{K+1}$) as the binary diversity loss

$$\mathcal{L}_b(\theta, \mathcal{T}) = \hat{q}_{K+1} \log \hat{q}_{K+1} + (1 - \hat{q}_{K+1}) \log(1 - \hat{q}_{K+1}). \tag{24}$$

By minimizing this binary diversity loss (or maximizing the corresponding binary entropy loss), we can avoid the trivial solution where the unknown class may dominate in the final predictions.

3.4   Final Approach

Integrating all things together, the proposed OSDA-EM takes its final form of

$$\min_{\theta} \mathcal{L}(\theta, \mathcal{S}, \mathcal{T}) = \mathcal{L}_s(\theta, \mathcal{S}) + \sum_{v \in \{e,d,u,b\}} \lambda_v \mathcal{L}_v(\theta, \mathcal{T}), \tag{25}$$

where $\lambda_v > 0, v \in \{d, u, e, b\}$ are positive weight factors.

4   Experiments

We evaluate the proposed OSDA-EM method with state-of-the-art methods. Open set domain adaptation tasks over both Office-31 and the cross-dataset benchmark of [19] are investigated.

4.1   Accuracy Metrics

There are three accuracy metrics for evaluation of open-set domain adaptation tasks, denoted as ALL, OS and OS*.

The common "ALL" accuracy over all classes (including the unknown class) is simply computed as the ratio of correctly-classified samples among all target samples.

Accuracy averaged over all classes is denoted as OS, where $OS = \frac{1}{K+1} \sum_{k=1}^{K+1} Acc_k$ with Acc_k denoting the ratio of correctly-classified k-th samples among all target samples of the k-th class.

Table 1. Average OS and OS* accuracies (%) and their deviations of each method in 20 shared class situation.

Method	A-D			A-W			D-A		
	OS	OS*	ALL	OS	OS*	ALL	OS	OS*	ALL
OSVM	73.6 ± 0.4	75.8 ± 0.6	57.6	72.0 ± 0.5	74.1 ± 0.5	58.0	44.9 ± 0.1	43.9 ± 0.1	51.1
MMD + OSVM	72.1 ± 0.9	73.9 ± 1.0	57.8	69.1 ± 0.8	71.2 ± 0.9	54.9	29.8 ± 0.6	26.5 ± 0.6	50.3
BP+OSVM	70.4 ± 0.2	72.1 ± 0.3	57.1	70.9 ± 0.5	72.9 ± 0.4	57.6	30.9 ± 0.2	27.6 ± 0.2	51.3
OSDA-BP	74.8 ± 0.5	74.6 ± 0.5	73.9	66.8 ± 3.5	66.1 ± 3.7	69.7	64.6 ± 1.2	65.9 ± 4.9	68.5
OSDA-EM (Ours)	$\mathbf{83.9 \pm 0.9}$	$\mathbf{84.4 \pm 0.9}$	**77.9**	$\mathbf{82.2 \pm 0.8}$	$\mathbf{82.2 \pm 0.8}$	**81.0**	$\mathbf{67.2 \pm 0.4}$	$\mathbf{66.5 \pm 0.4}$	**71.9**

Method	D-W			W-A			W-D			AVG		
	OS	OS*	ALL	OS	OS*	ALL	OS	OS*	ALL	OS	OS*	ALL
OSVM	63.1 ± 1.1	61.9 ± 1.2	69.9	34.0 ± 0.9	31.8 ± 1.3	48.3	82.9 ± 2.3	82.9 ± 1.7	84.2	61.8	61.7	61.5
MMD + OSVM	58.3 ± 0.6	56.6 ± 0.6	68.8	39.7 ± 2.1	37.1 ± 2.4	55.9	84.5 ± 1.2	84.2 ± 1.3	87.2	58.9	58.2	62.3
BP+OSVM	63.2 ± 2.8	61.7 ± 3.0	71.3	40.0 ± 2.7	37.4 ± 3.0	56.0	83.5 ± 0.8	83.1 ± 0.8	86.4	59.8	59.1	63.2
OSDA-BP	83.1 ± 0.5	82.5 ± 0.5	84.9	65.9 ± 3.5	65.3 ± 3.7	69.0	92.8 ± 1.2	93.3 ± 4.9	90.3	74.7	74.6	76.1
OSDA-EM (Ours)	$\mathbf{97.5 \pm 0.2}$	$\mathbf{98.3 \pm 0.2}$	**92.6**	$\mathbf{67.7 \pm 0.6}$	$\mathbf{67.0 \pm 0.6}$	**72.3**	$\mathbf{98.2 \pm 0.3}$	$\mathbf{98.8 \pm 0.3}$	**94.1**	**82.8**	**82.8**	**81.6**

Method	B - C	B - I	B - S	C - B	C -I	C - S
TCA	62.8 ± 3.8	56.6 ± 4.5	29.6 ± 4.2	38.9 ± 1.9	60.2 ± 1.4	29.7 ± 1.6
GFK	66.2 ± 4.0	58.3 ± 3.1	23.8 ± 2.0	40.2 ± 1.8	62.2 ± 1.5	28.5 ± 1.0
SA	66.0 ± 3.4	57.8 ± 3.2	24.3 ± 2.6	40.3 ± 1.7	62.5 ± 0.8	29.0 ± 1.5
CORAL	68.8 ± 3.3	60.9 ± 2.6	27.2 ± 3.9	40.7 ± 1.5	64.0 ± 2.6	31.4 ± 0.8
ATI	71.4 ± 2.3	69.0 ± 2.8	37.4 ± 2.6	45.7 ± 3.0	67.9 ± 4.2	37.5 ± 2.7
OSDA-BP	76.2 ± 1.7	70.9 ± 3.2	57.3 ± 1.1	63.5 ± 2.1	73.5 ± 0.8	60.5 ± 0.8
D-FRODA	74.6 ± 5.5	71.4 ± 2.0	55.4 ± 2.7	67.6 ± 1.2	75.0 ± 1.8	$\mathbf{61.7 \pm 2.1}$
OSDA-EM (Ours)	$\mathbf{82.0 \pm 1.0}$	$\mathbf{86.7 \pm 0.3}$	$\mathbf{61.0 \pm 1.2}$	$\mathbf{69.2 \pm 0.7}$	$\mathbf{79.3 \pm 0.4}$	58.0 ± 1.4

Accuracy measured only on the known classes of the target domain is deonted as OS*, where $OS^* = \frac{1}{K} \sum_{k=1}^{K} Acc_k$.

4.2   Office Dataset

Office-31 is a standard benchmark dataset for visual domain adaptation, which has 4652 images and 31 categories collected from three domains, Amazon (A), Webcam (W) and DSLR (D). We consider all 6 domain combinations.

Table 2. Average "ALL" accuracy (%) and its standard deviation on BCIS dataset.

Method	I - B	I - C	I - S	S - B	S - C	S - I	Avg
TCA	40.9 ± 2.9	68.6 ± 1.8	34.5 ± 3.8	19.4 ± 2.1	32.0 ± 3.9	31.1 ± 4.6	42.0
GFK	42.6 ± 2.4	73.3 ± 3.6	32.7 ± 3.6	16.9 ± 1.5	28.6 ± 3.8	26.4 ± 1.1	41.6
SA	43.1 ± 1.6	72.8 ± 3.1	32.2 ± 3.7	17.5 ± 1.6	29.2 ± 4.2	27.1 ± 1.3	41.8
CORAL	44.6 ± 2.5	74.5 ± 3.4	35.4 ± 4.4	18.7 ± 1.2	33.6 ± 5.3	31.3 ± 1.3	44.3
ATI	48.8 ± 2.3	77.5 ± 2.2	43.4 ± 4.8	23.2 ± 3.2	47.3 ± 2.9	33.0 ± 1.1	50.2
OSDA-BP	66.3 ± 0.9	78.1 ± 0.9	59.4 ± 1.4	56.5 ± 2.6	59.6 ± 3.1	63.2 ± 1.3	65.4
D-FRODA	$\mathbf{66.4 \pm 1.7}$	80.5 ± 1.5	59.8 ± 1.2	55.5 ± 2.4	61.2 ± 1.9	59.6 ± 2.2	65.7
OSDA-EM (Ours)	63.9 ± 0.8	$\mathbf{81.2 \pm 1.1}$	$\mathbf{63.0 \pm 0.9}$	$\mathbf{57.1 \pm 0.5}$	$\mathbf{66.1 \pm 0.6}$	$\mathbf{64.3 \pm 1.4}$	$\mathbf{69.3}$

Implementation Details. The network and training parameters are kept similar across all pre-trained architectures and domain adaptation tasks. Specifically, we use stochastic gradient descent with an initial learning rate of $\eta_0 = 0.005$ and Nesterov momentum of 0.9, a batch size of 32. During training, the learning rate η_p is dynamically-adjusted according to the formula $\eta_p = \frac{\eta_0}{(1+\mu p)^\nu}$ [7], where p is the training progress linearly changing from 0 to 1, $\mu = 10$ and $\nu = 0.75$. The scale layer employs $s = 16$ in Fig. 2. The weighting factors are set as $\lambda_e = 1, \lambda_d = 0.5, \lambda_u = 0.5, \lambda_b = 0.5$. In all experiments, we train each model for 200 epochs. We run 10 experiments for computing average accuracy and its deviation. All of these parameter settings are considered default settings.

We report the test accuracy results of our method, which are compared with the published results of the following baseline methods, an open set SVM (OSVM) [11], a combination of Maximum Mean Discrepancy (MMD) based training method for neural networks and OSVM (MMD+OSVM) [17], a combination of a domain classifier based method, BP and OSVM (BP+OSVM) [17], a combination of Assign-and-Transform-Iteratively (ATI) [4] and OSVM (ATI+OSVM) [17], and an open set domain adaptation with BP (OSDA-BP) [17].

Result on 21 Class Classification. We evaluate our method over pretrained VGG network when 20 classes in Office-31 are considered as the known classes in both domains just as did in [17]. With regard to other details of the experiment, we followed the setting of [17]. The results are shown in Table 1 by further including "ALL" accuracy for a complete comparison with [17]. As shown, our method performs significantly better than OSDA-BP in all three accuracy metrics.

4.3   Dense Cross-Dataset Benchmark

We also evaluate our approach on the challenging dense cross-dataset benchmark of [19]. This dataset was built using images depicting 40 object categories and coming from four datasets, namely Bing (B), Caltech256 (C), ImageNet (I) and SUN (S), hence referred to as BCIS. Following [4], we consider the samples from the first 10 classes as known instances, while the samples with class labels 26–40 are taken to be the unknown samples in the target domain. We follow the unsupervised protocol of [4], which relies on 50 source samples per class and 30 target images per class, except when the target data is coming from SUN, in which case only 20 images per class are employed.

Implementation Details. Just like in [4], we directly employ the 4096-dimensional DeCAF7 features extracted from a pretrained neural net [5] for both the source and target samples. Hence, the pre-trained network shown in Fig. 2 is simply omitted in this scenario. By taking the DeCAF7 features as input, we then use a simple neural network with just one fully-connected layer of 1024 units and a final classification layer. No batch normalization is employed here. The training scheduling is just the same as the previous setting, where the initial learning rate is set to $\eta_0 = 0.002$ and the batch size is 64. The weighting factors are just the same as the previous settings except that $\lambda_u = 0.3$.

Result. We compare our method with the baseline methods in Table 2: Transfer Component Analysis (TCA) [15], Geodesic Flow Kernel (GFK) [8], Subspace Alignment SA [6], CORrelation ALignment (CORAL) [18], Assign-and-Transform-Iteratively (ATI) [4], OSDA-BP [17], Discriminative FRODA (D-FRODA) [1]. Our method performs the best and achieves the average accuracy of 69.3%, which improves 3.6% compared to D-FRODA [1].

4.4   Ablation Studies

We consider BCIS dataset and focus on the domain adaptation task from Caltech256 (C) to SUN (S).

Trivial One-Class Solution. By setting $\lambda_d = 0$ instead of 0.5, we show that OSDA-EM simply results into a trivial solution, where class 4 dominates among other classes.

Table 3. The sensitivity of λ_u on the accuracy (%).

λ_u	0.1	0.2	0.3	0.4	0.5	0.6	0.7
–	57.8	58.4	57.2	58.2	58.2	57.8	56.8

Trivial All-Unknown-Class Solution. By setting $\lambda_b = 0$, we also show that OSDA-EM simply results into a trivial solution, where unknown class (class 11) dominates among other classes.

Sensitivity of λ_u. It is also interesting to investigate the choice of λ_u on the final accuracy. As shown in Table 3, OSDA-EM performs very stable when λ_u varies from 0.1 to 0.7.

5   Conclusion

We developed a novel end-to-end training approach with entropy minimization for open-set domain adaptation. With an aggressive use of unknown target samples in training, we show it is possible to learn a boundary between known and unknown samples by a cooperative use of binary cross entropy loss over a batch of target samples and supervised loss over a batch of source samples. Extensive experiments shows its superiority among various baseline methods.

References

1. Baktashmotlagh, M., Faraki, M., Drummond, T., Salzmann, M.: Learning factorized representations for open-set domain adaptation. In: ICLR (2019)
2. Ben-David, S., Blitzer, J., Crammer, K., Pereira, F.: Analysis of representations for domain adaptation. In: NIPS (2007)
3. Blitzer, J., Crammer, K., Kulesza, A., Pereira, F., Wortman, J.: Learning bounds for domain adaptation. In: NIPS (2008)
4. Busto, P.P., Gall, J.: Open set domain adaptation. In: ICCV (2017)
5. Donahue, J., et al.: DeCAF: a deep convolutional activation feature for generic visual recognition. In: ICML (2013)
6. Fernando, B., Habrard, A., Sebban, M., Tuytelaars, T.: Unsupervised visual domain adaptation using subspace alignment. In: ICCV (2013)
7. Ganin, Y., Lempitsky, V.S.: Unsupervised domain adaptation by backpropagation. In: ICML (2015)
8. Gong, B., Shi, Y., Sha, F., Grauman, K.: Geodesic flow kernel for unsupervised domain adaptation. In: CVPR (2012)
9. Haeusser, P., Frerix, T., Mordvintsev, A., Cremers, D.: Associative domain adaptation. In: ICCV (2017)
10. Ian, G., et al.: Generative adversarial nets. In: NIPS (2014)
11. Jain, L.P., Scheirer, W.J., Boult, T.E.: Multi-class open set recognition using probability of inclusion. In: Fleet, D., Pajdla, T., Schiele, B., Tuytelaars, T. (eds.) ECCV 2014. LNCS, vol. 8691, pp. 393–409. Springer, Cham (2014). https://doi.org/10.1007/978-3-319-10578-9_26
12. Konstantinos, B., George, T., Nathan, S., Dilip, K., Dumitru, E.: Domain separation networks. In: NIPS (2016)
13. Long, M., Cao, Y., Wang, J., Jordan, M.I.: Learning transferable features with deep adaptation networks. In: ICML (2015)
14. Chen, M., Weinberger, K.Q., Blitzer, J.: Co-training for domain adaptation. In: NIPS (2011)

15. Pan, S., Tsang, I., Kwok, J., Yang, Q.: Domain adaptation via transfer component analysis. IEEE Trans. Neural Netw. **22**, 199–210 (2011)
16. Pietro, M., Jacopo, C., Vittorio, M.: Minimal-entropy correlation alignment for unsupervised deep domain adaptation. In: ICLR (2018)
17. Saito, K., Yamamoto, S., Ushiku, Y., Harada, T.: Open set domain adaptation by backpropagation. In: CVPR (2018)
18. Sun, B., Saenko, K.: Deep coral: correlation alignment for deep domain adaptation. In: ICCV Workshop on Transferring and Adapting Source Knowledge in Computer Vision (2016)
19. Tommasi, T., Tuytelaars, T.: A testbed for cross-dataset analysis. In: Agapito, L., Bronstein, M.M., Rother, C. (eds.) ECCV 2014. LNCS, vol. 8927, pp. 18–31. Springer, Cham (2015). https://doi.org/10.1007/978-3-319-16199-0_2
20. Tzeng, E., Hoffman, J., Saenko, K., Darrell, T.: Adversarial discriminative domain adaptation. In: CVPR (2017)
21. Tzeng, E., Hoffman, J., Zhang, N., Saenko, K.: Deep domain confusion: maximizing for domain invariance. arXiv:1412.3474 (2014)
22. Wu, X., Zhang, S., Zhou, Q., Yang, Z., Zhao, C., Latecki, L.J.: Minimal-entropy diversity maximization for unsupervised domain adaptation. arXiv:2002.01690 (2020)

An Adversarial Learned Trajectory Predictor with Knowledge-Rich Latent Variables

Caizhen He, Biao Yang[✉], Lanping Chen, and Guocheng Yan

Changzhou University, Changzhou 2131641, Jiangsu, China
1771501144@qq.com, yb6864171@cczu.edu.cn

Abstract. Forecasting human trajectories is critical for different applications, such as autonomous driving and social robot. Recent works predict future trajectories by using a generative model, in which human motion is encoded with recurrent neural network. However, the latent variable needed in the generative model is always either a random Gaussian noise or encoded from a scene. In this work, we focus on generating the latent variable from the trajectory itself. Specifically, we propose a latent variable predictor, which can bridge the gap between latent variable distributions of observed and ground truth trajectories. We evaluate the proposed method on several benchmarking datasets. Results demonstrate that the proposed method outperforms state-of-the-art methods in average and final displacement errors. In addition, the ablation study indicates that the prediction performance will not dramatically decrease as sampling times decline during tests.

Keywords: Trajectory forecasting · Generative model · Latent variable

1 Introduction

Forecasting pedestrians' future trajectories is a strong demand for different applications, such as autonomous driving and social robot. For example, a self-driving car can make a safe route planning if it can foresee surrounding pedestrians' future positions in a few seconds. Unlike humans who have the innate ability to understand motions of surrounding people, intelligent machines cannot do the same thing because these machines cannot easily understand common sense rules, and social interactions exist in complex real-world environments. As indicated in social generative adversarial network (SGAN) [1], predicting the behaviors of humans is challenging due to the following inherent human properties, including interpersonal, socially acceptable, and multi-modal properties.

Pioneering works related to trajectory prediction focused on designing robust motion models, such as constant velocity and constant acceleration models [2]. Great efforts are devoted into modeling the interactions among pedestrians. Such interactions can be defined by several hand-crafted rules, such as social forces [3]

© Springer Nature Switzerland AG 2020
Y. Peng et al. (Eds.): PRCV 2020, LNCS 12307, pp. 42–53, 2020.
https://doi.org/10.1007/978-3-030-60636-7_4

and stationary crowds' influence [4]. Such methods are effective in modeling the motion patterns of vehicles or moving robots. However, these methods cannot model pedestrians' motion patterns due to nonlinearity and complexity. To cope with complicated scenarios, researchers have proposed many advanced learning-based models, such as Gaussian mixture regression [5], hidden Markov models [6], Gaussian process [7], random tree searching [8], and dynamic Bayesian networks (DBNs) [9]. Among these learning methods, DBNs are commonly used because they simultaneously infer the joint latent dynamical state conditioned on observed data and learn the corresponding system dynamics.

With developments in deep learning, pedestrians' motion patterns are always modeled by a data-driven method, namely, recurrent neural network (RNN) [10]. Specifically, the long-short term memory (LSTM) network is used to encode pedestrians' motion patterns, and their future trajectories are generated through decoding [11]. To address the problem of social interactions, a social pooling layer is proposed to aggregate the information of surrounding people. Later, an generative adversarial network (GAN) structure is proposed to generate socially acceptable future trajectories. In addition, multi-modal is guaranteed by sampling the latent variable from a random Gaussian noise [1]. On the basis of these two baseline methods, many improvements are proposed, and a detail review is discussed in the next section. Amirian et al. [12] replaced the traditional GAN with info-GAN to alleviate the model collapse problem. Sadeghian et al. [13] proposed SoPhie, which blends a social attention mechanism with a physical attention that helps the GAN model learn where to look in a large scene and extract the most salient parts of the image relevant to the path. Kosaraju et al. [14] introduced graph attention networks into a bicycle-GAN for multi-modal trajectory forecasting. Ma et al. [15] proposed TrafficPredict that can predict the trajectories of heterogeneous traffic agents, such as vehicles, pedestrians, bicycles, etc. A 4D graph was used to model the spatio-temporal interactions between homogeneous and heterogeneous traffic agents. The graph model can better capture the social interactions between humans and their physical interactions with the scene than the pooling strategy used in SGAN.

Despite tremendous recent interest in trajectory prediction, only few works have concentrated on the latent variable which is essential for accurate trajectory prediction. Most studies have sampled the latent variable from a random Gaussian noise to accommodate future uncertainties. Certain works have sampled the latent variable from the embedding of a scene layout, which is obtained through semantic segmentation or object detection. However, such manipulation on the whole scene heavily increases the computing burden, therefore imposing restrictions on applications in edge computing equipments.

To fully utilize the latent variable with little additional overhead, we propose a novel method to learn the latent variable from the trajectory itself. The trajectory contains rich information about a scene and a pedestrian. For example, trajectory positions reflect the potential scene layout. Trajectory velocities and accelerations represent pedestrians' motion patterns and radicalness. After extracting these information from trajectories, we propose a latent variable predictor that learns how to estimate the latent variable from observed and ground truth trajectories. Specifically, the latent variable is sampled from ground truth trajectories with a feed-forward neural network in the training stage. In the testing stage, such variable is sampled from observed trajectories. A learning mechanism is used to guarantee that the latent variable sampled from observed trajectories is similar to that sampled from ground truth trajectories. The learned latent variable is beneficial to accurate trajectory prediction through comparisons with several state-of-the-art methods in benchmarking datasets. In addition, the proposed method can estimate accurate future trajectories with few attempts.

The proposed method contains an RNN encoder-decoder generator and an RNN based encoder discriminator. Our main contributions are listed as follows: (1) we propose a latent variable predictor, which bridges the gap between latent variable distributions of observed and ground truth trajectories. Multiple inputs, including positions, velocities, and accelerations, are used to train the latent variable predictor. (2) We embed the latent variable predictor into a GAN-based trajectory predictor to generate socially acceptable trajectories. (3) We achieve the state-of-the-art performance on commonly used trajectory forecasting benchmarks, including ETH [16] and UCY [17] datasets.

The rest of the paper is listed as follows. Section 2 describes the proposed method in detail. Section 3 presents the experimental results. Section 4 provides the discussion.

2   Proposed Method

In this work, we develop a model that can generate multiple future trajectories of all agents in a scene with high accuracy. Figure 1 illustrates the pipeline of the proposed model called SGAN-MLP (multi-input latent variable predictor).

2.1   Problem Definition

The trajectory prediction problem is a time-series analysis. For pedestrian i, we first denote his position (x_i^t, y_i^t) at time step t as p_i^t. The goal of trajectory prediction is to estimate his future trajectory $T_i = \left(p_i^{t+1}, \ldots, p_i^{t+T_{obs}} \right)$, considering his motion history $\mathcal{H}_i = \left(p_i^0, \ldots, p_i^t \right)$ and interactions with other pedestrians or objects. Then, the trajectory prediction problem is converted into finding a parametric model that predicts future trajectory T_i, which can be formulated as follows:

$$\arg\max_{\Theta} P_\theta \left(T_i | \mathcal{H}_0, \ldots, \mathcal{H}_n \right), \tag{1}$$

where Θ represents learnable parameters, and n represents the number of pedestrians. Recently, the above-mentioned formulation is always converted into a sequence-to-sequence prediction problem, which can be addressed by the data-driven RNN module.

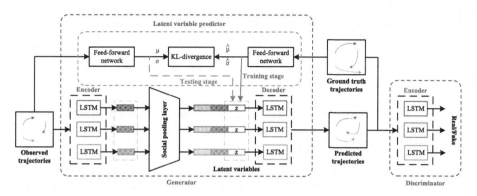

Fig. 1. System pipeline. Our model contains three key components: a generator, a discriminator, and a latent variable predictor. The generator takes input observed trajectories and encodes them. A social pooling layer is then used to aggregate information, and a latent variable is estimated by the latent variable predictor. The predicted trajectories are generated by decoding the concatenation of the trajectory embedding, social embedding, and learned latent variable. The latent variable predictor explores the correlations between observed and future trajectories at the training stage, and estimates accurate latent variables for trajectory prediction by using observed trajectories only at the testing stage. The discriminator takes the input ground truth and predicted trajectories and classifies them as socially acceptable or not (best viewed in color).

2.2   Structure of SGAN

SGAN is commonly used as the baseline model for trajectory prediction problem because of its ability in aggregating neighbors' information and generating multiple future trajectories. We briefly introduce the generator and the discriminator as follows:

Generator: The generator consists of a shared encoder-decoder and a social pooling layer used to aggregate social interactions of pedestrians in a scene. The motion history of pedestrian i is first embedded with a single layer MLP to obtain a fixed length vector e_i^t. Then, the embedding is fed into the LSTM-based encoder to generate the hidden state of pedestrian i at time t as follows:

$$e_i^t = \phi \left(x_i^t, y_i^t; W_{ee} \right)$$
$$h_{ei}^t = LSTM \left(h_{ei}^{t-1}, e_i^t; W_{encoder} \right),$$

(2)

where $\phi(\cdot)$ is a MLP function with ReLU nonlinearity. W_{ee} and $W_{encoder}$ are the learnable weights of $\phi(\cdot)$ and the encoder function $LSTM(\cdot)$, respectively.

The social pooling layer takes the input hidden states of all pedestrians in the scene, and then generates their social interactions on the basis of their velocities and relative positions. The output of the social pooling layer is denoted as P_i^t.

An LSTM-based decoder is used to predict the future trajectories of pedestrian i on the basis of the concatenation of hidden state h_{ei}^t, pooling output P_i^t, and Gaussian noise z_i^t, which is used to generate multiple outputs. The decoding is formulated as follows:

$$h_{di}^t = LSTM\left(h_{di}^{t-1}, [h_{ei}^t, P_i^t, z_i^t]; W_{\text{decoder}}\right)$$
$$(\hat{x}_i^t, \hat{y}_i^t) = \gamma\left(h_{di}^t\right) \tag{3}$$

where $\gamma(\cdot)$ is an MLP function with ReLU nonlinearity to predict future trajectories $(\hat{x}_i^t, \hat{y}_i^t)$. W_{decoder} is the learnable weight of the decoder, which is shared by all pedestrians in the scene.

Discriminator: The discriminator is used to classify input trajectories, including predicted and ground truth ones, as socially acceptable or not. The discriminator uses an LSTM-based encoder to embed input trajectories, and then perform classification with a Softmax classifier.

2.3   Latent Variable Predictor

As we discuss before, the latent variable used in generative trajectory predictors is either a random Gaussian noise or encoded scene information. The former utilizes little prior information, whereas the latter increases considerable computing overhead. We propose a novel latent variable predictor to generate an improved latent variable for accurate trajectory prediction. Latent variable distributions are learned from observed and ground truth trajectories, and their KL-divergence is minimized during training. Therefore, the latent variable learned from observed trajectories is similar to that learned from ground truth trajectories. Such latent variable is more suitable to describe future trajectories than a random Gaussian noise. Input into the latent variable predictor is trajectory itself with no scene image, thus increasing little computing overhead.

As illustrated in Fig. 1, the latent variable predictor consists of two feed-forward networks, which are formulated as follows:

$$(\mu_i^k, \sigma_i^k) = \Psi\left(T_i^k; W_{LP}^k\right)$$
$$(\hat{\mu}_i^k, \hat{\sigma}_i^k) = \hat{\Psi}\left(\hat{T}_i^k; \hat{W}_{LP}^k\right) \tag{4}$$

where $\Psi(\cdot)$ and $\hat{\Psi}(\cdot)$ are the feed-forward networks that take the observed and ground truth trajectories as input, respectively. W_{LP}^k and $\hat{W}_{LP}^k$ are the learnable weights of both networks. T_i^k and $\hat{T}_i^k$ represent the kth pattern we draw from observed and ground truth trajectories, respectively. In this work, we use three patterns, which represent positions, velocities, and accelerations of each trajectory. Velocities reflect the motion patterns of different pedestrians and thus are commonly used in trajectory prediction tasks. In addition, positions reveal the potential scene layout, and accelerations indicate pedestrians' radicalness. (μ_i^k, σ_i^k) and $(\hat{\mu}_i^k, \hat{\sigma}_i^k)$ are the distributions of the kth pattern estimated by $\Psi(\cdot)$ and $\hat{\Psi}(\cdot)$, respectively. Finally, the latent variable is generated by concatenating the estimated distributions with the random Gaussian noise, which is used to handle future uncertainties. In the training stage, estimated distributions

$\left(\hat{\mu}_i^k, \hat{\sigma}_i^k\right)$ are used, and $\left(\mu_i^k, \sigma_i^k\right)$ are used in the testing stage. We expect that the latent variable predictor can estimate similar distributions from observed and ground truth trajectories after training.

2.4 Loss Function

In this work, the loss function contains three parts, namely, adversarial, variety, and latent distribution losses. The training procedure of GAN is similar to a two-player min-max game with the following objective function:

$$\min_G \max_D V(G, D) = \\ \mathbb{E}_{x \sim p_{\text{data}}(x)}[\log D(x)] + \mathbb{E}_{z \sim p_{(z)}}[\log(1 - D(G(z)))] \tag{5}$$

The latent variable z is learned from the trajectory in the training stage with the proposed latent variable predictor. Thus, the adversarial loss is reformulated as follows:

$$\mathcal{L}_{adv} = \\ \mathbb{E}_{x \sim p_{\text{data}}(x)}[\log D(x)] + \mathbb{E}_{z \sim p_{(z|\mathcal{T}_i, \mathcal{H}_i)}}[\log(1 - D(G(z|\mathcal{T}_i, \mathcal{H}_i)))] \tag{6}$$

The variety loss is defined as that in SGAN as follows: for each pedestrian, the model predicts multiple trajectories by randomly sampling the stochastic part in the latent variable from a random Gaussian noise. Then, the L2 loss between the ground truth and the best predicted trajectory (closest to the ground truth) is calculated as follows:

$$\mathcal{L}_{\text{variety}} = \min_m \left\| \hat{\mathcal{T}}_i - \mathcal{T}_i^m \right\|_2, \tag{7}$$

where $\hat{\mathcal{T}}_i$ and $\mathcal{T}_i^m$ are ground truth and predicted trajectories, respectively. m is a hyper-parameter and is set to 20 in this work.

The latent distribution loss is calculated by the KL-divergence between the distributions estimated by the two feed-forward networks in the latent variable predictor. The loss is formulated as follows:

$$\mathcal{L}_{\text{LD}} = D_{KL}((\mu_i^k, \sigma_i^k) \,\|\, (\hat{\mu}_i^k, \hat{\sigma}_i^k)), \tag{8}$$

The total loss is formulated in a weighted manner as follows:

$$\mathcal{L}_{\text{total}} = \mathcal{L}_{adv} + \alpha \times \mathcal{L}_{\text{variety}} + \beta \times \mathcal{L}_{\text{LD}}, \tag{9}$$

where α is set to 1 following SGAN, and β is set to 10 by cross validation across different benchmarking datasets.

2.5 Implementation Details

The dimensions of the hidden states for encoder and decoder are 32. For the latent variable predictor, positions, velocities, and accelerations are embedded as three two-dimensional vectors and then are concatenated together, with a two-dimensional random Gaussian noise. We iteratively train the generator and discriminator with a batch size of 64 for 600 epochs using Adam [18], with the initial learning rate of 0.001.

3   Experimental Results

The proposed method is evaluated on two publicly available datasets, namely ETH [16] and UCY [17]. Both of them contain real world pedestrian trajectories with rich human-human and human-object interaction scenarios. Following the setting used in Social-LSTM, all the trajectory data are converted to real world coordinates, which are sampled every 0.4 s through the interpolation operation. In total there are 5 sets of data, namely ETH, HOTEL, UNIV, ZARA1, and ZARA2 which consists of 1,536 pedestrians in challenging scenarios such as people crossing each other, groups forming and dispersing, and collision avoidance.

Similar to most of the prior works [1,12], we evaluate the proposed method with two error metrics as follows:

1. *Average Displacement Error (ADE)*: Average L2 distance between the ground truth trajectory and the predicted trajectory over all predicted time steps.
2. *Final Displacement Error (FDE)*: The Euclidean distance between the true final destination and the predicted final destination at the last step of prediction.

We follow the similar evaluation methodology as that proposed in Social-LSTM. We use the leave-one-out approach, more specifically, we train models on 4 sets and test them on the remaining set. We observe the trajectory for 8 time steps (3.2 s) and show prediction results for 8 (3.2 s) and 12 (4.8 s) time steps. We use T to denote the prediction horizon.

3.1   Quantitative Evaluations

We compare the proposed method against the following methods. The first three are commonly used baselines, and the latter three are state-of-the-art approaches. For generative model based methods, 20 times are sampled from the generator at test time and the best prediction in L2 sense is used for quantitative evaluation.

1. *Linear*: A linear regressor is used to estimate linear parameters through minimizing the least square error.
2. *LSTM*: A simple LSTM is used to learn the motion characteristics of observed trajectories. Future trajectories are estimated on the basis of the learned motion patterns. Social interactions among pedestrians are not considered.
3. *SGAN*: Future trajectories are predicted by a generator, which is jointly trained with a discriminator through adversarial learning. Gaussian noises are used in hidden states to generate multiple outputs in consideration of pedestrians' future uncertainties.
4. *SR-LSTM* [19]: A data-driven state refinement module is proposed for LSTM, which activates the utilization of the current intention of neighbors, and jointly and iteratively refines the current states of pedestrians in the scene through message passing.

5. *Sophie* [13]: Social and physical attention modules are added into the SGAN framework for improved trajectory prediction performance.
6. *Social-BiGAT* [14]: The bicycle-GAN is used to train the generator used for trajectory prediction, and social interactions are modeled by a graph attention network.

Table 1. Quantitative results between the proposed method and the above mentioned methods across five datasets. We report ADE and FDE for $T = 12$ in meters. Our method outperforms others and is specifically good for long-term predictions (low is preferred and is labeled with bold fonts).

Metric	Dataset	Linear	LSTM	SGAN	Sophie	Social-BiGAT	SR-LSTM	Ours
ADE	ETH	1.33	1.09	0.87	0.70	0.69	**0.63**	0.67
	HOTEL	0.39	0.86	0.67	0.70	0.49	**0.37**	0.44
	UNIV	0.82	0.61	0.76	0.54	0.55	0.51	**0.45**
	ZARA1	0.62	0.41	0.35	0.30	0.30	0.41	**0.24**
	ZARA2	0.77	0.52	0.42	0.38	0.36	0.32	**0.21**
AVG			0.79	0.70	0.61	0.54	0.48	0.45	**0.40**
FDE	ETH	2.94	2.41	1.62	1.43	1.29	1.25	**1.13**
	HOTEL	**0.72**	1.91	1.37	1.67	1.01	0.74	0.91
	UNIV	1.59	1.31	1.52	1.24	1.32	1.10	**0.69**
	ZARA1	1.21	0.88	0.68	0.63	0.62	0.90	**0.42**
	ZARA2	1.48	1.11	0.84	0.78	0.75	0.70	**0.36**
AVG			1.59	1.52	1.21	1.15	1.00	0.94	**0.70**

Table 1 demonstrates the quantitative results between the proposed method and the above mentioned methods across five datasets. SGAN-MLP almost outperforms all baseline methods in ADE and FDE. The superiority of our method to SGAN in accurate trajectory prediction indicates the effectiveness of the proposed latent variable predictor. In addition, our method outperforms the state-of-the-art methods in UNIV, ZARA1, and ZARA2 datasets. SR-LSTM performs better than our method in ETH and HOTEL datasets by using refinement mechanism. Attention mechanisms are employed in Sophie and Social-BiGAT, but the results they report are inferior to that of ours. Moreover, gaps are still observed in terms of average ADE and FDE between ours and state-of-the-art methods. Such comparisons indicate that our method can benefit from the learned prior information from multiple inputs, namely, positions, velocities, and accelerations.

3.2 Qualitative Evaluations

Benefiting from the proposed latent variable predictor, SGAN-MLP can learn contextual environments, pedestrians' motions, and radicalness from the trajectory itself. Thus, SGAN-MLP can perform accurate trajectory prediction.

Figure 2 illustrates the trajectory prediction results by using SGAN, SGAN-LP, and SGAN-MLP in different datasets. SGAN-LP represents that the latent variable is learned from a single input, namely, the velocity. Each sub-figure represents a scene with multiple pedestrians. For each pedestrian, the predicted trajectory is the best one that has the lowest ADE value among the 20 samples generated by each method. In Figs. 2(a) and 2(d), SGAN-MLP successfully forecasts the sudden motion changes whereas two other methods generate future trajectories far away from the ground truth. In Fig. 2(b), SGAN-MLP recognizes the still pedestrians, whereas SGAN and SGAN-LP take them as moving pedestrians. In Fig. 2(c), SGAN-MLP outperforms others by closely predicting future trajectory to ground truth for the nethermost pedestrian.

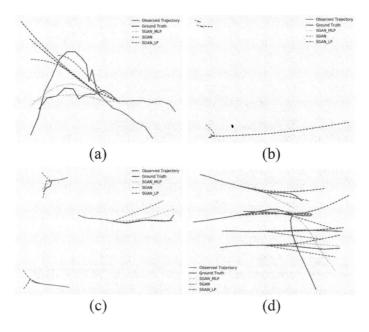

Fig. 2. Path prediction results using SGAN, SGAN-LP, and SGAN-MLP in (a) ETH, (b) HOTEL, (c) ZARA1, and (d) ZARA2 datasets. Red and blue lines represent observed and ground truth trajectories, respectively. Green, purple, and orange dashed lines represent estimated trajectories of SGAN, SGAN-LP, and SGAN-MLP, respectively. We show the best trajectory with the lowest ADE value from 20 predicted samples (best viewed in color and zoom-in).

As mentioned above, SGAN-MLP can predict accurate future trajectories with the proposed latent variable predictor and can still maintain diverse outputs due to the random Gaussian noise used in the predicted latent variable. Figure 3 demonstrates the density maps of trajectory prediction results in ZARA1 dataset. The upper and lower parts represent the results generated

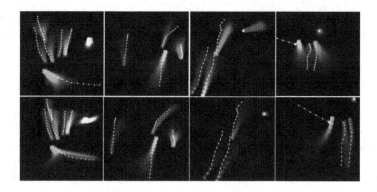

Fig. 3. Density maps of trajectory prediction results in ZARA1 dataset. The upper and lower parts represent the results generated using SGAN and SGAN-MLP respectively. The density maps are generated by sampling 300 times of the learned generators. The white stars represent the ground truth future trajectories, and different colors indicate the density distributions of different pedestrians (best viewed in color).

using SGAN and SGAN-MLP, respectively. As revealed by the blue density distribution in the first scene, SGAN-MLP can generate accurate output while maintaining the diversity. Both methods fail in the last scene due to sudden motion changes, which are difficult to predict even when using the proposed predictor.

3.3   Comparison with SGAN

The proposed SGAN-MLP can be termed as an improved SGAN by incorporating a latent variable predictor into the generator. Table 1 demonstrates the

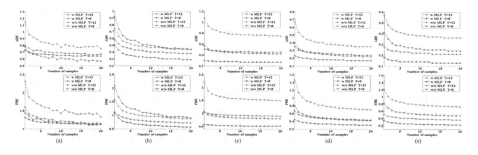

Fig. 4. Comparison results of ADE and FDE values between our method and SGAN when using different numbers of samples across (a) ETH, (b) HOTEL, (c) UNIV, (d) ZARA1, and (e) ZARA2 datasets. The upper and lower parts are comparison results of ADE and FDE, respectively. The star marker represents the proposed method (w MLP), and the diamond marker represents SGAN (w/o MLP). The red and blue lines (including the dashed) represent the prediction results for $T = 12$ and $T = 8$ in meters, respectively (best viewed in color and zoom-in.)

superiority of SGAN-MLP in accurate trajectory prediction. Another advantage of SGAN-MLP is the ability of accurate trajectory prediction with few attempts, specifically, few sampling times during test. Figure 4 illustrates the comparison results of ADE and FDE between SGAN-MLP and SGAN when using different numbers of samples across five datasets. Except the ADE and FDE for $T = 12$ in the HOTEL dataset, SGAN-MLP greatly outperforms SGAN, especially with few sampling times. We can observe that ADE and FDE values of SGAN-MLP gently increase while decreasing sampling times. However, those of SGAN drastically increase when the number of samples is close to 1. The difference indicates the power of SGAN-MLP in predicting accurate future trajectories with few attempts. Therefore, SGAN-MLP has learned useful information from observed and ground truth trajectories.

4   Conclusion and Discussion

In this work, we design a novel latent variable predictor by using two simple feed-forward neural networks, which can be easily embedded into generative model-based future trajectory generators. We use SGAN as our base model and propose SGAN-MLP, in which latent variables are learned from multiple inputs of trajectories, including positions, velocities, accelerations, and a random Gaussian noise. The first three inputs are used to encode information, such as contextual environments, pedestrians' motions, and radicalness. The random Gaussian noise is employed to handle trajectory multi-modalities. Evaluations are performed in two commonly used metrics, namely, ADE and FDE, across five benchmarking datasets. Comparisons with baseline methods and state-of-the-art approaches indicate the effectiveness of the proposed latent variable predictor. Ablation studies reveal the necessity of learning information from multiple inputs and the superiority of accurate trajectory prediction with few sampling times. In addition, the proposed method only learns knowledge from trajectories, and thus avoid the usage of whole scenes, which demands additional computing expense.

References

1. Gupta, A., Johnson, J., Fei-Fei, L., Savarese, S., Alahi, A.: Social GAN: socially acceptable trajectories with generative adversarial networks. In: 2018 IEEE/CVF Conference on Computer Vision and Pattern Recognition, pp. 2255–2264. IEEE, Salt Lake City (2018). https://doi.org/10.1109/CVPR.2018.00240
2. Zernetsch, S., Kohnen, S., Goldhammer, M., Doll, K., Sick, B.: Trajectory prediction of cyclists using a physical model and an artificial neural network. In: 2016 IEEE Intelligent Vehicles Symposium (IV), pp. 833–838 IEEE (2016)
3. Helbing, D., Molnar, P.: Social force model for pedestrian dynamics. Phys. Rev. E **51**(5), 4282 (1995)
4. Yi, S., Li, H., Wang, X.: Understanding pedestrian behaviors from stationary crowd groups. In: 2015 IEEE Conference on Computer Vision and Pattern Recognition (CVPR), pp. 3488–3496. IEEE, Boston (2015). https://doi.org/10.1109/CVPR.2015.7298971

5. Li, J., Zhan, W., Tomizuka, M.: Generic vehicle tracking framework capable of handling occlusions based on modified mixture particle filter. In: 2018 IEEE Intelligent Vehicles Symposium (IV), pp. 936–942 IEEE Suzhou (2018). https://doi.org/10.1109/IVS.2018.8500626
6. Wang, W., Xi, J., Zhao, D.: Learning and inferring a driver's braking action in car-following scenarios. IEEE Trans. Veh. Technol. **67**(5), 3887–3899 (2018)
7. Laugier, C., et al.: Probabilistic analysis of dynamic scenes and collision risks assessment to improve driving safety. IEEE Intell. Transp. Syst. Mag. **3**(4), 4–19 (2011)
8. Aoude, G., Joseph, J., Roy, N., How, J.: Mobile agent trajectory prediction using Bayesian nonparametric reachability trees. In: AIAA Infotech Aerospace Conference 2011, p. 1512 (2011)
9. Kasper, D., et al.: Object-oriented Bayesian networks for detection of lane change maneuvers. IEEE Intell. Transp. Syst. Mag. **4**(3), 19–31 (2012)
10. Lee, N., Choi, W., Vernaza, P., Choy, C.B., Torr, P.H., Chandraker, M.: Desire: distant future prediction in dynamic scenes with interacting agents. In: Proceedings of the IEEE Conference on Computer Vision and Pattern Recognition, pp. 336–345 (2017)
11. Alahi, A., Goel, K., Ramanathan, V., Robicquet, A., Fei-Fei, L., Savarese, S.: Social LSTM: human trajectory prediction in crowded spaces. In: Proceedings of the IEEE Conference on Computer Vision and Pattern Recognition, pp. 961–971 (2016)
12. Amirian, J., Hayet, J.-B., Pettré, J.: Social ways: learning multi-modal distributions of pedestrian trajectories with GANs. In: Proceedings of the IEEE Conference on Computer Vision and Pattern Recognition Workshops (2019)
13. Sadeghian, A., Kosaraju, A., Sadeghian, A., Hirose, N., Rezatofighi, H., Savarese, S.: Sophie: an attentive GAN for predicting paths compliant to social and physical constraints. In: Proceedings of the IEEE Conference on Computer Vision and Pattern Recognition, pp. 1349–1358 (2019)
14. Kosaraju, V., Sadeghian, A., Martín-Martín, R., Reid, I., Rezatofighi, H., Savarese, S.: Social-BiGAT: multimodal trajectory forecasting using bicycle-GAN and graph attention networks. In: Advances in Neural Information Processing Systems, pp. 137–146 (2019)
15. Ma, Y., Zhu, X., Zhang, S., Yang, R., Wang, W., Manocha, D.: TrafficPredict: trajectory prediction for heterogeneous traffic-agents. In: Proceedings of the AAAI Conference on Artificial Intelligence, pp. 6120–6127 (2019). https://doi.org/10.1609/aaai.v33i01.33016120
16. Pellegrini, S., Ess, A., Van Gool, L.: Improving data association by joint modeling of pedestrian trajectories and groupings. In: Daniilidis, K., Maragos, P., Paragios, N. (eds.) ECCV 2010. LNCS, vol. 6311, pp. 452–465. Springer, Heidelberg (2010). https://doi.org/10.1007/978-3-642-15549-9_33
17. Leal-Taixé, L., Fenzi, M., Kuznetsova, A., Rosenhahn, B., Savarese, S.: Learning an image-based motion context for multiple people tracking. In: Proceedings of the IEEE Conference on Computer Vision and Pattern Recognition, pp. 3542–3549 (2014)
18. Kingma, D.P., Ba, J.: Adam: a method for stochastic optimization (2014). arXiv:1412.6980
19. Zhang, P., Ouyang, W., Zhang, P., Xue, J., Zheng, N.: SR-LSTM: state refinement for LSTM towards pedestrian trajectory prediction. In: 2019 IEEE/CVF Conference on Computer Vision and Pattern Recognition (CVPR), pp. 12085–12094. IEEE Long Beach (2019). https://doi.org/10.1109/CVPR.2019.01236

Top-Down Fusing Multi-level Contextual Features for Salient Object Detection

Mingyuan Pan, Huihui Song[✉], Junxia Li, Kaihua Zhang, and Qingshan Liu

Jiangsu Key Laboratory of Big Data Analysis Technology (B-DAT) and Jiangsu Collaborative Innovation Center on Atmospheric Environment and Equipment Technology (CICAEET), Nanjing University of Information Science and Technology, Nanjing 210044, China
songhuihui@nuist.edu.cn

Abstract. Recently, benefiting from the fast development of deep convolutional neural networks, salient object detection (SOD) has achieved gratifying performance in a variety of challenging scenarios. Among them, how to learn more discriminative features plays a key role. In this paper, we propose a novel network architecture that progressively fuses the rich multi-level contextual features from top to bottom to learn a more effective feature presentation for robust SOD. Concretely, we first design a multi-receptive field block (MRFB) to capture multi-scale contextual information. Then, we develop a feature fusion block that progressively fuses different outputs of MRFBs from top to bottom, which can effectively filter out the non-complementary parts of the high-level and low-level features. Afterwards, we leverage a refinement residual block to refine the results further. Finally, we leverage an edge-aware loss as an aid to guide the network to learn more sharpen details of the salient objects. The whole network is trained end-to-end without any pre-processing and post-processing. Exhaustive evaluations on six benchmark datasets demonstrate superiority of the proposed method against state-of-the-arts in terms of all metrics.

Keywords: Salient object detection · Deep learning · Multi-scale fusion · Boundary information

1 Introduction

Given an image, salient object detection (SOD) aims to detect the most visually distinctive objects or regions in it, which has attracted wide attention recently.

M. Pan—He is currently working towards the Master degree.

H. Song—This work is supported in part by National Major Project of China for New Generation of AI (No. 2018AAA0100400), in part by the Natural Science Foundation of China under Grant nos. 61872189, 61876088, 61702272, in part by the Natural Science Foundation of Jiangsu Province under Grant nos. BK20191397, BK20170040, in part by Six talent peaks project in Jiangsu Province under Grant nos. XYDXX-015, XYDXX-045, in part by the 333 High-level Talents Cultivation Project of Jiangsu Province under Grant nos. BRA2020291.

© Springer Nature Switzerland AG 2020
Y. Peng et al. (Eds.): PRCV 2020, LNCS 12307, pp. 54–65, 2020.
https://doi.org/10.1007/978-3-030-60636-7_5

SOD is a fundamental problem in computer vision, and serves as an effective pre-processing step for a variety of computer vision tasks, including semantic segmentation [6], object detection [35], visual tracking [12,16], video SOD [8,30], to name a few.

The traditional SOD methods utilize hand-crafted features (e.g, color, texture, and contrast) or heuristic priors [3,37,42] that are incapable of capturing high-level semantic and context information, leading to an unsatisfying prediction. Luckily, fully CNNs [27] greatly promote the performance of SOD models because their learned features have a strong semantical and spatial preservation capability. However, a series of convolutional and pooling layers cause the low-resolution of image, leading to the loss of fine structures.

There is evidence that integrating multi-level features plays a crucial role in SOD according to some previous works [13,38]. Multi-scale fusion mechanisms can enhance communication of hierarchical deep features and spatial details, where skip-connections [34], short-connections [13] and feature aggregations [38] are three main strategies. Specifically, the top deeper layers contain global contextual knowledge and are capable of locating the salient objects, while the bottom shallower layers often capture spatial details to sharpen object boundaries. Despite being studied actively, how to effectively fuse multi-level features to learn more discriminative feature representation remains a huge challenge for SOD. Moreover, the salient object edge information is still not explicitly modeled. Some existing methods [5,13,14,20] use pre-processing or post-processing to preserve object boundaries, which are time-consuming and unsatisfactory.

To address above issues, we propose a novel network architecture that effectively fuses Multi-level Contextual Features from top to bottom for SOD. The network is termed as MCFNet, which can achieve accurate and sharpened SOD results. First, motivated by receptive field block (RFB) applied to object detection [21], we design an effective module named multi-receptive field block (MRFB) to capture multi-scale information. MRFB is a multi-branch structure that can reinforce the feature representation extracted by the backbone network. Second, we design a feature fusion block (FFB) to effectively and efficiently fuse features of different stages step by step which can remove background noises from low-level layers and solve the problem of coarse boundaries from high-level layers to some extent. It has the ability to combine the advantages of high-level features and low-level features, which complements each other. Afterwards, we leverage a refinement residual block (RRB) to further optimize its results. The widely-used binary cross-entropy loss for SOD treats all pixels equally. However, pixels at the boundary are more important and should be assigned with larger weights. Therefore, we use the edge detection operator Laplace [41] to construct an edge-aware loss that guides the network to learn more edge information without any time-consuming post-processing. In this way, the network can produce saliency maps with sharpen boundaries. Extensive experiments on six popular SOD datasets have demonstrated favorable performance of the proposed method over state-of-the-arts.

Our main contributions are summarized as follows:

- We present a novel MCFNet that has three novel block designs, i.e., MRFB, FFB and RRB, to produce accurate and sharpened saliency maps for SOD.
- We design an edge-aware loss that can effectively guide the network to learn more sharpened details of the salient objects.
- The proposed MCFNet has achieved state-of-the-art performance on six widely-used benchmark datasets.

2   Our Method

In this section, we detail architecture of the proposed framework for SOD as illustrated in Fig. 1, which composes of MRFM, FFM and RRM. Each of the three modules contains five blocks. The MRFM is an effective context module inspired by the RFB [21], which can capture rich contextual information. The FFM can effectively and efficiently fuse different outputs of the MRFBs step by step. The RRM is designed to refine the results further. And we use the edge detection operator Laplace as an aid to guide network to focus more on boundary information. In the following, we will describe these in detail.

2.1   Overview of Network Architecture

We firstly use ResNeXt-101 [33] to extract features. Then these feature maps from different layers go through corresponding MRFBs. After that, features with rich contextual information from different layers are fused progressively by a series of FFBs. It should be noted that the features from the last convolutional layers in feature extraction network go through the ASSP module proposed in [1] to encode global context as a guide and it fuses the corresponding MRFB's output through FFBs. Finally, the feature maps of FFBs go through the RRBs which are inspired by ResNet [10,11] and each of RRBs' output is as the previous FFB's one input. The last RRB's output through 3×3 convolutional layers is our final saliency map. For every stage, we use loss function to supervise learning.

2.2   Multi-receptive Field Module

Visual context is crucial to SOD. Most CNN models stack multiple convolutional and pooling layers to get discriminative feature representation. However, under these circumstances that the salient objects vary greatly in size, shape and location, these methods mostly cannot work very well. Motivated by the RFB applied to object detection [21], we design the MRFM, which composes of five MRFBs as shown in Fig. 2. It can enhance the discriminability and robustness of features. We elaborate the architecture of it in the following.

To be more specific, compared to the original RFB, we add two more branches to get more contextual information. Our MRFB composes of five branches $\{b_m, m = 1, \ldots, 5\}$. In each branch, we use a 1×1 convolutional layer to reduce channel number for acceleration. For $\{b_m, 1 < m < 5\}$, we add two

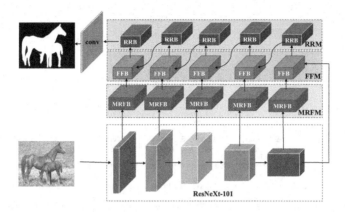

Fig. 1. Pipeline of our MCFNet. The MRFM, FFM and RRM are composed of 5 MRFBs, FFBs and RRBs, respectively.

layers: one 3×3 convolutional layer and one 3×3 convolutional layer with $(2m - 3) \times (2m - 3)$ dilation. For b_5, we use a larger kernel 5×5 and set the dilated rate to 7. Then, we concatenate the outputs of five branches and a 3×3 convolutional layer is followed. In addition, a shortcut layer is added by a 1×1 convolutional layer, which can maintain the performance of previous layer. Finally, we obtain the discriminative and robust feature representation through the ReLU activation function.

2.3 Feature Fusion Module

Using MRFBs enhances the feature discriminability and robustness of different stages from the feature extraction network. However, how to effectively merge different level features is also a challenging problem. In some previous works, they just concatenate high-level and low-level features progressively after going through the convolution layers. This is very rough. To this end, we put forward FFB that is illustrated in Fig. 3.

We represent the enhanced features of each stage as $f_i \in \mathbb{R}^{W \times H \times C}$, $i = 1, \ldots, 5$. First, we concatenate high-level features and low-level features directly. Then, we use average pooling layers with downsampling rate 2 and further use the upsampling operation to recover the size same as the original. The outputs of it go through one 1×1 convolutional layer to reduce channel number to an half. In addition, we directly multiply the corresponding position values of the output of one 1×1 convolutional layer and low-level features. Finally, we add the high-level features and the last operation output to enhance the merged features representation. This operation can be formulated as

$$f_i = f_{low} \odot \text{Conv}[\text{Avgpool}(\text{Concate}(f_{low}, f_{high}))] + f_{high}, i \in [1, \ldots, 5] \quad (1)$$

where $\odot$ is element-wise multiplication, Conv$(.)$ is the operation including two 1×1 convolutional layers and upsampling layer, Avgpool is an average pooling

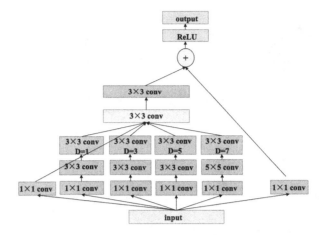

Fig. 2. Architecture of MRFB.

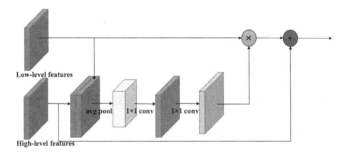

Fig. 3. Architecture of FFB. $\otimes$ and $\oplus$ mean element-wise multiplication and addition.

layer and Concate is concatenation operation. Besides, f_{low} denotes low-level features and f_{high} denotes high-level features.

2.4 Refinement Residual Module

Inspired by the architecture of ResNet [10,11], we design the RRB to enhance the recognition ability of each stage to get better results, which is depicted in Fig. 4. First, we use a 1×1 convolution to reduce channel number to an half. Then a basic residual block is applied, which can refine the feature map. Finally, we can get more discriminative features to guide network learning step by step.

2.5 Loss Function

We apply the Laplace operator together with the classification cross-entropy loss to get sharpened and refined boundaries. The classification cross-entropy loss is defined as:

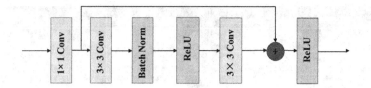

Fig. 4. Architecture of the RRB.

$$L_c^n = -\sum_{(x,y)} [G^n(x,y)\log(S^n(x,y)) + (1 - G^n(x,y))\log(1 - S^n(x,y))] \quad (2)$$

where $n = 1, \ldots, 5$ denotes different stages, L_c^n denotes the value of classification cross-entropy loss in n-th stage, $S(x,y)$ is the predicted saliency map and $G(x,y)$ is the ground-truth label. However, the boundaries of the saliency maps generated under this loss function are not well-defined. To this end, we apply the Laplace operator to get boundary-aware results. This operation is defined as follows

$$f_{laplace} = relu(tanh(conv(P))) \quad (3)$$

where P denotes an image input, $conv(.)$ remarks the Laplace edge detection operator, $tanh(\cdot)$ represents the tanh activation function and $relu(\cdot)$ denotes the ReLU activation function. Given the saliency map S and the corresponding mask G, let L_{edge}^n denote the loss to supervise the generation of salient object boundaries defined as

$$
\begin{aligned}
L_{edge}^n = -\sum_{(x,y)} &[f_{laplace}(G^n(x,y))\log(f_{laplace}(S^n(x,y))) \\
&+ (1 - f_{laplace}(G^n(x,y)))\log(1 - f_{laplace}(S^n(x,y)))]
\end{aligned}
\quad (4)
$$

Finally, the total loss function is defined as

$$L = \sum_{n=1}^{5} \beta L_c^n + (1 - \beta)L_{edge}^n \quad (5)$$

where $\beta = 0.7$ is a balance parameter that balances the cross-entropy and the edge detection loss.

3 Experiments

Implementation Details. The proposed MCFNet is implemented based on PyTorch 1.0.1 framework and a GeForce GTX 2080Ti GPU is used for acceleration. We train our model on the training set of DUTS [25] dataset, which contains $10,553$ images selected from the ImageNet DET train/val set [4]. All

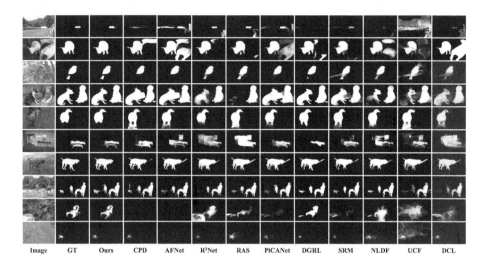

Fig. 5. Qualitative comparison of the proposed method with other ten methods.

the experiments are conducted using the Adam optimizer [15]. The batch size is set to 10 and the initial learning rate is set as 10^{-4} which is divided by 10 when training loss reaches convergence. The parameters of the feature extraction network are initialized by the pre-trained ResNeXt network on ImageNet [33], while the other convolutional layers are randomly initialized. All training and test images are resized to 352×352. In order to alleviate the over-fitting problem, we utilize simple random horizontal flipping for data augmentation during the training.

Datasets and Evaluation Metrics. We evaluate our model on six widely used benchmark datasets, including ECSSD [36], HKU-IS [17], PASCAL-S [19], SOD [23], DUT-OMRON [37] and DUTS [25]. Then, we compare the proposed method with 16 state-of-the-arts in terms of three metrics including maximum F-measure (F_β), mean absolute error (MAE) and structure measure (S_m) [7].

3.1 Comparisons to State-of-the-Arts

We compare our MCFNet with other 16 state-of-the-art deep SOD methods in recent three years, including DCL [18], RFCN [26], DSS [13], NLDF [22], UCF [39], Amulet [38], SRM [28], DGRL [29], PiCANet [20], RAS [2], R^3net [5], PAGR [40], PAGENet [31], CPD [32], AFNet [9] and BASNet [24]. For fair comparison, we directly evaluate saliency maps provided by authors or run their released models under the same settings.

Quantitative Evaluation. As listed by Table 1, our method achieves excellent performance in terms of three evaluation metrics compared with other 16 state-of-the-arts. In particular, our method has a significant performance improvement compared to the other methods for DUT-TE (2.2% gain in terms of

Table 1. Comparisons of our method and other 16 methods on six benchmark datasets, where red, green and blue indicate the best, second best and third best performance, respectively.

Datasets	ECSSD			DUT-OMRON			PASCAL-S			HKU-IS			DUTS-TE			SOD		
Metircs	F_β^{max}	S_m	MAE	F_β^{max}	S_m	MAE	F_β^{max}	S_m	MAE	F_β^{max}	S_m	MAE	F_β^{max}	S_m	MAE	F_β^{max}	S_m	MAE
DCL [18]	.896	.868	.080	.733	.771	.094	.805	.796	.115	.893	.877	.063	.786	.796	.081	.831	.747	.131
RFCN [26]	.898	.860	.097	.742	.774	.095	.837	.808	.118	.892	.858	.079	.784	.792	.091	.805	.732	.161
DSS [13]	.906	.882	.064	.760	.790	.074	.821	.798	.101	.900	.879	.050	.813	.824	.065	.834	.751	.125
NLDF [22]	.903	.875	.065	.753	.770	.079	.795	.822	.098	.902	.879	.048	.815	.816	.065	.837	.759	.125
UCF [39]	.908	.883	.069	.735	.760	.120	.820	.805	.115	.874	.888	.062	.771	.782	.116	.798	.753	.164
Amulet [38]	.915	.894	.059	.737	.780	.098	.837	.818	.098	.895	.886	.052	.778	.803	.085	.799	.757	.146
SRM [28]	.916	.895	.056	.769	.798	.069	.838	.834	.084	.906	.887	.046	.826	.836	.058	.840	.741	.126
DGRL [29]	.921	.906	.043	.774	.810	.062	.844	.839	.072	.910	.897	.036	.828	.842	.049	.843	.771	.103
PiCANet [20]	.931	.914	.047	.794	.826	.068	.868	.850	.077	.921	.906	.042	.851	.861	.054	.855	.789	.108
RAS [2]	.921	.893	.056	.786	.814	.062	.837	.795	.104	.913	.887	.045	.831	.839	.060	.810	.764	.124
R^3net [5]	.935	.906	.040	.805	.817	.063	.845	.803	.100	.916	.893	.036	.827	.836	.066	.847	.761	.124
PAGR [40]	.924	.889	.064	.771	.775	.071	.847	.749	.089	.919	.887	.047	.855	.838	.053	.838	.720	.145
PAGENet [31]	.931	.912	.042	.791	.825	.062	.848	.841	.076	.918	.903	.037	.838	.858	.051	.837	.775	.110
CPD [32]	.939	.918	.037	.797	.825	.056	.864	.848	.072	.925	.906	.034	.865	.872	.043	.857	.771	.110
AFNet [9]	.935	.914	.042	.797	.826	.057	.868	.850	.071	.923	.905	.036	.862	.866	.046	-	-	-
BASNet [24]	.942	.916	.037	.805	.836	.056	.854	.838	.076	.928	.909	.032	.860	.869	.047	.851	.772	.114
Ours	.943	.919	.040	.813	.838	.054	.870	.857	.068	.933	.914	.033	.882	.885	.041	.871	.796	.099

maximum F-measure) and SOD (2% gain in terms of maximum F-measure) datasets, which possess complex scenes that make them very challenging. We can observe that our approach improves structure measure S_m by a gain of $0.3\%, 0.2\%, 1.9\%, 0.5\%, 1.6\%, 2.4\%$ on ECSSD, DUT-OMRON, PASCAL-S, HKU-IS, DUTS-TE and SOD datasets, respectively.

Qualitative Evaluation. Figure 5 illustrates visual comparison results of our method against other state-of-the-arts. We can observe that our results are very close to the ground-truths. For the first and the last samples, in which the salient object of each image is very small, our method still performs very well while the other counterparts suffer from background interferences or lack the enough semantic information. For the next-to-last sample, in which the color of the salient object is close to the background, our model achieves the best result among all methods. For the eighth sample, it could localize and segment multiple salient objects accurately. In conclusion, our MCFNet performs well in challenging scenarios, e.g., for low contrast between object and background (e.g., first, ninth and last rows), small salient object (first and last rows), and multiple salient objects (eighth row). Simultaneously, our approach can maintain salient objects' sharpened boundaries to a certain degree due to its use of edge information without any post-processing.

3.2   Ablation Studies

In this subsection, we conduct ablation studies on PASCAL-S and DUTS-TE datasets to investigate the effectiveness of different modules, including MRFM, FFM and RRM. Table 2 lists the results in terms of maximum F-measure (F_β), mean absolute error (MAE) and structure measure (S_m). First, without MRFM,

Table 2. Ablative studies of the proposed modules on two datasets. The best statistic results are highlighted in red.

No.	Modules				PASCAL-S			DUTS-TE		
	MRFM	FFM	RRM	Edgeloss	F_β^{max}	S_m	MAE	F_β^{max}	S_m	MAE
1		✓	✓	✓	0.861	0.849	0.073	0.871	0.874	0.046
2	✓		✓	✓	0.858	0.850	0.070	0.879	0.881	0.041
3	✓	✓		✓	0.865	0.851	0.071	0.875	0.879	0.042
4	✓	✓	✓		0.858	0.849	0.072	0.873	0.878	0.043
5	✓	✓	✓	✓	0.870	0.857	0.068	0.882	0.885	0.041

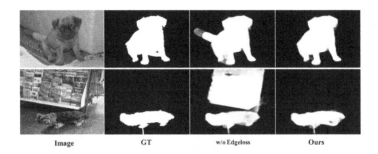

Fig. 6. Visual comparison results with and without the edgeloss. w/o Edgeloss means only using the classification entropy loss function.

the performance of the proposed model significantly drops in terms of three metrics on two datasets. Especially on DUTS-TE, F_β^{max} and S_m drop from 0.882 to 0.871 by 1.1%, from 0.885 to 0.874 by 1.1%, and MAE increase from 0.041 to 0.046 by 0.5%. It demonstrates the importance of the visual context. Then, without FFM, our model suffers from performance drop. Specifically, F_β^{max} and S_m on PASCAL-S are reduced from 0.870 to 0.858 by 1.2%, from 0.857 to 0.850 by 0.7% respectively. It proves that the proposed high-level and low-level features fusion strategy is effective to saliency detection. Furthermore, in absence of RRM, we can observe that RRM could improve the results in three evaluation indicators, showing the effectiveness of the RRBs. The RRM enables our network to enhance the feature representation further, which is also significant to improve the results.

Finally, we compare our loss function with the common binary cross entropy. We give some visual comparison results in Fig. 6. From Fig. 6, we can see that the proposed edge detection loss can sharpen salient object boundaries and thus result in accurate and refined results. Therefore, we can observe that using the edge detection loss as supervision can boost the performance on PASCAL-S and DUTS-TE datasets in terms of three metrics as listed in Table 2 (see the 4nd row and 5th row). These experiments further verify that the edge detection loss is helpful for SOD.

4 Conclusion

In this paper, we have proposed a novel MCFNet for SOD. The MCFNet is an encoder-decoder architecture, which can obtain accurate and robust results. We have designed two novel modules: MRFM and FFM. The MRFM is designed to capture the rich contextual information which is essential for SOD while the FFM aims to effectively fuse the multi-level and multi-scale information step by step. Besides, we produce boundary-aware saliency maps by using the edge detection operator Laplace. Extensive experimental results on widely-used six benchmark datasets have demonstrated that the proposed method significantly outperforms the other 16 state-of-the-art methods in terms of maximum F-measure, mean absolute error and structure measure.

Acknowledgements. This work is supported in part by National Major Project of China for New Generation of AI (No. 2018AAA0100400), in part by the Natural Science Foundation of China under Grant nos. 61872189, 61876088, 61702272, in part by the Natural Science Foundation of Jiangsu Province under Grant nos. BK20191397, BK20170040. in part by Six talent peaks project in Jiangsu Province under Grant nos. XYDXX-015, XYDXX-045.

References

1. Chen, L.C., Papandreou, G., Schroff, F., Adam, H.: Rethinking atrous convolution for semantic image segmentation. arXiv preprint arXiv:1706.05587 (2017)
2. Chen, S., Tan, X., Wang, B., Hu, X.: Reverse attention for salient object detection. In: Proceedings of the European Conference on Computer Vision, pp. 234–250 (2018)
3. Cheng, M.M., Mitra, N.J., Huang, X., Torr, P.H., Hu, S.M.: Global contrast based salient region detection. IEEE Trans. Pattern Anal. Mach. Intell. **37**(3), 569–582 (2014)
4. Deng, J., Dong, W., Socher, R., Li, L.J., Li, K., Fei-Fei, L.: ImageNet: a large-scale hierarchical image database. In: 2009 IEEE Conference on Computer Vision and Pattern Recognition, pp. 248–255. IEEE (2009)
5. Deng, Z., et al.: R^3Net: recurrent residual refinement network for saliency detection. In: Proceedings of the 27th International Joint Conference on Artificial Intelligence, pp. 684–690. AAAI Press (2018)
6. Donoser, M., Urschler, M., Hirzer, M., Bischof, H.: Saliency driven total variation segmentation. In: 2009 IEEE 12th International Conference on Computer Vision, pp. 817–824. IEEE (2009)
7. Fan, D.P., Cheng, M.M., Liu, Y., Li, T., Borji, A.: Structure-measure: a new way to evaluate foreground maps. In: Proceedings of the IEEE International Conference on Computer Vision, pp. 4548–4557 (2017)
8. Fan, D.P., Wang, W., Cheng, M.M., Shen, J.: Shifting more attention to video salient object detection. In: Proceedings of the IEEE Conference on Computer Vision and Pattern Recognition, pp. 8554–8564 (2019)
9. Feng, M., Lu, H., Ding, E.: Attentive feedback network for boundary-aware salient object detection. In: Proceedings of the IEEE Conference on Computer Vision and Pattern Recognition, pp. 1623–1632 (2019)

10. He, K., Zhang, X., Ren, S., Sun, J.: Deep residual learning for image recognition. In: Proceedings of the IEEE Conference on Computer Vision and Pattern Recognition, pp. 770–778 (2016)
11. He, K., Zhang, X., Ren, S., Sun, J.: Identity mappings in deep residual networks. In: Leibe, B., Matas, J., Sebe, N., Welling, M. (eds.) ECCV 2016. LNCS, vol. 9908, pp. 630–645. Springer, Cham (2016). https://doi.org/10.1007/978-3-319-46493-0_38
12. Hong, S., You, T., Kwak, S., Han, B.: Online tracking by learning discriminative saliency map with convolutional neural network. In: International Conference on Machine Learning, pp. 597–606 (2015)
13. Hou, Q., Cheng, M.M., Hu, X., Borji, A., Tu, Z., Torr, P.H.: Deeply supervised salient object detection with short connections. In: Proceedings of the IEEE Conference on Computer Vision and Pattern Recognition, pp. 3203–3212 (2017)
14. Hu, P., Shuai, B., Liu, J., Wang, G.: Deep level sets for salient object detection. In: Proceedings of the IEEE Conference on Computer Vision and Pattern Recognition, pp. 2300–2309 (2017)
15. Kingma, D.P., Ba, J.: Adam: a method for stochastic optimization. arXiv preprint arXiv:1412.6980 (2014)
16. Lee, H., Kim, D.: Salient region-based online object tracking. In: 2018 IEEE Winter Conference on Applications of Computer Vision, pp. 1170–1177. IEEE (2018)
17. Li, G., Yu, Y.: Visual saliency based on multiscale deep features. In: Proceedings of the IEEE Conference on Computer Vision and Pattern Recognition, pp. 5455–5463 (2015)
18. Li, G., Yu, Y.: Deep contrast learning for salient object detection. In: Proceedings of the IEEE Conference on Computer Vision and Pattern Recognition, pp. 478–487 (2016)
19. Li, Y., Hou, X., Koch, C., Rehg, J.M., Yuille, A.L.: The secrets of salient object segmentation. In: Proceedings of the IEEE Conference on Computer Vision and Pattern Recognition, pp. 280–287 (2014)
20. Liu, N., Han, J., Yang, M.H.: PiCANet: learning pixel-wise contextual attention for saliency detection. In: Proceedings of the IEEE Conference on Computer Vision and Pattern Recognition, pp. 3089–3098 (2018)
21. Liu, S., Huang, D., et al.: Receptive field block net for accurate and fast object detection. In: Proceedings of the European Conference on Computer Vision, pp. 385–400 (2018)
22. Luo, Z., Mishra, A., Achkar, A., Eichel, J., Li, S., Jodoin, P.M.: Non-local deep features for salient object detection. In: Proceedings of the IEEE Conference on Computer Vision and Pattern Recognition, pp. 6609–6617 (2017)
23. Movahedi, V., Elder, J.H.: Design and perceptual validation of performance measures for salient object segmentation. In: 2010 IEEE Computer Society Conference on Computer Vision and Pattern Recognition-Workshops, pp. 49–56. IEEE (2010)
24. Qin, X., Zhang, Z., Huang, C., Gao, C., Dehghan, M., Jagersand, M.: BASNet: boundary-aware salient object detection. In: Proceedings of the IEEE Conference on Computer Vision and Pattern Recognition, pp. 7479–7489 (2019)
25. Wang, L., et al.: Learning to detect salient objects with image-level supervision. In: Proceedings of the IEEE Conference on Computer Vision and Pattern Recognition, pp. 136–145 (2017)
26. Wang, L., Wang, L., Lu, H., Zhang, P., Ruan, X.: Saliency detection with recurrent fully convolutional networks. In: Leibe, B., Matas, J., Sebe, N., Welling, M. (eds.) ECCV 2016. LNCS, vol. 9908, pp. 825–841. Springer, Cham (2016). https://doi.org/10.1007/978-3-319-46493-0_50

27. Wang, L., Wang, L., Lu, H., Zhang, P., Ruan, X.: Salient object detection with recurrent fully convolutional networks. IEEE Trans. Pattern Anal. Mach. Intell. **41**(7), 1734–1746 (2018)

28. Wang, T., Borji, A., Zhang, L., Zhang, P., Lu, H.: A stagewise refinement model for detecting salient objects in images. In: Proceedings of the IEEE International Conference on Computer Vision, pp. 4019–4028 (2017)

29. Wang, T., et al.: Detect globally, refine locally: a novel approach to saliency detection. In: Proceedings of the IEEE Conference on Computer Vision and Pattern Recognition, pp. 3127–3135 (2018)

30. Wang, W., Shen, J., Guo, F., Cheng, M.M., Borji, A.: Revisiting video saliency: a large-scale benchmark and a new model. In: Proceedings of the IEEE Conference on Computer Vision and Pattern Recognition, pp. 4894–4903 (2018)

31. Wang, W., Zhao, S., Shen, J., Hoi, S.C., Borji, A.: Salient object detection with pyramid attention and salient edges. In: Proceedings of the IEEE Conference on Computer Vision and Pattern Recognition, pp. 1448–1457 (2019)

32. Wu, Z., Su, L., Huang, Q.: Cascaded partial decoder for fast and accurate salient object detection. In: Proceedings of the IEEE Conference on Computer Vision and Pattern Recognition, pp. 3907–3916 (2019)

33. Xie, S., Girshick, R., Dollár, P., Tu, Z., He, K.: Aggregated residual transformations for deep neural networks. In: Proceedings of the IEEE Conference on Computer Vision and Pattern Recognition, pp. 1492–1500 (2017)

34. Xie, S., Tu, Z.: Holistically-nested edge detection. In: Proceedings of the IEEE International Conference on Computer Vision, pp. 1395–1403 (2015)

35. Xu, K., et al.: Show, attend and tell: Neural image caption generation with visual attention. In: International Conference on Machine Learning, pp. 2048–2057 (2015)

36. Yan, Q., Xu, L., Shi, J., Jia, J.: Hierarchical saliency detection. In: Proceedings of the IEEE Conference on Computer Vision and Pattern Recognition, pp. 1155–1162 (2013)

37. Yang, C., Zhang, L., Lu, H., Ruan, X., Yang, M.H.: Saliency detection via graph-based manifold ranking. In: Proceedings of the IEEE Conference on Computer Vision and Pattern Recognition, pp. 3166–3173 (2013)

38. Zhang, P., Wang, D., Lu, H., Wang, H., Ruan, X.: Amulet: aggregating multi-level convolutional features for salient object detection. In: Proceedings of the IEEE International Conference on Computer Vision, pp. 202–211 (2017)

39. Zhang, P., Wang, D., Lu, H., Wang, H., Yin, B.: Learning uncertain convolutional features for accurate saliency detection. In: Proceedings of the IEEE International Conference on Computer Vision, pp. 212–221 (2017)

40. Zhang, X., Wang, T., Qi, J., Lu, H., Wang, G.: Progressive attention guided recurrent network for salient object detection. In: Proceedings of the IEEE Conference on Computer Vision and Pattern Recognition, pp. 714–722 (2018)

41. Zhao, T., Wu, X.: Pyramid feature attention network for saliency detection. In: Proceedings of the IEEE Conference on Computer Vision and Pattern Recognition, pp. 3085–3094 (2019)

42. Zhu, W., Liang, S., Wei, Y., Sun, J.: Saliency optimization from robust background detection. In: Proceedings of the IEEE Conference on Computer Vision and Pattern Recognition, pp. 2814–2821 (2014)

Path Aggregation and Dual Supervision Network for Scene Text Detection

Shuyang Feng[1], Na Zhang[1], and Cairong Zhao[1,2(✉)]

[1] Department of Computer Science and Technology, Tongji University, Shanghai, China
zhaocairong@tongji.edu.cn
[2] Key Laboratory of Embedded System and Service Computing (Tongji University),
Ministry of Education, Shanghai 201804, China

Abstract. In recent years, instance segmentation-based scene text detection has been widely concerned by academics and industry. However, these segmentation methods based on the coding-decoding paradigm are limited by the loss of information caused by subsampling, which is the root cause of pixel misclassification in the instance segmentation task. In this paper, we propose an effective approach for scene text detection, which named Path Aggregation and Dual Supervision Network (PADSNet). To introduce the from coarse to fine detection idea into the one-stage segmentation algorithm, a single-task multi-level supervision method is designed. Meanwhile, deformable convolution is used to break through the limits of CNN's rectangular receptive field, so that it can better adapt to arbitrary shape scene text. The experimental results show that our method can effectively reduce pixel misclassification, and achieve f-measure 85.4% and 83.19% on the ICDAR2015 dataset and CTW1500 dataset respectively.

Keywords: Scene text detection · Instance segmentation · Deep learning

1 Introduction

In recent years, approaches based on deep learning have become the mainstream in the field of text detection. Unlike the detection of general objects, text detection, as a new area of research, certainly has some unique challenges. First of all, the text has distinct stroke characteristics. Besides, It has a large aspect ratio and scale variance, which puts forward higher requirements for the commonly used object detection method, and requires greater support from CNN receptive field. Last but not least, there are many different granularities in the method of detecting text objects, such as character level, text segment level, and word level. Whether a word or a sentence is made up of every single letter, the margin between the letters is the key to distinguish words or sentences, which is affected by the text size and style. Therefore, the text object has fuzzy boundary properties, so that the detection model has put forward a higher precision requirement.

At present, to cope with the needs of various scenes, curved text detection has attracted much attention. Since instance segmentation based methods can model curved text naturally, they are becoming the dominant method in scene text detection filed.

Y. Peng et al. (Eds.): PRCV 2020, LNCS 12307, pp. 66–77, 2020.
https://doi.org/10.1007/978-3-030-60636-7_6

However, there are still some problems with these methods. First of all, they often rely on complex post-processing processes, which greatly influence the speed of detection. Secondly, compared with the method of boundary box regression, the coding-decoding segmentation method needs more storage resources to do the more complex calculation. Finally, to balance model complexity and segmentation performance, it is inevitable to subsample features. However, the subsampling will cause a certain degree of information loss, which can result in misclassification of pixels in challenging scenarios.

In this work, we have been inspired by PANet [1], and introduced the idea of coarse-to-fine classification, proposing a scene text detection network called PADSNet. Specifically, because features in low levels are typically used to represent object textures, the ability for segmentation networks to accurately predict the edges of instances depends on the characterization of object textures. We design a bottom-up feature fine-tuning network and added the feature residuals of the network shallow in the process of feature fusion. The above practice can effectively shorten the deep feature learning path of the low-level structure to the top level of the network. So, It can obtain more accurate instance location information. Intuitively, there is an iterative fusion relationship in our feature fusion method, which is enriched and enhanced based on containing the original features. Based on this hypothesis, we supervise both the original and fusion features and propose a single task multi-level supervision idea (i.e., the dual supervision module). Finally, the deformable convolution is introduced, which can adaptively select feature sampling points, and enable the model's receptive field to adapt to the arbitrary shape scene text more efficiently.

In summary, our main contributions are as follows:

- Drawing on the two-stage detector classification idea from coarse to fine, a single-task multi-level supervision method is proposed, and this method is applied to text detection of arbitrary shape.
- The robustness of FPN [2] features is enhanced by introducing shallow residuals and feature fine-tuning networks. At the same time, the asymmetry of feature fusion can be compensated to some extent.
- Experiments have shown that our model can effectively enhance the perception of arbitrary shape instance positioning with the help of deformable convolution [3]. Our framework has obtained comparable experimental results on several benchmarks.

2 Related Work

2.1 Character-Based Text Detection

Due to the high cost of labeling training samples at the character level, character-based text detection methods are usually trained in a weak supervision manner. Hu, Han et al. [4] generated a character mask iteratively based on the object detection framework, and used it to synthesize the labels of the training samples for semi-supervised learning and regress a single character bounding box. Youngmin Baek et al. [5] introduce Gaussian distribution to enhance the model's central attention to each character. Minghui Liao et al. [6] and Linjie Xing et al. [7] associate mask predictions with character tag information, which can segment and recognize character at the same time.

2.2 Segment-Based Text Detection

Since the text has a large aspect ratio and its size scale is variable, regression-based text detection methods particularly rely on CNN's perception field. To solve this problem, some researchers have come up with the idea of slicing long text, detecting each text segment individually. CTPN [8] modifies anchors in Faster R-CNN [9] to fix its width, predicts its vertical offset, and finally generates detection results based on the dependency between the vertical and horizontal coordinates of the candidate boxes. Shi, B. et al. [10] also follow this idea, detecting text segments and their links on multi-scale feature maps.

2.3 Word-Based Text Detection

Since most datasets are labeled based on words, the mainstream scene text detection methods are usually word-based. Textboxes++ [11] directly detect the inclined text by modifying the aspect ratio of detection anchors, using rectangular convolution cores, and increasing the output parameters of the boundary box rotation angle. EAST [12] is an anchor-free based model, which regress the inclined bounding box in a pixel-level manner.

To facilitate arbitrary shape text detection, the segmentation-based text detection methods are more popular. Textsnake [13] predicts the centerline of text based on the idea of multiscale skeleton symmetry and covers the text area with circular objects. PSENet [14] predicts a set of text instance masks with different shrink scales, expanding in turn by pixel-by-pixel search from the smallest shrink map. TextField [15] change the previous bit map to a weighted mask map, focusing on the center area of the text so that it can clearly distinguish the edge of the text area to implement instance segmentation.

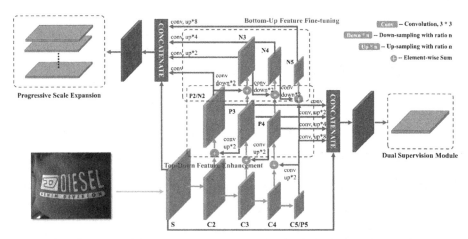

Fig. 1. The network architecture of our proposed method. It includes a PAFPN basic network, which is consists of a top-down feature enhancement module and bottom-up feature fine-tuning module, dual supervision module, and progressive scale expansion post-processing module.

3   Methodology

3.1   Path Aggregation Feature Pyramid Network

Liu S. et al. believe that adding a bottom-up convolutional pathway can enhance the high-level generalization ability of neurons in high layers responding to local textures and activation patterns captured by shallow neurons [1, 16]. The proposed method is essentially aimed at the segmentation problem. Even if instance segmentation is achieved by shrinking and expanding the edge of the object, we still rely on the strong response of the network to the low-level patterns extracted from the target region.

The classic FPN network, using the characteristics of the fully convolutional network feature map from large to small and semantic information coding intensity from low to high, constructs the feature pyramid structure with high-level semantics throughout. Although this top-down feature fusion method can effectively utilize the advantages of texture robustness of features in low-level and semantic robustness of features in high-level, the feature fusion pyramid network lacks a structural symmetry. That is, the subsampling and up-sampling of the full convolution network are not aligned, the subsampling on the backbone network is often as many as dozens or hundreds of layers, and the up-sampling is composed of simple bilinear interpolation and feature fusion, this asymmetry may be the most important reason for FPN used to segmentation task, which may exacerbate the loss of information subsampling. So, the proposed network (shown in Fig. 1) extends the structural characteristics of the FPN network and constructs a structure iterative relationship through the bottom-up pyramid structure.

Compared with FPN, the PAFPN network compensates for the nonlinear mapping asymmetry caused by simple up-sampling via feature finetuning fusion. And by the top-down and bottom-up fusion, the framework can aggregate the path of the two-way conduction features. As shown in Fig. 2, we choose the fusion feature layer N3 to compare with the original P3 feature layer and observe the feature enhancement performance of the new structure in the backpropagation process.

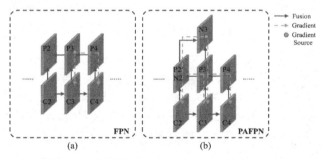

Fig. 2. Comparison of FPN vs. PAFPN backpropagation flow. Select the P3 and N3 feature layers as the gradient source points and compare the gradient paths during backpropagation.

Specifically, we implemented the PAFPN network architecture based on ResNet [17]. To more clearly represent the iterative relationship of the double pyramid structure, we specifically named the first pyramid structure group as the top-down feature augmentation, labeling each layer in the module with P_2, P_3, P_4, P_5. We also used bottom-up feature finetune module to represent the second pyramid structure group and each fusion feature layer is denoted by N_2, N_3, N_4, N_5.

Mathematically, if we consider $D_n(\cdot)$ as down-sampling function with ratio factor n and $C(\cdot)$ represents a set of 3*3 convolutions, Batch-Norm regular method, and Relu activation function, N_i feature map can be calculated as:

$$N_i = \begin{cases} P_2, i = 2 \\ C(D_2(N_{i-1}) + P_i), 2 < i \le 5 \end{cases} \tag{1}$$

The insightful point [17] that the introduction of residual blocks can reduce the side effects caused by the increase of the network depth, and can improve the model's ability to learn shallow feature representations. Therefore, we use the feature map S of the fully convolutional network part as a shortcut to directly communicate with the PSE module and DSM and fuse with deep features.

Progressive scale expansion is a simple and effective post-processing method, and here we follow the implementation of Wenhai Wang et al. [14]. At the same time, we follow Zhu et al. 2019 [3] using modulated deformable convolutions to replace conv3, conv4, and conv5 in ResNet-50 [17] backbone, making better progress.

3.2 Dual Supervision Module

Drawing on the two-stage detection from coarse to fine classification idea and Utilizing the characteristics of the network's pathway iterative structure, we propose a dual supervision module, which uses the original size kernel mask to supervise the homomorphic structure in the middle of the network and iteratively enhances the ultimate performance of the model. Double supervision is reflected in our simultaneous study of object mask prediction on the top-down feature enhancement module and the bottom-up feature fine-tuning module.

Intuitively, there is an internal connection in our network framework, that is, the feature map P_i is mainly the features of the feature map C_i, and N_i continues to fuse

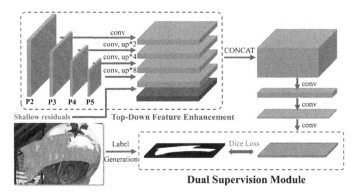

Fig. 3. Dual supervision module.

the features of P_i to further characterize the captured maximum response. Therefore, we believe that the features captured between the C, P, and N feature maps of the same index have greater correlation, and the ability to abstract features is gradually enhanced.

Based on this assumption, we use top-down feature augmentation for all feature maps {P2, P3, P4, P5} and shallow residuals for feature fusion, and use the original scale bitmap generated by ground truth for supervised learning. Following the idea of classification from coarse to fine, we propose a single-task multi-layered iterative supervision method, which designs a supervision module similar to the network output task and names it a double supervision module (DSM), as shown in Fig. 3. Here we verify that the dual supervision module can improve the performance of the segmentation step by step, and details are in Fig. 4.

3.3 Loss Function Based on Dual Supervision

Mathematically, we designed the following loss function to train our method:

$$L = \lambda L_c + \xi L_s + (1 - \lambda - \xi) L_d \qquad (2)$$

where L_c, L_s and L_d represent the losses for the original scale text instance, the shrunk bitmaps, and supervision loss for top-down feature augmentation module. Meanwhile, λ and ξ are balancing hyper-parameters to control the trade-off between the three losses.

Here we use DiceLoss [18] for experiments. The Dice coefficient is equivalent to the intersection ratio of the prediction result area and the ground truth area. It uses all pixels of a class as a whole to calculate Loss. Because Dice loss directly uses the segmentation effect evaluation index as loss function to supervise the network and also ignores a large number of background pixels when calculating the crossover ratio, it solves the problem of imbalance between positive and negative samples, so the convergence speed is fast. It can be mathematically expressed as:

$$Dice(P_i, G_i) = 1 - 2 \times \frac{\Sigma_{x,y}\left(P_{i,x,y} \times G_{i,x,y}\right)}{\Sigma_{x,y}P^2_{i,x,y} + \Sigma_{x,y}G^2_{i,x,y}} \qquad (3)$$

where $P_{i,x,y}$ and $G_{i,x,y}$ represent the value of each pixel (x, y) on the prediction segmentation map and ground truth.

$$L_c = Dice(P_n \cdot M, G_n \cdot M) \qquad (4)$$

$$L_d = Dice(C \cdot M, G_n \cdot M) \qquad (5)$$

$$L_s = \frac{\Sigma_{i=1}^{n-1} Dice(B(P_i), B(G_i))}{n-1} \qquad (6)$$

where P and G are the network prediction mask and ground truth, respectively, M represents the bitmap used for selecting pixel by the Online Hard Example Mining (OHEM) [19] after balancing the positive and negative samples, C is the original scale double supervision mask and $B(\cdot)$ is a function that can set a threshold to convert a mask map on a continuous range into a 0/1 bitmap.

4   Experiments

4.1   Benchmark Datasets

ICDAR 2015 [20] is proposed in Incidental Scene Text Detection of ICDAR 2015 Robust Reading Competition challenge 4. It consists of 1000 training samples and 500 test samples and is usually used as a standard evaluation method for evaluating horizontal text detection algorithms with directions.

ICDAR 2017 MLT [21] acts as pre-training data here. MLT is a large-scale multilingual text dataset, which contains 7200 training images, 1800 validation images, and 9000 test images. It contains a large number of complex pictures, and the text content comes from nine different languages, such as English, Chinese, Japanese, etc. This undoubtedly makes it a difficult benchmark or as effective pre-training data.

SCUT-CTW1500 [22] is a text-line based dataset with both English and Chinese instances, which is usually used as a benchmark dataset for measuring text detection algorithms to detect text of arbitrary shapes. It includes 1000 training images and 500 testing images and each image contains at least 1 curved text.

4.2   Implementation Details

First of all, the data augmentation for the training data includes: (1) Randomly resize the image with a scale ratio within (0.5, 1.0, 2.0, 3.0), while ensuring that the short edge of the image is greater than a preset value. (2) Flip horizontally at a 50% probability. (3) Random rotation with an angle range of $\left(-10^{\circ}, 10^{\circ}\right)$. (4) Random crop to get a 640×640 image for better training efficiency.

We use ResNet-50 pre-trained on ImageNet [23] as our backbone and use two different training strategies: (1) training from scratch. (2) fine-tuning the model trained on the MLT dataset. If we start training from scratch, we only train the model on the corresponding real-world datasets with batch size 10 to train 600 epochs on two 2080Ti. The initial learning rate is 1×10^{-3} and is divided by 10 at 200, 400 epochs. If we use another strategy, we first use the training and validation sets of MLT as training data. During pre-training, the batch-size is set to 15, the initial learning rate is 1×10^{-3}. We train 300 epochs and the learning rate is divided by 10 at the 100 and 200 epochs respectively. Then, we need to finetune the model on the corresponding real-world datasets with a batch size of 10 to train 400 epochs and is divided by 10 at 200 epochs. The difference is that the initial learning rate is 1×10^{-4}. Meanwhile, we use 5×10^{-4} weight decay and 0.99 momentum.

In the inference period, we keep the aspect ratio of the test images, and We resize the image so that its maximum edge length does not exceed a fixed value, which is set accordingly to different benchmark. We set batch-size to 1 with a single 2080ti.

4.3   Ablation Study

In Sect. 3, We propose a dual supervision method and apply deformable convolution to adapt to the structural characteristics of curved texts. Table 1 experiments on the sequential ablation of DSM modules and Deformable Convolution on CTW1500 and

ICDAR2015 standard benchmark. Taking the cost of calculation into consideration, we only compare the training from scratch results of the experiment.

Table 1. Detection results on the CTW1500 dataset with different settings. "DCN" indicates deformable convolution. "DSM" indicates the dual supervision module.

Backbone	DCN	DSM	CTW1500			ICDAR2015		
			Precision	Recall	Hmean	Precision	Recall	Hmean
ResNet-50	×	×	80.57	75.55	78.00	83.72	76.79	80.11
ResNet-50	×	✓	83.28	77.28	80.17	85.35	78.53	81.80
ResNet-50	✓	×	86.00	77.09	81.30	84.23	80.25	82.19
ResNet-50	✓	✓	86.36	78.42	82.20	84.31	81.51	82.89

Dual Supervision Module. In Table 1, By using the experimental comparison without deformable convolution, we can see that adding DSM can improve the detection results on the above two datasets by 2.17% and 1.69% Hmean respectively. However, in the experimental comparison using deformable convolution, the elevation of DSM is not as obvious as the former, which can achieve about 1% performance gain. Moreover, DSM does not take up any time in the inference period.

Deformable Convolution. As shown in Table 1, in a set of comparative experiments without DSM, we can see that deformable convolution can result in a performance

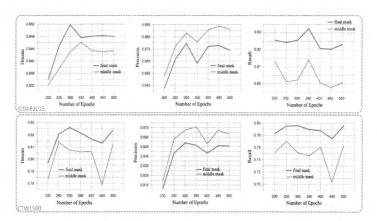

Fig. 4. Comparison between the middle DSM mask and the final output mask. The blue folds in the figure represent the result of the former, while the red folds represent the result of the latter. The orange dotted box and the green dotted box represents the results tested on ICDAR2015 and CTW1500 datasets, respectively. Results sampled from several progressive training epochs. (Color figure online)

Table 2. Results on ICDAR2015. "DCN" indicates the use of deformable convolution, and "Ext" means the pre-training model with ICDAR2017 MLT.

Approaches	Ext	Precision	Recall	F-measure
CTPN [8]	×	74.22	51.56	60.85
EAST [12]	×	83.57	73.47	78.2
RRPN [24]	×	82.0	73.0	77.0
PSENet [14]	×	81.49	79.68	80.57
PADSNet(ours)	×	**85.35**	78.53	81.8
PADSNet-DCN (ours)	×	84.31	**81.51**	**82.89**
SegLink [10]	√	73.1	76.8	75.0
SSTD [25]	√	80.23	73.86	76.91
Lyu et al. [26]	√	94.1	70.7	80.7
RRD [27]	√	85.6	79.0	82.2
TextSnake [13]	√	84.9	80.4	82.6
PSENet [14]	√	87.56	**83.38**	**85.42**
PADSNet-DCN (ours)	√	**88.04**	82.91	85.40

improvement of 2–3%. Besides, when we do the ablation experiment of deformable convolution on the DSM, we can see that deformable convolution can result in a performance improvement of 1–2%.

Table 3. Results on CTW1500. "DCN" indicates the use of deformable convolution, and "Ext" means the pre-training model with ICDAR2017 MLT.

Approaches	Ext	Precision	Recall	F-measure
SegLink [10]	×	42.3	40.0	40.8
CTPN [8]	×	60.4	53.8	56.9
EAST [12]	×	78.7	49.1	60.4
PSENet [14]	×	80.57	75.55	78.0
PADSNet (ours)	×	85.04	76.50	80.54
PADSNet-DCN (ours)	×	**86.36**	**78.42**	**82.20**
TextSnake [13]	√	67.9	85.3	75.6
PSENet [14]	√	84.84	79.73	82.2
PADSNet-DCN (ours)	√	**86.44**	**80.18**	**83.19**

Comparison Between DSM Mask and the Final Mask. As shown in Fig. 4, the two sets of contrast charts in the vertical direction represent performance indicators on the

ICDAR2015 and CTW1500 datasets, respectively. We represent the detection results under the DSM mask constraint and the detection results under the network final output constrained by different color folds. Overall, the hmean value under the final output constraint is always higher than the DSM in several different stages of network training. The performance improvement mainly depends on the increase in recall value. This shows that DSM can effectively increase the sensitivity of the model to small scene text and some hard samples by conducting gradients through the middle layer and introducing residuals. We can see the effect of small or hard scene text detection intuitively from Fig. 5.

Fig. 5. Scene text detection results from comparison on CTW1500. The first and second lines of each dashed box represent PSENet and our test results respectively. These green, blue, purple, and red dotted boxes represent a comparison of the occluded environment, small samples, large targets, and recall/precision visualization respectively. (Color figure online)

4.4 Comparisons with Previous Methods

Multi-oriented Scene Text Detection. We evaluate multi-oriented scene text detection on ICDAR2015, as shown in Table 2. In the inference period, we resize the input images to a maximum edge length of 2240 pixels. We can see that without MLT extra pre-trained data, the improvement of our method is very obvious, and it can achieve about 2.3% f-measure value improvement comparing with PSENet.

Arbitrary-Shape Scene Text Detection. We conduct experiments on CTW1500, the results of which are shown in Table 3. Specifically, in the inference period, we resize the input images to a maximum edge length of 1280 pixels. The "PADSNet" outperforms "PSENet" by 2.54%, which are both using ResNet-50 as the backbone and without pre-trained data. With the same experimental setup and using deformable convolution, our method can outperform "PSENet" by 4.20%. Furthermore, our models perform better than "PSENet" with a pre-trained model, increasing hmean by about 1%.

4.5 Qualitative Results

Some qualitative results of PADSNet are shown in Fig. 5. The experimental results show that our method can effectively detect oriented text and arbitrary shape text.

5 Conclusion

This paper introduces Path Aggregation and Dual Supervision Network (PADSNet) for arbitrary shape scene text detection, which includes the proposed dual supervision module (DSM) in a segmentation network. The experiments have verified that our approach can effectively improve the performance of the model, especially in a single domain environment. In the future, we will continue to try to adopt a more adaptive multiple supervision schemes in a network architecture with an iterative structure, and combine the text recognition algorithm to try an end-to-end text detection and recognition.

References

1. Liu, S., et al.: Path aggregation network for instance segmentation. In: Computer Vision and Pattern Recognition, pp. 8759–8768 (2018)
2. Lin, T., et al.: Feature pyramid networks for object detection. In: Computer Vision and Pattern Recognition, pp. 936–944 (2017)
3. Zhu, X., et al.: Deformable ConvNets V2: more deformable, better results. In: Computer Vision and Pattern Recognition, pp. 9308–9316 (2019)
4. Hu, H., et al.: WordSup: exploiting word annotations for character based text detection. In: International Conference on Computer Vision, pp. 4950–4959 (2017)
5. Baek, Y., et al.: Character region awareness for text detection. In: Computer Vision and Pattern Recognition, pp. 9365–9374 (2019)
6. Liao, M., et al.: Mask TextSpotter: an end-to-end trainable neural network for spotting text with arbitrary shapes. IEEE Trans. Pattern Anal. Mach. Intell. 1 (2019)

7. Xing, L., et al.: Convolutional character networks. In: International Conference on Computer Vision, pp. 9126–9136 (2019)

8. Tian, Z., Huang, W., He, T., He, P., Qiao, Yu.: Detecting text in natural image with connectionist text proposal network. In: Leibe, B., Matas, J., Sebe, N., Welling, M. (eds.) ECCV 2016. LNCS, vol. 9912, pp. 56–72. Springer, Cham (2016). https://doi.org/10.1007/978-3-319-46484-8_4

9. Ren, S., et al.: Faster R-CNN: towards real-time object detection with region proposal networks. IEEE Trans. Pattern Anal. Mach. Intell. 1137–1149 (2017)

10. Shi, B., Xiang, B., Serge, B.: Detecting oriented text in natural images by linking segments. In: Computer Vision and Pattern Recognition, pp. 3482–3490 (2017)

11. Liao, M., Shi, B., Bai, X.: Textboxes ++: a single- shot oriented scene text detector. IEEE Trans. Image Process. 3676–3690 (2018)

12. Zhou, X., et al.: EAST: an efficient and accurate scene text detector. In: Computer Vision and Pattern Recognition, pp. 2642–2651 (2017)

13. Long, S., Ruan, J., Zhang, W., He, X., Wu, W., Yao, C.: textsnake: a flexible representation for detecting text of arbitrary shapes. In: Ferrari, V., Hebert, M., Sminchisescu, C., Weiss, Y. (eds.) ECCV 2018. LNCS, vol. 11206, pp. 19–35. Springer, Cham (2018). https://doi.org/10.1007/978-3-030-01216-8_2

14. Wang, W., et al.: Shape robust text detection with progressive scale expansion network. In: Computer Vision and Pattern Recognition, pp. 9336–9345 (2019)

15. Xu, Y., et al.: TextField: learning a deep direction field for irregular scene text detection. IEEE Trans. Image Process. 5566–5579 (2019)

16. Zeiler, M.D., Fergus, R.: Visualizing and understanding convolutional networks. In: Fleet, D., Pajdla, T., Schiele, B., Tuytelaars, T. (eds.) ECCV 2014. LNCS, vol. 8689, pp. 818–833. Springer, Cham (2014). https://doi.org/10.1007/978-3-319-10590-1_53

17. He, K., et al.: Deep residual learning for image recognition. In: Computer Vision and Pattern Recognition, pp. 770–778 (2016)

18. Milletari, F., Nassir, N., Seyedahmad, A.: V-Net: Fully convolutional neural networks for volumetric medical image segmentation. In: International Conference on 3d Vision, pp. 565–571 (2016)

19. Shrivastava, A., Abhinav, G., Ross, G.: Training region-based object detectors with online hard example mining. In: Computer Vision and Pattern Recognition, pp. 761–769 (2016)

20. Karatzas, D., Gomez-Bigorda, L., Nicolaou, A., et al.: ICDAR 2015 competition on robust reading. In: ICDAR 2015

21. Icdar2017 competition on multi-lingual scene text detection and script identification. http://rrc.cvc.uab.es/?ch=8&com=introduction

22. Liu, Y., Jin, L., Zhang, S., Zhang, S.: Detecting curve text in the wild: New dataset and new solution. CoRR, abs/1712.02170 (2017)

23. Deng, Jia, et al.: ImageNet: a large-scale hierarchical image database. In: Computer Vision and Pattern Recognition, pp. 248–255 (2009)

24. Ma, J., et al.: Arbitrary-oriented scene text detection via rotation proposals. IEEE Trans. Multimedia, pp. 3111–3122 (2018)

25. He, P., et al.: Single shot text detector with regional attention. In: International Conference on Computer Vision, pp. 3066–3074 (2017)

26. Lyu, P., et al.: Multi-oriented scene text detection via corner localization and region segmentation. In: Computer Vision and Pattern Recognition, pp. 7553–7563 (2018)

27. Liao, M., et al.: Rotation-sensitive regression for oriented scene text detection. In: Computer Vision and Pattern Recognition, pp. 5909–5918 (2018)

Semantic Inpainting with Multi-dimensional Adversarial Network and Wasserstein Distance

Haodi Wang[1], Libin Jiao[2], Rongfang Bie[1], and Hao Wu[1(✉)]

[1] College of Artificial Intelligence, Beijing Normal University, Beijing, China
wuhao@bnu.edu.cn
[2] Institute of Remote Sensing and Digital Earth (RADI),
Chinese Academy of Science (CAS), Beijing, China

Abstract. Inpainting represents a procedure which can restore the lost parts of an image based upon the residual information. We present an inpainting network that consists of an Encoder-Decoder pipeline and a multi-dimensional adversarial network. The Encoder-Decoder pipeline extracts features from the input image with missing area and learns these features. Through unsupervised learning, the pipeline can predict and fill the missing region with the most reasonable content. Meanwhile the multi-dimensional adversarial network identifies the difference between the ground truth and the generated images both in detail and in general. Compared with the traditional training procedure, our model combines with Wasserstein Distance that enhances the stability of network training. The network is training specifically on street view images and not only performs a satisfying outcome, but also shows competitiveness when comparing with existing methods.

Keywords: Inpainting · Multi-dimensional discriminator · Wasserstein distance

1 Introduction

INPAINTING is known as a procedure which is used to complete the missing part of the images [22]. While the structure and content of the pictures in our real world are complicated, it is natural for human beings to understand the meaning of the images without compromising. By the analogy of this kind of behavior, in the region of computer science, extracting and learning the feature of the input images, especially focusing on the context of incomplete part is

This research is sponsored by National Natural Science Foundation of China (No. 61571049, 61371185, 61401029, 11401028, 61472044, 61472403, 61601033) and the Fundamental Research Funds for the Central Universities (No. 2014KJJCB32, 2013NT57) and by SRF for ROCS, SEM and China Postdoctoral Science Foundation Funded Project (No. 2016M590337).

Y. Peng et al. (Eds.): PRCV 2020, LNCS 12307, pp. 78–88, 2020.
https://doi.org/10.1007/978-3-030-60636-7_7

Fig. 1. An example of image inpainting.

essential to accomplish inpainting. Several methods are applied on the task of Inpainting such as Nearest Neighbor based scene completion [11], textures synthesis methods [5] and so on. These approaches achieved a great result when the missing area is relatively small. However, different from the situation when we are required to fill in the narrow blank of a broken image or video, the task in this paper is more difficult, where the missing region is large. This kind of circumstance makes it demanding on a more efficient algorithm as well as a more formidable structure of the network to extract high frequency of features. After convolutional neural network was put forward, quantities of models was proposed basing on it [15]. Thanks to the enhanced ability of CNNs, those structures like [13,16], inpainting approaches attaching to the visual attention model [14] etc. are capable of completing the missing part based on the features from residual input. Yet they still have shortcomings in some of the results and stabilities while training. Context Encoders [16], which is adopted as a one of the benchmark of this paper, only has a single discriminator and is found difficult while training due to the properties of Generative Adversarial Network [9]. Y. Li et al. [13] apply two discriminators to accomplish face completion and acquire marvelous results, while they still remain the problem during training, not mention that their model is designed only for human faces. Different from those works, we settle the drawbacks such as model collapse and unstable training by combining with Wasserstein Distance and adopt multi-dimensional discriminators to the model, which is trained specifically for street view dataset (Fig. 1).

We draw experience from Autoencoder [7] and present a network consists with an encoder-decoder pipeline with a multi-scale discriminator. Given an image with missing region, our network is able to construe the content and deduct the blank part of the pictures. The auto-encoder is in responsible for the feature learning and extracting by compassing the input images with multiple features. It is an unsupervised procedure which have the ability to represent the input image veraciously.

While this convolutional neural network is under training, we anticipate that it will achieve a stable and swift processing, which is nasty especially in adversarial network. Therefore, we draw lessons from Wasserstein generative adversarial network (WGANs)[2,21] and proved that combining with Wasserstein Distance, the velocity of network is distinctly increased and obviously ameliorate the stability.

We evaluate the network to accomplish inpainting and the stability by training it on Paris Dataset. we also compare our model with Context Encoders [16] and other structures to prove that our work achieves an impressive result.

The main work and contributions of this paper are as follows:

- We used multi-dimensional adversarial network to distinguish the real and fake images both in detail and in general, which is more powerful than single one.
- During the training, we combined our structure with Wasserstein Distance so that the stability of the model is prominently enhanced.
- We evaluate our model on a street-view dataset and achieved satisfiable results.

2 Methodology

In this section we will introduce the structure of our network. The construction of our model is shown in Fig. 2.

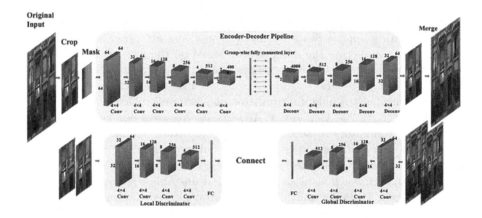

Fig. 2. The structure of our network.

2.1 Generative Pipeline

The generative pipeline is constituted with an encoder and a decoder. We will introduce those portions separately.

Encoder. The Encoder is comprised by 6 convolutional layers, with leaky-relu as its activation function. It is designed to represent those images with as few features as possible. On the other hand, if an image can be expressed by limited features, those features can be understood as the core content of a specific image and valid enough to represent it. Encoder extracts those features by means of multiple convolutional neural networks, exports those feature maps for decoders to learn and decompress.

Decoder. The encoder has ability to extract features, it can not make sure that those features are appropriate and valid, however. In order to guarantee that those features encoder has learned are significant and serviceable, they would be transferred to a subsequent architecture which is known as decoder. Decoder receives the features as a simplified form of the original input images, and decompress them to examine those features encoder learned are whether proper and sufficient.

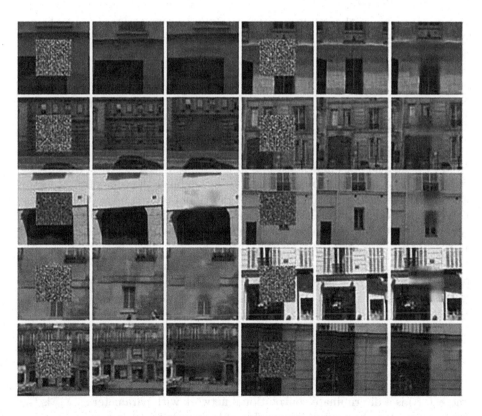

Fig. 3. Results of our method.

2.2 Multi-dimensional Discriminators

The encoder-decoder pipeline can generate the anticipating content of the input images with missing region, it will be kind of far-fetched to rely on the unsupervised procedure merely. In fact, as a consequence of using Tikhonov Matrix [8] as loss function of Encoder-Decoder pipeline, the structure always tends to average all the possible distributions so that it can acquire minimum loss. Therefore, it is crucial for us to initial a structure which is able to "select" the most proper distribution from the general possibilities. In this paper, we propose a multi-dimensional discriminator, which is composed of two different size of discriminators. The original discriminator which targets at the inpainting part is defined as the local discriminator, while the bigger one which aims at the whole input image is defined as global discriminator. By working together, our experiments prove that this procedure can achieve a better result than those structure with a solo discriminator.

2.3 Loss Function

In order to measure the validity of the inpainting content, we adopt Tikhonov Matrix as the loss function:

$$L^{'} = \min \|Ax - b\|^2 + \|\Gamma x\|^2 \tag{1}$$

where Γ signifies the Tikhonov Matrix. We determine the Tikhonov Matrix as $\Gamma = mI$, where I is the identity matrix, m is the parameter. Combining with the data preprocessing, the reconstruction loss can be shown as:

$$L_{E-D} = \|M \odot (x - f(1 - M) \odot x)\|_2^2 \tag{2}$$

where $\odot$ is element-wise multiplication. M is the mask used to create the missing region and $f(.)$ is a function initialized to accomplish the inpainting. On the other hand, we have two different size of discriminators to revise the outcome of encoder-decoder pipeline. We coalesce the multi-dimensional discriminators by merging the two outcome vectors together, with hyper-parameters α_{adv} and β_{adv}:

$$L_{adv} = \alpha_{adv} L_{local} + \beta_{adv} L_{global} \tag{3}$$

To enhance the stability of the structure during training, we adopt Wasserstein distance to modify the original GANs loss function, which will be discussed in detail in Sect. 3.2.

$$L_{dis} = \mathbb{E}_{x \sim P_{E-D}}[f_\omega(x)] - \mathbb{E}_{x \sim P_r}[f_\omega(x)]$$
$$+ \lambda_{gp} \mathbb{E}_{\hat{x} \sim P_{\hat{x}}}[(\| \nabla_{\hat{x}} D(\hat{x})\|_2 - 1)^2] \tag{4}$$

where $f_\omega(.)$ is a discriminate convolutional network with parameter ω, λ_{gp} is the hyper-parameter. As a result, we combined those loss function together:

$$L_{joint} = \lambda_{E-D} L_{E-D} + \lambda_{dis} L_{dis} \tag{5}$$

where λ_{E-D} and λ_{dis} are hyper-parameters.

3   Training

In this section, we will illustrate the procedure of the training.

Table 1. Comparison with other methods

Methods	PSNR	MSE
Context encoders [16]	16.7236	647.61
Content aware fill [3]	12.8399	837.87
Ours	18.6943	488.49

3.1   Implementation Details

The input images need to be cropped before we drag them into the encoder-decoder pipeline to fit the purpose of our experiments. We determine to set the central part as the missing area, with a quarter proportion of the whole image. During implementation, the missing region is represented by a mask which is composed with 0 and 1, where 0 means the corresponding pixel ought to be removed.

We select TensorFlow [1] framework as the basis of the implementation. During the training, there were 10,000 epochs with batch size 100, and learning rate is set as 0.002. Hyper-parameters mentioned in Sect. 2.2 is determined as $\lambda_{E-D} = 0.999$, $\lambda_{dis} = 0.001$.

Table 2. The mean and variance of generator's loss

Methods	PSNR	MSE
W/OWD	MEAN LOSS	VARIANCE
$WITH$	191.08	48.41
$WITHOUT$	200.18	102.37

3.2   Wasserstein-Distance Training

During the training of GANs-based deep learning structure, it can be apparently observed that the training process is unstable and depends largely on the initial parameters, which is randomly given usually. Besides, it also suffers from mode collapse issue. As analyzed in Wasserstein GANs [2, 10], both of the loss functions of GANs have shortcomings. The loss function can be derived as:

$$V(G, D) = \int_x p_{data}(x) \log(D(x)) + p_g \log(1 - D(x)) \mathrm{d}x \qquad (6)$$

where the G represents generator while D represents discriminator. According to Wasserstein GANs, we can calculate that the optimal solution $C(G)$ which is achieved when $p_g = p_{data}$:

$$C(G) = -\log 4, D_{*G}(x) = \frac{1}{2} \tag{7}$$

With this solution, the derivation formula is as follows:

$$C(G) = -\log 4 + 2JSD(p_{data}\|p_g) \tag{8}$$

Based on those conclusions, we combine Wasserstein distance with our model during the training. We establish a structure with parameter ω which is able to achieve discriminating steadier. ω, must satisfy the Lipschitz property. With Wasserstein Distance replacing the original loss function as GANs, the network performs a more stationary characteristics during our experiments.

4   Experiments

In this section, we will exhibit some outcomes of our experiments.

4.1   The Results of the Structure

Figure 3 are some results of our structure on Paris Dataset. The original input is an incomplete image with central missing area which is of a quarter of the whole. In Fig. 3, the first and fourth columns of each row are the residual input, the second and fifth column is the ground truth while the third and last columns are the results of our network.

4.2   Comparisons

Moreover, we also compare our results with some baselines, including Context Encoders and Content Aware Fill which Adobe Photoshop adopts. The outcomes of those algorithms are shown below in Fig. 4. In Table 1, we calculated the PSNR and MSE of Context Encoders, Content Aware Fill and our model. It can be seen that our structure is more reliable in semantic inpainting comparing with those algorithms we mentioned as benchmarks.

4.3   Hyper-Parameters Sensitivity

As introduced in Sect. 2.3, we set hyper parameters when combing local discriminator and global discriminator with α_{adv} and β_{adv}. What's more, there are also λ_{E-D} and λ_{dis} which are used to calculate the union loss of the structure, known as the optimize target. On the other hand, because we add the Wasserstein Distance into our training procedure, there is also a penalty term representing as λ_{gp}. Figure 5 is the results as we adjust the value of hyper-parameters. We tried on several combinations by controlling the variate and finally acquired three most representative outcomes as shown in Fig. 5.

Fig. 4. Comparison of our method and other networks. In each row, the first column is the original ground truth with incomplete input in the second column. The third, fourth and last columns are the results of Context Encoders, the Content Aware Fill and our structure respectively.

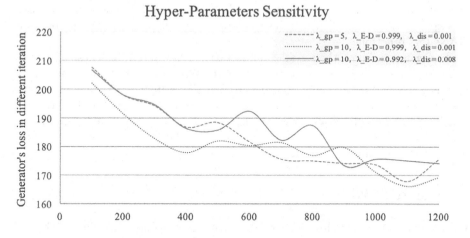

Fig. 5. Results when we change the value of hyper-parameters.

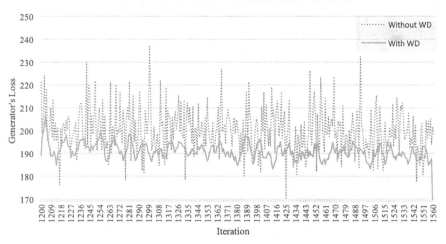

Fig. 6. The loss of multi-dimensional discriminators.

4.4   Training Stability

In this paper, we replace the Jason-Shannon divergence with Wasserstein Distance, expecting to acquire a more stable training procedure targeting at the arduous training relating to generative adversarial network. Therefore, we take an experiment to verify the efficiency of this attempt by simply using original GANs loss function.

In Fig. 6, we choose the results from iteration 1200 to 1561. In these figures, it is obvious that when training with the help of Wasserstein Distance, the procedure is faster and more stable, considering that the orange line is generally below the blue one and the amplitude of fluctuation is far less than the latter. This conclusion can also be drawn from the numerical indices shown in Table 2. From these experiments, we can conclude that Wasserstein Distance can prominently enhance the stability of training.

5   Related Work

Generative Adversarial Network [9]. At present, more and more scholars turn their focus to generative-models-field in which one of the most impressive outcome is Generative Adversarial Network, as known as GANs [9]. In 2014, Goodfellow proposed GANs which composed of a discriminate network and a generative one. During the training, Generator tries it best to produce images as real as the ground truth while the Discriminator distinguishes the differences between the former and the latter. GANs laid the foundation for image restoration for a certain degree, and led the wave of deep learning research based on it [4,20].

Image Inpainting. The appearance of convolutional neural network prominently pushed forward the ability for computer to do those tasks and lots of works [12] proved that those architectures can be effective in Inpainting. Approaches applied in the region of inpainting formed a dichotomy including Traditional approaches and CNN-Based approaches. The basis of most Traditional approaches is image interpolation, image feature extraction, diffusion equation [18], Markov Random Fields [6], Bayes Theories [19] and theory of wavelet [17] etc. Those methods are limited performance because of restrictive capability in mending large missing area.

6   Conclusions

In this paper, we propose a convolutional neural network targeting image inpainting and acquiring a satisfying outcome on Paris Dataset. Our structure consists of an encoder-decoder pipeline and a multi-dimensional adversarial network. The pipeline oversees extracting and learning features from the residual input and predict the mighty inpainting content of it. On the other hand, the multi-dimensional adversarial network determines to pick the most proper distribution which can be represented as completing image from all the possibilities the pipeline provides. Specifically speaking, the global discriminator supervises the whole consistence of the reconstruction while local discriminator monitors the vividness in detail. The structure is trained combining with Wasserstein distance and perform a stable and reasonable results. Yet there are still some undesirable results which may due to the unfit parameters or construction of our network. Furthermore, the stability of the training can still be improved if we make some progress about Wasserstein Distance.

References

1. Abadi, M., et al.: Tensorflow: a system for large-scale machine learning. In: 12th {USENIX} Symposium on Operating Systems Design and Implementation ({OSDI} 2016), pp. 265–283 (2016)
2. Arjovsky, M., Chintala, S., Bottou, L.: Wasserstein GAN (2017)
3. Bedi, A., Gupta, S., Gupta, S.: Content aware fill based on similar images (Jul 4 2017), uS Patent 9,697,595
4. Chen, X., Duan, Y., Houthooft, R., Schulman, J., Sutskever, I., Abbeel, P.: Infogan: interpretable representation learning by information maximizing generative adversarial nets. In: Advances in Neural Information Processing Systems, pp. 2172–2180 (2016)
5. Efros, A.A., Leung, T.K.: Texture synthesis by non-parametric sampling. In: Seventh IEEE International Conference on Computer Vision (2002)
6. Ganapathi, V., Vickrey, D., Duchi, J., Koller, D.: Constrained approximate maximum entropy learning of Markov random fields (2012)
7. Ghasedi Dizaji, K., Herandi, A., Deng, C., Cai, W., Huang, H.: Deep clustering via joint convolutional autoencoder embedding and relative entropy minimization. In: The IEEE International Conference on Computer Vision (ICCV), October 2017

8. Golub, G.H., Hansen, P.C., O'Leary, D.P.: Tikhonov regularization and total least squares. SIAM J. Matrix Anal. Appl. **21**(1), 185–194 (1999)
9. Goodfellow, I.J., et al.: Generative adversarial nets. In: International Conference on Neural Information Processing Systems (2014)
10. Gulrajani, I., Ahmed, F., Arjovsky, M., Dumoulin, V., Courville, A.C.: Improved training of Wasserstein GANs. In: Advances in Neural Information Processing Systems, pp. 5767–5777 (2017)
11. Hays, J., Efros, A.A.: Scene completion using millions of photographs **26**(3), 4 (2007)
12. Jiao, L., Wu, H., Wang, H., Bie, R.: Multi-scale semantic image inpainting with residual learning and GAN. Neurocomputing **331**, 199–212 (2019)
13. Li, Y., Liu, S., Yang, J., Yang, M.: Generative face completion. CoRR abs/1704.05838 (2017). http://arxiv.org/abs/1704.05838
14. Ma, L., Jiang, W., Jie, Z., Wang, X.: Bidirectional image-sentence retrieval by local and global deep matching. Neurocomputing (2019). https://doi.org/10.1016/j.neucom.2018.11.089
15. Park, Y., Yang, H.S.: Convolutional neural network based on an extreme learning machine for image classification. Neurocomputing **339**, 66–76 (2019). https://doi.org/10.1016/j.neucom.2018.12.080
16. Pathak, D., Krähenbühl, P., Donahue, J., Darrell, T., Efros, A.: Context encoders: feature learning by inpainting (2016)
17. Patwardhan, K.A., Sapiro, G.: Projection based image and video inpainting using wavelets. In: International Conference on Image Processing (2003)
18. Tschumperlé, D., Deriche, R.: Vector-valued image regularization with PDE's: a common framework for different applications. IEEE Trans. Pattern Anal. Mach. Intell. 27 (2002)
19. Wen, T., Yang, F., Gu, J., Wang, L.: A novel Bayesian-based nonlocal reconstruction method for freehand 3D ultrasound imaging. Neurocomputing **168**, 104–118 (2015). https://doi.org/10.1016/j.neucom.2015.06.009
20. Zhang, H., et al.: StackGAN: text to photo-realistic image synthesis with stacked generative adversarial networks. In: Proceedings of the IEEE International Conference on Computer Vision, pp. 5907–5915 (2017)
21. Zhang, L., Zhang, Y., Gao, Y.: A Wasserstein GAN model with the total variational regularization. CoRR abs/1812.00810 (2018)
22. Zhao, Y., Price, B., Cohen, S., Gurari, D.: Guided image inpainting: replacing an image region by pulling content from another image (2018)

Interpretable Neural Computation for Real-World Compositional Visual Question Answering

Ruixue Tang and Chao Ma[✉]

MoE Key Lab of Artificial Intelligence, AI Institute, Shanghai Jiao Tong University,
Shanghai, China
{alicetang,chaoma}@sjtu.edu.cn

Abstract. There are two main lines of research on visual question answering (VQA): compositional model with explicit multi-hop reasoning, and monolithic network with implicit reasoning in the latent feature space. The former excels in interpretability and compositionality but fails on real-world images, while the latter usually achieves better performance due to model flexibility and parameter efficiency. We aim to combine the two to build an interpretable framework for real-world compositional VQA. In our framework, images and questions are disentangled into scene graphs and programs, and a symbolic program executor runs on them with full transparency to select the attention regions, which are then iteratively passed to a visual-linguistic pre-trained encoder to predict answers. Experiments conducted on the GQA benchmark demonstrate that our framework outperforms the compositional prior arts and achieves competitive accuracy among monolithic ones. With respect to the validity, plausibility and distribution metrics, our framework surpasses others by a considerable margin.

Keywords: VQA · Interpretable reasoning · Neural-symbolic reasoning

1 Introduction

The advances in deep representation learning and the development of large-scale dataset [4] have inspired a number of pioneering approaches in visual question answering (VQA). Though neural networks are powerful, flexible and robust, recent work has repeatedly demonstrated their flaws, showing how they struggle to generalize in a systematic manner [15], overly adhere to superficial and potentially misleading statistical associations instead of learning true causal relations [1]. The statistical nature of these models that supports robustness and versatility is also what hinders their interpretability, modularity, and soundness.

This work was supported by NSFC (60906119) and Shanghai Pujiang Program.

Y. Peng et al. (Eds.): PRCV 2020, LNCS 12307, pp. 89–101, 2020.
https://doi.org/10.1007/978-3-030-60636-7_8

Indeed, humans are particularly adept at making abstractions of various kinds. We instantly recognize objects and their attributes, parse complicated questions, and leverage such knowledge to reason and answer the questions. We can also clearly explain how we reason to obtain the answer. To this end, researchers consider how best to design a model that could imitate the reasoning procedure of humans while take advantages of neural networks. In particular, recent studies designed new VQA datasets, CLEVR [12] and GQA [11], in which each image comes with intricate, compositional questions generated by programs, and the programs exactly represent the human reasoning procedure. They facilitate us to learn an interpretable model by the supervision of programs.

Later, compositional models [3,8,19] show a promising direction in conferring reasoning ability for the end-to-end design by composing neural modules from a fixed predefined collection. However, the behaviors of the attention-based neural executor are still hard to explain. NS-VQA [24] moves one step further proposing a neural-symbolic approach for visual question answering that fully disentangles vision and language understanding from reasoning. However, these compositional models which designed for synthetic images in CLEVR are not capable of generalizing on real-images in GQA, where real images are much more semantic and visual richness than the synthetic ones and make it challenge to inferring objects, their interactions and subtle relations.

Drawing inspiration from NS-VQA, we further design a model for real-world visual reasoning and compositional question answering that incorporate the symbolic program execution with a vision-and-language pre-trained encoder, LXMERT [20]. We use neural networks as powerful tools for parsing – generating scene graph from images, and programs from questions. Next, we incorporate the symbolic program executor with the LXMERT by running the programs on the scene graphs to locate attention on object regions, which are then iteratively fed to LXMERT to finally get the answer predictions.

The combination of symbolic program executor and the visual-linguistic encoder offers two advantages. First, the use of symbolic representation offers robustness to long, complex and compositional questions. It endows our proposed model with transparent and interpretable reasoning process. Second, the visual-linguistic encoder, LXMERT, offers great cross-modality (image and text) representations to compensate the noisy scene graph. By conducting experiments on GQA dataset, results show that our model achieves competitive accuracy among prior arts, and notably, outperforms state-of-the-art models concerning the essential qualities (i.e. validity, plausibility and distribution) which are necessarily evaluated in GQA datasets.

To summarize, our main contributions are:

– We propose an interpretable framework for real-world visual reasoning and compositional question answering, where images and questions are disentangled into scene graphs and programs, respectively, and by incorporating with a vision-and-language pre-trained encoder LXMERT [20], we do a soft logic reasoning over the scene graphs.

- We extend the seq2seq [5] to predict two tokens at each step to generate the programs from questions.
- Our model achieves competitive accuracy among prior arts on GQA dataset, and notably, outperforms state-of-the-art models with respect to the essential qualities by a considerable margin.

2   Related Work

VQA. There have been numerous prominent models that address the VQA task. By and large they can be partitioned into two groups: 1) monolithic approaches [10,18,20], which embed both the image and question into a feature space and infer the answer by feature fusion; 2) neural module approaches [3,8,19], which first parse the question into a program assembly of neural modules, and then execute the modules over the image features for visual reasoning.

Scene Graph. This task is to produce graph representations of images in terms of objects and their relationships. Scene graphs have been shown effective in boosting several vision-language tasks [13,21,25]. However, scene graph detection is far from satisfactory compared to object detection [16,22,26]. To this end, we utilize a large-scale vision-and-language pre-trained encoder to compensate the noisy predicted scene graph.

3   Method

In this section, we first briefly summarize the LXMERT model (Sect. 3.1) and then describe how we incorporate symbolic program executor with it (Sect. 3.2).

3.1   Preliminary: LXMERT Background

LXMERT [20](Learning Cross-Modality Encoder Representations from Transformers) is a model for learning task-agnostic joint representations of image content and natural language. It is a large-scale Transformer model that consists of three encoders: an object relationship encoder, a language encoder, and a cross-modality encoder. As shown in Fig. 1, LXMERT takes two inputs: an image and its related sentence (e.g., a caption or a question). Each image is represented as a sequence of objects, and each sentence is represented as a sequence of words. Via careful design and combination of these self-attention and cross-attention layers, LXMERT is able to generate language representations, image representations, and cross-modality representations from the inputs.

The **object-relationship encoder** and **language encoder** are two transformer models and each of them only focuses on a single modality (i.e., language or vision). Each layer (left dashed blocks in Fig. 1) in a single-modality encoder contains a self-attention ('Self') sub-layer and a feed-forward ('FF') sub-layer. The ('Self') sub-layer at k-th layer could be formulated as:

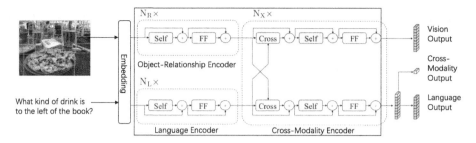

Fig. 1. The LXMERT model for learning vision-and-language cross-modality representations. 'Self' and 'Cross' are abbreviations for self-attention sub-layers and cross-attention sub-layers, respectively. 'FF' denotes a feed-forward sub-layer. The components in the solid block which consist of an object-relation encoder, a language encoder and a cross-modality encoder are applied in our interpretable framework introduced in the following.

$$\check{h}_i^k = \text{SelfAtt}_{\text{L} \to \text{L}} \left(h_i^{k-1}, \left\{ h_1^{k-1}, ..., h_n^{k-1} \right\} \right) \tag{1}$$

$$\check{v}_i^k = \text{SelfAtt}_{\text{R} \to \text{R}} \left(v_i^{k-1}, \left\{ v_1^{k-1}, ..., v_m^{k-1} \right\} \right) \tag{2}$$

where $\left\{ \hat{h}_i^k \right\}$ are language features and $\left\{ \hat{v}_i^k \right\}$ are vision features. We take N_L and N_R layers in the language encoder and the object-relationship encoder, respectively. A residual connection and layer normalization (annotated by the '+' sign in Fig. 1) is added after each sub-layer. Each cross-modality layer in the **cross-modality encoder** consists of one bi-directional cross-attention sub-layer, two self-attention sub-layers, and two feed-forward sub-layers. We stack N_X these cross-modality layers in our encoder implementation. Inside the k-th layer, the bi-directional cross-attention sub-layer ('Cross') is first applied, which contains two uni-directional cross-attention sub-layers: one from language to vision and one from vision to language, which are formulated as:

$$\hat{h}_i^k = \text{CrossAtt}_{\text{L} \to \text{R}} \left(h_i^{k-1}, \left\{ v_1^{k-1}, ..., v_m^{k-1} \right\} \right) \tag{3}$$

$$\hat{v}_i^k = \text{CrossAtt}_{\text{R} \to \text{L}} \left(v_i^{k-1}, \left\{ h_1^{k-1}, ..., h_n^{k-1} \right\} \right) \tag{4}$$

A residual connection and layer normalization are added after each sub-layer as in single-modality encoders.

LXMERT is pretrained on the large scale of datasets via five diverse representative pre-training tasks: masked language modeling, masked object prediction (feature regression and label classification), cross-modality matching, and image question answering. These tasks help in learning both intra-modality and cross-modality relationships.

3.2 The Interpretable Neural Computation

Our framework has three components: a scene parser (de-renderer), a question parser (program generator), and a symbolic program executor with LXMERT.

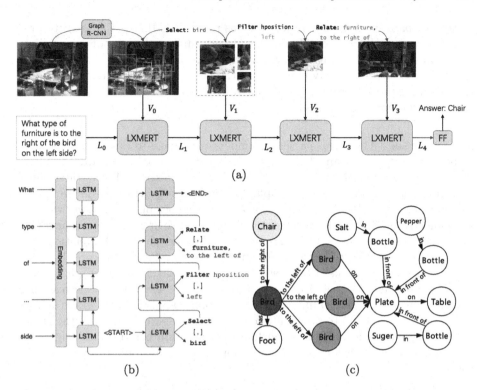

Fig. 2. Our interpretable framework has three components: first, a scene parser (Graph R-CNN [23]) that generates a scene graph (c) of each image; second, a question parser (b) that converts a question in natural language into a program; third, a neural-symbolic program executor incorporated with a neural module (LXMERT) (a), which utilizes the generated programs and scene graphs to perform soft logical reasoning. (Color figure online)

Given an image-question pair, the scene parser de-renders the image to obtain a scene graph (Fig. 2(c)), the question parser generates a program from the question (Fig. 2(b)), and the executor runs the program on the scene graph and passes the proposals to LXMERT to predict an answer (Fig. 2(a)).

Our scene parser generates a structural and disentangled representation of the scene in the image (Fig. 2(c)), based on which we can perform interpretable symbolic reasoning. We use a state-of-the-art method Graph R-CNN [23] to generates the scene graphs, which classifies the object, its attributes and relationships.

The question parser maps an input question in natural language (Fig. 2(b)) to a latent program. The program has a hierarchy of functional modules, each fulfilling an independent operation on the scene graph. Using a hierarchical program as our reasoning backbone naturally supplies compositionality and interpretability power.

The program executor takes the program output from the question parser, applies these functional modules on the scene graph of the input image, and iteratively pass the attention object regions to the LXMERT (Fig. 2(a)) to predict the answers. The executable program performs purely symbolic operations on its input throughout the execution process, and by the cooperation with LXMERT, it could not only compensate the noisy scene graph but also endow the reasoning process with interpretability. In the following section, we introduce the three components in detail.

Scene Parser. The scene parser de-renders the image to obtain a structural scene representation, named scene graph (see Fig. 2(c)). It generates a number of region proposals, and for each region, classifies the objects, attributes and their relationships. We use Graph R-CNN [23] to generate scene graphs for each image. Graph R-CNN is the prior art on scene graph generation, which is both effective and efficient at detecting objects and their relations in images. It utilizes Faster R-CNN [17] to localize a set of object regions, and a relation proposal network (RePN) to learn to efficiently compute relatedness scores between object pairs which are used to intelligently prune unlikely scene graph connections (as opposed to random pruning in prior work). Then, given the resulting sparsely connected scene graph candidate, it applies an attentional graph convolution network (aGCN) to propagate higher-order context throughout the graph – updating each object and relationship representation based on its neighbors. As for attributes of each object, we additionally train a simple CNN to classify them.

Question Parser. In GQA, each question could be represented as a program which is viewed as a sequence of functions $P = f_0, f_1, ...f_T$. Each function then sequentially executes on the output of the previous one to finally obtain the answer. There are 12 different categories of functions based on their coarse-grained functionality (e.g., "relate, verify, filter, choose, or"). In total, there are 139 fine-grained functions (e.g., "verify material, filter color, choose left|right"). For example, in Fig. 2, f_2 is `Relate: furniture, to the right of, [1]`, the functionality of which is to find a furniture which is to the right if the objects returned by f_1: `Filter hposition: left [0]`. `Relate` and `Filter` are called "operation". `[1]` is the "dependency" which implies that function f_2 depends on the second execution results and `furniture, to the right of` is the "arguments".

Our question parser is to generate operation and arguments of each function from question sentence (dependency could be inferred from the generated function sequence, so we need not predict it). We apply an attention-based sequence to sequence (seq2seq) model with an encoder-decoder structure similar to that in [5]. The encoder is a bidirectional LSTM [7] that takes as input a question of variable lengths and outputs an encoded vector e_i at time step i as

$$e_i = [e_i^F, e_i^B] \tag{5}$$

$$e_i^F, h_i^F = \text{LSTM}(\Phi_E(x_i), h_{i-1}^F) \quad e_i^B, h_i^B = \text{LSTM}(\Phi_E(x_i), h_{i+1}^B) \tag{6}$$

Here Φ_E is the jointly trained encoder word embedding. (e_i^F, h_i^F), (e_i^B, h_i^B) are the outputs and hidden vectors of the forward and backward networks at time step i. The decoder is a similar LSTM that generates a vector q_t from the previous token of the output sequence. In this paper, we extend the decoder LSTM to have two heads where output operation tokens and arguments tokens, respectively (see Fig. 2(b)). We concatenate the embedding of operation o_{t-1} and arguments g_{t-1} as the input of LSTM at step t. q_t is then fed to an attention layer to obtain a context vector c_t as a weighted sum of the encoded states via

$$q_t = \mathrm{LSTM}([\Phi_D(o_{t-1}), \Phi_D(g_{t-1})]), \quad \alpha_{t_i} \propto \exp(q_t^\top W_A e_i), \quad c_t = \sum_i \alpha_{t_i} e_i \quad (7)$$

where Φ_D is the decoder word embedding. For simplicity we set the dimensions of vectors q_t, e_i to be the same and let the attention weight matrix W_A to be an identity matrix. Finally, the context vector, together with the decoder output, is passed to a fully connected layers with softmax activation to obtain the distribution for the predicted token $o_t \sim \mathrm{softmax}(W_O[q_t, c_t])$ and $g_t \sim \mathrm{softmax}(W_G[q_t, c_t])$. Both the encoder and decoder have two hidden layers with a 256-dim hidden vector. We set the dimensions of both the encoder and decoder word vectors to be 300.

The Soft Logic Program Execution. Previous neural-symbolic based work [24] implements the program executor as a collection of deterministic, generic functional modules in Python, designed to host all logic operations on the scene graphs of synthetic images. However, the state-of-the-art scene graph generation of real images is far from practical to support all logical operations (the actual R@20 results of scene graph generation methods are around 25% while the desired are near 90%). Therefore, we apply a soft logic reasoning process that incorporates the symbolic program executor into a neural module (LXMERT [20]) which learns a strong vision-and-language representation to compensate the noisy scene graphs and on the other side, the program executor endows the LXMERT with the interpretability and sound attention regions.

The Selection of Functions. The symbolic program executor performs purely symbolic operations on its input. For example, given a scene graph (see Fig. 2(c)), Select: bird is to find the bounding boxes that contain bird – the four red circles. Filter hposition: left [0] is to pick the one that locates on the left side (the darker red circle). Relate: furniture, to the right of, [1] is to find the furniture that is to the right of the picked bird – the green circle. The functions output values could be *List of Objects*, *Boolean* or *String* (we call these function sets $\mathcal{F}_O$, $\mathcal{F}_B$ and $\mathcal{F}_S$, respectively, for simplicity), where *Object* specifically refers to the detected bounding box and *String* could refer to object name, attributes, relations, etc. Generally, $\mathcal{F}_O$ would re-locate the attention of the object regions while $\mathcal{F}_B$ and $\mathcal{F}_S$ would not, and $\mathcal{F}_O$ is always at the front of the function sequence and followed $\mathcal{F}_B$ and $\mathcal{F}_S$. To help LXMERT locate attention on proper regions, $\mathcal{F}_O$ is chose to incorporate with LXMERT and others are ignored. For example, in Fig. 2, the functions that with operation

`Select`, `Filter` and `Relate` are selected to perform re-locating regions in our framework.

Input Embeddings. We need to convert the inputs of LXMERT (i.e., an image and a question) into two sequences of features: word-level question embeddings and object-level image embeddings. The question embeddings are $\{h_i\}$:

$$\hat{w}_i = \text{WordEmbed}(w_i), \quad \hat{u}_i = \text{IdxEmbed}(i), \quad h_i = \text{LayerNorm}(\hat{w}_i + \hat{u}_i) \quad (8)$$

where w_i is a word in question sentence $\{w_1, ..., w_n\}$, i is w_i's absolute position in the sentence. The object-level image embeddings are $\{v_j\}$:

$$\hat{r}_j = \text{LayerNorm}(W_F r_j + b_F), \quad \hat{p}_j = \text{LayerNorm}(W_P p_j + b_P), \quad v_j = (\hat{r}_j + \hat{p}_j)/2 \quad (9)$$

where each object o_j is represented by its position feature (i.e., bounding box coordinates) p_j and its 2048-dimensional region-of-interest (RoI) feature r_i. We learn a position-aware embedding v_j by adding outputs of 2 fully-connected layers.

The Layout. As depicted in Fig. 2(a), firstly, object-level image embeddings of all the objects in each image ($V_0 = \{v_j\}$) and question embeddings ($L_0 = \{h_i\}$) are fed to LXMERT. Then, the function $f_t \in \mathcal{P}_O$ selects a list of objects at every step $t \in \{0, ..., T\}$ via our program executor, and the embeddings of selected object V_{t+1}, together with previous language representation output of LXMERT L_{t+1}, are passed to LXMERT to output the next language representation L_{t+2}. These could be formulated as:

$$L_0 = \{h_i\}, \; V_0 = \{v_j\}, \; V_{t+1} = \text{ImEmb}(\text{Exe}(f_t, V_t)), \; L_{t+1} = \text{LXMERT}(V_t, L_t) \quad (10)$$

where ImEmb() is the object-level image embeddings formulated in Eq. 9, Exe() is the symbolic executor. We only pass the hidden representation via the language output of LXMERT. Note that the LXMERT modules share the parameters. Finally, the language output at the last step is passed to a feed-forward network with softmax activation to obtain the distribution for the predicted answers.

4   Experiment

In this section, we conduct the following experiments: we evaluate our proposed model and its components on GQA v1.1 dataset [11].

4.1   Dataset

We demonstrate the value and performance of our model on the "balanced-split" of GQA v1.1, which contains 1M questions over 140K images with a more balanced answer distribution. Compared with the VQA v2.0 dataset [4], the questions in GQA are designed to require multi-hop reasoning to test the reasoning skills of developed models. Compared with the CLEVR dataset [12], GQA greatly increases the complexity of the semantic structure of questions, leading to a more diverse function set. The real-world images in GQA also bring in a bigger challenge in visual understanding. Following [11], the main evaluation metrics used in our experiments are accuracy, plausibility, validity and distribution.

4.2   Implementation Details

Parser. There are 1702 object classes and 310 relation classes in GQA dataset, and it has a long tail. Therefore, to train the Graph R-CNN, we only use the most frequent 500 object categories which account for 93.1% of the total instances and 50 relation categories which account for 95.9%. We use Faster R-CNN [17] associated with ResNet101 [6] as the backbone based on the PyTorch re-implementation. During training, the number of proposals from RPN is 256. For each proposal, we perform ROI align pooling, to get a 7×7 response map, which is then fed to a two-layer MLP to obtain each proposal's representation. We perform stage-wise training – we first pre-trained Faster R-CNN for object detection, and then fix the parameters in the backbone to train the scene graph generation model. SGD is used as the optimizer, with initial learning rate 1e-2 for both training stages. For question parser, we train with learning rate 7×10^{-4} for 20,000 iterations. The batch size is fixed to be 64.

Program Executor with LXMERT. For the LXMERT module, we set the number of layers N_L, N_X, and N_R to 9, 5, and 5 respectively. We initialize the weights of LXMERT using the model pre-trained on the large aggregated dataset[1]. To train the executor, we use a learning rate of $1e - 5$, a batch size of 32, and fine-tune the model from pre-trained parameters for 4 epochs.

4.3   Results

VQA. We compare our performance both with baselines, as appear in [11], as well as with other prior arts of VQA model. Apart from the standard accuracy metric and the more detailed type-based diagnosis (i.e. Binary, Open), we get further insight into reasoning capabilities by reporting three more metrics [11]:

Validity, Plausibility and **Distribution.** The validity metric checks whether a given answer is in the question scope, e.g. responding some color to a color question. The plausibility score goes a step further, measuring whether the answer is reasonable, or makes sense, given the question (e.g. elephant usually do not eat, say, pizza). The distribution score measures the overall match between the true answer distribution and the model predicted distribution (for this metric, lower is better). As Table 1 shows, our model achieves competitive accuracy among

---

[1] https://github.com/airsplay/lxmert.

Table 1. VQA results for single-model settings. The models with * are submissions to the GQA server but without published paper. For distribution score, lower is better.

Model	Binary	Open	Validity	Plausibility	Distribution↓	Accuracy
Local Prior [11]	47.90	16.66	84.33	84.31	13.98	31.24
Language [11]	61.90	22.69	96.39	87.30	17.93	41.07
Vision [11]	36.05	1.74	35.78	34.84	19.99	17.82
Lang+Vis [11]	63.26	31.80	96.02	84.25	7.46	46.55
BottomUp [2]	66.64	34.83	96.18	84.57	5.98	49.74
MAC [10]	71.23	38.91	96.16	84.48	5.34	54.06
NMN [3]	72.88	40.53	-	-	-	55.70
LCGN [9]	73.77	42.33	96.48	84.81	4.70	57.07
BAN [14]	76.00	40.41	96.16	85.58	10.52	57.10
SK T-Brain*	77.42	43.10	96.26	85.27	7.54	59.19
PVR*	77.69	43.01	96.45	84.53	5.80	59.27
LXMERT [20]	77.16	45.47	96.35	84.53	5.69	60.33
Ours	75.62	41.07	**96.87**	**87.94**	**2.72**	58.50

Table 2. The accuracy (%) of our question parser and symbolic executor. Program Acc. represents the accuracy of generated program, which is evaluated by the accuracy of operation token, arguments token and the function (It is positive when both operation and arguments in a function are correct). Executor Acc. represents the accuracy of the answers obtained by our deterministic part of program executor executed on the ground-truth scene graph, by using ground-truth (G.T.) and generated (Gen.) program.

Data split	Program Acc.			Executor Acc.	
	Operation	Arguments	Function	G.T.	Gen.
Testdev	97.31	82.52	81.76	-	-
Val	99.01	83.20	83.06	97.71	91.46

published approaches. Notably, our model outperforms state-of-the-art models (especially, LXMERT) with respect to the three metrics, which indicates that our model has more a comprehensive understanding of questions and does not learn from the data bias. NMN [3] is also a compositional method that uses the program supervision, but lack of cross-modality learning. Its poor performance implies the complex content in real images and question induces challenge to multi-hop reasoning. The strong image and language representations play a crucial role in our framework. More visualizations of the reasoning process in our method are provided in the supplementary material.

The Performance of Each Components. Since each component in our framework has essential impacts on final prediction, we also report the individual performance of them. Our question parser could reach the accuracy of 83.06% with respect to the function instances, specifically, 99.01% for "operation", 83.2% for "arguments" on val set (see Table 2). It implies our generated programs could recover the semantics of questions and provide sound interpretable reasoning skill.

We evaluate the scene graph generation via widely adopted metrics SGDet@K – the Recall@K of predicting objects and their relationships from scratch. We obtain 17.43, 22, 24.61 on SGDet@20, @50, @100, respectively.

We evaluate our deterministic symbolic program executor by applying it on ground-truth scene graph. Due to the incomplete and ambiguous annotations of scene graphs in GQA, the ground truth programs execute on the ground-truth scene graph results in a VQA accuracy of 97.71%. It revealing the performance upper-bound of models for GQA dataset. The accuracy of answers obtained by generated programs is 91.46%. These results suggest that the noisy visual recognition hinders the "high-level" logical reasoning in our model leading to the marginal decrease on the accuracy, but our interpretability enhanced design indeed helps our model to predict more valid and plausible answers.

5   Conclusion

In this paper, we have proposed an interpretable model for real-world compositional visual question answering, which combines the compositional and monolithic model to leverage the merits of both. In our method, images and questions are disentangled into scene graphs and programs, and a symbolic program executor runs on them with full transparency to locate the attention regions, which are then iteratively passed to a visual-linguistic pre-trained encoder to predict answers. The proposed model can explain its reasoning steps with a sequence of image attentions because of the symbolic nature of the execution. Experimental results demonstrate that our method not only achieves competitive accuracy among previous works, but also could predict the answers with more validity and plausibility.

References

1. Agrawal, A., Batra, D., Parikh, D.: Analyzing the behavior of visual question answering models. arXiv preprint arXiv:1606.07356 (2016)
2. Anderson, P., et al.: Bottom-up and top-down attention for image captioning and visual question answering. In: Proceedings of the IEEE Conference on Computer Vision and Pattern Recognition, pp. 6077–6086 (2018)
3. Andreas, J., Rohrbach, M., Darrell, T., Klein, D.: Neural module networks. In: Proceedings of the IEEE Conference on Computer Vision and Pattern Recognition, pp. 39–48 (2016)
4. Antol, S., et al.: VQA: visual question answering. In: Proceedings of the IEEE International Conference on Computer Vision, pp. 2425–2433 (2015)
5. Bahdanau, D., Cho, K., Bengio, Y.: Neural machine translation by jointly learning to align and translate. arXiv preprint arXiv:1409.0473 (2014)

6. He, K., Zhang, X., Ren, S., Sun, J.: Deep residual learning for image recognition. In: Proceedings of the IEEE Conference on Computer Vision and Pattern Recognition, pp. 770–778 (2016)
7. Hochreiter, S., Schmidhuber, J.: Long short-term memory. Neural Comput. **9**(8), 1735–1780 (1997)
8. Hu, R., Andreas, J., Rohrbach, M., Darrell, T., Saenko, K.: Learning to reason: end-to-end module networks for visual question answering. In: Proceedings of the IEEE International Conference on Computer Vision, pp. 804–813 (2017)
9. Hu, R., Rohrbach, A., Darrell, T., Saenko, K.: Language-conditioned graph networks for relational reasoning. In: Proceedings of the IEEE International Conference on Computer Vision, pp. 10294–10303 (2019)
10. Hudson, D.A., Manning, C.D.: Compositional attention networks for machine reasoning. arXiv preprint arXiv:1803.03067 (2018)
11. Hudson, D.A., Manning, C.D.: GQA: A new dataset for real-world visual reasoning and compositional question answering. arXiv preprint arXiv:1902.09506 (2019)
12. Johnson, J., Hariharan, B., van der Maaten, L., Fei-Fei, L., Lawrence Zitnick, C., Girshick, R.: CLEVR: a diagnostic dataset for compositional language and elementary visual reasoning. In: Proceedings of the IEEE Conference on Computer Vision and Pattern Recognition, pp. 2901–2910 (2017)
13. Johnson, J., et al.: Image retrieval using scene graphs. In: Proceedings of the IEEE Conference on Computer Vision and Pattern Recognition, pp. 3668–3678 (2015)
14. Kim, J.H., Jun, J., Zhang, B.T.: Bilinear attention networks. In: Advances in Neural Information Processing Systems, pp. 1564–1574 (2018)
15. Lake, B.M., Baroni, M.: Generalization without systematicity: On the compositional skills of sequence-to-sequence recurrent networks. arXiv preprint arXiv:1711.00350 (2017)
16. Li, Y., Ouyang, W., Zhou, B., Shi, J., Zhang, C., Wang, X.: Factorizable net: an efficient subgraph-based framework for scene graph generation. In: Ferrari, V., Hebert, M., Sminchisescu, C., Weiss, Y. (eds.) ECCV 2018. LNCS, vol. 11205, pp. 346–363. Springer, Cham (2018). https://doi.org/10.1007/978-3-030-01246-5_21
17. Ren, S., He, K., Girshick, R., Sun, J.: Faster R-CNN: towards real-time object detection with region proposal networks. In: Advances in Neural Information Processing Systems, pp. 91–99 (2015)
18. Santoro, A., et al.: A simple neural network module for relational reasoning. In: Advances in Neural Information Processing Systems, pp. 4967–4976 (2017)
19. Shi, J., Zhang, H., Li, J.: Explainable and explicit visual reasoning over scene graphs. In: Proceedings of the IEEE Conference on Computer Vision and Pattern Recognition, pp. 8376–8384 (2019)
20. Tan, H., Bansal, M.: LXMERT: learning cross-modality encoder representations from transformers. arXiv preprint arXiv:1908.07490 (2019)
21. Teney, D., Liu, L., van Den Hengel, A.: Graph-structured representations for visual question answering. In: Proceedings of the IEEE Conference on Computer Vision and Pattern Recognition, pp. 1–9 (2017)
22. Xu, D., Zhu, Y., Choy, C.B., Fei-Fei, L.: Scene graph generation by iterative message passing. In: Proceedings of the IEEE Conference on Computer Vision and Pattern Recognition, pp. 5410–5419 (2017)
23. Yang, J., Lu, J., Lee, S., Batra, D., Parikh, D.: Graph R-CNN for scene graph generation. In: Ferrari, V., Hebert, M., Sminchisescu, C., Weiss, Y. (eds.) ECCV 2018. LNCS, vol. 11205, pp. 690–706. Springer, Cham (2018). https://doi.org/10.1007/978-3-030-01246-5_41

24. Yi, K., Wu, J., Gan, C., Torralba, A., Kohli, P., Tenenbaum, J.: Neural-symbolic VQA: disentangling reasoning from vision and language understanding. In: Advances in Neural Information Processing Systems, pp. 1031–1042 (2018)
25. Yin, X., Ordonez, V.: Obj2text: Generating visually descriptive language from object layouts. arXiv preprint arXiv:1707.07102 (2017)
26. Zellers, R., Yatskar, M., Thomson, S., Choi, Y.: Neural motifs: Scene graph parsing with global context. In: Proceedings of the IEEE Conference on Computer Vision and Pattern Recognition. pp. 5831–5840 (2018)

Attention-Based Network for Semantic Image Segmentation via Adversarial Learning

Xinnan Ding[1], Ying Tian[1], Chenhui Wang[2(✉)], Yilong Li[1], Haodong Yang[1], and Kejun Wang[1(✉)]

[1] College of Automation, Harbin Engineering University, Harbin 150001, China
heukejun@126.com
[2] Department of Statistics, University of California, Los Angeles, CA 90095-1554, USA
harbin0451@g.ucla.edu

Abstract. As a fundamental research, semantic image segmentation is widely used in the computer vision system. In this paper, we explore the attention mechanism for semantic segmentation to improve the extraction and recovery of information efficiently. Mixed attention modules are designed for the segmentation task, and the attention-based network is the combination by the encoder of Xception and the decoder of residual connections. Experiments are conducted on the PASCAL VOC dataset, and the proposed method outperforms DeepLabV3Plus. In addition, the adversarial training is deployed based on the attention-based segmentation network, and the experimental results show the performance is further advanced with the addition of adversarial learning.

Keywords: Semantic image segmentation · Attention mechanism · Adversarial learning · Convolutional neural network

1 Introduction

Semantic image segmentation is a fundamental technology in computer vision, whose essence is a pixel-level image classification [1]. In the field of robotic vision and self-driving automobile [2], the semantic segmentation technology is applied for unmanned equipment to understand and analyze the surrounding environment; in the medical field, it is helpful to recognize abnormal or diseased parts in slice images [3]; in other fields such as security and graphics software, it also plays an irreplaceable role [4]. It can be seen that the semantic segmentation has substantial practical merit with the society requirement and technology development. Therefore, semantic segmentation has become a hot issue that appeals to more and more researchers.

The difficulty of making accurate segmentation lies in the complexity of images in natural scenes and the existence of multiple objects at multiple scales. In most of the existing semantic segmentation algorithms, many contributions are made in the structural improvement on the network [3, 5]. Moreover, the amount of training data has a critical influence on the segmentation results. The difficulty of getting enough annotated data for training further affects the performance of segmentation [6]. To overcome the hurdles

© Springer Nature Switzerland AG 2020
Y. Peng et al. (Eds.): PRCV 2020, LNCS 12307, pp. 102–114, 2020.
https://doi.org/10.1007/978-3-030-60636-7_9

in multiple scales of different object classes and the complicated background [7], the attention mechanism and the adversarial learning are explored in this work [8, 9], with advance in the network structure and training method. Although there are some existing works employing attention method in segmentation task [10], the application is simple and direct, neglecting the comprehensive means (positions and types) of introduction of attention. Additionally, we adopt the adversarial learning to further improve the effect of segmentation based on the attention-based network. In this paper, we have made the following contributions:

- The mixed domain attention module, combined with spatial domain attention and channel domain attention, is designed for the segmentation task, and we explore where is the suitable position to put different attention modules.
- An encoder based on Xception network, feature fusion, atrous convolution, and the mixed domain attention module is proposed. A residual decoder based on channel domain attention is designed to recover more details of the original information.
- We apply the method of adversarial learning to guide output results of the attention-based network near to the ground truth.
- Comprehensive experiments are provided on the PASCAL VOC 2012 dataset. In particular, the segmentation accuracy of this paper outperforms DeepLabV3Plus that is an authoritative model with remarkable segmentation performance.

2   Related Work

In 2014, Long et al. [1] employed the end-to-end fully convolutional networks (FCN), which is the first to employ deep learning method for semantic segmentation. With the remarkable ability to data representations of deep convolution networks, such as ResNet [2] and XceptionNet [3], the performance of semantic segmentation model is also improved. Google first proposed DeepLabV1 [5], based on the deep neutral network and the probabilistic model of conditional random field. From 2016 to 2018, Google improved DeepLabV1 every year, proposed a series of DeepLab (DeepLabV2 [11], DeepLabV3 [12] and DeepLabV3plus [13]), removing the probabilistic model, and replacing the atrous convolution instead of pooling to reduce the loss of feature.

2.1   Semantic Segmentation Models Based on Attention Mechanism

Attention mechanism is a method of selective focus based on human vision. It has been widely used in sequential tasks and computer vision in recent years [8, 9]. Some semantic segmentation models also involved the attention mechanism. Li et al. [10] proposed a feature pyramid attention network (PAN) to extract high-dimensional feature maps with more key information. The global attention module is used to recover the detail information in upsampling, but the application of attention is relatively simple. Similarly, Kong et al. [14] applied the global pyramid attention module (GPAM) and pyramid decoder module for semantic segmentation. Fu et al. [15] present the dual attention network (DAN), where channel attention is employed to learn the channel interdependence but ignoring information from the local features.

2.2   Semantic Segmentation Models Based on Improvement of Training

Hung et al. [16] enabled semi-supervised learning by using an adversarial network, utilizing weakly-labeled images to enhance the segmentation model. Zhan et al. [17] proposed a hybrid and matching self-supervised semantic segmentation model by adding a mixed-and-matching tuning stage in the self-supervised training process, to reduce the amount of annotated training data used. To overcome the negative impact of imbalanced semantic annotations distribution, Liu et al. [18] explored the data enhancement methods to balance the distribution of data, using generative adversarial network (GANs) [19, 20]. This approach improved the segmentation performance of low-accuracy classes, and could be easily applied to any other segmentation models.

3   Methods

3.1   Overview

As shown in Fig. 1, the semantic segmentation network is mainly divided into two parts: an encoder and a decoder, and the attention method is deployed in both the encoder and the decoder. The encoder is based on Xception and the mixed domain attention module. Xception can capture information efficiently, and the attention module is able to help the model learn the effective features. The decoder network is based on the channel attention module in upsampling of residual skip-connections to recover the pixel position of the original image more accurately.

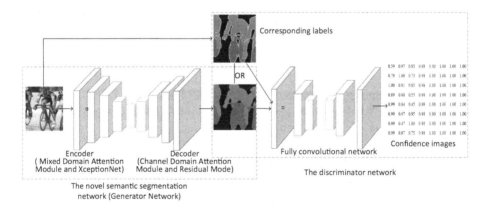

Fig. 1. Main structure of the proposed model.

Furthermore, the method of adversarial learning is employed in training to guide the segmentation network to predict near to the ground truth. In adversarial learning, we need to add a discriminator, which is a fully convolutional network. The input of discriminator is the ground truth or the result of a semantic segmentation network as illustrated in Fig. 1. The output is a single channel confidence map with the same resolution, in which each pixel of the output indicates the possibility that the classification result of this pixel is from the ground truth.

3.2   Mixed Domain Attention Module

The attention model is able to make the network capture semantic information better by paying more attention to useful features while ignoring irrelevant features [8]. For the semantic segmentation task, images are always with complicated backgrounds, multiple semantic classes, and multiple image resolutions. Existing attention mechanism can be divided into two categories: spatial domain attention module, channel domain attention module. We explore the fusion of them, and design mixed domain attention modules for semantic segmentation.

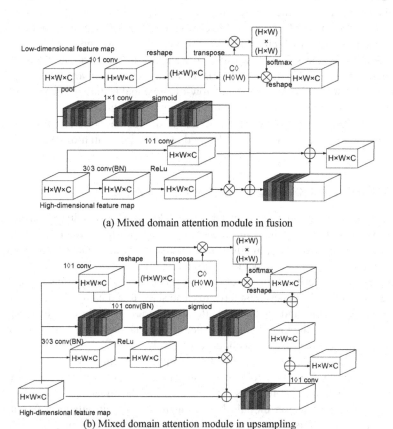

(a) Mixed domain attention module in fusion

(b) Mixed domain attention module in upsampling

Fig. 2. Mixed domain attention modules.

The spatial domain attention module is to capture the critical information from the input image by various spatial transformations. The method of the spatial domain attention is to make the weight of the key features increasing, and the weight of irrelevant features decreasing by evaluating the importance of pixel features [21]. Channel domain attention is different, and it emphasizes to evaluate the importance of each filter for the feature map [9]. The weight of each channel is computed according to the contribution to the effective information.

Mixed domain attention module compromises the merits of spatial domain attention and channel domain attention, and compensates for their shortcomings. Spatial domain attention only focuses on the local features in the two-dimensional space, ignoring the internal relationship between channels, while the channel domain attention is too direct and simple, neglecting the pixel features in each channel. A union of both is a dual-attentional approach, focusing on the effective features in both the spatial domain and the channel domain. Therefore, we advocate the fusion of the two mentioned attention modules, as the mixed domain attention module.

We design two kinds of mixed domain attention modules for fusion and upsample, the detailed structures of which are illustrated Fig. 2. The mixed domain attention module of fusion is provided in Subfigure (a). Mixed domain attention is applied to the fusion of the two feature maps, in which spatial weights and channel weights are obtained from low-dimensional features. These two sorts of weights can help estimate the importance of each pixel and channel in the high-dimensional features respectively. Then, the feature map with spatial weights is contacted with low-dimensional feature maps on the channel. The mixed domain attention module of the upsampling is illustrated as subfigure (b) of Fig. 2. The designing principle is similar to that of the fusion module. The difference is that the spatial and channel weights are learned from the input high-dimensional feature map.

3.3 Attention-Based Semantic Segmentation Network

The encoder with Xception backbone and the decoder based on residual connections are proposed with attention mechanism, illustrated as Fig. 3. The mixed domain attention module can be employed to capture information efficiently and reduce influence related to the multiple scales in the encoder. Additionally, the estimating of the importance of each channel is more critical for the decoder, as each layer produces feature maps with numerous channels. The experimental results also show that the mixed attention module is the best in the fusion, and the channel attention module is the best in the upsampling (Sect. 4.1). Therefore, the mixed attention module and the channel attention module are employed in the encoder and the decoder respectively.

We design an encoder structure based on Xception and the mixed domain attention module, combining Xception, feature fusion, atrous convolution and mixed domain attention to extract effective features. The encoder has the advantages of XceptionNet. A multi-scale feature fusion module based on mixed domain attention is put in the encoder network to focus on the objects of different scales in each image.

Multi-scale feature fusion module consists of five branches. The first one is to capture image-level global information. The second is to preserve the original information of the input feature map and refine the edge partly through 1×1 convolution. The last three branches are used to extract features on different scales through three convolutional layers (3×3, 5×5, and 7×7). In addition, the mixed domain attention module is applied in the last three branches to pay dual special attention to the space domain and the channel domain. Output of last three branches is fused as an attention weight vector, and it is multiplied with the produced feature map of the second branch, which is equivalent to the local feature map with attention on multiple image resolutions. Then this local feature map is merged with the global features from the first branch. Therefore, attention

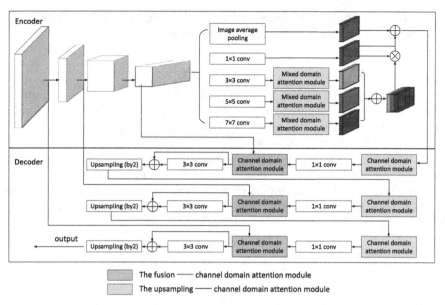

Fig. 3. Attention-based semantic segmentation network.

module is adopted in the encoder to fuse the global information, feature maps of different scales, and the local features.

It is essential to recover and locate the original information in upsampling of the decoder for semantic segmentation, and the low-dimensional features are helpful to recover the valuable details effectively. The number of channels of the feature map produced is very large in the decoder, so it is critical to evaluate the contribution of each filter. The spatial position information is not accurate in the decoder, so it is more reasonable to employ the channel domain attention in the decoder.

The details of structure are illustrated as the decoder of Fig. 3. The decoder consists of three decoder modules, each of which is the same process. The feature map is input into the channel attention module and the convolutional layer (1 × 1) to reduce the number of output channels of the encoder. Then, the produced feature map is fused with the low-dimensional feature map corresponding to the encoder, and the fused features are sent to the convolutional layer (3 × 3) and residual skip-connections, to fuse the features from the both high and low dimensions. Finally, the feature map is available to the next decoder module by a bilinear interpolation with a sampling factor of two. It is fed into the three decoder modules in the same process as described above to gain the segmentation result of the same size as the original input.

3.4 Adversarial Training for Semantic Segmentation

Both the network structure and the training method affect the final performance. The adversarial training method is adopted in to drive the segmentation result to the ground truth [16, 22]. Drawing on the method of generative adversarial networks [20], the attention-based semantic segmentation network proposed in this paper is deployed as a generator, with a fully convolutional network as a discriminator to differentiate the segmentation results from the network or manual annotations.

3.4.1 Network Architecture

The model of adversarial training for semantic segmentation in this paper is illustrated as Fig. 4. The network structure contains two parts: discriminator and generator, similar to the typical GAN model. The semantic segmentation network proposed in Sect. 3.3 is adopted as the generator, and we design a fully convolutional network as the discriminator. The semantic pixel label of the image or the output of the segmented network is sent to the discriminator in one-hot encoding. The discriminator produces a single-channel confidence map with the same resolution as the input, where each pixel indicates the probability of the segmentation result from the ground truth (denoted as1) or the network (denoted as 0).

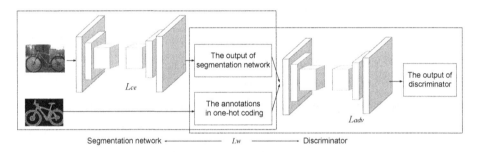

Fig. 4. The model in adversarial training.

3.4.2 Loss Function

The loss function of the semantic segmentation adversarial training is mainly composed of the basic semantic segmentation loss and the adversarial loss. The adversarial loss can establish linkages between the generator and the discriminator. In this way, they can share the learned information.

The basic semantic segmentation loss function is a multi-class cross-entropy loss:

$$L_{ce} = -\sum_{h,w}\sum_{c \in C} Y_n^{(h,w,c)} \log(S(X_n)^{(h,w,c)}) \tag{1}$$

where X_n is the input image, and Y_n is the corresponding one-hot coded with pixel labels. C is the total number of semantic classes of the dataset, and the network output, the segmentation result, is $S(X_n)$.

The task of the discriminator is to determine whether the input comes from the ground truth or the segmentation network [19]. If the segmentation result of the coordinate (h,w) is from the network, the discriminator output y_n will be expected to be 0. Otherwise, y_n

will be expected to be 1. The adversarial loss is expressed as:

$$L_{adv} = - \sum_{h,w} \log(D(S(X_n))^{(h,w)})$$

(2)

Therefore, the loss function with adversarial training is a weighted sum of the multi-class cross entropy loss L_{ce} and the adversarial loss L_{adv}:

$$L_w = L_{ce} + \lambda_{adv} L_{adv}$$

(3)

where λ_{adv} is the constant used to balance the two losses. Through the loss, the segmentation network is combined with the discriminator.

4   Experiments

All experiments are conducted in the GeForce GTX1080 hardware environment and the dataset of PASCAL Visual Object Classes 2012 (PASCAL VOC 2012) [18]. Due to he limitation of hardware, the batch size of the entire experiments is set to be 4. Moreover, this paper adopts the polynomial attenuation learning rate update strategy. The initial learning rate is 7e−3, and the minimum is 1e−6. The momentum optimizer is applied in training with γ as 0.9.

4.1   Impact of Attention Modules

Attention method can enhance the network's attention to the key features, which may overcome the difficulty caused by the complex background or multiple scales in natural scenes. Mixed domain modules are designed for the segmentation network.

Different attention modules are added to the structure of DeepLabV3plus to evaluate performance in the provided experiments. Fusion attention modules are placed to the pyramid fusion with the atrous convolution, and the fusion of the low-dimensional feature map and the high-dimensional. The upsampling attention modules are put to the first upsampling of DeepLabV3plus. Six attention modules are adopted for the structure to compare the performance of different types (spatial, channel, and mixed) and different positions (fusion and upsampling).

It can be seen from Table 1, both mIOU and PA have been improved with the attention module added. All attention modules in fusion lead to better segmentation performance, and mixed domain attention is the best. However, the results are worse when the spatial attention module is put alone in upsampling. The reason may be that the input information in the spatial domain is derived from upsampling, features without accurate details. Accordingly, adding spatial attention in upsampling reduces the accuracy of segmentation. In contrast, channel domain attentions can play a positive role due to the large number of channels in upsampling. The mixed attention is a combination of the spatial and the channel, so the results are improved slightly.

It can be concluded that the mixed domain attention module is best in fusion, and the channel domain attention module is satisfactory, especially in the upsampling.

Table 1. Performance comparison among attention modules.

Spatial domain attention module		Channel domain attention module		Mixed domain attention module		mIOU (%)	PA (%)
Fusion	Upsampling	Fusion	Upsampling	Fusion	Upsampling		
						65.2	91.0
√						70.0	92.2
	√					65.1	90.8
		√				70.8	92.3
			√			67.9	91.4
				√		71.2	93.0
					√	66.9	91.2
√	√					68.0	91.4
		√	√			72.0	93.8
				√	√	68.7	91.5

4.2 Impact of Encoder and Decoder Structure

The mixed domain attention mechanism can capture the useful information more effectively in the encoder, while estimating the importance of each filter is more critical in the decoder due to the large number of channels of the produced feature maps. Therefore, it is reasonable to adopt mixed attention module in the fusion of the encoder, and the channel attention module in the upsampling of the decoder.

Table 2. Impact of encoder and decoder structure.

DeepLabV3Plus (encoder or decoder)	Attention-based encoder of Xception	Attention-base decoder of residual connections	mIOU (%)	PA (%)
√			65.2	91.0
√	√		74.2	94.2
√		√	74.8	94.6
	√	√	76.5	95.0

We design an encoder based on the fusion domain attention module and Xception network, and a decoder based on the residual connections and channel domain attention module. The proposed encoder and the proposed decoder are used to replace the encoder and the decoder in DeepLabv3plus respectively in the experiments, to test the effectiveness of the designed structures. The experimental results are reported in Table 2. It can be seen that the encoder increases mIOU by 0.09 and PA by 0.032. For the decoder, mIOU is enhanced by 0.096 and PA is enhanced by 0.036. The attention-based semantic segmentation network, with Xception and residual connections, yields the best improvement in both mIOU and PA, by 0.113 and 0.04 respectively. We also can obverse that the detailed object boundary recovery is improved visibly in Fig. 5. The attention-based semantic segmentation network has attained the expected results.

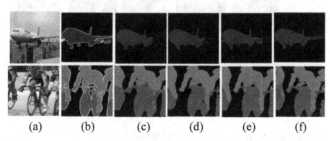

(a)   (b)   (c)   (d)   (e)   (f)

Fig. 5. Visualization examples of different networks. ((a) original image (b) ground truth (c) DeepLabV3Plus (d) attention-based encoder + DeepLabV3Plus decoder (e) DeepLabV3Plus encoder + attention-based decoder (f) attention-based network)

4.3 Impact of Adversarial Training

The adversarial training method is employed to guide the network to predict the segmentation near to the ground truth to improve the proposed network. The adversarial training is applied to optimize DeepLabV3Plus and the attention-based segmentation network in experiments. We compare mIOU of different semantic segmentation networks with adversarial training in Table 3 (λ_{adv} defaults to 0.01). For all networks, the segmentation performance with adversarial training exceeds that of the original network, and adversarial training yields 0.026 and 0.013 improvement of mIOU respectively. However, it is noteworthy that the proposed network is superior, even compared with DeepLabV3Plus under adversarial training. The best results are obtained for the segmentation model with adversarial training, with mIOU of 0.778.

Table 3. Impact of different segmentation networks with adversarial training.

Network	mIOU(%)
DeepLabV3Plus	65.2
DeepLabV3Plus+ adversarial training	67.8
The attention-based segmentation network	76.5
The attention-based segmentation network + adversarial training	77.8

Visualization examples with adversarial training are shown in Fig. 6. The proposed segmentation network with adversarial training attains the best results visibly, with obvious improvements in both the sharp boundaries and the pixel classification.

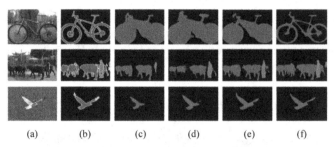

Fig. 6. Visualization examples of adversarial training ((a) original images (b) ground truth (c) DeepLabV3Plus (d) DeepLabV3Plus with adversarial training (e) the attention-based segmentation network (f) the attention-based segmentation network)

4.4 Comparisons with State-of-the-Art Methods

The proposed method is compared with state-of-the-art methods: DeepLabV3Plus [13], AL [16], GPAM [14], DAN [15], and PAN [10]. DeepLabV3Plus is a classic and authoritative algorithm. GPAM, DAN, and PAN all employ attention mechanism for segmentation, but the approaches of introducing it into the network are different. AL uses the method of GAN to implement semi-supervised learning.

Table 4. Comparisons with state-of-the-art methods on the PASCAL VOC dataset.

Methods	mIOU(%)
DeepLabV3Plus [13]	65.2
AL [16]	74.9
GPAM [14]	72.3
DAN [15]	74.1
PAN [10]	75.8
Attention-based network (Ours)	76.5
Attention-based network+ adversarial training (Ours)	77.8

As illustrated in Table 4, the proposed attention-based network yields the best result, and the performance is further improved with adversarial training. Compared with GPAM [14], DAN [15], and PAN [10], mIOU is 0.042, 0.024, 0.013 higher, respectively. The reason is that GPAM, DAN, and PAN exploit attention mechanism simply, without exploring the suitable type and position of attention module in segmentation network. PAN and GPAM only apply the global attention, ignoring capturing contextual information from the local features. DAN utilizes spatial attention module and channel attention module, but they are set to fuse the features from the encoder. In this paper, the mixed domain attention module and the channel domain attention module are deployed in the encoder and the decoder respectively, and the structure is determined by theoretical analysis and experiment, so the better effect is obtained. In addition, the purpose of AL [16] is to employ adversarial learning to realize semi-supervised learning, and the used network is simple. We can find that the original proposed network achieves better results than AL, and the mIOU is further increased by adapting the method of adversarial training.

5 Conclusion

We have done a comprehensive study about the attention mechanism for semantic segmentation, and designed mixed attention modules that can be used for semantic segmentation in fusion or upsampling. Moreover, the mixed domain attention module is combined with Xception to build the encoder, and the decoder is based on the channel domain attention module with residual skip-connections. The experimental results show an outstanding segmentation effect of the proposed model. Furthermore, the segmentation performance is further improved by adversarial training.

References

1. Badrinarayanan, V., Handa, A., Cipolla, R.: SegNet: a deep convolutional encoder-decoder architecture for robust semantic pixel-wise labelling. IEEE Trans. Pattern Anal. Mach. Intell. **39**(12), 2481–2459 (2017)
2. Lateef, F., Ruichek, Y.: Survey on semantic segmentation using deep learning techniques. Neurocomputing **338**(21), 321–348 (2019)
3. Mo, J., Lei, Z., Feng, Y.: Exudate-based diabetic macular edema recognition in retinal images using cascaded deep residual networks. Neurocomputing **290**, 161–171 (2018)
4. Dai, J., Li, Y., He, K., Su, J.: R-FCN: object detection via region-based fully convolutional networks. In: Proceedings of the Advances in Neural Information Processing Systems, pp. 379–387 (2016)
5. Chen, L.C., Papandreou, G., Kokkinos, I., Murphy, K., Yuille, A.L.: Semantic image segmentation with deep convolutional nets and fully connected CRFs. In: Proceedings of the IEEE Conference Computer Vision and Pattern Recognition (CVPR), pp. 357–361 (2014)
6. Everingham, M., Eslami, S.M.A., Gool, L.V., Williams, C.K.I., Winn, J., Zisserman, A.: The Pascal visual object classes challenge a retrospective. Int. J. Comput. Vis. **111**(1), 98–136 (2015)
7. Chen, L.C., Yang, Y., Wang, J., Xu, W., Yuille, A.L.: Attention to scale: scale-aware semantic image segmentation. In: Proceedings of the IEEE Conference Computer Vision and Pattern Recognition (CVPR) (2017)
8. Wang, X., Girshick, R., Gupta, A., He, K.: Non-local neural networks. In: Proceedings of the IEEE Conference Computer Vision and Pattern Recognition (CVPR), pp. 7794–7803 (2018)
9. Jie, H., Shen, L., Sun, G.: Squeeze-and-excitation networks. In: Proceedings of the IEEE Conference Computer Vision and Pattern Recognition (CVPR), pp. 7132–7141 (2018)
10. Li, H., Xiong, P., An, J., Wang, L.: Pyramid Attention Network for Semantic Segmentation. arXiv:1805.10180 (2016)
11. Chen, L.C., Papandreou, G., Kokkinos, I., Yuille, A.L.: DeepLab: semantic image segmentation with deep convolutional nets, atrous convolution, and fully connected CRFs. IEEE Trans. Pattern Anal. Mach. Intell. **40**(4), 834–848 (2018)
12. Chen, L.C., Papandreou, G., Schroff, F., Adam, H.: Rethinking atrous convolution for semantic image segmentation. arXiv:706.05587 (2017)
13. Chen, L.C., Zhu, Y., Papandreou, G., Schroff, F., Adam, H.: Encoder-decoder with atrous separable convolution for semantic image segmentation. arXiv:1706.05587 (2017)

14. Kong, H., Hu, J., Fan, L., Zhang, X., Fang, Y.: Encoder–decoder with double spatial pyramid for semantic segmentation. J. Electron. Imaging **28**(6), 063007 (2019)
15. Fu, J., Liu, J., Tian, H., Li, Y., Bao, Y., Fang, Z.: Dual attention network for scene segmentation. In: Proceedings of the IEEE Conference Computer Vision and Pattern Recognition (CVPR) (2019)
16. Hung, W.C., Tsai, Y.H., Liou, Y.T., Lin, Y.Y., Yang, M.H.: Adversarial learning for semi-supervised semantic segmentation. In: British Machine Vision Conference (2018)
17. Zhan, X., Liu, Z., Luo, P., Tang, X., Chen, C.L.: Mix-and-match tuning for self-supervised semantic segmentation. In: AAAI Conference on Artificial Intelligence (2018)
18. Liu, S., Zhang, J., Chen, Y., Liu, Y., Qin, Z., Wang, T.: Pixel Level Data Augmentation for Semantic Image Segmentation using Generative Adversarial Networks. arXiv:1811.00174 (2018)
19. Goodfellow, I.J., et al.: Generative adversarial networks. In: Proceedings of the Advance Neural Information Processing Systems (NIPS), pp. 2672–2680 (2014)
20. Isola, P., Zhu, J.Y., Zhou, T., Alexei, A.E.: Image-to-image translation with conditional adversarial networks. In: Proceedings of the IEEE Conference Computer Vision and Pattern Recognition (CVPR), pp. 5967–5976 (2017)
21. Hu, J., Shen, L., Albanie, S., Sun, G., Wu, E.: Squeeze-and-excitation networks. IEEE Trans. Pattern Anal. Mach. Intell. (Early Access) (2019)
22. Luc, P., Couprie, C., Chintala, S., Verbeek, J.: Semantic segmentation using adversarial networks. In: Workshop on Adversarial Training, Neural Information Processing Systems, Barcelona (2016)

Efficient Single Shot Object Detector Towards More Accurate and Faster Prediction

Shengxiang Qi[(⊠)] and Jiarong Yang

Shanghai Electric Group Co., Ltd. Central Academe, Shanghai 200070, China
shengxiang.qi@gmail.com

Abstract. Although a series of refinements on single shot object detector (SSD) are presented recently for better precision, most come at the cost of increased inference time. Inspiringly, we propose a very efficient SSD (ESSD) towards more accurate and faster detection. It could not only significantly optimize the detection accuracy, but also greatly improve the computational efficiency. The core lies in the proposed neighbor-scale feature fusion, a simple but effective way, to reduce the channel dimensionality followed by integrating neighbor-scale feature layers in the network. That is the key to characterize the principal component expression of objects in fewer dimensions and strengthen the abstraction of objects on both the current and higher feature layers, which evidently decrease the inference time while improving the performance. Experimental results show that the mean average precision (mAP) of ESSD on Pascal VOC 2007 and 2012 evaluations achieves 81.2 and 79.1, respectively, as well as the average speed reaches 52.9 fps for a 512 × 512 input, which actually outperform many state-of-the-art methods.

Keywords: Object detection · Computer vision · Convolutional neural network · Deep learning

1 Introduction

As an important task in computer vision, object detection aims to accurately identify the interested objects from natural scenes, and correspondingly give the coordinates of the bounding boxes where these objects are located. The existing object detection techniques according to their applications could be mainly divided into two types, the specific target detection and generic object detection [1]. The former focuses on some special object tasks in specific scenarios, such as the infrared target detection [2] and the satellite target detection [3]. These models are generally highly customized whose scope of application is often limited. In contrast, the latter does not develop according to the characteristics of the objects, but pays more attention to the generalization of the algorithm models. So it is widely considered to be more adaptable for complex scenes, which brings us a great challenge in object detection research.

In general, the research on generic object detection often use the publicly available datasets consisting of large amounts of images with natural scenes containing up to dozens of objects as the evaluation benchmark [4, 5]. Facing this task, the early models

© Springer Nature Switzerland AG 2020
Y. Peng et al. (Eds.): PRCV 2020, LNCS 12307, pp. 115–124, 2020.
https://doi.org/10.1007/978-3-030-60636-7_10

based on artificial feature are not only difficult in characteristic expression, but also perform poorly when dealing with multi-object detection tasks in pan-natural scenes [6]. Encouragingly, the development of convolutional neural network (CNN) in the recent five years has boosted a number of milestone breakthroughs for generic object detection [7–15]. Up to now, majorly two solutions have been formed for the task based on CNN, namely the two-stage models and one-stage models [16]. The two-stage models, such as Faster R-CNN [7], R-FCN [8] and FPN [9], are prone to coarsely extract candidate regions with proposals and then proceeds to fine prediction by integrating their respective frameworks of CNN. They generally obtain better scores in accuracy but require more cost on inference time. In view of the fact that the computational efficiency of the two-stage scheme is difficult to meet the scenarios with high real-time requirement, the one-stage models then emerged at the historic moment. Concisely, these models like YOLO [10, 11] and SSD [12] construct a single framework of CNN as the unique backbone to directly classify the objects and regress their bounding boxes from inputs. The deep network is performed only once so that this kind of models often has satisfactory computational efficiency, while the precision is somehow lost. Regarding to remedy this deficiency, numerous improved techniques have been recommended successively. Among them, as one of the classical one-stage model, the single shot detector (SSD) is made up for its precision by a series of refinements including DSSD [13], FSSD [14] and RSSD [15] via adding more complex layers to the network. However, the increments would always result in the degradation of computational efficiency as well.

Towards more accurate and faster object detection, we propose a very efficient SSD, named ESSD, in this paper. Although it is also derived from the SSD model, ours is inspiring for the improvement on both the detection accuracy and the computational efficiency, which are different from others [13–15]. To achieve the goal, we creatively provide a simple but effective way, namely the neighbor-scale feature fusion. It contains two crucial operations for feature layers in the network, the channel dimensionality reduction and the neighbor-scale integration. The former is used to characterize the principal component expression for objects in fewer dimensions, and the latter promotes to strengthen the abstraction of objects on the current and higher feature layers. That is the key to greatly decrease the inference time while improving the prediction accuracy. Finally, experiments are performed on the publicly available Pascal VOC 2007 and 2012 benchmarks [4, 5], and the results validate the effectiveness of our proposed model, which actually outperforms the state-of-the-art methods in both the precision and the efficiency.

2 Efficient Single Shot Object Detector

Although the traditional SSD [12] model has shown effective performance when dealing with natural scenes, its structure of a single network exposes an inevitable flaws as well. The simple cascade of feature layers makes it impossible to fully mine and correlate the information in feature layers, while the further complication for the network would also result in a degradation in computational efficiency. To change the contradiction, we propose a novel model, the ESSD, by combining the channel dimensionality reduction and neighbor-scale integration for feature layers in the network, called the neighbor-scale feature fusion. Instead of increasing the calculation burden, it significantly optimizes the detection accuracy while greatly improving the computational efficiency.

2.1 SSD Network

SSD [12] is a classical one-stage object detection model. It adopts the VGG16 [17] network as the backbone and uses small convolution filters to predict the scores of a series of default prior boxes belonging to each class and the offsets relative to real truth bounding regions in multi-scale feature layers, to realize the object classification and location. In details, the structure of a typical SSD network mainly consists of two parts, the backbone VGG16 convolutional network (without the classification layer) and the extra convolutional network. The front VGG16 is used to extract preliminary features from the images, and the extra module is used to further extract the feature maps generated from the former. By a cascade manner, SSD is to increase the extra convolutional layers to the end of VGG16. These feature layers gradually decrease in resolution, that is, the model allows prediction from extracted features under multiple scales. There is only once calculation on the deep convolutional network in the inference of SSD. In addition, the classification for object recognition and the regression for bounding box location are all performed on each feature map by full convolution, so that SSD could achieve competitive speed in most real-time tasks and has prediction ability for multi-scale complex scenarios.

2.2 Proposed ESSD Network

The proposed ESSD network is mainly composed of two parts, the basic backbone network and the neighbor-scale feature fusion module. The backbone network adopts the SSD architecture with a 512×512 input in our model. Conventionally, the feature maps in SSD are extracted by stepwise downscaling the cascade convolution layers through the network, and then provided for prediction on multiple different scales (totally 7 feature layers are extracted for a 512×512 input). Compared with SSD, our ESSD model does not directly adopt these feature layers to make predictions. Instead, we use them for neighbor-scale feature fusion by channel dimension reduction and neighbor-scale integration, as shown in Fig. 1. The purpose is that: (1) channel dimensionality reduction helps to characterize the principal component expression of the objects in fewer feature dimensions, so as to highlight the effective components for object features while decreasing the calculation amount for subsequent prediction; (2) neighbor-scale fusion helps to integrate the feature abstraction of the objects on both the current and deeper convolution layer, so as to strengthen the semantic expression ability for the object features in related scales. Afterwards, the predictions are inferred on the neighbor-scale fused feature maps by a series of default prior boxes as in [11–15]. As a result, the proposed ESSD requires fewer but more effective feature dimensions for prediction, which plays an important role in achieving faster speed and better accuracy.

2.3 Neighbor-Scale Feature Fusion

Let f_i be the i-th feature layer obtained by SSD backbone network, then its corresponding neighbor-scale fused feature layer F_i in ESSD can be expressed as follows:

$$F_i = \begin{cases} \mathbf{C}_i\{\mathbf{R}_i(f_i), \mathbf{S}_i[\mathbf{R}_i(f_{i+1})]\}, & \text{if } i \neq \text{top layer} \\ \mathbf{R}_i(f_i), & \text{if } i = \text{top layer} \end{cases}, \tag{1}$$

ESSD Network Structure

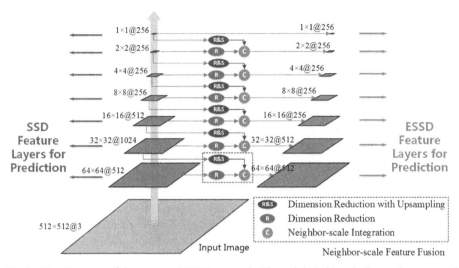

Fig. 1. The Structure of the proposed ESSD network. The red dotted box indicates the proposed neighbor-scale feature fusion including the channel dimensionality reduction and the neighbor-scale integration. The features for prediction extracted from SSD and ESSD are colored by blue and orange, respectively. Layers not used for prediction are ignored in the figure. (Color figure online)

where R_i represents the channel dimension reduction corresponding to the i-th layer, that is, to decrease the original feature dimension from (d_i, d_{i+1}) in (f_i, f_{i+1}) to $(D_i/2, D_{i+1}/2)$ so that the new feature F_i has a dimension of D_i. S_i is the upsampling to resize the feature map f_{i+1} to the same scale with f_i. C_i indicates the integration of neighbor-scale features.

We can see that the newly constructed feature map F_i (when i is not the top layer) is formed via the operations of dimension reduction and integration by the i-th feature map f_i and $i + 1$-th feature map f_{i+1} from the original SSD backbone network. Therefore, for the fused i-th feature layer: on one hand, it contains the dual information of the original i-th feature layer and its deeper feature layer that strengthens the semantic abstraction of the object features; on the other hand, the dimension reduction of the i-th and $i + 1$-th feature channels during the process highlights the principal component characterization of the objects.

In practice, numerous techniques for the dimension reduction R, upsampling S and integration C could be taken into account in formula (1). Generally, non-linear transformation networks would bring us better results. However, for our ESSD, in order to guarantee the high real-time efficiency, we just adopt a set of very simple solutions that will be demonstrated to be effective enough, namely: the 1×1 convolution followed by a relu process for R_i, the bilinear interpolation for S_i, and the concat operation for C_i, when i is not the top layer. Since the top layer does not have a corresponding deeper neighbor-scale layer, we directly use it as the top for newly constructed feature layers.

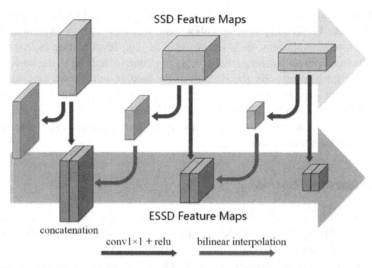

Fig. 2. The details of our neighbor-scale feature fusion in ESSD. The channel dimensionality reduction consists of a 1 × 1 convolution and a relu process, and the neighbor-scale integration contains a bilinear interpolation and a concatenation. All these operations are very simple but effective, bringing high detection accuracy and computational efficiency.

Table 1 lists the processing information for each layer in ESSD in details. Obviously, our model has fewer dimensions than the original features (labeled in bold in Table 1), making it more advantageous in accelerating predictions. Figure 2 shows a schematic diagram of our operations. The high efficiency of ESSD will be verified in subsequent experiments.

Table 1. Processing information for each feature layer in ESSD.

Feature layer	Map scale	$\mathbf{R}_i$	$\mathbf{S}_i$	$\mathbf{C}_i$	d_i	D_i
F_1	64 × 64	conv1 × 1×256 + relu	bilinear 64 × 64	concat	512	256 + 256
F_2	32 × 32		bilinear 32 × 32		**1024**	**256 + 256**
F_3	16 × 16	conv1 × 1×128 + relu	bilinear 16 × 16		**512**	**128 + 128**
F_4	8 × 8		bilinear 8 × 8		256	128 + 128
F_5	4 × 4		bilinear 4 × 4		256	128 + 128
F_6	2 × 2		bilinear 2 × 2		256	128 + 128
F_7	1 × 1	no			256	256

2.4 Differential Analysis with Other Refinements

The proposed method provides a new solution to promote both the accuracy and efficiency. We just adopt the 1 × 1 convolution to accelerate the speed and the neighbor-scale concatenation to improve the precision, which are absolutely different with others

[13–15]. Furthermore, most models would like to adopt the multi-layer fusion process [9, 13–15], while ESSD only fuse neighbor-scale features. This is explained that for objects with lower resolutions, their information in high-level feature layers may disappear, so the multi-layer fusion probably not only contribute little to the performance, but also cause false results. By the reason, to the best of our knowledge, we are the first time to adopt only the neighbor-scale features because it contains both the finer resolution information (in the current feature layer) and deeper abstraction information (in the neighbor-scale feature layer). Encouragingly, the final experimental results will demonstrate our perspective well.

3 Experimental Results

The publicly available benchmarks, Pascal VOC 2007 and 2012 [4, 5], are used to validate the effectiveness of our model. For Pascal VOC 2007, there are 5011 and 4952 natural images in trainval2007 and test2007, respectively. For Pascal VOC 2012, there are 11540 and 10991 natural images in trainval2012 and test2012, respectively. When evaluating the 2007 dataset, trainval2007 and trainval2012 are used for training, and test2007 are used for testing. We set the learning rate to 10-3 for the first 100k iterations, and decay it to 10-4 and 10-5 for training another 20k and 20k iterations, respectively. When evaluating the 2012 dataset, trainval2007, trainval2012 and test2007 are used for training, and test2012 are used for testing. We set the learning rate to 10-3 for the first 120k iterations, and decay it to 10-4 and 10-5 for training another 30k and 30k iterations, respectively. The default batch size is 16, and a single NVIDIA RTX 2080Ti GPU is performed in our experiments.

3.1 Comparison Under Different Configurations

In order to evaluate the performance of our model under different configurations, we set up 5 sets of experiments, they are: ESSD[1] with the original SSD512; ESSD[2] with only dimension reduction (to the half of the original dimensions); ESSD[3] with the 3×3 convolution instead of 1×1 convolution in dimension reduction; ESSD[4] with the input of 300×300 (based on the SSD300 network); and ESSD[5] with both the dimension reduction and neighbor-scale fusion (the proposed ESSD). The test is performed on Pascal VOC 2007 and the results are shown in Table 2 (with all best scores labeled in bold). It can be seen that both the ESSD[3] and ESSD[5] have the best score in mAP, indicating that the performance of 1×1 convolution in dimension reduction is equivalent to 3×3 convolution, while the former is obviously simpler and faster. The fact that ESSD[2] also performs better than ESSD[1] demonstrates that the dimension reduction could not only increase the speed but also improve the accuracy. Meanwhile, the results of ESSD[1], ESSD[2] and ESSD[5] gradually validate the effectiveness of our proposed dimension reduction and neighbor-scale fusion. Furthermore, although the smaller input scale like ESSD[4] may sacrifice some precision, it can get up to a speed of 92.5 fps that meets the high real-time requirements.

Table 2. Comparison under different configurations.

Model configurations	Input size	Reduction convolutions	Feature dimension	FPS	mAP
ESSD^1	512×512	no	d	27.4	79.8
ESSD^2	512×512	$1 \times 1 \times d/2$	$d/2$	51.1	80.6
ESSD^3	512×512	$3 \times 3 \times D/2$	D	50.0	**81.2**
ESSD^4	300×300	$1 \times 1 \times D/2$	D	**92.5**	78.3
ESSD^5	512×512	$1 \times 1 \times D/2$	D	52.9	**81.2**

3.2 Comparison with State-of-the-Art Models

Many state-of-the-art methods are compared with ESSD on Pascal VOC 2007 and 2012, by which only models with input scales not smaller than 512×512 are adopted for fair comparison since our network input is set to 512×512. The experimental results on these two benchmarks are shown in Table 3 and Table 4, respectively. It is notable that all the time performance is derived from their corresponding literatures and is only for objective reference. Overall, from Table 3 and Table 4 (with all best scores labeled in bold), we can see that the proposed ESSD has evident advantages in both the prediction accuracy and computational efficiency that actually outperforms the state-of-the-art models. In addition, several instances of the detected results by our ESSD from Pascal VOC 2012 test dataset are shown in Fig. 3 for visualization.

Table 3. Comparison with state-of-the-arts models on Pascal VOC 2007.

Models	Backbone	Input size	FPS	mAP
Faster R-CNN [7]	VGG16	~600 × 1000	7.0	73.2
Faster R-CNN [7]	ResNet101	~600 × 1000	2.4	76.4
ION [18]	VGG16	~600 × 1000	1.25	76.5
MR-CNN [19]	VGG16	~600 × 1000	0.03	78.2
R-FCN [8]	ResNet101	~600 × 1000	5.8	79.5
YOLOv2 [11]	Darknet19	544 × 544	40.0	78.6
SSD [12]	VGG16	512 × 512	19.0	79.8
STDN [20]	DenseNet169	513 × 513	28.6	80.9
MLKP [21]	VGG16	~600 × 1000	10	80.6
R-DAD [22]	ResNet101	~600 × 1000	1.88	**81.2**
ESSD	VGG16	512 × 512	**52.9**	**81.2**

Table 4. Comparison with state-of-the-arts models on Pascal VOC 2012.

Models	aero	bike	bird	boat	bottle	bus	car	cat	chair	cow	table	dog	horse	mbike	person	plant	cheep	sofa	train	tv	mAP
Faster R-CNN[7]	86.5	81.6	77.2	58.0	51.0	78.6	76.6	**93.2**	48.6	80.4	59.0	92.1	85.3	84.8	80.7	48.1	77.3	66.5	84.7	65.6	73.8
ION[18]	87.5	84.7	76.8	63.8	58.3	82.6	79.0	90.0	57.8	82.0	64.7	88.9	86.5	84.7	82.3	51.4	78.2	69.2	85.2	73.5	76.4
MR-CNN[19]	85.5	82.9	76.6	57.8	**62.7**	79.4	77.2	86.6	55.0	79.1	62.2	87.0	83.4	84.7	78.9	45.3	73.4	65.8	80.3	74.0	73.9
R-FCN[8]	86.9	83.4	**81.5**	63.8	62.4	81.6	81.1	93.1	58.0	83.8	60.8	**92.7**	86.0	84.6	84.4	59.0	80.8	68.6	86.1	72.9	77.6
YOLOv2[11]	88.8	**87.0**	77.8	64.9	51.8	**85.2**	79.3	93.1	**64.4**	81.4	**70.2**	91.3	88.1	87.2	81.0	57.7	78.1	**71.0**	**88.5**	**76.8**	78.2
SSD[12]	**90.0**	85.3	77.7	64.3	58.5	85.1	**84.3**	92.6	61.3	83.4	65.1	89.9	88.5	**88.2**	85.5	54.4	82.4	70.7	87.1	75.6	78.5
MLKP[21]	87.1	85.1	79.0	64.2	60.3	82.1	80.6	92.3	57.4	81.8	61.6	92.1	86.3	85.3	84.3	**59.1**	81.7	69.5	85.0	70.1	77.2
ESSD	89.8	86.9	80.3	**66.3**	62.4	83.7	82.9	93.0	61.0	**84.2**	62.1	90.9	**89.6**	88.1	**86.8**	57.2	**84.0**	67.3	88.1	76.4	**79.1**

Fig. 3. Instances of the detection results by ESSD from Pascal VOC 2012 test dataset.

3.3 Comparison with Refinement Models of SSD

In order to further uniformly compare the performance and efficiency of ESSD with other typical refinements of SSD, we finally execute all the models on the same platform of Pytorch 1.0 by a single NVIDIA RTX 2080Ti GPU. The detailed results are listed in Table 5. According to it, ESSD is nearly twice faster than SSD, and more than twice as fast as other methods. Although its accuracy is not as good as DSSD, which increases the network complex by applying a number of deconvolution and multi-layer fusion, the overall performance of ESSD is quite outstanding, especially for the computational efficiency.

Table 5. Comparison with refinement models of SSD.

Models	Backbone	Input size	GPU	FPS	mAP
SSD [12]	VGG16	512 × 512	RTX 2080Ti	27.4	79.8
FSSD [14]	VGG16	512 × 512		21.3	80.9
RSSD [15]	VGG16	512 × 512		23.9	80.8
DSSD [13]	ResNet101	513 × 513		7.9	**81.5**
ESSD	VGG16	512 × 512		**52.9**	81.2

4 Conclusion

A novelly simple way refined from SSD to greatly improve the object detection accuracy and computational efficiency is provided in this paper. By the proposed neighbor-scale feature fusion with the channel dimensionality reduction and neighbor-scale integration, our model has been demonstrated to be more efficient and accurate than many state-of-the-art methods. Meanwhile, the result also inspiringly gives a new way to improve multi-layer based detection models in the future.

References

1. Liu, L., Ouyang, W., Wang, X., et al.: Deep learning for generic object detection: a survey. Int. J. Comput. Vis. **128**, 261–318 (2020). https://doi.org/10.1007/s11263-019-01247-4
2. Qi, S., Ma, J., Tao, C., et al.: A robust directional saliency-based method for infrared small-target detection under various complex backgrounds. IEEE Geosci. Remote Sens. Lett. **10**(3), 495–499 (2012)
3. Qi, S., Ma, J., Lin, J., et al.: Unsupervised ship detection based on saliency and S-HOG descriptor from optical satellite images. IEEE Geosci. Remote Sens. Lett. **12**(7), 1451–1455 (2015)
4. Everingham, M., Van Gool, L., Williams, C.K.I., et al.: The Pascal visual object classes (VOC) challenge. Int. J. Comput. Vis. **88**(2), 303–338 (2010)
5. Everingham, M., Eslami, S.M.A., Van Gool, L., et al.: The Pascal visual object classes challenge: a retrospective. Int. J. Comput. Vis. **111**(1), 98–136 (2015)
6. Felzenszwalb, P.F., Girshick, R.B., McAllester, D., et al.: Object detection with discriminatively trained part-based models. IEEE Trans. Pattern Anal. Mach. Intell. **32**(9), 1627–1645 (2009)

7. Ren, S., He, K., Girshick, R., et al.: Faster R-CNN: towards real-time object detection with region proposal networks. In: Advances in Neural Information Processing Systems, pp. 91–99 (2015)

8. Dai, J., Li, Y., He, K., et al.: R-FCN: object detection via region-based fully convolutional networks. In: Advances in Neural Information Processing Systems, pp. 379–387 (2016)

9. Lin, T.Y., Dollar, P., Girshick, R., et al.: Feature pyramid networks for object detection. In: Proceedings of the IEEE Conference on Computer Vision and Pattern Recognition, pp. 2117–2125. IEEE (2017)

10. Redmon, J., Divvala, S., Girshick, R., et al.: You only look once: unified, real-time object detection. In: Proceedings of the IEEE Conference on Computer Vision and Pattern Recognition, pp. 779–788. IEEE (2016)

11. Redmon, J., Farhadi, A.: YOLO9000: better, faster, stronger. In: Proceedings of the IEEE Conference on Computer Vision and Pattern Recognition, pp. 7263–7271. IEEE (2017)

12. Liu, Wei, et al.: SSD: single shot multibox detector. In: Leibe, Bastian, Matas, Jiri, Sebe, Nicu, Welling, Max (eds.) ECCV 2016. LNCS, vol. 9905, pp. 21–37. Springer, Cham (2016). https://doi.org/10.1007/978-3-319-46448-0_2

13. Fu, C.Y., Liu, W., Ranga, A., et al.: DSSD: deconvolutional single shot detector. arXiv preprint arXiv:1701.06659 (2017)

14. Li, Z., Zhou, F.: FSSD: feature fusion single shot multibox detector. arXiv preprint arXiv:1712.00960 (2017)

15. Jeong, J., Park, H., Kwak, N.: Enhancement of SSD by concatenating feature maps for object detection. arXiv preprint arXiv:1705.09587 (2017)

16. Zhao, Z.Q., Zheng, P., Xu, S., et al.: Object detection with deep learning: a review. IEEE Trans. Neural Netw. Learn. Syst. **30**(11), 3212–3232 (2019)

17. Simonyan, K., Zisserman, A.: Very deep convolutional networks for large-scale image recognition. arXiv preprint arXiv:1409.1556 (2014)

18. Bell, S., Lawrence Zitnick, C., Bala, K., et al.: Inside-outside net: detecting objects in context with skip pooling and recurrent neural networks. In: Proceedings of the IEEE Conference on Computer Vision and Pattern Recognition, pp. 2874–2883. IEEE (2016)

19. Gidaris, S., Komodakis, N.: Object detection via a multi-region and semantic segmentation-aware CNN model. In: Proceedings of the IEEE International Conference on Computer Vision, pp. 1134–1142. IEEE (2015)

20. Zhou, P., Ni, B., Geng, C., et al.: Scale-transferrable object detection. In: Proceedings of the IEEE Conference on Computer Vision and Pattern Recognition, pp. 528–537. IEEE (2018)

21. Wang, H., Wang, Q., Gao, M., et al.: Multi-scale location-aware kernel representation for object detection. In: Proceedings of the IEEE Conference on Computer Vision and Pattern Recognition, pp. 1248–1257. IEEE (2018)

22. Bae, S.H.: Object detection based on region decomposition and assembly. arXiv preprint arXiv:1901.08225 (2019)

Student Performance Prediction Based on Multi-view Network Embedding

Jianian Li[2], Yanwei Yu[1(✉)], Yunhong Lu[2], and Peng Song[2]

[1] Ocean University of China, Qingdao 266100, Shandong, China
yuyanwei@ouc.edu.cn
[2] Yantai University, Yantai 264005, Shandong, China

Abstract. Predicting student performance is a very important but yet challenging task in education. In this paper, we propose a Multi-View Network Embedding (MVNE) method for student performance prediction, which effectively fuses multiple data sources. We first construct three networks to model three different types of data sources correlated with student performance, ranging from class performance data, historical grades, to students' campus social relationships. Then we use joint network embedding to learn the embedding representation of students and questions based on the proposed separated random walk sampling. Student performance is predicted based on both student and question similarities in the low-dimensional representation. Experimental results on the real-world datasets demonstrate the effectiveness of the proposed method.

Keywords: Student performance prediction · Network embedding · Heterogeneous networks · Multi-source data

1 Introduction

Education is the foundation of a nation. Students' performance plays a significant role in a country's social and economic growth by producing creative graduates, innovators and entrepreneurs. In recent years, the phenomenon of failing examinations in universities has become more serious, which has already affected the students' enthusiasm for learning, even the smooth graduation for some students. Predicting students' academic performance in advance has become more important to both students and teachers. On the one hand, educators can strengthen the management of students who do not perform well in predicted results, improving the enthusiasm for the students to learn, and thus reducing the probability of students hanging out. On the other hand, according to the predicted student performance, teachers can adjust the teaching plan in time and facilitate personalized education to enhance the learning efficiency and effect of all students.

Therefore, there are varieties of studies have been conducted to predict student performance. A line of methods use traditional machine learning methods to

© Springer Nature Switzerland AG 2020
Y. Peng et al. (Eds.): PRCV 2020, LNCS 12307, pp. 125–136, 2020.
https://doi.org/10.1007/978-3-030-60636-7_11

predict student performance, such as decision tree [17], linear regression [12,13], Bayesian classification [14], neural network [21], and SVM [1]. Another line of studies use matrix decomposition [18] and collaborative filtering [19] for student performance prediction. The major challenge of performance prediction is to reveal important factors that affect students' academic performance. Several methods [5,23] are conducted to explore the impact of varieties of potential information on students' academic performance. It has been demonstrated that programming behavior [4], friend relationship [23], and personal behavior [22] are correlated with students' academic performance. There are several studies focus on exploring the effects of multiple variables on student performance, such as the impact of multi-regression model [10] and multi-relational factorization model [18] on student performance prediction. Most of these approaches are supervised learning or semi-supervised learning, which requires plenty of labelled data. Additionally, existing methods only consider a single data source or independently consider the impact of each data source on student performance prediction. But fortunately, thanks to the progress of modern network and information technology, lots of data in the process of teaching and learning has been recorded and collected, such as learning management system data [7], campus behaviors [22] and programming behaviors [4]. Recently, emerging network embedding techniques [8] provide a way to learn features from networks automatically. The basic idea is to learn the low-dimensional representation of nodes in a network by preserving the network structure. There have been many studies on how to embed nodes into a low-dimensional space, such as random walk based methods [11,15,24,25], matrix factorization based methods [2,16], Random projection based methods [6,26], and deep learning based methods [3,20]. However, none of them can handle multi-view network data from multiple different data sources.

In this paper, we propose a multi-view network embedding method for student performance prediction, which supports to predict student performance using multiple data sources. More specifically, we consider students' class practice test records, historical grade data, and campus social relationships as input data. First, we construct a heterogeneous network and two homogeneous networks to model the relationships between students, questions, and students and questions from the three types of data sources. Second, we design a separated random walk sampling for the heterogeneous network, and use joint network embedding to learn the low-dimensional representation of students and questions. Third, we implement a similarity-based performance prediction to estimate students' academic performance using student similarity and question similarity in the low-dimensional representation. Finally, experiments on the real-world datasets demonstrated the effectiveness of our proposed method.

2   Problem Definition

In this section, we first introduce the data used in the paper and then formulate the problem of student performance prediction.

Online Judge (OJ) system is an online test and evaluation platform, which compiles and executes the source code (e.g., C, C++) submitted by users, and verifies the correctness of the program source code through the pre-designed test data. It collects all records of practice tests for all students in the programming courses. We define a practice test record as follows:

Definition 1 (practice test record). *A practice test record is a three tuple $\langle s_i, q_j, t \rangle$ that represents student s_i taking the time t to finish the exercise question q_j in OJ system.*

The practice test records reflect the performance of students in class. In addition, the historical grade information of students is also easily available, and thus is often used to predict student performance. We next define a historical grade record as:

Definition 2 (Historical grade record). *A historical grade record is a three tuple $\langle s_i, c_j, g \rangle$ that represent student s_i achieving the score g when he/she took the course c_j.*

Moreover, the campus social relationships also influence students' learning activities, which in turn may affect students' performance. We define the campus social relationship network of students as follows:

Definition 3 (Campus Social Relationship Network). *The campus social network is defined as an undirected graph $\mathcal{G}_s = (V, E_s)$, where V is the set of students, and E_s is the set of edges between the students. Each edge $e_{ij} \in E_s$ represents the relationship between students s_i and s_j and is associated with weight $w_{ij} > 0$, which indicates their interaction behavior in learning activities (i.e., the interaction frequency).*

In fact, in college life, there are many student activities that may affect students' performance, such as co-participating academic competition, co-completing study topics, co-involving in club activities, and often co-attending self-studies.

One simple but intuitive measure for relationship strength between students is the interaction frequency. Specifically, let $A = \{a_1, a_2, \dots\}$ denote the set of all activities that both students s_i and s_j participate in. Then the weight w_{ij} of edge e_{ij} in graph $\mathcal{G}_s$ is the cardinality of A.

Then we formally define our student performance prediction problem as follows:

Problem (Student Performance Prediction Problem). *At semester Γ, given the set of practice test records of all student in the semester, the historical grade records, and the campus social network $\mathcal{G}_s$, our goal is to predict the students' academic performance rank at this semester.*

3 Method

3.1 Overview

Figure 1 shows the overall framework of our proposed model based on multi-view network embedding, which includes three major modules as follows: *Multi-view heterogeneous network construction* module builds a heterogeneous network that involves students and tested questions to capture all relationships among students, questions, and student and questions from input data. *Network embedding* module learns the low-dimensional representations for students and questions using our proposed separated random walk sampling from the constructed heterogeneous network. *Similarity-based performance predictor* module finally predicts students' academic performance based on both student similarity and question similarity in the low-dimensional vector space.

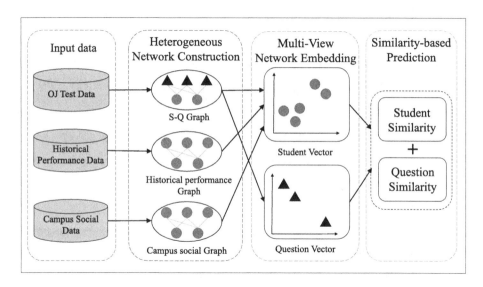

Fig. 1. Overview of the proposed multi-view embedding based student performance prediction model.

3.2 Heterogeneous Network Construction

We first introduce our student-question (or in short *S-Q*) graph as follows:

Definition 4 (Student-Question Graph). *Student-Question (S-Q) graph is a bipartite graph $\mathcal{G}_{sq} = (S \cup Q, E_{sq})$, where S is the set of students and Q is the set of tested questions. E_{sq} is the set of edges between students and questions. If student s_i did tested question q_j, there will be an edges e_{ij} between them, otherwise none. The weight w_{ij} on edge e_{ij} is set to t according to each practice test record $\langle s_i, q_j, t \rangle$.*

The S-Q graph is designed to capture all information of students' class performance in this semester.

Next we also build a historical information network to capture the student similarities from student historical performance data. Specifically, the historical information network is an undirected graph $\mathcal{G}_h = (S, E_h)$, where S is the set of all students, and E_h is the set of edges between students. If two students achieve relative equivalent scores (e.g., less than 5 % points) in the same course, we regard they are similar once. The weight w_{ij} on edge $eij \in E_h$ is the sum of similarities between students s_i and s_j performed in the historical grade records.

The three types of graphs above (i.e, S-Q graph, historical graph, and campus social graph) can well capture the class performance influence, historical performance effect and campus social relationship effect, respectively. Therefore, we propose to learn embeddings from the three graphs jointly to estimate the student similarity and question similarity.

3.3 Multi-view Network Embedding

The three graphs collaboratively model the similarity relationships between students from multiple perspectives. Inspired by the recent graph embedding techniques [11,15], we propose a multi-view network embedding method based on random walk sampling.

Actually, our constructed heterogeneous graph is not a pure similarity graph. S-Q graph only captures the information that students taking how long time to finish the tested questions, which does not represent the similarity relationships between students and questions, and thus can not indicate the similarity between students. Therefore, existing random walk sampling strategies are not applied into our graph directly.

To capture the similarities among students and among questions in S-Q graph, we design a separated walk sampling strategy which guides the generation of random walks in S-Q graph: Consider a random walk that just traversed edge (s_1,q), and now stays at node q (Fig. 2). The walk now needs to decide on the next node so it evaluates the transition probabilities $Pr(q, s_i)$ on edges (q,s_i) starting from q. We set the transition probability $Pr(q, s_i)$ as follows:

$$Pr(q, s_i) = \begin{cases} 1 & s_i = s_1 \\ \exp(\lambda \frac{\min(w(s_1,q),w(q,s_i))}{\max(w(s_1,q),w(q,s_i))}) & |w(s_1,q) - w(q, s_i)| < r \\ \exp(-\frac{\max(w(s_1,q),w(q,s_i))}{\min(w(s_1,q),w(q,s_i))}) & otherwise \end{cases} \quad (1)$$

Intuitively, parameters r and λ flexibly control how to explore the student neighbors of node q. In particular, r controls the walk to tend to visit the student nodes who take similar time with s_1 w.t.r. question q. λ allows the search to differentiate between similar nodes and dissimilar nodes by scaling the transition probability. But even if there no similar student node in the next step, the return weight (i.e.,1) also ensures the walk to backtrack a step, rather than going to the dissimilar student nodes.

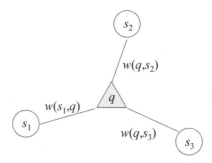

Fig. 2. An example of walk sampling in S-Q graph.

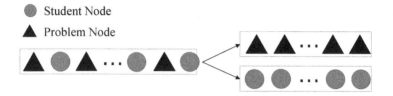

Fig. 3. Illustration of the separated random walk sampling in S-Q graph.

Note that, $Pr(q, s_i)$ is not real transition probability in the strict sense, but an updated transition weight, hence the transition probability will be computed based on the updated weights.

By sampling the random walks in S-Q graph, we can collect the walks in which student node and question node alternate. However, the sampled walks are not suitable for being used directly to learn the embedding vectors of students and questions. First, it is not necessary to map students and questions into the same vector space. That is, we need not learn the similarity between students and questions (i.e., the first-order proximity in the walks). Second, directly applying such walks actually hurts the prediction accuracy, because such walks invisibly closes the representations between dissimilar student nodes. For example, two completely dissimilar students may have done the same questions. Because they take relatively large time differences, they may not appear in the same walks. However, in different walks, both student nodes may have first-order proximity with the same question, and thus their representations tend to be similar during the training process.

To address these issues, we propose a separated random walk sampling strategy. As shown in Fig. 3, we generate two walks from an original walks sampled from S-Q graph, namely, each walk only contains one kind of nodes. In this way, we cut off the similarity between students and questions, and thus effectively differentiates the vector representations between dissimilar student nodes, and between dissimilar question nodes.

To obtain the multi-view embedding representations, we again generate random walks in historical information graph $\mathcal{G}_h$ and campus social graph $\mathcal{G}_s$, and then jointly learn the embeddings of student nodes and question nodes using the sampled random walks from the three graphs.

Actually, we can easily tune the weights for the three views in the embedding learning by setting different number of sampled walks on three graphs in the implementation. More specifically, we fix the number of sampled walks on historical graph $\mathcal{G}_h$, and set α and β times the number of walk samples for S-Q graph and $\mathcal{G}_s$, respectively. By default, we set $\alpha = \beta = 1$.

3.4 Similarity-Based Performance Prediction

After embedding different types of information into the representation, we use the cosine distance to measure the similarity in the embedding space.

To predict the performance rank of students, we predict the total time took by students to finish random selected questions, and use the time to get students' performance ranking.

Given a selected question q, the time spent $t_i(q)$ by student s_i is predicted by:

$$t_i(q) = \omega \frac{\sum_{s_j \in N_k(s_i)} t_j(q)}{k} + (1 - \omega) \frac{\sum_{q_j \in N_k(q)} t_i(q_j)}{k}, \tag{2}$$

where $N_k(s_i)$ represents the kNNs of s_i in the embedding space, and $N_k(q)$ denotes the most similar k questions of q. By default, ω is set to 0.5.

4 Experiment

4.1 Datasets

We collected the data of nearly two thousand students from one university in China during 2016/09/01 to 2018/07/15. The dataset consists of three types of data, which are described as follows:

- OJ practice test data: This data contains almost 2.1 millions test records from more than 5,000 students.
- Historical performance data: This data contains all historical course grades for the selected students in their first two years of college. Specifically, the data includes the grade information of 24 subjects, such as advanced mathematics, analog circuits, and linear algebra.
- Campus social data: We collect 25 campus activities of the selected students reflecting the campus social relationships among students, such as subject competitions, lab-mates, learning group.

We divide the data into two datasets, one containing the above three types of data, denoted Data A. It includes more than 300 students from two majors. Another dataset includes only the first two types of data, denoted Data B, which consists of more than 1400 students from two grades.

4.2   Baselines and Metrics

We compare our method with the following baselines:

- Average-based methods: This baseline uses average time spent to estimate the performance of students. We compare two average-based methods: one is using the average time spent per student on all his/her answered questions, the other one is using the average time spent of each student on the questions that are similar with examinations to predict ranking, which are referred to as Global-Avg and Neighbor-Avg, respectively.
- Matrix Factorization (MF) [19]: We perform MF on student-question matrix instead of the user-item matrix, and complete the student-question matrix by matrix decomposition.
- Collaborative Filtering (CF) based methods [19]: This baseline contains two methods: User-CF and Item-CF.

Our embedding method has three kinds of variations:

- Single-view variations: We have three single-view variations, that is, OJ-view, History-view, and Social-view.
- Dual-view variations: We also have three dual-view variations, each variation considers both two different data sources.
- MVNE/s: MVNE/s directly use the original random walk sampling in MVNE, rather than the separated random walks.

Finally, we predict the results of all students from two majors and use RMSE (root mean square error) to evaluate the effectiveness of our proposed method, which was also used as an assessment metric in previous work [5,9,18,19].

Table 1. Experimental results of all methods

Method	Data A		Data B	
	Major I	Major II	Grade I	Grade II
Global-Avg	0.3219	0.3184	0.3795	0.3651
Neighbor-Avg	0.3109	0.3073	0.3755	0.3342
User-CF	0.3023	0.3287	0.3545	0.3604
Item-CF	0.2945	0.2743	0.3504	0.3434
MF	0.2901	0.2895	0.3277	0.3012
Social-view	0.2962	0.2740	–	–
History-view	0.2619	0.2431	0.2586	0.2565
OJ-view	0.2195	0.2173	0.2456	0.2286
Social-History-view	0.2342	0.2201	–	–
Social-OJ-view	0.1934	0.1945	–	–
OJ-History-view	0.1756	0.1843	0.2258	0.2056
MVNE/s	0.2975	0.2886	0.3456	0.3256
MVNE	0.1691	0.1703	–	–

4.3   Experimental Results

Overall Performance. Table 1 shows the experimental results of our method compared to all baselines.

As we can see, our proposed Multi-View Network Embedding (MVNE) method significantly outperforms all baselines on two datasets. The main reasons may be: First, MVNE effectively combines three different types of data sources (i.e., historical performance data, campus social data, and class performance records), while all existing methods consider only a single data source. Second, MVNE uses a heterogeneous networks to clearly reflect the relationships between students and questions in the real-world datasets, and uses joint network embedding to encode all data source information into a low-dimensional representation for each student. Last but most important, MVNE uses the proposed separated random walk sampling in S-Q graph to significantly improve the embedding representations of students and questions in predicting student performance.

Variation Study. From Table 1, we also observe that OJ-view performs better than other two single-view methods (i.e., Social-view and History-view). This may be because the class performance has greater impact on students' final performance in this semester compared to historical grade and campus relationship. Among the three views, campus social relationship has the weakest impact on student performance. However, Social-view method using network embedding is still better than other baselines.

Moreover, dual-view methods perform better than corresponding either of single-view methods on both two datasets. And MVNE achieves the best performance on both two majors. This also demonstrates that our proposed multi-view embedding method maximally fuses the information from multiple data sources.

Additionally, MVNE performs significantly better than MVNE/s on two majors, which also confirms that our proposed separated random walk sampling is much more useful in learning the representations of students and questions.

Parameter Sensitivity. First, we study the impact of each view on the prediction performance by varying the weights of the three views in the embedding learning. The results of parameters α and β on two datasets are shown in Fig. 4. We vary α and β from 0.1 to 5 respectively. We use the grid search method to find the best parameter settings. As we can see, the RMSE of MVNE first decreases to the minimal value and then increases as the weight parameters increasing. This is intuitive because both class performance and social relationships are essential for a precise prediction. As shown in Fig. 4(a), the RMSE reaches minimum value when α and β fall around 1 and 0.3, respectively.

Similarly, the RMSE achieves minimum value when α is 1 in Fig. 4(b). In addition, it is clear that the prediction error decreases rapidly with α increasing from 0. This suggests the class performance contributes a lot to the overall prediction accuracy.

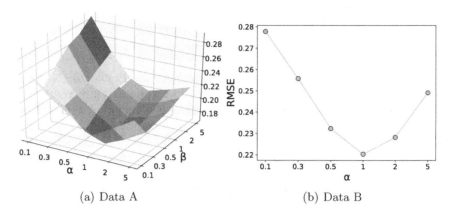

(a) Data A   (b) Data B

Fig. 4. Results of varying the weight parameters

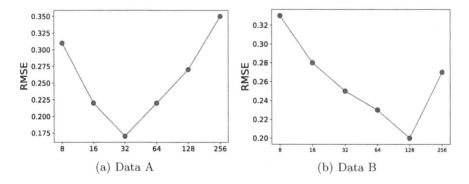

(a) Data A   (b) Data B

Fig. 5. Performance w.r.t. the embedding dimension

Second, we explore how the performance of MVNE changes with respect to embedding dimension. The results on two datasets are shown in Fig. 5. As expected, the performance of MVNE first increases as embedding dimension increases, and then drops when the dimension becomes too large. We also observe that our MVNE achieves the best results when selecting 32 dimensions on the small dataset (Fig. 5(a)), and the best performance when adopting 128 dimensions on the large dataset (Fig. 5(b)).

5   Conclusions

Predicting student performance is a very important and challenging task in education. This paper proposes a multi-view based network embedding method for student performance prediction. Specifically, we use joint network embedding to learn the similarities between students, questions, and students and questions from three different types of data sources. We also design a separated random walk sampling in the heterogeneous graph to improve the prediction performance. Finally, the superiority of the proposed model is confirmed by experiments on the real-world datasets.

Acknowledgments. This work is partially supported by the National Natural Science Foundation of China under grant Nos. 61773331, 61403328 and 61703360. The views and conclusions contained in this paper are those of the authors and should not be interpreted as representing any funding agencies.

References

1. Al-Shehri, H., et al.: Student performance prediction using support vector machine and k-nearest neighbor. In: 2017 IEEE 30th Canadian Conference on Electrical and Computer Engineering (CCECE), pp. 1–4. IEEE (2017)
2. Cao, S., Lu, W., Xu, Q.: Grarep: learning graph representations with global structural information. In: Proceedings of the 24th ACM International on Conference on Information and Knowledge Management, pp. 891–900 (2015)
3. Cao, S., Lu, W., Xu, Q.: Deep neural networks for learning graph representations. In: Thirtieth AAAI Conference on Artificial Intelligence (2016)
4. Carter, A.S., Hundhausen, C.D., Adesope, O.: The normalized programming state model: Predicting student performance in computing courses based on programming behavior. In: Proceedings of the eleventh annual International Conference on International Computing Education Research, pp. 141–150 (2015)
5. Cetintas, S., Si, L., Xin, Y.P., Tzur, R.: Probabilistic latent class models for predicting student performance. In: Proceedings of the 22nd ACM International Conference on Information & Knowledge Management, pp. 1513–1516 (2013)
6. Chen, H., Sultan, S.F., Tian, Y., Chen, M., Skiena, S.: Fast and accurate network embeddings via very sparse random projection. In: Proceedings of the 28th ACM International Conference on Information and Knowledge Management, pp. 399–408 (2019)
7. Conijn, R., Snijders, C., Kleingeld, A., Matzat, U.: Predicting student performance from LMS data: a comparison of 17 blended courses using Moodle LMS. IEEE Trans. Learn. Technol. **10**(1), 17–29 (2017)
8. Cui, P., Wang, X., Pei, J., Zhu, W.: A survey on network embedding. IEEE Trans. Knowl. Data Eng. **31**(5), 833–852 (2018)
9. Elbadrawy, A., Polyzou, A., Ren, Z., Sweeney, M., Karypis, G., Rangwala, H.: Predicting student performance using personalized analytics. Computer **49**(4), 61–69 (2016)
10. Elbadrawy, A., Studham, R.S., Karypis, G.: Collaborative multi-regression models for predicting students' performance in course activities. In: Proceedings of the Fifth International Conference on Learning Analytics and Knowledge, pp. 103–107 (2015)
11. Grover, A., Leskovec, J.: node2vec: scalable feature learning for networks. In: Proceedings of the 22nd ACM SIGKDD International Conference on Knowledge Discovery and Data Mining, pp. 855–864. ACM (2016)
12. Huang, S., Fang, N.: Predicting student academic performance in an engineering dynamics course: a comparison of four types of predictive mathematical models. Comput. Educ. **61**, 133–145 (2013)
13. Kabakchieva, D.: Predicting student performance by using data mining methods for classification. Cybern. Inf. Technol. **13**(1), 61–72 (2013)

14. Mayilvaganan, M., Kalpanadevi, D.: Comparison of classification techniques for predicting the performance of students academic environment. In: 2014 International Conference on Communication and Network Technologies, pp. 113–118. IEEE (2014)
15. Perozzi, B., Al-Rfou, R., Skiena, S.: Deepwalk: online learning of social representations. In: Proceedings of the 20th ACM SIGKDD International Conference on Knowledge Discovery and Data Mining, pp. 701–710. ACM (2014)
16. Qiu, J., et al.: Netsmf: large-scale network embedding as sparse matrix factorization. In: The World Wide Web Conference, pp. 1509–1520 (2019)
17. Quadri, M.M., Kalyankar, N.: Drop out feature of student data for academic performance using decision tree techniques. Glob. J. Comput. Sci. Technol. (2010)
18. Thai-Nghe, N., Drumond, L., Horváth, T., Schmidt-Thieme, L., et al.: Multirelational factorization models for predicting student performance. In: KDD Workshop on Knowledge Discovery in Educational Data (KDDinED), pp. 27–40 (2011)
19. Thai-Nghe, N., Drumond, L., Krohn-Grimberghe, A., Schmidt-Thieme, L.: Recommender system for predicting student performance. Procedia Comput. Sci. 1(2), 2811–2819 (2010)
20. Wang, D., Cui, P., Zhu, W.: Structural deep network embedding. In: Proceedings of the 22nd ACM SIGKDD International Conference on Knowledge Discovery and Data Mining, pp. 1225–1234 (2016)
21. Wang, T., Mitrovic, A.: Using neural networks to predict student's performance. In: Proceedings of International Conference on Computers in Education, pp. 969–973. IEEE (2002)
22. Yao, H., Lian, D., Cao, Y., Wu, Y., Zhou, T.: Predicting academic performance for college students: a campus behavior perspective. arXiv preprint arXiv:1903.06726 (2019)
23. Yao, H., Nie, M., Su, H., Xia, H., Lian, D.: Predicting academic performance via semi-supervised learning with constructed campus social network. In: Candan, S., Chen, L., Pedersen, T.B., Chang, L., Hua, W. (eds.) DASFAA 2017. LNCS, vol. 10178, pp. 597–609. Springer, Cham (2017). https://doi.org/10.1007/978-3-319-55699-4_37
24. Yu, Y., Wang, H., Li, Z.: Inferring mobility relationship via graph embedding. In: Proceedings of the ACM on Interactive, Mobile, Wearable and Ubiquitous Technologies, vol. 2, no. 3, pp. 1–21 (2018)
25. Yu, Y., Yao, H., Wang, H., Tang, X., Li, Z.: Representation learning for large-scale dynamic networks. In: Pei, J., Manolopoulos, Y., Sadiq, S., Li, J. (eds.) DASFAA 2018. LNCS, vol. 10828, pp. 526–541. Springer, Cham (2018). https://doi.org/10.1007/978-3-319-91458-9_32
26. Zhang, Z., Cui, P., Li, H., Wang, X., Zhu, W.: Billion-scale network embedding with iterative random projection. In: 2018 IEEE International Conference on Data Mining (ICDM), pp. 787–796. IEEE (2018)

Hierarchical Matching and Reasoning for Action Localization via Language Query

Tianyu Li and Xinxiao Wu[✉]

Beijing Laboratory of Intelligent Information Technology, School of Computer Science, Beijing Institute of Technology, Beijing 100081, People's Republic of China
{3120181002,wuxinxiao}@bit.edu.cn

Abstract. This paper strives for temporal localization of actions in untrimmed videos via natural language queries. Prevailing methods represent both query sentence and video as a whole and perform sentence-video matching via global features, which neglects local correspondence between sentence and video. In this work, we aim to move beyond this limitation by delving into the fine-grained local sentence-video matching, such as phrase-motion matching and word-object matching. We propose a hierarchical matching and reasoning method based on deep conditional random field to integrate hierarchical matching between visual concepts and textual semantics for temporal action localization via query sentence. Our method decomposes each sentence into textual semantics (i.e., phrases and words), obtains multi-level matching results between the textual semantics and the visual concepts in a video (i.e., results of phrase-motion matching and word-object matching), and then reasons relations between multi-level matching via pairwise potentials of conditional random field to achieve coherence in hierarchical matching. By minimizing the overall potential, the final matching score between a sentence and a video is computed as the conditional probability of the conditional random field. Our proposed method is evaluated on public Charades-STA dataset and the experimental results verify its superiority over the state-of-the-art methods.

Keywords: Action localization via language query · Hierarchical matching · Conditional random field

1 Introduction

Temporal action localization via language query aims to localize actions consistent with a given language query, and has attracted much attention in recent years, due to its wide range of applications such as video question answering and

---

This work was supported in part by the Natural Science Foundation of China (NSFC) under grants No. 61673062.

Y. Peng et al. (Eds.): PRCV 2020, LNCS 12307, pp. 137–148, 2020.
https://doi.org/10.1007/978-3-030-60636-7_12

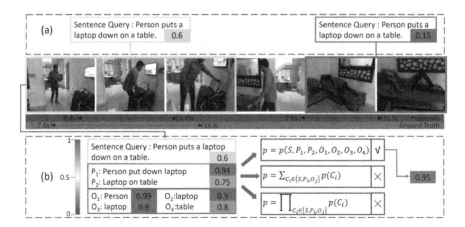

Fig. 1. (a) Previous methods match global sentence with video. (b) Our method matches textual semantics with video then aggregates matching results by reasoning their hierarchical relations.

video content retrieval. Many existing methods [5, 6, 18] adopt a two-stage strategy that first generates temporal action proposals by sliding window method or proposal generator and then matches proposals and sentences by cross-modal matching. Some methods [3, 5, 7] focus on global-level matching that directly maps a sentence and a video into a common embedding space, and ignore the local correspondence between textual semantics and visual concepts such as phrase in sentence corresponds to motion in video, and word in phrase corresponds to object in video. Exploiting these fine-grained correspondences can boost sentence-video matching. Thus, several recent methods [11, 12, 21] seek to explore local matching that maps textual semantics and visual concepts into a common embedding space. These methods simply aggregate the local matching by extracting sentence-attended visual feature or video-attended textual feature to generate the final matching score, without considering the interaction between different local matchings (Fig. 1).

In this paper, we investigate reasoning relations between multi-level matchings (i.e., high-level sentence-video matching, mid-level phrase-motion matching, low-level word-object matching) to achieve coherence in the hierarchical matching. From the top-down view, since the sentence contains phrases, if a sentence matches with a video, its phrases should also be matched with the motions in the video. We denote this matching relation as top-down matching coherence. From the bottom-up view, if one phrase mismatches with motions, the whole sentence should also be mismatched with the video. We denote this matching relation as bottom-up matching coherence. Taking the sentence "A person throws a paper ball into a trash can" for example, when considering the top-down matching coherence, if the sentence matches with a video, the phrases of "person throw paper ball" and "person throw into trash can" should match with motions in the video. When considering the bottom-up matching coherence, if the phrase of "person throws paper ball" or the phrase of "person throws into trash can" mismatches with motions, the sentence should mismatch with the video.

We propose a HIerarchical Matching and Reasoning (HIMR) method that explores fine-grained multi-level local matching and reasons both top-down and bottom-up matching coherence relations for temporal action localization via language query. A hierarchical matching paradigm is adopted to perform the multi-level local matching between a sentence and a video. Specifically, the sentence is decomposed to relation phrases and words by scene graph parser, and then the sentence matches with the video, phrases match with motions in the video, words match with objects in frames. The relations between multi-level local matching are modeled by the Conditional Random Field (CRF) that specializes in modeling statistical dependency between nodes in the Markov field. The Markov field has a tree-like topological structure: each root node represents the fused feature of the sentence feature and the sentence-attended video feature, each intermediate node represents the fused feature of the phrase feature and the phrase-attended motion feature, each leaf node represents the fused feature of the word feature and the word-attended object feature. Based on the Markov field, conditional random field models the matching coherence by pairwise potentials. By maximizing the overall potential, the final matching score between a sentence and a video is computed as the conditional probability of the conditional random field. Our main contributions are summarized as follows:

(1) We propose a hierarchical matching and reasoning method. It performs the fine-grained sentence-video matching at hierarchical levels with superior matching coherence.
(2) We design deep conditional random field to model and reason the matching relations between different evels.
(3) Experiments on Charades-STA dataset demonstrate the effectiveness of our method.

2 Related Work

2.1 Temporal Action Localization via Language Query

Most existing methods of temporal action localization via language query can be roughly divided into two categories: two-stage localization and one-stage localization. Two-stage localization methods firstly generate temporal action proposals by sliding window method [5,6,11,12] or proposal generator [3,18], then match proposals with query sentence by matching module. Liu et al. [11] compute query-based visual attention to obtain attended visual feature, Liu et al. [12] compute video-based textual attention to obtain attended textual feature. Xu et al. [18] interact query with video word-by-word to learn a fine-grained similarity metric. One-stage localization methods [7,19,20] firstly fuse query with video then predict regression offsets or boundary confidence at each timestamp. Yuan et al. [20] predict the temporal coordinates of a query sentence based on temporal attention sequence. Ghosh et al. [7] directly predicts the probability with each timestamp as start time and end time.

2.2 Deep Conditional Random Field

Deep conditional random field has been applied to various tasks in computer vision. Schewing et al. [15] attempt to express the fully-connected conditional random field as recurrent neural networks and led to interesting applications in image segmentation. Chandra et al. [2] construct a deep Gaussian conditional random field on a densely connected spatio-temporal graph in video segmentation. Sigurdsson et al. [16] reason temporally about multiple aspects of activities by Asynchronous Temporal Field. Dai et al. [4] infer the labels of (subject, action, object) triplet by modeling spatial configuration and statistical dependency. Tsai et al. [17] introduce a novel gated energy function parametrization that learns adaptive relations conditioned on visual observations.

We make the first attempt to apply deep conditional random field to action localization via language query. We model the hierarchical matching coherence by the pairwise potential and formulate the final matching score between a sentence and a video as the conditional probability of conditional random field.

3 Method

Given an untrimmed video $V = \{f_t\}_{t=1}^T$ and a query sentence $S = \{w_n\}_{n=1}^N$, where f_t and w_n represent the t-th frame of the video and the n-th word of the sentence respectively, the goal of temporal action localization via language query is to predict the start time t^s and end time t^e of one video segment that semantically consists with the sentence. In this paper, we focus on the visual-semantic matching, so we extract action proposals using off-the-shelf proposal extractor. An action proposal set is denoted as $\{t_i^s, t_i^e\}_{i=1}^{N_{proposal}}$. We propose a HIerarchical Matching and Reasoning method (HIMR) that consists of three modules: an encoding module, a hierarchical matching module, and a reasoning module, shown in Fig. 2.

3.1 Encoding Module

Textual Encoding. We decompose each query sentence into several phrases and words by Stanford scene graph parser [14]. For a query sentence $S = \{w_n\}_{n=1}^N$, the extracted phrase set is denoted as $P = \{P_i\}_{i=1}^{N_p}$, where $P_i = (subject_i, predicate_i, object_i)$, represents the i-th extracted phrase, N_p is the number of extracted phrased. The extracted word set is denoted as $\{O_j\}_{j=1}^{N_p \times 2}$, where O_j is the subject or the object of extracted phrases. The sentence S is represented as hidden states $\{h_n^s\}_{n=1}^N$, each phrase P_i is represented as the last hidden state h_i^p by LSTM, each word w_j is represented as h_j^w by word embedding via Glove [10].

Visual Encoding. For a video $\{f_t\}_{t=1}^T$, I3D [1] feature sequence $\{v_t\}_{t=1}^{T_c}$ are extracted in the whole video, where v_t is the I3D feature of the t-th video clip, T_c is the number of video clips. Resnet-50 [9] features $\{v_t^o\}_{t=1}^T$ are extracted

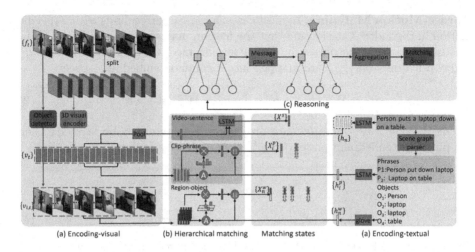

(a) Encoding-visual   (b) Hierarchical matching   Matching states   (a) Encoding-textual

Fig. 2. Method Overview. Our proposed method HIMR contains three modules: (a) The encoding module generates hierarchical representation of a sentence and a video. (b) The hierarchical matching module matches each textual semantics with visual features at levels separately. (c) The reasoning module integrates local matching by reasoning hierarchical coherence relations based on conditional random field.

to represent objects detected by Mask R-CNN [8], where $\boldsymbol{v}_t^o = \{\boldsymbol{v}_{j,t}\}_{j=1}^{N^o}$, $\boldsymbol{v}_{j,t}$ represents the j-th object feature in the t-th frame, N^o represents the number of detected objects in each frame.

3.2 Hierarchical Matching Module

After obtaining hierarchical representations of a sentence and a video, they are matched at three hierarchical levels: sentence-video matching, phrase-motion matching, and word-object matching. In each matching, the textual feature and the matched visual feature are fused as the observation feature of the conditional random field in the reasoning module. Fused features in tree hierarchical levels are named as sentence-video observation feature, phrase-motion observation feature, and word-object observation feature respectively. We detail matchings at three levels in this section.

Sentence-Video Matching: The sentence-video matching adopts the Early Fusion Retrieval Model (EFRM) proposed in [18]. EFRM matches sentence with video word-by-word by a two-layer LSTM. The first LSTM encodes sentence $S = \{w_n\}_{n=1}^N$ to hidden states sequence $\{\boldsymbol{h}_n^s\}_{n=1}^N$, then the second LSTM encodes each hidden state $\boldsymbol{h}_n^s$, along with pooled proposal feature $\hat{\boldsymbol{v}}$ progressively:

$$\boldsymbol{H}_{n+1}^s = \text{LSTM}(\boldsymbol{H}_n^s, \boldsymbol{h}_{n+1}^s, \hat{\boldsymbol{v}}). \tag{1}$$

The last hidden state of the second LSTM $\boldsymbol{H}_N^s$ is represented as the sentence-video observation feature $\boldsymbol{X}^s$.

Phrase-Motion Matching. In most cases, a phrase corresponds with a specific motion in the video. Considering that the motion may span multiple video clips, it is matched with the phrase by soft attention mechanism. Phrase feature h_i^p and clip features $\{v_t\}_{t=t_s}^{t_e}$ are mapped into a common embedding space:

$$\tilde{h}_i^p = W^{pl}(h_i^p) + b^{pl}, \qquad \tilde{v}_t^p = W^{pv}(v_t) + b^{pv}, \tag{2}$$

where W^{pl}, b^{pl}, W^{pv} and b^{pv} are projection parameters to be learned. Then the phrase-attended motion feature $\bar{v}_i^p$ is computed by attention mechanism:

$$\bar{v}_i^p = \sum_{t=t_s}^{t_e} a_{i,t} \tilde{v}_t^p, \tag{3}$$

$$a_{i,t} = (\tilde{v}_t^p)^T \tilde{h}_i^p, \qquad a_i = \text{Softmax}(a_i). \tag{4}$$

Then the phrase feature $\tilde{h}_i^p$ and the attended motion feature $\bar{v}_i^p$ are concatenated as the phrase-motion observation feature $X_i^p = \tilde{h}_i^p || \bar{v}_i^p$.

Word-Object Matching. In word-object matching, a word is matched with an object in a frame by hard attention mechanism. Concretely, word features $\{h_n^w\}$ and object features $\{v_{i,t}\}_{i=1}^{N_o}$ are mapped into a common embedding space:

$$\tilde{h}_n^w = W^{wl}(h_n^w) + b^{wl}, \qquad \tilde{v}_{i,t}^w = W^{wv}(v_{i,t}^w) + b^{wv}, \tag{5}$$

where W^{wl}, b^{wl}, W^{wv} and b^{wv} are projection parameters to be learned. Then the index of the object feature $v_{i,t}$ which matches mostly with the word feature h_n^w in the t-th frame is computed as

$$j_{n,t} = \text{argmax}_i((\tilde{h}_n^w)^T \cdot \tilde{v}_{i,t}^w). \tag{6}$$

Then the word feature $\tilde{h}_n^w$ and the matched object feature $\tilde{v}_{j_{n,t},t}^w$ are concatenated in each frames, and are pooled along time to obtain the word-object observation feature X_n^w:

$$X_{n,t}^w = (\tilde{h}_n^w || \tilde{v}_{j_{n,t},t}^w), \tag{7}$$

$$X_n^w = \text{Pool}(X_{n,t_s}^w, ..., X_{n,t_e}^w). \tag{8}$$

3.3   Reasoning Module

Matching coherence relations between hierarchical matching are reasoned based on the Conditional Random Field (CRF) to comprehensively measure the overall matching. According to the basic theorem of CRF, given structured observation $X = \text{graph}(X_1, ..., X_N)$, the probability of structured prediction $Y = \text{graph}(Y_1, ..., Y_N)$ is computed as:

$$P(Y|X) = \frac{1}{Z(X)} \exp(-E(Y|X)), \tag{9}$$

$$E(\mathbf{Y}|\mathbf{X}) = \sum_{i=1}^{N^{node}} \psi_i(Y_i|\mathbf{X}) + \sum_{\{i,j\}\in Set^r} \phi_{i,j}(Y_i, Y_j|\mathbf{X}), \qquad (10)$$

where $E(\mathbf{Y}|\mathbf{X})$ represents the potential conditioned on the pair of observation $\mathbf{X}$ and prediction Y, ψ_i represents unary potential of Node i, $\phi_{i,j}$ represents pairwise potential between Node i and Node j, Set^r represents the set of neighbouring nodes. In traditional prediction task, given structured observation $\mathbf{X} = \mathrm{graph}(X_1, ..., X_N)$, the structured prediction $\mathbf{Y} = \mathrm{graph}(Y_1, ..., Y_N)$ is the one which maximize the conditional probability $P(\mathbf{Y}|\mathbf{X})$. The structured prediction $\mathbf{Y}$ takes into account interactions between neighbour observations and predictions in the Markov field.

To apply CRF to hierarchical matching of sentence and video, we formulate the Markov field of CRF as a tree-like topological structure: the observation in the root node is represented by sentence-video observation feature $\mathbf{X}^s$, the observation in each intern node is represented by phrase-motion observation feature $\mathbf{X}_m^p$, the observation in each leaf node is represented by word-object observation feature $\mathbf{X}_n^w$. Prediction Y_k in each node k is the binary classification label, Y_k with label 0 indicates that the textual semantics mismatches with the visual concept, Y_k with label 1 indicates that the textual semantics matches with the visual concepts in the corresponding matching. Upon the Markov field, the unary potential $\psi(Y_i|\mathbf{X})$ is formulated as

$$\psi(Y_i|\mathbf{X}) = f_\theta^\psi(\mathbf{X}_i, i, Y_i) = <\mathbf{w}_\theta^{l_i}(\mathbf{X}_i)>_{Y_i}, \qquad (11)$$

where $\mathbf{w}_\theta^{l_i}$ is a two-layer fully connected layers, $<\cdot>_{Y_i}$ denotes the Y_ith element, l_i represents the level of the node i. The pairwise potential $\phi_{i,j}$ is formulated as

$$\phi_{i,j}(Y_i, Y_j|\mathbf{X}) = f_\theta^\phi(\mathbf{X}_i, \mathbf{X}_j, Y_i, Y_j) = <(\mathbf{r}_\theta^{l_i l_j}(\mathbf{X}_i))^T \mathbf{h}_\theta^{l_i l_j}(\mathbf{X}_j)>_{Y_i, Y_j}, \qquad (12)$$

where $\mathbf{r}_\theta^{l_i l_j}(\cdot)$, $\mathbf{h}_\theta^{l_i l_j}(\cdot) \in \mathrm{R}^{r\times 2}$ represent the r-rank projection, which is modeled by a two-layer fully connected network and a resize operation. In the above formulation, pairwise potentials are determined by labels and observation features.

After formulating the unary potential and the pairwise potential, final binary classification results of all nodes can be predicted by maximizing the conditional probability $P(\mathbf{Y}|\mathbf{X})$ as in Eq. (10). To make the maximizing process end-to-end, the conditional probability $P(\mathbf{Y}|\mathbf{X})$ is approximated and factorized to $P \approx Q = \prod Q_i$. Each factor Q_i is computed as

$$Q(Y_i) \propto \exp(-\psi(Y_i|\mathbf{X})) \prod_{\{i,j\}\in Set_i^r} m_{j,i}(Y_i|\mathbf{X}), \qquad (13)$$

$$m_{j,i}(Y_i|\mathbf{X}) = \exp(-\sum_{Y_i} \phi_{i,j}(Y_i, Y_j|\mathbf{X})Q(Y_j|\mathbf{X})). \qquad (14)$$

In the above factorization, each factor Q_i approximates prediction Y_i that considers hierarchical interactions. So by choosing Y_i which maximizes factor Q_i, the approximated prediction $\mathbf{Y}$ is obtained. To select the segment which semantically consists with the query sentence, the conditional probability $P(\mathbf{Y}^1|\mathbf{X})$ is formulated as similarity score, where $\mathbf{Y}^1$ represents the structured prediction where each node's binary classification label is 1.

3.4   Training and Inference

Training: Each raw training sample d_i consists of four elements: the query sentence S_i, the video V_i, the boundary (t_i^s, t_i^e) of the ground-truth segment and the binary classification labels $\boldsymbol{Y}_i$. For convenience, d_{ij} denotes the generated training sample with the query sentence S_i, the video V_j, the boundary (t_j^s, t_j^e) and the binary classification labels $\boldsymbol{Y}_{i,j}$, where $\boldsymbol{Y}_{i,j}$ is computed by comparing $\boldsymbol{Y}_i$ and $\boldsymbol{Y}_j$: if one textual semantics (sentence, phrase or word) of the sentence S_j appears in the sentence S_i, the corresponding binary classification label of Y_{ij} is 1, otherwise 0. During training, each training samples d_i, along with another randomly sampled training sample d_j are used to generate two positive training samples d_{ii} and d_{jj}, two negative training samples d_{ij} and d_{ji}. Then the training object of one minibatch is computed as

$$L = \frac{1}{B}\left(\sum_{b,k,m} \text{CrossEntropy}(\psi_{b,k}^m, \hat{y}_{b,k}^m) + \sum_{b,k,m} \text{CrossEntropy}(Q_{b,k,m}^m, \hat{y}_{b,k}^m)\right), \quad (15)$$

where b denotes training batch, m denotes training samples generated by b-th sample, $\psi_{b,k}^m$ represents the vector of unary potential of node k, $\hat{y}_{b,k}^m$ represents the one-hot ground-truth vector of node k, $Q_{b,j}^m$ is the vector of binary classification results of node k after reasoning the hierarchical relations between nodes.

Inference: During inference, action proposals are generated by action proposal generator [18]. The matching score of each proposal with a given query sentence is computed as the conditional probability $P(\boldsymbol{Y}^1|\boldsymbol{X})$. Proposals are filtered by non-maximum suppression with a threshold of 0.7.

4   Experiments

4.1   Dataset and Implementation Details

To evaluate the proposed method, the Charades-STA dataset [5] is employed for experiments, which focus on complicated human activities in daily life. There are annotations of 12,408 sentence-segment pairs for training, and 3,720 for testing. Following [5], we use "$R@n, IoU@m$" as evaluation metrics, which is defined as the percentage of the testing queries having at least one hitting retrieval (with IoU larger than m) in the top-n retrieved segments.

Video frames are sampled at the frame rate of 5. Action proposals are extracted by proposal extractor in [18]. I3D [1] features are extracted in the whole video. We use a fine-tuned version for Charades available here. Object features are extracted by Mask R-CNN [8]. Word embedding with the vector dimension of 300 is initialized by Glove word embedding [13]. The dimension of the hidden state in LSTM is set to 512, and the maximum sentence length is set to 10. The dimension of the hidden layer of potential function is set to 512. The rank in pairwise potential is set to 2. The Adam optimizer is used for training with a learning rate of 0.00002.

Table 1. Comparison of our HIMR method with state-of-the-art two-stage localization methods.

Method	R@1 IoU@0.3	R@5 IoU@0.3	R@1 IoU@0.5	R@5 IoU@0.5	R@1 IoU@0.7	R@5 IoU@0.7
CTRL [5]	-	-	23.63	58.92	8.89	29.52
MAC [6]	-	-	26.47	61.51	11.23	33.25
SAP [3]	-	-	27.42	66.37	13.36	38.15
Xu et al. [18]	54.70	95.60	35.60	79.40	15.80	45.40
HIMR	59.73	95.02	41.78	85.32	18.68	51.37

4.2 Comparison with State-of-the-art

We compare our model with several state-of-the-art methods. Since our method adopts two-stage localization framework, we only compare it with the two-stage methods. Table 1 shows the comparison results between our HIMR and existing two-stage localization methods. Our method achieves better results than global-level matching methods [3,5,6]. Though matching method in [18] implicitly takes into account the local semantic information by early fusion of textual and visual features, it does not model interactions between matching results at different levels. Through reasoning the relations between multiple matching at different levels, our HIMR achieves better results than [18], which validates the superior of matching coherence in HIMR.

4.3 Ablation Study

We perform ablation studies to validate the effectiveness of individual module in HIMR. The compared models are listed as follows:

- Matching-x: perform sentence-video matching at level x, where $x \in \{s,p,w\}$.
- HIMR-x: perform hierarchical matching and reasoning at multiple levels x, where $x \in \{sp,sw,spw\}$.
- Average-x: perform hierarchical matching and average matching scores at all levels, where $x \in \{sp,sw,spw\}$.
- Product-x: perform hierarchical matching and multiply matching score at all levels, where $x \in \{sp,sw,spw\}$.

In the above definitions, the denotations "s", "p" and "w" represent the sentence-video matching, the phrase-motion matching, and the word-object matching, respectively. The denotations "sp", "sw" and "spw" represent the hierarchical matching and reasoning at the corresponding levels.

The results of ablation studies are reported in Table 2. It is interesting to observe that: (1) Result of the Matching-s method outperforms the Matching-p method and the Matching-w method, the possible reason is that the phrase losses some temporal information in the sentence, the word losses some relation information in the phrase. (2) Though the Matching-w method and the Matching-p

Table 2. Ablation study of our method.

Method	R@1,IoU@0.5	Method	R@1,IoU@0.5
Matching-s	39.25	Average-sp	39.14
Matching-p	38.28	Average-sw	35.43
Matching-w	26.43	Average-spw	39.41
HIMR-sp	41.41	Product-sp	39.41
HIMR-sw	40.52	Product-sw	35.60
HIMR-spw	41.78	Product-spw	39.22

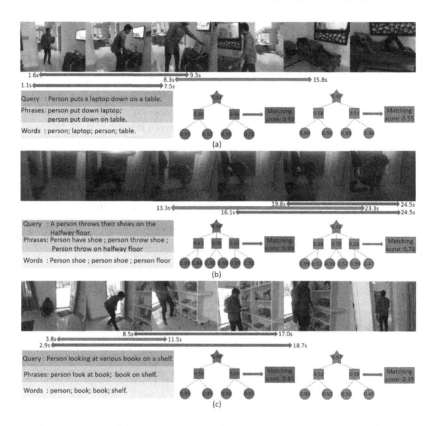

Fig. 3. Visualization of hierarchical matching and reasoning results. (Color figure online)

method have relatively low results, the HIMR-sw method, the HIMR-sp method and the HIMR-spw method achieve better performance than the Matching-s method by a gain of 1.1%, 2.1%, and 2.5% respectively, which demonstrates that exploiting fine-grained correspondences can boost sentence-video matching. (3) Results of the Average-spw method and Product-sp method have little improvement upon the Matching-s method, while results of the Average-sp method, the Average-sw method, the Product-sw method, and the Product-spw method are lower than the Matching-s method, which demonstrates that improvements of HIMR are not caused by stacking of matching at levels, but by exploiting hierarchical interactions between local matching.

4.4   Visualization Results

Several examples of action localization results of our method are shown in Fig. 3. For each example, the red line represents the ground-truth video segment, the green line represents the video segment localized by our HIMR method and the blue line represents the video segment localized by only sentence-video matching of our HIMR method. Number in five-pointed star, square, and circle represent sentence-video matching score, phrase-motion matching score, and word-object matching score respectively. Considering only the sentence-video matching, the matching score of the green segment (closer to ground truth segment) is lower than the blue segment. After reasoning coherence relations between local matching, the score of green segment surpasses the blue segment.

5   Conclusion

We have presented a hierarchical matching and reasoning method for temporal action localization via language query. It matches textual semantics and visual concepts at multiple levels, and fuses the multi-level matching by reasoning their relations via deep conditional random field. Our method can achieve coherence in hierarchical fine-grained matching between sentences and videos. Experiments results on the Charades-STA datasets demonstrate the effectiveness and interpretability of our method.

References

1. Carreira, J., Zisserman, A.: Quo vadis, action recognition? a new model and the kinetics dataset. In: proceedings of the IEEE Conference on Computer Vision and Pattern Recognition, pp. 6299–6308 (2017)
2. Chandra, S., Couprie, C., Kokkinos, I.: Deep spatio-temporal random fields for efficient video segmentation. In: Proceedings of the IEEE Conference on Computer Vision and Pattern Recognition, pp. 8915–8924 (2018)
3. Chen, S., Jiang, Y.G.: Semantic proposal for activity localization in videos via sentence query. In: Proceedings of the AAAI Conference on Artificial Intelligence, vol. 33, pp. 8199–8206 (2019)
4. Dai, B., Zhang, Y., Lin, D.: Detecting visual relationships with deep relational networks. In: Proceedings of the IEEE Conference on Computer Vision and Pattern Recognition, pp. 3076–3086 (2017)
5. Gao, J., Sun, C., Yang, Z., Nevatia, R.: Tall: temporal activity localization via language query. In: Proceedings of the IEEE International Conference on Computer Vision, pp. 5267–5275 (2017)

6. Ge, R., Gao, J., Chen, K., Nevatia, R.: MAC: mining activity concepts for language-based temporal localization. In: 2019 IEEE Winter Conference on Applications of Computer Vision (WACV), pp. 245–253 (2019)

7. Ghosh, S., Agarwal, A., Parekh, Z., Hauptmann, A.G.: ExCL: extractive clip localization using natural language descriptions, pp. 1984–1990 (2019)

8. He, K., Gkioxari, G., Dollár, P., Girshick, R.: Mask R-CNN. In: Proceedings of the IEEE International Conference on Computer Vision, pp. 2961–2969 (2017)

9. He, K., Zhang, X., Ren, S., Sun, J.: Deep residual learning for image recognition. In: Proceedings of the IEEE Conference on Computer Vision and Pattern Recognition, pp. 770–778 (2016)

10. Hendricks, L.A., Wang, O., Shechtman, E., Sivic, J., Darrell, T., Russell, B.: Localizing moments in video with temporal language. In: Proceedings of the 2018 Conference on Empirical Methods in Natural Language Processing, pp. 1380–1390 (2018)

11. Liu, M., Wang, X., Nie, L., He, X., Chen, B., Chua, T.S.: Attentive moment retrieval in videos. In: The 41st International ACM SIGIR Conference on Research and Development in Information Retrieval, pp. 15–24 (2018)

12. Liu, M., Wang, X., Nie, L., Tian, Q., Chen, B., Chua, T.S.: Cross-modal moment localization in videos. In: Proceedings of the 26th ACM International Conference on Multimedia, pp. 843–851 (2018)

13. Pennington, J., Socher, R., Manning, C.: Glove: global vectors for word representation. In: Proceedings of the 2014 Conference on Empirical Methods in Natural Language Processing (EMNLP), pp. 1532–1543 (2014)

14. Schuster, S., Krishna, R., Chang, A., Fei-Fei, L., Manning, C.D.: Generating semantically precise scene graphs from textual descriptions for improved image retrieval. In: Proceedings of the Fourth Workshop on Vision and Language, pp. 70–80 (2015)

15. Schwing, A.G., Urtasun, R.: Fully connected deep structured networks. arXiv preprint arXiv:1503.02351 (2015)

16. Sigurdsson, G.A., Divvala, S., Farhadi, A., Gupta, A.: Asynchronous temporal fields for action recognition. In: Proceedings of the IEEE Conference on Computer Vision and Pattern Recognition, pp. 585–594 (2017)

17. Tsai, Y.H.H., Divvala, S., Morency, L.P., Salakhutdinov, R., Farhadi, A.: Video relationship reasoning using gated spatio-temporal energy graph. In: Proceedings of the IEEE Conference on Computer Vision and Pattern Recognition, pp. 10424–10433 (2019)

18. Xu, H., He, K., Plummer, B.A., Sigal, L., Sclaroff, S., Saenko, K.: Multilevel language and vision integration for text-to-clip retrieval. In: Proceedings of the AAAI Conference on Artificial Intelligence, vol. 33, pp. 9062–9069 (2019)

19. Yuan, Y., Ma, L., Wang, J., Liu, W., Zhu, W.: Semantic conditioned dynamic modulation for temporal sentence grounding in videos. In: Advances in Neural Information Processing Systems, pp. 534–544 (2019)

20. Yuan, Y., Mei, T., Zhu, W.: To find where you talk: temporal sentence localization in video with attention based location regression. In: Proceedings of the AAAI Conference on Artificial Intelligence, vol. 33, pp. 9159–9166 (2019)

21. Zhang, Z., Lin, Z., Zhao, Z., Xiao, Z.: Cross-modal interaction networks for query-based moment retrieval in videos, pp. 655–664 (2019)

Semi-supervised Uncertain Linear Discriminant Analysis

Guowan Shao[1]([✉]), Fanmao Liu[2], and Chunjiang Peng[1]

[1] College of Mechanical and Electrical Engineering,
Hunan University of Science and Technology,
Xiangtan 411201, Hunan, People's Republic of China
gwshao_ezhou@163.com
[2] Engineering Research Center for Advanced Mine
Equipment of Ministry of Education, Hunan University of Science and Technology,
Xiangtan 411201, People's Republic of China

Abstract. Linear discriminant analysis (LDA) is a popular supervised method for dimensionality reduction for its simplicity and effectiveness. However, its performance may significantly deteriorate in the situation that labeled training samples are very scarce and many semi-supervised methods are presented to solve the problem with a large amount of unlabeled samples available. In this paper, inspired by the uncertainty idea, we propose a semi-supervised uncertain linear discriminant analysis (SULDA). First, we present a fractional-step label propagation to reliably label the unlabeled samples. Secondly, we use all training samples and their labels to construct double-layer Gaussian mixture models. Finally, we utilize the originally labeled samples and the obtained models to define expected between-class and within-class scatter matrices. Experimental results illustrate that our method is superior to some state-of-the-art semi-supervised methods with respect to the discriminative power.

Keywords: Discriminant analysis · Dimensionality reduction · Semi-supervised.

1 Introduction

It is difficult to analyze high-dimensional data directly and dimensionality reduction (DR) facilitates the task greatly. In general, dimensionality reduction includes two kinds of techniques: unsupervised and supervised ones. The most representative unsupervised technique is principal component analysis (PCA) [1]. Among the supervised techniques, linear discriminant analysis (LDA) [2] is a basic method. For the supervised methods, the performance may deteriorate when labeled training samples are not sufficient. In this case, unlabeled samples,

Supported by Hunan Provincial Natural Science Foundation of China (Grant No. 2018JJ2133).

Y. Peng et al. (Eds.): PRCV 2020, LNCS 12307, pp. 149–160, 2020.
https://doi.org/10.1007/978-3-030-60636-7_13

which are easily accessible, are generally used to improve the performance and thus the supervised methods turn into semi-supervised ones.

LDA suffers from overfitting when there are only a few labeled samples and the optimal subspace may not be obtained. Many semi-supervised methods enhance its performance using unlabeled samples [2–5]. Semi-supervised discriminant analysis (SDA) [3] uses labeled and unlabeled samples to construct a geometrically based regularizer and then defines a new objective function to prevent the overfiting. However, the objective function is actually a determinant ratio problem, i.e., a ratio trace problem, and thus the solution is suboptimal. Moreover, SDA is a linear method which is not suitable for dealing with samples from a nonlinear manifold. Trace ratio based flexible semi-supervised discriminant analysis (TR-FSDA) [4] reformulates the ratio trace problem into a trace ratio one and relaxes the constraint that training samples are linearly mapped into the subspace. Label information can be quantitatively utilized using a ridge regression function and then similar to SDA, a manifold regularization term is added to construct an objective function [5]. However, it may be overstrict to directly utilize label information by mean of the linear regression function. Flexible manifold embedding (FME) [6] introduces the predicted labels to relax it and directly utilizes label information and manifold structure by the predicted labels. Semi-supervised orthogonal discriminant analysis (SODA) [7] uses the trick of label propagation to obtain the soft label of each unlabeled sample and redefines the scatter matrices with the soft label. Then the optimal subspace can be obtained by solving the trace ratio problem. The problem can be transformed into a constrained trace maximization one whose solution can be efficiently obtained by dealing with a weighted and regularized least squares problem [8]. However, label propagation suffers from three problems: Firstly, it may not reliable when the input data are high-dimensional. Secondly, label propagation is independent of sequent linear discriminant analysis. Thirdly, it may become unreliable when there are only very scarce labeled samples. To avoid the former two problems, semi-supervised linear discriminant analysis [9] constructs an objective function to calculate the label and projection matrices simultaneously.

The performance of LDA becomes poor when the input data are distorted or contaminated by noise. Since the ℓ_1-norm is more robust to noisy data than ℓ_2-norm, some methods apply ℓ_1-norm to improve its performance [10,11]. Recently, uncertain linear discriminant analysis (ULDA) [12] is proposed to deal with the noisy data. It assumes that each training sample comes from a corresponding Gaussian distribution and obtains the expected between-class and within-class scatter matrices. The method reduces to LDA when the data are free of noise. However, it is impossible to attain the posterior distribution corresponding to each labeled training sample without the information on uncertainty of the sample.

In this paper, inspired by the uncertainty idea behind ULDA, we propose a novel semi-supervised learning method, semi-supervised ULDA (SULDA). A fractional-step label propagation is first presented to label the unlabeled samples in order to cope with the third problem for label propagation mentioned previously. Then double-layer Gaussian mixture models are constructed using all training samples and their labels. Finally, the originally labeled samples and the means and covariances from the double-layer Gaussian mixture models are used to define new expected between-class and within-class scatter matrices. It can achieve good classification performance when the input data include few labeled samples and large quantities of unlabeled ones. Experimental results on the synthetic data sets and two publicly available real datasets show that SULDA achieves better classification performance than some state-of-the-art semi-supervised methods.

2   Related Work

In this section, we briefly review LDA, ULDA and label propagation. For supervised dimensionality reduction, its goal is to obtain an optimal subspace using class label information. More specifically, given a data set $X = [X_L, X_U]$, where $X_L = [x_1, \cdots, x_l]$, $X_U = [x_{l+1}, \cdots, x_n]$, $x_j \in \mathbb{R}^m$, $j = 1, 2, \cdots, n$, X_L includes l labeled data points from c classes and X_U includes $n - l$ unlabeled ones. Let x_{ij} denote the jth point from class i in X_L and n_i be the number of labeled data points from class i. A supervised method is to construct an objective function using labeled data points and then get a transformation matrix $W \in \mathbb{R}^{m \times d}$, namely a d-dimensional subspace, with which the objective function is optimal.

2.1   Linear Discriminant Analysis

LDA is the most popular method for supervised dimensionality reduction and has been extended into many different methods with more excellent performance. Its objective function involves two matrices, namely the between-class scatter matrix S_b and the within-class scatter matrix S_w, which are defined as follows:

$$S_b = \sum_{i=1}^{c} (\mu_i - \mu)(\mu_i - \mu)^T \tag{1}$$

$$S_w = \sum_{i=1}^{c} \sum_{j=1}^{n_i} n_i (x_{ij} - \mu_i)(x_{ij} - \mu_i)^T \tag{2}$$

where μ_i denotes the mean of class i and is generally empirically estimated as $\mu_i = \frac{1}{n_i} \sum_{j=1}^{n_i} x_{ij}$, and μ denotes the mean of all the classes and is estimated as $\mu = \frac{1}{l} \sum_{j=1}^{l} x_j$. There are several forms for the objective function of LDA, and here we formulate it as the trace ratio problem:

$$\max_{W} \frac{tr(W^T S_b W)}{tr(W^T S_w W)} \tag{3}$$

Problem (3) can be transformed into the ratio trace problem and a suboptimal solution can be obtained by generalized eigenvalue decomposition. In real applications, the input data are generally corrupted by noise and the performance of LDA may become poor.

2.2 Uncertain Linear Discriminant Analysis

ULDA is presented to deal with observation uncertainties from noise and takes the probabilistic description of each labeled sample into account [12]. The method assumes that each labeled sample comes from a Gaussian distribution, denoted as $x_{ij} \sim \mathcal{N}(\mu_{ij}, \Sigma_{ij})$, $i = 1, 2, \cdots, c$, $j = 1, 2, \cdots, n_i$, and it assumes the distributions can be obtained by the available prior information. Moreover, ULDA assumes that all the distributions are independent each other. Therefore, the means of class i and all the classes can be formulate as

$$\mu_i \sim \mathcal{N}\left(\frac{1}{n_i} \sum_{j=1}^{n_i} \mu_{ij}, \frac{1}{n_i^2} \sum_{j=1}^{n_i} \Sigma_{ij} \right) \tag{4}$$

$$\mu \sim \mathcal{N}\left(\frac{1}{l} \sum_{i=1}^{c} \sum_{j=1}^{n_i} \mu_{ij}, \frac{1}{l^2} \sum_{i=1}^{c} \sum_{j=1}^{n_i} \Sigma_{ij} \right) \tag{5}$$

and the expected between-class and within-class scatter matrices can be derived as follows [12]:

$$\widehat{S_b} = S_b + \sum_{i=1}^{c} \left(\frac{n_i}{l^2} \sum_{k=1}^{c} \sum_{j=1}^{n_i} \Sigma_{kj} + \frac{l - 2n_i}{n_i l} \sum_{j=1}^{n_i} \Sigma_{ij} \right) \tag{6}$$

$$\widehat{S_w} = S_w + \sum_{i=1}^{c} \frac{n_i - 1}{n_i} \sum_{j=1}^{n_i} \Sigma_{ij} \tag{7}$$

After replacing S_b and S_w in problem (3) with $\widehat{S_b}$ and $\widehat{S_w}$, the optimal subspace can be obtained by solving the problem. The method reduces to LDA when the training samples are free of uncertainties. For ULDA, it is a key step to find the Gaussian distribution corresponding to each labeled training sample. However, there is no available information to obtain the distributions when only the labeled samples are provided and thus the method becomes invalid.

2.3 Label Propagation

In real applications, it is time-consuming and costly to obtain labeled samples. In contrast, abundant unlabeled samples are available. In this case, label propagation is presented to cope with the scarcity of labeled samples using the manifold structure of labeled and unlabeled samples [7]. In general, a neighbor weighted graph must be constructed first. There are many strategies to construct the graph and here we only present a popular strategy [7]: if x_i is among the k nearest neighbors of x_j or x_j is among the k nearest neighbors of x_i, then the weight between x_i and x_j is defined as $A_{ij} = \exp(-\|x_i - x_j\|^2/\sigma^2)$, where σ is the variance, otherwise, $A_{ij} = 0$.

An additional class $c+1$ is introduced to find the outliers in X and thus the performance of label propagation may be improved. Let $Y = [Y_1^T, \cdots, Y_n^T] \in \mathbb{R}^{n \times (c+1)}$ be the initial label matrix, where $Y_i \in \mathbb{R}^{1 \times (c+1)}$, $i = 1, 2, \cdots, n$, and $Y_{ij} = 1$ if x_i is labeled as class j, $j = 1, 2, \cdots, c+1$, otherwise, $Y_{ij} = 0$. Let $F = [F_1^T, \cdots, F_n^T] \in \mathbb{R}^{n \times (c+1)}$ be the predicted label matrix, where $F_i \in \mathbb{R}^{1 \times (c+1)}$, $i = 1, 2, \cdots, n$, and $0 \leqslant F_{ij} \leqslant 1$, $j = 1, 2, \cdots, c+1$.

A diagonal matrix D is obtained using the weight matrix A, i.e., $D_{ii} = \sum_{j=1}^{n} A_{ij}$, and $P = D^{-1}A$ is a stochastic matrix. Label information is propagated through an iterative process based on the principle that the label of each unlabeled sample at time $t+1$ is weighted by both its label and the labels from its neighbors at time t. More specifically,

$$F(t+1) = I_\alpha P F(t+1) + I_\beta Y \tag{8}$$

where I_α is a diagonal matrix with each element being α_i, $0 \leqslant \alpha_i \leqslant 1$, and $I_\beta = I - I_\alpha$. For our fractional-step label propagation in Subsect. 3.1, let $\alpha_i = 0$ and $\alpha_j = 1$ for the labeled and unlabeled samples x_i and x_j, respectively. The iterative process converges to

$$F = (I - I_\alpha P)^{-1} I_\beta Y \tag{9}$$

and $\sum_{j=1}^{c+1} F_{ij} = 1$, namely, F_{ij} is the posterior probability of x_i affiliated to class j [7]. As mentioned previously, the popular method for label propagation may become unreliable when labeled samples are much scarce. Therefore, we present a fractional-step label propagation to alleviate the difficulty.

3   Semi-supervised Uncertain Linear Discriminant Analysis

LDA is a classical supervised method for dimensionality reduction and its performance may become poor when the input data are contaminated by noise. In this case, ULDA is presented to solve the problem. The uncertain idea behind the method: The noisy data is deemed to be the uncertain data, more specifically, each labeled sample is deemed to come from a corresponding Gaussian distribution. Based on the uncertain idea, we use unlabeled samples to deal with the other problem that the performance of LDA may greatly deteriorate with much scarce labeled training samples.

3.1   Fractional-Step Label Propagation

We give fractional-step label propagation to enhance the performance of the popular method for label propagation mentioned previously. After obtaining the weight matrix A, the label information is propagated in fractional steps. More explicitly, we first select all the k nearest neighbors of the initial labeled samples and remove the duplicate items. Then a dataset is constructed with the initial labeled samples and the selected ones. We apply the popular method for label propagation to obtain the labels of the unlabeled samples in the dataset. In the next step, we select all the k nearest neighbors of the selected samples and remove the duplicate ones. A new dataset is constructed with the newly selected samples and the last dataset. Then we apply the label propagation to obtain the labels of the newly selected unlabeled samples. We repeat the above procedures until all the samples are labeled.

Algorithm 1 summarizes the idea of the fractional-step label propagation in Table 1. The predicted label matrix in the tth step is calculated as follows: We obtain the weight matrix $A^t \in \mathbb{R}^{n_t \times n_t}$ from $A \in \mathbb{R}^{n \times n}$ and the predicted label matrix $Y^t \in \mathbb{R}^{n_t \times (c+1)}$ corresponding to the dataset X_l^t and then obtain the stochastic matrix $P^t = (D^t)^{-1} A^t$, where $D^t \in \mathbb{R}^{n_t \times n_t}$ is a diagonal matrix, more specifically, $D_{ii}^t = \sum_{j=1}^{n_t} A_{ij}^t$, then

$$F^t = (I^t - I_\alpha^t P^t)^{-1} I_\beta^t Y^t \tag{10}$$

The fractional-step label propagation may obtain more reliable labels when the initial labeled samples are very scarce. It is because that labeled samples may play a more important part in label propagation within a small scope, namely, their neighborhood.

Table 1. Algorithm 1. Fractional-step label propagation

Input : X_L – labeled data matrix, $X_L \in \mathbb{R}^{m \times l}$;
  X_U – unlabeled data matrix, $X_U \in \mathbb{R}^{m \times (n-l)}$;
  X – data matrix, $X = [X_L, X_U] \in \mathbb{R}^{m \times n}$;
Output : F – predicted label matrix, $F \in \mathbb{R}^{n \times (c+1)}$.
Procedure :
  Calculate the weight matrix $A \in \mathbb{R}^{n \times n}$ according to the
    description in subsection 2.3;
  Set $t=1$, $X_l^1 = X_L$, $X_a^1 = \{x_i \mid x_i \in X_U, x_j \in X_L, A_{ij} \neq 0\}$,
    $X_u^1 = X_U$;
  while $X_a^t \neq \emptyset$
    Let $t=t+1$;
    Let $X_l^t = [X_l^{t-1}, X_a^{t-1}]$, n_i is the number of samples
      in X_l^t;
    Compute the predicted label matrix $F^t \in \mathbb{R}^{n_t \times (c+1)}$
      according to (10);
    Let $X_a^t = \{x_i \mid x_i \in X_u^t, x_j \in X_l^t, A_{ij} \neq 0\}$, where $X_u^t = X - X_l^t$;
  end

3.2   Semi-supervised Uncertain Linear Discriminant Analysis

As mentioned previously, the performance of LDA may become poor when the labeled samples are very scarce. Fortunately, there are large quantities of unlabeled samples in reality. Inspired by the uncertain idea behind ULDA, we use the unlabeled samples to obtain the Gaussian distributions corresponding to some labeled samples. In other words, the distributions contain the discriminative information from the unlabeled samples and can be used to improve the performance of LDA. More explicitly, we utilize the labeled samples and the obtained distributions to construct the expected between-class and within-class scatter matrices and thus the optimal subspace can be obtained.

Let $\mathcal{N}(\mu_{ij}, \Sigma_{ij})$ is the jth Gaussian distribution belong to class i, $i = 1, 2, \cdots, c$, $j = 1, 2, \cdots, l_i$, where l_i is the number of the Gaussian distributions belong to class i, then the Gaussian mixture model being to class i is formulated as $\sum_{j=1}^{l_i} \pi_{ij} \mathcal{N}(\mu_{ij}, \Sigma_{ij})$, where π_{ij} is a mixing coefficient, $0 \leqslant \pi_{ij} \leqslant 1$, and $\sum_{j=1}^{l_i} \pi_{ij} = 1$. Let $\mathcal{A}_i = \{\pi_{ij}\}_{j=1}^{l_i}$, $\mathcal{B}_i = \{\mu_{ij}\}_{j=1}^{l_i}$, $\mathcal{C}_i = \{\Sigma_{ij}\}_{j=1}^{l_i}$, $\Theta_i = \{\mathcal{A}_i, \mathcal{B}_i, \mathcal{C}_i\}$, $\Theta = \{\Theta_i\}_{i=1}^{c}$. A superposition of c Gaussian mixture densities are defined as

$$p(x_k \mid F, \Theta) = \sum_{i=1}^{c} F_{ki} \sum_{j=1}^{l_i} \pi_{ij} p(x_k \mid \mu_{ij}, \Sigma_{ij}) \tag{11}$$

where $k = 1, 2, \cdots, n$, which is referred to a double-layer mixture of Gaussians. Then the likelihood function is given by

$$p(X \mid F, \Theta) = \prod_{k=1}^{n} \sum_{i=1}^{c} F_{ki} \sum_{j=1}^{l_i} \pi_{ij} p(x_k \mid \mu_{ij}, \Sigma_{ij}) \tag{12}$$

Therefore, the following objective function is given by

$$\max_{\pi_{ij}, \mu_{ij}, \Sigma_{ij}} \ln p(X \mid F, \Theta)$$

Namely,

$$\max_{\pi_{ij}, \mu_{ij}, \Sigma_{ij}} \sum_{k=1}^{n} \ln \left(\sum_{i=1}^{c} F_{ki} \sum_{j=1}^{l_i} \pi_{ij} p(x_k \mid \mu_{ij}, \Sigma_{ij}) \right) \tag{13}$$

The solution to problem (13) can be obtained using the expectation maximization algorithm (EM) [13] and here we directly give the iterative formulae of the parameters at time t:

$$\pi_{ij}^t = \frac{\sum_{k=1}^{n} p(ij \mid x_k, \Theta^{t-1})}{\sum_{z=1}^{l_i} \sum_{k=1}^{n} p(iz \mid x_k, \Theta^{t-1})} \tag{14}$$

$$\mu_{ij}^t = \frac{\sum_{k=1}^{n} x_k p(ij \mid x_k, \Theta^{t-1})}{\sum_{k=1}^{n} p(ij \mid x_k, \Theta^{t-1})} \tag{15}$$

$$\Sigma_{ij}^t = \frac{\sum_{k=1}^{n} p(ij \mid x_k, \Theta^{t-1})(x_k - \mu_{ij}^t)(x_k - \mu_{ij}^t)^T}{\sum_{k=1}^{n} p(ij \mid x_k, \Theta^{t-1})} \tag{16}$$

where

$$p(ij \mid x_k, \Theta^{t-1}) = \frac{F_{ki} \pi_{ij}^{t-1} p(x_k \mid \mu_{ij}^{t-1}, \Sigma_{ij}^{t-1})}{\sum_{e=1}^{c} F_{ke} \sum_{z=1}^{l_i} \pi_{ez}^{t-1} p(x_k \mid \mu_{ez}^{t-1}, \Sigma_{ez}^{t-1})} \tag{17}$$

Problem (13) is actually a semi-supervised clustering one. More specifically, it can accomplish the clustering within each class simultaneously with label information. In other words, the Gaussian distributions extract the information from unlabeled samples corresponding to different classes and thus can be used for the improvement of the performance of LDA.

Based on the obtained parameters and the initial labeled samples, we redefine the mean of each class and that of all the classes. Let $\bar{\mu}_i$ is the mean of class i, then

$$\bar{\mu}_i = \frac{1}{(n_i + l_i)} \left(\sum_{j=1}^{n_i} x_{ij} + \sum_{j=1}^{l_i} \mu_{ij} \right) \tag{18}$$

Let $\bar{\mu}$ is the mean of all the classes, then

$$\bar{\mu} = \frac{1}{\sum_{i=1}^{c}(n_i + l_i)} \sum_{i=1}^{c} \left(\sum_{j=1}^{n_i} x_{ij} + \sum_{j=1}^{l_i} \mu_{ij} \right) \tag{19}$$

Therefore, the between-class and within-class scatter matrices are formulated as

$$\bar{S}_b = \sum_{i=1}^{c} (\bar{\mu}_i - \bar{\mu})(\bar{\mu}_i - \bar{\mu})^T \tag{20}$$

$$\bar{S}_w = \sum_{i=1}^{c} (n_i + l_i) \left\{ \sum_{j=1}^{n_i} (x_{ij} - \bar{\mu}_i)(x_{ij} - \bar{\mu}_i)^T \right.$$
$$\left. + \sum_{j=1}^{l_i} (\mu_{ij} - \bar{\mu}_i)(\mu_{ij} - \bar{\mu}_i)^T \right\} \tag{21}$$

Let $h = \sum_{i=1}^{c}(n_i + l_i)$, the expected between-class and within-class scatter matrices are formulated as

$$\widehat{S}_b = \bar{S}_b + \sum_{i=1}^{c} \left(\frac{n_i + l_i}{h^2} \sum_{k=1}^{c} \sum_{j=1}^{l_i} \Sigma_{kj} + \frac{h - 2(n_i + l_i)}{n_i h} \sum_{j=1}^{l_i} \Sigma_{ij} \right) \tag{22}$$

$$\widehat{S}_w = \bar{S}_w + \sum_{i=1}^{c} \frac{n_i + l_i - 1}{n_i + l_i} \sum_{j=1}^{l_i} \Sigma_{ij} \tag{23}$$

It is worthwhile to point out that all the initial labeled samples are regarded as the Gaussian distributions with the covariance being zero matrix. Finally, the optimal subspace can be obtained by solving problem (3) when $\widehat{S}_b$ and $\widehat{S}_w$ are substituted for S_b and S_w, respectively.

4   Experiments

In this section, we evaluate the classification error rate of the proposed method, and LDA, SDA, SODA, FME and TR-FSDA are run respectively on the synthetic data sets and two real datasets, namely COIL-20 dataset [14] and USPS

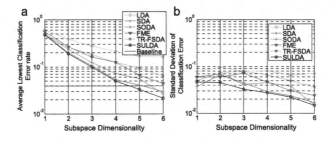

Fig. 1. Comparisons of (a) average lowest classification error rates and (b) standard deviations of the error rates on the synthetic data sets.

database [15]. For the real datasets the grey scale of images is normalized to $[0, 1]$ and then PCA is used to reduce the dimensionality to 10 for simplicity. The nearest neighbor classifier (1NN) is adopted to evaluate the classification performance. Moreover, the classifier is directly used in the original data or the preprocessed data by PCA as the baseline method. The weight matrix involved in SDA, SODA, FME, TR-FSDA and SULDA is constructed according to [9]. For the former four semi-supervised methods, the two regularization parameters involved are chosen from the set $[10^{-9}, 10^{-6}, 10^{-3}, 10^{0}, 10^{+3}, 10^{+6}, 10^{+9}]$, respectively, and the best classification performance is reported. For SULDA, we set $l_i = 1$, $i = 1, 2, \cdots, c$.

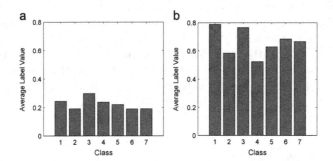

Fig. 2. Comparisons of (a) traditional label propagation and (b) fractional-step label propagation.

4.1 Synthetic Data Sets

In this subsection, we test the classification performance of SULDA on the synthetic data sets. The data sets involve two types of Gaussian distributions. The first type only includes a distribution whose mean and covariance are the zero vector and the identity matrix I_{10}, respectively. The second type consists of seven homoscedastic distributions whose covariance is the matrix $4I_{10}$ and their means are seven random sample vectors from the first type of distribution. The

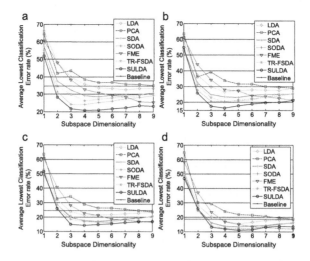

Fig. 3. Average lowest classification error rates on the COIL-20 database. (a) 2 labeled samples; (b) 3 labeled samples; (c) 4 labeled samples; and (d) 6 labeled samples.

data sets include 20 synthetic data sets and each data set consists of the samples from the second type of distributions. More specifically, there are 200 training samples and 100 testing samples from each distribution and among the training samples, there are only two labeled ones. In this experiment, testing samples are projected into subspaces obtained by training samples. Figure 1 gives the average lowest classification error rates and the standard deviations of the average error rates. As shown in the figure, our method greatly outperforms SODA, FME, and TR-FSDA and slightly outperforms SDA. In addition, we randomly select a synthetic data set to test the performance of the fractional-step label propagation. As shown in Fig. 2, it greatly outperforms the traditional label propagation method in terms of the average label value of samples in each class affiliated to their own class.

4.2 COIL-20 Database

There are 1440 grayscale images in the COIL-20 database and the images are taken at every $5°$ when 20 objects are rotating [14]. That is to say, each object has 72 images. In this experiment, the images have been down-sampled and their size is 32×32 pixels. Training samples consist of randomly selected 54 samples from each object and 2, 3, 4 and 6 samples are labeled for each object in the selected samples, respectively. Testing samples consist of the corresponding rest samples of each object. We repeat the procedure 10 times to obtain average lowest classification error rates. As shown in Fig. 3, our method greatly outperforms other semi-supervised ones in most cases.

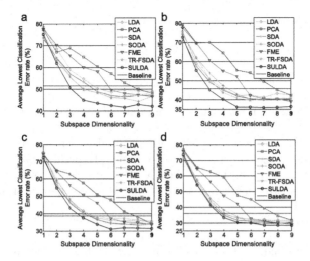

Fig. 4. Average lowest classification error rates on the USPS database. (a) 2 labeled samples; (b) 3 labeled samples; (c) 4 labeled samples; and (d) 6 labeled samples.

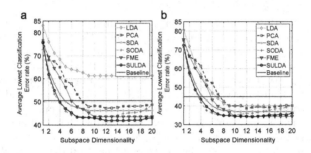

Fig. 5. Average lowest classification error rates on the USPS database. (a) 2 labeled samples; (b) 3 labeled samples.

4.3 USPS Database

The USPS database consists of 9298 grayscale images of digits from envelopes and their size is 16×16 pixels, namely, each image can be described as a 256-dimensional vector [15]. For each digit, we randomly select 100 samples from the database and thus a subset is constructed. Further more, for each digit in the subset, we randomly select 75 samples for training and the rest for testing. Similar to the experiment on the COIL-20 dataset, only 2, 3, 4 and 6 samples are labeled for each digit in the training samples, respectively. The experiment is run 10 times and average lowest classification error rates are obtained. As shown in Fig. 4, SULDA performs much better than other semi-supervised methods in most cases. However, our method is only compared to some semi-supervised ones when PCA is used to reduce the dimensionality of the original data to 20, as shown in Fig. 5.

5 Conclusions

In this paper, we propose a semi-supervised method for dimensionality reduction, semi-supervised uncertain linear discriminant (SULDA). Fractional-step label propagation is proposed to reliably propagate label information from labeled samples to unlabeled ones when the labeled samples are very scarce. Meanwhile, double-layer Gaussian mixture modes are defined to extract the discriminative information from unlabeled samples. With the obtained modes and the labeled samples, the expected between-class and within-class scatter matrices are constructed and an optimal subspace can be obtained. Experiments on the synthetic data sets, the COIL-20 database and the USPS database show that our method is more discriminative than some state-of-the-art semi-supervised methods.

References

1. Turk, M., Pentland, A.: Eigenfaces for recognition. J. Cogn. Neurosci. **3**(1), 71–86 (1991)
2. Belhumeur, P.-N., Hespanha, J.-P., Kriegman, D.-J.: Eigenfaces vs. Fisherfaces: recognition using class specific linear projection. IEEE Trans. Pattern Anal. Mach. Intell. **19**(7), 711–720 (1997)
3. Cai, D., He, X., Han, J.: Semi-supervised discriminant analysis. In: Proceedings of IEEE 11th International Conference on Computer Vision, pp. 1–7 (2007)
4. Huang, Y., Xu, D., Nie, F.: Semi-supervised dimension reduction using trace ratio criterion. IEEE Trans. Neural Netw. Learn. Syst. **23**(3), 519–526 (2012)
5. Sindhwani, V., Niyogi, P., Belkin, M., Keerthi, S.: Linear manifold regularization for large scale semi-supervised learning. In: Proceedings of the 22nd ICML Workshop on Learning with Partially Classified Training Data, pp. 1–7 (2005)
6. Nie, F., Xu, D., Tsang, I.-W.-H., Zhang, C.: Flexible manifold embedding. IEEE Trans. Image Process. **19**(7), 1921–1932 (2010)
7. Nie, F., Xiang, S., Jia, Y.: Semi-supervised orthogonal discriminant analysis via label propagation. Pattern Recogn. **42**(11), 2615–2627 (2009)
8. Zhao, M., Zhang, Z., Chow, T.-W., Li, B.: A general soft label based linear discriminant analysis for semi-supervised dimensionality reduction. Neural Netw. **55**, 83–97 (2014)
9. Wang, S., Lu, J., Gu, X., Du, H., Yang, J.: Semi-supervised linear discriminant analysis for dimension reduction and classification. Pattern Recogn. **57**, 179–189 (2016)
10. Li, C.-N., Shao, Y.-H., Deng, N.-Y.: Robust L1-norm two-dimensional linear discriminant analysis. Neural Netw. **65**, 92–104 (2015)
11. Wang, H., Lu, X., Hu, Z., Zheng, W.: Fisher discriminant analysis with L1-norm. IEEE Trans. Cybern. **44**(6), 828–842 (2014)
12. Saeidi, R., Ramón, F.-A., Kolossa, D.: Uncertain LDA: including observation uncertainties in discriminative. IEEE Trans. Pattern Anal. Mach. Intell. **38**(7), 1479–1488 (2016)
13. Bishop, C.-M.: Pattern Recognition and Machine Learning, 2nd edn. Springer, Heidelberg (2006)
14. Nene, S.-A., Nayar, S.-K., Murase, H.: Columbia object image library (coil-20). Columbia University, Department of Computer Science, New York (1996)
15. Hull, J.-J.: A database for handwritten text recognition research. IEEE Trans. Pattern Anal. Mach. Intell. **16**(5), 550–554 (1999)

Adaptive Attributed Network Embedding for Community Detection

Mengqing Luo and Hui Yan[✉]

Nanjing University of Science and Technology, Nanjing 210094, China
yanhui@njust.edu.cn

Abstract. Community detection, which discovers densely-connected groups of nodes in networks, is a fundamental task in machine learning and data mining. Compared with plain network, community detection in attributed network presents more challenges. Several recent embedding-based methods have achieved promising community detection performance on some real attributed networks. However, there is limited understanding of how to effectively learn the combination of heterogeneity in the joint space of topology and attribute in unsupervised scenarios. In this paper, we propose an end-to-end network embedding method. By employing the high order graph convolutional networks, our method encodes the topological structure and node attributes to learn compact representations, i.e., community membership. The decoder on the other side, we reconstruct the global topological structure based on the learned community membership and stochastic block model. We further employ a self-training module, which takes the "confident" link assignments as soft labels to guide the optimizing procedure. Experiments show our method has achieved the sate-of-the-art performance on three popular datasets.

Keywords: Community detection · Attributed network · Unsupervised learning

1 Introduction

Network data is ubiquitous in the real world, and it is naturally represented in graph format. Graph characterizes complex relationships among objects, which generally consists of a node set and an edge set which captures the pairwise relationships. Besides edges, each node is often associated with a rich set of attributes in attributed networks such as social networks, citation networks, protein-protein interaction networks, etc.

Community detection (graph clustering) algorithms serve as the fundamental analysis tools for analyzing and understanding the structure of complex networks [20], which aim to partition the nodes in the network into disjoint groups. Attribute-only community detection methods such as some classical clustering methods [21], only deal with

---

The first author is a student.

This work was supported in part by NSF of China (Grant no. 61773215, no. 61772273, no. 61703209), National Defense Preresearch Foundation (Grant no. 41412010101), NSF (Grants III-1526499, III-1763325, III-1909323, SaTC-1930941), and CNS-1626432.

Y. Peng et al. (Eds.): PRCV 2020, LNCS 12307, pp. 161–172, 2020.
https://doi.org/10.1007/978-3-030-60636-7_14

node attributes. Topology-only methods [1, 2, 15, 22] merely leverage network connection patterns, e.g., user friendships in social networks, paper citation links in citation networks, and genetic interactions in protein-protein interaction networks.

In recent years, various topology-plus-attribute methods [16, 17, 23, 24] based on embedding-based models [4, 18, 26] have attracted a large amount of attention. For example, [19] is under the framework of non-negative matrix factorization (NMF). [27] introduces the stacked denoising autoencoder, which is a deep learning model, to generate a low dimensional vector for each node, upon which classic clustering methods like k-means or spectral clustering algorithms are applied. In particular, methods based on graph convolutional neural network (GCN) such as graph autoencoder (GAE) [9], adversarially regularized graph autoencoder (ARGA) [10], have demonstrated state-of-the-art performance on several attributed graph clustering tasks. Compared with the two-step framework, which usually leads to suboptimal performance, [11] and [12] are goal-directed, i.e., designed for the specific clustering task. Nevertheless, it remains to be solved that is how to learn "confident" community membership or other effective node representations as soft labels to guide the entire optimization procedure in a unified framework.

In this paper, we propose an adaptive attributed network embedding method for community detection (AANE for short). We employ our high order graph convolutional network as an encoder to integrate rich node attribute information with network topological structure. We design two branches for decoder to reconstruct the global and local topological structure, respectively. Our contributions can be summarized as follows:

- We propose a new end-to-end network embedding framework, which simultaneously optimizes the node embedding learning and community detection.
- To obtain effective community membership as pseudo labels to guide node embedding leaning, we reconstruct the topological structure based on stochastic block model involving learnable parameters to measure the correlation among difference communities.
- We introduce a positive and negative sampling strategy based on the similarity measurement in the space of node embedding. After sampling, we employ a self-training module, which takes the "confident" link assignments as soft labels to guide the optimizing procedure.
- We compare our algorithm with some state-of-the-art community detection methods, and the results show the superiority of our algorithm.

2 Related Work

For community detection in attributed networks, an important but challenging issue is how to combine attribute information and network topology in unsupervised scenarios. To address the problems, more recent community detection has resorted to network embedding learning.

One group of methods learns compact node embeddings, upon which classic clustering methods like k-means or spectral clustering algorithms are applied. For example, inspired by GCN [13] which has shown its effectiveness for graph-structured data, some methods [26, 27] adopt GCN as encoder. And [30] adopt a symmetric stable decoder for graph convolutional encoder to reconstruct the node attributes. [3] designed two decoders to reconstruct node attributes and topological structure respectively but share a graph convolutional encoder. [14] adopt a graph convolutional autoencoder with a modularity module and a self-clustering module to learn cluster-oriented node representations. Autoencoder is an alternative solution for this kind of embedding-based approaches [27], as the autoencoder based hidden representation learning approaches can be applied to purely unsupervised environments. Therefore, all these methods are two-step. The learned embeddings may not be the best fit for the subsequent clustering task, and the result of graph clustering is not beneficial to the embeddings. To achieve mutual benefit for these two steps, a goal-directed training framework is proposed recently such as [11] and [12]. [11] conducts the particular k-order graph convolution for different graphs to obtain smooth node representations, and performs spectral clustering on the learned representations to cluster the nodes. [12] employs an attention network as encoder to learn the compact representation for each node, on which an inner product decoder is trained to reconstruct the graph structure.

Another group of community detection methods in attributed network learns two kinds of node representations from the topological structure and node attributes respectively. For example, [5] introduces maximizing likelihood estimation based strategy to guarantee their consistency between the topology and node attributes.

3 The Proposed Model

3.1 Problem Formulation

Consider an undirected attributed graph $G = (V, E, X)$, where $V = \{v_i\}_{i=1,...,n}$ is a set of n nodes, $E \subseteq V \times V$ denotes the set of edges, and x_i is the i-th row of attribute matrix $X \in R^{n \times d}$, which denotes attribute vector of the i-th node. The topological structure of graph can be represented by an adjacency matrix A, where $A_{ij} = 1$ if there is an edge between node v_i and the node v_j; otherwise $A_{ij} = 0$. Given the number of communities c, the community detection problem studied in this paper is to find c groups of nodes $G = \{G_1, G_2, \ldots, G_c\}$. Note that the communities studied in this paper are not allowed to overlap, i.e., $G_i \cap G_j = \phi$.

3.2 Network Architecture

Our framework is shown in Fig. 1 and consists of two parts: a high order graph convolutional based encoder and a self-training clustering module. We design two branches for decoder. The first branch is based on joint stochastic block model and the learned community membership matrix Z to reconstruct the topological structure, which can capture the global topological structure. The second branch is to reconstruct the direct link, which can preserve the proximity of nodes in the same community with high confidence.

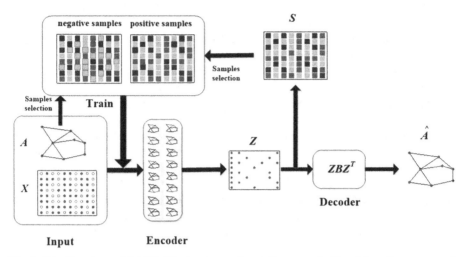

Fig. 1. The flowchart of AANE. The inputs are the attribute matrix X and the adjacency matrix A. AANE learns the community membership matrix Z through high order GCN, and reconstructs adjacency matrix A. Furthermore, it selects "confident" links based on positive and negative samples as soft labels to guide the optimizing procedure. Samples depicted in the red boxes represent the positive samples and samples depicted in the orange boxes represent the negative samples.

3.3 Graph Convolution Based Encoder

To combine the attribute information X and network topology A in our framework, we introduce k-order graph convolution model to learn the representations of nodes.

Generally speaking, the first-order neighborhood of a node v_i influence v_i through the directed edges, and GCN only considers the first-order neighborhood. We plot the proportion of k-order neighbors within community on three real datasets in Fig. 2. From Fig. 2, we can see that the influence of neighbors of higher orders becomes smaller. In citeseer dataset, the proportion of edges within community in second-order adjacency is higher than that in first-order one. As graphs have complex structure relationships, we propose to exploit weighted high-order adjacency matrix M in our encoder:

$$M = wA + w^2A^2 + \ldots + w^kA^k \tag{1}$$

where w is a learnable weight parameter, and k could be chosen flexibly for different datasets to balance the precision and efficiency of the model. As k increases, k-order graph convolution will make the node embeddings smoother on each dimension of attributes.

The core idea of graph convolution is based on the spectral decomposition of the graph Laplacian matrix $\tilde{L} \in R^{n \times n}$:

$$\tilde{L} = \tilde{D}^{-\frac{1}{2}}\tilde{A}\tilde{D}^{-\frac{1}{2}} \tag{2}$$

Where $\tilde{A} \in R^{n \times n}$ is the adjacency matrix with self-loop, i.e., $\tilde{A} = A + I$ where I denotes the identity matrix and $\tilde{D}$ is the degree matrix of $\tilde{A}$. Since we use high-order adjacency matrix M in our encoder to improve the performance of our model, Eq. (2) can be rewritten as:

$$\tilde{L} = \tilde{D}^{-\frac{1}{2}} M \tilde{D}^{-\frac{1}{2}} \tag{3}$$

We have $H^0 = X$ as the input for our model, and stack several graph layers to learn the node embeddings, which are implemented by convolution operation by multiplying with the normalized graph Laplacian matrix. It can be formulated as follows:

$$H^l = \sigma\left(\tilde{L} H^{l-1} W^l\right) \tag{4}$$

where $H^l \in R^{n \times d_l}$ is the output node representations of the l-th layer. $W^l \in R^{d_{l-1} \times d_l}$ is the trainable parameter of the l-th layer and $\sigma(\cdot)$ is the nonlinear activation function. Note that even if we use untrained GCN and randomly initialized weights $\{W^l\}_{l=1,\ldots,nl}$ where nl is the number of GCN layers, our model can get passable community membership, as Kipf et al. argued in [13].

In the last encoder layer, we obtain $H \in R^{n \times c}$. Then, the softmax function is used to obtain the node embedding matrix $Y \in R^{n \times c}$:

$$Y = softmax(H) \tag{5}$$

Since we hope the i-th row vector of Y indicates the probability that node v_i belongs to each community, $||Y(i,:)||_2 = 1$ and $Y_{ij} \geq 0$ should be satisfied. Thus we map Y into $[0, 1]$, and we will have the community membership Z:

$$Z_{ij} = e^{Y_{ij} - max(Y(i,:))} \tag{6}$$

$$Z_{ij} = \frac{Z_{ij}}{||Z(i,:)||_2} \tag{7}$$

where $Y(i,:)$ denotes the i-th row of Y and $Z(i,:)$ denotes the i-th row of Z.

There are various kinds of decoders, which reconstruct either the graph structure, the attribute value, or both. As our latent embedding Z already contains both attribute and structure information, we choose two decoders to reconstruct the links between nodes globally and locally in the next section.

3.4 Reconstruct First-Order Proximity

To preserve the first-order proximity in the topological structure, we model joint probability between the node v_i and the node v_j as r_{ij}, i.e., $r_{ij} = 1$ if v_i and v_j are in the same community, otherwise $r_{ij} = 0$. Due to the lack of ground-truth label information, r_{ij} is unknown. Therefore we can define r_{ij} based on the community membership matrix Z. In practice, $z_i = Z(i,:)$ is not one-hot vector, so we try to get binary r_{ij} by a simple threshold method as following:

$$r_{ij} = \begin{cases} 1, & \text{if } g(z_i, z_j) > \theta_1 \text{ and } A_{ij} = 1 \\ 0, & \text{if } g(z_i, z_j) < \theta_2 \text{ and } A_{ij} = 0 \\ 0.5, & \text{otherwise} \end{cases} \tag{8}$$

where $g(z_i, z_j)$ is a function to measure the similarity of z_i and z_j. We choose a simple inner product decoder $g(z_i, z_j) = z_i z_j^T$, which would be efficient and flexible. $\theta_1 = \mu(\lambda)$ and $\theta_2 = l(\lambda)$, λ is the parameter to control the change of threshold. Because the model prediction is the most unreliable at the beginning of training, θ_1 at the beginning should be the maximum value and gradually decrease with training; similarly, θ_2 also reaches the minimum value at the beginning of training and gradually increase with training until the value of θ_2 is equal to θ_1. In our experiments, $\theta_2 = b_1 + k_1\lambda, \theta_2 = b_2 + k_2\lambda, \lambda = \lambda + \eta(k_1 + k_2)$, where b_1 and b_2 control the initial value of threshold, k_1, k_2 and η control the rate of change of threshold.

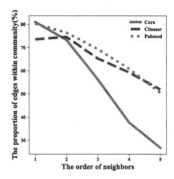

Fig. 2. The proportion of k-order neighbors within community on cora, citeseer and pubmed datasets.

Moreover, as illustrated in Fig. 2, the proportion of edges within community in the first order adjacency matrix of the three datasets are very high, above 70%. The intuition is that the node pairs with direct links and high confidence may be in the same community, and meanwhile the node pairs without direct links with low confidence may be in different communities. To this end, we introduce an efficient most positive and negative sampling strategy, which is based on the similarity measurement in the space of node embedding, to make the loss function robust. Based on Eq. (8), we select some positive pairwise samples (v_i, v_j) if $r_{ij} = 1$ and negative pairwise samples (v_i, v_j) if $r_{ij} = 0$. The loss function is:

$$L_c = \sum_{i,j} -r_{ij} \log(g(z_i, z_j)) - (1 - r_{ij}) \log(1 - g(z_i, z_j)) \tag{9}$$

3.5 Reconstruct Network Topology

Since it is well known that an ideal similarity matrix, i.e., ZZ^T, based on membership matrix is supposed to be block diagonal regularized, which has exactly c connected components [25]. Unfortunately, due to the fact that a node could be connected with other nodes from different but related communities, this nature of communities can lead the blocks to appear in non-diagonal of similarity matrix. Therefore, we incorporate probabilistic generative model. We define matrix $B \in R^{c \times c}$ as learnable parameters such that the matrix element B_{rs} denotes the probability of an edge between vertex v_i belonging to G_r and vertex v_j belonging to G_s.

Algorithm 1 Adaptive Attributed Network Embedding for Community Detection

---

Input: $X \in R^{n \times d}$, $A \in R^{n \times n}$, k, *maxiter, epochs*, $u(\lambda)$, $l(\lambda)$, λ
Output: The label c_i of node i, $i = 1, \ldots, n$
1:    Randomly initialize the learnable parameters of model
2:    **for** *iter* = 0 to *maxiter* − 1 **do**
3:       Calculate high order adjacency matrix M according to Eq.(1)
4.   Calculate the community membership Z according to Eq.(6) and Eq.(7)
5:       Sample positive and negative samples according to Eq.(8)
6:       **for** *epoch* = 0 to *epochs* − 1 **do**
7:         Update the whole framework by minimizing Eq.(12).
8:       **end for**
9:       Update θ_1 and θ_2 according to $u(\lambda)$ and $l(\lambda)$.
10: **end for**
11: Return the predict label c_i according to Eq.(13).

Inspired by recent study [28] of equivalence of stochastic block model (SBM), the connection probability of node v_i and v_j can be written as

$$\hat{A}_{ij} = z_i B z_j^T \tag{10}$$

Our goal is to maximize the probability of observed graph A given the parameters B and the learned community membership matrix Z [29]. We minimize the reconstruction error by measuring the difference between A and $\hat{A}$:

$$L_r = \sum_{i=1}^{n} loss(A_{ij}, \hat{A}_{ij}) \tag{11}$$

We define our total objective function as:

$$L = L_c + \gamma L_r \tag{12}$$

where $\gamma \geq 0$ is a coefficient that controls the balance between proximity and topology reconstruction.

Finally, we could assign the community label c_i for each node v_i directly from Z:

$$c_i = \arg \max_j (Z_{ij}), j = 1, 2, \ldots, c \tag{13}$$

The overall procedure of our algorithm is shown in Algorithm 1.

4 Experiments

4.1 Datasets and Metrics

In our experiments, we evaluate the performance of our model on three popular network datasets, including cora, citeseer, and pubmed. These three datasets are citation networks where each node represents an article and the edges are the citations among different articles. More details about datasets are in Table 1. We use three metrics to evaluate the performance of community detection methods: Accuracy (ACC), Normalized Mutual Information (NMI) and Macro F1-score (Macro).

Table 1. Datasets summary.

Dataset	#Nodes	#Features	#Edges	#Classes
Cora	2708	1433	5429	7
Citeseer	3327	3703	4732	6
Pubmed	19717	500	44338	3

4.2 Experiment Settings

Baseline Methods. We compared our method with 10 algorithms, including:

1) K-means that only uses attribute information.
2) Methods that only use topology information including DeepWalk [6], deep neural networks for learning graph representations (DNGR) [7] and modularized nonnegative matrix factorization (M-NMF) [8].
3) Methods that combine topology information and attribute information including GAE, graph variational auto-encoder(VGAE) [9], ARGA, adversarially regularized graph variational autoencoder (ARVGA) [10], adaptive graph convolution(AGC) method [11] and deep attentional embedded graph clustering (DAEGC) [12].

Parameter Settings. For methods that are not targeted at community detection task, including DeepWalk, DNGR, GAE, VGAE, ARGA and ARVGA, we applied k-means on the representations learned by these models. For the sake of fairness, we run k-means 20 times to get the average score for the above graph embedding methods. For all of the baseline methods, we use the implementations provided by their authors and the parameter settings are the same as those in original papers. And as for AGC, we directly use the results in [11] because the authors do not provide the code of AGC. For our method, we use the second order neighbors ($k = 2$ in Eq. (1)) as adjacency matrix in GCN and the number of GCN layers in our model is 3, and the number of hidden units of the first two layers of GCN is 256 and 128 respectively. The maximum number of iterations is 100.

4.3 Experimental Results

In each dataset, we run each method 10 times and take the average value as the final results in Table 2, where the bold values indicate the best performance. The results show that our proposed method performs better than other baselines in most cases.

We can see from Table 2, that the methods combining attribute information and network topology generally outperform those using only attribute information or network topology. Therefore, the experimental results prove that both attribute information and network topology are beneficial to community detection.

Table 2. Community detection performance (%).

Methods	Cora			Citeseer			Pubmed		
	ACC	NMI	Macro	ACC	NMI	Macro	ACC	NMI	Macro
K-means	31.80	15.07	29.50	45.39	22.31	42.87	59.47	31.34	58.11
DeepWalk	48.38	36.40	43.56	37.23	10.10	30.58	61.47	17.24	52.42
DNGR	39.87	31.85	34.55	32.73	17.98	31.27	46.10	15.32	43.29
M-NMF	42.30	25.60	32.00	33.50	10.82	25.58	47.27	9.01	43.78
GAE	52.34	40.23	40.58	42.92	19.33	31.58	64.41	22.42	51.28
VGAE	55.60	41.53	44.36	44.38	23.88	33.05	65.49	26.51	52.65
ARGA	66.40	41.50	66.14	57.80	29.71	55.59	64.81	23.14	64.90
ARVGA	67.50	48.4	66.89	60.80	32.97	58.39	59.36	14.60	59.30
AGC	68.92	53.68	65.61	67.00	41.13	62.48	69.78	**31.59**	**68.72**
DAEGC	70.40	52.80	68.20	67.20	39.70	63.60	67.10	26.60	65.90
AANE	**72.40**	**55.57**	**68.29**	**69.53**	**42.87**	**63.97**	**70.59**	31.12	67.33

GAE, VGAE, ARGA and ARVGA all use auto-encoders to reconstruct the adjacency matrix to learn the node representations while both ARGA and ARVGA add adversarial model to learn more accurate node representations. Thus ARGA and ARGVA perform better than GAE and VGAE. Because they are two-step frameworks and their auto-encoders are merely dedicated to reconstructing topology, there is still room for improvement in community detection task. The performance of goal-directed methods AGC and DAEGC is better than ARGA and ARGVA.

While our method performs better than AGC and DAEGC in most cases, the reasons are that: (1) we take the "confident" link assignments as soft labels to guide the optimizing procedure, such that the model is trained in "supervised" way; (2) Our model reconstructs network topology based on learnable random block module to model the correlation among communities.

To validate the effectiveness of reconstructing network topology and using high-order neighbors in our framework, we conduct ablation study on three datasets and the results are in Table 3. As we can see, the correlation between communities is considered to reconstruct network topology in our model, which is better than simply considering the cosine similarity of node embedding. In addition, reconstructing network topology and using high-order neighbors in GCN are both beneficial to community detection task.

We vary the value of γ as $\{0.0, 0.2, 0.4, 0.6, 0.8, 1.0, 1.2, 1.4, 1.6, 1.8, 2.0\}$ to study the effects of γ, which controls the influence of L_r. We conduct experiments on cora, citeseer and pubmed dataset, respectively, and results are shown in Fig. 3. As shown in Fig. 3 (a), ACC, NMI and Macro increase with the increase of γ until $\gamma = 1.0$ and then decrease gradually with the increase of γ. And when $\gamma = 1.4$ ANNE achieves best

Table 3. Ablation study

	$\hat{A}_{ij} = z_i B z_j^T$	$\hat{A}_{ij} = z_i z_j^T$	L_r	M	ACC (%)	NMI (%)	Macro (%)
Cora	✓		✓	✓	72.40	55.57	68.29
		✓	✓	✓	68.76	52.80	63.23
				✓	66.10	51.99	56.09
					43.94	25.69	38.04
Citeseer	✓		✓	✓	69.53	42.87	63.97
		✓	✓	✓	67.27	35.66	59.17
				✓	57.73	31.77	51.23
					49.86	24.51	43.58
Pubmed	✓		✓	✓	70.59	30.12	67.33
		✓	✓	✓	67.24	25.70	62.12
				✓	61.56	20.89	53.28
					51.79	12.01	48.26

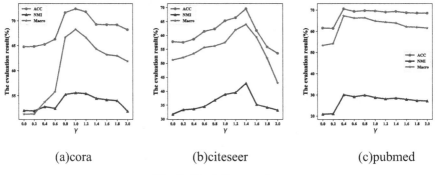

(a)cora   (b)citeseer   (c)pubmed

Fig. 3. The influence of γ.

performance on citeseer dataset as shown in Fig. 3(b); when $\gamma = 0.4$, AANE performs best on pubmed dataset as shown in Fig. 3(c).

5   Conclusion

In this paper, we propose an adaptive attributed network embedding method for community detection, to jointly perform community detection and learn the community membership as node embedding in a unified frame. We reconstruct the global topological structure based on the learned community membership and stochastic block model. To further effectively guide the optimizing procedure, we propose most positive and negative sampling strategy based on binary classification. Experimental results of our model compared with other state-of-the-art algorithms on three datasets demonstrate the effectiveness of our model on community detection task.

References

1. Cao, S.S., Lu, W.: GraphRep: learning graph representation with global structural information. In: CIKM, Melbourne, VIC, Australia, pp. 891–900 (2015)
2. Ye, F.H., Chen, C., Zheng, Z.B.: Deep autoencoder-like nonnegative matrix factorization for community detection. In: CIKM, Torino, Italy, pp. 1393–1402 (2018)
3. Jin, D., Li, B.Y., Jiao, P.F., He, D.X., Zhang, W.X.: Network-specific variational auto-encoder for embedding in attribute networks. In: IJCAI, Macao, China, pp. 2663–2669 (2019)
4. Zhang, Z., et al.: ANRL: attributed network representation learning via deep neural networks. In: IJCAI, Stockholm, Sweden, pp. 3155–3161 (2018)
5. Gao, H.C., Huang, H.: Deep attributed network embedding. In: IJCAI, Stockholm, Sweden, pp. 3364–3370 (2018)
6. Perozzi, B., Al-Rfou, R., Skiena, S.: DeepWalk: online learning of social representations. In: KDD, New York, USA, pp. 701–710 (2014)
7. Cao, S.S., Lu, W., Xu, Q.K.: Deep neural networks for learning graph representations. In: AAAI, Phoenix, Arizona, USA, pp. 1145–1152 (2017)
8. Wang, X., Cui, P., Wang, J., Pei, J., Zhu, W.W., Yang, S.Q.: Community preserving network embedding. In: AAAI, San Francisco, California, USA, pp. 203–209 (2017)
9. Kipf, T.N., Welling, M.: Variational graph auto-encoders. In: NIPS (2016)
10. Pan, S.R., Hu, R.Q., Long, G.D., Jiang, J., Yao, L.N., Zhang, C.Q.: Adversarially regularized graph autoencoder for graph embedding. In: IJCAI, Stockholm, Sweden, pp. 2609–2615 (2018)
11. Zhang, X.T., Liu, H., Li, Q.M., Wu, X.M.: Attributed graph clustering via adaptive graph convolution. In: IJCAI, Macao, China, pp. 4327–4333 (2019)
12. Wang, C., Pan, S.R., Hu, R.Q., Long, G.D., Jiang, J., Zhang, C.Q.: Attributed graph clustering: a deep attentional embedding approach. In: IJCAI, Macao, China, pp. 3670–3676 (2019)
13. Kipf, T.N., Welling, M.: Semi-supervised classification with graph convolutional networks. In: ICLR (2017)
14. Sun, H.L., et al.: Network embedding for community detection in attributed networks. ACM TKDD **14**(3), 36:1–36:25 (2020)
15. Sun, F.Y., Qu, M., Hoffmann, J., Huang, C.W., Tang, J.: vGraph: a generative model for joint community detection and node representation learning. In: NeurIPS, Canada, pp. 512–522 (2019)
16. He, D.X., Feng, Z.Y., Jin, D., Wang, X.B., Zhang, W.X.: Joint identification of network communities and semantics via integrative modeling of network topologies and node contents. In: AAAI, San Francisco, California, USA, pp. 116–124 (2017)
17. Bojchevski, A., Gunnemann, S.: Bayesian robust attributed graph clustering: joint learning of partial anomalies and group structure. In: AAAI, New Orleans, Louisiana, USA, pp. 2738–2745 (2018)
18. Yang, C., Liu, Z.Y., Zhao, D.L., Sun, M.S., Chang, E.Y.: Network representation learning with rich text information. In: IJCAI, Buenos, Aires, Argentina, pp. 2111–2117 (2015)
19. Li, Y., Sha, C.F., Huang, X., Zhang, Y.C.: Community detection in attributed graphs: an embedding approach. In: AAAI, New Orleans, Louisiana, USA, pp. 338–345 (2018)
20. Wang, F., Li, T., Wang, X., Zhu, S., Ding, C.: Community discovery using nonnegative matrix factorization. Data Min. Knowl. Discov. **22**(3), 493–521 (2011). https://doi.org/10.1007/s10618-010-0181-y

21. Ng, A.Y., Jordan, M.I., Weiss, Y.: On spectral clustering: analysis and an algorithm. In: NIPS, pp. 849–856 (2002)
22. Yang, J., Leskovec, J.: Defining and evaluating network communities based on groundtruth. Knowl. Inf. Syst. **42**(1), 181–213 (2015). https://doi.org/10.1007/s10115-013-0693-z
23. Yang, J., McAuley, J., Leskovec, J.: Community detection in networks with node attributes. In: ICDM, Dallas, TX, USA, pp. 1151–1156 (2013)
24. Huang, X., Cheng, H., Yu, J.X.: Attributed community analysis: global and ego-centric views. IEEE Data Eng. Bull. **39**(3), 29–40 (2016)
25. Lu, C.Y., Feng, J.S., Mei, T., Lin, Z.C., Yan, S.C.: Subspace clustering by block diagonal representation. TPAMI **41**(2), 487–501 (2018)
26. Wu, Z.H., Pan, S.R., Chen, F.W., Long, G.D., Zhang, C.Q., Yu, P.S.: A comprehensive survey on graph neural networks. arXiv:1901.00596 (2019)
27. Cao, S.S., Lu, W., Xu, Q.K.: Deep neural networks for learning graph representations. In: AAAI, Phoenix, Arizona, USA, pp. 1145–1152 (2016)
28. Zhang, Z.Y., Gai, Y.J., Wang, Y.F.: On equivalence of likelihood maximization of stochastic block model and constrained nonnegative matrix factorization. Phys. A Stat. Mech. Appl. **503**, 687–697 (2017)
29. Karrera, B., Newman, M.E.: Stochastic blockmodels and community structure in networks. Phys. Rev. E **83**(1), 016107 (2011)
30. Park, J., Lee, M., Chang, H.J., Lee, K., Choi, J.Y.: Symmetric graph convolutional autoencoder for unsupervised graph representation learning. In: ICCV, Seoul, Korea, pp. 6518–6527 (2019)

Single-View 3D Shape Reconstruction
with Learned Gradient Descent

Guanglun Zhang and Lu Yang[✉]

School of Automation Engineering, University of Electronic Science and Technology
of China, Chengdu 610054, China
yanglu@uestc.edu.cn

Abstract. Reconstructing the 3D shape from single image has become a
popular research topic imputed to the end-to-end learning ability of deep
convolutional networks. In this paper, we show that, the 3D-2D geometry
knowledge can be explicitly incorporated into the deep convolutional
network to regularize the reconstruction task. Leveraging recent advances
in learned gradient descent, we pass the gradient components directly to
the learning network during learning to enable a sequence of update
CNNs, which can generate updates to the predicted 3D shape. Hence,
we can explicitly regularize the learnable 3D reconstruction with the
projective constraint between 2D view and 3D shape. We show that our
method can outperform the state-of-the-art results on the ShapeNet test
dataset as our network has learned a 2D-3D prior.

Keywords: Deep learning · 3D shape reconstruction · Learned
gradient descent

1 Introduction

Reliable and robust generation of 3D data has become an essential basis of many
applications related to robotics, rendering and modeling. Hence, understanding
the 3D world is a fundamental problem in computer vision. However, traditional
methods based on multi-view geometry such as Structure from motion [5,22]
or simultaneous localization and mapping [6], often have many restrictions. It
has been demonstrated [16] that it is difficult to establish feature correspondences when the viewpoints are separated by a large baseline. Moreover, it is
also problematic to do feature matching when the object's texture is absent [18].

In recent years, with the release of large scale datasets of 3D object models
such as ShapeNet [7], methods using deep learning techniques have been attract-
ing increasing attention in the research community. Among them, the methods
for 3D shape generation from a single RGB image using deep learning techniques
have achieved great success [8,11]. However, these methods usually take advantage of the learning capability of CNN in order to estimate 3D shape, without
considering geometric constraints between 3D shape output and 2D image input.
Recently, a new method called learned gradient descent (LGD) was proposed by

© Springer Nature Switzerland AG 2020
Y. Peng et al. (Eds.): PRCV 2020, LNCS 12307, pp. 173–184, 2020.
https://doi.org/10.1007/978-3-030-60636-7_15

the optimization community [1–3]. This method uses a deep network to generate parameter updates, instead of simple gradient descent update rule, allowing the updated network to learn a prior on the model parameters while only a few iterations are required for the network to converge.

In this paper, we present a new method for 3D shape reconstruction from a single image with learned gradient descent. Our approach takes the correspondence between 3D shape output and 2D image input into account by passing the gradient components to LGD network, enabling the network to learn a prior on model parameters. The experiments show that our method can generate high-quality 3D shape on ShapeNet datasets.

2   Related Work

In this section, we will provide a brief overview of the related works on 3D reconstruction. In addition, we will introduce a new method called learned gradient descent (LGD) [12], which is built on recent ideas from optimization community.

2.1   3D Reconstruction

Traditional 3D reconstruction methods based on multi-view geometry (MVG) has been well studied. Structure from motion (SfM) [5,20,22] based methods recover the 3D structure by extracting the features in images and estimating camera motion. Visual simultaneous localization and mapping (vSLAM)[6,10] problem can be viewed as a specific case of SfM, which estimates a map of the 3D environment as well as localizing the agent at the same time. However, these methods are often restricted by large baselines and texture-less regions.

In Recent years, with the release of large-scale 3D shape datasets such as ShapeNet [7] and KITTI [13], the deep-learning based approaches have drawn much attention and achieved good progress. Learning based methods usually consider single or a few images as input, and aim to learn the shape priors from data. Fan et al. [11] propose a conditional generative network (PSGN) to infer the point positions. Soltani et al. [4] recovered 3D shape from silhouettes. However, their methods are not applicable for the real-world scenarios because these methods require strong presumptions. Choy et al. [8] introduce 3D Recurrent Reconstruction Network (3D-R2N2) based on long-short term memory (LSTM)[15], which learns the 3D representation of an object from a single view or multiple views. Tatarchenko et al. [21] propose an octree representation and in their network the representation is gradually up-sampled by learned filters. However, these methods often focus on the representation of 3D shapes, without considering the constraints of geometry between 3D shape and 2D image. Therefore, Wang et al. [23] propose Pixel2mesh, which generate the desired shape from an initial ellipsoid via a coarse-to-fine strategy. They designed a series of reasonable loss functions to constrain the property of the output shape in order to guarantee appealing results. However, it may be useful as well to take advantage of 3D-2D geometric constraints of 3D-2D correspondence. Shen et al. [19] build a deep network to predict the thickness map from the input image by exploiting the edge and silhouette constraints but it takes up too much memory while the 3D voxel's resolution is high. Dai et al. introduce Scan2Mesh [9], a generative approach that transforms a range scan of a 3D object into a structured 3D mesh representation. Nevertheless, this method is still computationally expensive and can not guarantee a closed mesh. Gkioxari et al. [14] propose Mesh R-CNN, which generates promising combinations of voxels and meshes, but results are still coarse. Most relevant to our method is Perspective Transformer Nets [24]. In this paper, Yan et al. propose an encoder-decoder network with a 3D-2D projection loss defined by the perspective transformation. This method takes the correspondences built via 3D-2D projection as a kind of likelihood rather than a prior.

2.2 Learned Gradient Descent

Inspired by recent ideas from optimization community [1–3], Flynn et al. present DeepView [12], a new method for novel view synthesis by using learned gradient descent. This method uses a sequence of update CNNs to generate e updates to the MPIs [25] (kind of scene representation) through manipulation of the gradient components and achieves high-quality results.

The outstanding performance of DeepView shows the promise of learned gradient descent for solving non-linear inverse problems. When it comes to single-view 3D shape reconstruction problem, which is also an ill-posed inverse problems, we hope that we could pass gradient components that encodes the correspondence between 3D shape and 2D projection into the learned gradient descent network. We reasonably speculate that the use of learned gradient descent would enable the network to learn a prior on the model parameters and generate high-quality 3D shape as well. In addition, compared to standard gradient descent, the network would only take a few iterations to converge, because it learns to take larger and parameter-specific steps. Hence, in this paper, we adopt this learned gradient descent method to solve the single-image based 3D reconstruction problem.

3 Method

In this section, we will first introduce the details of the learned gradient descent process. Then, we will present the architecture of our network and show how we use the learned gradient descent to optimize our network's parameters. At last, we will show the Implementation details of our experiments. The framework of our method is illustrated in Fig. 1.

3.1 3D-2D Projection

As Fig. 2 shows, for 3D point set $X_{3D} = \{X_1, X_2, ..., X_n\}$ in 3D world frame, we can compute its corresponding 2D coordinates $X_{2D} = \{x_1, x_2, ..., x_n\}$ on

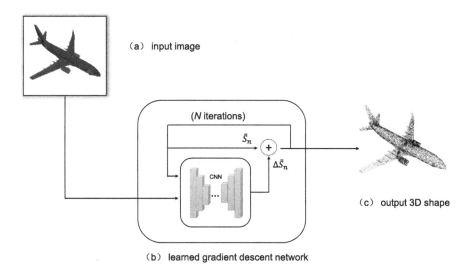

(a) input image

(N iterations)

CNN

(c) output 3D shape

(b) learned gradient descent network

Fig. 1. The architecture of our learned gradient descent network for single-view 3D reconstruction. (a) The network takes a single RGB image of an object as input. (b) The 3D shape of the object is updated iteratively using learned gradient descent. (c) The final 3D shape is reconstructed after N iterations.

image plane, using the inverse of perspective transformation matrix: $X_{2D} \sim Proj_P(X_{3D})$ where $Proj_P$ is the projection function.

Under the central projection assumption, we have

$$Proj_P = \begin{bmatrix} K & 0 \\ 0 & 1 \end{bmatrix} \cdot \begin{bmatrix} R & t \\ 0 & 1 \end{bmatrix} \tag{1}$$

where K is camera calibration matrix and (R, t) is extrinsic parameters So, Therefore, for a three-dimensional shape S, we can use perspective transformation to project it to 2D image coordinates J from the viewpoint α : $J = Proj_P(S; \alpha)$. a

3.2 Learned Gradient Descent for 3D Shape Reconstruction

As an Inverse problem, 3D reconstruction problems are often solved by minimization, e.g: $\arg\min_{\sim S} L(S_{gt}, \sim S) + \phi(\sim S)$, where $\sim S = f(I; \omega)$. S_{gt} is the ground truth 3D shape, $\sim S$ is the shape predicted by a deep network parameterized by a set of weights ω, I is the input image and ϕ is a prior on the predicted shape. What's more, L represents the loss function that measuring the disagreement between the predicted and ground truth 3D shape . We usually use iterative methods (e.g., gradient descent) to solve this non-linear optimization, as Eq. 2 shows.

$$\sim S_{n+1} = \sim S_n - \lambda\left(\frac{\partial L(S_{gt}, \sim S_n)}{\partial \sim S_n} + \frac{\partial \phi(\sim S_n)}{\partial \sim S_n}\right) \tag{2}$$

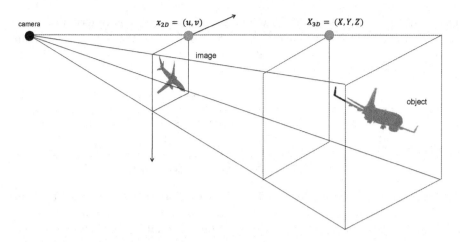

Fig. 2. Camera projection from X_{3D} to X_{2D}.

Recently, works on learned gradient descent (LGD) propose replacing the simple gradient descent update rule with a neural network that generates parameter updates, as Eq. 3 shows:

$$\sim S_{n+1} =\sim S_n + F_\theta\left(\frac{\partial L(S_{gt}, \sim S_n)}{\partial \sim S_n}, \sim S_n\right) \tag{3}$$

where F_θ is a neural network with a set of weights θ. As we have folded λ and ϕ into F_θ, the network is able to learn a prior on $\sim S_n$ and learn a parameter-specific and suitable step size. In order to train the network, we unroll the N-iteration network F_θ obtaining the full network N_θ. We compute a loss L_f comparing the predicted shape and the corresponding ground truth shape S_{gt}. The optimization of the network's weights θ is performed over a series of training tuples (I, S_{gt}), using stochastic gradient descent: arg min

$$\underset{\theta}{\arg\min}\, L_f(S_{gt}, N_\theta(I)) \tag{4}$$

3.3 3D Shape Reconstruction Gradients

LGD requires the gradients of the loss $L(S_{gt}, \sim S)$ at each iteration. We can pass the gradients components directly into the update networks, instead of defining a specific loss function. As we have $\sim J = Proj_P(\sim S; \alpha)$, through the chain rule, we can reduce the gradient components to a simple form:

$$\frac{\partial L(S_{gt}, \sim S_n)}{\partial \sim S_n} = \frac{\partial L(S_{gt}, Proj_P^{-1}(\sim J_n))}{\partial \sim S_n} \tag{5}$$

The gradient of any loss function w.r.t to $\sim S_n$ will be some function of its 2D projection $\sim J_n$, the input image I and $\sim S_n$ itself. Thus, though we don't define a specific loss function, we can write its gradient as some function G of these inputs:

$$\frac{\partial L(S_{gt}, \sim S_n)}{\partial \sim S_n} = G(\sim J_n, I, \sim S_n) \tag{6}$$

When using LGD, we pass the computed gradients directly into the network F_θ, as G is redundant because it can be included by F_θ:

$$\sim S_{n+1} = \sim S_n + F_\theta(\sim J_n, I, \sim S_n) \tag{7}$$

It is unnecessary to specifying the loss in each iteration. We only need to define a final training loss L_f. The network could be able to compute the needed gradients, as we provide it with enough prior information. The pipeline of our learned gradient descent network is visualized in Fig. 3. We first generate a initial 3D shape from the image input via an initialization CNN. Then, there are a sequence of CNNs, which are used to generate updates to the predicted shape and we can get a final predicted shape after multiple iterations.

3.4 Implementation

• **3D Representation:** In this paper, we choose point cloud as the 3D shape representation. A point cloud is a uniform structure and is easy to learn. Additionally, when it comes to geometric transformations and deformations, a point cloud allow simple manipulations as it doesn't have to update the connectivity. Therefore, it is easy to do the 3D-2D projection.

• **Network Architecture:** As in Fig. 3, our update CNN have an encoder stage and a predictor stage. The encoder takes three inputs, which are an imageI , last updated output $\sim S_n$ and its projection $\sim J_n$ (for the initialization CNN, we only have the input imageI as input). We first map $\sim S_n$ into an embedding space.The way we deal with the point cloud is borrowed from the method in PointNet [17]. Then we concatenate I and $\sim J_n$ and map them into another embedding space. For the predictor stage, we have two parallel branches, i.e., a deconvolution and a fully-connected branch. The deconvolution branch predicts a 3 channel image output, the size of which is $H \times W$ and the pixel's value of the three channel are the X, Y, Z coordinates respectively. The fully-connected branch predicts N_1 points. In total, the update outputs $(N_1 + H \times W)$ points for the current iteration. This update CNN will be repeated several times as Fig. 3 shows. At inference time, our network iteratively computes gradients of the current predicted shape and process the gradients with a CNN to generate an update shape. After several iterations, the network outputs a final shape.

• **Losses:** In order to guarantee appealing results. it is important to design appropriate losses, which should be differentiable and calculated efficiently. We adopt the Chamfer distance [11] and Earth Mover's distance to constrain the

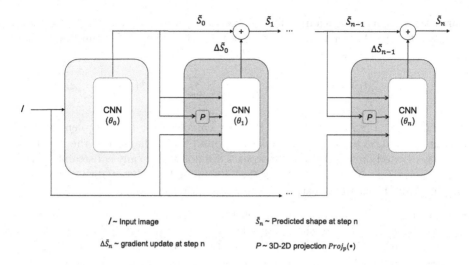

Fig. 3. The pipeline of our learned gradient descent network. An initialization CNN generates an initial 3D shape from the input image. Then, a sequence of update CNNs generates updates to the predicted shape based on the computed gradients components. All the CNNs are trained with different weights but have the same architecture, as Fig. 4 shows.

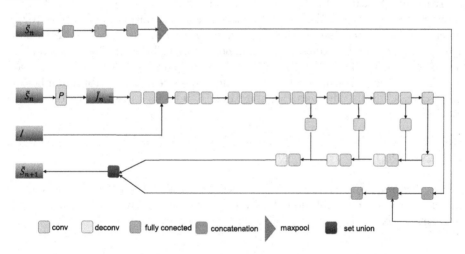

Fig. 4. The architecture of the predicted shape update CNN.

location of the point set. Chamfer distance measures the distance of each point to the other set. Chamfer distance between $\sim S$ and S_{gt} are defined as:

$$d_{CD}(\sim S, S_{gt}) = \sum_{x \in \sim S} \min_{y \in S_{gt}} \|x - y\|_2^2 + \sum_{y \in S_{gt}} \min_{x \in \sim S} \|x - y\|_2^2 \qquad (8)$$

Earth Mover's distance is a measure between two probability distributions, which is also called the Wasserstein metric in mathematics. The EMD definition is valid only when the two distributions have the same integral, as shown below:

$$d_{EMD}(\sim S, S_{gt}) = \min_{\Phi:\sim S \to S_{gt}} \sum_{x \in \sim S} \|x - \Phi(x)\|_2 \tag{9}$$

where $\Phi :\sim S \to S_{gt}$ is a bijection. We only calculate the loss between the final output of the last update CNN and the ground truth shape. For the predicted shape generated during the update process, we don't place any constraints. Ablation experiments in Sect. 4.2 shows that it will reduce the quality of the final output shape if we add constraints before the iteration ends.

• **Training Data:** We take the approach of rendering 2D views from 3D CAD object models to generate the dataset for training and testing. We use a subset of the ShapeNet [7] dataset and it consists of 50, 000 models and 13 major categories. For each model, we normalized the radius of its bounding hemisphere to unit 1 . Then we choose a random point on the bounding hemi-sphere as the viewpoint of the camera and each model was render into 2D images. The calibration matrix K and extrinsic parameters (R, t) were recorded and will be used in the operation $Proj_P$ in the network .

• **Training Details:** Our network takes the input images of 224×224. The number of the update CNNs is 3. The number of the output point set is 1024, which is sufficient to preserve the major structures of an objects. The projection operation $Proj_P$ is differentiable so our network can be trained end to end. In our experiments, the network is implemented in pytorch and we use Adam as the optimizer, with learning rate $5e - 5$. The batch size is 32; the total number of training epoch is 40. The total training time is 40 hours on two GPUs of Nvidia 2080Ti.

4   Evaluation

In this section, we first compare our method to serval state-of-the-art methods. Then we do some ablation studies to prove the effectiveness of our learned gradient descent network

4.1   Comparison to State-of-the-Art

Specifically, we choose four state-of-art 3d reconstruction methods for comparison, which are 3D-R2N2 [8], PSGN [11] and Pixel2Mesh [23]. We trained these four methods on our own datasets. Qualitative results are shown as Fig. 5. In addition, the results are compared under two different metrics CD and EMD for all 13 categories in Table 1. We can see that our approach outperforms the other methods in most categories and achieves the best mean score as well. We attribute this to our learned gradient descent network, which is capable to learn a prior from the gradient components passed into the update CNNs.

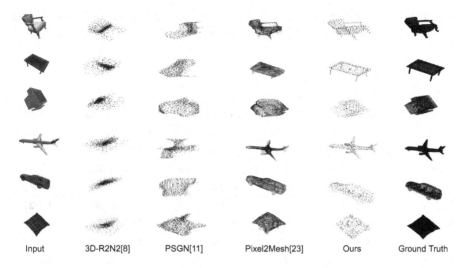

| Input | 3D-R2N2[8] | PSGN[11] | Pixel2Mesh[23] | Ours | Ground Truth |

Fig. 5. Visual comparison to state-of-the-art methods.

4.2 Ablation Study

• **Gradient Components:** In this experiment, we set one or more of the gradient components $(\sim J_n, I, \sim S_n)$ to zero, in order to measure their importance to our LGD network. As the result in Table 2 shows, the output shape achieve the best performance only when all the gradients all included. When $\sim S_n$ and $\sim J_n$ are removed, the full network can be viewed as a residual network.

• **Number of Iterations:** We measured the effect of the number of LGD iterations from 1 to 4 as well, as Table 3 shows. A single iteration means that we just use the initialization CNN to generate 3D shape and the performance is poor as expected. As the increasing of the number of iterations, the output results improve. However, memory usage has also increased. We notice that four iteration don't improve significantly, so three iteration is a good choice.

• **Additional Constraints:** We calculate the loss between S_0 or S_1 (3 iterations in total) and ground truth shape S_{gt} to check what effect it will have on the network. The result in Table 4 shows that it will have a serious negative effect on the final output of the network. We think that constraining the output in the middle of the network is not helpful for the final output of the network, but it will affect the flexibility of the update of network's parameters, so that the final output will be worse. Therefore, we only calculate the final loss in our method.

Table 1. CD and EMD (smaller is better) on our ShapeNet test set. Best results under each threshold are bolded.

Category	CD				EMD			
	3DR2N2	PSGN	Pixel2Mesh	Ours	3DR2N2	PSGN	Pixel2Mesh	Ours
Plane	0.955	0.855	**0.284**	0.546	1.072	1.052	1.173	**0.649**
Bench	0.953	0.952	1.311	**0.914**	1.269	1.271	**0.795**	1.150
Cabinet	1.941	1.972	**1.590**	1.952	1.503	1.508	**0.792**	1.386
Car	2.650	2.572	2.182	**1.326**	1.327	1.312	1.058	**1.041**
Chair	2.023	1.973	**1.121**	2.352	1.455	1.443	**0.996**	1.056
Monitor	1.011	1.097	1.213	**0.723**	1.566	1.559	1.318	**1.249**
Lamp	1.781	1.717	1.225	**1.176**	1.923	1.911	1.238	**1.027**
Speaker	1.305	1.123	1.902	**1.004**	1.695	1.719	**1.033**	1.280
Firearm	1.713	1.590	1.532	**0.965**	1.492	1.452	1.286	**1.152**
Couch	1.370	1.325	**1.232**	1.323	1.239	1.227	**0.808**	1.111
Table	2.758	2.732	2.030	**1.808**	1.571	1.568	**1.041**	1.143
Cellphone	2.483	2.282	1.575	**1.313**	1.528	1.519	1.302	**0.993**
Watercraft	1.330	1.315	1.611	**0.714**	1.472	1.463	1.293	**0.697**
Mean	1.713	1.654	1.447	**1.239**	1.470	1.462	1.087	**1.072**

Table 2. The influence of gradient components on network's performance.

Gradient components	Mean CD	Mean EMD
$(\sim J_n, I, \sim S_n)$	**1.239**	**1.072**
$(\sim J_n, I)$	1.322	1.096
$(\sim J_n, \sim S_n)$	1.303	1.238
$(I, \sim S_n)$	1.373	1.304
I	1.397	1.362

Table 3. The influence of the number of LGD iterations on network's performance.

Number of LGD iterations	Mean CD	Mean EMD
1	1.502	1.496
2	1.305	1.286
3	**1.239**	**1.072**
4	1.212	0.994

Table 4. The influence of final loss design on network's performance.

Total loss	Mean CD	Mean EMD
$L_f(\sim S_2, S_{gt})$	**1.239**	**1.072**
$L_f(\sim S_2, S_{gt}) + L_f(\sim S_1, S_{gt})$	1.463	1.286
$L_f(\sim S_2, S_{gt}) + L_f(\sim S_0, S_{gt})$	1.452	1.269

5   Conclusion

We have presented a novel approach for 3D reconstruction from a single image with learned gradient descent. The explicit correspondence relationship between

2D projection of the 3D shape was embedded in the learning network to better capture the geometry prior. The resulting approach exhibited competitive performance on the ShapeNet dataset. In the future we would like to extend the potential of proposed approach to other 2.5D/3D reconstruction problems such as stereo matching and optical flow estimation.

Acknowledgement. This research was partially supported by NSFC (No. 61871074).

References

1. Adler, J., Öktem, O.: Solving ill-posed inverse problems using iterative deep neural networks. Inverse Prob. **33**(12), 124007 (2017)
2. Adler, J., Öktem, O.: Learned primal-dual reconstruction. IEEE Trans. Med. Imaging **37**(6), 1322–1332 (2018)
3. Andrychowicz, M., et al.: Learning to learn by gradient descent by gradient descent. In: Advances in Neural Information Processing Systems, pp. 3981–3989 (2016)
4. Arsalan Soltani, A., Huang, H., Wu, J., Kulkarni, T.D., Tenenbaum, J.B.: Synthesizing 3D shapes via modeling multi-view depth maps and silhouettes with deep generative networks. In: Proceedings of the IEEE Conference on Computer Vision and Pattern Recognition, pp. 1511–1519 (2017)
5. Brown, M., Lowe, D.G.: Unsupervised 3D object recognition and reconstruction in unordered datasets. In: Fifth International Conference on 3-D Digital Imaging and Modeling (3DIM 2005), pp. 56–63. IEEE (2005)
6. Cadena, C., Carlone, L., Carrillo, H., Latif, Y., Scaramuzza, D., Neira, J., Reid, I., Leonard, J.J.: Past, present, and future of simultaneous localization and mapping: toward the robust-perception age. IEEE Trans. Rob. **32**(6), 1309–1332 (2016)
7. Chang, A.X., et al.: ShapeNet: an information-rich 3D model repository. arXiv preprint arXiv:1512.03012 (2015)
8. Choy, C.B., Xu, D., Gwak, J.Y., Chen, K., Savarese, S.: 3D-R2N2: a unified approach for single and multi-view 3D object reconstruction. In: Leibe, B., Matas, J., Sebe, N., Welling, M. (eds.) ECCV 2016. LNCS, vol. 9912, pp. 628–644. Springer, Cham (2016). https://doi.org/10.1007/978-3-319-46484-8_38
9. Dai, A., Nießner, M.: Scan2Mesh: from unstructured range scans to 3D meshes. In: Proceedings of the IEEE Conference on Computer Vision and Pattern Recognition, pp. 5574–5583 (2019)
10. Engel, J., Schöps, T., Cremers, D.: LSD-SLAM: large-scale direct monocular SLAM. In: Fleet, D., Pajdla, T., Schiele, B., Tuytelaars, T. (eds.) ECCV 2014. LNCS, vol. 8690, pp. 834–849. Springer, Cham (2014). https://doi.org/10.1007/978-3-319-10605-2_54
11. Fan, H., Su, H., Guibas, L.J.: A point set generation network for 3D object reconstruction from a single image. In: Proceedings of the IEEE Conference on Computer Vision and Pattern Recognition, pp. 605–613 (2017)
12. Flynn, J., et al.: Deepview: view synthesis with learned gradient descent. In: Proceedings of the IEEE Conference on Computer Vision and Pattern Recognition, pp. 2367–2376 (2019)
13. Geiger, A., Lenz, P., Urtasun, R.: Are we ready for autonomous driving? The KITTI vision benchmark suite. In: 2012 IEEE Conference on Computer Vision and Pattern Recognition, pp. 3354–3361. IEEE (2012)

14. Gkioxari, G., Malik, J., Johnson, J.: Mesh R-CNN. In: Proceedings of the IEEE International Conference on Computer Vision, pp. 9785–9795 (2019)
15. Hochreiter, S., Schmidhuber, J.: Long short-term memory. Neural Comput. **9**(8), 1735–1780 (1997)
16. Lowe, D.G.: Distinctive image features from scale-invariant keypoints. Int. J. Comput. Vision **60**(2), 91–110 (2004). https://doi.org/10.1023/B:VISI.0000029664.99615.94
17. Qi, C.R., Su, H., Mo, K., Guibas, L.J.: Pointnet: deep learning on point sets for 3D classification and segmentation. In: Proceedings of the IEEE Conference on Computer Vision and Pattern Recognition, pp. 652–660 (2017)
18. Saponaro, P., Sorensen, S., Rhein, S., Mahoney, A.R., Kambhamettu, C.: Reconstruction of textureless regions using structure from motion and image-based interpolation. In: 2014 IEEE International Conference on Image Processing (ICIP), pp. 1847–1851. IEEE (2014)
19. Shen, W., Jia, Y., Wu, Y.: 3D shape reconstruction from images in the frequency domain. In: Proceedings of the IEEE Conference on Computer Vision and Pattern Recognition, pp. 4471–4479 (2019)
20. Snavely, N., Seitz, S.M., Szeliski, R.: Photo tourism: exploring photo collections in 3D. In: ACM SIGGRAPH 2006 Papers, pp. 835–846 (2006)
21. Tatarchenko, M., Dosovitskiy, A., Brox, T.: Octree generating networks: efficient convolutional architectures for high-resolution 3D outputs. In: Proceedings of the IEEE International Conference on Computer Vision, pp. 2088–2096 (2017)
22. Ullman, S.: The interpretation of structure from motion. Proc. R. Soc. London. Ser. B. Biol. Sci. **203**(1153), 405–426 (1979)
23. Wang, N., Zhang, Y., Li, Z., Fu, Y., Liu, W., Jiang, Y.-G.: Pixel2Mesh: generating 3D mesh models from single RGB images. In: Ferrari, V., Hebert, M., Sminchisescu, C., Weiss, Y. (eds.) ECCV 2018. LNCS, vol. 11215, pp. 55–71. Springer, Cham (2018). https://doi.org/10.1007/978-3-030-01252-6_4
24. Yan, X., Yang, J., Yumer, E., Guo, Y., Lee, H.: Perspective transformer nets: learning single-view 3D object reconstruction without 3D supervision. In: Advances in Neural Information Processing Systems, pp. 1696–1704 (2016)
25. Zhou, T., Tucker, R., Flynn, J., Fyffe, G., Snavely, N.: Stereo magnification: learning view synthesis using multiplane images. arXiv preprint arXiv:1805.09817 (2018)

Joint Self-expression with Adaptive Graph for Unsupervised Feature Selection

Aihong Yuan[1,3,4(✉)], Xiaoyu Gao[1], Mengbo You[1,3,4], and Dongjian He[2,3,4]

[1] College of Information Engineering, Northwest A&F University,
YangLing, Xianyang 712100, China
{ahyuan,2017013078,ymb}@nwafu.edu.cn
[2] College of Mechanical and Electronic Engineering, Northwest A&F University,
YangLing, Xianyang 712100, China
hdj168@nwsuaf.edu.cn
[3] Key Laboratory of Agricultural Internet of Things,
Ministry of Agriculture and Rural Affairs, Yangling, Beijing 712100, China
[4] Shaanxi Key Laboratory of Agricultural Information Perception and Intelligent
Service, Yangling, Xianyang 712100, China

Abstract. Feature selection usually takes unsupervised way to preprocess the data before clustering. In the unsupervised feature selection, the embedding based method can capture more discriminative information contained in data compared to the other methods. Considering many existing methods learn a cluster indicator matrix which may bring noise, and at the same time, these kinds of methods does not make good use of the geometry structure of the data. In order to address the existing problems, we propose a novel model based on joint self-expression model with adaptive graph constraint. The joint self-expression module is utilized to explore the relationship between features. Different from the conventional self-expression, our joint self-expression module contains two types self-expression, *i.e.*, conventional self-expression and the *convex non-negative matrix factorization* (CNMF) which can extract more representative features. Furthermore, we introduce manifold learning to maintain the structural characteristics of the original data. Adaptive graph regularization term is also incorporated based on the principle of maximum entropy into our model. In order to solve the final model, an alternative algorithm is well designed. Finally, experiment is well designed on five benchmark datasets and the experimental results show that the model proposed in this paper is more effectiveness than the state-of-the-art comparison models.

Keywords: Unsupervised feature selection · Self-expression ·
Adaptive graph constraint · Maximum entropy

Supported in part by the Natural Science Foundation of Shaanxi Province under Grant 2020JQ-279, in part by the Doctoral Start-up Foundation of Northwest A&F University under Grant Z1090219095, and Grant Z109021803.

Y. Peng et al. (Eds.): PRCV 2020, LNCS 12307, pp. 185–196, 2020.
https://doi.org/10.1007/978-3-030-60636-7_16

1   Introduction

Data in machine learning, data mining and computer vision are always represented with high-dimensionality. Processing high-dimensional data directly will cause problems such as computational difficulties and storage overflow, which is so-called the curse of dimensionality. To address the curse of dimensionality, some dimensionality reduction techniques, such as *principal component analysis* (PCA) [19], manifold learning [17] and data compression [9], has been proposed. *Feature selection* (FS) is also such technique for dimensionality reduction. However, unlike PCA, manifold learning and data compression, which alter the representation of the original data, FS reduces the data dimensionality via selecting an effective subset from the original data.

The core idea of FS is that the high-dimensional data contains many redundant and irrelevant information, which is useless or even increase the difficulty of learning task. Therefore, FS aims to select the most representative features and remove the redundant and irrelevant features. According to the training data whether has label information, FS can be roughly classified into two categories: *supervised feature selection* (SFS) and *unsupervised feature selection* (UFS). In practical applications, obtaining label information is time consuming and laborious. So UFS is more valuable in practical applications. At the same time, UFS is more challenging. Recently, UFS has attracted extensive attention and many UFS methods have been proposed. The methods can be classified into three groups, *i.e.*, filter based methods [4,5,7], wrapper based methods [1,8,14] and embedding based methods [3,6,12]. And the embedding based methods are most popular in recent years. Among the embedding based methods, sparse regularization is the most common in the FS models. This is mainly consistent with the sparsity of feature selection.

1.1   Motivation and Overview

Most of the embedding methods exploit the spectral analysis and mainly contain two steps. Firstly, the data structure is explored by spectral analysis of manifold learning. Secondly, the feature selection matrix is optimized by sparsity regularization module. In the first step, the most important purpose is to learn the cluster indicator matrix or the pseudo label matrix. Therefore, the learned cluster indicator matrix is critical for spectral analysis based methods. However, most spectral analysis based methods use the regression learning scheme. Specifically, they use continuous pseudo label matrix to approximate the true label matrix which is discrete in the truly data. **This inevitably introduces estimation error and noise into the cluster indicator matrix.** Furthermore, during the constructing of pseudo label matrix, if we mark the pseudo label matrix as Y_p and the true label matrix as Y, the constraint $Y_p^T Y_p = I$ is always used [11]. However, it is not true for the practical data. In fact, for the true label matrix Y, it satisfies the following equation: $Y^T Y = \Lambda$, where Λ is a diagonal matrix and the i-th diagonal element denotes the number of data samples of the i-th class. Therefore, **using the regression learning scheme** with the $Y_p^T Y_p = I$ constraint term **is not very suitable for the real data**.

To address the aforementioned limitations, a novel joint self-expression with adaptive graph model is proposed in this paper for UFS. Generally speaking, the proposed model contains two types of self-expression modules and two corresponding types of adaptive graph constraint modules. Specifically, conventional self-expression and *convex nonnegative matrix factorization* (CNMF) are used as the two types of self-expression modules. Conventional self-expression not only can dig up the correlation between the data samples, but also can avoid the estimation error and noise caused by regression learning scheme. Meanwhile, CNMF also can be seen as a special self-expression scheme. Compared with conventional self-expression, CNMF requires self-expression matrix to be nonnegative and the self-expression matrix is factored into two nonnegative matrices. CNMF is a partial-based data representation method which increases the interpretability of the corresponding data, and it suitable for both nonnegative and general data. Besides, to unify the two self-expression into one model and capture the local structure of the original data, two adaptive graph constraint terms are embedded into the proposed method. When the whole model is constructed, an efficient alternative iterative scheme is designed to optimize the model and the convergence of our algorithm are rigorously proved.

1.2 Contributions

The key contributions can be summarized as follows:

1. Two types of self-expression modules are jointly embedded for UFS. The two modules are mutually reinforcing and can not only explore the relationship between the data samples, but also avoid the estimation error and noise introduced by regression learning scheme.
2. Two adaptive graph constraint terms are designed to keep the local structure of the original data and unify the two self-expression modules into one model. The adaptive graph constraints help our method remove the redundant features of the original data.
3. The effectiveness of the proposed model are evaluated on the benchmark datasets. All experimental results have shown that the proposed model gains the best performance among the state-of-the-art UFS methods.

1.3 Organization

The rest of this paper is organized as follows. In Sect. 2, some previous works are briefly introduced. Section 3 presents the process of our model construction and model optimization. To validate the proposed method, the experimental results are shown in Sect. 4. At last, Sect. 5 makes a brief conclusion for this paper.

2   Related Work

In recent years, the embedding methods for feature selection have gained the promising performance, and therefore, these methods have attracted wide attention. In this section, the related embedding methods is briefly presented. Zhao et al. devoted themselves to exploring the inherent attributes and connections between many feature selection algorithms (supervised and unsupervised), and developed a unified framework based on spectral graph theory [20]. Afterwards, a new robust method was proposed, focusing on joint l_{21}-norm minimization in both the loss function and the regularization step. This method gained good performance on bioinformatics dataset [15]. Similarly, the UDFS [18] model combines discriminant analysis and l_{21}-norm minimization, and aims to use batch processing to find the most distinctive feature subset. MCFS proposed a UFS model to preserve the multi-cluster structure of the raw data [2]. NDFS model proposed by Li et al. [13] can complete the synchronization of spectral clustering and feature selection. The PCA based method [16] solves the problem that many robust PCA use the 2 norm distance incorrectly in order to achieve a more effective method of reducing the data dimension. Zhu et al. [21] embedded a graph regularizer in the joint sparse regression framework in order to retain the important information of the data-local structural features. The SCE model [10] proposed for data partitioning emphasizes the structural information of the original data. According to the previous works, keeping the local structure is important for UFS.

3   Proposed Approach

This paper presents a novel FS method. The self-expression and convex NMF are associated and constrained by an adaptive graph. In this section, the methods presented in this article will be described in detail. In addition, the convergence of the method will be theoretically analyzed.

3.1   Model Constructing

Suppose the input original data matrix is $X = \{x_1, x_2, x_3, \cdots, x_n\} \in \mathbb{R}^{d \times n}$, where x_i is the i-th sample, and each sample has d dimensions. The self-expression is to take into account the correlation between each feature in the original data, and to linearly express each feature with all features. The expression of the model is $X^T = X^T W$, which $W = [w_{ij}] \in \mathbb{R}^{d \times d}$ is self-expression matrix and w_{ij} means the coefficient of the i-th feature to express the j-th feature. Generally, we want to minimize the self-expression error and we use F-norm to measure the size of the residual. Therefore, the objective function can be represented as follows:

$$\min_{W} \left\| X^T - X^T W \right\|_F^2 + \lambda \|W\|_p, \tag{1}$$

where λ is a hyper-parameter and $\|\bullet\|_p$ denotes the p-norm. The second term is a regular constraint for W. To ensure that the selected feature are representative with low dimensionality, the matrix W should have property of row sparsity. In this paper, $l_{2,1}$-norm is used to constrain the matrix W and Eq. (1) can be rewritten as follows:

$$\min_{W} \left\| X^T - X^T W \right\|_F^2 + \lambda \|W\|_{2,1}. \tag{2}$$

In order to preserve the local manifold structure, the reconstructed data points should keep their nearest neighbor relationships in the original data space. In other words, if the raw data pairs x_i and x_j are close in the original space, the re-expression of the data pairs (i.e., $W^T x_i$ and $W^T x_j$) also should be closed. And vice versa. We define $S = [S_{ij}] \in \mathbb{R}^{n \times n}$ as the similarity matrix of the original data. Based on this hypothesis, Eq. (2) is added by the graph regular term and the objective function can be rewritten as follows:

$$\min_{W} \left\| X^T - X^T W \right\|_F^2 + \lambda \|W\|_{2,1} + \frac{\alpha}{2} \sum_{i,j} \left\| W^T x_i - W^T x_j \right\|^2 S_{ij}, \tag{3}$$

where α is a weight factor. We define $L_S = D_S - S$ as the Laplacian graph of the similarity matrix S and $D_S \in \mathbb{R}^{n \times n}$ is a diagonal matrix corresponding to S. The calculation formula of D_S is as follows:

$$D_{ii} = \sum_{j=1}^{n} S_{ij}. \tag{4}$$

After introducing L_S, Eq. (3) can be rewritten as follows:

$$\min_{W} \left\| X^T - X^T W \right\|_F^2 + \lambda \|W\|_{2,1} + \alpha \mathrm{Tr} \left(W^T X L_S X^T W \right), \tag{5}$$

where $\mathrm{Tr}(\cdot)$ denotes the trace of the corresponding matrix.

NMF can automatically lead to the parts-based representation of the data which is closely related to the perception mechanism. Additionally, considering that the data in the real world are not all non-negative, CNMF is used in this paper to improve the performance of the model. Furthermore, Laplacian graph regularizer is also added to keep the local manifold structure of the original data. This idea can be represented as the following formula:

$$\min_{U,V} \|X - XUV\|_F^2 + \gamma Tr \left(V L_S V^T \right), \tag{6}$$

where γ is the weight factor, $U \in \mathbb{R}_+^{n \times k}$ denotes the basis matrix and $V \in \mathbb{R}_+^{k \times n}$ represents the low-dimensional embedding of data matrix X.

In many previous works, S is fixed when the data matrix X is given. However, when the S is fixed, Eq. (5) and Eq. (6) have no interaction. In order to combine the two graph constraint in Eq. (5) and Eq. (6) into one model, information entropy is used to optimize the similarity matrix S. The objective function for S is:

$$\max_S \sum_{i=1}^{n} \sum_{j=1}^{n} -S_{ij} \log S_{ij}, \; s.t. \; \sum_{j=1}^{n} S_{ij} = 1, S_{ij>0}. \tag{7}$$

Combining Eq. (5)–(7), the whole loss function in this paper can be written as follows:

$$\begin{aligned} \mathcal{O}(W,G,V,S) &= ||X^T - X^T W||_F^2 + ||X - XGV||_F^2 \\ &+ \gamma Tr\left(VL_SV^T\right) + \alpha Tr\left(W^T XL_S X^T W\right) + \lambda ||W||_{2,1} \\ &+ \beta \sum_{i,j} S_{ij} \log S_{ij}, \; s.t. \; G \geq 0, V \geq 0, \sum_{j=1}^{n} S_{ij} > 0. \end{aligned} \tag{8}$$

The whole model is presented and the next section will introduce the specific steps of optimization.

3.2 Model Optimizing

Fix W, U, V and Update S. When W, U and V are fixed, Eq. (8) is transformed as follows:

$$\begin{aligned} \mathcal{O}_1 &= \gamma Tr\left(VL_SV^T\right) + \alpha Tr\left(W^T XL_S X^T W\right) \\ &+ \beta \sum_{i,j} S_{ij} \log S_{ij}, \; s.t. \; \sum_{j=1}^{n} S_{ij} = 1, S_{ij} \geq 0. \end{aligned} \tag{9}$$

The Lagrangian function of Eq. (9) can be represented as follows:

$$\begin{aligned} \mathcal{L}_1 &= \gamma \mathrm{Tr}\left(VL_SV^T\right) + \alpha \mathrm{Tr}\left(W^T XL_S X^T W\right) \\ &+ \beta \sum_{i,j} S_{ij} \log S_{ij} - \sum_{i,j} \pi_{ij} S_{ij} - \sum_{i=1}^{n} \mu_i \left(\sum_{j=1}^{n} S_{ij} - 1\right), \end{aligned} \tag{10}$$

where π_{ij} and μ_i are Lagrangian multipliers. Using the KKT conditions, the optimal solution of the relevant parameters should satisfy the following equation:

$$\begin{cases} \frac{\partial \mathcal{L}_1}{\partial S_{ij}} = \gamma ||v_i - v_j||_2^2 + +\beta\left(\log S_{ij} + 1\right) - \pi_{ij} - \mu_i = 0, \\ S_{ij} \geq 0, \; \pi_{ij} \geq 0, \; \mu_i \geq 0, \; \sum_{j=1}^{n} S_{ij} = 1, \; \pi_{ij} S_{ij} = 0, \; \mu_i S_{ij} = 0, \end{cases} \tag{11}$$

where v_i represents the i-th column of V. By solving the Eq. (11), we can get the calculating formula for S as follows:

$$S_{ij} = \frac{\exp\left(-\frac{\gamma||v_i - v_j||_2^2 + \alpha ||W^T x_i - W^T x_j||_2^2}{\beta}\right)}{\sum\limits_{j=1}^{n} \exp\left(-\frac{\gamma||v_i - v_j||_2^2 + \alpha ||W^T x_i - W^T x_j||_2^2}{\beta}\right)}. \tag{12}$$

Fix W, S and update G and V. When W, S are fixed, Eq. (8) is equivalent to solving the following formula:

$$\mathcal{O}_2 = \|X - XUV\|_F^2 + \gamma \mathrm{Tr}\left(VL_S V^T\right), \; s.t. \; U \geq 0, \; V \geq 0, \qquad (13)$$

The Lagrangian function of Eq. (13) can be represented as follows:

$$\mathcal{L}_2 = \|X - XUV\|_F^2 + \gamma \mathrm{Tr}\left(VL_S V^T\right) - Tr\left(\Phi U^T\right) - Tr\left(\Psi V^T\right), \qquad (14)$$

where $\Phi \in \mathbb{R}_+^{n \times k}$ and $\Psi \in \mathbb{R}_+^{k \times n}$ are Lagrangian multiply matrices. Using the KKT conditions, the optimal solution of Eq. (14) should satisfy the following formula:

$$\begin{cases} \frac{\partial \mathcal{L}_2}{\partial U} = -2X^T X V^T + 2X^T XUVV^T + \Phi = 0, \\ \frac{\partial \mathcal{L}_2}{\partial V} = -2U^T X^T X + 2UX^T XUV + 2\gamma VL_S + \Psi = 0, \\ U_{ij} \geq 0, \; V_{ij} \geq 0, \; \Phi_{ij} \geq 0, \; \Psi_{ij} \geq 0, \; \Phi_{ij}U_{ij} = 0, \; \Psi_{ij}V_{ij} = 0. \end{cases} \qquad (15)$$

According to Eq. (15), we can obtain the updating rules of U and V according to multiplicative iterative optimization:

$$\begin{cases} U \leftarrow U \odot \frac{X^T X V^T}{X^T XUVV^T}, \\ V \leftarrow V \odot \frac{U^T X^T X + \gamma VS}{\gamma VD + U^T X^T XUV}, \end{cases} \qquad (16)$$

where $\odot$ means multiplication by elements, and division is also calculated by elements.

Fix U, V, S and Update W. When U, V and S are fixed, Eq. (8) is transformed to:

$$\mathcal{O}_3 = \left\|X^T - X^T W\right\|_F^2 + \alpha \mathrm{Tr}\left(W^T XL_S X^T W\right) + \lambda \|W\|_{2,1}. \qquad (17)$$

Setting the derivative of $\mathcal{O}_3$ respect to W to be zero, we have

$$\frac{\partial \mathcal{O}_3}{\partial W} = -2XX^T + 2XX^T W + 2\alpha XL_S X^T W + \lambda D^w W = 0, \qquad (18)$$

where D^w is a diagonal matrix and it can be represented as follows:

$$D^w = diag\left(\frac{1}{\|w^1\|_2}, \frac{1}{\|w^2\|_2}, \cdots, \frac{1}{\|w^d\|_2}\right), \qquad (19)$$

where $\|w^i\|_2$ represents the l_2-norm of the i-th row of W.

Because the D^w is corresponding to W, Eq. (18) cannot obtain an analytical solution. However, we can get an alternative iterative form as follows:

$$W \leftarrow \left(XX^T + \alpha XL_S X^T + \lambda D^w\right)^{-1} XX^T. \qquad (20)$$

After obtaining the W, we use $\|w^i\|_2$ to represent the l_2-norm of the i-th row of W and we can sort all features according to $\|w^i\|_2$ in descending order and select the top K ranked features. The whole procedures of our optimization algorithm is given in Algorithm 1.

4   Experiments

In this section, we evaluate our model on five popular datasets, $i.e.$, Isolet, USPS, COIL20, MNIST and TOX_171. The clustering accuracy (ACC) and normalized mutual information (NMI) are used to evaluate the performance of the proposed model.

Algorithm 1. Alternative iterative algorithm to solve problem (8)

Input:
   The Data matrix $\mathbf{X} \in \mathbb{R}^{d \times n}$, the coefficients α, β, λ and γ . Number of iterations niter.
Output:
   K selected features.
   Initialize a random matrix $\mathbf{W} \in \mathbb{R}^{d \times d}$, a random matrix $\mathbf{U} \in \mathbb{R}^{n \times k}$ and random matrix $\mathbf{V} \in \mathbb{R}^{k \times n}$.
   Repeat
     1: Update S by Eq. (12).
     2: Update G and V by Eq. (16).
     3: Update W by Eq. (20).
   Until Convergence.
   Sort all features according to $\left\| w^i \right\|_2$ in descending order and select the top K ranked features.

4.1   Datasets

The proposed model is evaluated on five datasets, including one spoken letter recognition dataset ($i.e.$, Isolet), three image datasets ($i.e.$, COIL20, MNIST and USPS) and one biological dataset ($i.e.$, TOX_171). Table 1 gives a summary of the aforementioned datasets.

Table 1. Introduction of the datasets.

Dataset	# of samples	# of features	# of classes
Isolet	1560	617	26
USPS	9298	256	10
COIL20	1440	1024	20
MNIST	3000	784	10
TOX_171	171	5748	4

4.2   Experimental Setup

Competitors. To evaluate the effectiveness of the proposed model, we compare our model with four state-of-the-art approaches ($i.e.$, LS, MCFS, UDFS, NDFS) and one baseline approach ($i.e.$, All-Fea, which all original features are used).

Comparison Schemes. There are four hyper-parameters in our model, they are α, β, γ, and λ. In this paper, grid search strategy is used for these hyper-parameter setting. The four hyper-parameters are set from $\{10^{\pm 3}, 10^{\pm 2}, 10^{\pm 1}, 1\}$. The number of selected features are set as $\{40, 80, 120, 160, 200\}$ for all the datasets. In order to evaluate the performance of the selected features by the comparison model, K-means algorithm is used to cluster the datasets.

4.3   Performance Comparison of Clustering

The clustering experiment is designed and the clustering results are showed to evaluate the performance of the selected features by the comparison model. Table 2 shows the results on all the five datasets. Considering the K-means algorithm is sensitive to initialization, all cluster sub-experiment are repeated 10 times (including the comparison models) and we report the average result with *standard deviation* (Std). From the results, we can draw a conclusion that the embedding models can obtain a better performance on most datasets than All-Fea and LS. Among the embedding model, the proposed model in this paper almost get the highest ACC and NMI scores on all the datasets which confirms the truth that the UFS model proposed in this paper is most effective and robust. Specifically, our model has more than 6% (ACC) improvement on MNIST and 8% (NMI) improvement on TOX_171. Furthermore, our model has relative low Std among the five datasets. Therefore, our model can select the more representative and robust features than the comparison models.

Table 2. Clustering results (ACC/NMI %± Std) of the proposed approach and five representative unsupervised feature selection methods on the benchmark datasets. The best results are highlighted in bold.)

Datasets	Isolet	USPS	COIL20	MNIST	TOX_171
ACC (%)					
All-Fea	65.08 ± 1.41	69.39 ± 2.16	54.33 ± 3.67	40.78 ± 2.18	42.26 ± 3.71
LS [7]	57.45 ± 1.35	71.03 ± 2.25	61.00 ± 2.38	41.78 ± 2.30	46.18 ± 1.52
MCFS [2]	60.38 ± 3.25	72.20 ± 1.48	61.70 ± 4.05	56.60 ± 2.86	47.39 ± 6.58
UDFS [18]	49.22 ± 2.39	69.51 ± 1.74	61.65 ± 3.74	45.41 ± 3.37	36.67 ± 6.72
NDFS [13]	69.23 ± 0.41	68.80 ± 0.03	61.60 ± 3.62	43.31 ± 3.13	43.10 ± 6.10
Ours	$\mathbf{70.99 \pm 3.17}$	$\mathbf{74.68 \pm 1.50}$	$\mathbf{65.41 \pm 2.88}$	$\mathbf{62.44 \pm 2.34}$	$\mathbf{50.35 \pm 2.37}$
NMI (%)					
All-Fea	71.68 ± 1.27	60.36 ± 0.93	71.33 ± 2.01	34.85 ± 2.87	24.79 ± 5.67
LS [7]	65.19 ± 0.69	61.36 ± 1.39	73.43 ± 2.01	34.94 ± 1.79	24.91 ± 0.82
MCFS [2]	67.69 ± 1.33	63.11 ± 1.22	76.07 ± 2.11	45.79 ± 1.62	25.26 ± 6.25
UDFS [18]	56.25 ± 1.18	59.62 ± 0.92	71.78 ± 2.44	37.10 ± 2.24	11.43 ± 9.25
NDFS [13]	$\mathbf{81.03 \pm 2.64}$	63.51 ± 0.06	74.96 ± 1.86	36.72 ± 2.89	19.04 ± 9.95
Ours	79.51 ± 1.43	$\mathbf{63.95 \pm 1.90}$	$\mathbf{76.21 \pm 1.65}$	$\mathbf{52.58 \pm 1.42}$	$\mathbf{33.44 \pm 2.62}$

4.4   Parameter Sensitivity

The sensitive of the hyper-parameters (*i.e.*, α, β, γ and λ) are investigated in Fig. 1. According to Fig. 1, the ACC results is sensitive to the hyper-parameters. Furthermore, for different datasets, the optimal value of the hyper-parameter is also different. Therefore, how to select the value of hyper-parameter is still an open question in UFS. Furthermore, form Fig. 1, we can also draw a conclusion each constraint term has the potential for improving the performance of the UFS model.

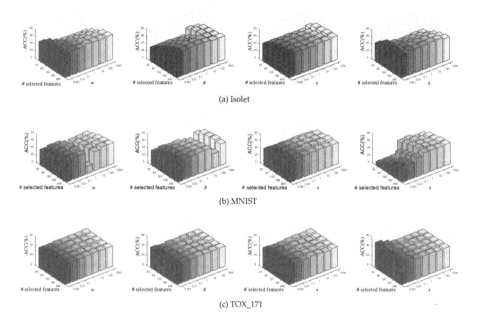

Fig. 1. The sensitivity of hyper-parameters. The four sub-figures in the same row demonstrate sensitivity of four hyper-parameters on the same dataset. The x-axis represents α, β, γ and λ, respectively, while y-axis represents the number of selected features, and z-axis represents the clustering accuracy. Specifically, the four sub-figures in the first column apply setting: $\alpha = 0.001$, $\beta = 100$, $\gamma = 1000$ and $\lambda = 0.001$. The second column: $\alpha = 0.1$, $\beta = 1000$, $\gamma = 0.001$ and $\lambda = 1$. The third column: $\alpha = 0.1$, $\beta = 10$, $\gamma = 1$ and $\lambda = 100$. Best view in color.

5   Conclusion

In this paper, we propose a novel UFS model based on joint self-expression with adaptive graph. The joint self-expression module two type of self-expression form, which can well explore the relationship between data. The adaptive graph constraint is also used, which can keep the local manifold structure of the original data. Practically, clustering experiments have been carried out, and the experimental results have shown the excellent performance of the proposed model.

References

1. Bermejo, P., Gámez, J.A., Puerta, J.M.: Speeding up incremental wrapper feature subset selection with Naive Bayes classifier. Knowl.-Based Syst. **55**, 140–147 (2014)
2. Cai, D., Zhang, C., He, X.: Unsupervised feature selection for multi-cluster data. In: Rao, B., Krishnapuram, B., Tomkins, A., Yang, Q. (eds.) Proceedings of the ACM SIGKDD International Conference on Knowledge Discovery and Data Mining, pp. 333–342. ACM (2010)
3. Du, X., Nie, F., Wang, W., Yang, Y., Zhou, X.: Exploiting combination effect for unsupervised feature selection by $l_{2,0}$ norm. IEEE Trans. Neural Netw. Learn. Syst. **30**(1), 201–214 (2019)
4. Duda, R.O., Hart, P.E., Stork, D.G.: Pattern Classification. Wiley, Hoboken (2012)
5. Gu, Q., Li, Z., Han, J.: Generalized fisher score for feature selection. arXiv preprint arXiv:1202.3725 (2012)
6. Han, X., Chai, H., Liu, P., Li, D., Wang, L.: A new graph-preserving unsupervised feature selection embedding LLE with low-rank constraint and feature-level representation. Artif. Intell. Rev. **53**(4), 2875–2903 (2020). https://doi.org/10.1007/s10462-019-09749-w
7. He, X., Cai, D., Niyogi, P.: Laplacian score for feature selection. In: Advances in Neural Information Processing Systems, pp. 507–514 (2006)
8. Kabir, M.M., Islam, M.M., Murase, K.: A new wrapper feature selection approach using neural network. Neurocomputing **73**(16–18), 3273–3283 (2010)
9. Lee, Y., Hirakawa, K., Nguyen, T.Q.: Camera-aware multi-resolution analysis for raw image sensor data compression. IEEE Trans. Image Process. **27**(6), 2806–2817 (2018)
10. Li, X., Lu, Q., Dong, Y., Tao, D.: SCE: A manifold regularized set-covering method for data partitioning. IEEE Trans. Neural Netw. Learn. Syst. **29**(5), 1760–1773 (2017)
11. Li, X., Zhang, H., Zhang, R., Liu, Y., Nie, F.: Generalized uncorrelated regression with adaptive graph for unsupervised feature selection. IEEE Trans. Neural Netw. Learn. Syst. **30**(5), 1587–1595 (2019)
12. Li, X., Zhang, H., Zhang, R., Nie, F.: Discriminative and uncorrelated feature selection with constrained spectral analysis in unsupervised learning. IEEE Trans. Image Process. **29**, 2139–2149 (2020)
13. Li, Z., Yang, Y., Liu, J., Zhou, X., Lu, H.: Unsupervised feature selection using nonnegative spectral analysis. In: Twenty-Sixth AAAI Conference on Artificial Intelligence (2012)
14. Maldonado, S., Weber, R.: A wrapper method for feature selection using support vector machines. Inf. Sci. **179**(13), 2208–2217 (2009)
15. Nie, F., Huang, H., Cai, X., Ding, C.H.: Efficient and robust feature selection via joint $l_{2,1}$-norms minimization. In: Advances in Neural Information Processing Systems, pp. 1813–1821 (2010)
16. Nie, F., Yuan, J., Huang, H.: Optimal mean robust principal component analysis. In: International Conference on Machine Learning, pp. 1062–1070 (2014)
17. Yang, L., Guo, Y., Cheng, J.: Manifold distance-based over-sampling technique for class imbalance learning. In: The Thirty-Third AAAI Conference on Artificial Intelligence, AAAI 2019, The Thirty-First Innovative Applications of Artificial Intelligence Conference, IAAI 2019, The Ninth AAAI Symposium on Educational Advances in Artificial Intelligence, EAAI 2019, Honolulu, Hawaii, USA, 27 January–1 February 2019, pp. 10071–10072. AAAI Press (2019)

18. Yang, Y., Shen, H.T., Ma, Z., Huang, Z., Zhou, X.: $l_{2,1}$-norm regularized discriminative feature selection for unsupervised. In: Twenty-Second International Joint Conference on Artificial Intelligence (2011)
19. Zhao, X., Guo, J., Nie, F., Chen, L., Li, Z., Zhang, H.: Joint principal component and discriminant analysis for dimensionality reduction. IEEE Trans. Neural Netw. Learn. Syst. **31**(2), 433–444 (2020)
20. Zhao, Z., Liu, H.: Spectral feature selection for supervised and unsupervised learning. In: Proceedings of the 24th International Conference on Machine Learning, pp. 1151–1157. ACM (2007)
21. Zhu, X., Li, X., Zhang, S., Ju, C., Wu, X.: Robust joint graph sparse coding for unsupervised spectral feature selection. IEEE Trans. Neural Netw. Learn. Syst. **28**(6), 1263–1275 (2016)

Fast Hyper-walk Gridded Convolution on Graph

Xiaobin Hong[1], Tong Zhang[1(✉)], Zhen Cui[1], Chunyan Xu[1], Liangfang Zhang[2], and Jian Yang[1]

[1] Key Laboratory of Intelligent Perception and Systems for High-Dimensional Information of Ministry of Education, Nanjing University of Science and Technology, Nanjing, China
{xbhong,tong.zhang,zhen.cui,cyx,csjyang}@njust.edu.cn
[2] East Route Shandong Trunk Line co. LTD., Jinan, China
george_5876@163.com

Abstract. The existing graph convolution methods usually suffer high computation burden, large memory requirement and intractable batch-process. In this paper, we propose a high-efficient hyper-walk gridded convolution (hyper-WGC) method to encode non-regular graph data, which overcomes all these aforementioned problems. To high-efficient capture graph topology structures, we propose random hyper-walk by taking advantages of random-walks as well as node/edge encapsulation. The random hyper-walk could greatly mitigate the problem of exponentially explosive sampling times occurred in the original random walk, while well preserving graph structures to some extent. To efficiently encode local hyper-walks around one reference node, we project hyper-walks into an order space to form image-like grid data, which more favors those conventional convolution networks. We experimentally validate the efficiency and effectiveness of our proposed hyper-WGC, which has high-efficient computation speed, and comparable or even better performance when compared with those baseline GCNs.

Keywords: Hyper walk · Gridding · Graph convolution · Node classification

1 Introduction

In recent years, convolutional neural networks (CNNs) [16] had achieved great success in variety of machine learning tasks such as object detection [28], machine translation [19] and speech recognition [12]. The basic motivation of CNNs is to explore the local correlation through neighborhood convolution. CNNs are rather sophisticated to encode Euclidean structure data w.r.t. shape-gridded images and videos. In real-world applications, however, there is a large amount of non-Euclidean structure data such as social networks [23], citation networks [15],

---

Student Paper.

Y. Peng et al. (Eds.): PRCV 2020, LNCS 12307, pp. 197–208, 2020.
https://doi.org/10.1007/978-3-030-60636-7_17

protein-protein interaction [5] and knowledge graphs [34], which are usual non-grid data and cannot be habitually encoded with the conventional convolution.

As graph is natural also frequently-used to describe non-grid data, recently numerous literatures attempt to introduce convolution filtering into graph, called graph convolution or graph convolutional network (GCN). Generally, they fall into two categories: spectral based approaches [6,9,14,17] and spatial based approaches [2,3,10,11]. Spectral based approaches employed the recent emerging spectral graph theory to filter signals in the frequency domain of graph topology. This kind of methods are well-supported by the strong theory of graph signals, but they usually suffer high computation burden because of the eigenvalue decomposition on graph topology. To mitigate this problem, the fast approximation algorithm [8,18,29] defines convolution filtering as a recursive calculation on graph topology, which actually may be attributed to the category of spatial convolution. Spatial based approaches often use explicitly spatial edge-connection relations to aggregate those nodes locally adjacent to one reference node. The local aggregation with mean/sum/max operation on neighbor nodes cannot yet satisfy Weisfeiler-Lehman (WL) test [35], where non-isomorphism graph structures need different filtering responses. The critical reason is that graph topology structures are degraded to certain-degree confusion after aggregation, even though the recent graph attention networks (GAT) [33] attempt to adaptively/discriminatively aggregate local neighbor nodes with different weights learned by the attention mechanism between one central node and its neighbor nodes. Moreover, spatial based GCNs usually need to optimize the entire graph during training as the intractability with batch-process, which will result into high-memory requirement for large-scale graphs and thus cannot run on the plain platforms. It means, when graph structures change with new-added/deleted nodes or links, the GCN models should be well-restarted or even re-trained for new structures. In addition, the time complexity of spatial based GCNs will be exponentially increased with the receptive field size (w.r.t. the hop steps l), i.e., $\mathcal{O}(Nm^l d^2)$ in each convolution layer, where N is the number of nodes, m denotes average degree of nodes, and d is the dimension of input signal.

In this paper, we propose a fast hyper-walk gridded convolution (hyper-WGC) method with high-computation efficiency, low-memory cost, easy batch-process, and comparable or even better performance when compared with the baseline GCNs. To efficiently capture local structures, we introduce the random sampling strategy through random walks, which can well preserve graph topology under randomly sample sufficient walks. As the quantity of walks has the exponentially-explosive increase with the walk step, i.e., $\mathcal{O}(Nm^l)$, the burden of sampling sufficient walks tends to overwhelm the entire algorithm especially for the larger node degree $m \gg 2$. Instead of the original random walk, specifically, we propose hyper-walk to reduce sampling times. The strategy of hyper-walk can efficiently reduce traversal edges through random combination (to form hyper-edge) of connection edges during walking. The hyper-walk balances the advantages of random walk as well as node aggregation. Under the fixed hyper-edge number $\widetilde{m}$, the random hyper-walk will fall into a deep-first traversal on $\widetilde{m}$-tree, whose height may be limited in the radius of graph to cover the global receptive field. In view of the limited height as well as small $\widetilde{m}$ value, a small amount of sampling times could well preserve most information of topology structures as well as node signals.

To efficiently encode local hyper-walks around each reference node, we project hyper-walks into an order space to form image-like grid-shape data, which more favors those conventional convolution networks. Thus a 2-D convolution filtering can be performed in the normalized hyper-walk space to encode the correlation of within-walk adjacencies and cross adjacent walks. The proposed hyper-WGC can be framed in an end-to-end neural network with high-efficient running speed even on those large-scale graphs.

We summarize our contributions from three-fold:

- We propose random hyper-walk to describe local topology structure of graph, which can efficiently mitigate the problem of exponentially-explosive sampling times occurred in the original random walk.
- We design to project hyper-walks into the grid-shape space and then introduce 2-D convolution to describe the uncertainty of latent features, which makes the convolution operation on graph more efficient and flexible like on images, and well support batch-process.
- We experimentally validate the efficiency and effectiveness of our proposed hyper-WGC, which has high-efficient computation speed, and comparable or even better performance when compared with those baseline GCNs.

2   Related Work

In this section, we will introduce some previous works which are related with our work. In conclusion there are semi-supervised graph learning, graph convolution neural networks and random walk there parts.

2.1   Semi-supervised Graph Learning

Among the various graph related tasks, semi-supervised graph learning has achieved increasing attention recently, and various approaches have been proposed to deal with these problems, including explicit graph Laplacian regularization [4,14,39,40] and graph embedding methods [1,25,26,32,37]. The task of semi-supervised node classification is to learn a model of associating data and labels on partially labels nodes, and to enable the model to obtain the best generalization ability in label prediction of unlabeled nodes. According to whether the data to be predicted can be known from the model in training stage, it can be divided into transductive learning [7] and inductive learning [20]. For transductive learning, the data to be predicted is the unlabeled data in training stage. While for inductive learning, the data needs to be predicted is not access to model when training, and the data of the model may be an "open world".

2.2   Graph Convolutional Neural Networks

With the rapid development of deep learning, more and more graph convolutional neural network models [13, 22, 31, 36] are proposed to deal with the irregular data structure of graphs. Compared with regular convolutional neural networks on structured data, there is a challenge since each node's neighborhood size is varied in graphs while the regular convolutional operation requires fixed local neighborhood. To address this problem, the graph convolutional neural networks fall into two categories, spectral-based convolution and spatial-based convolution. Spectral-based filtering method was first proposed by Bruna et al. [6]. It defines the filter operators in spectral domain, and then implement a series of convolution operations through the Laplace decomposition of graphs. Because the spectrum filter includes the process of matrix eigenvalue decomposition, the computational complexity is generally high, especially for graphs with large number of nodes. To alleviate the computation burden, Defferrard et al. [9] proposed a local spectral filtering method, which approximated the frequency responses as Chebyshev polynomial. Spatial-based filtering method simulates the image processing approach of regular convolutional neural networks, it employs convolution operator based on node's spatial relations. The general approach of spatial convolution is to construct the regular neighborhood of nodes through sampling (discard part of nodes if neighbors number exceeds, repeat part of nodes if neighbors number is insufficient), and then carry out convolution operation with the convolution kernel of rules.

2.3   Random Walk

Random walk is an effective method to get graph embedding. It is especially useful in the situation that the graph is partial visible or the graph is too large to measure in its entirety. Graph is composed of nodes and the connection between nodes, select the start nodes, and execute random walk with some strategies to get walk path. The commonly used random walk strategies generally include truncated random walk [24, 25, 38] and second-order random walk [1]. Analogous to tasks in natural language processing, all the nodes in graph constitute a dictionary, walk path is regarded as a sentence, and the node in the path is regarded as word. Graph embedding can be learned by adopting Continuous Bag-Of-Words (CBOW) model [27] or Skip-gram model [21]. Specifically, the CBOW model uses context to predict the central node embedding, while the Skip-gram model predict the context nodes based on the central node embedding.

3   Hyper-WGC

In this section, we will introduce our hyper-WGC in detail. We first define the notations used in this paper and overview the entire architecture of hyper-WGC, then introduce the main modules of hyper-WGC, including random hyper-walk and gridding.

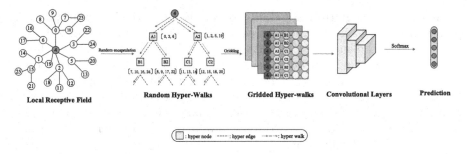

Fig. 1. The framework of our proposed hyper-WGC, the introduction can be find in Sect. 3.3

3.1   Notations

We use $\mathcal{G} = \{\mathcal{V}, \mathcal{E}, \mathbf{X}\}$ to represent a graph, where $\mathcal{V}$ denotes the set of $|\mathcal{V}| = N$ nodes, and $\mathcal{E}$ is the set of $|\mathcal{E}| = e$ edges. Each node is associated with a d-dimension signal/feature vector, so the signals of graph $\mathcal{G}$ form a matrix $\mathbf{X} \in \mathbb{R}^{N \times d} = [\mathbf{x}_1^\mathsf{T}; \cdots ; \mathbf{x}_N^\mathsf{T}]$ where $\mathbf{x}_i$ is the signal vector of the i-th node, and d is the signal dimension. For the semi-supervised node classification, the expected output is a label matrix $\mathbf{Y} \in \mathbb{R}^{N \times c}$ in which c is the total class number. To describe the adjacent relationship among nodes, the adjacency matrix is defined as $\mathbf{A} \in \mathbb{R}^{N \times N}$ where the element $A^{(i,j)}$ located at the i-th row and j-th column indicates the connection weight between the i-th and j-th nodes. In random hyper-walk, we use L to represent the maximum walk steps, T for the sampling times from each starting nodes, $\widetilde{m}$ for the maximum number of hyper-edges for every hyper-node. The average quantity of node degrees is denoted by m. Besides, in convolutional layers, the 2-D kernel size of convolutional filters is denoted as $k_1 \times k_2$.

3.2   Overview

The overall network framework is shown in Fig. 1, where the input is graph-structured data. To illustrate the convolution process, we take the corresponding local subgraph (i.e., local receptive field) around one node as an example. To capture the local structures, the proposed random hyper-walk (in Sect. 3.3) is used to sample hyper-walks through the revision of random walk. The hyper-walks are generated by randomly traversing along those hyper-nodes and hyper-edges, which are encapsulated after random partition. Intuitively, the random hyper-walk models the adjacent nodes of one precursor vertex as a m-tree by randomly dividing these neighbors into m clusters. For each cluster, node and edge combinations are further used to form hyper-node and hyper-edge. Through random division and efficient aggregation, the random hyper-walk could effectively mitigate the problem of exponentially-explosive increase of sampled walks incurred in the original random walk, as sufficient sampling could well guarantee to cover graph structures. Next, the sampled hyper-walks are adaptively gridded into an ordered space through the computation of correlation to the first principal component of hyper-walks, please refer to Sect. 3.4. The gridding hyper-walks are spanned to a 2-D plane of $T \times L$, which thus favors the conventional convolution operations. If stacking multi-dimensional signals, the gridded representation of local subgraph is a 3-D tensor of $d \times T \times L$. Thus, the high-efficient and powerful CNNs run on images can be extended for this case to encode the correlation of within-walk adjacencies and cross adjacent walks. Finally, the output features of convolutional layer are passed through a fully connected layer and a softmax function for node classification.

3.3   Hyperwalks

The random sampling strategy is introduced to characterize the topology structure of local receptive fields. There are two critical problems need to be solved: i) random sampling should well preserve topology property of original graph, and ii) sampling times should be as few as possible for high-efficient computation as well as low-memory requirement. The first condition dedicates to the accuracy of representation, while the second one focuses on the efficiency of learning. Random walk can well satisfy the first condition under the sufficient samplings, but the sampling complexity heavily depends on node degrees during traversal on graph. To address this problem, we extend the original random walk to random hyper-walk by leveraging the powerful topology preservation ability of random walk and the high-efficiency of random aggregation. During random walking, concretely, the connection edges (w.r.t. adjacent nodes) of each node are randomly partitioned into (less than) $\widetilde{m}$ clusters. Then we encapsulate each cluster consisting of some edges and the corresponding nodes into one hyper-edge and corresponding hyper-node. The encapsulation may be taken from those conventional aggregation strategies (e.g., the sum operation). Therefore, the constructed random-walk (i.e, random hyper-walk) actually performs on a $\widetilde{m}$-tree, whose nodes/edges correspond to hyper-nodes/hyper-edges. As the maximum selection number of one-hop walk at each node is constrained to m, the combinatorial number of walks is $\widetilde{m}^t$ for walk length t. In practical, $\widetilde{m} = 2$ can work well, i.e., $\widetilde{m} \ll m$. It's worth noting that the aggregation operation in the conventional GCNs is just a specific case of our random hyper-walk when $\widetilde{m} = 1$. This means that our random hyper-walk can efficiently mitigate the problem of exponentially-explosive increase of walks incurred in the original random-walk.

3.4   Gridding

One problem of the classic random walk is the irregularity along different paths caused by random sampling, which makes it rather challenging to exploit the underlying local correlation across adjacent walks. To solve this problem, we perform gridding on the output features of random hyper-walk to project them into an ordered space. Based on this operation, the gridding hyper-walks are spanned to a 2-D plane based on two axes, i.e. T and L, representing sampling times and the numbers of walk step, respectively. The operation of gridding brings one notable benefit that the high-efficient and powerful CNNs run on images can be extended for the random hyper-walk to jointly encode the correlation of within-walk adjacencies and cross adjacent walks. And for multi-dimensional signals, the gridded representation of local subgraph may be a 3-D tensor of $d \times T \times L$, which is also suitable to apply CNN. To adaptively capture the correlation among random paths, we conduct gridding from the perspective of distribution and consider each sampled path based on its correlation to the first principal component of hyper-walks. For the hyper-walk on one node with the representation denoted as $\mathcal{D} \in \mathbb{R}^{d \times T \times L}$, we first split it into a set of path samples denoted as $\{\mathbf{d}_1, \cdots, \mathbf{d}_T\}$ along the sampling time axis T, where $\mathbf{d}_i \in \mathbb{R}^{(d \times L)}$ is the vectorized representation of the i-th path sample. For gridding, the clustering center of path samples is first calculated as:

$$\mathbf{d}_c = \frac{1}{T} \sum_{i=1}^{T} \mathbf{d}_i. \tag{1}$$

Then, the correlation between the i-th path sample and the cluster centre is defined as follows:

$$S_i = \frac{\mathbf{d}_i^T \mathbf{d}_c}{\|\mathbf{d}_i\| \cdot \|\mathbf{d}_c\|} \tag{2}$$

Then, the hyper-walk of each node is gridded based on its corresponding correlation value related to the cluster center.

4   Experiments

In this section, we comprehensively evaluate the effectiveness of our method on four widely used public datasets named Cora, Citeseer, Pubmed [30] and Nell [37]. We first briefly introduce these datasets, then report our experimental results on them and compare the performances with those state-of-the-art methods. Finally, we conduct ablation study to dissect the proposed model.

4.1   Datasets

Four public graph-structured datasets are employed to evaluate our proposed method, including three citation network datasets (i.e., Cora, Citeseer, Pubmed) and one knowledge graph dataset (i.e., Nell). For the three citation networks, we selected 20 samples for each category as the training set, 500 samples as the validation set, and 1000 samples as the testing set. For Nell dataset, we split the training \ validation \ testing by 500 \ 500 \ 1000 randomly. The overall information about these four datasets is listed in Table 1.

4.2   Baseline Methods

To verify the superiority of our proposed hyper-WGC model, various state-of-the-art baseline methods are involved for performance comparison, which including **DeepWalk** [25], **Planetoid** [37], **Chebyshev** [9], **GCN** [14], **GAT** [33] and

Table 1. Graph datasets information

Dataset	Nodes	Edges	Degrees	Features	Labels
Cora	2,708	5,429	4	1,433	7
Citeseer	3,327	4,732	3	3,703	6
Pubmed	19,717	44,338	5	500	3
NELL	65,755	266,144	4	61,278	210

Table 2. Performances of graph node classification, compared with DeepWalk, Planetoid, Chebyshev, GCN, GAT and DGCN methods

Method	Cora	Citeseer	Pubmed	NELL
DeepWalk [25]	67.2%	43.2%	65.3%	58.1%
Planetoid [37]	75.7%	64.7%	77.2%	61.9%
Chebyshev [9]	81.2%	69.8%	74.4%	–
GCN [14]	81.4%	70.5%	79.0%	66.0%
GAT [33]	**83.0%**	72.5%	79.0%	–
DGCN [41]	82.5%	**72.6%**	79.3%	74.9%
Hyper-WGC	82.9%	71.7%	**81.4%**	**79.5%**

DGCN [41]. Basically, the results of these baseline methods are obtained either according to their reported performances in previously literatures, or through conducting the experiments based on their released public codes. For those baseline methods of our implementation, sophisticated hyper-parameters fine-grained tuning are performed to report their performances.

4.3 Experiment Setting

The parameters of our hyper-WGC model are traversed in certain ranges and finally set when obtaining the best performance on the validation sets. For the basic architecture of the hyper-WGC model, in the hyper-walk process, the number of walks, denoted as T, is set to 15, and the hyper-walk length L is 5. For the two convolutional layers, the sizes of convolution kernels are set to 5×3. During the training process, we run the model for 500 epochs with the learning rate of 0.01 and dropout rate of 0.5 for tuning the network parameters.

4.4 Experiment Results

The experimental results of our proposed hyper-WGC on the three citation datasets (Cora, Citeseer and Pubmed) and one large-scale dataset of knowledge graph (NELL) are reported in Table 2. These performances are also compared with various state-of-the-art methods, where the metric of accuracy is employed

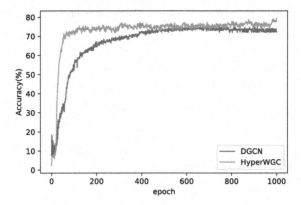

Fig. 2. The convergence on Nell datasets, compared with DGCN.

for quantitative evaluation of the semi-supervised node classification. Our hyper-WGC obtains the best results on Pubmed and NELL datasets (there are 2.1% gain on Pubmed, and 4.6% gain on NELL), and achieves the competitive performances on Cora and Citerseer datasets. Besides the competitive performance, it should be especially noticed that our model is more advantageous in computation efficiency comparing with all those baseline methods.

We record the time costs of our hyper-WGC for running one epoch on Cora and Pubmed datasets in Table 3, and compare them with GAT, DGCN and GCN. For the smallest dataset Cora, GAT takes about 7 s per epoch while its sparse version takes 1 s, and DGCN takes about 0.5 s per epoch. The time consumed by our hyper-WGC is 0.05 s, which is much less than those of GAT and DGCN while almost the same as GCN. However, on the large graph Pubmed (19,717 nodes), our hyper-WGC takes about 0.04 s per epoch, and is the fastest comparing with the sparse GAT of 2.5 s per epoch, DGCN of 3.2 s, and GCN of 0.6 s.

The convergence of our hyper-WGC on the Nell datasets is shown in Fig. 2, and is compared with that of DGCN which also achieves considerable performances. Both hyper-WGC and DGCN are trained 1000 epochs on NELL dataset. According to Fig. 2, our hyper-WGC can converge faster and meantime obtain better performances. In terms of running time and accuracy comparisons, our hyper-WGC takes about 6 min with the accuracy of 79.5%. In contrast, DGCN takes about 2.8 h which are 29.2 times as hyper-WGC, while obtains the accuracy of 74.9% which is about 5% lower.

4.5 Ablation Study and Parameter Sensitivity

As the proposed hyper-WGC achieves promising performance with high computational efficiency, it is interesting for us to dissect the model to evaluate the contribution of hyper walks. To verify the superiority of the proposed hyper-walk over random walk, we simply replace the hyper-walks unit with random-walks

Table 3. Each epoch time cost on Cora and Pubmed, compared with GAT, DGCN and GCN.

Method	Cora	Pubmed
GAT	7 s	10 s
GAT_sparse	1 s	2.5 s
DGCN	0.5 s	3.2 s
GCN	0.05 s	0.6 s
Hyper-WGC	**0.05 s**	**0.04 s**

Table 4. Comparison between hyper-walk and random-walk.

Dataset	Random-walk	Hyper-walk
Cora	81.8%	**82.5%**
Citeseer	71.0%	**71.5%**
Pubmed	79.9%	**81.4%**
NELL	77.9%	**79.5%**

on the original graph, and test the performance on the four public datasets. The results are shown in Table 4.

Hyper-walk outperforms classic random walk and promotes the node classification performance. On all the four evaluated datasets, the classification accuracies of our hyper-walk are higher than those of random walk. The performances gain verifies the effectiveness of our hyper-walk, which constructs coarsening graph meanwhile avoids the explosive growth of walk paths increasing with walk steps.

5   Conclusion

In this paper, we proposed Hyper-Walk Gridded Convolution networks for graph semi-supervised learning. We design the hyper-walks for random walk, which effectively avoids the bad situation that the number of possible walk paths explodes exponentially as the path length increases, and can cover the whole neighborhood by hyper-node. In order to maintain the permutation invariance of the input hyper-walks belong to same node of each epoch, we sorted them by projection to mean vector and constructed a grid-like feature map for 2-D convolution. Hyper-WGC learns the aggregation pattern of node topological neighborhood in an inductive way, which can be easily extended to the inference problem of unknown nodes. And hyper-WGC can process large scale graphs fast with tensor graph structure and consumes less memory. Experiments on a variety of public datasets illustrate the effectiveness of our method for solving classification task.

References

1. Grover, A., Leskovec, J.: node2vec: scalable feature learning for networks (2016)
2. Atwood, J., Towsley, D.: Diffusion-convolutional neural networks. In: Advances in Neural Information Processing Systems, pp. 1993–2001 (2016)
3. Battaglia, P.W., et al.: Relational inductive biases, deep learning, and graph networks. arXiv preprint arXiv:1806.01261 (2018)

4. Belkin, M., Niyogi, P.: Laplacian eigenmaps and spectral techniques for embedding and clustering. In: Advances in Neural Information Processing Systems, pp. 585–591 (2002)
5. Borgwardt, K.M., Kriegel, H.P., Vishwanathan, S., Schraudolph, N.N.: Graph kernels for disease outcome prediction from protein-protein interaction networks. In: Biocomputing 2007, pp. 4–15. World Scientific (2007)
6. Bruna, J., Zaremba, W., Szlam, A., LeCun, Y.: Spectral networks and locally connected networks on graphs. arXiv preprint arXiv:1312.6203 (2013)
7. Ceci, M., Appice, A., Barile, N., Malerba, D.: Transductive learning from relational data. In: Perner, P. (ed.) MLDM 2007. LNCS (LNAI), vol. 4571, pp. 324–338. Springer, Heidelberg (2007). https://doi.org/10.1007/978-3-540-73499-4_25
8. Dai, H., Kozareva, Z., Dai, B., Smola, A., Song, L.: Learning steady-states of iterative algorithms over graphs. In: International Conference on Machine Learning, pp. 1114–1122 (2018)
9. Defferrard, M., Bresson, X., Vandergheynst, P.: Convolutional neural networks on graphs with fast localized spectral filtering. In: Advances in Neural Information Processing Systems, pp. 3844–3852 (2016)
10. Franco, S., Marco, G., Ah Chung, T., Markus, H., Gabriele, M.: The graph neural network model. IEEE Trans. Neural Netw. 20(1), 61 (2009)
11. Hamilton, W.L., Ying, R., Leskovec, J.: Inductive representation learning on large graphs (2017)
12. Hinton, G., et al.: Deep neural networks for acoustic modeling in speech recognition. IEEE Sig. Process. Mag. 29, 82–97 (2012)
13. Kashima, H., Tsuda, K., Inokuchi, A.: Marginalized kernels between labeled graphs. In: Proceedings of the 20th International Conference on Machine Learning (ICML-2003), pp. 321–328 (2003)
14. Kipf, T.N., Welling, M.: Semi-supervised classification with graph convolutional networks (2017)
15. Kleinberg, J.M., Kumar, R., Raghavan, P., Rajagopalan, S., Tomkins, A.S.: The web as a graph: measurements, models, and methods. In: Asano, T., Imai, H., Lee, D.T., Nakano, S., Tokuyama, T. (eds.) COCOON 1999. LNCS, vol. 1627, pp. 1–17. Springer, Heidelberg (1999). https://doi.org/10.1007/3-540-48686-0_1
16. LeCun, Y., Bottou, L., Bengio, Y., Haffner, P., et al.: Gradient-based learning applied to document recognition. Proc. IEEE 86(11), 2278–2324 (1998)
17. Li, R., Wang, S., Zhu, F., Huang, J.: Adaptive graph convolutional neural networks. In: Thirty-Second AAAI Conference on Artificial Intelligence (2018)
18. Li, Y., Tarlow, D., Brockschmidt, M., Zemel, R.: Gated graph sequence neural networks. arXiv preprint arXiv:1511.05493 (2015)
19. Luong, M.T., Pham, H., Manning, C.D.: Effective approaches to attention-based neural machine translation. arXiv preprint arXiv:1508.04025 (2015)
20. Michalski, R.S.: A theory and methodology of inductive learning. In: Michalski, R.S., Carbonell, J.G., Mitchell, T.M. (eds.) Machine Learning. SYMBOLIC, pp. 83–134. Springer, Heidelberg (1983). https://doi.org/10.1007/978-3-662-12405-5_4
21. Mikolov, T., Sutskever, I., Chen, K., Corrado, G.S., Dean, J.: Distributed representations of words and phrases and their compositionality. In: Advances in Neural Information Processing Systems, pp. 3111–3119 (2013)
22. Morris, C., Kersting, K., Mutzel, P.: Glocalized Weisfeiler-Lehman graph kernels: global-local feature maps of graphs. In: 2017 IEEE International Conference on Data Mining (ICDM), pp. 327–336. IEEE (2017)
23. Orsini, F., Baracchi, D., Frasconi, P.: Shift aggregate extract networks. Front. Robot. AI 5, 42 (2018)

24. Pan, S., Wu, J., Zhu, X., Zhang, C., Wang, Y.: Tri-party deep network representation. Network **11**(9), 12 (2016)
25. Perozzi, B., Al-Rfou, R., Skiena, S.: DeepWalk: online learning of social representations. In: Proceedings of the 20th ACM SIGKDD International Conference on Knowledge Discovery and Data Mining, pp. 701–710. ACM (2014)
26. Perozzi, B., Kulkarni, V., Skiena, S.: Walklets: multiscale graph embeddings for interpretable network classification. arXiv preprint arXiv:1605.02115 (2016)
27. Qiu, L., Cao, Y., Nie, Z., Yu, Y., Rui, Y.: Learning word representation considering proximity and ambiguity. In: Twenty-Eighth AAAI Conference on Artificial Intelligence (2014)
28. Redmon, J., Divvala, S., Girshick, R., Farhadi, A.: You only look once: unified, real-time object detection. In: Proceedings of the IEEE Conference on Computer Vision and Pattern Recognition, pp. 779–788 (2016)
29. Scarselli, F., Gori, M., Tsoi, A.C., Hagenbuchner, M., Monfardini, G.: The graph neural network model. IEEE Trans. Neural Netw. **20**(1), 61–80 (2008)
30. Sen, P., Namata, G., Bilgic, M., Getoor, L., Galligher, B., Eliassi-Rad, T.: Collective classification in network data. AI Mag. **29**(3), 93–93 (2008)
31. Shervashidze, N., Vishwanathan, S., Petri, T., Mehlhorn, K., Borgwardt, K.: Efficient graphlet kernels for large graph comparison. In: Artificial Intelligence and Statistics, pp. 488–495 (2009)
32. Tang, J., Qu, M., Wang, M., Zhang, M., Yan, J., Mei, Q.: LINE: large-scale information network embedding. In: Proceedings of the 24th International Conference on World Wide Web, pp. 1067–1077. International World Wide Web Conferences Steering Committee (2015)
33. Veličković, P., Cucurull, G., Casanova, A., Romero, A., Liò, P., Bengio, Y.: Graph attention networks. In: International Conference on Learning Representations (2018). https://openreview.net/forum?id=rJXMpikCZ. Accepted as poster
34. Xu, D., Zhu, Y., Choy, C.B., Fei-Fei, L.: Scene graph generation by iterative message passing. In: Proceedings of the IEEE Conference on Computer Vision and Pattern Recognition, pp. 5410–5419 (2017)
35. Xu, K., Hu, W., Leskovec, J., Jegelka, S.: How powerful are graph neural networks? arXiv preprint arXiv:1810.00826 (2018)
36. Yanardag, P., Vishwanathan, S.: Deep graph kernels. In: Proceedings of the 21th ACM SIGKDD International Conference on Knowledge Discovery and Data Mining, pp. 1365–1374. ACM (2015)
37. Yang, Z., Cohen, W.W., Salakhutdinov, R.: Revisiting semi-supervised learning with graph embeddings. arXiv preprint arXiv:1603.08861 (2016)
38. Zhang, H., Shang, X., Luan, H., Wang, M., Chua, T.S.: Learning from collective intelligence: feature learning using social images and tags. ACM Trans. Multimedia Comput. Commun. Appl. (TOMM) **13**(1) (2017). Article no. 1
39. Zhou, D., Bousquet, O., Lal, T.N., Weston, J., Schölkopf, B.: Learning with local and global consistency. In: Advances in Neural Information Processing Systems, pp. 321–328 (2004)
40. Zhu, X., Ghahramani, Z., Lafferty, J.D.: Semi-supervised learning using gaussian fields and harmonic functions. In: Proceedings of the 20th International Conference on Machine Learning (ICML-2003), pp. 912–919 (2003)
41. Zhuang, C., Ma, Q.: Dual graph convolutional networks for graph-based semi-supervised classification. In: Proceedings of the 2018 World Wide Web Conference, pp. 499–508. International World Wide Web Conferences Steering Committee (2018)

UDenseNet: A Universal Dense Convolutional Network for Image Recognition

Liang Wang[1]($\boxtimes$), Changshuang Zhao[1], Ling Shao[2], and Yihong Wu[3]

[1] Faculty of Information Technology, Beijing University of Technology, Beijing 100124, China
wangliang@bjut.edu.cn
[2] Inception Institute of Artificial Intelligence, Abu Dhabi, UAE
[3] National Laboratory of Pattern Recognition, Institute of Automation, Chinese Academy of Sciences, Beijing 100080, China

Abstract. Densely connected convolutional networks (DenseNet) have reached unprecedented parameter-performance efficiencies and alleviated problems of vanishing gradients by concatenating each layer to every other layer. However, with the increase in network depth, the cross-channel interaction of dense blocks has become increasingly complex. Hence, it is now more difficult to optimize networks. Moreover, the way combining features in DenseNet restricts its flexibility and scalability in learning more expressive combination strategies. In this study, we aim to answer the question of how to simultaneously ensure the benefits of feature reuse, reduce the complexity of cross-channel interactions, and increase the flexibility of the network. Hence, the components of DenseNet are refined and then used as a basis to develop a universal densely connected convolutional network (UDenseNet). Based on the proposed architecture, the impact of different component configurations on the network performance is empirically analyzed to determine the optimal architectural configuration. Extensive experiments are conducted to validate the proposed UDenseNet on benchmark datasets (CIFAR, SVHN and ImageNet). Results show that, compared to most other methods, the proposed UDenseNet can significantly improve performance in image recognition tasks.

Keywords: Deep learning · Neural networks · Dense connection · Image recognition

1 Introduction

Deep convolutional networks have achieved promising results in many visual recognition tasks [1–3], with significantly improved feature representations. High-level semantic information is known to play a crucial role in this. One simple and intuitive way to extract more high-level information is to increase the network depth. Residual network (ResNets) [4] trains a much deeper network architecture by leveraging the concept of

This work was partially supported by the National Natural Science Foundation of China under grant numbers of 61772050 and 61836015.

shortcut connections. However, when the depth exceeds 1000 layers, the performance of ResNets reaches saturation owing to information loss caused by the simple summation-based feature aggregation. This occurs because the information carried by prior feature maps becomes corrupted or washed out by later features.

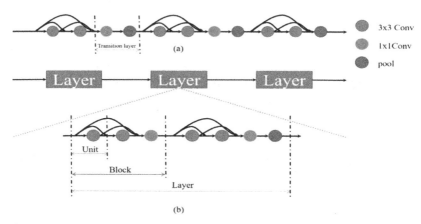

Fig. 1. Comparison of network architecture of (a) DenseNet and (b) the proposed UDenseNet.

To resolve this problem faced by ResNets, the densely connected convolutional network (DenseNet) [5] was proposed. Dense connections allow each convolutional layer to connect to every other layer in a feed-forward way. Then, a series of concatenations is used to integrate semantic information from different layers into one entity as the final input. The better parameter-performance efficiency of DenseNet over ResNets may be due to aggregation style, which combines features via direct concatenation, while preserving their original form. However, concatenation increases the complexity of cross-channel interactions and the difficulty of optimization, respectively. Moreover, the way DenseNet combines features restricts its flexibility and scalability to learn more expressive combination strategies.

In this study, we revisit DenseNet and propose a universal densely connected convolutional network (UDenseNet) to extend network flexibility and versatility, while preserving the efficiency of feature reuse. As shown in Fig. 1, unlike DenseNet, the proposed UDenseNet consists of three main components: *unit*, *block*, and *layer*. Hierarchically, a *unit* is not only the most fundamental part of the network but also the minimal entity of dense connections. A *block* consists of a series of units followed by a 1 × 1 convolution, which can produce cross-channel interactions. Finally, a *layer* comprises several layers of *blocks*, followed by a 2 × 2 average pooling layer, which fulfils the task of down-sampling. The entire network resembles a building made of Lego bricks; it is built step-by-step from the most fundamental *unit*. The feature maps produced by each *block* have the same size as the input. Additionally, the neuron of a *layer* encodes higher-level semantics by processing larger receptive fields with the pooling layers. The three components perform distinct roles and combine for desirable outcomes. The difference between the proposed UDenseNet and DenseNet is shown in Fig. 1. The proposed UDenseNet (Fig. 1(b)) is an extension of DenseNet (Fig. 1(a)), which is a combination of multiple *units*, *blocks*, and *layers*. This hierarchy significantly expands the flexibility of the network's construction. It is worth noting that, unlike DenseNet, the last layer of UDenseNet has a 1 × 1 Conv. The proposed UDenseNet is evaluated on several benchmark datasets (CIFAR [6], SVHN [7], and ImageNet [8]) for image recognition and significantly outperforms the state-of-the-art methods on most.

The main contributions of this paper can be summarized as follows:

- A universal densely connected convolutional network is proposed, which can reasonably extend network flexibility and versatility, while preserving efficient feature reuse.
- The proposed UDenseNet architecture enhances the performance of dense connections, enabling it to achieve high performance and dramatically improve accuracy and effectiveness in comparison with existing deep convolutional networks.
- To the best of our knowledge, this is the first time that an optimal architectural configuration is provided for a densely connected convolutional network. This was achieved by fixing the total number of network layers and performing extensive experiments with varying number of network components.

The remainder of this paper is organized as follows. Section 2 reviews related works. In Sect. 3, the proposed model and its components are illustrated in more detail. Extensive experiments are reported in Sect. 4 and Sect. 5 concludes the paper.

2 Related Works

Since AlexNet [1] won the 2012 ImageNet Challenge [8], deep convolutional networks have become an important machine learning method in computer vision. With the development of hardware and the emergence of large-scale datasets, it is now possible to train very deep neural networks. In the last few years, the number of network layers has gradually increased. From the initial LeNet5 [9] of only 5 layers, to the later VGG [10] and Inception [11] of dozens of layers as well as the more recent highway networks [12], ResNets [4] and DenseNet [5] which have hundreds of layers, the performance of deep convolutional networks has steadily and dramatically improved for many image recognition tasks. This reveals that network depth is crucial. However, it does not mean that learning better networks is as easy as simply adding more layers. One reason for this is the notorious problems of vanishing/exploding gradients [13], which hinders convergence from the start. Furthermore, with increasing network depth, difficulties with feature reuse have been highlighted, thereby resulting in accuracy saturation. Many recent publications have addressed related issues [13, 14]. In the following paragraphs, we review several works that are closely related to this present study from micro and macro perspectives.

To alleviate the problems of deep convolutional networks, earlier works adopted better initialization schemes. For example, [13] proposed that a properly scaled uniform distribution should be adopted for initialization. Unfortunately, this initialization scheme is only valid for linear activations, whereas ReLU and PReLU are nonlinear. Because of this dilemma, [14] proposed a better, more theoretically sound initialization by considering ReLU/PReLU, and this enabled very deep models to converge where [13] method failed. A recently proposed, notable contribution for training extremely deep networks is BN [15], which can standardize each mini-batch hidden layer's mean and variance. It not only decreases the vanishing gradients problem, but also yields a strong regularizing effect. However, dataset distributions are generally uneven, especially for a mini-batch of data taken from a dataset. In these situations, batch normalization fails to adapt to some data.

On the other hand, some works have focused on the macro design of the network structure. Most of them improved information flow during forward and backward propagation by introducing extra skip connections. Typical works include highway networks [12], ResNets [4], and many other residual networks [16–18]. Highway networks [12] introduce gating units to regulate the information flow of the networks, thereby allowing information to propagate unimpeded on information highways across several layers. Unlike highway networks, ResNets [4] combine features through direct summation defined by identity shortcut connections before features are passed into a layer. This is performed instead of the gated summation defined by shortcut connections with the gating function. This simplification significantly improves training efficiency, simplicity, and scalability. Instead of focusing on the depth, wide residual networks [17] focus on the width of the network. [18] analyses the success of highway networks and ResNets, which may owe to the dropout mechanism applied on network layers during training. This makes it possible that the resulting networks are short during training but deep during tests. In summary, these findings enable information flow to bypass some dropped layers via skip connections. Afterward, DenseNet [5] was proposed by building shorter paths from early layers to later layers, which concatenates all layers together in a feed-forward way. This has allowed DenseNet to attain high parameter-performance efficiency. Since its original construction, several extensions of DenseNet have been proposed [19, 20]. The notion of local dense connectivity was introduced in [19], which suggests that less connectivity can achieve more efficient feature reuse and higher accuracy in dense architectures, thereby allowing for an increased growth rate at a fixed network capacity. The closest study to ours is [20], which explores a key architectural aspect of densely connected convolutional networks, dense feature aggregation, including the summing scheme of ResNets and concatenating scheme of DenseNet. However, it mainly focused on the skip layer connections instead of the entire architecture of densely connected convolutional networks.

In this paper, we separate the fully-dense connectivity of dense block by introducing 1×1 Conv and redefine the components of densely connected convolutional network. A universal densely connected convolutional network is proposed. Based on this, the impact on network performance of different component configurations is empirically analyzed to determine the optimal architectural configuration. To the best of our knowledge, this is the first study that provides an optimal configuration for the densely connected convolutional network architecture, when the total number of layers, i.e., the depth, is fixed.

3   Universal Densely Connected Convolutional Network

In DenseNet, each layer that is densely connected by concatenation receives the feature maps of all previous layers. In contrast to common connection methods, dense connections ensure maximum information flow between network layers, which is beneficial for information transmission in the network. Consequently, the feature maps of the ith layer can be represented by the following formula:

$$x_i = H_i\big([x_0, x_1, \cdots, x_{i-1}]\big) \tag{1}$$

where $x_j (0 \leq j \leq i)$ is the output of the jth layer, $[\cdot]$ refers to the concatenation of the feature maps, and $H_i (\cdot)$ denotes the non-linear transformation function corresponding to the ith layer. In [5], DenseNet consists of sequentially stacked dense blocks, as shown in Fig. 1(a). A detailed description is as follows. DenseNet is divided into three dense blocks, each of which has an equal number of layers. There is a transition layer between dense blocks to reduce the number of accumulated channels per concatenation while one 2×2 average pooling operation is used for down-sampling to increase the size of the network's receptive field.

In the remaining parts of this section, we introduce the network architecture of UDenseNet. A schematic illustration is shown in Fig. 1(b) to facilitate an understanding of the network architecture. Each component of the network is now described.

3.1   Unit

A *unit* refers to the minimal dense connection in the network, which connects the input with its output by concatenation to ensure the benefits of feature reuse (see Fig. 1(b)). Following DenseNet [5], two types of *units* are used in UDenseNet:

Basic - BN and ReLU are followed by one 3×3 convolution: BN-ReLU-3 $\times$ 3 Conv, with which the network is denoted as UDenseNet.

Bottleneck - one 1×1 convolution is added before the 3×3 convolution of the **Basic** *unit* to reduce the feature dimension: BN-ReLU-1 $\times$ 1 Conv-BN-ReLU-3 $\times$ 3 Conv, with which the networks is denoted as UDenseNet-B.

As in [5], the 3×3 convolution kernel is adopted here without considering other convolutional kernels with different sizes.

3.2   Block

Skip connections allow useful features to be transferred from shallower layers to deeper layers, where each layer is directly supervised by the final output layer. DenseNet implements skip connections by concatenating outputs of all previous layers. However, a potential drawback is that aggregation by concatenation results in the isolation between feature maps. Therefore, to learn complex cross channel interactions, an additional convolutional operation with a kernel size of 1×1 is added before down-sampling in transition layers. Thus, the 1×1 Conv is a necessary component of a *block*. In an ablation study, we performed extensive experiments to show the effect of 1×1 Conv, as described in Sect. 4.2. In UDenseNet, the 1×1 Conv in the transition layer in the original DenseNet was moved to the end of the *block*. Then, we redefined the concept of the *block*, that is, a group of dense connections ending with one 1×1 Conv form the new *block*. Note that the 1×1 Conv is connected in a traditional way rather than as a dense connection. Further, a *unit* factor *u*, which is the number of *units* (including both **Basic** and **Bottleneck**) in each *block*, was also introduced.

3.3 Layer

Inspired by residual networks, in which multiple residual blocks process feature maps of the same scale, we took advantage of a few dense *blocks* for this. The down-sampling layer is essential for changing the size of feature maps in the network. As in [5], the pooling operation was also used. Here, we introduced the concept of a *layer*, which consists of several serially connected *blocks* followed by one 2×2 pooling layer (see Fig. 1(b)). Additionally, two factors, *block* factor *b* and *layer* factor *l*, were also introduced, where *b* is the number of *blocks* in each *layer* and *l* is the number of *layers* in UDenseNet. From the perspective of UDenseNet, the original densely connected convolutional network (i.e., 40-layer DenseNet [5]) has 3 *layers*, where each *layer* has 1 *block*, and each *block* has 12 *units*, but the last *layer* has no 1×1 Conv.

3.4 The General Expression and Structure

Various components of the densely connected convolutional network are refined above. In this section, we will present a concrete mathematical expression that indicates the relationship between the total number of network layers and the number of components. Additionally, to express the network architecture, we present a description to clarify the specific general structure of the network.

A list is used to express an N-layer densely connected network, as follows:

$$[N(u_1, b_1)(u_2, b_2) \cdots (u_l, b_l)] \tag{2}$$

where *l* refers to the number of *layers* in the network. Each *layer* is in the form of parentheses with two elements, where the first element, i.e., $u_i (1 \leqslant i \leqslant l)$, is the number of *units* in each *block*, and the second element, i.e., $b_j (1 \leqslant j \leqslant l)$, is the number of *blocks* within each *layer*. The relationship between the total number of network *layers* and the number of *units* and *blocks* can be represented by the following formula:

$$N = \sum_{i=1}^{l} (\alpha u_i + 1) \times b_i + 2 \tag{3}$$

where the coefficient $\alpha = 1$ for UDenseNet and $\alpha = 2$ for UDenseNet-B.

Several variants of the network structure can be obtained for different *l*, *b*, and *u*, respectively. The above analysis shows that the architecture of UDenseNet more flexible for learning more expressive merge strategies. For example, a UDenseNet version of original DenseNet [5], which is a 40-layer DenseNet, can be described as follows:

$$[40(5, 1)(7, 2)(7, 2)] \tag{4}$$

From Eq. (3), it can be seen that Eq. (4) is not the sole UDenseNet architecture corresponding to the original 40-layer DenseNet. For example, [40(4, 2)(6, 2)(6, 2)] and [40(9, 1)(6, 2)(6, 2)] are also corresponding UDenseNet architectures. This shows that UDenseNet has more flexibility than DenseNet.

Table 1 illustrates the general structure of UDenseNet. It consists of an initial convolution Conv; 3 sequential layers L1, L2, and L3, each of which is followed by average pooling, which is not shown in this table; and the final classification layer, which is also omitted for clarity. In the example shown, the network uses a **Basic** *unit*. As in [5], we also introduced the compression factor r to scale the channel of the 1×1 Conv in the last *block* of one *layer*, and the growth rate k to describe the number of feature maps (or channels) added by per dense connection. A UDenseNet with compression factor r is called UDenseNet-C, and in the following experiments, it is set to $r = 0.5$. When both the bottleneck and compression factor r are used, the corresponding UDenseNet is called UDenseNet-BC. We analyzed the impacts of the *unit*, *block*, and *layer* on the performance of dense connections through experiments. Several modifications of the densely connected network architecture are further reported and compared in the following section of experiments.

Table 1 Structure of universal densely connected convolutional networks. The number of *units* in each *block* is denoted by factor u_i; the parameters k and r are the growth rate and the compression ratio of the network, respectively; and groups of convolutions are shown in brackets, where b_i is the number of *blocks* in each *layer*.

Group	Input size	Output size	Layer type
Conv	32×32	32×32	$(3 \times 3, 2k)$
L1	32×32	16×16	$\begin{pmatrix} (3 \times 3, k) \times u_1 \\ 1 \times 1, r \end{pmatrix} \times b_1$
L2	16×16	8×8	$\begin{pmatrix} (3 \times 3, k) \times u_2 \\ 1 \times 1, r \end{pmatrix} \times b_2$
L3	8×8	1×1	$\begin{pmatrix} (3 \times 3, k) \times u_3 \\ 1 \times 1, r \end{pmatrix} \times b_3$

4 Experiments

4.1 Implementation Details

We empirically validated UDenseNet on a series of benchmark datasets (including CIFAR [6], and SVHN [7]) for image recognition tasks. Comparisons with the state-of-the-art methods were also performed. The main purpose of Subsect. 4.2 is to explore the internal structure of the dense convolutional network, i.e., the relationship between *unit*, *block*, and *layer*, and its impact on network performance, rather than to focus on higher precision. In contrast, Subsect. 4.3 focuses on the high precision. In the experiments, the DenseNet [5] was taken as the reference network. For all datasets, we compared the results of the reference network with those of the proposed UDenseNet.

Similar to [5], for the CIFAR datasets [6], the training and test sets have 50,000 and 10,000 images, respectively, and 5,000 training images were taken as a validation set. A standard data augmentation scheme (mirroring/shifting) was adopted, and a "+" mark after the dataset name denotes this data augmentation in the following tables. For the Street View House Numbers (SVHN) dataset [7], the training set contains 73,257 images and additional 531,131 images, and 6,000 images were used as a validation set. The test set contains 26,302 images. No data augmentation was adopted for this dataset. Each UDenseNet has three dense layers. For the CIFAR dataset, networks did not adopt the dropout, whereas the dropout rate is 0.2 for the SVHN. Further, we also verified the proposed UDenseNet on the ImageNet2012 [8] dataset and compared it with the DenseNet. In the experiments on ImageNet, we used a 121-layer UDenseNet-BC structure. And UDenseNet-BC has four dense layers.

As in [5], all networks utilize stochastic gradient descent (SGD) with a weight decay of 10^{-4} as a learning optimizer and adopt the parameter initialization introduced by [14]. For the CIFAR and SVHN datasets, the batch size of the network is set to 64 and is trained for 4 and 5 epochs, respectively. The initial learning rate is set to 0.1, and is divided by 10 at 50% and 70% of the total number of training epochs. For the ImageNet, model is trained for 90 epochs with a batch size of 256. The initial learning rate of the model is 0.1 and every 30 rounds divided by 10 until 90 epochs. Our implementations were performed in Pytorch [21].

4.2   Trade-Off Between Unit and Block

First, experiments were performed to explore the relationship between unit factor u and block factor b and its impact on network performance. The comparison was performed among networks of equal depths, thus we established networks with different u and b to ensure that the total number of convolutional layers were equal. This means, for instance, that u should increase while b decreases. Results are shown in Table 2, where the total number of convolutional layers of UDenseNet, 38, is fixed, and several networks with different unit factors u and block factors b were trained and tested. Further, results of a UDenseNet with the same depth as the original 40-layer DenseNet and a UDenseNet with similar layer type (12, 1)(12, 1)(12, 1) as the original DenseNet are also shown in Table 2. It can be seen that both significantly outperformed the original DenseNet. Notably, the difference in network architectures makes that UDenseNet and DenseNet unable to have the same depth and similar layer type simultaneously. Considering that UDenseNet outperformed the corresponding DenseNet with the same depth, 38-layer UDenseNet were used here for perform analysis.

As seen in Table 2, [38(5, 2)(5, 2)(5, 2)] and [38(3, 3)(3, 3)(3, 3)] turn out to be the better, whereas [38(11, 1)(11, 1)(11, 1)] and [38(16)(1, 6)(1, 6)] have the poorer performances. This is probably due to the increased difficulty in optimization as a result of the increased number of dense connections in [38(11, 1)(11, 1)(11, 1)]. Similarly, it is speculated that feature extraction may not be sufficient in [38(1, 6)(1, 6)(1, 6)]. Thus, when the depth of the network is fixed, too many or too few units in each block result in poor network performance. This means that the optimal architecture of UDenseNet can be obtained when the unit factor u and block factor b reach the best trade-off. Further, we also discuss the impact of the last layer, with and without the 1×1 convolution, on network performance. Table 2 shows that [41(12, 1)(12, 1)(12, 1)] outperformed the reference network. On CIFAR-10, the error dropped from 5.24% to 5.13%. Following a similar trend, the error dropped from 24.42% to 23.23% on CIFAR-100. Notably, the performance of the proposed UDenseNet with 38 layers exceeded that of the reference network everywhere except for [38(1, 6)(1, 6)(1, 6)]. The number of network layers, meanwhile, was smaller, which increased the compactness of the densely connected network. From the point of view of the number of FLOPs, it is also consistent with the above conclusion. For networks listed from top to bottom in Table 2, the number of FLOPs is 0.29, 0.29, 0.30, 0.18, 0.26, 0.24, 0.22, 0.20, and 0.15, respectively. It can be seen that UDenseNet can improve the network performance with similar FLOPs and parameters in comparison with DenseNet.

Similar to the case of the 40-layer UDenseNet stated in Sect. 3.4, there are some other 38-layer UDenseNet. They have similar performances with the ones reported. The relationship between u and b and its impact on network performance of them follow the trend summarized above, too. For clarity and space limitation, we do not list them here.

Table 2 Test error on CIFAR-10+ and CIFAR-100+ of dense convolutional network with varying u and b. The overall best results are in blue, and the best results of the networks with the same depth are in bold.

Network	Depth	Params	FLOPs (10^9)	CIFAR-10+	CIFAR-100+
DenseNet [5]	40	1.0M	0.29	5.24	24.42
Our implementation	40	1.0M	0.29	5.38	24.47
UDenseNet [41(12, 1)(12, 1)(12, 1)]	41	1.2M	0.30	5.13	23.23
UDenseNet [40(5, 1)(7, 2)(7, 2)]	40	1.1M	0.18	4.74	**22.88**
UDenseNet [38(11, 1)(11, 1)(11, 1)]	38	1.0M	0.26	5.18	23.64
UDenseNet [38(5, 2)(5, 2)(5, 2)]	38	1.0M	0.24	4.84	22.83
UDenseNet [38(3, 3)(3, 3)(3, 3)]	38	0.9M	0.22	**4.83**	22.61
UDenseNet [38(2, 4)(2, 4)(2, 4)]	38	0.8M	0.20	5.07	23.20
UDenseNet [38(1, 6)(1, 6)(1, 6)]	38	0.6M	0.15	5.93	25.80

4.3 Performance Evaluation

Experiments were also performed to evaluate the UDenseNet architecture. To make comparisons, the DenseNet and other state-of-the-art methods were also applied on benchmark datasets. Experiments were performed on datasets of CIFAR-10, CIFAR-100 and SVHN. The top1 error rate was used to evaluate the performance. Experimental results are shown in Table 3, which shows that UDenseNet-BC [250(11, 4) (13, 3)(12, 3)] with depth = 250 and k = 24 outperformed the existing DenseNet and other state-of-the-art methods on all CIFAR datasets. Its error rates of 3.56% on CIFAR-10+ and 17.48% on CIFAR-100+ are significantly lower than the error rates achieved by the variations of ResNets. Notably, the performance of UDenseNet is improved in comparison with the corresponding DenseNet variant structure.

Table 3 Comparisons of test error (%) of UDenseNet and existing methods. The overall best results are in blue. The symbol+ in the dataset name indicates standard data augmentation (translation and/or mirroring).

Network	Depth	Params	CIFAR-10+	CIFAR-100+	SVHN
Network in network [22]	–	–	8.81	–	2.35
All-CNN [23]	–	–	7.25	33.71	–
Highway network [12]	–	–	7.72	32.39	–
Scalable BO [24]	–	–	6.37	27.40	1.77
FractalNets [25]	21	38.6M	5.22	23.30	2.01
Wide ResNets [17]	16	11.0M	4.81	22.07	–
ResNets [4]	110	1.7M	6.41	27.22	2.01
ResNets (pre-activation) [16]	164	1.7M	5.46	24.33	–
ResNets with stochastic depth [18]	110	1.7M	5.23	24.58	1.75
DenseNet [5]	40	1.0M	5.24	24.42	1.79
DenseNet [5]	100	7.0M	4.10	20.20	**1.67**
DenseNet-BC [5]	100	0.8M	4.51	22.27	1.76
DenseNet-BC (k = 24) [5]	250	15.3M	3.62	17.60	1.74
UDenseNet-BC [40(5, 1)(7, 2)(7, 2)]	40	1.1M	4.74	22.88	1.80
UDenseNet-BC [100(12, 2)(8, 4)(8, 4)]	100	10.25M	3.83	19.17	1.74
UDenseNet-BC [100(7, 2)(8, 2)(8, 2)]	100	0.9M	4.40	21.31	1.88
UDenseNet-BC [250(11, 4)(13, 3)(12, 3)]	250	21.99M	**3.56**	**17.48**	1.71

For example, the DenseNet with depth = 100 and k = 12 obtained a competitive error rate of 4.10% on the test dataset of CIFAR-10+. Meanwhile, the test error of the UDenseNet [100(12, 2)(8, 4)(8, 4)] with depth = 100 and k = 12 reached 3.83% on CIFAR-10+, which is a relative improvement of 6.59% with respect to the aforementioned DenseNet. On CIFAR-100+, we observed a similar trend. However, the UDenseNet performed poorer than the DenseNet on SVHN. This was partly because the content of the SVHN was comparatively simple, thus overfitting to the training dataset might have occured. In summary, the proposed UDenseNet surpassed most state-of-the-art methods on CIFAR-10, CIFAR-100, and SVHN.

Table 4. The top1 and top5 errors (%) of UDenseNet and DenseNet on ImageNet validation set, with single-crop testing. All the networks have the same growth rate k = 32 and depth 121. The overall best results are in blue.

Network	Params	FLOPs (10^9)	top1	top5
DenseNet-BC	7.98M	0.57	25.02	7.71
UDenseNet [121(12, 1)(7, 2)(7, 2)(8, 2)]	7.99M	0.50	**24.69**	**7.30**
UDenseNet [121(7, 2)(7, 2)(5, 3)(6, 2)]	8.29M	0.61	24.75	7.38
UDenseNet [121(5, 3)(7, 2)(7, 2)(6, 2)]	8.01M	0.68	24.80	7.36

To show efficiency on a larger-scale dataset, the different configurations of UDenseNet were tested and compared with DenseNet on ImageNet [8]. All models had the same preprocessing methods and hyperparameters during training. The validation error for ImageNet2012 is reported in Table 4. These results show that the better accuracy exhibited by UDenseNet over DenseNet extended to ImageNet. UDenseNets have similar numbers of parameters to those of state-of-the-art DenseNets, while obtain significantly higher precision. For example, UDenseNet-BC (k = 32) [121(12, 1) (7, 2)(7, 2)(8, 2)] (7.99 M params) yielded lower validation error to DenseNet-BC (k = 32) (7.98 M params). Table 4 shows it can be seen that different network structures can be constructed by controlling u and b when the network depth remains unchanged, which can also reflects the flexibility of the UDenseNet.

5 Conclusions

In this study, DenseNet was revisited, and components of densely connected convolutional networks were refined to propose a universal dense convolutional network, UDenseNet. The proposed UDenseNet guarantees the benefits of feature reuse while reducing the complexity of cross-channel interactions and increasing network flexibility. Additionally, it can also significantly improve the performance of the densely connected convolutional networks. Based on the proposed network architecture, the impact of different component configurations on network performance was analyzed empirically to investigate the optimal architecture configuration of the densely connected convolutional networks. Extensive experiments proved the feasibility of the proposed UDenseNet. Moreover, the proposed UDenseNet also outperforms most state-of-the-art methods on the datasets of CIFAR-10, CIFAR-100, SVHN, and ImageNet. We believe that these results will help the further study of densely connected convolutional networks. In a future study, we plan to focus on the optimal configuration of densely connected convolutional networks in theory and apply the proposed UDenseNet for various purposes.

References

1. Krizhevsky, A., Sutskever, I., Hinton, G.E.: ImageNet classification with deep convolutional neural networks. In: Proceedings of NIPS 2012, Lake Tahoe, NV, USA, pp. 1106–1114 (2012)
2. Hu, H., Ma, B., Shen, J., Sun, H., Shao, L., Porikli, F.: Robust object tracking using manifold regularized convolutional neural networks. IEEE Trans. Multimedia 21(2), 510–521 (2019)
3. Hsu, Y.C., Lv, Z., Schlosser, J., Odom, P., Kira, Z.: Multiclass classification without multi-class labels. In: Proceedings of ICLR 2019, New Orleans, LA, USA, pp. 1–16 (2019)
4. He, K., Zhang, X., Ren, S., Sun, J.: Deep residual learning for image recognition. In: Proceedings of CVPR 2016, Seattle, WA, USA, pp. 770–778 (2016)
5. Huang, G., Liu, Z., Weinberger, K.Q., Van Der Maaten, L.: Densely connected convolutional networks. In: Proceedings of CVPR 2017, Honolulu, HI, USA, pp. 2261–2269 (2017)
6. Krizhevsky, A.: Learning multiple layers of features from tiny images. Technical report, Department of Computer Science, University of Toronto (2009)
7. Netzer, Y., Wang, T., Coates, A., Bissacco, A., Wu, B., Ng, A.: Reading digits in natural images with unsupervised feature learning. In: NIPS Workshop on Deep Learning and Unsupervised Feature Learning (2011)
8. Deng, J., Dong, W., Socher, R., Li, L.-J., Li, K., Li, F.F.: ImageNet: a large-scale hierarchical image database. In: Proceedings of CVPR 2009, Miami, FL, USA, pp. 248–255 (2009)
9. Sermanet, P., Chintala, S., LeCun, Y.: Convolutional neural networks applied to house numbers digit classification. In: Proceedings of ICPR 2012, Tsukuba, Japan, pp. 3288–3291 (2012)
10. Simonyan, K., Zisserman, A.: Very deep convolutional networks for large scale image recognition. In: Proceedings ICLR 2015, Vancouver, BC, Canada, pp. 1–14 (2015)
11. Szegedy, C., et al.: Going deeper with convolutions. In: Proceedings of CVPR 2015, Boston, MA, USA, pp. 1–9 (2015)
12. Srivastava, R.K., Greff, K., Schmidhuber, J.: Highway networks. arXiv:1505.00387 (2015)
13. Glorot, X., Bengio, Y.: Understanding the difficulty of training deep feed forward neural networks. In: Proceedings of International Conference on Artificial Intelligence and Statistics, PMLR, vol. 9, pp. 249–256 (2010)
14. He, K., Zhang, X., Ren, S., Sun, J.: Delving deep into rectifiers: surpassing human-level performance on imagenet classification. In: Proceedings ICCV 2015, Santiago, Chile, pp. 1026–1034 (2015)
15. Ioffe, S., Szegedy, C.: Batch normalization: accelerating deep network training by reducing internal covariate shift. In: Proceedings of ICML 2015, Lille, France, pp. 448–456 (2015)
16. He, K., Zhang, X., Ren, S., Sun, J.: Identity mappings in deep residual networks. In: Leibe, B., Matas, J., Sebe, N., Welling, M. (eds.) ECCV 2016. LNCS, vol. 9908, pp. 630–645. Springer, Cham (2016). https://doi.org/10.1007/978-3-319-46493-0_38
17. Zagoruyko, S., Komodakis, N.: Wide residual networks. In: Proceedings of BMVC 2016, York, UK, pp. 87.1–87.12 (2016)
18. Huang, G., Sun, Yu., Liu, Z., Sedra, D., Weinberger, K.Q.: Deep networks with stochastic depth. In: Leibe, B., Matas, J., Sebe, N., Welling, M. (eds.) ECCV 2016. LNCS, vol. 9908, pp. 646–661. Springer, Cham (2016). https://doi.org/10.1007/978-3-319-46493-0_39
19. Hess, A.: Exploring feature reuse in DenseNet architectures. arXiv:1086.01935v1 (2018)
20. Zhu, L., Deng, R., Maire, M., Deng, Z., Mori, G., Tan, P.: Sparsely aggregated convolutional networks. In: Ferrari, V., Hebert, M., Sminchisescu, C., Weiss, Y. (eds.) ECCV 2018. LNCS, vol. 11216, pp. 192–208. Springer, Cham (2018). https://doi.org/10.1007/978-3-030-01258-8_12
21. Paszke, A., et al.: Automatic differentiation in PyTorch. In: AutoDiff Workshop of NIPS 2017, Long Beach, CA, USA (2017)

22. Lin, M., Chen, Q., Yan, S.: Network in network. In: Proceedings of ICLR 2014, Banff, Canada (2014)
23. Springenberg, J.T., Dosovitskiy, A., Brox, T., Riedmiller, M.: Striving for simplicity: the all convolutional net. In: Proceedings of ICLR 2015, San Diego, CA, USA (2015)
24. Shoek, J., et al.: Scalable Bayesian optimization using deep neural networks. In: Proceedings of ICML 2015, Lille, France, pp. 2171–2180 (2015)
25. Larsson, G., Maire, M., Shakhnarovich, G.: FractalNet: ultra-deep neural networks without residuals. In: Proceedings of ICLR 2017, Toulon, France (2017)

End-to-End Blurry Template Matching Method Based on Siamese Networks

Wenhao Li and Nong Sang[(⊠)]

National Key Laboratory of Science and Technology on Multispectral Information
Processing, School of Artificial Intelligence and Automation,
Huazhong University of Science and Technology, Wuhan, China
{ewenlee,nsang}@hust.edu.cn

Abstract. Template matching is a classic problem in computer vision,
but most matching methods simply assume the ideal inputs without real-
world degradation, such as blur. For blurry template matching, existing
methods either have low accuracy or low time efficiency, this paper proposes an end-to-end network BMNet based on siamese networks. When
the blurry template image and the clear reference image are input in
pairs, the siamese networks are used to extract features respectively,
then the two feature maps are transformed and sent to two branches
for the classification of the target scene/background and the regression
of the coordinates' offsets. Through the multi-task learning, a trained
BMNet can accurately output the coordinates of the template image
in the reference image. Extensive experiments demonstrate that our
method significantly outperforms state-of-the art on accuracy, speed and
robustness.

Keywords: Blurry template matching · Siamese networks · Multi-task
learning

1 Introduction

Template matching mainly studies how to calculate the coordinates of a small-
size template image from a large-size reference image. In guidance applications'
imaging of high-speed aircraft in the atmosphere, the heat generated by the
friction between the aircraft and the airflow causes the airflow density to become
uneven, coupled with the effects of noise and the limitations of the sensor, the
obtained template image often has a blur degradation, which brings template
matching a challenge. Existing blurry template matching methods can be divided
into the following three categories:

1) The two-stage method of restoration and matching. Performing template
   matching between the reference image and what reconstructed from the
   blurry template image through a deblurring method.

The first author of this paper is a graduate student.

N. Sang—This work is supported by the National Natural Science Foundation of China
under grant 61433007 and 61773389.

Y. Peng et al. (Eds.): PRCV 2020, LNCS 12307, pp. 222–233, 2020.
https://doi.org/10.1007/978-3-030-60636-7_19

2) The matching method based on blur invariant features. Performing template matching based on the similarity measure between the blur invariant features extracted from the template image and the local candidate regions of the reference image.

3) The joint image restoration and matching method based on sparse representation. Using sparse representation joint image restoration and image matching to promote each other. Alternating iteration to solve a joint optimization formula to get the final matching results.

The two-stage method includes a blind deblurring method and a template matching method. In 2006, Fergus et al. proposed to use the heavy-tailed distribution as a prior information and introduce Bayesian formula to deblur based on the maximum posterior probability model (MAP) [7]. In 2015, Zhu et al. used the L_0 and L_1 distributions to perform sparse prior constraints for deblurring on the blur kernel and the blur image respectively [22]. In 2016, Pan et al. introduced sparse priors for dark channels and achieved a good deblurring performance [13].

In recent years, many CNN-based deblurring methods have emerged. In 2018, Tao et al. proposed a multi-scale recursive network SRN-DeblurNet, which uses auto-encoders with multi-scale recursive loop to achieve a better deblurring performance [21]. Kupyn et al. proposed DeblurGAN based on the generative adversarial network, which achieved a excellent deblurring performance with the naked eye benefiting from the perceptual loss [9]. In 2019, Kupyn proposed an improved version of the predecessor DeblurGAN-v2 [10]. By introducing a feature pyramid network and a relative condition GAN based on a dual-scale discriminator, DeblurGAN-v2 achieved a balance between deblurring performance and efficiency.

Template matching methods are generally divided into two categories: gray-based methods and feature-based methods. The former match based on the similarity calculated between the pixel gray values of the two images to be matched, common methods include Normalized Cross Correlation (NCC) [17] and Sequential Similarity Detection Algorithm (SSDA) [1]. While the latter match base on the similarity of the features (such as edges, contours, straight lines, corners, etc.) extracted from the images to be matched, common methods include SUSAN [19], SIFT [12], SURF [2] etc. The matching performance of the two-stage methods depend heavily on the restoration quality of the deblurring methods, while the blind deblurring is a serious ill-conditioned problem, which exists numerous optimal solutions and results in the unstable performance of the two-stage methods.

On the other side, Flusser et al. first proposed a symmetric blur invariant feature in 1996 through the analysis of the image geometric moments and frequency domain characteristics [8]. In 2003, on the basis of the previous work, Flusser et al. introduced the affine invariant moments and proposed a both blur and affine invariant feature [20]. In 2010, Zhu et al. proposed a Zernike blur invariant feature orthogonal to the unit circle, which has invariance to various blur degradations and rotation transformations [23]. In 2012, Dai et al. proposed a blur invariant feature based on Pesude-Zernike combined moments, and got stronger discriminating ability in pattern recognition [6]. The construction of blur invariant features is generally based on statistical analysis of the blur degradation models, which has the disadvantage of being applicable only to specific degradation, and the anti-blur robustness of which also fluctuates greatly with the setting of parameters. .

In the joint image restoration and matching methods based on sparse representation, Shao et al. first proposed the joint method based on distance-weighted sparse representation JRM-DSR [18], which employs sparse representation as the driving force to make image restoration and image matching iterative in the process, mutual promotion promotes better results. However, JRM-DSR has a speed problem. Li et al. used PCA and K-means to cluster the dictionary based on feature similarity to generate a two-layer dictionary with size much smaller than that of the original dictionary, to perform a coarse-to-fine matching and realized a substantial increase in speed [11]. Peng et al. used 2D PCA to extract features from the template images and the dictionary atoms, and performed sparse representation in the feature space, which achieved both time efficiency and performance improvements [15].

In this paper, we propose an end-to-end model BMNet based on siamese networks. In the training of the paired template image-reference image, BMNet introduces the idea of correlation filtering and target detection, through the cross-correlation convolution between the template feature map and the reference feature map, supervising the classification of the target scene/background and the regression of the target scene coordinates to realize the multi-task learning. The trained BMNet can directly output the coordinates of the template image in the reference image. In summary, the contributions of this paper are as follows:

1) Aiming at the blurry template matching, a single model BMNet is proposed to avoid solving the ill-conditioned problem of image deblurring. The end-to-end training and testing is implemented based on siamese networks.
2) Extensive experiments prove that BMNet has strong anti-scale change and anti-blur degradation robustness, matching performance reaches SOTA, and speed reaches real-time level.

2   Proposed Method

Image matching tasks are similar to target tracking tasks, but blur degradation and pixel-level accuracy demand without the limit of a target makes blurry image matching tasks more challenging. Inspired by the widespread application of siamese networks in target tracking tasks [3,4], we propose BMNet for bluryy image matching tasks. In this chapter we will introduce the structure of BMNet in detail. As shown in Fig. 1, the structure of BMNet is divided into two parts: the first is the feature extraction network, and the second is the coordinates positioning network. BMNet carries out end-to-end training on pairs of blurry template image-reference image, and supervises the two score maps to obtain a stable generalized model.

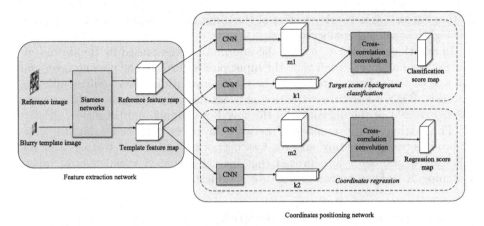

Fig. 1. The architecture of BMNet

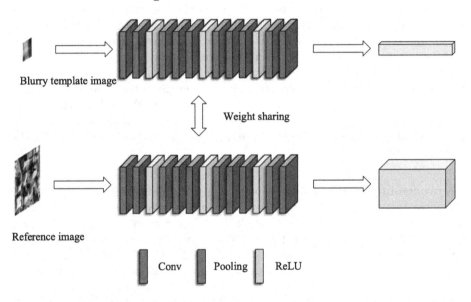

Fig. 2. The architecture of the feature extraction network.

2.1 Feature Extraction Network

The feature extraction network consists of siamese networks with shared weights, which are fully convolutional networks, as is shown in Fig. 2. There are all $3 * 3$ convolution kernels with step size of 1 and the input is filled with 1 pixel during convolution. A total of three pooling layers, which are the maximum pooling layers using $2 * 2$ convolution kernels with step size of 2, and each pooling layer will go through a ReLU activation function before it. After passing through the feature extraction network, the size of the input sample will be downsampled to one-eighth of the original size.

In addition, in order to reduce the information loss caused by the downsampling of pooling layers, each time the input passes through the pooling layer and the size of the output is reduced, the next convolutional layer will double the channels. BMNet's feature extraction network has only 10 layers, which ensures the lightweight of the network and the speed of training and testing.

The setting of the number of network layers is borrowed from [14]. The 10-layer network structure ensures fast network training and testing, and the following experiments also proved that for the low-level visual task of image matching, a 10-layer network structure is sufficient.

2.2   Coordinates Positioning Network

After obtaining the features of the template image and the reference image through the feature extraction network, enters the coordinates positioning network, which is divided into two parts, the first is the preprocessing of the feature maps: four convolution kernels are used to perform convolution operation on the template feature map and the reference feature map to obtain the two sets of convolution kernels and feature maps required for the next step. The second part is the cross-correlation convolution, which includes target scene/background classification branch and coordinates regression branch. We will use the $50 * 50$ template image and the $600 * 600$ reference image as en example to show the intermediate results and outputs of the coordinates positioning network in the following content.

Preprocessing of the Feature Maps. After passing through the feature extraction network, two features, one large and one small are obtained, which are the $6*6*128$ template feature and the $75*75*128$ reference feature. First, we use two $2*128*3*3$ convolution kernels to perform unfilled convolution operation on the template feature to obtain $4 * 4 * 128 * 2$ classification convolution kernel k_1 and $4 * 4 * 128 * 2$ regression convolution kernel k_2 respectively. Then use two $128 * 3 * 3$ convolution kernels to perform unfilled convolution operations on the reference feature to obtain $73 * 73 * 128$ classification feature map m_1 and $73*73*128$ regression feature map m_2 respectively. k_1 and m_1 are used as paired convolution kernel and feature map for classification branch, while k_2 and m_2 are for regression branch.

Cross-Correlation Convolution. Next enters the cross-correlation convolution operation of classification and regression branches. The so-called cross-correlation convolution is to use a small-size feature map as a convolution kernel to perform convolution operation on a large-size feature map. Corresponding to BMNet, the template image feature map k_1 is used as the convolution kernel to perform convolution operation on the reference image feature map m_1, and the template image feature map k_2 is used as the convolution kernel to perform the convolution operation on the reference image feature map m_2. Then the classification score map and regression score map of $70 * 70 * 2$ are obtained respectively. This process adopts the idea of the cross-correlation information in deep learning to obtain the response position of the template image on the reference image.

As shown in Fig. 3, the outputs of each grid in the classification score map are the confidences of which local area this pixel mapped back to the reference image belongs to the target scene and the background respectively. While the outputs of each grid in the regression score map are the horizontal and vertical offsets between the local area and the ground truth position. The horizontal and vertical offsets B_x, B_y are shown as Eq. 1.

$$B_x = (x - x_a)/w_m, \ B_y = (y - y_a)/w_n \tag{1}$$

Where x and y are the horizontal and vertical coordinates of ground truth, x_a and y_a are the horizontal and vertical coordinates of the local area's center the target scene score map indicates. w_m, w_n are the length and width of the template image.

Generally speaking, the classification score map indicates the rough local area of the template image in the reference image, and the regression score map indicates the relative position of the template image in the local area.

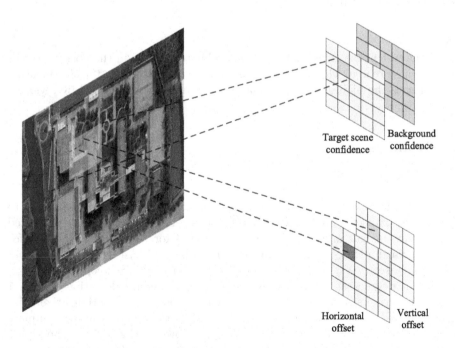

Fig. 3. The physical meaning of each output pixel on the score maps

2.3 Loss Function

The goal of BMNet is multi-task learning, so the loss function is divided into regression loss and classification loss. Here we refer to the practice in Faster R-CNN [16], the classification task uses the cross entropy loss, which is shown in Eq. 2, and the regression task uses *smooth L_1* loss, the loss function is shown in Eq. 3 and Eq. 4.

$$L_{cls} = \frac{1}{N} \sum_i - [y_i \cdot log(p_i) + (1 - y_i) \cdot log(1 - p_i)] \tag{2}$$

Where y_i is the label, p_i is the confidence output as the target scene in the score map.

$$smooth \; L_1 = \{0.5\sigma^2 x^2, |x| \leq \frac{1}{\sigma^2}; |x| - \frac{1}{2\sigma^2}, |x| \geq \frac{1}{\sigma^2}. \tag{3}$$

$$L_{reg} = \sum_{i=0}^{1} smooth \; L_1(\delta\,[i]\,,\sigma) \tag{4}$$

The loss function of BMNet is shown in Eq. 5, λ is a balance parameter that adjusts the ratio of regression loss.

$$L = L_{cls} + \lambda L_{reg} \tag{5}$$

In the test phase, according to the coordinates' offsets in the position of the regression score map where the confidence of the target scene in the classification score map is the highest, the final matching result can be obtained by reversely solving Eq. 1.

3 Training

3.1 Dataset

We selected 56 remote sensing street scene images in WHU-RS19 Dataset [5] to prepare the dataset. Firstly, these 56 street scene images are gray-scale processed as reference images and six of them are selected for testing, and the rest for training. Parts of the reference images are shown in Fig. 4. Randomly extract 400 locations on each reference image for $50 * 50$ image interception, perform 4 different degrees of Gaussian blur processing (standard deviation σ from 1 to 4, blur kernel size is $6 * \sigma + 1$), and then randomly add multiplicative noise with standard deviation randomly between 0.01–0.03 to prepare blurry template images. The 4° of blurry template images are shown in Fig. 5. Since the inputs of BMNet is pairs of images, the training set contains a total of 80,000 pairs of template images-reference images, and the test set contains 9,600 pairs of that.

Fig. 4. Parts of the reference images

Sharp   Sigma=1   Sigma=2   Sigma=3   Sigma=4

Fig. 5. The $4°$ of blurry template images

3.2 Environment and Parameters

We conducted experiments under the PyTorch 1.0 framework, using two GPUs of GeForce GTX 1080 Ti. The model parameters are set as follow: The balance parameter of regression loss $\lambda = 1$, the batch size of training $batchsize = 16$, the number of iterations of training $epoch = 200$, the network optimizer we select the SGD optimizer, and the learning rate lr from 10^{-2} decay exponentially to 10^{-6}.

4 Experiments

The experiments in this chapter are mainly divided into three parts. The first is the comparison of matching accuracy between BMNet and other methods, and the second is the comparison of algorithm speed, the last is the comparison of matching accuracy under scale variation's influence. In order to test the performance of BMNet, we selected some blurry image matching methods appeared in recent years and compared them with BMNet in every experiment, the involved methods are as follow: deblur first and then match method: DNCC (deblur+NCC) where we assemble the dark channel blind deblurring method [13] and cross-correlation information method [17], the joint image restoration and matching method based on distance-weighted sparse representation JRM-DSR [18], the joint image restoration and matching method based on hierarchical sparse representation JRM-HSR [11], the joint image deblurring and matching method with feature-based sparse representation JDM-FSR [15] and the blurry template matching method based on cascaded networks BCN [14].

4.1 Comparison of Matching Accuracy

The comparison of matching accuracy between BMNet and other methods under various degrees of blur are shown in Table 1. With the increase of Gaussian blur kernel σ, that is, with the increase of the degree of blur, the matching accuracy of the traditional methods have fallen sharply, while the CNN-based methods BCN and BMNet still maintain good performance, which shows both methods have strong anti-blur robustness. In addition, under all degrees of blur, the performance of JRM-DSR and JRM-HSR are similar, while JDM-FSR's performance is slightly better than the two, and BMNet showes the best matching performance. DNCC performs the worst under all degrees of blur, which is due to the uncertainty brought by solving the blind deblurring problem.

Table 1. Comparison of matching accuracy between BMNet and other methods

Blur degree	$\sigma = 1$	$\sigma = 2$	$\sigma = 3$	$\sigma = 4$
DNCC	64	14.33	2.33	0.33
JRM-DSR	**100**	85.67	34.67	21.67
JRM-HSR	**100**	85.17	35.33	22.33
JDM-FSR	**100**	88.17	63.17	34.33
BCN	**100**	95.83	94.67	93.50
BMNet	**100**	**96.67**	**96.17**	**94.50**

4.2 Comparison of Speed

We conducted the speed comparison experiment between BMNet and the other methods, the results of which are shown in Table 2.

In terms of the preparation time, the three integrated methods and DNCC need to perform sliding window on the reference image to make the dictionary in advance, and JRM-HSR needs to cluster the dictionary based on feature similarity, of which the preparation time is much longer than that of JRM-DSR and DNCC, and JDM-FSR requires to prepare a PCA feature dictionary, which

Table 2. Comparison of speed between BMNet and other methods.

Time	Preparation time (s)	Test time (s)	Total time (s)
DNCC	552	1.05	553.05
JRM-DSR	552	20.39	572.39
JRM-HSR	673	6.93	682.35
JDM-FSR	575	8.78	583.78
BCN	–	0.57	0.57
BMNet	–	**0.36**	**0.36**

takes longer than JRM-DSR and DNCC as well. However, BCN and BMNet do not need to spend preparation time in advance, and both can directly match when the template image and the reference image are given at the same time.

In terms of the test time, due to the simplicity of the method, DNCC is very fast, with a single image matching speed of only 1.05 s. JRM-HSR benefits from the use of a small-sized hierarchical dictionary for sparse representation, the test speed is three times that of JRM-DSR. JDM-FSR benefits from the sparse representation based on feature dictionary, the test speed is slower than JRM-HSR but much faster than JRM-DSR. The test time of BCN and BMNet both reach the real-time level. Due to the lightweight single model structure, BMNet only takes 0.36 s to test a pair of images, better than BCN which is made up of cascaded networks.

4.3   Comparison of Scale Variation's Influence

Contrast experiments under multi-size template images are used to analyze the robustness of each algorithm to scale variation. We compare the matching performance of each method under Gaussian blur kernel $\sigma = 3$, three sizes of template images are set, as $40 * 40$, $50 * 50$ and $60 * 60$. Among them, BCN and BMNet are only trained with the $50 * 50$ template images and the $600 * 600$ reference images, and the results are shown in Table 3. In addition, due to the poor performance, DNCC was excluded in this experiment.

Table 3. Comparison of the matching accuracy between BMNet and other methods with different sized template images.

Template image size	$40 * 40$	$50 * 50$	$60 * 60$
JRM-DSR	29.17	34.67	70.67
JRM-HSR	30.00	35.33	70.17
JDM-FSR	57.50	63.17	71.00
BCN	91.17	94.67	96.50
BMNet	**92.00**	**96.17**	**97.50**

It can be seen from Table 3, as the size of the template image decreases, the information that can be obtained decreases. The matching performance of JRM-DSR and JRM-HSR decreases in a similar way, and the performance of JDM-FSR is slightly better than the other two integrated methods, that indicates JDM-FSR has a certain degree of robustness to scale variation which benefits from its feature-based matching strategy. The matching accuracy of BMNet still maintains leading, and that of BCN is also relatively good. This result shows BMNet has strong anti-scale-variation robustness.

5   Conclusion

In this paper, we have presented a blurry template matching method BMNet based on siamese networks, which absorbs the idea of the cross-correlation information and target detection, through multi-task learning of a single model, end-to-end outputs the coordinates of the template image in the reference image. The experimental results and analysis demonstrate BMNet significantly outperforms state-of-the art in terms of matching accuracy, speed and robustness.

References

1. Barnea, D.I., Silverman, H.F.: A class of algorithms for fast digital image registration. IEEE Trans. Comput. **100**(2), 179–186 (1972)
2. Bay, H., Ess, A., Tuytelaars, T., Van Gool, L.: Speeded-up robust features (SURF). Comput. Vis. Image Underst. **110**(3), 346–359 (2008)
3. Bertinetto, L., Valmadre, J., Henriques, J.F., Vedaldi, A., Torr, P.H.S.: Fully-convolutional siamese networks for object tracking. In: Hua, G., Jégou, H. (eds.) ECCV 2016. LNCS, vol. 9914, pp. 850–865. Springer, Cham (2016). https://doi.org/10.1007/978-3-319-48881-3_56
4. Bo, L., Yan, J., Wei, W., Zheng, Z., Hu, X.: High performance visual tracking with siamese region proposal network. In: 2018 IEEE/CVF Conference on Computer Vision and Pattern Recognition (CVPR) (2018)
5. Dai, D., Yang, W.: Satellite image classification via two-layer sparse coding with biased image representation. IEEE Geosci. Remote Sens. Lett. **8**(1), 173–176 (2010)
6. Dai, X., Liu, T., Shu, H., Luo, L.: Pseudo-Zernike moment invariants to blur degradation and their use in image recognition. In: Yang, J., Fang, F., Sun, C. (eds.) IScIDE 2012. LNCS, vol. 7751, pp. 90–97. Springer, Heidelberg (2013). https://doi.org/10.1007/978-3-642-36669-7_12
7. Fergus, R., Singh, B., Hertzmann, A., Roweis, S.T., Freeman, W.T.: Removing camera shake from a single photograph. In: ACM SIGGRAPH 2006 Papers, pp. 787–794 (2006)
8. Flusser, J., Suk, T., Saic, S.: Recognition of blurred images by the method of moments. IEEE Trans. Image Process. **5**(3), 533–538 (1996)
9. Kupyn, O., Budzan, V., Mykhailych, M., Mishkin, D., Matas, J.: DeblurGAN: blind motion deblurring using conditional adversarial networks. In: Proceedings of the IEEE Conference on Computer Vision and Pattern Recognition, pp. 8183–8192 (2018)

10. Kupyn, O., Martyniuk, T., Wu, J., Wang, Z.: DeblurGAN-v2: deblurring (orders-of-magnitude) faster and better. In: Proceedings of the IEEE International Conference on Computer Vision, pp. 8878–8887 (2019)

11. Li, W., Sang, N., Gao, C., Shao, Y.: Joint image restoration and matching based on hierarchical sparse representation. In: 2019 IEEE International Conference on Image Processing (ICIP), pp. 4494–4498. IEEE (2019)

12. Lowe, D.G.: Distinctive image features from scale-invariant keypoints. Int. J. Comput. Vis. **60**(2), 91–110 (2004). https://doi.org/10.1023/B:VISI.0000029664.99615.94

13. Pan, J., Sun, D., Pfister, H., Yang, M.H.: Blind image deblurring using dark channel prior. In: Proceedings of the IEEE Conference on Computer Vision and Pattern Recognition, pp. 1628–1636 (2016)

14. Peng, J., Sang, N., Gao, C., Li, L.: Blurred template matching based on cascaded network. In: Zhao, Y., Barnes, N., Chen, B., Westermann, R., Kong, X., Lin, C. (eds.) ICIG 2019. LNCS, vol. 11901, pp. 480–492. Springer, Cham (2019). https://doi.org/10.1007/978-3-030-34120-6_39

15. Peng, J., Shao, Y., Sang, N., Gao, C.: Joint image deblurring and matching with feature-based sparse representation prior. Pattern Recogn. **103**, 107300 (2020)

16. Ren, S., He, K., Girshick, R., Sun, J.: Faster R-CNN: towards real-time object detection with region proposal networks. In: Advances in Neural Information Processing Systems, pp. 91–99 (2015)

17. Rosenfeld, A.: Digital Picture Processing. Academic Press, New York (1976)

18. Shao, Y., Sang, N., Gao, C., Lin, W.: Joint image restoration and matching based on distance-weighted sparse representation. In: 2018 24th International Conference on Pattern Recognition (ICPR), pp. 2498–2503. IEEE (2018)

19. Smith, S.M., Brady, J.M.: SUSAN–a new approach to low level image processing. Int. J. Comput. Vis. **23**(1), 45–78 (1997). https://doi.org/10.1023/A:1007963824710

20. Suk, T., Flusser, J.: Combined blur and affine moment invariants and their use in pattern recognition. Pattern Recogn. **36**(12), 2895–2907 (2003)

21. Tao, X., Gao, H., Shen, X., Wang, J., Jia, J.: Scale-recurrent network for deep image deblurring. In: Proceedings of the IEEE Conference on Computer Vision and Pattern Recognition, pp. 8174–8182 (2018)

22. Zhu, C., Zhou, Y.: A map framework for single-image deblurring based on sparse priors. In: 2015 Chinese Automation Congress (CAC), pp. 701–706. IEEE (2015)

23. Zhu, H., Liu, M., Ji, H., Li, Y.: Combined invariants to blur and rotation using Zernike moment descriptors. Pattern Anal. Appl. **13**(3), 309–319 (2010). https://doi.org/10.1007/s10044-009-0159-9

Training Wide Residual Hashing
from Scratch

Yang Li$^{(\boxtimes)}$ ⓘ, Jiabao Wangⓘ, Zhuang Miaoⓘ, Jixiao Wangⓘ,
and Rui Zhangⓘ

Command and Control Engineering College, Army Engineering University of PLA,
Nanjing 210007, China
`solarleeon@outlook.com`

Abstract. Deep supervised hashing aims to encode high-dimensional
data into low-dimensional compact hash codes, which is important for
solving large-scale image retrieval problems. In recent years, deep supervised hashing methods have achieved some positive outcomes. However,
these methods can not meet expectations without fine-tuning from the
off-the-shelf networks pre-trained on large-scale classification dataset. To
cope with this problem, we rethink the paradigm of fine-tuning on deep
supervised hashing and propose training deep supervised hashing from
scratch. Based on this new perspective, we propose a wide residual hashing model trained from scratch, which can greatly improve the training
time and reduce the model size. To the best of our knowledge, our method
is the first framework that can train deep hashing networks from scratch
without losing performance. By training from scratch, the parameters of
the model are more less and our results are superior to state-of-the-art
hashing algorithms. We hope the insights in this paper will open a new
avenue for learning deep hash codes from scratch and transfer to further
tasks not explored in this work.

Keywords: Image retrieval · Deep hashing · Convolutional neural
network

1 Introduction

In the recent years, with the rapid growth of image data, learning efficient image
features with high accuracy have become a hot research topic in the field of
image retrieval [1–4]. However, for efficient image retrieval tasks in the real
world, the efficiency is actually reflected in two aspects: feature efficiency and
model efficiency. For feature efficiency, image features must have low storage cost,

This work was supported by the National Natural Science Foundation of China under
Grant 61806220 and the Frontier Science and Technology Innovation Project of Army
Engineering University of PLA.

Y. Peng et al. (Eds.): PRCV 2020, LNCS 12307, pp. 234–248, 2020.
https://doi.org/10.1007/978-3-030-60636-7_20

fast query speed and impressive retrieval performance. For model efficiency, the training process and the speed of image feature extraction need to be efficient.

For the first problem (feature efficiency), deep supervised hashing has been widely studied over the past years [5–15]. Hashing aims to encode high-dimensional data into low-dimensional compact hash codes, in which only similar data preserving smaller Hamming distance [16]. This challenging task is important for solving large-scale image retrieval [17], video retrieval [18,19] and bioinformatics [20] problems due to its low storage cost and fast query speed.

In order to further improve the representation ability of hash features, the fine-tuning paradigm is widely used during deep hashing learning. It is commonly believed that fine-tuning can transfer "dark knowledge" containing privileged information to enhance hashing learning [21–23]. Being able to better handle the domain gap, fine-tuning deep hashing methods typically achieve higher performance. And the current state-of-the-art deep hashing methods [10–12] are generally fine-tuned from pre-trained classification networks on ImageNet [24] dataset, e.g., AlexNet [25], VGGNet [26], and ResNet [27].

However, there is no such thing as a free lunch. As illustrated in Fig. 1, fine-tuning pre-trained networks to deep supervised hashing has some critical limitations for model efficiency. First, it is inefficient to resize images and fine-tune on the pre-trained network. For example, the input size of ResNet is 224×224. If the training image size is 32×32, resize all training images to 224×224 and fine-tune the network requiring higher computational cost. Second, most existing deep hashing methods are designed based on the backbone networks that are pre-trained on a classification dataset [24]. These pre-trained networks are fairly heavy on parameters and inefficient for many embedded devices such as mobile phones. Third, the loss functions between classification and supervised hashing tasks are different, this may lead to different optimization spaces and produce a local minimum solution [28]. For instance, most existing deep hashing methods adopt triplet or pairwise losses to fine-tune deep network underlying a new dataset, but their training methods are difficult and less efficient because $O(n^3)$ triplets pairs and $O(n^2)$ data pairs are involved.

Therefore, in this work, we want to answer the following two questions. First, is it possible to train deep supervised hashing networks from scratch directly without the pre-trained parameters? Second, if the first answer is positive, are there any methods to design a resource efficient network structure for image hashing, meanwhile keeping high retrieval accuracy?

To cope with these questions, in this paper, we rethink the paradigm of fine-tuning on deep supervised hashing and propose training deep supervised hashing from scratch. Learning from scratch means we directly train the deep hashing model on the target dataset without involving extra fine-tuning process. Moreover, we proposed to re-examine the image hash learning problem from two aspects: feature efficiency and model efficiency. This new perspective simplifies the complex retraining process to a simple deep model learning problem.

Specifically, the simplification mechanism of this paper is reflected in two aspects. First, the training process is simplicity from scratch without the need

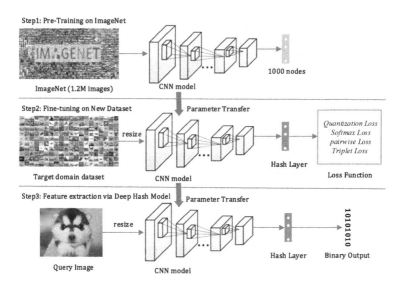

Fig. 1. Fine-tuning deep hash learning methods consist of three main steps. The first stage is to learn a deep convolutional neural network on ImageNet. In the second stage, it is needed to modify the pre-trained model and add a hash layer, then the new dataset need to be resized to the input of the pre-trained network and a complex loss function is used to fine-tune the pre-trained network. Finally, in the third stage, the fine-tuned model is used to extract binary features, but the input image is also need to resize.

for transfer learning and image rescaling. Second, the loss function is a primitive classification loss which reducing the complexity to $O(n)$. By training from scratch, the parameters of the model are more less and our results are better than state-of-the-art hashing algorithms.

To sum up, the major contributions of this work are comprised as follows:

- We propose a wide residual hashing model trained from scratch, which can greatly improve the training speed and reduce the model size. To the best of our knowledge, our method is the first framework that can train deep hashing networks from scratch without losing performance.
- We introduce a new intuitive view for efficient image retrieval tasks, which help us understand the feature efficiency and model efficiency during hashing learning.
- Extensive experiments on public benchmarks demonstrate the advantages of our method. Moreover, the results show that our method can outperform the state-of-the-art pre-trained based methods.

The remainder of this paper is organized as follows. In Sect. 2, we briefly make an overview of the related works. In Sect. 3, we elaborate the proposed method and its learning scheme in detail. In Sect. 4, we conduct various experiments and compare with other methods on popular benchmark datasets. Finally, we draw a conclusion in Sect. 5.

2   Related Work

In this section, we first briefly overview existing deep supervised hashing methods based on different loss functions. Then, we introduce the network architectures for hashing and learning from scratch deep learning methods.

2.1   Deep Supervised Hashing

Recently, the computer vision community has witnessed continuous studies on deep supervised hashing. These methods can simultaneously learn deep neural networks as well as hash functions at the same time. However, most of these CNN based deep supervised hashing methods are fine-tuned from pre-trained networks on ImageNet. Generally, based on different loss functions, we can divide these methods into three groups: triplet loss hashing, pairwise loss hashing and pointwise loss hashing.

For example, CNNH [5], NINH [6], DRSCH [9] and DTSH [11] used triplet loss, which calculated on the triplet of training samples from two different classes. Triplet loss requires the anchor point and a similar example should be smaller than that between the anchor point and a dissimilar example by a large margin. DPSH [10], DHN [7], HashNet [29] and DCH [30] proposed pairwise loss, which requires the distances from the same class small while those from different classes large. However, triplet loss methods require $O(n^3)$ triplets data and pairwise loss methods require $O(n^2)$ pair data. Both of these methods require a long computation time and a high storage cost for training. And it has been shown that pairwise or triplet loss is much more difficult to train for large scale image data in practice.

DARH [12] and SSDH [13] and (SCDH) [31] are based on pointwise loss with the complexity of $O(n)$, which assume that image labels can be implicitly represented by the binary codes. For model efficiency, our method is also built upon pointwise loss and thus it inherits the speed advantage with the complexity of $O(n)$. Differently, our method is trained from scratch which is more flexible than the fine-tuning methods.

2.2   Network Architectures for Hashing

Because designing an advanced neural network architecture is one of the most effective ways for improving the performance of image classification, many powerful network architectures are emerged recently, such as AlexNet [25], VGGNet [26], GoogLeNet [32], ResNet [27], DenseNet [33], to name just a few. Meanwhile, several advanced networks have been directly utilized as the backbone network for hashing learning task.

Most of these CNN based deep supervised hashing methods are fine-tuned from pre-trained networks on ImageNet [24]. As illustrated in Table 1, DHN [7], DSRH [8], and SSDH [13] were based on the pre-trained backbone of

Table 1. A general comparison of the most related works to our method. All of these methods are based on a pre-trained network. Most of these methods are based on pairwise or triplet loss.

Method	Training strategy	Loss function	Architecture	Model size
NINH [6]	Fine tune	Triplet loss	NIN	–
DSRH [8]	Fine tune	Pairwise loss	AlexNet	216.88 MB
DPSH [10]	Fine tune	Pairwise loss	VGG-F	216.62 MB
DARH [12]	Fine tune	Pointwise loss	ResNet	91.95 MB
SSDH [13]	Fine tune	Pointwise loss	AlexNet	216.88 MB
DBCH [14]	Fine tune	Pairwise loss	VGG-F	216.62 MB
Our method	Scratch	Pointwise loss	Wide ResNet	**58.13 MB**

AlexNet [25]. DPSH [10], DTSH [11], and DBCH [14] were based on the pre-trained backbone of VGGNet [26]. DARH [12] were based on the pre-trained backbone of ResNet [27].

As illustrated in Fig. 1, fine-tuning deep hash learning methods consist of three main steps. The first stage is to learn a deep convolutional neural network on ImageNet classification task. This dataset contains about 1.2 million training images with 1000 categories. In the second stage, it is needed to modify the pre-trained model and add a hash layer, then the new dataset need to be resized to the input of the pre-trained network and a complex loss function is used to fine-tune the pre-trained network. Finally, in the third stage, the fine-tuned model is used to extract binary features, but the input image is also need to resize. However, in this paper, the pre-training mechanism on ImageNet is no longer needed by our method.

2.3   Learning from Scratch Methods

It is worth to notice that the strategy of training from scratch has attempted to be applied in some fields. In object detection field, DSOD [34] proposed the first one-stage CNN detector trained from scratch. ScratchDet [35] integrated Batch-Norm to train SSD from scratch, which improved the detection accuracy. In natural language processing field, ScratchGAN [36] first proposed to train word-level language models successfully from scratch. In semantic segmentation, a well-designed DenseNets structure was proposed and outperformed state-of-the-art methods without using the pre-trained models [37]. Recently, He et al. [38] further point out that training from scratch can be no worse than its ImageNet pre-training counterparts under many circumstances. Bethge et al. [39] demonstrated binary neural networks can be trained from scratch with a simple training strategy.

However, in the deep hashing learning field, all state-of-the-art deep supervised hashing methods adopt the strategy of fine-tuning to get better hash codes.

And the accuracy of training from scratch methods [9] are much lower than fine-tuning hashing methods. To the best of our knowledge, our method is the first learning from scratch deep hashing method that can surpass the pre-training hashing methods.

3 Methodology

The purpose of this paper is to maintain the accuracy of the hash learning model without the pre-training parameters of ImageNet [24]. Under this goal, using complex loss functions to improve the accuracy is not our purpose. In fact, we only use the simplest classification loss function and a common model structure to achieve better results.

In this section, we first introduce some definitions that would be used in this paper. Then, we illustrate the whole framework of our deep hashing model, following by some important design principles. Finally, we describe the training settings and objective function in detail.

3.1 Problem Definition

Suppose we are given N training image samples $I = \{I_1, I_2, \cdots, I_N\}$, the corresponding set of labels can be represented as $Y = \{y_1, y_2, \cdots, y_N\}$, where $y_i \in \mathbb{R}^C$ is the ground-truth label of I_i, and C is the total number of image classes. The goal of deep supervised hashing is to learn similarity-preserving hash functions which can map the input images into binary codes.

To be specific, for arbitrary image I_i, we can extract its deep features denoted as $\mathbf{f}_i$ by:

$$\mathbf{f}_i = \Phi(I_i; \theta), i = 1, 2, \ldots N \tag{1}$$

where $\mathbf{f}_i \in \mathbb{R}^{C \times H \times W}$ is typical CNN feature maps with C channels. Φ is the network function and θ denotes the parameters of the network. This network function actually performs a series of linear and nonlinear transformations, including convolution, pooling, and nonlinear mapping.

Different from other pre-trained methods, the parameters of our method are initialized randomly from scratch. Subsequently, a hash layer is inserted to transfer the high-dimensional deep features into compact K-bit binary codes, which can be formulated as:

$$\mathbf{b}_i = \text{sgn}(\mathbf{f}_i) \tag{2}$$

where $\text{sgn}(\cdot)$ performs element-wise operations for a vector, i.e., $\text{sgn}(x) = 1$ if $x > 0$ and -1 otherwise. $\mathbf{b}_i$ is the K-bit binary codes associated with the I_i in Hamming space.

3.2   Network Architecture

As mentioned in the previous section, residual connections [27] are a very popular operation in convolutional neural network. Residual connections can make the parameter gradients propagate more easily from the output layer to the earlier layers, which makes it possible to train more deeper networks (*e.g.* with more than 1000 layers). An alternative to deeper topology is decreasing the depth and widening the layers channels. This architecture is called wide residual network [40].

Formally, residual block with identity mapping can be expressed as follow:

$$z_l = h\left(x_l\right) + \mathcal{F}\left(x_l, W_l\right)$$
$$x_{l+1} = f\left(z_l\right) \tag{3}$$

where x_{l+1} and x_l are the output and input of the l-th block. $\mathcal{F}$ represents the residual mapping function and W_l represents parameters of the block. $h\left(x_l\right)$ is an identity function and f is a ReLU function. Furthermore, residual connections can increase network depth which always results in higher accuracies on more difficult tasks. As an alternative to increase depth, decreasing the depth and widening the layers are our option in this paper.

As illustrated in Fig. 2, our wide residual hashing network use the identity mapping approach for residual connections. The residual network architecture consists of convolutional layers, batch normalization (BN), and ReLU layer connected sequentially. With different shortcut connections, our residual hashing networks consisted of two types of blocks: basic residual block and down sample residual block. The basic residual block is composed of two consecutive 3×3 convolutions with batch normalization and ReLU layer. The down sample residual block is performed with a stride of 2, which is based on the basic residual block with extra shortcut with 1×1 convolutional layer together with its batch normalization layer. Both of these two blocks can bypass the convolutional layers of the main branch. And the outputs of the convolutional units and residual connections are added element-wise. The final section of our network are composed of global average pooling, hashing layer, fully connective layer, and classification layer. Moreover, both binary hash codes and deep features are learned from the neural network during optimizing.

Furthermore, as illustrated in Table 2, our wide residual hashing architecture is not a very deep network. However, the net width which defined as the number of filters in the convolutional layers is very large. For example, in the middle stage, the net width is 320 or 640, which is larger than the normal residual network.

Although there are other residual blocks (*e.g.* BN-ReLU-conv order or bottleneck convolutional residual unit), but because this paper is to explore the importance of learning from scratch for hashing, so we do not discuss the structure of the model too much.

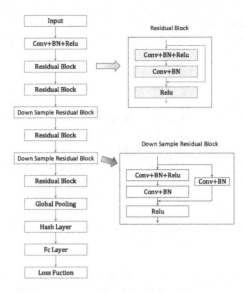

Fig. 2. Proposed wide residual hashing architecture for learning from scratch. On the left, our framework consists of several blocks. On the right, we show two types backbone blocks (residual block and down sample residual block) in detail.

Table 2. The configurations of our wide residual hashing architecture.

Layer name	Type	Activations
Input	Image input	32*32*3
Conv+BN+Relu	Convolution block	32*32*16
Residual block	Residual block	32*32*16
Residual block	Residual block	32*32*16
Down sample residual block	Down sample	16*16***320**
Residual block	Residual block	16*16***320**
Down sample residual block	Down sample	8*8***640**
Residual block	Residual block	8*8***640**
Global pooling	Average pooling	1*1*640
Hash layer	Fully connected	1*1*K
Fc layer	Fully connected	1*1*10
Loss Layer	Softmax	1*1*10

3.3 Loss Function

Compared to pointwise loss, pairs or triplets labels in the hash learning phase require a long computation time and a high storage cost for training. And it has been shown that pairwise or triplet loss is much more difficult to train in practice. Pointwise loss methods assume that image labels can be implicitly represented by the binary codes. Based on this assumption, we can construct the hash function as a hidden layer between image representations and classification outputs in a CNN, and the hash codes can be learned by minimizing an objective function defined by the classification loss.

To obtain a hash code of the input image, we feed the deep features $\mathbf{f}_i$ through one fully connected layer. The fully connected layer contains K neurons. Then, the outputs of K neurons pass through a *tanh* unit which can encourage the activations v_i to be -1 and 1. Finally, a fully connected layer with n nodes and softmax loss layer is connected, where n denotes the number of class in the training set. Therefore, it becomes a traditional image classification problem. A simple softmax loss function can be used to train the network [25]. The classification loss function can be formulated as follows:

$$L_c = -\sum_{i=1}^{m} \log \frac{e^{\mathbf{Q}_{p_i}^T \mathbf{v}_i + \mathbf{b}_{p_i}}}{\sum_{j=1}^{n} e^{\mathbf{Q}_j^T \mathbf{v}_i + \mathbf{b}_j}} \tag{4}$$

where $\mathbf{v}_i$ represents the correct output deep feature of this model, which belongs to the p_ith class. $\mathbf{Q}$ denotes the weights connecting the output and the fully-connected layer with n nodes. m is the size of mini-batch, $\mathbf{b}$ is the bias vector.

4   Experiments

In order to thoroughly evaluate the ideas proposed in this paper, in this section, we conduct several experiments on CIFAR-10[1] dataset.

4.1   Dataset and Experimental Setup

CIFAR-10 dataset contains 60,000 32×32 natural color images with 10 categories (6,000 images per category). And this dataset is widely used for evaluating the performance of hashing.

We implement our method in Matlab 2019a on an Intel I5-4690 3.50 GHz CPU with 16 GB RAM. During training, we randomly flip the training images along the vertical axis and randomly translate them up to four pixels horizontally and vertically. Data augmentation [41] can prevent the network from overfitting and memorizing the exact details of the training images. Adam optimizer [42] is used for training our model with a default parameters.

The experimental protocols and evaluation method are exactly the same as that in [10,11]. To study thoroughly the performance of our method, during the training stage, all the 50,000 dataset images are used as training images. During the testing stage, 10,000 samples (1,000 per class) were randomly selected as the query set, the remaining 50,000 images were selected as the database images.

In the query phase, we firstly rank all samples by computing the Hamming distance between the query sample and the database samples. Once obtaining the ranked list, we can get the average precision (AP) for each query image.

---

[1] http://www.cs.toronto.edu/~kriz/cifar.html.

Finally, the MAP can be computed via averaging the AP of all query images, which is defined as:

$$\text{MAP} = \frac{1}{|M|} \sum_{i=1}^{|M|} \frac{1}{n_i} \sum_{k=1}^{n_i} P_k \times pos_k \tag{5}$$

where $|M|$ is the volume of the query image set, n_i is the number of images relevant to i-th query image in the searching database, and P_k is the precision of the top-k retrieved image. The pos_k is an indicator, in which $pos_k = 1$ if the k-th returned image is relevant to the query.

4.2 Comparison with State-of-the-art Algorithms

We compare the proposed method with several state-of-the-art deep supervised hashing methods, including DPSH [10], DSRH [8], DRSCH [9], DSCH [9], and DTSH [11]. And we also compare our method with one deep unsupervised hashing method BGAN [43]. Please note that traditional hashing methods are not the focus of this paper and we only compare with deep learning based methods.

The results of our method and other previously published results are summarised in Table 3. And the first and second best results are highlighted by **bold** and underline.

Table 3. Performance comparison in mean average precision (MAP) with state-of-the-art deep hashing methods. The best and second best values are highlighted by **Bold** and Underline respectively.

Methods	16-bits	24-bits	32-bits	48-bits
Our method	**0.928**	**0.931**	**0.929**	**0.931**
DTSH [11]	0.915	0.923	0.925	0.926
DPSH [10]	0.763	0.781	0.795	0.807
DRSCH [9]	0.615	0.622	0.629	0.631
DSCH [9]	0.609	0.613	0.617	0.620
DSRH [8]	0.608	0.611	0.617	0.618
BGAN [43]	–	0.512	0.531	0.558

From Table 3, we can see that our method outperforms all state-of-the-art methods on all number of bits, which demonstrated the effectiveness of our method. To be specific, among the state-of-the-art methods in the literature, DTSH [11] achieves the best results. However, DTSH [11] method used pretrained VGGNet [26] and triplet labels, which suffers from data expansion when constituting the sample pairwise from the training set. Differently, our method is trained from scratch and uses more efficient pointwise loss, which can outperform

DTSH [11] over 1%. These results confirm the superiority of our proposed scheme in deep supervised hashing.

In addition, the MAP performance of our method with 16-bits can outperform the DTSH method [11] with 48-bits (ours 0.928 MAP vs. DTSH 0.926 MAP). As is well-known, if the binary codes are 3x lower, the storage cost will decrease 3x and the query speed will be significantly improved. Therefore, our method can significantly improve the effectiveness and adaptability of image retrieval systems. Our results suggest that training from scratch on deep supervised hashing is possible and can be no worse than its ImageNet pre-training counterparts.

4.3   Experimental Analysis

Analyses of Training Process in Hashing Learning. It is unfair to expect models trained from random initialization to converge as fast as those initialized from ImageNet pre-training. When we trained a model from scratch, the model has to learn high-level and low-level features at the same time, so more iterations may be necessary for it to converge well.

In Fig. 3, we show a from scratch case for learning 48-bit hash code. From Fig. 3, we can see that out random initial model can converge to a solution that is no worse than the fine-tuning counterpart. Therefore, for model efficiency, the training process of our method is more efficient.

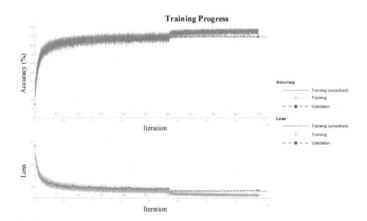

Fig. 3. The training progress for learning 48-bit hash codes embedding by random weights. We show the training accuracy and training loss for learning hash codes. The model is trained from scratch converges to a solution that is no worse than the fine-tuning counterpart.

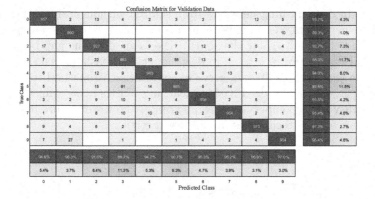

Fig. 4. The confusion matrix for validation data. Each row of the matrix represents the instances in a true class while each column represents the instances in a predicted class.

Analyses of Confusion Matrix. Based on the classification loss, our method can be viewed as a type of supervised classification learning task. Therefore, the confusion matrix is one of the most powerful tools for predictive analysis in machine learning. In Fig. 4, the confusion matrix showed the discrepancies between predicted and actual labels. The vast majority of the predictions end up on the diagonal (predicted label = actual label). However, there are a number of misclassifications, and it is interesting to see that these misclassified products belong to the under-represented classes.

Analyses of Model Size. Fine-tuning deep supervised hashing methods are designed based on the backbone networks that are pre-trained on classification datasets [24]. These pre-trained networks are fairly heavy on parameters and inefficient for many embedded devices such as mobile phones. In Table 1, we report model size of different methods. Compared to other fine-tuned methods, it is clear that our method is much more efficient than others. Specifically, our method is designed for a small model (only 58.13 MB), but it is still better than VGG-F model (216.62 MB) for higher computation cost.

5   Conclusion

This work shows how to train a wide residual hashing model from scratch in order to make hashing learning more efficient. Adding wide skip connections to deep supervised hashing alleviates the training difficulty which was impeding hash codes to further progress. A large number of experiments showed the benefit of our architecture by state-of-the-art performance.

Moreover, we introduce a new intuitive view for efficient image retrieval tasks, which help us to understand the feature efficiency and model efficiency during hashing learning. To the best of our knowledge, our method is the first framework that can train deep hashing networks from scratch without losing performance. Extensive experiments on public benchmarks demonstrate the advantages of our method. And the results show that our method can close the gap between pre-training and training from scratch in deep supervised hashing tasks.

We hope that our results can serve as an alternative method to supervised pre-training in deep supervised hashing learning. Further, we want to illustrate the practicality of deep supervised hash learning, and foster future researches to further advance these techniques in real world settings.

References

1. Smeulders, A.W.M., Worring, M., Santini, S., Gupta, A., Jain, R.: Content-based image retrieval at the end of the early years. IEEE Trans. Pattern Anal. Mach. Intell. **22**(12), 1349–1380 (2000)
2. Zheng, L., Yang, Y., Tian, Q.: SIFT meets CNN: a decade survey of instance retrieval. IEEE Trans. Pattern Anal. Mach. Intell. **40**(5), 1224–1244 (2017)
3. Li, Y., Miao, Z., Wang, J., Zhang, Y.: Nonlinear embedding neural codes for visual instance retrieval. Neurocomputing **275**, 1275–1281 (2018)
4. Zhang, X., Lai, H., Feng, J.: Attention-aware deep adversarial hashing for cross-modal retrieval. In: IEEE Conference on European Conference on Computer Vision, pp. 591–606 (2018)
5. Xia, R., Pan, Y., Lai, H., Liu, C., Yan, S.: Supervised hashing for image retrieval via image representation learning. In: International Joint Conference on Artificial Intelligence, pp. 2156–2162 (2014)
6. Lai, H., Pan, Y., Liu, Y., Yan, S.: Simultaneous feature learning and hash coding with deep neural networks. In: IEEE Conference on Computer Vision and Pattern Recognition, pp. 3270–3278 (2015)
7. Zhu, H., Long, M., Wang, J., Cao, Y.: Deep hashing network for efficient similarity retrieval. In: International Conference on Artificial Intelligence, pp. 3270–3278 (2016)
8. Zhao, F., Huang, Y., Wang, L., Tan, T.: Deep semantic ranking based hashing for multi-label image retrieval. In: IEEE Conference on Computer Vision and Pattern Recognition, pp. 1556–1564 (2015)
9. Zhang, R., Lin, L., Zhang, R., Zuo, W.: Bit-scalable deep hashing with regularized similarity learning for image retrieval and person re-identification. IEEE Trans. Image Process. **24**(12), 4766–4779 (2015)
10. Li, W.J., Wang, S., Kang, W.C.: Feature learning based deep supervised hashing with pairwise labels. In: International Joint Conference on Artificial Intelligence, pp. 1711–1717 (2015)
11. Wang, X., Shi, Y., Kitani, K.M.: Deep supervised hashing with triplet labels. In: Lai, S.-H., Lepetit, V., Nishino, K., Sato, Y. (eds.) ACCV 2016. LNCS, vol. 10111, pp. 70–84. Springer, Cham (2017). https://doi.org/10.1007/978-3-319-54181-5_5
12. Li, Y., Miao, Z., He, M., Zhang, Y., Li, H.: Deep attention residual hashing. IEICE Trans. Fundam. Electron. Commun. Comput. Sci. **101**(3), 654–657 (2018)
13. Yang, H.F., Lin, K., Chen, C.S.: Supervised learning of semantics-preserving hash via deep convolutional neural networks. IEEE Trans. Pattern Anal. Mach. Intell. **40**(2), 437–451 (2018)
14. Li, Y., Miao, Z., Wang, J., Zhang, Y.: Deep binary constraint hashing for fast image retrieval. Electron. Lett. **54**(1), 25–27 (2018)

15. Gui, J., Liu, T., Sun, Z., Tao, D., Tan, T.: Fast supervised discrete hashing. IEEE Trans. Pattern Anal. Mach. Intell. **40**(2), 490–496 (2017)
16. Gong, Y., Lazebnik, S.: Iterative quantization: a procrustean approach to learning binary codes. In: IEEE Conference on Computer Vision and Pattern Recognition, pp. 817–824 (2011)
17. Wang, J., Zhang, T., Song, J., Sebe, N., Shen, H.T.: A survey on learning to hash. IEEE Trans. Pattern Anal. Mach. Intell. **40**(4), 769–790 (2018)
18. Liong, V.E., Lu, J., Tan, Y.-P., Zhou, J.: Deep video hashing. IEEE Trans. Multimedia **19**(6), 1209–1219 (2016)
19. Song, J., Zhang, H., Li, X., Gao, L., Wang, M., Hong, R.: Self-supervised video hashing with hierarchical binary auto-encoder. IEEE Trans. Image Process. **27**(7), 3210–3221 (2018)
20. Zhao, Y., Guangyuan, F., Wang, J., Guo, M., Guoxian, Yu.: Gene function prediction based on gene ontology hierarchy preserving hashing. Genomics **111**(3), 334–342 (2019)
21. Weiss, K., Khoshgoftaar, T.M., Wang, D.: A survey of transfer learning. J. Big data **3**(1), 1–9 (2016). https://doi.org/10.1186/s40537-016-0043-6
22. Jie, L., Behbood, V., Hao, P., Zuo, H., Xue, S., Zhang, G.: Transfer learning using computational intelligence: a survey. Knowl.-Based Syst. **80**, 14–23 (2015)
23. Guth, F., de Campos, T.E.: Research frontiers in transfer learning-a systematic and bibliometric review. arXiv preprint arXiv:1912.08812 (2019)
24. Russakovsky, O., et al.: ImageNet large scale visual recognition challenge. Int. J. Comput. Vis. **115**(3), 211–252 (2015). https://doi.org/10.1007/s11263-015-0816-y
25. Krizhevsky, A., Sutskever, I., Hinton, G.E.: ImageNet classification with deep convolutional neural networks. In: International Conference on Neural Information Processing Systems, pp. 1106–1114 (2012)
26. Simonyan, K., Zisserman, A.: Very deep convolutional networks for large-scale image recognition. In: International Conference on Learning Representations, pp. 1–14 (2015)
27. He, K., Zhang, X., Ren, S., Sun, J.: Deep residual learning for image recognition. In: IEEE Conference on Computer Vision and Pattern Recognition, pp. 770–778 (2016)
28. Recht, B., Roelofs, R., Schmidt, L., Shankar, V.: Do imagenet classifiers generalize to imagenet? arXiv preprint arXiv:1902.10811 (2019)
29. Cao, Z., Long, M., Wang, J., Yu, P.S.: HashNet: deep learning to hash by continuation. In: IEEE International Conference on Computer Vision, pp. 5609–5618 (2018)
30. Cao, Y., Long, M., Liu, B., Wang, J.: Deep cauchy hashing for hamming space retrieval. In: IEEE Conference on Computer Vision and Pattern Recognition, pp. 1229–1237 (2018)
31. Zhang, S., Li, J., Bo, Z.: Semantic cluster unary loss for efficient deep hashing. IEEE Trans. Image Process. **28**(6), 1–17 (2019)
32. Szegedy, C., et al.: Going deeper with convolutions. In: IEEE Conference on Computer Vision and Pattern Recognition, pp. 1–9 (2015)
33. Huang, G., Liu, Z., Van Der Maaten, L., Weinberger, K.Q.: Densely connected convolutional networks. In: IEEE Conference on Computer Vision and Pattern Recognition, pp. 4700–4708 (2017)
34. Shen, Z., Liu, Z., Li, J., Jiang, Y.-G., Chen, Y., Xue, X.: DSOD: learning deeply supervised object detectors from scratch. In: IEEE International Conference on Computer Vision, pp. 1919–1927 (2017)

35. Zhu, R., et al.: ScratchDet: training single-shot object detectors from scratch. In: IEEE Conference on Computer Vision and Pattern Recognition, pp. 2268–2277 (2019)

36. de Masson d'Autume, C., Rosca, M., Rae, J.W., Mohamed, S.: Training language GANs from scratch. CoRR, abs/1905.09922 (2019)

37. Jégou, S., Drozdzal, M., Vazquez, D., Romero, A., Bengio, Y.: The one hundred layers tiramisu: fully convolutional densenets for semantic segmentation. In: IEEE Conference on Computer Vision and Pattern Recognition Workshops, pp. 11–19 (2017)

38. He, K., Girshick, R.B., Dollár, P.: Rethinking imagenet pre-training. CoRR, abs/1811.08883 (2018)

39. Bethge, J., Yang, H., Bornstein, M., Meinel, C.: Back to simplicity: how to train accurate BNNs from scratch? arXiv preprint arXiv:1906.08637 (2019)

40. Zagoruyko, S., Komodakis, N.: Wide residual networks. In: IEEE Conference on British Machine Vision Conference, pp. 1–12 (2016)

41. Xie, Q., Dai, Z., Hovy, E., Luong, M.-T., Le, Q.V.: Unsupervised data augmentation. arXiv preprint arXiv:1904.12848 (2019)

42. Kingma, D., Ba, J.: Adam: a method for stochastic optimization. In: International Conference on Learning Representations, pp. 1–15 (2015)

43. Song, J., He, T., Gao, L., Xu, X., Hanjalic, A., Shen, H.T.: Binary generative adversarial networks for image retrieval. In: Thirty-Second AAAI Conference on Artificial Intelligence, pp. 394–401 (2018)

H-AT: Hybrid Attention Transfer
for Knowledge Distillation

Yan Qu[✉], Weihong Deng, and Jiani Hu

School of Information and Communication Engineering,
Beijing University of Posts and Telecommunications, Beijing 100876, China
{quyan,whdeng,jnhu}@bupt.edu.cn

Abstract. Knowledge distillation is a widely applicable technique for supervising the training of a light-weight student neural network by capturing and transferring the knowledge of a high-capacity trained teacher neural network. However, the distillation performance is very sensitive to how the distilled knowledge and the distillation loss are defined. In this paper, we propose a novel channel-wise attention transfer loss with a corresponding channel selection method. Further, we develop a hybrid attention transfer loss. Extensive experiments on four public datasets demonstrate that the proposed channel-wise transfer method shows a complementary effect with other attention based methods, and the hybrid attention transfer achieves state-of-the-art performance on knowledge distillation tasks. Code for our experiments is available at https://github.com/somone23412/H-AT.

Keywords: Convolutional neural networks · Knowledge distillation · Neural network compression

1 Introduction

Deep neural network (DNN) models are being used to solve an increasingly wide array of problems, and providing state-of-the-art performance in many tasks, ranging from computer vision [1] to natural language processing [2]. The general trend in deep learning are towards deeper, wider, and more complex networks, which requires us to consider the computational cost of deploying deep learning solutions in the real world.

Knowledge distillation is a general technique for supervising the training of a light-weight "student" neural network by capturing and transferring the knowledge of a high-capacity trained "teacher" network. One of the first knowledge distillation works is introduced by [3] suggesting to adopting soft labels generated by teacher model as the supervision signal in addition to the regular labeled training data during the training phase. Although Hinton's traditional knowledge distillation (KD) training achieved improved accuracy over several datasets,

---

The first author is student.

© Springer Nature Switzerland AG 2020
Y. Peng et al. (Eds.): PRCV 2020, LNCS 12307, pp. 249–260, 2020.
https://doi.org/10.1007/978-3-030-60636-7_21

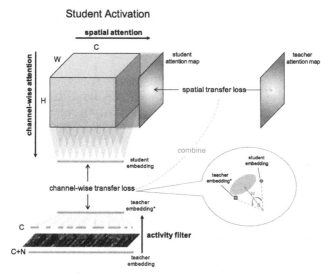

Fig. 1. *Hybrid attention transfer* guides the training procedure of a student network by using the channel-wise and spatial semantic information from teacher. Global average pooling and an activity filter is used to produce the channel-wise embeddings, and the spatial attention function is used to compute the spatial attention maps. Channel-wise cosine similarity and spatial L_2 distance are combined to be used as constraints and the extra supervision for the training procedure of student network.

it was reported that KD struggles to work if teacher and student are very deep or have different architecture. In fact, the knowledge distillation performance is very sensitive to how the distilled knowledge and the distillation loss are defined. How to best transfer the knowledge of the teacher to the student still remains an open question. In this paper, we proposed a hybrid attention transfer method for knowledge distillation, as shown in Fig. 1.

In traditional knowledge distillation, the softened class scores of the teacher are used as the extra supervisory signal, and the distillation loss encourages the student to mimic the scores of the teacher, while hint-based knowledge distillation [4] externs the traditional knowledge distillation by adding hints to guide the training of intermediate layers, and showing better accuracy on trained deep student network. In flow-based knowledge distillation [5], the extra supervisory signal comes from the inter-layer "flow" - how features are transformed between layers. The distillation loss encourages the student to mimic the teacher's flow matrices, which are derived from the inner product of feature maps in two layers, such as the first and last layers in a residual block. In similarity-preserving distillation [6], the extra supervisory signal comes from the similarities in the activations of the network as elicited by the images in the mini-batch. The distillation loss encourages the students to mimic the similarity matrices of the teacher. In attention transfer [7], the supervision for knowledge distillation is in the form of spatial attention, in which attention maps are computed by summing the

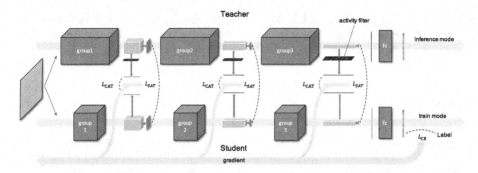

Fig. 2. The over-all procedure of transferring knowledge from teacher network to student network using the channel-wise and spatial semantic information. Each group consist of several CNN blocks. Teacher is running in inference mode. Distillation loss is used to constrain and to guide the training procedure of students' network. L_{CAT}, L_{SAT}, and L_{CE} are channel-wise attention distillation loss, spatial attention distillation loss, and usual cross entropy loss, respectively.

squared activations along the channel dimension. The distillation loss encourages the student to produce similar normalized spatial attention maps as the teacher, intuitively paying attention to similar parts of the image as the teacher.

Our approach was inspired by SCA-CNN [8], in which the network learns to pay attention to every feature entry of the multi-layer 3D feature maps during the training procedure, which indicated that in addition to spatial attention, the channel-wise attention can also be helpful to guide the training procedure of a neural network.

In the hybrid attention transfer method proposed in this paper, the extra channel-wise supervision signal comes from the channel-wise embeddings in vector form by applying the global average pooling (GAP) to each channel of activations of the network, as shown in Fig. 1. In order to solve the difficulty on transferring between networks with different widths, we develop an activity filter for the teacher network to select the same number of channels with the student network. Finally, our distillation loss is defined on the combination of spatial and channel-wise attention matrices, which encourages the student to mimic the matrices of teacher network from both spatial aspect and channel-wise aspect, so as to obtain more effective guidance from the teacher network during the training procedure. Figure 2 illustrates the overall procedure.

The contributions of this paper are:

- We introduce *channel-wise and spatial hybrid attention transfer*, a hybrid attention transfer method for knowledge distillation that uses the attention information from spatial aspect and channel-wise aspect to supervise the training procedure of a student network with a trained teacher network.
- We further propose a channel-wise selection method to select part of the most active channels of teacher network, which allows the channel-wise attention transfers between networks with different channel numbers.

– Extensive experiments on CIFAR-10, CUB, Scenes, and ImageNet databases show that channel-wise attention plays a unique role on knowledge distillation and the hybrid attention transfer achieves state-of-the-art performance on all databases.

2   Related Work

In this paper, several prior knowledge distillation works are described in the introduction. Besides knowledge distillation, there are also approaches for neural network compression. For example, weight pruning methods [9,10] remove unimportant weights from the network, sparsifying the network connectivity structure, while quantized networks [11–13] encode weights and/or activations using a small number of bits, or at lower precision.

3   Method

Our goal is to train a light-weight student network under the guidance of a trained teacher network, which acts as an extra source of supervision. The challenge is to determine how to encode and transfer the teacher's knowledge such that student performance is maximized.

3.1   Knowledge Distillation

It can be said that the traditional knowledge distillation (KD) [3] established the basic pattern of knowledge distillation, that is, in the total distillation loss, one term is usually the cross-entropy loss defined using data supervision (ground truth labels), while the other term encourage the student to mimic the characteristics of the teacher in some aspects.

In KD, the characteristic that student need to mimic is the softened class scores of the teacher:

$$\mathcal{L} = (1 - \alpha)\mathcal{L}_{CE}(\mathbf{y}, \sigma(\mathbf{z}_S)) + 2\alpha T^2 \mathcal{L}_{CE}(\sigma(\frac{\mathbf{z}_S}{T}), \sigma(\frac{\mathbf{z}_T}{T}))) \tag{1}$$

where $\mathcal{L}_{CE}(\cdot, \cdot)$ denotes the cross-entropy loss, $\sigma(\cdot)$ denotes the softmax function, $\mathbf{y}$ is the one-hot vector indicating the ground truth class, $\mathbf{z}_S$ and $\mathbf{z}_T$ are the output logits of the student and teacher networks, respectively, T and α are hyperparameters.

3.2   Spatial Attention Transfer

In spatial attention transfer (AT) [7], given the spatial attention map computed from the corresponding activation tensor $A \in R^{C \times H \times W}$, the characteristic that student need to mimic is the attentions maps of the teacher. When ignoring the same data supervision part as in the traditional KD, the spatial attention transfer loss can be defined as follows:

$$\mathcal{L}_{SAT}(Q_T, Q_S) = \|\frac{Q_T}{\|Q_T\|_2} - \frac{Q_S}{\|Q_S\|_2}\|_2 \tag{2}$$

where Q_T and Q_S are respectively the pair of student and teacher attention maps in vectorized form, which are computed by the attention mapping function:

$$Q = vec(\sum_{i=1}^{C} |A^i|^2) \tag{3}$$

3.3 Hybrid Attention Transfer

The spatial attention encourages the network to pay attention to important parts of the image intuitively. It is easy to speculate that for the same input picture, when the student network tries to focus on the same important area as the teacher network, its performance will be improved. However, a defect of the above spatial attention transfer method is that it summed the feature maps of all channels together. Thus, channel-wise information will be lost inevitably. More seriously, it is difficult to distill knowledge from the network with small feature map size (for example, the size of feature maps from the last several blocks of MobileNet is 1×1, which may result in insignificant spatial attention).

Based on the above analysis of spatial attention transfer, we start to think about how to make the student network make full use of the knowledge contained in the activation of the teacher network: we want the student network to observe and imitate the activation of the teacher network from more aspects intuitively. However, we can't let the student imitate the activation of the teacher network by rote, such excessive imitation will make students' performance decline. For example, the L_2 loss is used directly to constrain the activation of student networks and teacher networks as a baseline in [7], and the performance of student network is worse than that of spatial attention transfer. So we need to find a balance between excessive imitation and insufficient attention. Finally, we propose to use the channel-wise attention information as a supplement.

We use the embeddings produced by the global average pooling as the carrier of additional supplementary information, as shown in Fig. 1, which is actually a vector. Our goal is to let students learn the supplementary information from teacher network via the channel-wise embedding pairs, so we proposed to take the cosine similarity as a constraint, which is often used to measure the similarity of two vectors. In fact, it is to make the angle θ between students' embedding and teachers' embedding as small as possible, as shown in Fig. 3. Since the value range of cosine similarity is $[-1, 1]$, in order to make the training result convergence, we define the channel-wise attention loss as $(1 - \cos\theta)^2$, as follows:

$$\mathcal{L}_{CAT}(\mathbf{e}_T, \mathbf{e}_S) = \|1 - \frac{\mathbf{e}_T}{\|\mathbf{e}_T\|} * \frac{\mathbf{e}_S}{\|\mathbf{e}_S\|}\|_2^2 \tag{4}$$

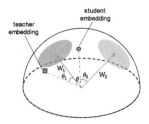

Fig. 3. Channel-wise attention transfer is to make the angle θ between students' embedding and teachers' embedding as small as possible.

where $\mathbf{e}_T = GAP(A_T)$ and $\mathbf{e}_S = GAP(A_S)$ are respectively the pair of student and teacher embeddings after global average pooling.

We define the channel-wise and spatial hybrid attention transfer loss as:

$$\mathcal{L}_{H-AT} = \sum_{j \in \mathcal{I}} \left[\beta_j \mathcal{L}_{CAT}(Q_T^j, Q_S^j) + \delta_j \mathcal{L}_{SAT}(\mathbf{e}_T^j, \mathbf{e}_S^j) \right] \tag{5}$$

where Q_T^j and Q_S^j are respectively the j-th pair of student and teacher attention maps in vectorized form, and $\mathbf{e}_T^j$ and $\mathbf{e}_S^j$ are respectively the j-th pair of student and teacher embeddings after global average pooling.

Finally, we define the total loss for training the student network as:

$$\mathcal{L} = \mathcal{L}_{CE}(\mathbf{y}, \sigma(\mathbf{z}_S)) + \mathcal{L}_{H-AT} \tag{6}$$

3.4   Channel-Wise Activity Filter

Our experiments show that the channel-wise and spatial hybrid attention transfer method can achieve good results. However, when the student network and the teacher network have different widths, the channel dimensions of the student and the teacher do not match, and the channel-wise attention information cannot be transferred. In order to solve this problem, we further propose a channel-wise aspect selection method: activity filter.

The idea is coming from an interesting phenomenon in our analysis of channel-wise attention output of neural network, that is, in the information transmission of neural network, not all channels' activation output is active, as shown in Fig. 4. We visualized the activation intensity of the samples in a batch on all channels, and sorted them according to the ground truth label categories, so that the samples of the same category are continuous together. It can be seen that some channels can give outputs with good distinguishing characteristics while some can hardly distinguish samples of different categories. Based on this observation, we try to choose the most active part of teacher network channel that matches the dimension number of student network channels (we default that the width of teacher network is wider than that of student network) to guide the training process of student network (Algorithm 1), and the measure

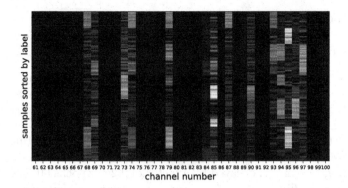

Fig. 4. Not all channels is active. This visualization shows part of the activation intensity on channel-wise aspect, produced by trained WideResNet-16-2 network on a CIFAR-10 batch (sorted by label). Some channels are active and can give outputs with good distinguishing characteristics (e.g. columns 93 to 97) while some can hardly distinguish samples of different categories (e.g. columns 61 to 67). The highlighted channels (64/128) are selected by the activity selection method in experiment.

Algorithm 1. Activity-based channel selection.

Require: $E_T \in R^{b \times n}$: The teacher embeddings after global average pooling in a batch, where b and n represent batch size and the number of channels of teacher network respectively; m: the number of students channels;

Ensure: The selected indexes of teacher channels, $I \in R^m$;

1: Calculating the standard deviation of E_T in batch dimension and express the result as $D_T \in R^n$.
2: Recording the original channel indexes corresponding to the element in D_T;
3: Sorting the elements of D_T in descending order;
4: Taking the channel indexes of the first m elements as the final result I.
5: **return** I;

---

of activity is the standard deviation of channel-wise activation values in a batch dimension.

The last step of channel selection can be simply expressed as:

$$\mathbf{e}'_T = \mathbf{e}_T[I] \tag{7}$$

where $\mathbf{e}_T \in R^n$ is the teacher embedding after global average pooling, and $I \in R^m$ is the list of indexes selected by the activity filter.

This is actually a further attention to the channel-wise information: we pay more attention to the active channels and give up those channels that are not active enough. On the one hand, it makes the channel-wise attention more focused. On the other hand, it allows the channel-wise attention transfers between networks with different widths.

4   Experiments

4.1   CIFAR-10

We start with CIFAR-10 dataset which consisits of 50,000 training images and 10,000 testing images at a resolution of 32×32. The dataset covers ten object classes, with each class having an equal number of images. We conducted experiments using wide residual networks (WideResNets, WR) [14] following [7]. We adopted the standard protocol [14] for training wide residual networks on CIFAR-10 (SGD with Nesterov momentum; 200 epochs; batch size of 128; and an initial learning rate of 0.1, decayed by a factor of 0.2 at epochs 60, 120 and 160). We use horizontal flips and random crops data augmentations. We performed baseline comparisons with respect to traditional knowledge distillation (softened class scores, KD), spatial attention transfer (AT) and similarity preserving distillation (correlation between embeddings in a batch, SP). For all these cases, the teacher is running in inference mode. We use $\alpha = 0.9$ and $T = 4$ for KD, and we use $\beta = 1000$ for AT for WideResNets transfers following the CIFAR-10 experiments in [7]. We set $\gamma = 3000$ and only using the activations collected from the last convolution layers of the student network and teacher network for SP following the CIFAR-10 experiments in [6]. In case of channel-wise and spatial hybrid attention transfer we apply losses to each of the three residual block groups. Considering that progressing deeper in the network, the channels encode increasingly specialized features, and deeper features may be more helpful to classification [15], we use the hyperparameters increasing according to the depth: $[\beta_1, \beta_2, \beta_3] = [10, 100, 1000]$ (β of the last residual block group is consistent with that in spatial attention transfer experiment), and we set $[\delta_1, \delta_2, \delta_3] = [0.1, 1, 10]$ by held-out validation on a subset of the training set.

Student and teacher with same widths. We firstly tested cases in which the student and teacher networks have the same width but different depth. Table 1 shows the results. In these cases, distilling the knowledge of the teacher network using channel-wise and spatial hybrid attention transfer improved student training outcomes. Compared to training with data supervision only, the student network obtained lower median error with no additional network parameters. Hybrid attention transfer also performed favorably with respect to the traditional KD (softened class scores), AT, and SP baselines, achieving the lowest error in five of the two cases. This validates our induction that the channel-wise and spatial hybrid attention transfer can extract more useful semantic information, and provide more effective guidance for knowledge distillation.

Different student and teacher widths. In case of student and teacher networks with different widths, we select part of the most active channels of the teacher network by activity filter (Alg. 1) to guide the student network in channel-wise aspect. Table 2 shows our results experimenting with three student-teacher network pairs with different widths, in which H-AT outperforms conventional training as well as the traditional KD, AT, and SP baselines. In this case the

Table 1. Experiments on CIFAR-10 with four different knowledge distillation losses: softened class scores (traditional KD), spatial attention transfer (AT), similarity preserving (SP), and channel-wise and spatial hybrid attention transfer (H-AT). Median of 5 runs test errors are reported. The best result for each experiment is shown in bold. Brackets indicate model size in number of parameters. "WR" refer to WideResNet [14].

Student	Teacher	Student	KD [3]	AT [7]	SP [6]	H-AT	Teacher
WR-16-1 (0.2M)	WR-40-1 (0.6M)	8.83	8.33	8.30	8.26	**7.86**	6.38
WR-16-2 (0.7M)	WR-40-2 (2.2M)	6.34	6.02	5.80	5.68	**5.51**	4.97

Table 2. Experiments on CIFAR-10 in case of teacher network with different width to student network, using activity filter to fit the size of teacher embedding to the same as student embedding. Median of 5 runs test errors are reported. The best result for each experiment is shown in bold. Brackets indicate model size in number of parameters.

Student	Teacher	Student	KD [3]	AT [7]	SP [6]	H-AT	Teacher
WR-16-1 (0.2M)	WR-16-2 (0.7M)	8.83	7.84	8.17	7.82	**7.74**	6.34
WR-16-2 (0.7M)	WR-16-8 (11.0M)	6.34	5.56	5.60	5.60	**5.48**	4.33
WR-40-2 (2.2M)	WR-16-8 (11.0M)	4.97	4.82	4.63	4.56	**4.55**	4.33

activity channel filter and the channel-wise transfer loss were applied to the last convolution layers of the student and teacher networks with $\delta = 10$, and the feature maps collected from the last convolution layers to computed spatial attention map were also selected by activity channel filter. We also evaluated the impact of different channel selection methods in H-AT, as shown in Table 3. Compared to random select and inactivity filter (to take the complementary set of indexes selected by the active filter), activity filter achieved the lowest error, which demonstrate the validity of this channel-wise selection approach.

Our results suggest the effectiveness for using H-AT distillation to compress large networks into more resource-efficient ones with minimal accuracy loss. In the third test in Table 2, for example, the knowledge of a trained WideResNet-16-8 network, which contains 11.0M parameters, is distilled into a smaller WideResNet-40-2 network, which contains only 2.2M parameters. This

Table 3. Transferring the knowledge from WideResNet-16-2 to WideResNet-16-1 with three different channel selection methods.

Method	WR-16-2 (0.7M) → WR-16-1 (0.2M)
Student	8.83
Inactivity	8.60 (−0.23)
Random	7.98 (−0.85)
Activity	**7.74 (−1.09)**
Teacher	6.38

is a 5× compression rate with only 0.2% loss in accuracy, using off-the-shelf PyTorch without any specialized hardware or software.

4.2 Transfer Learning

To see how channel-wise and spatial hybrid attention transfer works in finetuning we choose two datasets: Caltech-UCSD Birds-200–2011 fine-grained classification (CUB) [16], and MIT indoor scene classification (Scenes) [17] dataset, both containing around 5 K images training images. We took ResNet-18 and ResNet-34 pretrained on ImageNet and finetuned on Scenes datasets. On CUB we crop bounding boxes, rescale to 256 in one dimension, random rotate from $-45°$ to $45°$, and then take a random crop. Batch normalization layers are fixed for finetuning, and first group of residual blocks is frozen. We then took finetuned ResNet-34 networks and used them as teachers for ResNet-18 pretrained on ImageNet. In case of AT, apply spatial attention losses to the 2 last residual groups following the transfer learning experiment in [7]. In case of SP, apply loss to the last residual group. In case of H-AT, since the first group of residual blocks is frozen, losses were applied to the 3 last residual groups. All networks were trained using SGD with Nesterov momentum, a batch size of 8 (for better generalization ability), and for 60 epochs with an initial learning rate of 0.001 reduced to 0.0001 after 30 epochs. We used the standard training-validation-testing split and set the hyperparameters for H-AT and all baselines by held-out validation (KD: $\alpha = 0.9$; AT: $\beta = 500$; SP: $\gamma = 500$; H-AT: $[\beta_1, \beta_2, \beta_3] = [5; 50; 500]$ and $[\delta_1, \delta_2, \delta_3] = [0.05, 0.5, 5]$).

Table 4. Finetuning with H-AT error on CUB and Scenes datasets. The best result for each experiment is shown in bold.

Method	Model	ImageNet → CUB	ImageNet → Scenes
Student	ResNet-18	26.86	25.67
KD [3]	ResNet-18	25.35 (−1.51)	23.81 (−1.86)
AT [7]	ResNet-18	25.39 (−1.47)	23.88 (−1.79)
SP [6]	ResNet-18	25.44 (−1.42)	24.63 (−1.04)
H-AT	ResNet-18	**24.91 (−1.95)**	**23.66 (−2.01)**
Teacher	ResNet-34	24.82	23.58

Table 4 shows the results. In both cases H-AT provides significant improvements, closing the gap between ResNet-18 and ResNet-34 in accuracy. H-AT also performed favorably with respect to KD, AT, and SP baselines, achieving the lowest error in four of both cases.

4.3 ImageNet

To showcase channel-wise and spatial hybrid attention transfer on ImageNet [18], we took ResNet-18 as a student and ResNet-34 as a teacher trying to improve the student's accuracy, and compared with other baseline methods. The detailed experimental settings are: SGD with Nesterov momentum; 100 epochs; batch size of 256; and an initial learning rate of 0.1, decayed by a factor of 0.2 at epochs 30, 60 and 90. In this section, we didn't validate traditional knowledge distillation method because it can't achieve positive results on ImageNet, which was mentioned in [7]. In case of AT, we apply two losses to the last two residual block groups following the ImageNet experiments in [7]. We set $\beta = 500$ by held-out validation on a subset of the training set. In case of SP, we keep the same hyperparameter from CIFAR-10 experiment by held-out validation on a subset of the training set. In case of H-AT, losses were applied for each of the four residual block groups, we set $[\beta_1, \beta_2, \beta_3, \beta_4] = [0.5, 5, 50, 500]$ and $[\delta_1, \delta_2, \delta_3, \delta_4] = [0.005, 0.05, 0.5, 5]$ according to the ratio of spatial attention transfer loss to channel-wise attention transfer loss of the CIFAR-10 experiment in 4.1.

Table 5. Training ResNet-18 on ImageNet with three different knowledge distillation losses. Validation errors (single crop) are reported. The best result is shown in bold.

Model	Top1	Top5
ResNet18 (student)	30.43	10.76
ResNet18-AT [7]	29.29 (-1.14)	10.11 (-0.65)
ResNet-18-SP [6]	29.55 (-0.88)	10.31 (-0.45)
ResNet18-H-AT	**29.18 (-1.25)**	**9.89 (-0.91)**
ResNet34 (teacher)	26.72	8.74

Compared to training with data supervision only, ResNet-18 with channel-wise and spatial hybrid attention transfer consistently improved student training outcomes, achieving 1.25% top-1 and 0.91% top-5 better validation accuracy (as shown in Table 5), and achieved the lowest error with respect to AT and SP distillation baselines.

5 Conclusion

We proposed channel-wise and spatial hybrid attention transfer: a hybrid attention transfer method for knowledge distillation, and a channel-wise selection method to select part of the most active channels of teacher network, which allows the channel-wise attention transfers between networks wth different channel numbers. Our experiments on CIFAR-10, CUB, Scenes, and ImageNet databases shows that channel-wise attention transfer complements the spatial attention transfer method and captures teacher knowledge that is not fully encoded in spatial attention map, and the hybrid attention transfer achieves state-of-the-art performance on knowledge distillation tasks.

References

1. He, K., Zhang, X., Ren, S., Sun, J.: Deep residual learning for image recognition. In: Proceedings of the IEEE conference on computer vision and pattern recognition, pp. 770–778 (2016)
2. Antol, S., et al.: Vqa: visual question answering. In: Proceedings of the IEEE international conference on computer vision, pp. 2425–2433 (2015)
3. Hinton, G., Vinyals, O., Dean, J.: Distilling the knowledge in a neural network. arXiv preprint arXiv:1503.02531 (2015)
4. Romero, A., Ballas, N., Kahou, S.E., Chassang, A., Gatta, C., Bengio, Y.: Fitnets: hints for thin deep nets. arXiv preprint arXiv:1412.6550 (2014)
5. Yim, J., Joo, D., Bae, J., Kim, J.: A gift from knowledge distillation: Fast optimization, network minimization and transfer learning. In: Proceedings of the IEEE Conference on Computer Vision and Pattern Recognition, pp. 4133–4141 (2017)
6. Tung, F., Mori, G.: Similarity-preserving knowledge distillation. In: Proceedings of the IEEE International Conference on Computer Vision, pp. 1365–1374 (2019)
7. Zagoruyko, S., Komodakis, N.: Paying more attention to attention: Improving the performance of convolutional neural networks via attention transfer. arXiv preprint arXiv:1612.03928 (2016)
8. Chen, L., et al.: Sca-cnn: spatial and channel-wise attention in convolutional networks for image captioning. In: Proceedings of the IEEE conference on computer vision and pattern recognition, pp. 5659–5667 (2017)
9. Liu, Z., Xu, J., Peng, X., Xiong, R.: Frequency-domain dynamic pruning for convolutional neural networks. In: Advances in Neural Information Processing Systems, pp. 1043–1053 (2018)
10. Luo, J.H., Wu, J., Lin, W.: Thinet: a filter level pruning method for deep neural network compression. In: Proceedings of the IEEE international conference on computer vision, pp. 5058–5066. IEEE (2017)
11. Courbariaux, M., Bengio, Y., David, J.P.: Binaryconnect: training deep neural networks with binary weights during propagations. In: Advances in neural information processing systems, pp. 3123–3131 (2015)
12. Courbariaux, M., Hubara, I., Soudry, D., El-Yaniv, R., Bengio, Y.: Binarized neural networks: training deep neural networks with weights and activations constrained to + 1 or -1. arXiv preprint arXiv:1602.02830 (2016)
13. Rastegari, M., Ordonez, V., Redmon, J., Farhadi, A.: XNOR-Net: imagenet classification using binary convolutional neural networks. In: Leibe, B., Matas, J., Sebe, N., Welling, M. (eds.) ECCV 2016. LNCS, vol. 9908, pp. 525–542. Springer, Cham (2016). https://doi.org/10.1007/978-3-319-46493-0_32
14. Zagoruyko, S., Komodakis, N.: Wide residual networks. arXiv preprint arXiv:1605.07146 (2016)
15. Tzeng, E., Hoffman, J., Zhang, N., Saenko, K., Darrell, T.: Deep domain confusion: maximizing for domain invariance. arXiv preprint arXiv:1412.3474 (2014)
16. Wah, C., Branson, S., Welinder, P., Perona, P., Belongie, S.: The caltech-ucsd birds-200-2011 dataset. Computation & neural systems technical report. California Institute of Technology (2011)
17. Quattoni, A., Torralba, A.: Recognizing indoor scenes. In: 2009 IEEE Conference on Computer Vision and Pattern Recognition, pp. 413–420. IEEE (2009)
18. Russakovsky, O., et al.: Imagenet large scale visual recognition challenge. Int. J. Comput. Vision **115**(3), 211–252 (2015)

Cross-Domain Disentangle Network for Image Manipulation

Zhening Xing[1], Jinghuan Wen[2], and Huimin Ma[1(✉)]

[1] University of Science and Technology Beijing, Beijing, China
g20198883@xs.ustb.edu.cn, mhmpub@ustb.edu.cn
[2] TencentInc., Tsinghua University, Beijing, China
jinghuanwen@tencent.com

Abstract. Deep image-to-image translation networks have shown satisfying results on domain adaptive image generation tasks. In this paper, we make further progress on a new task of cross-domain image manipulation. We aim at generating a manipulated image that has a specified factor of the source-domain image and other factors of the target-domain image. We present a novel cross-domain disentangle network, which is capable of learning disentangled representation from data across multiple domains. This network extracts the latent representation of images on source and target domains, and disentangles the specified and unspecified factors of latent representation simultaneously on both domains. Image manipulation within and across domain can be realized by manipulating on the latent space. Empirical experiments show that our method is able to generate convincing intra-domain and cross-domain manipulated images.

Keywords: Representation disentanglement · Image-to-image manipulation

1 Introduction

Recent researches on image-to-image translation and domain adaptation have shown satisfying visual effects on generating images across different data domains. This provides a new possibility of cross-domain image manipulation, i.e. given a image from source domain image set $\{X_s\}$ and another image from target domain image set $\{X_t\}$ we aim at swapping their features shared in both domains and reserving features which is only belonged to their own domain. We call the former features as *domain-invariant factors* and call the latter features as *domain-specific factors*. Take digit datasets, MNIST and SVHN, as example, the domain-invariant factors in both domains are digit labels, and domain-specific factors are style, background, etc. The success of cross-domain manipulation requires extracting a domain-invariant factor of the common semantic information, as well as disentangling such factor with other domain-specific factors. Recent works [1–5] have presented several approaches on extracting disentangled

© Springer Nature Switzerland AG 2020
Y. Peng et al. (Eds.): PRCV 2020, LNCS 12307, pp. 261–272, 2020.
https://doi.org/10.1007/978-3-030-60636-7_22

latent space representations, but a cross-domain variant of such approaches is required for extracting common factors of multiple domains.

In this paper, we propose a novel approach on cross-domain image manipulation. We present a cross-domain disentangle network to extract the latent representation of images on source and target domains, and to disentangle the domain-invariant and domain-specific factors of the latent representation. Further, by replacing the domain-invariant factor of latent vector, the proposed network is capable of generating images from manipulated latent representations. A manipulated latent representation can be a combination of two images within the same domain, which realizes an intra-domain image manipulation, or a combination of two images from different domains, which realizes a cross-domain image manipulation. We examine our method and show its capacity on disentangling factors and manipulating images across multiple data domain.

To summarize, the major contributions of this paper are: (a) a novel approach on cross-domain image manipulation by combining disentangled latent representations on domain-specific and domain-invariant latent spaces, (b) a novel cross-domain disentangle network architecture that learns disentangled domain-specific and domain-invariant representations from data across multiple domains, (c) and task-specified training strategy that supplement the missing supervision in generating images of mixed latent representations.

2   Related Work

Variational Auto-Encoder [6] (VAE) and it's variants are used to learn disentangled latent factors of image variants. The works presented in [7,8] use semi-supervised learning to disentangle the features of label information. The works presented in [2–5] use adversarial training between encoder and latent classifier to ensure the disentanglement of latent vectors. In this paper, we use an adversarial VAE to learn latent factors, and disentangle the domain-specific and domain-invariant factors using adversarial latent classifier.

Generative adversarial network (GAN) introduced by Goodfellow *et al.* in [9] realize image generation via adversarial training between generator and discrimiantor. Later on, other methods improve the original GAN in terms of model structures [10], application fields [11–13] and mathematic principles [14–16]. For better training stability, the adversarial discriminators in this paper are based on WGAN-GP [15], which minimizes Wasserstein distance between generated and real distribution and uses gradient penalty to ensure Lipschitz continuity of discrimiantor.

Domain adaptation methods transfer data distribution from one (source domain) to another (target domain). Domain classifiers are used in [17,18] to ensure the feature similarity between two domains. It is worth noticing that the method by Liu *et al.* [19] views both data domains and image attributes as latent factors to be disentangled, our method considers data domains and image attributes separately, which realizes cross-domain image attribute manipulation.

Image-to-Image translation methods are another way to generate cross-domain images. Isola *et al.* [20] introduced conditional GAN to translate images using pairwise training data. Taigman *et al.* [21] introduced cross-domain feature consistency in domain transfer, which is also employed in our method. Cycle-consistency-like loss is introduced in [22–24] which restricts that the network reconstructs the original image by translating backwards. Further more, methods for multimodal image translation are introduced in [25–27]. Some other methods [12,28,29] are proposed to apply image-to-image translation between more than two domains. Although these methods have shown promising results and some of them present a disentangle between *style* and *content*, they do not take the meaning of latent feature presentation, which is crucial in cross-domain label manipulation tasks, into consideration.

3   Cross-Domain Disentangle Network

We present a novel network that disentangles the domain-invariant and domain-specific factors from multiple data domains, and swap the domain-invariant factors for cross-domain image manipulation. We adapt the same network structure on intra-domain and cross-domain disentangle tasks.

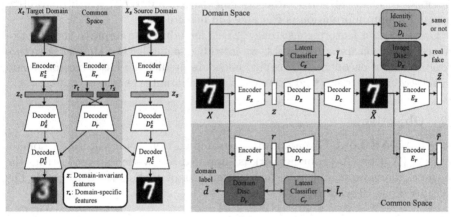

(a) Cross domain manipulation   (b) Intra domain manipulation

Fig. 1. (a) The process of cross domain image manipulation. Note that we swap domain invariant features of source and target domain before decoding them to RGB space. (b) Model structure for single domain. Note that for simplicity, the illustration only contain structure for a single domain.

3.1   Network Structure

The VAEs [6] and their combination with GANs [30] are able to learn representations of the image and generate image from latent representations. Our model uses VAEs to extract latent factors of source-domain and target-domain images, and use additional discriminators and classifiers to disentangle the domain-invariant factors r and domain-specific factors z. The overall structure of the proposed network is shown as Fig. 1b. To learn common features across domains, we apply a shared encoder E_r that encode the images x to latent vector r in common feature space. The complimentary features z are extracted by private encoder E_z in each domain. To ensure that the r and z contains all the information of the image, we use a decoder that takes the input of r and z, and reconstruct the image. The decoder consists of three parts, a domain-specific part D_z, a domain-invariant part D_r and a output part D_c which map feature map from feature space to RGB space.

Other than VAEs, we need extra structures to disentangle domain-invariant and domain-specific factors of the representations. In this paper, we use adversarial classifiers to separate these factors. Since the shared encoder E_r aims at learning domain-invariant features, we use a domain-invariant classifier C_r that takes feature r as input and infers the image attribute label l. C_r is co-trained with VAEs. In contrast, we use adversarial training for domain-specific classifier C_z to ensure that feature z does not contain the information of label l. Since the domain-invariant latent vector is supposed to be of the same distribution across domains, we adapt an adversarial domain discriminator D_r, which guarantees that no domain information is contained in feature r.

Cross-domain feature consistency [21] is introduced to improve the effect of image translation. In our network, we introduce a similar but simpler structure using a copy of encoders. The copied encoders predict the latent vectors $\tilde{r}$ and $\tilde{z}$. Well-trained encoders and decoders should guarantee that $\tilde{r} = r$ and $\tilde{z} = z$.

3.2   Objective

Original VAE Loss. Given an image x sampled from source or target domain datasets $\{X_s\}$ or $\{X_t\}$, our network is supposed to encode and reconstruct the image x, therefore a typical reconstruction loss of VAEs should be used. The VAE losses are defined as

$$
\begin{aligned}
\mathcal{L}_{rec} &= \mathbb{E}\left[\|\tilde{x} - x\|_2^2\right] \\
\mathcal{L}_{kld} &= D_{KL}\left[q(z|x)\|p(z)\right] + D_{KL}\left[q(r|x)\|p(r)\right],
\end{aligned}
\tag{1}
$$

where $\tilde{x}$ is the reconstructed image and D_{KL} is the Kullback-Leibler divergence that limits the deviation of latent distributions $q(z|x)$ and $q(r|x)$ to prior distributions $p(z)$ and $p(r)$ (as $z, r \sim \mathcal{N}(0, I)$).

Feature Classification Loss. The co-training of classifier C_r is crucial for learning domain-invariant features because C_r ensures r to have all the information needed for inferring the label. The classification loss for classifier C_r is defined as

$$
\mathcal{L}_{C_r} = -\mathbb{E}_{x \sim \mathbb{P}_r}\left[\log P(\tilde{l}_r = l|x)\right],
\tag{2}
$$

where l is the label of image, and $\mathbb{P}_r$ is the real image distribution of source or target domain. A similar loss can be applied to classifier C_z, except that the adversarial training of encoder E_z should also be considered:

$$\mathcal{L}_{C_z} = -\mathcal{L}_{C_z}^{adv} = -\mathbb{E}_{x \sim \mathbb{P}_r} \left[\log P(\tilde{l}_z = l | x) \right]. \tag{3}$$

Identity Loss. The identity discriminator D_l is used to restrict the identities (labels) of generated images. The identity discriminator takes two images as input, one from source domain and another from target domain. It learns whether or not the input images have the same label. It is useful in cross-domain manipulation, since no ground-truth image is available. The losses in the training of discriminator and the adversarial training of VAEs are defined as

$$\mathcal{L}_{D_l}^{adv} = -\mathbb{E}_{\tilde{x} \sim \mathbb{P}_g} \left[\log P(\tilde{l}_x = l | \tilde{x}) \right], \qquad \mathcal{L}_{D_l} = -\mathbb{E}_{x \sim \mathbb{P}_r} \left[\log P(\tilde{l}_x = l | x) \right]. \tag{4}$$

Domain Classification Loss. For better manipulation results, we hope that the domain-invariant factors r should be of the same distribution for both domains. Therefore, another discriminator D_r is used for adversarial training against the encoder E_r. For a two-domain disentangle task, we set the domain label $d = 1$ for source domain and $d = 0$ for target domain. A similar WGAN-GP model is applied with the loss defined as

$$\begin{aligned} \mathcal{L}_{D_r}^{adv} &= \mathbb{E}\left[D_r(r_s)\right] - \mathbb{E}\left[D_r(r_t)\right], \\ \mathcal{L}_{D_r} &= -\mathbb{E}\left[D_r(r_s)\right] + \mathbb{E}\left[D_r(r_t)\right] + \lambda \left(\|\nabla_{\hat{r}} D_r(\hat{r})\|_2 - 1\right)^2, \end{aligned} \tag{5}$$

where $r_s = E_r(x_s)$ and $r_t = E_r(x_t)$ are latent vectors encoded from source and target domain, respectively, and $\hat{r} = \epsilon r_s + (1 - \epsilon) r_t$ is the interpolation of r_s and r_t.

Latent Cycle Consistency Loss. Ideal encoders should output the same latent variables for original and reconstructed images, which requires latent consistency. To address these, we use a unified cross-domain latent consistency loss defined as

$$\mathcal{L}_{lc} = \|\tilde{r} - r\|_2^2 + \|\tilde{z} - z\|_2^2, \tag{6}$$

which is the L_2 distance between the latent vectors of the original and generated images. To be noted that, for optimal decoders with zero reconstruction loss, our latent consistency loss equals to original cycle consistency loss in image space. And in the training of deep convolution neural networks, the gradient of latent consistency loss directly acts on the encoders which are more important in disentangling latent factors.

Image Adversarial Loss. Moreover, in order to make generated images as realistic as possible, we introduce image discrimiantor D_x. For better training stability, the WGAN loss with gradient penalty [15] is used in the training process:

$$\begin{aligned} \mathcal{L}_{D_x}^{adv} &= -\mathbb{E}_{\tilde{x} \sim \mathbb{P}_g}\left[D_x(\tilde{x})\right], \\ \mathcal{L}_{D_x} &= -\mathbb{E}_{x \sim \mathbb{P}_r}\left[D_x(x)\right] + \mathbb{E}_{\tilde{x} \sim \mathbb{P}_g}\left[D_x(\tilde{x})\right] + \lambda \left(\|\nabla_{\hat{x}} D_x(\hat{x})\|_2 - 1\right)^2, \end{aligned} \tag{7}$$

where $\mathbb{P}_r$ and $\mathbb{P}_g$ are the real image distribution and generated image distribution respectively, and $\hat{x} = \epsilon x + (1 - \epsilon)\tilde{x}$, $\epsilon \in (0, 1)$, which is the interpolation of x and $\tilde{x}$. λ is the weight for gradient penalty and we set $\lambda = 10$ as suggested in [15].

The full objective of encoder-decoder structure is

$$\mathcal{L} = \lambda_{rec}\mathcal{L}_{rec} + \lambda_{kld}\mathcal{L}_{kld} + \lambda_{C_r}\mathcal{L}_{C_r} + \lambda_{C_z}^{adv}\mathcal{L}_{C_z}^{adv} + \\ \lambda_{D_x}^{adv}\mathcal{L}_{D_x}^{adv} + \lambda_{D_r}^{adv}\mathcal{L}_{D_r}^{adv} + \lambda_{D_l}^{adv}\mathcal{L}_{D_l}^{adv} + \lambda_{lc}\mathcal{L}_{lc}, \quad (8)$$

where λ_*^* are weight of corresponding loss term. In this paper, we have $\lambda_{rec} = 10$, $\lambda_{kld} = 10^{-4}$, $\lambda_{C_r} = 2$, $\lambda_{C_z}^{adv} = 2$, $\lambda_{D_x}^{adv} = 1$, $\lambda_{D_r}^{adv} = 1$, $\lambda_{D_l}^{adv} = 1$, $\lambda_{lc} = 1$.

To train the network, the components of VAEs are updated to minimize

$$\theta_{E_z}, \theta_{E_r}, \theta_{D_z}, \theta_{D_r}, \theta_{D_c} = \underset{\theta_{E_z}, \theta_{E_r}, \theta_{D_z}, \theta_{D_r}, \theta_{D_c}}{\arg\min} \mathcal{L} \quad (9)$$

with the adversarial training components being alternatively updated to minimize

$$\theta_{C_z}, \theta_{D_l}, \theta_{D_r}, \theta_{D_x} = \underset{\theta_{C_z}, \theta_{D_l}, \theta_{D_r}, \theta_{D_x}}{\arg\min} \mathcal{L}_{C_z} + \mathcal{L}_{D_l} + \mathcal{L}_{D_r} + \mathcal{L}_{D_x} \quad (10)$$

3.3 Sub-task Training Strategies

A typical training process utilizing these losses will result into several limitations. First, it is not guarantee that z should contain any information of the input image. As a counterexample, the network can reconstruct the image only using r. Second, the manipulation operations should be included in training, otherwise the manipulated results may not be satisfactory. However, the ground-truth of manipulated images is absent in training. Therefore, a proper combination of latent factors depend on the specific task is required. We examine our network on intra-domain and cross-domain disentangle tasks. The training strategy under each sub-task is discussed as following.

(a) Latent manipulation within domain.   (b) Latent manipulation across domain.

Fig. 2. An illustration of latent manipulation strategies. For intra-domain image manipulation, only (a) is used. For cross-domain image manipulation training, a combination of (a) and (b) is used.

For intra-domain image manipulation, we use the training strategy proposed in [1]. We sample three images $x^{(1)}$, $x^{(1')}$ and $x^{(2)}$ from the dataset, where $x^{(1)}$ and $x^{(1')}$ have the same label and different from $x^{(2)}$. Therefore $x^{(1')}$ and $x^{(1)}$ are expected to have the same latent factor, i.e. $r^{(1')} = r^{(1)}$. Therefore, we have

$$\tilde{x}^{(1'1)} := D_c\left(D_r(r^{(1')}), D_z(z^{(1)})\right) = D_c\left(D_r(r^{(1)}), D_z(z^{(1)})\right), \quad (11)$$

where the last equal sign is the reconstruction objective of VAEs. The overall loss of VAEs consists of reconstruction loss $\mathcal{L}_{rec}(\tilde{x}^{(11)}, \tilde{x}^{(1)})$, $\mathcal{L}_{rec}(\tilde{x}^{(1'1)}, \tilde{x}^{(1)})$, and adversarial loss $\mathcal{L}_{D_x}^{adv}(\tilde{x}^{(21)})$, as shown in Fig. 2(a). Although this latent manipulation strategy is originally designed for weakly-supervised disentanglement, we find it useful for accelerating the training process for supervised disentanglement as well.

In a cross-domain setting, we introduce two additional adversarial loss for manipulated images, $\mathcal{L}_{D_x}^{adv}(x_t^{(12)})$ and $\mathcal{L}_{D_x}^{adv}(x_s^{(21)})$, as shown in Fig. 2(b). This is crucial for the network to learn disentangled representations across domain. The intra-domain losses force the network to learn valid common space representations, and the cross-domain losses are for improving the qualities of manipulated images. In addition, we introduce identity discriminator losses $\mathcal{L}_{D_l}^{adv}(x_s^{(1)}, \tilde{x}_t^{(12)})$ and $\mathcal{L}_{D_l}^{adv}(x_s^{(21)}, \tilde{x}_t^{(2)})$ that determine whether or not the paired images have the same identity. These training strategies supplement the missing supervision for generated mix-feature images.

4 Experiments

4.1 Datasets

MNIST [31], USPS [32], MNIST-M [17], SVHN [33] datasets are used as benchmark datasets to evaluate our method. Each dataset is considered as a different domain. MNIST dataset contains 60,000/10,000 training/testing images of handwritten digits. USPS contains 7,291/2,007 training/testing images of handwritten digits. MNIST-M is an extension of MNIST with colored background randomly extracted from photos. SVHN (Street View House Numbers) dataset has 73,257/26,032 training/testing images of digits on house-number signs with complex background and distracting digits. For training common space encoders and decoders, we resize the images of both domain to the same size (the larger of the two domains). To be noted that, all these digit images have clear label identities and different styles, which can help us to evaluate the qualities of latent feature disentanglement and intra and cross-domain image manipulation.

4.2 Intra-Domain Image Manipulation

We first test our method within each domain. We train a network following the intra-domain training procedure as shown in Fig. 2(a). The results are shown in Fig. 3. The network is able to disentangle specified factors (digit label) and other factors such as digit style, background and neighboring digits. Most images (exclude images on diagonal) are generated using a mixed latent vector from two different images, and we observe that the generated results are convincing.

For quantitative results, we evaluate the classification error for disentangled latent factors r and z, and the results are in Table 1. A well trained classifier on r is expected to have zero classification error, while a classifier on z is expected to have an error of 90% on digit datasets. Results shown that the network is able to

Table 1. Intra-domain and cross-domain classification error of r and z classifiers on training and testing datasets. Error rates of r and z are expected to be 0% and 90%, respectively.

	r		z	
	train	test	train	test
MNIST	0.02%	0.42%	79.76%	76.73%
MNIST-M	0.02%	1.69%	82.79%	82.86%
USPS	0.07%	2.37%	80.38%	77.22%
SVHN	0.08%	5.57%	80.84%	80.48%
Expected	0%		90%	

Table 2. Intra-domain and cross-domain reconstruction PSNR. *Left:* Reconstruction PSNR of intra-domain models in Sect. 4.2. *Right:* Source-to-source and target-to-target reconstruction PSNR of cross-domain models in Sect. 4.3.

	Reconstruction PSNR (dB)	
	train	test
MNIST	24.93	23.26
MNISTM	21.49	20.16
USPS	23.35	19.42
SVHN	25.70	25.08

	Reconstruction PSNR (dB)			
	source-to-source		target-to-target	
	train	test	train	test
MNIST↔MNIST-M	23.17	22.43	19.56	18.76
MNIST↔SVHN	11.93	11.98	16.09	16.07
MNISTM↔SVHN	21.49	20.87	25.51	25.22
MNIST↔USPS	20.96	20.31	20.15	20.15

Table 3. Cross-domain classification error of r and z classifiers on training and testing datasets. Error rates of r and z are expected to be 0% and 90%, respectively. r_s, r_t are r of source and target domain, respectively. And so is z_s and z_t.

	r_s		r_t		z_s		z_t	
	train	test	train	test	train	test	train	test
MNIST↔MNIST-M	0.74%	1.26%	0.48%	2.64%	81.70%	75.73%	89.83%	91.01%
MNIST↔SVHN	1.46%	1.19%	8.84%	9.71%	89.45%	89.23%	91.61%	91.69%
MNISTM↔SVHN	4.89%	2.97%	6.88%	8.06%	86.13%	85.38%	88.99%	88.32%
MNIST↔USPS	4.56%	1.21%	1.28%	2.88%	91.70%	95.26%	85.20%	85.63%
Expected	0%				90%			

disentangle the specified factor of latent representation. Since we apply the same network configuration on each dataset, the results indicate that the complexity of dataset affects disentanglement. A difficult dataset, such as SVHN, requires an effective encoder E_r. While a simple dataset, such as MNIST, requires a weak encoder E_z, otherwise some of the domain-invariant factors may be contained in z, which results in a classification error on z lower than 90%. In a particular task, proper encoder E_r and E_z should be chosen wisely for better disentangle effect. We also evaluate the self-reconstruction error of VAEs, as shown in Table 2

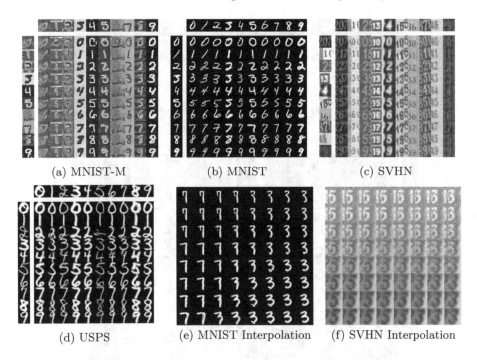

(a) MNIST-M   (b) MNIST   (c) SVHN

(d) USPS   (e) MNIST Interpolation   (f) SVHN Interpolation

Fig. 3. (a)-(d) Result of image manipulation within domains. The image of i-th row and j-th column in the matrix is composed of specified factor (digit label) from the i-th image (see left) and unspecified factors from the j-th image (see top). Each row in the matrix contains the images of the same digit and each column the same style, background and neighboring digits. Note that in SVHN the distracting digits remain unchanged for each column. (e)-(f) Result of latent space interpolation, showing the identity r changes horizontally and the style z changes vertically. The images on top-left and bottom-right right corner are from test datasets. Note the background gradually changes to foreground in (f).

(left). The VAEs are able to reconstruct the image from extracted feature, which indicates the information integrity of the encoders.

To show how the latent space manipulation can cause image changes, we perform an interpolation experiment. Given two images, we can generate images by interpolating alone r and z vectors, as shown in Fig. 3. We can see that the change in specified and unspecified latent vector can cause the image to change accordingly.

4.3   Cross-Domain Image Manipulation

The major task of cross-domain disentangle network is to manipulate target domain image given a reference source domain image, and vise versa. We train a network utilizing both the intra-domain training settings in Fig. 2(a) and the cross-domain training settings in Fig. 2(b). The results are shown in Fig. 4. The

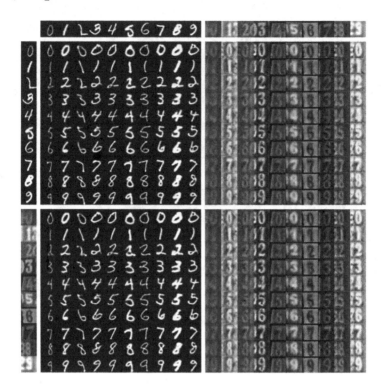

Fig. 4. Result of image manipulation across domains MNIST↔SVHN. There are four image matrices, and the image matrice on top-left, top-right, bottom-left and bottom-right are results of source-to-source, source-to-target, target-to-source and target-to-target, respectively. Images inside each matrix are organized as in Fig. 3. We show that our model can realize intra-domain (source-to-source and target-to-target) and cross-domain (source-to-target and target-to-source) image manipulations simultaneously.

cross-domain disentangle network is able to extract domain-invariant features (representing the label) and domain-specific features (representing background, digit style, etc.). The decoder successfully generates manipulated images using intra-domain and cross-domain combinations of latent factors.

We also perform quantitative evaluations similar to intra-domain experiments, as shown in Table 3 and Table 2 (right). The classification errors of r are slightly higher than intra-domain models, showing the interferences between multiple domains. In contrast, the classification errors of z is higher. The reconstruction PSNR of cross-domain model are lower than intra-domain models, which is limited by the shared decoder D_r.

5   Conclusion

We propose a cross-domain image manipulation method and the corresponding network architecture that disentangles domain-specific and domain-invariant factors on latent space. Our network is able to extract specified and unspecified latent representations. Using this architecture, we can generate desired target domain images by manipulating on the latent representation. We designed adversarial training losses and sub-task training strategies that supplement the missing supervision of mix-feature images. We examined the network on several datasets, and the results show that our method can generate convincing manipulated images across data domain.

References

1. Mathieu, M.F., Zhao, J.J., Zhao, J., Ramesh, A., Sprechmann, P., LeCun, Y.: Disentangling factors of variation in deep representation using adversarial training. In: Advances in Neural Information Processing Systems, pp. 5040–5048 (2016)
2. Lample, G., et al.: Fader networks: manipulating images by sliding attributes. In: Advances in Neural Information Processing Systems, pp. 5967–5976 (2017)
3. Hadad, N., Wolf, L., Shahar, M.: A two-step disentanglement method. In: Proceedings of the IEEE Conference on Computer Vision and Pattern Recognition, pp. 772–780. IEEE (2018)
4. Liu, Y., Wei, F., Shao, J., Sheng, L., Yan, J., Wang, X.: Exploring disentangled feature representation beyond face identification. In: Proceedings of the IEEE Conference on Computer Vision and Pattern Recognition, pp. 2080–2089. IEEE (2018)
5. Liu, Y., Wang, Z., Jin, H., Wassell, I.: Multi-task adversarial network for disentangled feature learning. In: Proceedings of the IEEE Conference on Computer Vision and Pattern Recognition, pp. 3743–3751. IEEE (2018)
6. Kingma, D.P., Welling, M.: Auto-encoding variational bayes. arXiv preprint arXiv:1312.6114 (2013)
7. Kingma, D.P., Mohamed, S., Rezende, D.J., Welling, M.: Semi-supervised learning with deep generative models. In: Advances in Neural Information Processing Systems, pp. 3581–3589 (2014)
8. Makhzani, A., Shlens, J., Jaitly, N., Goodfellow, I., Frey, B.: Adversarial autoencoders. arXiv preprint arXiv:1511.05644 (2015)
9. Goodfellow, I., et al.: Generative adversarial nets. In: Advances in neural information processing systems, pp. 2672–2680 (2014)
10. Mirza, M., Osindero, S.: Conditional generative adversarial nets. arXiv preprint arXiv:1411.1784 (2014)
11. Radford, A., Metz, L., Chintala, S.: Unsupervised representation learning with deep convolutional generative adversarial networks. arXiv preprint arXiv:1511.06434 (2015)
12. Choi, Y., Choi, M., Kim, M., Ha, J.W., Kim, S., Choo, J.: Stargan: unified generative adversarial networks for multi-domain image-to-image translation. arXiv preprint 1711 (2017)
13. Karras, T., Laine, S., Aila, T.: A style-based generator architecture for generative adversarial networks. In: Proceedings of the IEEE Conference on Computer Vision and Pattern Recognition, pp. 4401–4410. IEEE (2019)

14. Arjovsky, M., Chintala, S., Bottou, L.: Wasserstein generative adversarial networks. In: International conference on machine learning, pp. 214–223 (2017)
15. Gulrajani, I., Ahmed, F., Arjovsky, M., Dumoulin, V., Courville, A.C.: Improved training of wasserstein gans. In: Advances in Neural Information Processing Systems, pp. 5769–5779 (2017)
16. Mao, X., Li, Q., Xie, H., Lau, R.Y., Wang, Z., Paul Smolley, S.: Least squares generative adversarial networks. In: Proceedings of the IEEE International Conference on Computer Vision, pp. 2794–2802 (2017)
17. Ganin, Y., Lempitsky, V.: Unsupervised domain adaptation by backpropagation. arXiv preprint arXiv:1409.7495 (2014)
18. Tzeng, E., Hoffman, J., Darrell, T., Saenko, K.: Simultaneous deep transfer across domains and tasks. In: Proceedings of the IEEE International Conference on Computer Vision, pp. 4068–4076. IEEE (2015)
19. Liu, A., Liu, Y.C., Yeh, Y.Y., Wang, Y.C.F.: A unified feature disentangler for multi-domain image translation and manipulation. arXiv preprint arXiv:1809.01361 (2018)
20. Isola, P., Zhu, J.Y., Zhou, T., Efros, A.A.: Image-to-image translation with conditional adversarial networks. arXiv preprint (2017)
21. Taigman, Y., Polyak, A., Wolf, L.: Unsupervised cross-domain image generation. arXiv preprint arXiv:1611.02200 (2016)
22. Zhu, J.Y., Park, T., Isola, P., Efros, A.A.: Unpaired image-to-image translation using cycle-consistent adversarial networks. arXiv preprint (2017)
23. Kim, T., Cha, M., Kim, H., Lee, J.K., Kim, J.: Learning to discover cross-domain relations with generative adversarial networks. arXiv preprint arXiv:1703.05192 (2017)
24. Yi, Z., Zhang, H.R., Tan, P., Gong, M.: Dualgan: unsupervised dual learning for image-to-image translation. In: ICCV, pp. 2868–2876 (2017)
25. Huang, X., Liu, M.Y., Belongie, S., Kautz, J.: Multimodal unsupervised image-to-image translation. In: Proceedings of the European Conference on Computer Vision (ECCV), pp. 172–189 (2018)
26. Lee, H.Y., Tseng, H.Y., Huang, J.B., Singh, M., Yang, M.H.: Diverse image-to-image translation via disentangled representations. In: Proceedings of the European Conference on Computer Vision (ECCV), pp. 35–51 (2018)
27. Lee, H.Y., et al.: Drit++: diverse image-to-image translation via disentangled representations. arXiv preprint arXiv:1905.01270 (2019)
28. Choi, Y., Uh, Y., Yoo, J., Ha, J.W.: Stargan v2: diverse image synthesis for multiple domains. arXiv preprint arXiv:1912.01865 (2019)
29. Lee, D., Kim, J., Moon, W.J., Ye, J.C.: Collagan: collaborative gan for missing image data imputation. In: Proceedings of the IEEE Conference on Computer Vision and Pattern Recognition, pp. 2487–2496 (2019)
30. Larsen, A.B.L., Sønderby, S.K., Larochelle, H., Winther, O.: Autoencoding beyond pixels using a learned similarity metric. arXiv preprint arXiv:1512.09300 (2015)
31. LeCun, Y., Bottou, L., Bengio, Y., Haffner, P.: Gradient-based learning applied to document recognition. Proc. IEEE **86**(11), 2278–2324 (1998)
32. Hull, J.J.: A database for handwritten text recognition research. IEEE Trans. Pattern Anal. Mach. Intell. **16**(5), 550–554 (1994)
33. Netzer, Y., Wang, T., Coates, A., Bissacco, A., Wu, B., Ng, A.Y.: Reading digits in natural images with unsupervised feature learning. In: NIPS workshop on deep learning and unsupervised feature learning. vol. 2011, p. 5 (2011)

Multi-metric Joint Discrimination Network for Few-Shot Classification

Wei Wang[1], Zhijie Wen[1(✉)], Liyan Ma[2,3(✉)], and Shihui Ying[1]

[1] Department of Mathematics, College of Sciences, Shanghai University,
Shanghai, China
{lxywangwei,wenzhijie,shying}@shu.edu.cn
[2] School of Computer Engineering and Science, Shanghai University, Shanghai, China
liyanma@shu.edu.cn
[3] Shanghai Institute of Intelligent Science and Technology, Tongji University,
Shanghai, China

Abstract. Metric-based few-shot methods learn to recognize object categories from one or a few examples according to the distances between class features and query samples. The predicting labels of query samples are the same as those of the nearest class features. However, a single metric criterion can not model the distributions of different datasets very well. To get the more suitable metrics for a specified dataset, we propose a *Multi-Metric Joint Discrimination Network (MMJDN)* in this paper. Firstly, *Deep Metric Module (DMM)* is introduced to catch the complex relation between each pair of class features and query samples. Secondly, *Adaptive Weights Module (AWM)* is proposed to generate adaptive weights for different metric criteria. Our method is evaluated on three datasets: miniImageNet, Fewshot-Cifar100 (FC100) and Virus Texture Dataset (Virus15). The experimental results show that MMJDN provides positive performance for few-shot learning compared with some baselines.

Keywords: Deep metric · Multi-metric discrimination · Few-shot learning

1 Introduction

Though deep learning has made remarkable achievements in many fields, a large amount of labeled data is needed to train the supervised neural networks. However, many issues only have a small amount of data which is not enough for training the network. Even worse, the parameters of a deep learning network learned from a specific dataset have unsatisfactory performance on another dataset. In

The first author is a student.

This research is supported by the National Natural Science Foundation of China (11701357, 11971296, 81830058, 61976132), and The Capacity Construction Project of Local Universities in Shanghai under Grant (18010500600).

Y. Peng et al. (Eds.): PRCV 2020, LNCS 12307, pp. 273–285, 2020.
https://doi.org/10.1007/978-3-030-60636-7_23

contrast, humans can quickly learn new concepts by transferring knowledge of other domains [20, 26]. The task that only uses a small number of samples of each class to predict categories of some new samples is called few-shot learning [5, 9, 13]. Previously, many non-parametric methods were explored to tackle new examples [4, 14, 27]. With the development of meta learning [11, 18, 19, 24] and deep learning, the frameworks of the few-shot learning have been redefined [2, 10, 12, 15, 25, 29].

Few-shot learning methods only use a few samples of each class to learn a classifier. The dataset $\mathcal{D}$ is split into $\mathcal{D}_{meta-train}$ and $\mathcal{D}_{meta-test}$. Label sets $\mathcal{C}_{meta-train} \cap \mathcal{C}_{meta-test} = \varnothing$. $\mathcal{D}_{meta-train}$ is divided into a support set $\mathcal{S}_{train}$ and a query set $\mathcal{Q}_{train}$. If the support set $\mathcal{S}_{train}$ contains N examples from each K classes, this scenario is called $K-$way, $N-$shot. In the episodic training, the models are trained on the support set $\mathcal{S}_{train}$. The query set $\mathcal{Q}_{train}$ containing different examples from the same classes is used to minimize the loss function and update the parameters of models. We evaluate the trained models' generalization performance on $\mathcal{D}_{meta-test}$. The same as that in the training stage, $\mathcal{D}_{meta-test}$ is also divided into a support set $\mathcal{S}_{test}$ and a query set $\mathcal{Q}_{test}$. The samples from $\mathcal{S}_{test}$ and $\mathcal{Q}_{test}$ are fed into trained models.

Two main few-shot learning methods are identified in the literature. One class of few-shot methods is based on optimization. Andrychowicz et al. pointed out that they can learn to optimize neural networks by neural networks [1]. They found that the learned neural optimizers defeat many state-of-the-art hand-designed optimization methods. Following this work, Ravi and Larochelle [17] proposed a meta-learner to solve few-shot problems. They observed that the update rules for the cell state in LSTM [6] are similar to the ones in gradient descent used to train neural networks. Thus, the meta-learner LSTM is deployed to learn an update rule for neural networks. The meta-learner has a few advantages. First, not only the final optimized parameters are learned, but also the initial parameters are learned. Second, the final optimized parameters can avoid local optimum because of the forget gate. Third, there is no need to design the learning rate for the learner. These advantages ensure that the final optimized parameters are better than those by hand-designed optimizer. Different from the approaches in [1, 21], Finn et al. [3] aimed to learn good initial model parameters and fast learning new tasks.

The second category of the approaches is metric-based. Matching Networks [25] and prototypical networks [21] are in this family. They are all based on the metric over the embedding space. Differently, the matching networks [25] use the cosine distance and the prototypical networks [21] use the Euclidean distance. Matching networks [25] are composed of two full context embedding functions. One of the full context embedding functions is a bidirectional LSTM. The other is a LSTM with read-attention called attLSTM. These modules can be considered as feature embeddings functions. The query sets find a similar correlation through the attention kernel. Prototypical networks [21] involves an embedding module with an Euclidean distance. The prototypical networks [21] use an embedding module to compute features for support sets and query sets respectively. The prototype c_k is the mean vector of the support samples belonging to the class k. The prediction of the query sample is the category of the nearest prototype. Koch et al. proposed siamese networks [7] which have two embedding modules. These embedding modules share weights and bias vectors for each layer. The similarity of two feature vectors can be measured. For relation networks [23], Sung et al. used neural networks instead of traditional fixed metrics. Oreshkin et al. [16] demonstrated the scaling factor can improve performance for few-shot algorithms. Be different with the previous works, deep metric proposed in this paper can learn more complicated relationships between sample sets and query sets.

Many metric-based few-shot methods usually use only one metric criterion, such as the Euclidean distance or other hand-designed metrics. However, these metrics may not work well on all datasets. Multi-metric learning is a good way to solve this problem and Xu et al. [28] solve the text-independent speaker verification problem by multi-metric learning. They use three different metric learning loss functions to address their problem. Different from them, we propose a *Multi-Metric Joint Discrimination Network (MMJDN)* for few-shot learning. Inspired by [22], MMJDN aims to choose metric-based few-shot learning modules according to their performance. We design a meta learner, called Adaptive Weights Module (AWM), to generate weights for these metric modules. The bigger weight corresponds to, the better performance of the applied metric criterion on the faced task is. Further, Deep Metric Module (DMM), which is a complex nonlinear mapping of relations between class features and query samples, is introduced as a metric criterion. The differences between class features and query features are fed into DMM to generate deep metrics.

In summary, the contributions of our work are twofold.

- Deep Metric Module (DMM) is introduced to map the relations based on hand-designed metric criteria into more complex relations. These complex relations are called the deep metric criterion that can model many data distributions better.
- Multi-Metric Joint Discrimination Network (MMJDN) is proposed to solve the problem that a single metric criterion may not suitable for some specific data distributions. MMJDN can adaptively choose the metric criterion by the Adaptive Weights Module (AWM) to ensure the optimal performance of models.

2   Multi-metric Joint Discrimination Network

The architecture of the proposed method is presented in Fig. 1. We use a 5-way 1-shot problem as an example. First, five support samples and one query sample are all fed into E embedding modules $\mathcal{F} = \{f_{\theta_i}\}_{i=1}^{E}$, which are used to extract features (Sect. 2.1). Some metric criteria $\mathcal{M} = \{d_i\}_{i=1}^{E}$, e.g. Euclidean distance, are used to calculate the probability distributions (Sect. 2.2). Second, to integrate these predicting distribution maps, the meta learner AWM generates weights with these distribution maps as the input and gets the final distribution map to predict the label (Sect. 2.3). In Sect. 2.4, the training process is introduced in detail.

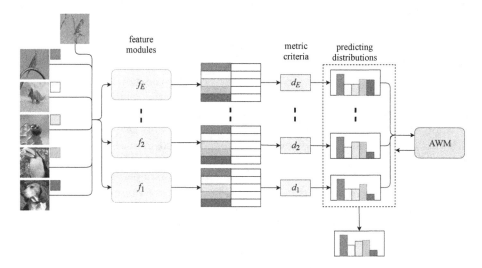

Fig. 1. The architecture of the proposed framework, MMJDN. MMJDN is composed of three modules: feature extractors, metric criteria and AWM.

2.1 Metric-Based Few-Shot Learning Modules

For these metric-based few-shot modules $\{f_{\theta_i}, d_i\}_{i=1}^E$ in the proposed architecture, we adopt the framework proposed in prototypical networks [21]. We first caculate a prototype c_k for each class k based on the features extracted via convolutional neural networks. Specifically, the prototypical c_k is chosen to be the mean vector of the support samples belonging to the class k. Then, a probability for each query sample x is provided by a softmax function under certain distance criterion d. To train the modules $\{(f_{\theta_i}, d_i)\}_{i=1}^E$, we utilize the cross-entropy loss which is defined as

$$\{(f_{\theta_i}, d_i)^*\}_{i=1}^E = \arg\min_{\{(f_{\theta_i}, d_i)\}} \sum_{i=1}^E \sum_{k=1}^N \mathcal{L}_k((f_{\theta_i}, d_i)) + \gamma R(\{(f_{\theta_i}, d_i)\}), \quad (1)$$

where

$$\mathcal{L}_k((f_{\theta_i}, d_i)) = \sum_{(x_i, y_i=k)\in \mathcal{Q}_{train}} d_i(f_\theta(x_i), c_k) + \log \sum_j \exp(-d_i(f_\theta(x_i), c_j)). \quad (2)$$

2.2 Deep Metric Module

The predicted labels can be determined by the maximum of the probabilities

$$p(y = k|x_i) = \frac{\exp(-d(f_\theta(x_i), c_k))}{\sum_j \exp(-d(f_\theta(x_i), c_j))}. \quad (3)$$

Most approaches use the Euclidean distance or other hand-designed metrics. However, these hand-designed metrics may fail to match between the feature $f_\theta(x_i)$ and the prototype $f_\theta(x_q)$. To address this limitation, we use a neural network to learn the metric, and define a nonlinear mapping $g : \mathbb{R}^n \to \mathbb{R}^+$. The following d_{DM} represents the deep metric.

$$d_{DM} = g(|f_\theta(x_i) - f_\theta(x_q)|), \tag{4}$$

where n is the dimensionality of features and θ is the parameters of f. Because many few-shot learning algorithms use the network with four convolutional blocks (4CONV), we design f based on 4CONV to provide fair comparisons.

A neural network, called Deep Metric Module (DMM), is used to learn the deep metric, that is $g(|f_\theta(x_i) - f_\theta(x_q)|; \Phi)$, where Φ is the parameters of DMM. The architecture of our deep metric network is CNN-based. As illustrated in Fig. 2, the input of the deep metric network is the difference between features and the output is the deep metric.

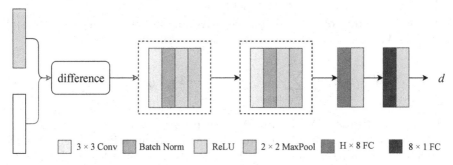

Fig. 2. The architecture of the deep metric module.

2.3 Adaptive Weights Module

The results shown in [21] demonstrate the performance of diverse metric criteria on the same dataset is different. Some metric criteria work well on one dataset and some work well on another dataset. To reduce this negative effect of metric criteria on the performance of metric-based methods, how to combine multiple metrics to make the algorithms work well on all datasets is a natural idea. So we consider generating adaptive weights for multiple metrics according to different tasks and design AWM to achieve it. AWM aims to generate adaptive weights to determine the reliabilities of results provided by some metric-based few-shot methods.

To implement AWM, we parametrize it as $\mathbf{W} \in \mathbb{R}^{M \times E}$. $M = N * E$, where N is the number of categories and E is the number of few-shot modules. We define ϕ as the function which maps the predicted probabilities P into the latent space.

Firstly, if ϕ is a linear transformation, the weight matrix $\mathbf{a}$ can be represented as

$$\mathbf{a} = P\mathbf{W}, \tag{5}$$

where $P \in \mathbb{R}^{B \times M}$ is the concatenation by the predicted results of all metric-based few-shot modules and B is the batch size of the test samples. If ϕ is a nonlinear transformation, Multilayer Perceptron (MLP) can be used to implement ϕ, that is

$$\mathbf{a} = \phi(P; \mathbf{W}), \tag{6}$$

where $\mathbf{W}$ is the parameters of MLP. Then, the column-wise normalization of $\mathbf{a} \in \mathbb{R}^{B \times E}$ is computed, which is denoted as $\hat{\mathbf{a}}$. The components of $\hat{\mathbf{a}}$ are weights for $\{(f_{\theta_i}, d_i)^*\}_{i=1}^E$. The more reliable the metric-based few-shot module is, the bigger the weight is. Finally, the predicted labels of query samples are given by P and $\mathbf{a}$.

In order to compute these predicted labels, we first reshape P into $\mathbb{R}^{B \times E \times N}$. $P = \{P_1, \cdots, P_B\}$ denotes the predicted probabilities of B samples. $P_i = \{P_{i1}, \cdots, P_{iE}\} \in \mathbb{R}^{E \times N}$ denotes the predicted probability distribution on each metric-based few-shot module and $P_{ij} = \{P_{ij1}, \cdots, P_{ijN}\}$ represents the predicted probability of each class. So the final predicted probabilities of the ith sample is $\hat{P}_{ij} = \sum_j a_{ij} P_{ij}$ and the label is the maximum of $\hat{P}_{ij}$.

The loss function of AWM is the negative log-probability and the optimal parameters $\mathbf{W}^*$ can be obtained by the following function

$$\mathbf{W}^* = \arg\min_{\mathbf{W}} \sum_{k=1}^N \sum_{(x_i, y_i = k) \in \mathcal{Q}_{train}} -\log \hat{P}_{ijk} + \lambda \|\mathbf{W}\|_2. \tag{7}$$

For a new dataset, AWM with $\mathbf{W}^*$ can produce weights for $\{(f_{\theta_i}, d_i)\}_{i=1}^E$ and choose the best metric criterion to achieve the classification. Thus, MMJDN effectively improves the performance of metric-based few-shot learning methods. Besides, it is more robust for different data distributions.

2.4   Algorithm

The training process of MMJDN is shown in Fig. 3. In the training stage, each pair of feature extractors and metric criteria (f_{θ_i}, d_i) is trained firstly. With $\{(f_{\theta_i}, d_i)\}_{i=1}^E$ as the input, AWM learns to determine the reliabilities of results provided by these metric-based few-shot modules. As shown in Fig. 3, AMW can be parameterized as $\mathbf{W}$ and be trained via minimizing the prediction error on query sets. The above process is summarized in Algorithm 1.

3   Experiments

3.1   Datasets and Implementation Details

miniImageNet: The miniImageNet proposed by Vinyals et al. [25] is a very popular dataset for few-shot learning. It consists of 60,000 images with size 84 × 84 belonging to 100 classes. Each class contains 600 images. All classes are divided into 64 training classes, 16 validation classes and 20 test classes. We follow the same splits introduced by Ravi and Larochelle [17].

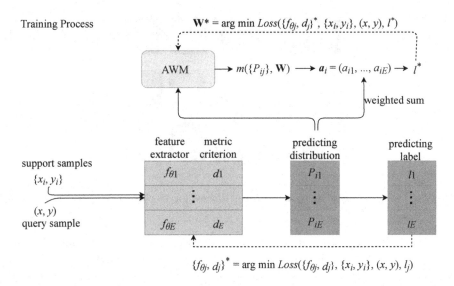

Fig. 3. The training process for MMJDN. The dashed line denotes the optimization process.

Algorithm 1: Training process

Input: $\mathcal{D}_{meta-train}$, $\{(f_{\theta_i}, d_i)\}_{i=1}^{E}$, AWM with $\mathbf{W}$
Output: $\{(f_{\theta_i}^*, d_i^*)\}_{i=1}^{E}$, $\mathbf{W}^*$

1: **while** not done **do**
2:     Sample $\mathcal{S}_{train}$, $\mathcal{Q}_{train}$ from $\mathcal{D}_{meta-train}$;
3:     Get $\{(f_{\theta_i}^*, d_i^*)\}_{i=1}^{E}$ by Eq. 1;
4: **end while**
5: **while** not done **do**
6:     Sample $\mathcal{S}_{train}$, $\mathcal{Q}_{train}$ from $\mathcal{D}_{meta-train}$;
7:     Get predicting probailites P;
6:     Get $\mathbf{W}^*$ by Eq. 7;
7: **end while**

Fewshot-CIFAR100: The Fewshot-CIFAR100 (FC100) which are based on CIFAR100 [8] was proposed by Oreshkin el at. in reference [17]. It consists of 60,000 images belonging to 100 different classes, thus each class has 600 images. The size of images in FC100, 32×32, is smaller than that in miniImageNet. They further split the 100 classes into 20 super-classes and consider 12/4/4 super-classes which contain 60/20/20 classes as the train/validation/test split. The information overlap between splits in FC100 is minimized which is a more difficult few-shot learning problem.

Virus15: We use Virus Texture Dataset v. 1.0 for few-shot learning. For simplicity, we call it Virus15. This data set is available at http://www.cb.uu.se/gustaf/virustexture/. The main motivation is that the dis-

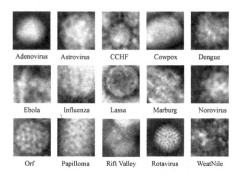

Fig. 4. Example virus images for 15 classes.

tribution of this dataset is different from natural images, i.e., miniImagNet and FC100. Many metric criteria cannot perform well on it even though they may work well on miniImagNet and FC100. The Virus15 contains 15 classes and 1500 virus images in total. In other words, there are 100 images in each class. The size of each image is 41 × 41 pixels. We show the example images of 15 virus types and their corresponding names in Fig. 4. We split the 15 classes into 5/5/5 classes for training/validation/testing.

Implementation Details: The codes are implemented based on PyTorch. For our experiments, we train 5-way 1-shot and 5-way 5-shot classification models respectively. In the test phase, we batch 15 query samples per class in 1-shot and 5-shot scenarios. The accuracies are computed by averaging 600 randomly test episodes and with 95% confidence intervals. We use Adam with initial learning rate 10^{-3}.

Architectures: For methods based on the hand-designed metric criteria, each convolutional block of the feature embedding includes a 64-filter 3 × 3 convolution, batch normalization, ReLU nonlinearity and 2 × 2 max-pool. Due to the sizes of the images in FC100 and Virus15 are smaller than that of miniImageNet, only the first block of the feature embedding module used in FC100 and Virus15 has a max-pool. For a deep metric module used in DMM, it includes two convolutional blocks and two fully connected layers. Each convolutional block is formed by a 64-filter 3 × 3 convolution, batch normalization, ReLU nonlinearity and 2 × 2 max-pool. For AWM, MLP with one hidden layer is used.

3.2　Results and Discussion

In this subsection, the results of our experiments are compared with some state-of-the-art baselines: metric-based baselines and optimization-based baselines. Further, we analyze the effects of the MMJDN framework. We highlight the top-1 result.

Table 1. Few-shot classification accuracies on miniImageNet.

	Methods	Metric	1-shot	5-shot
Metric-based	Matching Nets [25]	Cosine	38.00 ± 0.3	55.31 ± 0.7
Methods	ProtoNets [21]	Euclid	46.61 ± 0.8	65.77 ± 0.7
	Relation Nets [23]	Deep	**50.44 ± 0.8**	65.32 ± 0.7
Optimization-based Methods	MAML [3]		48.70 ± 1.8	63.11 ± 0.9
	Meta-LSTM [17]		43.56 ± 0.84	60.60 ± 0.7
	FOMAML [3]		45.53 ± 1.6	61.02 ± 1.1
	Meta-MinibatchProx [30]		48.51 ± 0.9	64.15 ± 0.9
Our methods	4CONV	Euclid	45.32 ± 0.8	62.45 ± 0.7
	4CONV	Deep	47.76 ± 0.8	64.17 ± 0.7
	MMJDN		49.47 ± 0.8	**66.04 ± 0.7**

The comparisons with baselines. In the experiments, two criteria that are the Euclidean distance and the deep metric, are considered in our method. From the results in Table 1, our method obtains second best performance for 1-shot (49.47%) and gets the best performance for 5-shot (66.04%). Although the performance of MMJDN is 0.97% lower than Relation Nets [23], the results of MMJDN is positive and the performance may be better than that when more metric criteria are considered. In Table 2, the results of MMJDN are the best.

For deep metric criteria, they can overcome the problem in which the feature extractors generate weakly discriminative features. So the performance of deep metric criteria in 1-shot is much better than that in 5-shot. Further, because deep metric criteria are also influenced by data distributions and the number of the training sample, only depending on deep metrics to calculate relations between samples is insufficient. Since utilizing multiple metric criteria, MMJDN is more robust and effective. The results of those comparisons are shown in Fig. 5a and Fig. 5b.

As we can be seen in the Table 1 and Table 2, the performance of the methods combining with multiple metrics is highly improved. On the one hand, the samples which are wrongly classified under one metric could be correctly classified under another metric. MMJDN can choose the right one by AWM. On the other hand, MMJDN reduces the impact of the insufficient feature discrimination to some certain. These comparisons are shown in Fig. 6. MMJDN improves the capability of recognition on the condition of a little labeled sample that only can be used.

The performance on Virus15. Because Virus15 is not a natural image dataset, the gaps of data distributions between Virus15 and two natural datasets are big. Table 3 shows that the performance on 1-shot of the deep metric is better than that of the Euclidean distance. However, the Euclidean distance is the better choice for 5-shot. This phenomenon is different from that in two natural datasets in which the best metric is the deep metric, but MMJDN can overcome this problem. MMJDN achieves the best result in 1-shot and 5-shot respectively, as shown in Table 3.

Table 2. Few-shot classification accuracies on FC100.

	Method	Metric	1-shot	5-shot
Metric-based	ProtoNets [21]	Euclid	40.8 ± 0.7	51.1 ± 0.2
Methods	Relation Nets [23]	Deep	41.6 ± 0.7	49.0 ± 0.7
Optimization-based	MAML [3]		38.1 ± 1.7	50.4 ± 1.0
Methods	MAML + HT [22]		39.9 ± 1.8	51.7 ± 0.9
Our methods	4CONV	Euclid	38.5 ± 0.7	49.8 ± 0.7
	4CONV	Deep	40.2 ± 0.7	53.4 ± 0.7
	MMJDN		**43.7 ± 0.7**	**53.7 ± 0.7**

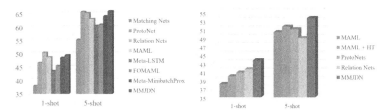

(a) The comparisons on miniImageNet.

(b) The comparisons on FC100.

Fig. 5. The comparisons with baselines.

Fig. 6. The comparison between MMJDN and other two metrics

The transferability of AWM. In this experiment, we evaluate the transferability of AWM. We have four settings: 1) AWM trained on FC100 is applied to test on miniImageNet; 2) AWM trained on miniImageNet is used to evaluate the performance of MMJDN on FC100; 3) AWM trained on miniImageNet is used to test on Virus15. 4) AWM trained on Virus15 is used to test on miniImageNet. The results are shown in Table 4. MMJDN* denotes the performance of MMJDN whose AWM is trained on another dataset. As we can see, the gaps between these results and the original results are very small for setting 1, 2, 3. It illustrates that the meta-learner AWM learns the meta-knowledge. Therefore

Table 3. The results of MMJDN on Virus15.

Method	Metric	1-shot	5-shot
4CONV	Euclid	47.67 ± 0.6	68.38 ± 0.4
4CONV	Deep	49.65 ± 0.6	63.70 ± 0.4
MMJDN		**50.48 ± 0.6**	**70.05 ± 0.4**

Table 4. The evaluation of the transferability of AWM.

(a) FC100 → miniImageNet			(b) miniImageNet → FC100		
	1-shot	5-shot		1-shot	5-shot
MMJDN*	49.35 ± 0.8	65.95 ± 0.7	MMJDN*	43.19 ± 0.7	53.57 ± 0.7
MMJDN	49.47 ± 0.8	66.04 ± 0.7	MMJDN	43.68 ± 0.7	53.66 ± 0.7
(c) Virus15 → miniImageNet			(d) miniImageNet → Virus15		
	1-shot	5-shot		1-shot	5-shot
MMJDN*	49.39 ± 0.7	66.09 ± 0.4	MMJDN*	50.04 ± 0.7	65.26 ± 0.4
MMJDN	49.47 ± 0.6	66.04 ± 0.4	MMJDN	50.48 ± 0.6	70.05 ± 0.4

MMJDN can solve different tasks by the same AWM. For the setting 4, the gap between MMJDN and MMJDN* is small in 1-shot. However, the gap is big in 5-shot. This suggests that the meta-knowledge which is generated by AWM is not completely independent of data distributions. In future, we will study this problem further.

4 Conclusion

In this paper, we proposed the Multi-Metric Joint Discrimination Network (MMJDN) to solve few-shot classification problems. MMJDN aims to adaptively generate the weights for metric-based few-shot methods by Adaptive Weights Module (AWM). The more reliable the metric-based few-shot methods is, the larger the weight is. Because of the limitation of the hand-designed metrics, we propose Deep Metric Module (DMM) to adapt more complicated data distributions. The experimental results demonstrate the good performance of the proposed method and DMM is more useful on miniImageNet. Further, AWM is little affected by data distributions. In the future, we will generalize MMJDN to other types of few-shot learning methods.

References

1. Andrychowicz, M., et al.: Learning to learn by gradient descent by gradient descent. In: NeurIPS, pp. 3981–3989 (2016)
2. Chen, M.T., et al.: Diversity transfer network for few-shot learning. AAAI **34**, 10559–10566 (2020)

3. Finn, C., Abbeel, P., Levine, S.: Model-agnostic meta-learning for fast adaptation of deep networks. ICML **70**, 1126–1135 (2017)
4. Goldberger, J., Hinton, G.E., Roweis, S.T., Salakhutdinov, R.: Neighbourhood components analysis. In: NeurIPS, pp. 513–520 (2004)
5. Hariharan, B., Girshick, R.: Low-shot visual recognition by shrinking and hallucinating features. In: ICCV, pp. 3037–3046 (2017)
6. Hochreiter, S., Schmidhuber, J.: Long short-term memory. Neural Comput. **9**(8), 1735–1780 (1997)
7. Koch, G.: Siamese neural networks for one-shot image recognition. Ph.D. thesis, University of Toronto (2015)
8. Krizhevsky, A.: Learning multiple layers of features from tiny images. Master's thesis, University of Tront (2009)
9. Lake, B.M., Salakhutdinov, R., Gross, J., Tenenbaum, J.B.: One shot learning of simple visual concepts. CogSci **33**(33), 2568–2573 (2011)
10. Lake, B.M., Salakhutdinov, R., Tenenbaum, J.B.: Human-level concept learning through probabilistic program induction. Sci. **350**(6266), 1332–1338 (2015)
11. Lake, B.M., Ullman, T.D., Tenenbaum, J.B., Gershman, S.J.: Building machines that learn and think like people. BBS **40**, e253 (2017)
12. Liu, Y., Lee, J., Park, M., Kim, S., Yang, Y.: Learning to propagate labels: transductive propagation network for few-shot learning. In: ICLR, pp. 1–14 (2019)
13. Miller, E.G., Matsakis, N.E., Viola, P.A.: Learning from one example through shared densities on transforms. In: CVPR, pp. 464–471 (2000)
14. Min, R., Stanley, D.A., Yuan, Z., Bonner, A., Zhang, Z.: A deep non-linear feature mapping for large-margin knn classification. In: ICDM, pp. 357–366 (2009)
15. Munkhdalai, T., Yu, H.: Meta networks. ICML **70**, 2554–2563 (2017)
16. Oreshkin, B.N., Rodriguez, P., Lacoste, A.: Tadam: task dependent adaptive metric for improved few-shot learning. In: NeurIPS, pp. 721–731 (2018)
17. Ravi, S., Larochelle, H.: Optimization as a model for few-shot learning. In: ICLR, pp. 1–11 (2016)
18. Santoro, A., Bartunov, S., Botvinick, M., Wierstra, D., Lillicrap, T.: Meta-learning with memory-augmented neural networks. ICML **48**, 1842–1850 (2016)
19. Schmidhuber, J., Zhao, J., Wiering, M.: Shifting inductive bias with success-story algorithm, adaptive levin search, and incremental self-improvement. Mach. Learn. **28**(1), 105–130 (1997)
20. Schmidt, L.A.: Meaning and compositionality as statistical induction of categories and constraints. Ph.D. thesis, MIT (2018)
21. Snell, J., Swersky, K., Zemel, R.S.: Prototypical networks for few-shot learning. In: NeurIPS, pp. 4080–4090 (2017)
22. Sun, Q.R., Liu, Y.Y., Chua, T.S., Schiele, B.: Meta-transfer learning for few-shot learning. In: CVPR, pp. 403–412 (2019)
23. Sung, F., Yang, Y., Zhang, L., Xiang, T., Torr, P.H., Hospedales, T.M.: Learning to compare: relation network for few-shot learning. In: CVPR, pp. 1199–1208 (2018)
24. Thrun, S., Pratt, L.: Learning to learn: Introduction and overview. In: Thrun, S., Pratt, L. (eds.) Learning to Learn, pp. 3–17. Springer, Boston, MA (1998). https://doi.org/10.1007/978-1-4615-5529-2_1
25. Vinyals, O., Blundell, C., Lillicrap, T., Kavukcuoglu, K., Wierstra, D.: Matching networks for one shot learning. In: NeurIPS, pp. 3630–3638 (2016)
26. Wang, Y.X., Girshick, R., Hebert, M., Hariharan, B.: Low-shot learning from imaginary data. In: CVPR, pp. 7278–7286 (2018)
27. Weinberger, K.Q., Blitzer, J., Saul, L.K.: Distance metric learning for large margin nearest neighbor classification. In: NeurIPS, pp. 1473–1480 (2005)

28. Xu, J.W., Wang, X.G., Feng, B., Liu, W.Y.: Deep multi-metric learning for text-independent speaker verification. Neurocomput. **410**(410), 394–400 (2020)
29. Yoon, J., Kim, T., Dia, O., Kim, S., Bengio, Y., Ahn, S.: Bayesian model-agnostic meta-learning. In: NeurIPS, pp. 7332–7342 (2018)
30. Zhou, P., Yuan, X.T., Xu, H., Yan, S.C., Feng, J.S.: Efficient meta learning via minibatch proximal update. In: NeurIPS, pp. 1534–1544 (2019)

LG-VTON: Fashion Landmark Meets Image-Based Virtual Try-On

Zhenyu Xie[1], Jianhuang Lai[1,2]([✉]), and Xiaohua Xie[1]

[1] School of Data and Computer Science, Sun Yat-sen University, Guangzhou, China
xiezhy6@mail2.sysu.edu.cn , xiexiaoh6@mail.sysu.edu.cn
[2] School of Information Science, Xinhua College of Sun Yat-Sen University,
Guangzhou, China
stsljh@mail.sysu.edu.cn

Abstract. Current leading algorithms of the image-based virtual try-on systems mainly model the deformation of clothes as a whole. However, the deformation of different clothes parts can change drastically. Thus the existing algorithms fail to transfer the clothes to the proper shape in cases, such as self-occlusion, complex pose, and sophisticated textures. Based on this observation, we propose a Landmark-Guided Virtual Try-On Network (LG-VTON), which explicitly divides the clothes into regions using estimated landmarks, and performs a part-wise transformation using the Thin Plate Spline (TPS) for each region independently. The part-wise TPS transformation can be calculated according to the estimated landmarks. Finally, a virtual try-on sub-network is introduced to estimate the composition mask to fuse the wrapped clothes and person image to synthesize the try-on result. Extensive experiments on the virtual try-on dataset demonstrate that LG-VTON can handle complicated clothes deformation and synthesize satisfactory virtual try-on images, achieving state-of-the-art performance both qualitatively and quantitatively.

Keywords: Virtual try-on · Image synthesis · Landmark prediction · Thin plate splines (TPS)

1 Introduction

Due to the great practicality and commercial potential for online shopping, the image-based virtual try-on has been wildly explored these years. [1–4] study the normal fixed pose image-based virtual try-on problem, while [5,6] explore the multi-pose virtual try-on problem. Also, [7] takes a step forward and proposes a flow-based method for the video virtual try-on.

All of the above virtual try-on tasks are confronted with the problem of how to warp the flat clothes to the target shape, which is the critical part of the virtual

Supported by the Key Field R & D Program of Guangdong Province (2019B010155003) and the National Natural Science Foundation of China (61876104).

© Springer Nature Switzerland AG 2020
Y. Peng et al. (Eds.): PRCV 2020, LNCS 12307, pp. 286–297, 2020.
https://doi.org/10.1007/978-3-030-60636-7_24

try-on systems. The existing works either utilize a model to fit the parameters of the TPS [8] transformation or directly estimate clothes flow between the source clothes and the target clothes by the flow regression network. Both of these methods directly use the same transformation function to warp the different clothes regions. However, the deformation of different clothes parts can diverge drastically. For instance, the sleeve region may have obvious deformation while the body region tends to deform less during the virtual try-on process. Simply applying single TPS transformation or clothes flow to warp clothes with various deformation degrees in different regions will lead to weird warping results.

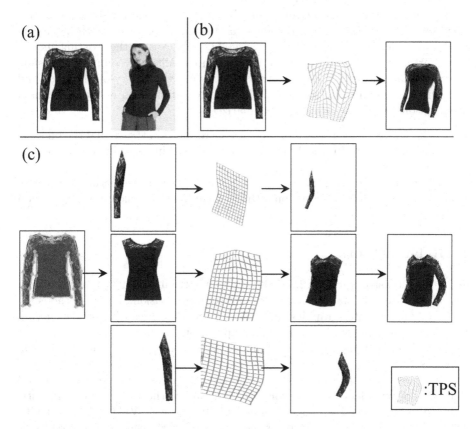

Fig. 1. (a) Shows the clothes image and the person image for the try-on task. (b) Directly warps the whole clothes image using the TPS transformation. (c) Warps different clothes regions independently by using the corresponding TPS transformations.

Taking the deformation discrepancy of different clothes regions into consideration, we propose the Landmark-Guided Virtual Try-On Network (LG-VTON) that models the geometric change of different clothes regions independently. Figure 1 compares the clothes deformation methods of LG-VTON and existing methods [1,2,4,5]. Specifically, LG-VTON consists of three modules: clothes landmark regression module, part-wise clothes warping module, and virtual try-on module. The clothes landmark regression module applies two sub-networks to regress the landmarks in the source clothes and predict the possible landmarks in the virtual try-on result, respectively. Given the clothes landmarks, the part-wise clothes warping module separates the clothes into several regions and then warp each part with TPS independently. All warped regions are merged to compose the whole warped clothes. The virtual try-on module introduces a sub-network to synthesize the coarse try-on result and predict the fusion mask simultaneously. We blend the warped clothes and the coarse try-on result using the fusion mask to get the final try-on result.

To demonstrate the effectiveness of LG-VTON, we conduct extensive experiments on the existing virtual try-on dataset and compare the clothes warping results and virtual try-on results between LG-VTON and the existing image-based virtual try-on methods. Quantitative and qualitative comparison results illustrate that LG-VTON outperforms the existing virtual try-on methods and can generate more precise warped clothes and realistic try-on results. The main contributions of this work can be summarized as:

- For the first time, clothes landmarks are introduced in the virtual try-on task, which enables learning clothes transformation within a specific region defined by landmarks.
- Compared to modeling the clothes wrapping as a whole, we perform part-wise clothes transformation based on estimated landmarks of the input clothes and the target try-on result.

2   Related Work

Recently, extensive works [1,2,5,7,9–11] about virtual try-on system have been done in the area of computer graphics and computer vision. Those methods [9–12] based on computer graphics can generate try-on images with precise clothes simulation but come with the price of computationally inefficient. Besides, these methods depend on high-quality 3D models which may not suitable for practical scenarios.

Compared with methods based on computer graphics, computer vision-based methods are with less computation cost and can synthesize the photo-realistic image directly from 2D images instead of 3D models. VITON [1] and CP-VTON [2] are both image-based virtual try-on network using warping strategy, in which VITON calculates the transformation mapping by the TPS warping directly while CP-VTON proposes a learning method to predict the transformation parameters. However, VITON and CP-VTON both model the deformation of clothes through TPS, which can only model limited geometric changes. Cloth-Flow [3] proposes a cascade method to learn an appearance flow, which can warp the clothes more naturally and seamlessly onto the target person. The above methods mainly target on fixed pose Virtual Try-on. MG-VTON [5] introduces a novel method to the problem of multi-pose virtual try-on, which is capable of handling arbitrary poses of target persons.

The above methods explore various ways to perform the transformation on target clothes and fit the wrapped clothes to the input persons. But as they consider the clothes transformation as a whole, complicated deformation is still challenging and can result in failure cases. In contrast, we propose a novel method that considers the transformation of clothes part by part. Besides, we carefully address the transformation of the shared boundary of two neighbor parts to mitigate boundary artifacts.

3   LG-VTON

Given a source person image and a target clothes, our Landmark Guided Virtual Try-on Network (LG-VTON) aims to generate a new image of the person wearing target clothes while preserving the pose and body in the source image. Similar to previous works [1,2], we first wrap the clothes with thin plate spline (TPS) transformation and then a virtual try-on module is utilized to integrate the wrapped clothes with person to obtain the final virtual try-on results. However, in contrast to wrapping the clothes as a whole, we introduce a part-independent warping to the clothes warping module. The main intuition lies that clothes deformation is closely related to the underlying person pose and clothes corresponding to different skeleton can result with independent transformation.

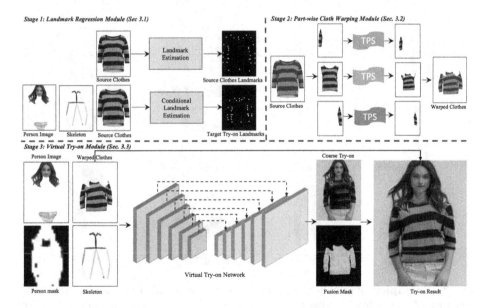

Fig. 2. Overview of LG-VTON. LG-VTON consists of three modules:(a) Landmark regression module (Sect. 3.1), (b) Part-wise clothes warping module (Sect. 3.2), (c) Virtual try-on module (Sect. 3.3).

Figure 2 illustrates the framework of the LG-VTON. We first estimate clothes landmarks in the target clothes image and predict the possible corresponding landmarks in the try-on result (Sect. 3.1). The landmark pairs are then used to guide the warping of the target clothes with TPS (Sect. 3.2). Finally, we use the wrapped clothes image together with the input person image, skeleton to synthesize the final try-on result (Sect. 3.3).

3.1 Landmark Regression Module

Recently, learning-based methods have achieved great success in human pose estimation. Adequate datasets [13–15] are provided and various algorithms [16–18] have been explored. Observing that clothes landmark estimation is essentially similar to pose estimation, we follow the network of state-of-the-art pose estimation method MSPN [16]. For supervising the clothes landmark estimation, we explore the fashion dataset with clothes annotations.

Fig. 3. Examples of clothes annotated with fashion landmarks. Under the guidance of the fashion landmarks, the short sleeve top and the long sleeve top are both divided into three clothes regions while the vest and the sling only contain one clothes region.

Deepfashion [19] and Deepfashion2 [20] are two famous fashion datasets with rich annotations of clothes. Here, we use the recently published Deepfahsion2 dataset for more diverse and precise annotations. Briefly, Deepfashion2 contains clothes in 13 categories and different categories have different landmarks annotations correspondingly. In this paper, we considered the common four clothes categories: short sleeve top, long sleeve top, vest, and sling, with 25, 33, 15, 15 clothes landmarks, respectively. Figure 3 gives an example of four kinds of clothes in the virtual try-on dataset with colored landmarks.

MSPN [16] performs multi-stage pose estimation in a coarse-to-fine manner. In more detail, it composes of two modules, each as a U-shape architecture. To alleviate the information loss during repeated up and downsampling in a multi-stage network, it adopts a cross-stage feature aggregation strategy, which combines the features of the same image scales at different stages together. Specifically, there are two last-stage information components for each downsample unit in the current state: the downsampling and upsampling units in the previous stage. Additionally, coarse-to-fine supervision at different image scales is used for better performance. We refer the readers to MSPN [16] for more details.

LG-VTON estimates clothes landmarks with the MSPN model. To cover the four clothes categories, we simply divide the clothes landmarks of different categories into corresponding output channels. However, the landmark regression of the clothes on the final try-on image is not straightforward, as the resulting try-on images can not be provided. Note that the clothes on the try-on image should keep the person pose, we thus feed the pose skeleton along with the person image to the regression module. Specifically, the inputs of the modified MSPN consist of three components: the source clothes image, the person image without clothes region, and the person skeleton image. As the clothes region of the input person image may disturb the target try-on clothes, we use the input person image without clothes region. For training the modified MSPN model, we follow the coarse-to-fine supervision training strategy in the original paper.

3.2 Part-Wise Clothes Warping

Leading algorithms of image-based virtual try-on follow the fashion to first warp the given clothes to the target pose and then synthesize the final try-on rendering from the wrapped clothes along with other components from the input person image. Thus the quality of the wrapped clothes is critical to the try-on results. While realistic image-based try-on have shown to be possible in recent works [1–3,5], clothes wrappings remains challenging when there is a big difference between the input clothes and target pose. One main issue lies that current wrapping methods consider the deformation of the clothes as a whole, which makes the wrapping modeling difficult when the deformation differs diversely across clothes regions.

Based on the above observation, LG-VTON explicitly separates the clothes into several regions and warps each region to the target shape independently. As pixels within one clothes region generally contain similar deformation, modeling the geometric change becomes much easier. In our virtual try-on dataset, we separate the short top sleeve and the long top sleeve categories into three regions:

left sleeve region, middle body region, and right sleeve region. For the vest and the sling categories, they contain only the middle body region part.

Given the estimated clothes landmarks, we first obtain the clothes region by cropping the region surrounded by the specific landmarks. Figure 3 gives an example of different clothes regions obtained according to the clothes landmarks in the four clothes categories. As the landmarks are dense enough, the cropped regions give a satisfactory boundary of the original clothes image. Furthermore, the clothes landmarks are utilized to calculate the parameters of the thin plate spline (TPS) [8] transformation. Specifically, given the source clothes landmarks and the target clothes landmarks for the same clothes region, we can fit a TPS interpolation function that transforms the source landmarks to the target landmarks.

Naive merging the warped clothes regions may cause artifact at the boundary of clothes parts, due to the independent transformations of clothes parts. The warping results of the landmarks in the intersection of two clothes parts may have variance under different TPS transformations and can result in blank space to the merged clothes. To address this problem, we first obtain the problem region through the warped results of the shared landmarks under two different TPS transformation. Then we fill the problem region by computing the warped clothes using the transform of the middle body region. Additionally, we ignore cloth wrapping at the backside of cloth for as it is invisible when the clothes are on people.

3.3   Virtual Try-On Module

The virtual try-on module is used to fuse the warped clothes and the target person seamlessly. Particularly, not only the color and the texture details of the clothes but the personal identity information need to be preserved as much as possible. Moreover, the fusion of the person and clothes must appear natural.

To meet this end, we introduce a virtual try-on network that takes the person representation and the warped clothes as inputs and outputs the coarse virtual try-on results along with the fusion mask. Similar to [1,2], the person representation consists of a person image, body shape mask, and the pose skeleton. Additionally, our person image contains only the head and the bottom body since these regions will not change during the virtual try-on process and taking these regions as inputs simplify the synthesis to focus on the clothes region in the try-on results. We generate the body shape mask from the human parsing map. To alleviate the effect of the original clothes in the input image, we downsample the human parsing map by 8 times and then upsample to the original image scale. In this work, the human parsing map is estimated by the human parser [21] while the human pose is predicted by the human pose extractor [22].

The fusion mask M is applied to blend the coarse virtual try-on results I_c and the warped clothes $\tilde{C}$ to obtain the final try-on results I_f, which can be formulated as followed:

$$I_f = M \otimes I_c + (1 - M) \otimes \tilde{C}. \tag{1}$$

The virtual try-on module adopts the U-Net like architecture with 6 down sampling layers and 6 up sampling layers.

For training, paired clothes image and the person wearing the target clothes are provided using the dataset [1]. As the input person representation is clothes unrelated, the learned virtual try-on module can be applied to arbitrary clothes image. We use the $L1$ loss between the coarse virtual try-on result I_c and the ground true target person image I to guide the learning procedure. VGG perceptual loss [23] is used for both the coarse virtual try-on results I_c and the final try-on result I. The VGG perceptual loss is formulated as followed:

$$L_p(I, \tilde{I}) = \sum_{k=0}^{5} \lambda_k ||\phi_k(I) - \phi_k(\tilde{I})||_1, \tag{2}$$

where $\phi_k(I)$ represents the k-th feature map from the VGG19 network. Finally, to encourage the fusion mask to select the warped clothes as much as possible, $L1$ loss between the fusion mask M and the warped clothes mask M_w is adopted. The total loss function for this module is:

$$L = ||I - I_c||_1 + L_p(I, I_c) + L_p(I, I_f) + \lambda ||M - M_w||_1, \tag{3}$$

where the value of λ is 5.0 in this work.

4   Experiments

4.1   Dataset and Training Details

Dataset. The experiments are mainly conducted on the virtual try-on dataset viton [1], which contains 16235 image pairs of front-view person image and the top clothes image. The images resolution are 256×192. The dataset is further divided into 14221 image pairs and 2032 image pairs for training and testing respectively. For training, the ground-truth try-on result is provided for supervision. However, at the testing stage, we randomly pick the target clothes for an input person image from the test set to simulate the try-on process in reality. The randomness choice of the input clothes shows the generability of our try-on module.

Training Details. We follow the training implementations of MSPN for our MSPN module and modified MSPN module. Both models are trained on 4 NVIDIA GTX 1080Ti GPUs with batch-size 20 per GPU. Adam optimizer is utilized and the weight decay is $1e - 5$. We train the modules with a learning rate of $4e - 4$ for the first 2400 iterations and gradually decrease the learning rate from $4e - 4$ to 0. Both modules converge after 19200 iterations.

We use Adam optimizer with $(\beta_1 = 0.5, \beta_2 = 0.999)$ for training the virtual try-on network. The initial learning rate is set to 1e-4 and the weight decay is $1e - 5$. The model is trained for 20 epochs. Batch size is set to 18 on one NVIDIA GTX 1080Ti graphics card.

4.2   Qualitative Results

Figure 4 displays the visual comparison with the baseline methods. VITON [1] performs poorly in the long sleeve try-on scenario, which fails to keep the texture characteristic and shape of the original clothes. Besides, VITON fails to synthesize the proper neckline region occasionally. Besides the problem faced by VITON, CP-VTON is unable to solve the problem of body occlusion. By considering clothes part warping independently, LG-VTON can warp each clothes region precisely and preserve the clothes texture feature as much as possible. Moreover, since the neckline region is removed under the guidance of landmarks in advance, the neckline region in LG-VTON results seems more natural.

Since the quality of the warped clothes directly influences the final try-on results, we provide a comparison of the wrapped clothes with the baseline methods in Fig. 5. VITON and CP-VTON warp the whole clothes using one TPS transformation, usually generating distorted warping results. Without explicitly removing the neckline region, VITON and CP-VTON generate a weird neckline region. In contrast, LG-VTON can solve the above two questions by the partwise warping and the removal of the neckline region. Besides, LG-VTON can eliminate the region occluded by the body part.

Fig. 4. Visual comparison among different methods on VITON dataset. Please zoom in for more details.

Fig. 5. Comparison of clothes warping results among different methods on VITON dataset. Please zoom in for more details.

4.3   Quantitative Results

Similar to VITON [1], we use Inception Score (IS) to measure the quality of the try-on results. In particular, IS is a common criterion to evaluate the synthesized image quality, whether the image is visually diverse and semantically reasonable. We compare the proposed method with state-of-the-art methods VITON and CP-VTON [2]. Table 1 shows that LG-VTON surpasses VITON and CP-VTON by 0.371 and 0.158 in terms of IS, meaning that LG-VTON produces more realistic try-on results.

Table 1. Comparison of IS among different methods on the VITON dataset.

Method	IS ↑
VITON (CVPR2018) [1]	2.514 ± 0.130
CP-VTON (CVPR2018) [2]	2.727 ± 0.126
LG-VTON (ours)	**2.885 ±0.130**

Table 2. Human evaluation results comparing pairs of methods.

Comparsion Method Pair	Human Evalution Score
Ours *vs* VITON (CVPR2018) [1]	**0.683** *vs* 0.317
Ours *vs* CP-VTON (CVPR2018) [2]	**0.734** *vs* 0.266

4.4   Human Evaluation

We conduct our human evaluation on the Amazon Mechanical Turk (AMT). Specifically, we randomly sample 100 image pairs from testing set of VITON dataset [1] and synthesize the virtual try-on results through LG-VTON, VITON, and CP-VTON [2], respectively. In each assignment, we provide the Amazon workers with a clothing image, a person image, and two virtual try-on results synthesized by the different methods. The workers are expected to pick a more realistic result with precise clothing warping. For each assignment, 5 workers randomly selected from the AMT platform will participate in the evaluation. Table 2 displays the human evaluation results. Compared with VITON, 68.3% AMT workers select the try-on results of LG-VTON while compared with CP-VTON, 73.4% AMT workers select the try-on results of LG-VTON, demonstarting the superiority of LG-VTON over VITON and CP-VTON.

5   Conclusion

We propose a Landmark-Guided Virtual Try-on Network in the field of image-based virtual try-on. Our main contribution lies in the part-wise clothes warping, which separates the clothes into pre-defined regions under the guidance of the clothes landmarks and each clothes region is wrapped under different TPS. Given the warped clothes, the virtual try-on module learns to synthesize realistic try-on results. We compare the clothes warping results and the synthesized images with state-of-the-art methods on the virtual try-on benchmark. The comparison results illustrate that LG-VTON outperforms the existing virtual try-on methods both qualitatively and quantitatively. Especially, the proposed method can better handle the failure cases of previous methods when the pose is complex or there exists self-occlusion.

References

1. Han, X., Wu, Z., Wu, Z., Yu, R., Davis, L.S.: Viton: an image-based virtual try-on network. In: Proceedings of the IEEE Conference on Computer Vision and Pattern Recognition (CVPR), pp. 7543–7552 (2018)
2. Wang, B., Zheng, H., Liang, X., Chen, Y., Lin, L., Yang, M.: Toward characteristic-preserving image-based virtual try-on network. In: Proceedings the European Conference on Computer Vision (ECCV), pp. 589–604 (2018)
3. Han, X., Hu, X., Huang, W., Scott, M.R.: Clothflow: a flow-based model for clothed person generation. In: Proceedings the IEEE International Conference on Computer Vision (ICCV), pp. 10471–10480 (2019)
4. Yu, R., Wang, X., Xie, X.: VTNFP: an image-based Virtual try-on network with body and clothing feature preservation. In: The IEEE International Conference on Computer Vision (ICCV), pp. 10511–10520 (2019)
5. Dong, H., Liang, X., Wang, B., Lai, H., Zhu, J., Yin, J.: Towards multi-pose guided virtual try-on network. In: The IEEE International Conference on Computer Vision (ICCV), pp. 9026–9035 (2019)
6. Zheng, N., Song, X., Chen, Z., Hu, L., Cao, D., Nie, L.: Virtually trying on new clothing with arbitrary poses. In: Proceedings of the 27th ACM International Conference on Multimedia (ACMMM), pp. 266–274 (2019)
7. Dong, H., Liang, X., Shen, X., Wu, B., Chen, B.-C., Yin, J.: FW-GAN: flow-navigated warping GAN for video virtual try-on. In: Proceedings the IEEE International Conference on Computer Vision (ICCV), pp. 1161–1170 (2019)

8. Bookstein, F.L.: Principal warps: thin-Plate Splines and the decomposition of deformations. IEEE Trans. Pattern Anal. Mach. Intell. **11**(6), 567–585 (1989)

9. Sekine, M., Sugita, K., Perbet, F., Stenger, B., Nishiyama, M.: Virtual fitting by single-shot body shape estimation. In: 3D Body Scanning Technologies, pp. 406–413 (2014)

10. Pons-Moll, G., Pujades, S., Hu, S., Black, M.J.: Clothcap: seamless 4D clothing capture and retargeting. ACM Trans. Graph. (TOG) **36**(4), 73 (2017)

11. Guan, P., Reiss, L., Hirshberg, D.A., Weiss, A., Black, M.J.: DRAPE: dressing any person. ACM Trans. Graph. **31**(4), 35 (2012)

12. Yang, S., et al.: Detailed garment recovery from a single-view image. arXiv preprint (2016). arXiv:1608.01250

13. Johnson, S., Everingham, M.: Clustered pose and nonlinear appearance models for human pose estimation. In: Proceedings of the British Machine Vision Conference (2010). https://doi.org/10.5244/C.24.12201

14. Andriluka, M., Pishchulin, L., Gehler, P., Schiele, B.: 2D human pose estimation: new benchmark and state of the art analysis. In: Proceedings the European Conference on Computer Vision (CVPR), pp. 3686–3693 (2014)

15. Lin, T.-Y.: Microsoft coco: common objects in context. In: Proceedings of European Conference on Computer Vision (ECCV), pp. 3686–3693 (2014)

16. Li, W., et al.: Rethinking on multi-stage networks for human pose estimation. arXiv preprint (2019). arXiv:1901.00148

17. Chen, Y., Wang, Z., Peng, Y., Zhang, Z., Yu, G., Sun, J.: Cascaded pyramid network for multi-person pose estimation. In: Proceedings of the IEEE Conference on Computer Vision and Pattern Recognition (CVPR), pp. 7103–7112 (2018)

18. He, K., Gkioxari, G., Dollár, P., Girshick, R.: Mask R-CNN. IEEE Trans. Pattern Anal. Mach. Intell. **42**(2), 386–397 (2020)

19. Liu, Z., Luo, P., Qiu, S., Wang, X., Tang, X.: DeepFashion: powering robust clothes recognition and retrieval with rich annotations. In: Proceedings of the IEEE Conference on Computer Vision and Pattern Recognition (CVPR), pp. 1096–1104 (2016)

20. Ge, Y., Zhang, R., Wu, L., Wang, X., Tang, X., Luo, P.: DeepFashion2: a versatile benchmark for detection, pose estimation, segmentation and re-identification of clothing images. In: Proceedings of the IEEE Conference on Computer Vision and Pattern Recognition (CVPR), pp. 5332–5340 (2019)

21. Gong, K., Gao, Y., Liang, X., Shen, X., Wang, M., Lin, L.: Graphonomy: universal human parsing via graph transfer learning. In: Proceedings of the IEEE Conference on Computer Vision and Pattern Recognition (CVPR), pp. 7442–7451 (2019)

22. Cao, Z., Simon, T., Wei, S.-E., Sheikh, Y.: OpenPose: realtime multi-person 2D pose estimation using part affinity fields. In: Proceedings of the IEEE Conference on Computer Vision and Pattern Recognition (CVPR), pp. 1302–1310 (2017)

23. Johnson, J., Alahi, A., Fei-Fei, L.: Perceptual losses for real-time style transfer and super-resolution. In: Proceedings the European Conference on Computer Vision (CVPR), pp. 694–711 (2016)

Deep Dependency Network for Multi-label Text Classification

Xiaodong Guo and Yang Weng[✉]

College of Mathematics, Sichuan University, Chengdu, China
wengyang@scu.edu.cn

Abstract. In multi-label text classification tasks, the effective extraction of text features and the use of correlations between labels are the main starting points to improve the performance of the tasks. This paper utilizes the powerful feature representation ability of deep learning, combined with the intuitionistic and easily extensible label correlations modeling method of conditional dependency network, to propose a Deep Dependency Network (DDN) framework based on label dependencies. The experimental results on a real-world dataset show that the framework proposed in this paper is effective and has good scalability.

Keywords: Multi-label · Text classification · Deep learning · Conditional dependency network · Label correlations

1 Introduction

Multi-label text classification (MLTC) is an important and valuable task in natural language processing (NLP), which can be applied in many real-world scenarios, including document indexing, tag suggestion and sentiment classification, etc. It refers to assigning more than one label to a given text instance, which is different from single-label classification and leads to be more complicated and challenging than the traditional classification task. A typical example is that news is often given many tags such as "social", "economic", "culture" and other tags so that searching or recommending more accurately.

Early work explores MLTC by traditional machine learning algorithms [1, 6,14,16]. Many of these algorithms capture the correlations between labels to improve the performance of multi-label classification (MLC) tasks. Probabilistic graphical model that is a powerful model framework to describe the correlations between variables has been applied in MLC, such as bayesian networks [4,18] and conditional random field [8]. However, these graphical models require complex learning and inference processes. Yuhong Guo *et al.* proposed a probabilistic graphical model, i.e. conditional dependency network (CDN), to model the correlations between labels in [9]. Although CDN builds multiple binary classifiers,

This work was supported by the National Key Research and Development Program of China under Grant 2018YFC0830300.

Y. Peng et al. (Eds.): PRCV 2020, LNCS 12307, pp. 298–309, 2020.
https://doi.org/10.1007/978-3-030-60636-7_25

it considers not only the features of sample but also the information from other labels simultaneously when it predicts one of labels. It supposes that each label is related to other labels and the degree of correlations is determined by the weight, which not only intuitively describes the dependencies between labels, but also simplifies the construction process of label correlations and is convenient for model extension.

In MLTC tasks, text data have complex semantic diversity and feature expression forms. However, the traditional MLC algorithms generally use word-level sparse features as text feature expressions and the feature extraction capability of these algorithms is insufficient. Therefore, it is difficult for these algorithms to fully utilize the text information. With the rapid development of deep learning, many deep learning network models have been used in MLTC tasks with their strong ability for text feature extraction and expression [2,11–13,17]. But many of these algorithms either do not explicitly consider the dependencies between labels, or even if the dependencies between labels are considered, these dependencies are not comprehensive. For example, it is sometimes not appropriate to use the serial structure of recurrent neural network (RNN) to construct serial label dependencies, because there may be multiple dependencies between labels. In addition, many deep learning models used for MLTC have a specific form, and it is not easy to expand. However, many new and powerful network models , such as the pre-training model bidirectional encoder representations from transformers (BERT) [5], can make full use of text information to improve the performance of text tasks, but many deep learning algorithms for MLTC are not easy to extend to these new network models, which makes these newer networks unable to be used simply and effectively in MLTC tasks.

Fortunately, we can obtain many effective ways to build dependencies between labels from traditional MLC algorithms. On the other hand, many deep learning networks can make more effective use of deep text structure features, but it is difficult for traditional MLC algorithms to have such feature extraction capabilities. Therefore, how to combine deep learning and some effective label correlations modeling ideas from traditional MLC algorithms, such as the idea of probabilistic graphical model, and give full play to the strengths of the two to improve the performance of MLTC tasks is very worth thinking.

In this paper, considering the intuitive and simple label dependencies modeling process and independent binary classification probability estimation of CDN, we find that it is easy to apply CDN in combination with neural networks. In order to give full play to the respective advantages of deep learning and CDN in MLTC tasks, we propose Deep Dependency Network (DDN) framework. DDN uses the idea of CDN to integrate the conditional dependency structure of labels into the output layer of neural network, that is, to add specific information implying the presence or absence of other labels to each label dimension of the output layer of neural network. The output of the DDN network is the conditional probability of each label under the condition of a given input text and other labels. The joint probability is inferred to obtain the label set that can maximize the joint probability of labels as the predicted labels.

The contributions of this paper are listed as follows:

- We propose DDN framework that combines conditional dependency network and deep learning to capture the dependency correlations between labels in deep learning.
- The experimental results on a real-world dataset show that DDN proposed in this paper is effective and has good scalability. DDN can be applied to a variety of neural networks, including pre-training model BERT, which improves the performance of MLTC tasks.

The whole paper is organized as follows. Section 2 introduces the related work. We describe conditional dependency network in Sect. 3. Based on Sect. 3, we propose our framework in Sect. 4. In Sect. 5, we design the experiments and give results. Finally in Sect. 6, we conclude this paper and explore the future work.

2 Related Work

The current models for the MLTC task can be classified into three main categories: problem transformation methods, algorithm adaptation methods, and deep learning neural network methods.

Problem transformation methods transform MLTC problems into problems that can be solved by using traditional classification algorithms [21]. The Binary Relevance (BR) algorithm [1] transforms multi-label problem into a series of separate binary classification problems by ignoring the correlations between labels. In order to model label correlations, Label Powerset (LP) [15], Random k Label sets (RAKLE) [16] and Classifer Chain (CC) [14] build traditional classifiers using the dependencies between labels. From the perspective of probabilistic graphical model, bayesian network [18] and conditional dependency network [9] are used to model the correlations between labels.

Algorithm adaptation methods improve existing algorithms or build new ones to enable them to handle multi-label problems directly [21]. Multi-label Decision Tree (ML-DT) [3], Rank Support Vector Machine (Rank-SVM) [6], Collective multi-label classifier (CML) [8] adjusted or proposed new strategies to fit the characteristics of MLC. Min-Ling Zhang *et al.* proposed Multi-label k-Nearest Neighbor (ML-KNN) [20], which is an improved algorithm of KNN.

In recent years, many neural networks have been applied to solve MLTC tasks. Min-Ling Zhang *et al.* proposed BP-MLL [19], which utilizes a fully connected neural network and a pairwise ranking loss function for MLTC. Jinseok Nam *et al.* showed that the binary-crossentropy loss function is a better loss function instead of the pairwise ranking loss function [13]. Jingzhou Liu *et al.* proposed using convolutional neural network (CNN) to solve extreme large-scale multi-label text classification [12]. In order to make better use of the correlations between labels, Gakuto Kurata *et al.* used the co-occurrence correlations between labels to initialize the output layer weights of CNN [11]. Guibin Chen *et al.* proposed CNN-RNN [2], which utilizes semantic information of text and

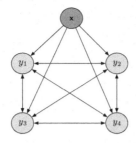

Fig. 1. The overview of CDN with four labels, i.e. y_1, y_2, y_3, y_4. It assumes that each label is related not only to the sample x but also to other labels.

model high-order label correlations by combining CNN with RNN. Pengcheng Yang *et al.* proposed SGM [17] , which uses the LSTM-based Seq2Seq structure with the attention mechanism to generate labels sequentially.

3   Conditional Dependency Network

Conditional dependency network (CDN) [9] is a directed probabilistic graphical model describing the dependencies between labels. As shown in Fig. 1, it originates from the dependency network [10]. Dependency network is also a directed probabilistic graphical model, which describes an unordered and direct dependency correlations between variables. The biggest difference between a dependency network and bayesian network or markov network is that the dependency network utilizes local conditional probability distribution that can be independently learned to build the dependency structure, and thus to obtain an approximate joint distribution. Although the dependency network cannot guarantee that the conditional probability distribution learnt independently specify a consistent joint distribution, when there are enough samples in the dataset, these conditional probability distributions can be approximately specified a consistent joint distribution [10].

Yuhong Guo *et al.* extended the general dependency network to CDN [9]. The CDN describes that under the condition of the observation feature, the labels depend on each other in the form of a dependency network, as shown in Fig. 1. Since there is generally no obvious order correlations between the labels, CDN is a dependency network form that is fully connected on all labels. This fully connected form also simplifies the complex process of structure learning and maintains a simple parameter learning process. The strength of correlations between labels and the importance of features for prediction results all appear in the form of model parameters. The CDN's simple and intuitive way of constructing label correlations is well worth using.

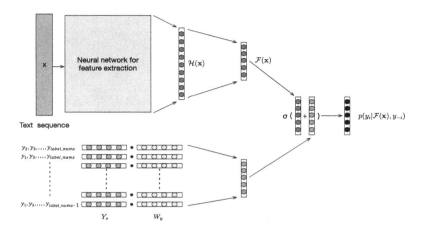

Fig. 2. The overview of DDN.

4   Proposed Framework

Given a text sequence $\mathbf{x}$ containing w words and a label space Y with L labels, $Y = \{y_1, y_2, ..., y_L\}$, the MLTC task is to assign a subset y containing $n(L \geq n \geq 1)$ labels in the label space Y to the text sequence $\mathbf{x}$. We use $\mathbf{y} = (y_1, y_2, ..., y_L)$ to express y corresponding to $\mathbf{x}$ for convenience of writing, which $y_i = \{1, 0\}, i = 1, ..., L$. $y_i = 1$ means that $\mathbf{x}$ has ith label and $y_i = 0$ means that has no.

CDN uses a probabilistic graphical model to describe the correlations between labels intuitively and concisely, but CDN is not a deep learning framework and cannot effectively extract text features. In order to give full play to the respective advantages of deep learning and CDN in MLTC tasks, we propose Deep Dependency Network (DDN) framework to improve the performance of deep neural networks in MLTC tasks.

The network of DDN is composed of two parts, as shown in Fig. 2, first is the feature extraction network at the front of the framework (the upper half in Fig. 2), and second is the label correlation network at the end of the framework (the lower half in Fig. 2). In DDN, all label classifiers are trained under the one network, which is different from CDN training multiple binary classifiers. DDN will make it easier to share features and learn parameters.

4.1   Feature Extraction Network

Many neural networks can be used as part of the feature extraction network in DDN, including CNN, RNN and BERT. After feature extraction through the network, a label prediction information vector $\mathcal{F}(\mathbf{x})$ with the same dimension as the number of labels can be obtained through a fully connected layer. Specifically, if we use the neural network $\mathcal{H}$ for feature extraction and expression, $\mathcal{H}(\mathbf{x})$ is the feature vector, and let $W_f \in \mathcal{R}^{L \times dim(\mathcal{H}(\mathbf{x}))}$ is the weight matrix, let $b_f \in \mathcal{R}^L$

is the bias, then the label prediction information vector can be calculated as the following:

$$\mathcal{F}(\mathbf{x}) = W_f \mathcal{H}(\mathbf{x}) + b_f \tag{1}$$

4.2   Label Correlation Network

Inspired by the dependency correlations between labels described by CDN, we use the idea of CDN to construct a structure for modeling the dependency correlations between labels in DDN. As shown in Fig. 2, the structure for capturing label dependencies is located behind the feature extraction network in DDN. We first suppose that each label is related to other labels, and the degree of correlations is determined by the weight. Of course, the prediction of each label also depends on the input text sequence $\mathbf{x}$. For the prediction of the ith label, in addition to containing the label information prediction vector $\mathcal{F}(\mathbf{x})$ given by the front neural network, the specific values indicating the presence or absence of other labels needs to be added. Let y_{-i} is the label set without ith label, we can calculate the new predicted information of ith label by adding the linear combination of label values (1 or 0) of labels from the label set y_{-i} to ith dimension of $\mathcal{F}(\mathbf{x})$, so as to obtain the final prediction information of the ith label, that is

$$\mathcal{F}(\mathbf{x})_i + w_{i1}y_1 + w_{i2}y_2 + \cdots + w_{ii-1}y_{i-1} + w_{ii+1}y_{i+1} + \cdots + w_{iL}y_L \tag{2}$$

where w_{ij} is the weight parameter that implies the correlation between ith label and jth label. Let $W_y \in \mathcal{R}^{L \times (L-1)}, W_y = (w_{ij})_{L \times (L-1)}$, we can get the final condition prediction information of labels:

$$\mathcal{F}(\mathbf{x}) + W_y \circ Y_s \tag{3}$$

where $\circ$ is Hadamard product, and $Y_s \in \mathcal{R}^{L \times (L-1)}$ is the matrix of labels. The ith line of Y_s is as the following:

$$(y_1, y_2, ..., y_{i-1}, y_{i+1}, ..., y_L) \tag{4}$$

Then we can use the sigmoid function σ to get the conditional prediction probability of each label:

$$p(y_i | \mathcal{F}(\mathbf{x}), y_{-i}) = \sigma(\mathcal{F}(\mathbf{x}) + W_y \circ Y_s)_i \tag{5}$$

For simplicity, W_y is omitted from the conditional part of the above conditional probability.

4.3   Loss Function

This is a binary probability prediction problem under certain conditions, so we use the binary-crossentropy loss function:

$$\mathcal{L} = -\sum^D \sum_{i=1}^L [y_i log p_i + (1 - y_i)log(1 - p_i)] \tag{6}$$

where D is the number of samples, and p_i is $p(y_i | \mathcal{F}(\mathbf{x}), y_{-i})$.

Algorithm 1. Gibbs Sampling for Inference of DDN

Input: Text sequence, $\mathbf{x}$;
    Number of labels, L;
    Burn-in iteration number, n_b;
    Instance collection iteration number, n_c.
Output: Predicted sequence of labels, $\hat{\mathbf{y}}$.
1: initialize $\mathbf{y} = (y_1, y_2, ..., y_L)$, $l = 0$;
2: choose a random ordering r over label space Y.
3: **for** $j = 1$ **to** $n_b + n_c$ **do**
4:    **for** $i = 1$ **to** L **do**
5:        $q = p(y_{r(i)} = 1 | \mathcal{F}(\mathbf{x}), y_{-r(i)})$;
6:        sample $u \sim uniform\ distribution\ of\ (0, 1)$;
7:        **if** $u \leq q$ **then** $y_{r(i)=1}$
8:        **else** $y_{r(i)=0}$
9:        **end if**
10:      **if** $j > n_b$ **then**
11:          $s = \prod_{i=1}^{L} p(y_i | \mathcal{F}(\mathbf{x}), y_{-i})$
12:        **if** $l < s$ **then**
13:          $l = s, \hat{\mathbf{y}} = \mathbf{y}$
14:        **end if**
15:      **end if**
16:    **end for**
17: **end for**

During the training process, after inputing the text sequence $\mathbf{x}$ in the front of the network, in order to get the predicted value of each label, we also need to input other label values corresponding to this sample $\mathbf{x}$, which is similar to the feature input of existing observations. The feature extraction network and the label correlation network are trained together. The entire training process is essentially the same as that of general neural networks.

4.4 Inference in Prediction

After finishing training, we can use the trained network to get the conditional probability $p(y_i | \mathcal{F}(\mathbf{x}), y_{-i})$, from which the dependency structure between labels can be obtained. Our goal is to find a optimal label set $\hat{\mathbf{y}}$, which make the conditional joint distribution $p(\mathbf{y}|\mathbf{x})$ obtain the maximum probability value, that is

$$\hat{\mathbf{y}} = arg \max_{\mathbf{y}} p(\mathbf{y}|\mathbf{x}) \tag{7}$$

We should first get the conditional joint distribution $p(\mathbf{y}|\mathbf{x})$, and then find the optimal $\hat{\mathbf{y}}$ as the predicted labels. However, this cannot be directly obtained from the trained network, so the prediction process of DDN is quite different.

    Gibbs sampling [7] is a Metropolis-Hastings sampling algorithm, which is often used in the inference problem of graph models. It is to sample one variable after fixing all other variables, which can be very suitably and conveniently used in the inference process of the DDN framework. Using the conditional probability given by the network in DDN, we can approximately get samples of $p(\mathbf{y}|\mathbf{x})$ by Gibbs sampling.

We expect that after a certain number of burn-in iteration steps during Gibbs sampling, the sampled samples can converge to a stationary distribution, and then these samples are approximated as samples of $p(\mathbf{y}|\mathbf{x})$. Further, we can see that the product of the conditional probability of each label $\prod_{i=1}^{L} p(y_i|\mathcal{F}(\mathbf{x}), y_{-i})$ and the conditional joint probability $p(\mathbf{y}|\mathbf{x})$ has the following relationship:

$$p(\mathbf{y}|\mathbf{x}) \approx \frac{1}{\mathbf{Z}} \prod_{i=1}^{L} p(y_i|\mathcal{F}(\mathbf{x}), y_{-i}) \tag{8}$$

Where $\mathbf{Z}$ refers to the sum of $\prod_{i=1}^{L} p(y_i|\mathcal{F}(\mathbf{x}), y_{-i})$ after traversing all sample cases. After the network parameters have been trained, $\mathbf{Z}$ is a fixed constant. Therefore, we use the sample that maximizes $\prod_{i=1}^{L} p(y_i|\mathcal{F}(\mathbf{x}), y_{-i})$ to approximate as the sample that maximizes $p(\mathbf{y}|\mathbf{x})$. After finishing sampling, we take the sample with the highest conditional probability product value as the final prediction result $\hat{\mathbf{y}}$. The detailed process of Gibbs sampling for DDN prediction inference is given in Algorithm 1.

5 Experiments

We conduct experiments with the real-world MLTC dataset to evaluate the effectiveness and scalability of our proposed framework.

5.1 Dataset

The dataset we use is CAIL2019 (Divorce), which is used for the extraction of the case element. All data in the dataset are from the legal documents published by China Judgment Document Network. Each data consists of the case description of a legal document, where each sentence is tagged with multiple corresponding category labels. The dataset is divided small and big dataset. In this paper, we use small dataset that is related to divorce and split the dataset, whose training set contains 10484 sentence samples, and the validation set contains 1201 sentence samples. There are 21 labels in total and the average number of labels per sample is 1.32.

5.2 Evaluation Metrics

The evaluation metrics of MLC tasks can be divided into binary evaluation metrics based on classification tasks and ranking evaluation metrics based on ranking tasks. Since the framework we proposed and the MLC task we solved only involved the classification problem, referring the review work [21], we choose Subset Accuracy, Hamming Loss, Micro-F_1 and Macro-F_1 as our main evaluation metrics. For reference, Micro-precision, Micro-recall, Macro-precision and Macro-recall are also recorded.

5.3   Experimental Models

We use two classical neural networks, i.e. CNN and RNN with a gated recurrent unit (GRU), and a pre-training model proposed recently, i.e. BERT [5], as feature extraction network in our proposed framework.

We use CNN consisted of a word embedding layer and one typical CNN layer with a convolution layer and a pooling layer. The convolution layer has multiple convolution kernels with different size and Max-pooling is applied in pooling layer. The output of pooling layer is concatenated into vector $\mathcal{H}(\mathbf{x})$ in (1), which is then as feature extraction part of DDN. As for embedding layer, we handle it by random word embedding and pre-training word embedding obtained by BERT respectively. We let CNN-DDN express DDN with CNN and random word embedding, while WCNN-DDN uses pre-training word embedding.

We use GRU consisted of a word embedding layer and a recurrent unit layer. The recurrent unit layer is unidirectional and has a gated recurrent unit. The last vector of output sequence from GRU is $\mathcal{H}(\mathbf{x})$ in (1), which is then merged into DDN. As for embedding layer, similar to CNN mentioned above, we let GRU-DDN express DDN with GRU and random word embedding, while WGRU-DDN refers to use pre-training word embedding.

We also want to test the actual effect of DDN on the typical pre-training model BERT. The final hidden state output of [CLS] token in BERT is $\mathcal{H}(\mathbf{x})$ in (1), which is then merged into DDN. We use two experimental ways on BERT, i.e. DDN with fixed BERT, which uses pre-training parameters of BERT and fixes those parameters during training, and DDN with tuned BERT, which use pre-training parameters of BERT and fine-tuning all parameters of model during training. We let BERT-DDN express the former way and FBERT-DDN express the later way.

All models mention above have their own baselines to compare. These baselines are the version of the above models without using DDN, which directly outputing the probability through the fully connected layer and the sigmoid function after the feature extraction. We let CNN-FL, WCNN-FL, GRU-FL, WGRU-FL, BERT-FL, FBERT-FL are the baselines compared network models mention above respectively.

All hyperparameters and network settings of models mention above are kept the same as respective baselines and no more adjustments.

5.4   Experimental Settings

We choose hyperparameters based on the performance of baselines on the validation set. The Chinese pre-training model of BERT used is $Chinese\_L - 12\_H - 768A - 12$[1], and the size of the pre-training word embedding from BERT is 768. The baselines settings are described as the following.

For CNN-FL, the size of convolution kernels is set to 3, 4 and 5, and the number of filters of each size is set to 128. The embedding size and the sequence length

---

[1] https://github.com/google-research/bert#pre-trained-models.

after word segmentation is set to 128 and 40 respectively. Out-of-vocabulary words and out-of-length words are replaced with *unk*. We set the number of epoch to 15. Beside, the learning rate is set to 0.001.

For WCNN-FL, since using the pre-trained word embedding, the sequence length of Chinese character is set to 128. The number of epoch and the learning rate is set to 25 and 0.001 respectively. The others are same as CNN-FL.

For GRU-FL, we set embedding size and hidden state size both to 128. The number of epoch, the sequence length and the learning rate are all same as CNN-FL.

For WGRU-FL, the hidden state size is set to 768, and the sequence length is same as WCNN-FL. The number of epoch and the learning rate are same as CNN-FL.

For BERT-FL, we use Chinese pre-training model of BERT to initialize the BERT network in BERT-FL. The sequence length of Chinese character, the number of epoch and the learning rate are all same as WCNN-FL.

For FBERT-FL, except that fine-tuning all parameters in FBERT-FL during 10 epoch and the learning rate is set to 0.00005, it's all the same with BERT-FL.

The batch size in all baselines is set to 32 and dropout with probability 0.5 is applied to avoid overfitting. We use Subset Accuracy as the reference metric for the final model selection, and the results with the highest Subset Accuracy are recorded.

5.5 Results and Discussion

We present the results of our proposed framework DDN with different typical neural networks on the Divorce validation set in Table 1. All results of all evaluation metrics mentioned in Sect. 5.2 in all experiments are reported. From Table 1, it can be found that whether or not to use pre-training word embedding or fine-tuning the pre-training model, three network models all make improvements in most evaluation metrics after using our proposed framework. Specially, some baselines can even make a little big improvement on some evaluation metrics. For example, the CNN-DDN achieves an improvement of 4.64% Subset Accuracy over the CNN-FL, and the FBERT-DDN achieves a reduction of 6.62% Hamming Loss over the FBERT-FL, and the BERT-DDN achieves an improvement of 2.85% Micro-F_1 over BERT-FL, and the GRU-DDN also achieves an improvement of 6.13% Macro-F_1 over GRU-FL.

In general, the results from experiments on real-word dataset Divorce show that our proposed framework is not only effective but also has good scalability, which achieve improvements on classical network CNN, GRU and pre-training model BERT. There also shows a similar improvement trend even with pre-training embedding and fine-tuning. With the emergence of various new network models, especially for pre-training models like BERT that are very effective in text tasks, this provides a simple but effective improvement idea for utilizing various deep neural network models in the field of MLTC, that is, better use of text semantic information and capturing the correlations between labels at the same time.

Table 1. Performance on the divorce validation set. SA, HL, MiP, MiR, MiF_1, MaP, MaR, and MaF_1denote Subset Accuracy, Hamming Loss, Micro-precision, Micro-recall, Micro-F_1, Macro-precision, Macro-recall, and Macro-F_1, respectively. The symbol "+" indicates that the higher the value is, the better the model performs. The symbol "−" is the opposite.

Models	SA(+)	HL(−)	MiP(+)	MiR(+)	MiF_1(+)	MaP(+)	MaR(+)	MaF_1(+)
CNN-FL	0.7177	0.02323	0.8528	0.7665	0.8071	0.5861	0.3835	0.4339
CNN-DDN	**0.7510**	**0.02256**	**0.8555**	**0.7759**	**0.8137**	**0.6126**	**0.3891**	**0.4398**
WCNN-FL	0.7777	0.01749	**0.8883**	0.8290	0.8576	0.7676	0.5718	0.6301
WCNN-DDN	**0.8018**	**0.01697**	0.8867	**0.8402**	**0.8628**	**0.8052**	**0.5879**	**0.6465**
GRU-FL	0.7202	0.02276	**0.8560**	0.7715	0.8116	0.5149	0.4225	0.4516
GRU-DDN	**0.7435**	**0.02236**	0.8460	**0.7921**	**0.8182**	**0.5968**	**0.4429**	**0.4793**
WGRU-FL	0.7968	0.01709	**0.8790**	0.8477	0.8630	0.7746	0.5938	0.6518
WGRU-DDN	**0.8027**	**0.01697**	0.8772	**0.8521**	**0.8645**	**0.7776**	**0.6186**	**0.6677**
BERT-FL	0.6536	0.02954	**0.8059**	0.7047	0.7519	0.5128	0.3769	0.4231
BERT-DDN	**0.6936**	**0.02815**	0.7915	**0.7559**	**0.7733**	**0.5827**	**0.4435**	**0.4785**
FBERT-FL	0.7910	0.01737	0.8712	0.8527	0.8618	**0.7170**	**0.5952**	**0.6276**
FBERT-DDN	**0.7985**	**0.01622**	**0.8749**	**0.8689**	**0.8719**	0.6811	0.5748	0.6019

6   Conclusion

In this paper, we propose a view that combines deep learning with label correlations modeling of conditional dependency network to make full use of the features extraction of deep learning and the advantages of describing the dependencies between labels in CDN. As a result, we establish a Deep Dependency Network (DDN) framework based on label dependencies. The experimental results on the real-word dataset show that our framework really do work and can be applied to many neural networks, which enables us to use more and better advanced deep networks to improve the performance of multi-label text classification.

The framework proposed in this paper has achieved good performance during the experiments, but there is room for further research. Future work will mainly focus on incorporating a more powerful and effective label correlation structure into the deep learning framework.

References

1. Boutell, M.R., Luo, J., Shen, X., Brown, C.M.: Learning multi-label scene classification. Pattern Recogn. **37**(9), 1757–1771 (2004)
2. Chen, G., Ye, D., Xing, Z., Chen, J., Cambria, E.: Ensemble application of convolutional and recurrent neural networks for multi-label text categorization. In: 2017 International Joint Conference on Neural Networks (IJCNN), pp. 2377–2383. IEEE (2017)
3. Clare, A., King, R.D.: Knowledge discovery in multi-label phenotype data. In: De Raedt, L., Siebes, A. (eds.) PKDD 2001. LNCS (LNAI), vol. 2168, pp. 42–53. Springer, Heidelberg (2001). https://doi.org/10.1007/3-540-44794-6_4

4. de Waal, P.R., van der Gaag, L.C.: Inference and learning in multi-dimensional bayesian network classifiers. In: Mellouli, K. (ed.) ECSQARU 2007. LNCS (LNAI), vol. 4724, pp. 501–511. Springer, Heidelberg (2007). https://doi.org/10.1007/978-3-540-75256-1_45

5. Devlin, J., Chang, M.W., Lee, K., Toutanova, K.: Bert: pre-training of deep bidirectional transformers for language understanding. arXiv preprint (2018). arXiv:1810.04805

6. Elisseeff, A., Weston, J.: A kernel method for multi-labelled classification. In: Advances in Neural Information Processing Systems, pp. 681–687 (2002)

7. Geman, S., Geman, D.: Stochastic relaxation, Gibbs distributions, and the bayesian restoration of images. IEEE Trans. Pattern Anal. Mach. Intell. PAMI **6**(6), 721–741 (1984)

8. Ghamrawi, N., McCallum, A.: Collective multi-label classification. In: Proceedings of the 14th ACM International Conference on Information and Knowledge Management, pp. 195–200 (2005)

9. Guo, Y., Gu, S.: Multi-label classification using conditional dependency networks. In: Twenty-Second International Joint Conference on Artificial Intelligence, pp. 1300–1305 (2011)

10. Heckerman, D., Chickering, D.M., Meek, C., Rounthwaite, R., Kadie, C.: Dependency networks for inference, collaborative filtering, and data visualization. J. Mach. Learn. Res. **1**(Oct), 49–75 (2000)

11. Kurata, G., Xiang, B., Zhou, B.: Improved neural network-based multi-label classification with better initialization leveraging label co-occurrence. In: Proceedings of the 2016 Conference of the North American Chapter of the Association for Computational Linguistics: Human Language Technologies, pp. 521–526 (2016)

12. Liu, J., Chang, W.C., Wu, Y., Yang, Y.: Deep learning for extreme multi-label text classification. In: Proceedings of the 40th International ACM SIGIR Conference on Research and Development in Information Retrieval, pp. 115–124 (2017)

13. Nam, J., Kim, J., Loza Mencía, E., Gurevych, I., Fürnkranz, J.: Large-scale multi-label text classification — revisiting neural networks. In: Calders, T., Esposito, F., Hüllermeier, E., Meo, R. (eds.) ECML PKDD 2014. LNCS (LNAI), vol. 8725, pp. 437–452. Springer, Heidelberg (2014). https://doi.org/10.1007/978-3-662-44851-9_28

14. Read, J., Pfahringer, B., Holmes, G., Frank, E.: Classifier chains for multi-label classification. Mach. Learn. **85**(3), 333 (2011)

15. Tsoumakas, G., Katakis, I.: Multi-label classification: an overview. Int. J. Data Warehousing Min. (IJDWM) **3**(3), 1–13 (2007)

16. Tsoumakas, G., Katakis, I., Vlahavas, I.: Random k-labelsets for multilabel classification. IEEE Trans. Knowl. Data Eng. **23**(7), 1079–1089 (2010)

17. Yang, P., Sun, X., Li, W., Ma, S., Wu, W., Wang, H.: SGM: sequence generation model for multi-label classification. In: Proceedings of the 27th International Conference on Computational Linguistics, COLING 2018, Santa Fe, New Mexico, USA, August 20–26, 2018, pp. 3915–3926 (2018)

18. Zhang, M.L., Zhang, K.: Multi-label learning by exploiting label dependency. In: Proceedings of the 16th ACM SIGKDD International Conference on Knowledge Discovery and Data Mining, pp. 999–1008. ACM (2010)

19. Zhang, M.L., Zhou, Z.H.: Multilabel neural networks with applications to functional genomics and text categorization. IEEE Trans. Knowl. Data Eng. **18**(10), 1338–1351 (2006)

20. Zhang, M.L., Zhou, Z.H.: Ml-knn: a lazy learning approach to multi-label learning. Pattern Recogn. **40**(7), 2038–2048 (2007)

21. Zhang, M.L., Zhou, Z.H.: A review on multi-label learning algorithms. IEEE Trans. Knowl. Data Eng. **26**(8), 1819–1837 (2013)

Soft-Root-Sign: A New Bounded Neural Activation Function

Dandan Li and Yuan Zhou[✉]

School of Electrical and Information Engineering, Tianjin University, Tianjin, China
zhouyuan@tju.edu.cn

Abstract. This paper proposes a new activation function, namely "Soft-Root-Sign" (SRS), which is smooth, non-monotonic, and bounded. The bounded property of SRS distinguishes itself from most state-of-the-art activation functions. It prevents the distribution of the output from being scattered in the non-negative real number space and corrects it to the positive real number space, providing a more stable distribution of output during network training. We evaluated SRS on deep networks applied to image classification task. Experimental results show that the proposed activation function SRS is superior to state-of-the-art nonlinearities.

Keywords: Activation function · Deep learning

1 Introduction

Deep learning is a branch of machine learning that uses multi-layer neural networks to identify complex features within the input data and solve complex real-world problems. It can be used for both supervised and unsupervised machine learning tasks [1]. Currently, deep learning is used in areas such as computer vision, video analytic, pattern recognition, anomaly detection, natural language processing, information retrieval, and recommender system, among other things. Also, it has widespread used in robotics, self-driving cars, and artificial intelligence systems in general [2].

Activation function is at the heart of any deep neural networks. It provides the non-linear property for deep neural networks and controls the information propagation through adjacent layers [3]. Therefore, the design of an activation function is crucial to the learning behavior and performance of neural networks. However, because of the unbounded output, many activation functions [4–8] have the problem of output scattered distribution, which makes the network difficult to train.

In this paper, we introduce the "Soft-Root-Sign" (SRS) which named by its appearance ("$\sqrt{}$"). The proposed SRS has smoothness, non-monotonicity, and boundedness (see Fig. 1). In fact, the bounded property of SRS distinguishes itself from most state-of-the-art activation functions. Our SRS avoids and rectifies the output distribution to be scattered in the non-negative real

© Springer Nature Switzerland AG 2020
Y. Peng et al. (Eds.): PRCV 2020, LNCS 12307, pp. 310–319, 2020.
https://doi.org/10.1007/978-3-030-60636-7_26

number space. This is desirable during inference, because it ensures a more stable distribution of output during network training. To validate the effectiveness of the proposed activation function, we evaluated SRS on deep networks applied to image classification task. Our SRS matches or exceeds models with state-of-the-art nonlinearities.

2   Related Work

Currently, the most popular and widely-used activation function for neural network is the rectified linear unit (ReLU) [4], defined as $ReLU(x) = max(0, x)$, which was first proposed for restricted Boltzmann machines and then successfully used for neural networks. On one hand, ReLU identically propagates all the positive inputs, which alleviates gradient vanishing and allows for much deeper neural networks. On the other hand, ReLU is computational efficient by just outputting zero for negative inputs.

In recent year, various activation functions have been proposed to improve the ReLU [9–24]. Leaky ReLU (LReLU) [6] replaces the negative part of the ReLU with a linear function have been shown to be superior to ReLU. Parametric ReLU (PReLU) [7] generalizes LReLU by learning the slope of the negative part which yielded improved learning behavior on large image benchmark datasets. Randomized leaky ReLU (RReLU) [8] randomly samples the slope of the negative part which raised the performance on image benchmark datasets and convolutional networks. However, non-hard rectification of these activation functions do not ensure a noise-robust deactivation state and will destroy sparsity. Other variants, i.e. shifted ReLU (SReLU) [25] and flexible ReLU (FReLU) [25], have flexibility of choosing horizontal shifts from learned biases, but they are not continuously differentiable might cause some undesired problems in gradient-based optimization.

More recently, the exponential linear unit (ELU) [5] has been proposed to capture negative values to allow for mean activations close to zero, but which saturates to a negative value with smaller arguments. Compared with LReLU, PReLU and RReLU, ELU not only provides fast convergence, but also has a clear saturation plateau in its negative region, allowing them to learn more important features. Building on this success, the variants of ELU [26–29] also demonstrate similar performance improvements. However, the incompatibility between these activation functions and batch normalization (BN) [30] has not been well treated. Another alternative to ReLU is scaled exponential linear unit (SELU) [31], which induces variance stabilization and overcomes the gradient-based problems like gradient vanishing or exploding. The main idea is to drive neuron activations across all layers to emit a zero mean and unit variance output. But there is still incompatibilities with BN. Besides, a special initialization method called LeCun Normal [32] is required to make a deep neural network with SELU remarkable.

Recently, Swish [33] opened up a new direction of bringing optimization methods including exhaustive search algorithm [34] and reinforcement learning [35] to activation function search. But one drawback is that the resulting nonlinearity is very dependent on the chosen network architecture.

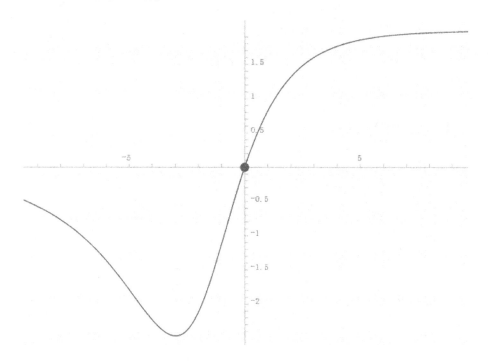

Fig. 1. SRS activation function.

3   Soft-Root-Sign Activation Function (SRS)

We propose the Soft-Root-Sign activation function (SRS), which is defined as

$$SRS(x) = \frac{x}{\frac{x}{\alpha} + e^{-\frac{x}{\beta}}} \tag{1}$$

with predetermined $\alpha = 2.0$ and $\beta = 3.0$.

Figure 1 shows the graph of the proposed SRS. In particular, SRS has non-monotonic region when $x < 0$ which helps capture negative information. Meanwhile, SRS is bounded output when $x > 0$ which avoids and rectifies the output distribution to be scattered in the non-negative real number space.

The derivative of SRS is defined as

$$SRS'(x) = \frac{(1 + \frac{x}{\beta})e^{-\frac{x}{\beta}}}{(\frac{x}{\alpha} + e^{-\frac{x}{\beta}})^2} \tag{2}$$

Figure 2 illustrates the first derivative of SRS, which gives nice continuity and effectivity.

Note that the proposed SRS activation function is bounded output with a range $[\frac{\alpha\beta}{\beta - \alpha e}, \alpha)$. Specifically, the minimum of SRS is observed to be at $x = -\beta$ with a magnitude of $\frac{\alpha\beta}{\beta - \alpha e}$; and the maximum of SRS is α when the network input $x \to +\infty$.

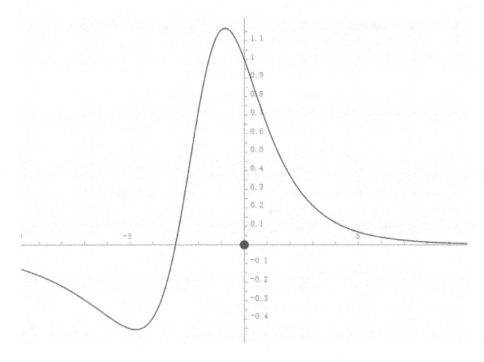

Fig. 2. First derivatives of SRS.

4 Experiments

This section presents a series of experiments to demonstrate that our Soft-Root-Sign activation function (SRS) improves performance in image classification task. Since many activation functions have been proposed, we choose the most common activation functions to compare against: the ReLU [4], the LReLU [6], the PReLU [7], the Softplus [36], the ELU [5], the SELU [31] and the Swish [33], and follow the following guidelines:

- Leaky ReLU (LReLU):

$$f(x) = \begin{cases} x & x \geq 0 \\ \alpha x & x < 0 \end{cases}$$

  where $\alpha = 0.2$. LReLU introduces a non-zero gradient for negative input.
- Parametric ReLU (PReLU):

$$f(x) = \begin{cases} x & x \geq 0 \\ \alpha x & x < 0 \end{cases}$$

PReLU is a modified version of LReLU that makes α trainable. Each channel has a shared α which is initialized to 0.1.

– Softplus:

$$f(x) = log(1 + e^x)$$

Softplus can be regarded as a smooth version of ReLU.

– Exponential Linear Unit (ELU):

$$f(x) = \begin{cases} x & x \geq 0 \\ \alpha(e^x - 1) & x < 0 \end{cases}$$

where $\alpha = 1.0$. ELU produces negative outputs, which helps the network push mean unit activations closer to zero.

– Scaled Exponential Linear Unit (SELU):

$$f(x) = \lambda \begin{cases} x & x \geq 0 \\ \alpha(e^x - 1) & x < 0 \end{cases}$$

with predetermined $\lambda \approx 1.0507$ and $\alpha \approx 1.6733$.

– Swish:

$$f(x) = \frac{x}{1 + e^{-\alpha x}}$$

where α can either be a trainable parameter or equal to 1.0.

4.1   Image Classification

We evaluate the proposed SRS on the image classification task. On CIFAR-10 and CIFAR-100, we compare the performance of SRS to that of different activation functions applied to the representative CNNs, i.e. VGG-16 [37] and MobileNet V1 [38].

Datasets. The CIFAR datasets, CIFAR-10 and CIFAR-100, consist of 32×32 colored images. Both datasets contain 60,000 images, which are split into 50,000 training images and 10,000 test images. CIFAR-10 dataset has 10 classes, with 6,000 images per class. CIFAR-100 dataset is similar to CIFAR-10 dataset, except that has 100 classes, each of which contains 600 images. The standard data-augmentation scheme, in which the images are zero-padded with 4 pixels on each side, randomly cropped to produce 32×32 images, and horizontally mirrored with probability 0.5 are adopted in our experiments, according to usual practice [39,40]. During training, we randomly sample 5% of the training images for validation.

Training Settings. We use exactly the same settings to train these models. All networks are trained using stochastic gradient descent (SGD) with a weight decay of 5×10^{-4} and momentum of 0.9. The weights initialized according to [41]. The biases are initialized with zero. On CIFAR-10 and CIFAR-100, we trained for 300 epochs, with a mini-batch size of 128. The initial learning rate is set to 0.1 and decayed by a factor of 0.1 after 120 and 240 epochs. Unless otherwise specified, we adopt batch normalization (BN) [30] right after each convolution, nonlinear activation is performed right after BN. Dropout regularization [42] is employed in the fully-connected layers, with a dropout ratio of 0.5.

Results. The results shown in Table 1 and 2 report the median of five different runs. As it can be seen, our SRS matches or exceeds models with state-of-the-art nonlinearities. In particular, SRS networks perform significantly better than ReLU networks. For example, on VGG, SRS performs well over ReLU with a 0.24% boost on CIFAR-10 and 0.99% on CIFAR-100 respectively. On MobileNet, SRS networks achieve up to 87.94% on CIFAR-10 and 60.60% on CIFAR-100, which are improvements of 2.33% and 4.36% above the ReLU baselines respectively. The observation in Fig. 3, clearly shows the learning behavior of SRS and ReLU networks. Networks with SRS show relatively lower validation error and lead for faster convergence, as compared to ReLU.

Table 1. CIFAR-10 accuracy (%). The red entries indicate the best, followed by blue.

Model	ReLU	LReLU	PReLU	Softplus	ELU	SELU	Swish	SRS
VGG$_{C10}$	93.10	93.34	92.85	93.16	93.23	93.08	93.13	93.34
MobileNet$_{C10}$	85.61	87.60	87.88	87.21	87.93	87.72	87.50	87.94

Table 2. CIFAR-100 accuracy (%). The red entries indicate the best, followed by blue.

Model	ReLU	LReLU	PReLU	Softplus	ELU	SELU	Swish	SRS
VGG$_{C100}$	72.23	72.86	71.13	72.21	73.20	72.08	72.43	73.22
MobileNet$_{C100}$	56.24	60.47	57.51	58.55	60.58	59.79	59.07	60.60

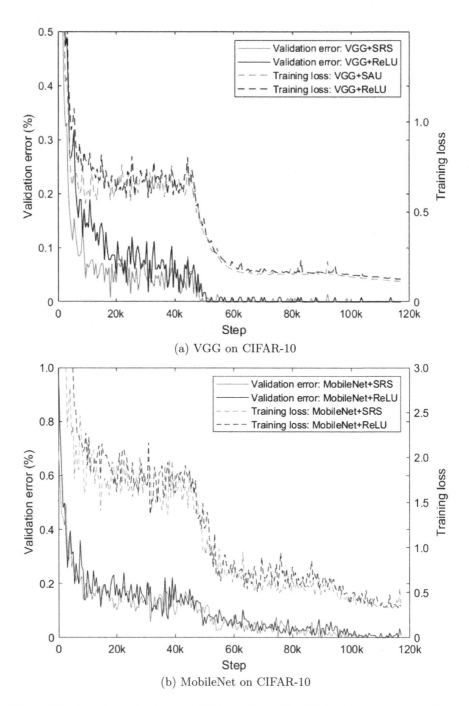

(a) VGG on CIFAR-10

(b) MobileNet on CIFAR-10

Fig. 3. The learning behavior of SAU (in red) and ReLU (in blue) networks. (Color figure online)

5   Conclusion

In this work, we have introduced a novel activation function called Soft-Root-Sign (SRS). The proposed SRS has smoothness, non-monotonicity, and boundedness. In fact, the bounded property of SRS distinguishes itself from most state-of-the-art activation functions. By defining a custom activation layer, SRS can be easily implemented in most deep learning framework. In experiments, we benchmarked SRS against several baseline activation functions on image classification task. Empirical results demonstrate that our SRS matches or exceeds all baselines. Finally, although SRS is computationally expensive because it involves complex mathematical operations, we expect that SRS implementations can be improved, e.g. by faster exponential functions. This remains one of the areas that warrants further exploration.

References

1. Bengio, Y., et al.: Learning deep architectures for AI. Found. Trends Mach. Learn. **2**(1), 1–127 (2009)
2. Schmidhuber, J.: Deep learning in neural networks: an overview. Neural Netw. **61**(1), 85–117 (2015)
3. LeCun, Y., Bengio, Y., Hinton, G.: Deep learning. Nature **521**(7553), 436–444 (2015)
4. Nair, V., Hinton, G.E.: Rectified linear units improve restricted Boltzmann machines. In: Proceedings of the International Conference on Machine Learning (ICML), pp. 807–814 (2010)
5. Clevert, D.A., Unterthiner, T., Hochreiter, S.: Fast and accurate deep network learning by exponential linear units. arXiv preprint arXiv:1511.07289 (2015)
6. Maas, A.L., Hannun, A.Y., Ng, A.Y.: Rectifier nonlinearities improve neural network acoustic models. In: Proceedings of the International Conference on Machine Learning (ICML), pp. 3–9 (2013)
7. He, K., Zhang, X., Ren, S., Sun, J.: Delving deep into rectifiers: surpassing human-level performance on ImageNet classification. In: Proceedings of the IEEE International Conference on Computer Vision (ICCV), pp. 1026–1034 (2015)
8. Xu, B., Wang, N., Chen, T., Li, M.: Empirical evaluation of rectified activations in convolutional network. arXiv preprint arXiv:1505.00853 (2015)
9. Misra, D.: Mish: a self regularized non-monotonic neural activation function. arXiv preprint arXiv:1908.08681 (2019)
10. Gulcehre, C., Moczulski, M., Denil, M., Bengio, Y.: Noisy activation functions. In: Proceedings of the International Conference on Machine Learning (ICML), pp. 3059–3068 (2016)
11. Basirat, M., Roth, P.M.: The quest for the golden activation function. arXiv preprint arXiv:1808.00783 (2018)
12. Jin, X., Xu, C., Feng, J., Wei, Y., Xiong, J., Yan, S.: Deep learning with S-shaped rectified linear activation units. In: 13th AAAI Conference on Artificial Intelligence (AAAI), pp. 1–8 (2016)
13. Agostinelli, F., Hoffman, M., Sadowski, P., Baldi, P.: Learning activation functions to improve deep neural networks. arXiv preprint arXiv:1412.6830 (2014)

14. Elfwing, S., Uchibe, E., Doya, K.: Sigmoid-weighted linear units for neural network function approximation in reinforcement learning. Neural Netw. **107**(1), 3–11 (2018)
15. Shang, W., Sohn, K., Almeida, D., Lee, H.: Understanding and improving convolutional neural networks via concatenated rectified linear units. In: Proceedings of the International Conference on Machine Learning (ICML), pp. 2217–2225 (2016)
16. Chen, T.Q., Behrmann, J., Duvenaud, D.K., Jacobsen, J.H.: Residual flows for invertible generative modeling. In: Advances in Neural Information Processing Systems (NeurIPS), pp. 9913–9923 (2019)
17. Wuraola, A., Patel, N.: SQNL: a new computationally efficient activation function. In: International Joint Conference on Neural Networks (IJCNN), pp. 1–7 (2018)
18. Carlile, B., Delamarter, G., Kinney, P., Marti, A., Whitney, B.: Improving deep learning by inverse square root linear units (ISRLUs). arXiv preprint arXiv:1710.09967 (2017)
19. Nicolae, A.: PLU: the piecewise linear unit activation function. arXiv preprint arXiv:1809.09534 (2018)
20. Eidnes, L., Nøkland, A.: Shifting mean activation towards zero with bipolar activation functions. arXiv preprint arXiv:1709.04054 (2017)
21. Hendrycks, D., Gimpel, K.: Gaussian error linear units (GELUs). arXiv preprint arXiv:1606.08415 (2016)
22. Godfrey, L.B., Gashler, M.S.: A continuum among logarithmic, linear, and exponential functions, and its potential to improve generalization in neural networks. In: 7th International Joint Conference on Knowledge Discovery, Knowledge Engineering and Knowledge Management (IC3K), pp. 481–486 (2015)
23. Alcaide, E.: E-swish: adjusting activations to different network depths. arXiv preprint arXiv:1801.07145 (2018)
24. Chieng, H.H., Wahid, N., Pauline, O., Perla, S.R.K.: Flatten-T Swish: a thresholded RElU-swish-like activation function for deep learning. Int. J. Adv. Intell. Inform. **4**(2), 76–86 (2018)
25. Qiu, S., Xu, X., Cai, B.: FReLU: flexible rectified linear units for improving convolutional neural networks. In: 24th International Conference on Pattern Recognition (ICPR), pp. 1223–1228 (2018)
26. Trottier, L., Gigu, P., Chaib-draa, B., et al.: Parametric exponential linear unit for deep convolutional neural networks. In: 16th IEEE International Conference on Machine Learning and Applications (ICMLA), pp. 207–214 (2017)
27. Li, Y., Fan, C., Li, Y., Wu, Q., Ming, Y.: Improving deep neural network with multiple parametric exponential linear units. Neurocomputing **301**(1), 11–24 (2018)
28. Cheng, Q., Li, H., Wu, Q., Ma, L., King, N.N.: Parametric deformable exponential linear units for deep neural networks. Neural Netw. **125**(1), 281–289 (2020)
29. Duggal, R., Gupta, A.: P-TELU: parametric tan hyperbolic linear unit activation for deep neural networks. In: Proceedings of the IEEE International Conference on Computer Vision Workshops (ICCV), pp. 974–978 (2017)
30. Ioffe, S., Szegedy, C.: Batch normalization: accelerating deep network training by reducing internal covariate shift. In: Proceedings of the International Conference on Machine Learning (ICML), pp. 448–456 (2015)
31. Klambauer, G., Unterthiner, T., Mayr, A., Hochreiter, S.: Self-normalizing neural networks. In: Advances in Neural Information Processing Systems (NeurIPS), pp. 971–980 (2017)
32. LeCun, Y.A., Bottou, L., Orr, G.B., Müller, K.R.: Efficient backprop. Neural Netw.: Tricks Trade **1**(1), 9–48 (2012)

33. Ramachandran, P., Zoph, B., Le, Q.V.: Searching for activation functions. arXiv preprint arXiv:1710.05941 (2017)
34. Liu, C., et al.: Progressive neural architecture search. In: Proceedings of the European Conference on Computer Vision (ECCV), pp. 19–34 (2018)
35. Schweighofer, N., Doya, K.: Meta-learning in reinforcement learning. Neural Netw. **16**(1), 5–9 (2003)
36. Glorot, X., Bordes, A., Bengio, Y.: Deep sparse rectifier neural networks. In: Proceedings of the 14th International Conference on Artificial Intelligence and Statistics, pp. 315–323 (2011)
37. Szegedy, C., et al.: Going deeper with convolutions. In: Proceedings of the IEEE Conference on Computer Vision and Pattern Recognition (CVPR), pp. 1–9 (2015)
38. Howard, A.G., et al.: MobileNets: efficient convolutional neural networks for mobile vision applications. arXiv preprint arXiv:1704.04861 (2017)
39. He, K., Zhang, X., Ren, S., Sun, J.: Identity mappings in deep residual networks. In: Leibe, B., Matas, J., Sebe, N., Welling, M. (eds.) ECCV 2016. LNCS, vol. 9908, pp. 630–645. Springer, Cham (2016). https://doi.org/10.1007/978-3-319-46493-0_38
40. Huang, G., Liu, Z., Van Der Maaten, L., Weinberger, K.Q.: Densely connected convolutional networks. In: Proceedings of the IEEE Conference on Computer Vision and Pattern Recognition (CVPR), pp. 4700–4708 (2017)
41. Glorot, X., Bengio, Y.: Understanding the difficulty of training deep feedforward neural networks. In: Proceedings of the 13th International Conference on Artificial Intelligence and Statistics, pp. 249–256 (2010)
42. Srivastava, N., Hinton, G., Krizhevsky, A., Sutskever, I., Salakhutdinov, R.: Dropout: a simple way to prevent neural networks from overfitting. J. Mach. Learn. Res. **15**(1), 1929–1958 (2014)

A Multi-level Equilibrium Clustering Approach for Unsupervised Person Re-identification

Fangyu Wang, Zhenyu Wang, Xuemei Xie$^{(\boxtimes)}$, and Guangming Shi

School of Artificial Intelligence, Xidian University, Xi'an 710071, China
xmxie@mail.xidian.edu.cn

Abstract. Unsupervised person re-identification (re-ID) has not achieved desired results because learning a discriminative feature embedding without annotation is difficult. Fortunately, the special distribution of samples in this task provides critical priority information for addressing this problem. On the one hand, the distribution of samples belonging to the same identity is multi-centered. On the other hand, distribution is distinct for samples of different levels that cropped from the images. According to the first property, we propose the equilibrium criterion, which provides a suitable measurement of dissimilarity between samples around a center or that from different centers. According to the second property, we introduce multi-level labels guided learning to mine and utilize the complementary information among different levels. Extensive experiments demonstrate that our method is superior to the state-of-the-art unsupervised re-ID approaches in significant margins.

Keywords: Person re-identification · Unsupervised learning · Clustering

1 Introduction

Person re-identification (re-ID) aims at retrieving the given person in a series of gallery pedestrian images captured by non-overlapping cameras. It has a broad application prospect in the field of surveillance security. Recently works mainly focus on supervised person re-ID [1–3]. However, achieving substantial pairwise labelled data needs costly manual effort. So, some new works turn into unsupervised person re-ID.

Some methods regard person re-ID problem as an unsupervised domain adaptation task (UDA) [4–10]. The main idea is to transform the prior knowledge learned from an external source dataset into the unlabelled target dataset. Nevertheless, the experience gained from the source domain is not always appropriate

F. Wang—Student.

This work was supported in part by the National Key R&D Program of China(No. 2018AAA0101400), the National Natural Science Foundation of China (No.61836008, 61632019).

Y. Peng et al. (Eds.): PRCV 2020, LNCS 12307, pp. 320–331, 2020.
https://doi.org/10.1007/978-3-030-60636-7_27

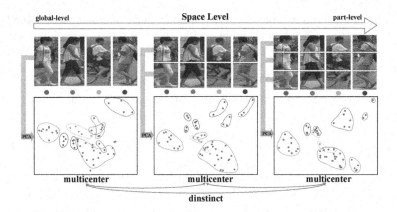

Fig. 1. Images of different space levels and the PCA results of them. The images are of 4 identities from the Market-1501 dataset [19], and dots with the same color represent samples of the same identity. The dotted line is used to circle adjacent identical samples. (Color figure online)

for the target domain. Besides, the source dataset still takes a large amount of annotation labour. Pure unsupervised methods are usually based on handcrafted features [11–14], dictionary learning [15,16] and deep learning [17,18]. However, these methods do not fully exploit the information according to the properties of the person re-ID data itself. So they are unable to effectively extract discriminative features from images.

By analyzing the data and its distribution, we notice two particular phenomena in person re-ID. As shown in Fig. 1, the distribution of samples belonging to the same identity is not spherical, but multi-centered. Some samples of different identities are mixed. Such distribution inspires us that we should not only focus on the similarity between samples but also the relationship among centers. Additionally, although coming from the same data, samples of different levels that cropped from the images are of distinct distribution. Such phenomenon is caused by the diversity of global and local differences between images. Thus, we can try to mine complementary information from this aspect for better identifying.

Based on the observation, we develop a **m**ulti-level **e**quilibrium **c**lustering approach (MEC) for unsupervised person re-ID. In our scheme, features extracted by a network are used to generate pseudo labels through clustering. Meanwhile, the network will learn to extract more discriminative features under the guidance of these labels. The process of generating pseudo labels is called clustering stage and the process of training the network by pseudo labels is called learning stage. We alternate these two stages for unsupervised learning of the network.

In the clustering stage, we propose equilibrium criterion based clustering which is competent for aggregating features of the same identity together under the multicenter distribution. Such clustering criterion can better measure the distance between scattered clusters under multicenter distribution and provide a trade-off between the completeness and homogeneity of clustering. In the learning stage, we propose multi-level labels guided learning. Not only global-level but also part-level features are extracted to generate multi-level labels by clustering. Multi-level labels could reflect multiple relationships of data samples and offer complementary supervised information for learning.

The main contributions of this work can be summarized as follows:(1) We exploit an inherent characteristic about the re-ID dataset and demonstrate how to use this prior knowledge to provide more reliable supervised information for unsupervised learning. (2) We propose a novel MEC for unsupervised person re-ID task, which iterates the process of multi-level labels guided learning and equilibrium criterion based clustering to get a discriminative feature embedding without any annotation. (3) We evaluate the proposed method on several benchmark datasets including Market-1501 [19], DuleMTMC-reID [20]. Extensive experimental results demonstrate that our approach is superior to the state-of-the-art methods in significant margins.

2   Related Work

2.1   Domain Transfer Person Re-identification

Some approaches treat the re-ID problem as UDA. It makes full use of additional source dataset to establish the relationship between the target domain and the source domain [4–7,10]. Wu *et al.* [9] propose soft multilabel learning in which each unlabeled person learns a soft multilabel by comparing itself with a set of reference people from an auxiliary dataset. Yang *et al.* [8] employ a patch-based framework to provide guidance for the target unlabelled dataset by learning local patch feature with an external dataset. However, the prior knowledge gained from the source dataset is not always useful for the target dataset. Additionally, these methods require an external abundant labelled dataset which still not reduce the workload of unsupervised re-ID annotation.

2.2   Unsupervised Person Re-identification

The traditional unsupervised person re-ID methods, mainly include learning with hand-crafted features [11–14] and dictionary learning based methods [15,16]. Yu *et al.* [21,22] propose asymmetric distance metric learning based on asymmetric K-means clustering to mine the latent information in unlabelled data. But these methods lack robustness and perform poorly on the large-scale re-ID dataset. Recently, Lin *et al.* [18] use an end-to-end convolutional framework, which alternatively trains the model with pseudo labels and merges similar data samples to form new pseudo labels. It mainly uses the minimum distance as the clustering criterion. However, applying such a clustering criterion may result in many large size clusters, which seriously destroys the homogeneity of clustering. Ding *et al.* [17] propose the validity guided dispersion criterion based on the bottom-to-up structure. This criterion consists of an inter-cluster dispersion term and intra-cluster dispersion term. It is greatly influenced by outliers and results in clustering errors. In a word, these methods do not consider the characteristics of the re-ID task itself. Therefore, they do not design a suitable clustering criterion.

3 Method

3.1 Problem Formulation and Overview

Given a training set $X = \{x_i\}_{i=1}^M$ composed of M images. Our goal is to obtain a feature embedding function $\varphi(x; \theta)$ learning from the training set, where parameters involved are collectively referred as θ. Supervised methods usually provide training set manual annotated labels $Z = \{z_i\}_{i=1}^M$ where $z_i \in \{1, 2, \ldots, C\}$ and C is the total number of identities. Under the guidance of labels, $\varphi(x; \theta)$ associated with the parameter ω constitutes a classifier $f(\varphi(x; \theta); \omega)$ to predict an identity. So the feature embedding parameter θ and classifier parameter ω can jointly be optimized by:

$$\min_{\theta, \omega} \sum_{i=1}^M l\left(f\left(\varphi\left(x_i; \theta\right); \omega\right), z_i\right) \tag{1}$$

where l is the loss function.

However, there are no annotation labels in unsupervised re-ID. We obtain the supervision information in a manner proposed by [18], which is similar to the hierarchical clustering. At first, all M images are regarded as different identities and assigned M individual labels to train the network $\varphi(x; \theta)$. After that, M features extracted from the images by $\varphi(x; \theta)$ are clustered into several clusters. The images whose features belong to the same cluster are regarded as the same identity and assigned the same new label. Then, the new labels are used to further train the network. The processes of training and clustering are alternated for several times T. The number of clusters which is also the number of labels will decrease in each iteration.

Obviously, the errors caused by unreliable labels will accumulate in the iteration. Thus, the reliability of supervision information and the fault tolerance of training significantly affect the performance of $\varphi(x; \theta)$ in discriminative feature extraction. Therefore, we propose a multi-level equilibrium clustering approach according to characteristics of data, which improves the reliability of labels and the fault tolerance of training with the equilibrium criterion based clustering and the multi-level labels guided learning, respectively. The overall illustration of the approach is shown in Fig. 2.

3.2 Equilibrium Criterion Based Clustering

In the iteration of clustering, if features belonging to the same identity do not merge gradually, they will generate unreliable labels that locate contradictory identities to the same person. Additionally, if there are many features of different identities merging into the same cluster, it will also result in unreliable labels.

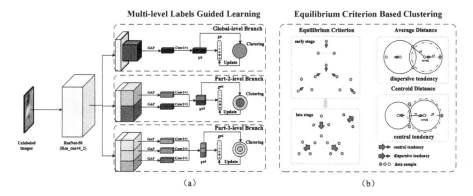

(a)   (b)

Fig. 2. An illustration of MEC. (a) The structure of our learning system. The global-level feature V^g and part-level features V^{p2}, V^{p3} are extracted to generate multi-level labels $\{Z^g, Z^{p2}, Z^{p3}\}$ by clustering. Specially, the labels and the clustering operation are only existing in the training phase. (b) The schematic of the clustering process. The proposed equilibrium criterion is composed of an average distance and a centroid distance, which reflect the dispersive tendency and central tendency between clusters respectively. The samples connected by the dotted lines are of the same cluster and r represents the distance between clusters.

Therefore, both the completeness and homogeneity of clustering are critical for obtaining reliable supervision information. By analyzing the images with PCA, we found that samples of the same identity follow a multicenter distribution (Fig. 1). If these samples are merging into the nearest center of them respectively, the formed clusters will lack completeness. Whereas, if pushing the samples around a center to samples near other centers, it may mistakenly merge some samples of different identities, which will influence the homogeneity. Thus, both the clustering of samples around a single center and various centers require to be considered in the clustering criterion. Hence, we propose a equilibrium criterion based clustering, which provides a good trade-off between completeness and homogeneity.

In our equilibrium criterion, dissimilarity between samples is measured by an average distance D^{average} and a centroid distance D^{centroid}. The average distance reflects the average dispersive tendency between clusters. The bigger is the value of the average distance, the higher is the dispersive tendency. Given two clusters A and B scattered in feature space, the average distance is calculated as follows:

$$D_t^{\text{average}}(A, B) = \frac{1}{N_A N_B} \sum_{a=1}^{N_A} \sum_{b=1}^{N_B} \|\overrightarrow{v_{t,a}} - \overrightarrow{v_{t,b}}\| \tag{2}$$

where N is the number of samples in the cluster. $\overrightarrow{v_t}$ is l_2 normalization of $\varphi_t(x_{t,i}; \theta)$. t is the current number of iteration and $t = 1, 2, 3 \ldots T$. As such, the centroid distance reflects the overall central tendency between clusters. The smaller is the value of the centroid distance, the higher is the central tendency.

The formulation of the centroid distance is:

$$D_t^{\text{centroid}}(A, B) = \|\overrightarrow{v_{t,A}} - \overrightarrow{v_{t,B}}\| \tag{3}$$

where

$$\overrightarrow{v_{t,A}} = \frac{1}{N_A} \sum_{a=1}^{N_A} \overrightarrow{v_{t,a}} \qquad \overrightarrow{v_{t,B}} = \frac{1}{N_B} \sum_{b=1}^{N_B} \overrightarrow{v_{t,b}}$$

The final distance metric we called equilibrium criterion is formulated as:

$$D_t^{\text{equilibrium}} = D_t^{\text{average}} + \lambda D_t^{\text{centroid}} \tag{4}$$

where λ is the trade-off parameter between these two kinds of distance.

As shown in Fig. 2, for samples around a cluster that of the same identity, the centroid distance between samples and the cluster is small which means the central tendency between them is high. If we measure the similarity between clusters by the centroid distance, the isolated samples will be merged into their nearest clusters, which is beneficial for forming a cluster of high completeness. However, because such measure will preferentially aggregate isolated samples into an existing cluster, it may result in a large but mixed cluster. Conversely, the average distance between isolated samples is usually lower than that between isolated samples and existing clusters which means the dispersive tendency between isolated samples is low. So the isolated samples are more likely to be clustered into a cluster under this measure. The characteristic of such measure will prevent samples from merging into a big and chaotic cluster, which guarantees the homogeneity of clustering. However, the characteristic also affects the aggregation of samples belonging to the same identity, which decreases the completeness.

As a result, our approach leverages the strengths of both to improve the effect of clustering. In the early iterative clustering, samples will merge into their nearest centers under the influence of the centroid distance. Meanwhile, isolated samples in the multi-center junction area are pushed by the average distance to form clusters between multiple centers instead of merging into the nearest centers. In the late iterative clustering, the centroid distance tends to gather the scattered clusters formed early to generate homogeneous clusters while the average distance will prevent the formation of excessive clusters. Thus, a result of high completeness and high homogeneity may be achieved under the joint action of both them. Meanwhile, the pseudo labels generated from such clustering results are closer to the real labels, which is beneficial for guiding the network to extract discriminative features.

3.3 Multi-level Labels Guided Learning

Although proper clustering will result in more reliable labels, it is impossible to avoid errors completely. Such error accumulation can not be automatically corrected in the iterative process if there are only single-level labels guiding the training. Therefore, if a set of complementary information can be introduced to the learning, the fault tolerance of the training framework will be improved so that the error accumulation effect will be weakened. Fortunately, the complementary information can also be achieved from the data itself. As shown in Fig. 1, features of different levels extracted from the same samples have different distributions. Specially, the confusing samples are also changed at these levels which means the wrong labels generated by the confusing samples will be different. Thus, the labels of different levels will provide complementary supervised information for learning.

Based on the above analysis, we propose multi-level labels guided learning. The framework of our scheme is shown in Fig. 2. The ResNet50 pre-trained on ImageNet is utilized as the backbone network. Specially, we maintain the front structure of Res_conv4_1 block and divide the subsequent part into three branches. The global-level branch down sample half in Res_conv5_1 block, and following a global max-pooling (GMP) and a 1×1 convolution layer. Inspired by many part-based methods in supervised person re-ID [1, 3, 23], the part-level branches have no down-sampling operation and directly split the feature maps into two or three stripes after Res_conv5_1 block. In this way, we could effectively extract the features of other spatial levels. These split feature maps follow the same operations as the global-level branch. Each unlabelled image $x_{t,i}$ is fed into all branches of the network to get the global-level feature $\overrightarrow{v_{t,i}^g}$, part-2-level feature $\overrightarrow{v_{t,i}^{p2}}$ and the part-3-level features $\overrightarrow{v_{t,i}^{p3}}$. After all images are processed, three sets of feature vectors are achieved:

The vectors in V_t^g, V_t^{p2} and V_t^{p3} are used for clustering, respectively. After that, each image $x_{t,i}$ is assigned three different level labels $z_{t,i}^g, z_{t,i}^{p2}, z_{t,i}^{p3}$ according to the clustering results. The relationship between images and labels is discribed as following:

$$\{X_t : Z\} = \left\{ x_{t,i} : \left(z_{t,i}^g, z_{t,i}^{p2}, z_{t,i}^{p3} \right) ; i = 1, 2, \ldots, M \right\} \qquad (5)$$

where $Z = (Z_t^g, Z_t^{p2}, Z_t^{p3})$ are sets of global-level labels, part-2-level labels and part-3-level labels, respectively.

Then, the multi-level labels are employed to training as supervision information. For each image, we use repelled loss function L^R [17, 18] to calculate the loss between it and three different labels, respectively. Finally, we sum up all losses as our loss. The full objective function is formulated as follows:

$$L_t^{\text{MEC}} = L_t^R (X_t; Z_t^g) + L_t^R \left(X_t; Z_t^{p2} \right) + L_t^R \left(X_t; Z_t^{p3} \right) \qquad (6)$$

By minimizing L^{MEC}, a discriminative feature embedding is automatically learned. In Fig. 3, we demonstrate the effect of multi-level labels guided learning. For similar people in a single-camera viewpoint, the global-level labels of them are the same while that of the same person in multiple camera viewpoints is different. Obviously, the global-level labels provide wrong guidance. But the training of our network will not be misled, because the other two kinds of part-level labels offer the right guidance.

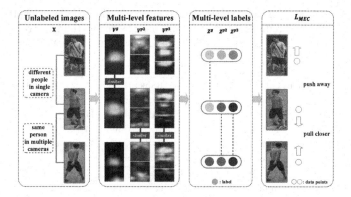

Fig. 3. Illustration of the effect of multi-level labels guided learning

---

Algorithm 1. Multi-level Equilibrium Clustering Algorithm

Input: training set $X = \{x_i\}_{i=1}^{M}$, merging percentage $m \in (0,1)$,
   trade-off parameter λ,CNN model $\varphi(x;\theta)$,
Output: Optimized model $\varphi(\mathrm{x};\hat{\theta})$
   Initialize: max iteration $T = 1/m - 1$
   current iteration $t = 1$, number of cluster $C = M$
   merge batch $k = \lceil M * m \rceil$, multi-level lable
   $\left\{ Z_t^g, Z_t^{p2}, Z_t^{p3} \right\} = \left\{ z_{1,i}^g = i, z_{1,i}^{p2} = i, z_{1,i}^{p3} = i \right\}_{i=1}^{M}$
   while $t <= T$ **do**
      Train model $\varphi(x;\theta)$ with X and $\left\{ Z_t^g, Z_t^{p2}, Z_t^{p3} \right\}$ by minimizing Eq. 6 with SGD
      Calculate the distance between any two clusters according to Eq. 4
      Respectively merge k pairs of clusters with the smallest distance
      $C \leftarrow C - k$, $t \leftarrow t + 1$
      Update $\left\{ Z_t^g, Z_t^{p2}, Z_t^{p3} \right\}$ with the new clusters
   end while
   Optimized model= $\varphi(x;\theta)$

The optimization of the network is iteratively carrying out the process of learning and clustering, which is described in Algorithm 1. The network is trained until the final number of clusters reaches the scale we set at the beginning.

4   Experiments

4.1   Datasets

Market-1501 [19] contains 32688 labelled images of 1501 identities, which is captured by 6 cameras in the university campus. The training set is composed of 12936 images of 751 identities while the testing set comprises 19732 images of 750 identities.

Table 1. Comparison with the state-of-the-art methods on image-based re-ID datasets. The column of "Labels" reflects the annotations used by the methods. "Transfer" means a additional labelled dataset is used. "None" denotes no annotation is used.

| Method | Publication | Labels | Market-1501 | | | | DukeMTMC-reID | | | |
			Rank1	Rank 5	Rank10	mAP	Rank1	Rank	Rank10	mAP
UMDL [6]	CVPR16	Transfer	34.5	52.6	59.6	12.4	18.5	31.4	37.6	7.3
PUL [4]	TOMM18	Transfer	44.7	59.1	65.6	20.1	30.4	46.4	50.7	16.4
MAR [9]	CVPR19	Transfer	67.7	81.9	–	40	67.1	79.8	–	48
PAUL [8]	CVPR19	Transfer	68.5	82.4	87.4	40.1	72	82.7	86	53.2
PAST [10]	ICCV19	Transfer	78.3	–	–	54.6	72.3	–	–	54.2
SSG [5]	ICCV19	Transfer	80	90	92.4	58.3	73	80.6	83.1	53.4
BOW [19]	ICCV15	None	35.8	52.4	60.3	14.8	17.1	28.8	34.9	8.3
LOMO [13]	CVPR15	None	27.2	41.6	49.1	8	12.3	21.3	26.6	4.8
UDML [6]	CVPR16	None	34.5	52.6	–	12.4	18.5	31.4	–	7.3
OIM [24]	CVPR17	None	38	58	66.3	14	24.5	38.8	46	11.3
BUC [18]	AAAI19	None	66.2	79.6	84.5	38.3	47.4	62.6	68.4	27.5
DBC [17]	BMVC2019	None	69.2	83	87.8	41.3	51.5	64.6	70.1	30
Ours		None	**83.8**	**92.7**	**95.2**	**62.1**	**64.5**	**76.8**	**81.1**	**42.6**

DukeMTMC-reID [20] is a subset of DukeMTMC dataset. It consists of 36411 labelled images of 1404 identities, among which 702 identities are used for training and the rest are for testing. There are 16522 training images, 2228 query images and 17661 gallery images.

4.2   Implementation Details

In our experiments, the network is initialized with the weights of ResNet50 pretrained on ImageNet. All input images are resized to 384×128. The dimensions of the three output vectors $\overrightarrow{v^g}, \overrightarrow{v^{p2}}, \overrightarrow{v^{p3}}$ are set as 2048, 2048 and 1536 respectively. During the training, m is set as $1/20$, so T is 19 and the final number of clusters is $M/20$. Epoch of training is 20 when t is 1 and reduced to 3, 2, 1 when t is 2, $3T/5$, $4T/5$. we set batch size as 16 and λ as 0.6. We use the SGD with a momentum of 0.9 to optimize the model. The learning rate is initialized to 0.1 and decays to 0.01 after 15 epochs. During the evaluation, the feature vectors extracted from the three branches of our network are concatenated into a long vector for identifying. We conduct the experiments on Pytorch platform with a NVIDIA TIAN X GPU.

4.3   Comparison with the State-of-the-art

We compare the proposed method with traditional algorithms and deep learning algorithms. The results of comparisons on Market-1501 dataset and DukeMTMC-reID dataset are reported in Table 1. Compared with other fully unsupervised methods, our method makes great progress. We also compare our

Table 2. Ablation study(%). The performance of re-ID models that clustered with different clustering criterion or trained with different level labels.

(b) Different level labels.

Method	Market-1501		DukeMTMC-reID	
	Rank1	mAP	Rank1	mAP
Global	76.3	53.9	55.8	36.3
Part-2	77.5	54.3	57.9	36.8
Part-3	77.1	54.0	60.6	38.4
Multi	**83.8**	**62.1**	**64.5**	**42.6**

(a) Different clustering criterion.

Method	Market-1501		DukeMTMC-reID	
	Rank1	mAP	Rank1	mAP
Average	77.1	51.4	54.4	31.3
Centriod	65.6	34.3	53.1	31.9
Equilibrium	**83.8**	**62.1**	**64.5**	**42.6**

method with the UDA transfer algorithms. Although these methods utilize additional re-ID dataset to provide more information about pedestrians, our method without any annotation can still surpass them on the Market-1501 dataset.

4.4 Ablation Study

The effectiveness of equilibrium criterion. In Table 2(a), Compared with clustering using only the average distance or the centroid distance, the proposed equilibrium criterion improves the performance significantly. And the result proves that our proposed equilibrium criterion could indeed improve the completeness and homogeneity of clustering to generate more reliable supervision information.

The effectiveness of multi-level labels. In Table 2(b), Comparing with the results of all single-level labels, ours proposed multi-level labels guided learning achieves better performance than any of them. This result means that multi-level labels indeed makes use of the complementarity between different levels of labels to improve the fault tolerance of the learning system and finally boosts the performance.

4.5 Further Analysis

Analysis on the Merging Percentage. The merging percentage m in Algorithm 1 is used to adjust the final cluster number and the total number of iterations T. We report the validation peformance mAP on the market-1501 dataset with varying m in Fig. 4(a). The best performance is obtained with $m = 0.05$. In this case, T is 19. When m is greater than or less than 0.05, the performances decrease.

Analysis on the Hyperparameter. The parameter λ in Eq. 4 is used to adjust the proportion of the average distance and the centroid distance. We report results on the market-1501 dataset with varying λ in Fig. 4(b). As λ is 0.6, the mAP achieves the best 62.1. In general, the performance is insensitive to the value of λ.

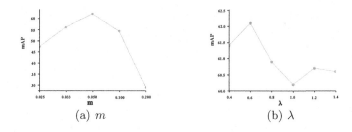

(a) m　　　　　　　　(b) λ

Fig. 4. Analysis of the hyperparameter

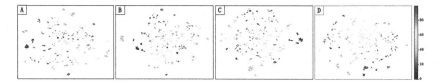

Fig. 5. A part of t-SNE visualization of feature embeddings on the DukeMTMC-reID dataset. There are 100 identities in total and the dots of same color represent the samples belonging to the same identity. A, B, C and D represent the feature embedding trained by global-level, part-2-level, part-3-level and multi-level labels respectively.

Analysis on the Multi-level Labels. To show the impact of multi-level labels on feature embedding function, we visualize the feature embedding in Fig. 5. The feature embedding with smaller intra-cluster distance and larger inter-cluster distance is more discriminative. The result of multi-level labels is more in line with the ideal situation.

5　Conclusion

In this paper, we propose a multi-level equilibrium clustering approach to tackle the unsupervised person re-ID task. The scheme can automatically generate supervised information by clustering to guide the learning of a discriminative feature embedding. According to the multicenter distribution of samples, we design an equilibrium criterion which can improve the completeness and homogeneity of clustering to generate reliable pseudo labels. Additionally, we propose multi-level labels guided learning and design a network with three branches, which fully exploits the complementary information between different spatial levels.

References

1. Fu, Y., et al.: Horizontal pyramid matching for person re-identification. In: AAAI (2019)

2. Sun, Y., Zheng, L., Yang, Y., Tian, Q., Wang, S.: Beyond part models: person retrieval with refined part pooling (and a strong convolutional baseline). In: ECCV (2018)
3. Wang, G., Yuan, Y., Chen, X., Li, J., Zhou, X.: Learning discriminative features with multiple granularities for person re-identification. In: ACMMM (2018)
4. Fan, H., Zheng, L., Yan, C., Yang, Y.: Unsupervised person re-identification: clustering and fine-tuning. TOMM **14**(4), 1–18 (2018)
5. Fu, Y., Wei, Y., Wang, G., Zhou, Y., Shi, H., Huang,T.S.: Self-similarity grouping: a simple unsupervised cross domain adaptation approach for person re-identification. In: ICCV (2019)
6. Peng, P., et al.: Unsupervised cross-dataset transfer learning for person re-identification. In: CVPR (2016)
7. Wang, J., Zhu, X., Gong, S., Li, W.: Transferable joint attribute-identity deep learning for unsupervised person re-identification. In: CVPR (2018)
8. Yang, Q., Yu, H.-X., Wu, A., Zheng, W.-S.: Patch-based discriminative feature learning for unsupervised person re-identification. In: CVPR (2019)
9. Yu, H.-X., Zheng, W.-S., Wu, A., Guo, X., Gong, S., Lai, J.-H.: Unsupervised person re-identification by soft multilabel learning. In: CVPR (2019)
10. Zhang, X., Cao, J., Shen, C., You, M.: Self-training with progressive augmentation for unsupervised cross-domain person re-identification. In: ICCV (2019)
11. Farenzena, M., Bazzani, L., Perina, A., Murino, V., Cristani, M.: Person re-identification by symmetry-driven accumulation of local features. In: CVPR (2010)
12. Gray, D., Tao, H.: Viewpoint invariant pedestrian recognition with an ensemble of localized features. In: ECCV (2008)
13. Liao, S., Hu, Y., Zhu, X., Li, S.Z.: Person re-identification by local maximal occurrence representation and metric learning. In: CVPR (2015)
14. Giuseppe, L., Iacopo, M., Bagdanov, A.D., Del Bimbo, A.: Person re-identification by iterative re-weighted sparse ranking. TPAMI **37**(8), 1629–1642 (2014)
15. Kodirov, E., Xiang, T., Gong, S.: Dictionary learning with iterative laplacian regularisation for unsupervised person re-identification. In: BMVC (2015)
16. Yan, C., Luo, M., Liu, W., Zheng, Q.: Robust dictionary learning with graph regularization for unsupervised person re-identification. MTA **77**(3), 3553–3577 (2018)
17. Ding, G., Khan, S., Tang, Z., Zhang, J., Porikli, F.: Dispersion based clustering for unsupervised person re-identification. In: BMVC (2019)
18. Lin, Y., Dong, X., Zheng, L., Yan, Y., Yang, Y.: A bottom-up clustering approach to unsupervised person re-identification. In: AAAI (2019)
19. Zheng, L., Shen, L., Tian, L., Wang, S., Wang, J., Tian, Q.: Scalable person re-identification: a benchmark. In: ICCV (2015)
20. Ristani, E., Solera, F., Zou, R., Cucchiara, R., Tomasi, C.: Performance measures and a data set for multi-target, multi-camera tracking. In: Hua, G., Jégou, H. (eds.) ECCV 2016. LNCS, vol. 9914, pp. 17–35. Springer, Cham (2016). https://doi.org/10.1007/978-3-319-48881-3_2
21. Yu, H.-X., Wu, A., Zheng, W.-S.: Cross-view asymmetric metric learning for unsupervised person re-identification. In: ICCV (2017)
22. Yu, H.-X., Wu, A., Zheng, W.-S.: Unsupervised person re-identification by deep asymmetric metric embedding. In: TPAMI (2018)
23. Cheng, D., Gong, Y., Zhou, S., Wang, J.: Person re-identification by multi-channel parts-based CNN with improved triplet loss function. In: CVPR (2016)
24. Xiao, T., Li, S., Wang, B., Lin, L., Wang, X.: Joint detection and identification feature learning for person search. In: CVPR (2017)

Deep Relevance Feature Clustering
for Discovering Visual Representation
of Tourism Destination

Qiannan Wang, Zhaoyan Zhu, Xuefeng Liang[(✉)], Huiwen Shi, and Pu Cao

School of Artificial Intelligence, Xidian University, Xi'an, China
xliang@xidian.edu.cn

Abstract. Discovering the visual representation(s) of a tourism destination is a challenging problem because it should be highly discriminating and frequently appeared in the travel photos of this destination. To address this issue, we propose a deep relevance feature clustering method (DRFC). To ensure the discrimination, DRFC uses layer-wise relevance propagvel feature maps to locate the region that contributes the most to network prediction. For frequency, DRFC clusters the extracted relevance features in a feature space according to their density, and selects highly dense instances for the visual representation. The experiments 100K photos of 20 tourism destinations show that DRFC can discover the discriminating and frequent visual representation, and outperforms the state-of-the-art methods.

Keywords: Visual representation · Layer-Wise Relevance Propagation · Density clustering

1 Introduction

Thanks to the development of Internet and social nation to extract high-level relevance features and propagates them back to low-leetworking sites, posting photos is becoming a common path of sharing travelers' experiences. These data are a gold mine to discover valuable information for the tourism industry [17,18]. For instance, these photos may depict the visual representations of a tourism destination, and can be further utilized for travel recommendation [3,16,20]. Among all visual elements in a travel photo set, the visual representation has two properties [6,24]: 1) *discrimination*, it represents only a particular tourism destination rather than the other destinations; 2) *frequency*, it appears in the scenic photo set frequently.

Actually, the visual representation of a tourism destination is a type of visual pattern, which represents the discernible regularity in the visual world and captures the essential nature of visual objects or scenes [6,13,14]. Many works have been done to understand and mordel visual patterns for object recognition or scene classification in the computer vision community. Handcrafted features

© Springer Nature Switzerland AG 2020
Y. Peng et al. (Eds.): PRCV 2020, LNCS 12307, pp. 332–341, 2020.
https://doi.org/10.1007/978-3-030-60636-7_28

[6,10,15,22] were firstly used for visual pattern mining, like SIFT [15] and HOG [6]. Due to the scale invariability and tolerating a certain distortion in a local space, they are regarded as low-level visual patterns. However, the local feature has a limited capability of expressing the semantic information of images.

Recently, Convolutional Neural Network (CNN) was often utilized as feature extractors [4,14,19,23], which are able to learn the hierarchical and high-level semantic representation of images. Li *et al.* [14] extracted features from image patches by a CNN model, and retrieved semantic patterns from these features based on association rules. Nevertheless, the discrimination of features from image patches is rather weak. Zhang *et al.* [23] employed a mean shift algorithm in the binary feature space of images to ensure the frequency, and enhanced the discrimination by leveraging contrast images. However, the outputs of their method are images instead of visual patterns. To address the above problems, Yang *et al.* [21] took advantage of the hierarchical abstraction of CNN and utilized unsupervised max-margin analysis to locate visual patterns in images. This method is effective but cannot guarantee the frequency. An emerging study [13] is able to mine visual patterns by only analyzing filter activations in CNN. Due to their empirical design of methodology, there is no solid theory to support the two aforementioned properties of visual representation, especially for the frequency. In addition, other studies [5,8,12] shown that the frequently occurring images could be found by clustering methods. However, they still face the challenge of maintaining the frequency and discrimination of the output images simultaneously.

In this work, we propose a deep relevance feature clustering (DRFC) method to mine the visual representations of tourism destinations from massive travel photos, which are discriminating and frequent. To this end, we firstly train a classification network to classify travel photos to their corresponding destinations. Please note that our first priority aims at the learned representations of destinations, rather than the best classification accuracy. To obtain and understand the learned representations, we utilize the Layer-wise Relevance Propagation (LRP) and relevance feature clustering. LRP helps us to know what relevance features in high-level layers and regions in low-level feature maps (even the pixels in the image) of the network contribute the most to the final prediction. It guarantees the discrimination of the corresponding region to locate the visual representation in photos. Meanwhile, clustering the relevance features according to the density in the feature space ensures a high frequency of the visual representation(s) in the photo set. Therefore, our contribution has twofold:

(1) DRFC is able to discover the visual representation that maintains discrimination and frequency simultaneously.
(2) Experiments show that DRFC outperforms existing state-of-the-arts.

2   The Proposed Method

In this section, we firstly design an image classification task for visual representation discovering, and then introduce a method to find the discriminating representation. Finally, we present an approach to discover the frequent representation. The schematic diagram of our method is illustrated in Fig. 1.

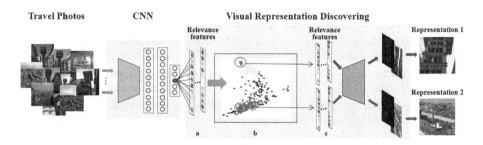

Fig. 1. The schematic diagram of our proposed DRFC. Firstly, a CNN (green box) is trained for travel photo classification. (a) The relevance features are extracted by LRP, in which ones with higher prediction probabilities are selected for subsequent processing. Then, (b) a density clustering is used to find the frequent instances in the relevance feature space. Finally, (c) LRP propagates the frequent relevance feature back to a region in the image to locate the visual representation. (Color figure online)

2.1   Formulation of Classification Task

In order to find the discriminating and frequent visual representations, we define a classification network with parameter θ as $f_\theta(\bullet)$. Given an image x and its label y, the network predicts its label $\hat{y} = f_\theta(x)$ that indicates which tourism destination x belongs to. To train the network, we minimize its loss $L(y, \hat{y})$ on a training dataset D,

$$\theta^* = \arg\min_\theta \sum_{(x,y)\in D} L\left(y, f_\theta(x)\right), \tag{1}$$

where θ^* denotes the optimal parameter. According to the classification result of new data, we select a set of photos with higher prediction probabilities, $> T_p$, for discovering visual representation, as shown in the green box of Fig. 1. This procedure is to ensure discrimination.

2.2   Discovering Discriminating Representations by Layer-Wise Relevance Propagation

Activation Maximization method [7] shows that the network learned features are generated by the visual patterns of inputs, which cause the maximization of neuron activation. Therefore, the activated neurons in the fully connected layer imply some specific patterns in the images, which play a key role in prediction. We believe the relevant neurons in each layer, which are associated with the prediction, can be used to find the visual representations. Here, we call them *relevance feature*.

Specifically, we propagate the final probability of prediction back to each layer of the network until the input layer (the input image), i.e. Layer-wise Relevance Propagation (LRP) [1], as shown in Fig. 1(a) and (c). LRP can help us to identify which region in the image is important for the classification [2], thus ensures the discrimination of expected visual representation. To obtain the relevance features, we follow the layer-wise conservation principle, which states that the total relevance associated with each layer of the network is equal to the prediction of the network,

$$\sum_i R_i^{(l)} = \sum_j R_j^{(l+1)} = f_{\theta^*}(x), \qquad (2)$$

where $R_i^{(l)}$ and $R_j^{(l+1)}$ denote the relevances associated with the i-th neuron of l-layer and the j-th neuron of the next layer, respectively.

2.3 Discovering Frequent Representations by Density Clustering

It has been known that the learned feature in the high-level layers of network has more semantic information. Hence, we employ high-level relevance features to discover the frequently appeared visual representations. Since a frequently appeared object/content can be considered as a highly-dense cluster in the feature space, the density based clustering algorithm is feasible for the mining task.

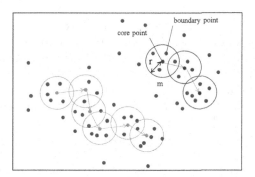

Fig. 2. Description of the density based clustering algorithm. The yellow point and green point are core points. (Color figure online)

Specifically, as shown in Fig. 2, we set an appropriate scan radius r and a number m. Given a feature point t who is the center of a circle, if the number of other feature points in the circle is greater than m, then t is a core point. If the number is less than m and the circle includes another core point t', then t is a boundary point of t'. The scan is performed on all feature points. We group core points, whose distance between each other is less than the radius r, to form a cluster. This cluster is a frequent feature of the set of photos. Please note that the number of clusters grouped by clustering may be greater than one. For example, Fig. 1(b) shows two visual representations: one is taken under the tower, another is taken on the tower. In this study, we choose n most dense feature points in a cluster to locate the visual representation in images. With these relevance features ready, the back-propagation of LRP projects them to low-level layers to locate the discriminating region in the image. Therefore, these regions become the visual representation.

3   Experiments

In this section, we compare our proposed DRFC with four state-of-the-arts on a newly collected dataset for performance evaluation.

3.1   Experimental Setup

Dataset. We used the popular travel website, TripAdvisor[1], to collect the travel photos, which includes 101,131 photos from 20 tourism destinations. Each destination has more than 3,500 photos. All data are divided into two parts for the experiments: (1) Testing set with 20000 photos: 1000 photos from each destination are used for discovering the visual representation(s); and (2) Training set with 81,131 photos: the remaining photos with destination label are used for training the CNN model.

Implementation Details. In this work, all the experiments were implemented by PyTorch on an NVIDIA 2080ti with 11 GB of on-board memory. We fine-tuned the pre-trained AlexNet [11] for the classification of travel photos. The AlexNet was trained by cross-entropy loss and adaptive moment estimation (Adam) with an initial learning rate of 0.0001. In order to prevent over-fitting, the training was stopped at 100 epochs where there was no significant reduction of the validation error. The threshold of selecting the higher discriminating photos was set to $T_p = 0.95$. For feature clustering, the number of relevance features with the highest density was set as $n = 20$. Thus, 20 visual instances would be discovered for each visual representation of a tourism destination.

Competing Methods. The recent study [14] reported that the CNN based visual patterns mining methods have largely outperformed the traditional hand-crafted based methods. Therefore, we compared our DRFC with four state-of-the-arts for performance evaluation, which are all CNN based methods. They are (1) Mid-level Deep Pattern Mining (MDPM) [14], (2) Contrastive Binary Mean Shift (CBMS) [23], (3) Part-level Convolutional Neural Network model (P-CNN) [21] and (4) PatternNet [13].

---

[1] https://www.tripadvisor.com.

Since only the code of MDPM [14] is available from authors, we implement other methods according to their papers. The CNNs in P-CNN [23] and PatternNet [13] were fine-tuned using the collected training set for the classification of tourism destinations. P-CNN [23] was trained with cross-entropy loss and Stochastic Gradient Descent with an initial learning rate of 0.001. While PatternNet [13] was trained with MSE loss and Adam with an initial learning rate of 0.0001.

Evaluation Metrics. Previous works for visual pattern mining [13, 14] used the image classification task as a proxy to evaluate their results. Thus, we followed their protocol and trained a Resnet50 [9] for classifying travel photos to the corresponding tourism destinations, which is for evaluating the discrimination of the discovered visual representations. The result is an average classification accuracy of those 20 photos retrieved by the clustering step. Since MDPM [14] divides the input image to a set of patches for subsequent processing, it is evaluated on the retrieved visual instances. Intuitively, classification accuracy cannot evaluate the frequency of discovered visual representation directly. Few previous studies explicitly measured it either. In this paper, we proposed a new metric (Frequency rate, FR) to compute the percentage of the images who are similar to the discovered visual representations in the high-level feature space. This can be defined as,

$$FR = \frac{1}{N_w \times N_u} \sum_{w=1}^{N_w} \sum_{u=1}^{N_u} \sum_{v=1}^{N} \left\| S_{u,v}^w \geq T_f \right\|_0, \tag{3}$$

where, $S_{u,v}^w = \cos\left(p_u^w, p_v^w\right)$ is a cosine similarity, p_u^w and p_v^w are the feature maps coming from the last convolution layer of above ResNet50. p_u^w is the feature map of one image from w-th tourism destination, p_v^w is the feature map of an instance of discovered visual representation from w-th tourism destination. N_w, N_u, N are the number of destinations, the number of retrieved instances of visual representation(s), and the number of images in each tourism destination, respectively. T_f denotes the similarity threshold.

3.2   Results and Analysis

To subjectively evaluate the performance of DRFC, we list ten instances of each discovered visual representation from five tourism destinations in Fig. 3. One can see that they contain the symbolic content and well represent these destinations. Interestingly, the number of discovered visual representations may be greater than one. Figure 3(a), (c) and (e) show the symbolic statue, tram and pagoda, respectively. However, Fig. 3(b) and (d) have two visual representations from each destination, which are marked by red and green boxes, respectively. Figure 3(b) shows two different perspectives including looking up to the lift and looking down from the top of the lift, while Fig. 3(d) shows the day time and night time views of the symbolic statue – Merlion. To illustrate the mechanism behind this result, we visualize the clusters of relevance features of Santa Justa Lift in

Fig. 3. Instances of discovered visual representations by DRFC from five tourism destinations: (a) *The Little Mermaid*, (b) *Santa Justa Lift*, (c) *Lisbon District Central Portugal*, (d) *Merlion Park Singapore*, and (e) *Kiyomizu Dera Temple*.

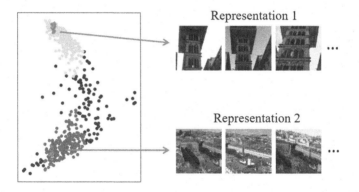

Fig. 4. Left side shows two clusters of relevance features of Santa Justa Lift, where the red dots are the most dense feature points. Right side shows the corresponding pictures of these most dense feature points. (Color figure online)

Fig. 4 by PCA dimension reduction. The red dots in each cluster are the most dense feature points of instances of a visual representation. Three corresponding pictures of these most dense feature points are demonstrated in Fig. 4 as well.

For the qualitative comparison, we list ten instances of visual representation discovered by five approaches in Fig. 5. One can observe that MDPM [14] produces the worst result in the blue box because it utilizes image patches that may merely have a part of the symbolic object. CBMS [23] only finds the frequent images in the yellow box instead of the visual representation in the images. P-CNN [21] and PatternNet [13] are able to discover the visual representation but

Fig. 5. Instances of visual representation of *Manneken Pis* discovered by (a) MDPM [14], (b) CBMS [23], (c) P-CNN [21], (d) PatternNet [13], and (e) DRFC (ours), respectively.

include a few off-target errors marked in the red boxes. By contrast, our DRFC can retrieve consistent instances of visual representation.

For the quantitative comparison, we first evaluate the classification accuracies of five approaches and list the result in Table 1. We can see DRFC outperforms the other four competing approaches. MDPM [14] performs the worst again because it samples the image into patches, which would lose the discriminating information. Surprisingly, PatternNet [13] concentrates on mining discriminating patterns, but achieves a worse performance. The reason might be the discriminating information of their result is only provided by one max-pooling layer (last convolution), which lacks adequate high-level semantic features. On the contrary, DRFC employs LRP to backpropagate the relevance feature from high-level layers to low-level layers, thus achieves the best accuracy. Meanwhile, it improves the accuracy 4.79% and 2.79% compared with CBMS [23] and P-CNN [21], respectively.

Table 1. Comparison of five approaches on classification accuracy using discovered representations.

Method	MDPM	CBMS	P-CNN	PatternNet	DRFC
mAcc(%)	84.08	94.75	96.75	90.00	99.54

Secondly, we compare the frequency of discovered visual representations at a varied threshold, T_f. The result is similar to the classification evaluation, and shown in Table 2. The visual representations discovered by our proposed DRFC reaches the highest frequency at all T_f. Although MDPM uses a frequent pattern mining algorithm, it still performs the worst. CBMS mainly targets at frequent images using the mean shift algorithm, but its result is worse than our DRFC and P-CNN. PatternNet and P-CNN focus on mining the discriminating patterns, while their results also have considerable high frequencies. All the above results demonstrate that DRFC is able to discover the discriminating and frequent visual representations of destinations.

Table 2. Comparison of five approaches on Frequency of discovered representations at varied thresholds T_f of cosine similarity.

Method	0.866 (30°)	0.883 (28°)	0.906 (25°)	0.940 (20°)
MDPM [14]	172.96	86.17	17.48	0.04
CBMS [23]	441.19	305.49	145.52	17.91
P-CNN [21]	466.05	348.01	187.08	30.52
PatternNet [13]	395.14	254.53	109.21	12.05
DRFC(ours)	**532.99**	**417.17**	**230.05**	**33.82**

4   Conclusion

In this work, we proposed a deep relevance feature clustering method (DRFC) to address the problem of discovering visual representations from tourism destinations. Unlike previous studies focused on either the discriminating patterns or frequent patterns, DRFC can maintain both the discrimination and frequency of discovered visual representations simultaneously. Both experiments of classification and frequency demonstrate that DRFC achieves the highest accuracy and frequency on a newly collected dataset compared with four state-of-the-art methods. These results show the effectiveness of our proposed DRFC on the task of visual representation discovery.

Acknowledgments. This work is supported by the Science and Technology Plan of Xi'an (20191122015KYPT011JC013) and the Fundamental Research Funds of the Central Universities of China (No. JX18001).

References

1. Bach, S., Binder, A., Montavon, G., Klauschen, F., Müller, K.R., Samek, W.: On pixel-wise explanations for non-linear classifier decisions by layer-wise relevance propagation. PLoS One **10**(7), e0130140 (2015)
2. Binder, A., Montavon, G., Lapuschkin, S., Müller, K.-R., Samek, W.: Layer-wise relevance propagation for neural networks with local renormalization layers. In: Villa, A.E.P., Masulli, P., Pons Rivero, A.J. (eds.) ICANN 2016. LNCS, vol. 9887, pp. 63–71. Springer, Cham (2016). https://doi.org/10.1007/978-3-319-44781-0_8
3. Bronner, F., De Hoog, R.: Vacationers and eWOM: who posts, and why, where, and what? J. Travel Res. **50**(1), 15–26 (2011)

4. Chen, Z., Maffra, F., Sa, I., Chli, M.: Only look once, mining distinctive landmarks from convnet for visual place recognition. In: IROS, pp. 9–16 (2017)

5. Chum, O., et al.: Large-scale discovery of spatially related images. IEEE TPAMI **32**(2), 371–377 (2009)

6. Doersch, C., Singh, S., Gupta, A., Sivic, J., Efros, A.A.: What makes Paris look like Paris? Commun. ACM **58**(12), 103–110 (2015)

7. Erhan, D., Bengio, Y., Courville, A., Vincent, P.: Visualizing higher-layer features of a deep network. Univ. Montreal **1341**(3), 1 (2009)

8. Gong, Y., Pawlowski, M., Yang, F., Brandy, L., Bourdev, L., Fergus, R.: Web scale photo hash clustering on a single machine. In: CVPR, pp. 19–27 (2015)

9. He, K., Zhang, X., Ren, S., Sun, J.: Deep residual learning for image recognition. In: CVPR, pp. 770–778 (2016)

10. Kim, S., Jin, X., Han, J.: DisiClass: discriminative frequent pattern-based image classification. In: KDD Workshop, p. 7 (2010)

11. Krizhevsky, A., Sutskever, I., Hinton, G.E.: ImageNet classification with deep convolutional neural networks. In: NIPS, pp. 1097–1105 (2012)

12. Lapuschkin, S., Binder, A., Montavon, G., Muller, K.R., Samek, W.: Analyzing classifiers: fisher vectors and deep neural networks. In: CVPR, pp. 2912–2920 (2016)

13. Li, H., Ellis, J.G., Zhang, L., Chang, S.F.: PatternNet: visual pattern mining with deep neural network. In: ICMR, pp. 291–299 (2018)

14. Li, Y., Liu, L., Shen, C., Van Den Hengel, A.: Mining mid-level visual patterns with deep CNN activations. IJCV **121**(3), 344–364 (2017)

15. Lowe, D.G., et al.: Object recognition from local scale-invariant features. In: ICCV, pp. 1150–1157 (1999)

16. Memon, I., Chen, L., Majid, A., Lv, M., Hussain, I., Chen, G.: Travel recommendation using geo-tagged photos in social media for tourist. Wirel. Pers. Commun. **80**(4), 1347–1362 (2015)

17. Michaelidou, N., Siamagka, N.T., Moraes, C., Micevski, M.: Do marketers use visual representations of destinations that tourists value? Comparing visitors' image of a destination with marketer-controlled images online. J. Travel Res. **52**(6), 789–804 (2013)

18. Pan, S., Lee, J., Tsai, H.: Travel photos: motivations, image dimensions, and affective qualities of places. Tourism Manage. **40**, 59–69 (2014)

19. Simonyan, K., Zisserman, A.: Very deep convolutional networks for large-scale image recognition. arXiv:1409.1556 (2014)

20. Vu, H.Q., Li, G., Law, R., Ye, B.H.: Exploring the travel behaviors of inbound tourists to Hong Kong using geotagged photos. Tourism Manage. **46**, 222–232 (2015)

21. Yang, L., Xie, X., Lai, J.: Learning discriminative visual elements using part-based convolutional neural network. Neurocomputing **316**, 135–143 (2018)

22. Zhang, B., Gao, Y., Zhao, S., Liu, J.: Local derivative pattern versus local binary pattern: face recognition with high-order local pattern descriptor. IEEE TIP **19**(2), 533–544 (2009)

23. Zhang, W., Cao, X., Wang, R., Guo, Y., Chen, Z.: Binarized mode seeking for scalable visual pattern discovery. In: CVPR, pp. 3864–3872 (2017)

24. Zheng, Y.T., Zha, Z.J., Chua, T.S.: Mining travel patterns from geotagged photos. ACM T. Intel. Syst. Tech. **3**(3), 56 (2012)

Balanced Loss for Accurate Object Detection

Qi Cheng, Yingjie Wu[✉], Fei Chen, and Yilong Guo

College of Mathematics and Computer Science, Fuzhou University,
Fuzhou 350108, China
yjwu@fzu.edu.cn

Abstract. In object detection, the imbalance problem often occurs when the number of training samples of different categories varies greatly, or multiple loss functions need to be minimized which is harmful to the performance of the detector. In this paper, we consider that the imbalance problem can be implied by the imbalance of gradient distribution. To address these imbalance issues, we analyze the gradient of cross-entropy loss and propose balanced cross-entropy (BLCE) loss and balanced binary cross-entropy (BBCE) loss for solving objective imbalance and class imbalance issues respectively. The BLCE loss significantly reduces the overall classification loss and keeps the classification loss and regression loss balanced. Furthermore, the BBCE loss automatically down-weight the contribution of inliers during training and rapidly focus the model on outliers. Ablation studies on object detection and image classification demonstrate the effectiveness of our loss function. We replace the corresponding losses in Libra R-CNN and evaluate our detector on the COCO test-dev. Our results show that Libra R-CNN can surpass the accuracy of many existing state-of-the-art detectors when training with our balanced loss.

Keywords: Object detection · Imbalance problems · Loss function

1 Introduction

Object detection is one of the fundamental problems and challenging tasks in computer vision, which has been widely used in intelligent video surveillance, industrial inspection, aerospace, and many other fields [9,18,29]. Reducing the consumption of human capital through computer vision has important practical significance. Especially with the development of deep learning, the research of object detection algorithms has developed rapidly.

In object detection, the architecture and training process of the model plays a key role in the final detection performance. However, in the training process, the

Student Paper. This work is supported by the National Natural Science Foundation of China (61771141) and the Natural Science Foundation of Fujian Province of China (2018J01799).

Y. Peng et al. (Eds.): PRCV 2020, LNCS 12307, pp. 342–354, 2020.
https://doi.org/10.1007/978-3-030-60636-7_29

performance of the detector is often limited by the imbalance problem [18,20]. In this paper, we focus on two of the imbalance issues in object detection: class imbalance and objective imbalance. Class imbalance occurs when the number of positive and negative samples or easy and hard samples varies greatly during training. Objective imbalance occurs when there are multiple loss functions to minimize, e.g. classification and regression losses.

In the two-stage detector, region proposals are generated through the region proposal network using specific anchor strategies. And we define the positive samples for the case where the IoU (Intersection over Union) of the anchor with ground truth exceeds 0.5. Due to the particularity of generating anchor strategy, the number of negative samples is much larger than the number of positive samples. During the training, there are always exists some samples that are difficult to classify correctly. We call these samples hard samples (outliers). Hard samples are more valuable as they can more effectively improve the performance of the detector [20]. However, the random sampling scheme usually results in the selection of easy samples [20]. Due to a large number of easy samples, their cumulative contribution plays a dominant role in the model parameter update. These samples can already be well classified by the model, so these samples will not improve the performance of the model, which makes the training process inefficient.

Object detection requires multiple loss functions to solve classification and regression tasks. If they are not properly balanced, one goal may be compromised, resulting in poor performance overall [20]. [18] pointed out that under normal circumstances, there is a huge imbalance between classification and regression losses, and classification losses often dominate the entire gradient. A common method is to balance the loss term by using additional hyperparameters as weighting factors between the two losses. Libra R-CNN [20] observes the regression loss function smooth L1 loss [5], starting from the demand, wants the sample to produce a slightly larger gradient when the regression error is less than 1.0, proposes balanced L1 loss. The purpose of the loss function is to increase the gradient of inliers in regression to balance the classification and regression loss.

In this paper, we consider that the imbalance problem can be implied by the imbalance of gradient distribution. Different objects make different contributions to the gradient so that the gradient is dominated by easy ones, resulting in the model learning process focusing more on one object, which is harmful to the performance of the detector.

To mitigate the adverse effects of objective imbalances, we propose a balanced cross-entropy loss (BLCE) to suppress the gradient of inliers during classification. We observe that our balanced cross-entropy loss function encourages the model to reduce the loss of easy samples and promotes the loss of hard samples, which makes the model pay more attention to the hard samples, as shown in Fig. 1. In this paper, we combine with the balanced L1 loss to reduce classification loss and promote regression loss to rebalance the classification and regression tasks (see Fig. 2).

To address the class imbalance, we generalize the proposed balanced cross-entropy loss to the binary classification task, inspired by anchor loss [26] and propose a balanced binary cross-entropy loss (BBCE). The loss function can automatically down-weight the contribution of easy examples (inliers) during training and rapidly focus the model on hard examples (outliers), which can also balance the contribution of easy samples and hard samples (see Fig. 3).

To demonstrate the effectiveness of the proposed loss function, we conduct experiments on image classification and object detection. The experimental analysis shows significant improvements in classification performance on the MNIST, CIFAR, ImageNet datasets. Without bells and whistles, our detector achieves 0.8 points higher AP than Libra R-CNN [20] baseline on COCO [16] Val-2017. With the 1×schedule in [19], our balanced loss on the ResNet-101 Libra R-CNN detector further improved the AP on COCO test-dev from 40.3 to 43.0.

2   Related Works

2.1   Object Detection

At present, deep learning based object detection model can generally be divided into two categories: the one is two-stage detector, such as R-CNN [6], Fast R-CNN [5], Faster R-CNN [24], Mask R-CNN [7]. The other is one-stage detector, such as YOLO [1, 21–23], SSD [15, 17], FPN [14], RetinaNet [15]. The two-stage detector divides object detection into two stages, RPN (Region Proposal Network) and ROI (Region of Interest) layers, which accuracy the localization and object recognition but result in long inference time. Furthermore, the one-stage detectors directly predict the boxes from input images, thus they are time efficient.

2.2   Class Imbalance

An effective way to solve the class imbalance issue is hard negative mining [27] methods, e.g. OHEM [2], can help drive the detector focus towards hard samples, however, they are usually sensitive to noise labels. RetinaNet [15] proposed focal loss by adding a weight factor to the cross-entropy loss so that the model can dynamically assign more/less weight to the hard/easy examples, but it is not suitable for two-stage detectors. GHM [13] introduced a novel gradient harmonizing mechanism to calculate the weight of the loss function through the distribution of gradients. [26] proposes anchor loss that dynamically adjusts the cross-entropy based on the prediction difficulty. Our balanced loss was inspired by the anchor loss, where encourage the model to focus more on hard samples during training.

2.3   Objective Imbalance

Object detection generally includes two tasks: classification and bounding box regression. [18] shows that the classification loss often dominates the overall gradient, which hampers the consistent and balanced optimization of the tasks.

The most common solution is to introduce a weighting factor to balance the two losses. However, the introduction of hyper-parameters increases the difficulty of the experiment. Therefore, researches have proposed several methods for adaptively adjusting the weighting factors during training, such as CARL [3]. Some research attempts to adopt some strategies to ensure the consistency of the multiple loss function ranges, such as AP loss [4], smooth L1 loss [5], GIoU loss [25].

3   Methodology

Our goal is to balance the gradient of the loss function during the training process, thus alleviating the class/objective imbalance issue during training. In this section, we first introduce a balanced cross-entropy loss (BLCE) for classification and object detection. Then the balanced cross-entropy loss is generalized to the binary classification task, and propose the balanced binary cross-entropy loss for region proposal network.

3.1   Balanced Cross-Entropy Loss (BLCE)

We introduce the balanced cross-entropy loss staring from the softmax cross-entropy (CE) loss for n-classification:

$$L_{CE} = \frac{1}{N} \sum_{i=1}^{N} \left(-\sum_{c=1}^{n} y_{ic} \log(p_{ic}) \right) \tag{1}$$

where N represents the number of samples, $\boldsymbol{y}$ is a one-hot encoded vector for the labels. $\boldsymbol{p}$ indicates the probability predicted by the model and is calculated by the softmax function s. For simplicity, we set $N = 1$ in subsequent calculations. The softmax function s takes as input an n-dimensional vector $\boldsymbol{z}$ and outputs an n-dimensional vector $\boldsymbol{p}$ of real values between $\boldsymbol{0}$ and $\boldsymbol{1}$. Softmax function defined as:

$$\boldsymbol{p} = s(\boldsymbol{z}) = \frac{e^{\boldsymbol{z}}}{\sum_{i=1}^{n} e^{z_i}} \tag{2}$$

So, the derivative of the output p_c of the softmax function with respect to its input z_j can be calculated as:

$$\frac{\partial p_c}{\partial z_j} = \begin{cases} p_c(1 - p_c) &, \text{if } c = j \\ -p_c p_j &, \text{if } c \neq j \end{cases} \tag{3}$$

The derivative of the cross-entropy loss function concerning the softmax input z_c can be calculated as:

$$\frac{\partial L_{CE}}{\partial z_c} = p_c - y_c \tag{4}$$

We plot cross-entropy loss and its gradient curve in Fig. 1. It can be observed that the gradient of cross-entropy is linear with classification error. That is, the

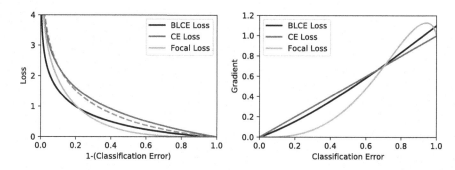

Fig. 1. Balanced cross-entropy loss (left) and gradient (right) compared to the cross-entropy loss and focal loss. BLCE loss reduces the relative loss/gradient for well-classified examples, putting more focus on misclassified examples (dashed line and black curves). Best viewed in electronic form.

greater the gap between the predicted value and ground-truth, the greater the gradient. This is reasonable. During training, when a sample has been predicted correctly, the model does not need to make larger adjustments to the parameters, thus reducing the gradient. When the gap between the prediction result of a sample and the ground-truth is large, the model can quickly find the optimal value by increasing the gradient value. However, this linear relationship will bring a series of problems such as model overfitting. Therefore, we try to introduce some parameters based on cross-entropy, through which we can adjust the steepness of the loss curve and change the gradient, as follows:

$$L^* = -\sum_{c=1}^{n} y_c \log\left(a + b p_c\right) \tag{5}$$

There are two parameters a and b that control the steepness and shift of the loss curve. When $a = 0$, $b = 1$, L^* is equivalent to cross-entropy loss. Since this form does not satisfy the nature of the loss function (when $p_c = 1$, the loss value needs to be 0, when $p_c = 0$, the loss value is infinite, and the loss value increases as p_c decreases), so change as follow:

$$L^* = -\sum_{c=1}^{n} y_c \log\left(p_c\left(a + b p_c\right)\right) \tag{6}$$

Let $a = 2$, $b = -1$, we have $p_c(2 - p_c) = 1 - (1 - p_c)^2$. Then, combining with cross-entropy loss by introducing the weighting factors $\alpha > 0$ and $\beta > 0$, we define the balanced cross-entropy loss as:

$$L_{BLCE} = -\sum_{c=1}^{n} y_c \left[\alpha \log\left(p_c\right) + \beta \log\left(1 - (1 - p_c)^2\right)\right] \tag{7}$$

The gradient of balanced cross-entropy loss is:

$$\frac{\partial L_{BLCE}}{\partial z_c} = \left[\alpha\left(p_c - y_c\right) - \beta\left[\frac{2\left(1 - p_c\right)\left(y_c - p_c\right)}{2 - p_c}\right]\right], c = 1, ..., n \qquad (8)$$

Figure 1 shows the gradient of cross-entropy, focal loss, and balanced cross-entropy loss. Compared with cross-entropy, when the classification error is small, BLCE loss and gradient are smaller than cross-entropy, and BLCE loss encourages the model to pay more attention to hard samples by increasing the loss and gradient of hard samples. This can significantly reduce the overall classification loss, making the classification loss and regression loss balanced (see Fig. 2).

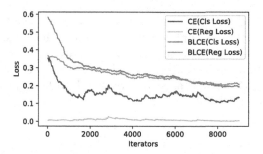

Fig. 2. Illustration of the gap between classification and regression when training Libra R-CNN detectors with different classification losses. These results indicate that using BLCE for training leads to a smaller gap between classification and regression loss compare with cross-entropy, meaning that the classification and regression are more balanced.

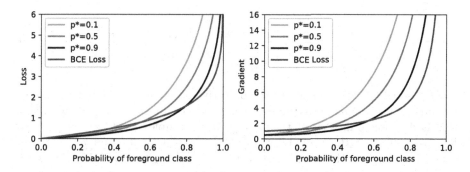

Fig. 3. BBCE increases the loss for hard samples ($d_i > 1$) while reducing the loss for easy samples ($d_i < 1$). This means that BLCE loss can automatically adjust the loss according to the classification difficulty of positive samples to achieve the balance between hard samples and easy samples.

3.2   Balanced Binary Cross-Entropy Loss (BBCE)

In the two-stage object detector, a larger number of anchors are generated by RPN, and the region proposals that may contain the object are selected through classification and regression branches. This step is critical to the accuracy of the object detector. Since a large number of anchors belong to the background, RPN will also be affected by class imbalance during training. The loss function used by the classification task in RPN is the binary cross-entropy loss (BCE), as follows:

$$L_{BCE} = -\frac{1}{N} \sum_{i=1}^{N} (y_i \log(p_i) + (1 - y_i) \log(1 - p_i)) \tag{9}$$

where p_i represents the probability that sample i is predicted as a background (assume that the positive sample label is $y = 0$ and the negative sample label is $y = 1$) and is calculated by the sigmoid function s. The sigmoid function maps the input z to output between 0 and 1. Note that p is not a vector here. If $p_i < 0.5$, we classify the sample as a positive sample, otherwise negative samples. The sigmoid function defined as:

$$s(z) = \frac{1}{1 + e^{-z}} \tag{10}$$

We have the gradient about z:

$$\frac{\partial L_{BCE}}{\partial z} = \frac{\partial L_{BCE}}{\partial p} \frac{\partial p}{\partial z} = p - y \tag{11}$$

When BLCE loss is applied to the binary classification problem, the loss function (7) is equivalent to:

$$L_{BLCE} = -\frac{1}{N} \sum_{i=1}^{N} \left[y_i \left[\alpha \log(p_i) + \beta \log\left(1 - (1 - p_i)^2\right) \right] \right. $$
$$\left. + (1 - y_i) \left[\alpha \log(1 - p_i) + \beta \log\left(1 - p_i^2\right) \right] \right] \tag{12}$$

We propose BLCE loss to address the objective imbalance issue, but the ability to handle class imbalance is limited. Inspired by anchor loss [26], we define the classification difficulty of the i-th positive samples as $d_i = 1 + p_i - p_i^*$, where $p_i \in [0, 1]$ is the probability predicted by the model and $p_i^* = 1 - p_i$, that is $d_i = 2p_i$. So the classification difficulty of positive samples means the divergence between the probabilities of the true and false predictions. We use the classification difficulty of positive samples as the weighting factor of BLCE, and the positive sample loss is as follows:

$$L_{BBCE}^{+} = -\frac{1}{N} \sum_{i=1}^{N} (1 - y_i) \left[\alpha \log(1 - p_i) + d_i^{\gamma} \log\left(1 - p_i^2\right) \right] \tag{13}$$

where $\gamma \geq 0$ is a hyperparameter that controls the influence of d_i in loss function. Negative sample loss is cross-entropy:

$$L_{BBCE}^{-} = -\frac{1}{N} \sum_{i=1}^{N} y_i \log{(p_i)} \tag{14}$$

With consideration of the classification difficulties, we propose the balanced binary cross-entropy loss function as follows:

$$L_{BBCE} = -\frac{1}{N} \sum_{i=1}^{N} [y_i \log{(p_i)} + (1 - y_i)[\alpha \log{(1 - p_i)} + d_i^{\gamma} \log{(1 - p_i^2)}]] \tag{15}$$

The gradient of balanced binary cross-entropy loss with respect to p_i:

$$\frac{L_{BBCE}}{\partial p_i} = -\left[\frac{y_i}{p_i} + (1 - y_i) \left[d_i^{\gamma-1} \left[\gamma \log{(1 - p_i^2)} - \frac{2p_i d_i}{1 - p_i^2} \right] - \frac{\alpha}{1 - p_i} \right] \right] \tag{16}$$

We divide the classification difficulty into three levels: easy, moderate, and hard:

- **Easy**($d_i < 1$): $p_i^* > 0.5$, indicating that the prediction is correct. Therefore, the loss value can be suppressed by the classification difficulty d_i.
- **Moderate**($d_i = 1$): $p_i^* = 0.5$, indicating that the prediction probability of negative samples and positive samples are equal, and the BBCE loss is slightly larger than the cross-entropy, so we do not need a margin variable δ as proposed in anchor loss [26] to penalize the output variables.
- **Hard**($d_i > 1$): $p_i^* < 0.5$, indicating that misclassify positive sample as a negative sample. Hence, the classification difficulty d_i increases the penalty of the loss function.

As a result, we apply different loss functions for each sample [26] as shown in Fig. 3. And BBCE loss can automatically adjust the loss according to the classification difficulty of the positive samples. For positive samples that are difficult to classify, the BBCE loss will increase the loss value and the gradient compared to the cross-entropy loss. For positive samples that are easy to classify, BBCE loss will reduce the loss value and gradient.

4   Experiments

4.1   Datasets

To demonstrate the effectiveness of balanced cross-entropy loss, we apply BLCE loss in image classification tasks and evaluate on three of the most popular

Table 1. The error rate (%) of the MNIST test set in different networks.

Model	LeNet	VGG	ResNet
Baseline (CE)	0.962	0.363	0.378
BLCE	**0.843**	**0.360**	**0.373**

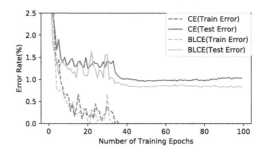

Fig. 4. The error plots are shown for training on the MNIST dataset using LeNet. BLCE improves the generalization ability of LeNet, and has better recognition ability for unseen data.

image classification datasets, i.e., MNIST [12], CIFAR-10 [10], CIFAR-100 [10] and Tiny ImageNet. We also conduct experiments on the MS COCO [16] dataset to analyze the contribution of BLCE and BBCE for object detection.

4.2   Experiment Setting

For MNIST, we train LeNet [12], VGG [28], ResNet [8] with balanced cross-entropy loss and compare with cross-entropy loss. And we train AlexNet [11] with BLCE loss on CIFAR and ImageNet. Our goal here is not to establish a new state-of-the-art, but to make a fair comparison with cross-entropy loss and demonstrate the performance gain with BLCE loss. Hence, we do not use data augmentation, regularization, and other tricks in our experiments. All experimental results are the average of three repetitions under the same conditions.

For the task of object detection, we use the Libra R-CNN [20] as a baseline and only replace the loss function with BLCE and BBCE during training. We train detectors with four GPUs, all other hyper-parameters follow the settings in PaddleDetection [19] if not specifically noted.

Table 2. Classification accuracy on CIFAR-10, CIFAR-100 and ImageNet.

Models	CIFAR-10	CIFAR-100	ImageNet-Top-1	ImageNet-Top-5
Baseline	73.723	37.228	29.634	55.184
Baseline with L2	73.745	36.028	30.320	56.030
Baseline with L1	73.660	34.313	30.333	55.617
BLCE	**74.068**	**39.218**	**32.360**	**57.927**

4.3   Image Classification Results

MNIST. We train and test the network three times and report the mean in Table 1. We also plot the error rate curve as shown in Fig. 4. The experimental results show that the balanced cross-entropy loss achieves a significant reduction in error on the MNIST dataset compare with cross-entropy loss.

CIFAR and ImageNet. For CIFAR and Tiny ImageNet datasets, we train and test AlexNet [30] and report the classification accuracy to compare cross-entropy loss functions and L1/L2 regularization in Table 2. As we can see, our loss function shows the improvement of the overall methods we evaluated. For CIFAR-10, the balanced cross-entropy loss improves the classification accuracy from 73.723% to 74.068%. For CIFAR-100, it is noted that when we used BLCE loss we achieved a 1.990% improvement over the baseline. For Tiny ImageNet, we also achieved a significant improvement in the classification accuracy of both in Top-1 and Top-5. Experimental results prove the effectiveness of BLCE loss in image classification.

Table 3. Ablation studies of balanced loss on COCO Val-2017.

BLCE	BBCE	AP	AP_{50}	AP_{75}	AP_s	AP_m	AP_l
–	–	29.4	50.5	30.8	16.9	32.7	36.6
$\alpha = 0.5, \beta = 0.7$	–	29.8	50.8	30.8	**18.1**	32.8	37.4
$\alpha = 0.5, \beta = 0.8$	–	29.6	50.6	30.5	**18.1**	32.6	36.8
$\alpha = 0.5, \beta = 0.9$	–	29.8	50.9	30.9	17.5	33.0	37.0
$\alpha = 0.5, \beta = 0.7$	$\alpha = 0.5, \gamma = 1.0$	29.7	50.9	30.9	17.6	32.9	37.4
$\alpha = 0.5, \beta = 0.7$	$\alpha = 0.5, \gamma = 2.0$	**30.2**	**51.3**	**31.3**	18.0	**33.4**	**37.7**
$\alpha = 0.5, \beta = 0.7$	$\alpha = 0.5, \gamma = 3.0$	30.0	51.0	31.2	17.8	33.1	37.5

4.4   Ablation Studies

In this section, we report the overall ablation studies on the COCO Val-2017 in Table 3. We gradually add BLCE loss and BBCE loss on the Libra R-CNN baseline. We first replace the cross-entropy in the ROI head with our BLCE loss. To compare with tuning loss weight directly, we validate the effectiveness of balanced cross-entropy loss when $\alpha = 0.5$. And we found that when $\beta = 0.7$, balanced cross-entropy loss can bring 0.4 points higher AP and 1.2 points higher AP on small than baseline. Then we replace the binary cross-entropy loss in the PRN with our BBCE loss. Libra R-CNN finally achieves 30.2 AP, which is 0.8 points higher than the baseline. Note that there are no parameters added during this process.

4.5   Comparison to State-of-the-Art

We evaluate our balanced loss on COCO test-dev and compare results to recent state-of-the-art methods. The results are represented in Table 4. To emphasize the effectiveness of balanced loss, we train a Libra R-CNN with the standard

Table 4. Comparisons with state-of-the-art methods on COCO test-dev.

Method	Backbone	AP	AP$_{50}$	AP$_{75}$	AP$_s$	AP$_m$	AP$_l$
RetinaNet [12]	ResNet-101-FPN	39.1	59.1	42.3	21.8	42.7	50.2
YOLOv3 [10]	DarkNet-53	33.0	57.9	34.4	18.3	35.4	41.9
GHM [23]	ResNet-101-FPN	39.9	60.8	42.5	20.3	43.6	**54.1**
Faster R-CNN [6]	ResNet-101-FPN	36.2	59.1	39.0	18.2	39.0	48.2
Mask R-CNN [7]	ResNet-101-FPN	38.2	60.3	41.7	20.1	41.1	50.2
Deformable R-FCN [32]	Inception-ResNet-v2	37.5	58.0	40.8	19.4	40.1	52.5
Libra R-CNN	ResNet-101-FPN	40.3	61.3	43.9	22.9	43.1	51.0
+ BLCE	ResNet-101-FPN	42.9	64.7	**47.0**	25.7	**45.9**	53.2
+ BLCE & BBCE	ResNet-101-FPN	**43.0**	**64.8**	**47.0**	**26.0**	**45.9**	53.3

cross-entropy loss as the baseline. Then, we replace the cross-entropy loss in the ROI head with our BLCE loss. It can be observed that BLCE loss improves AP from 40.3% to 42.9%. Finally, the best performance can be obtained by combining the two proposed loss function, and it confirms that BLCE loss and BBCE loss can handle the imbalance issue in detection better than standard cross-entropy loss.

5   Conclusion

In object detection, the performance of the detector is often limited by the imbalance issue. We focus on two of the imbalance issues in object detection: class imbalance and objective imbalance. And it is considered that the imbalance problem can be implied by the imbalance of gradient distribution. To address this, we proposed balanced cross-entropy loss and balanced binary cross-entropy loss to replace the standard cross-entropy loss in ROI head and RPN, respectively. With the help of balanced loss, Libra R-CNN brings significant improvements on COCO dataset. And it confirms that BLCE loss and BBCE loss can handle the imbalance issue in detection better than standard cross-entropy loss.

References

1. Bochkovskiy, A., Wang, C., Liao, H.M.: YOLOv4: optimal speed and accuracy of object detection. CoRR abs/2004.10934 (2020)
2. Bucher, M., Herbin, S., Jurie, F.: Hard negative mining for metric learning based zero-shot classification. In: Hua, G., Jégou, H. (eds.) ECCV 2016. LNCS, vol. 9915, pp. 524–531. Springer, Cham (2016). https://doi.org/10.1007/978-3-319-49409-8_45
3. Cao, Y., Chen, K., Loy, C.C., Lin, D.: Prime sample attention in object detection. CoRR abs/1904.04821 (2019)
4. Chen, K., et al.: Towards accurate one-stage object detection with AP-loss. In: CVPR 2019, pp. 5119–5127. Computer Vision Foundation/IEEE (2019)
5. Girshick, R.B.: Fast R-CNN. In: ICCV 2015, pp. 1440–1448. IEEE Computer Society (2015)

6. Girshick, R.B., Donahue, J., Darrell, T., Malik, J.: Rich feature hierarchies for accurate object detection and semantic segmentation. In: CVPR 2014, pp. 580–587. IEEE Computer Society (2014)

7. He, K., Gkioxari, G., Dollár, P., Girshick, R.B.: Mask R-CNN. In: ICCV 2017, pp. 2980–2988. IEEE Computer Society (2017)

8. He, K., Zhang, X., Ren, S., Sun, J.: Deep residual learning for image recognition. In: CVPR 2016, pp. 770–778. IEEE Computer Society (2016)

9. Jiao, L., et al.: A survey of deep learning-based object detection. IEEE Access **7**, 128837–128868 (2019)

10. Krizhevsky, A., Hinton, G., et al.: Learning multiple layers of features from tiny images (2009)

11. Krizhevsky, A., Sutskever, I., Hinton, G.E.: ImageNet classification with deep convolutional neural networks. Commun. ACM **60**(6), 84–90 (2017)

12. LeCun, Y., Bottou, L., Bengio, Y., Haffner, P.: Gradient-based learning applied to document recognition. Proc. IEEE **86**(11), 2278–2324 (1998)

13. Li, B., Liu, Y., Wang, X.: Gradient harmonized single-stage detector. In: AAAI 2019, pp. 8577–8584. AAAI Press (2019)

14. Lin, T.Y., Dollár, P., Girshick, R., He, K., Hariharan, B., Belongie, S.: Feature pyramid networks for object detection. CVPR **2017**, 2117–2125 (2017)

15. Lin, T., Goyal, P., Girshick, R.B., He, K., Dollár, P.: Focal loss for dense object detection. In: ICCV 2017, pp. 2999–3007. IEEE Computer Society (2017)

16. Lin, T.-Y., et al.: Microsoft COCO: common objects in context. In: Fleet, D., Pajdla, T., Schiele, B., Tuytelaars, T. (eds.) ECCV 2014. LNCS, vol. 8693, pp. 740–755. Springer, Cham (2014). https://doi.org/10.1007/978-3-319-10602-1_48

17. Liu, W., et al.: SSD: single shot MultiBox detector. In: Leibe, B., Matas, J., Sebe, N., Welling, M. (eds.) ECCV 2016. LNCS, vol. 9905, pp. 21–37. Springer, Cham (2016). https://doi.org/10.1007/978-3-319-46448-0_2

18. Oksuz, K., Cam, B.C., Kalkan, S., Akbas, E.: Imbalance problems in object detection: a review. CoRR abs/1909.00169 (2019)

19. PaddlePaddle: Object detection and instance segmentation toolkit based on PaddlePaddle (2019). https://github.com/PaddlePaddle/PaddleDetection. Acessed [Insert date here]

20. Pang, J., Chen, K., Shi, J., Feng, H., Ouyang, W., Lin, D.: Libra R-CNN: towards balanced learning for object detection. In: CVPR 2019, pp. 821–830. Computer Vision Foundation/IEEE (2019)

21. Redmon, J., Divvala, S.K., Girshick, R.B., Farhadi, A.: You only look once: unified, real-time object detection. In: 2016 IEEE Conference on Computer Vision and Pattern Recognition, CVPR 2016, pp. 779–788. IEEE Computer Society (2016)

22. Redmon, J., Farhadi, A.: YOLO9000: better, faster, stronger. In: CVPR 2017, pp. 6517–6525. IEEE Computer Society (2017)

23. Redmon, J., Farhadi, A.: YOLOv3: an incremental improvement. CoRR abs/1804.02767 (2018)

24. Ren, S., He, K., Girshick, R.B., Sun, J.: Faster R-CNN: towards real-time object detection with region proposal networks. IEEE Trans. Pattern Anal. Mach. Intell. **39**(6), 1137–1149 (2017)

25. Rezatofighi, H., Tsoi, N., Gwak, J., Sadeghian, A., Reid, I.D., Savarese, S.: Generalized intersection over union: a metric and a loss for bounding box regression. In: CVPR 2019, pp. 658–666. Computer Vision Foundation/IEEE (2019)

26. Ryou, S., Jeong, S., Perona, P.: Anchor loss: modulating loss scale based on prediction difficulty. In: ICCV 2019, pp. 5991–6000. IEEE (2019)

27. Shrivastava, A., Gupta, A., Girshick, R.B.: Training region-based object detectors with online hard example mining. In: CVPR 2016, pp. 761–769. IEEE Computer Society (2016)
28. Simonyan, K., Zisserman, A.: Very deep convolutional networks for large-scale image recognition. In: Bengio, Y., LeCun, Y. (eds.) ICLR 2015 (2015)
29. Zou, Z., Shi, Z., Guo, Y., Ye, J.: Object detection in 20 years: a survey. CoRR abs/1905.05055 (2019)

Nuclear-Norm-Based Jointly Sparse Regression for Two-Dimensional Image Regression

Haosheng Su[1], Zhihui Lai[1,2(⊠)], Ning Liu[1], and Jun Wan[1,2]

[1] College of Computer Science and Software Engineering,
Shenzhen University, Shenzhen 518060, China
2017151013@email.szu.edu.cn, lai_zhi_hui@163.com,
ningliu_cs@foxmail.com, junwan2014@whu.edu.cn
[2] Shenzhen Institute of Artificial Intelligence and Robotics for Society, Shenzhen, China

Abstract. As a typical manifold learning method, two-dimensional Locality Preserving Projections (2DLPP) can perverse the intrinsic manifold structure of the data, and it has been widely used in dimensionality reduction. However, 2DLPP is sensitive to noise and outliers since 2DLPP uses the Frobenius norm to measure the reconstruction error. In order to address the robustness problem in 2DLPP, this paper proposes a novel framework, called nuclear-norm-based jointly sparse regression (NJSR). NJSR characterizes the reconstruction error by using the nuclear norm as the measurement and the $L_{2,1}$-norm as the regularized term to derive jointly sparse solutions for feature extraction and selection. Moreover, we propose a bilateral extension over NJSR called Bilateral NJSR (BNJSR). BNJSR learns the projection matrices in both the row and the column directions simultaneously. Both the NJSR and BNJSR can be solved through an iterative algorithm by computing a set of eigenfunctions. Two face databases are used to verify the effectiveness of the proposed methods, and the experimental results show BNJSR outperformed the compared methods.

Keywords: Dimensionality reduction · 2DLPP · Nuclear norm · $L_{2,1}$ norm · Image feature extraction and recognition

1 Introduction

Dimensionality reduction is essential in computer vision, data mining and pattern recognition. Principal component analysis (PCA) [1–3] and linear discriminant analysis (LDA) [4] are the most classical unsupervised and supervised methods, respectively. PCA projects the data to the subspace by maximizing the variance while LDA maximizes the ratio of the between-class and the within-class scatter to preserve the discriminative information as much as possible. PCA and LDA are simple and effective but only can perverse the global structure of data. However, Roweis [5] and Tenenbaum [6] *et al.* found that high-dimensional data can be embedded into a low-dimensional manifold space. Therefore, manifold learning methods have been paid attention and many different manifold learning methods are proposed to exploit the intrinsic manifold structure of

© Springer Nature Switzerland AG 2020
Y. Peng et al. (Eds.): PRCV 2020, LNCS 12307, pp. 355–368, 2020.
https://doi.org/10.1007/978-3-030-60636-7_30

the data. The representative ones are locality preserving projections (LPP) [7–9], neighborhood preserving projection (NPP) [10]. NPP and LLE assume that the sample can be linearly represented by its k nearest neighbors while LPP utilizes a nearest-neighbor graph which is computed by original data.

PCA, LDA, LPP, NPP, LLE and ISOMAP are vector-based representation methods, which means that the two-dimensional data such as images need to be converted to be a high-dimensional vector. This vectorization may lose the topology structures of data such that these 1-D methods may perform badly. Additionally, these 1-D methods may encounter some problems such as small sample size problem and the curse of dimensionality dilemma. Therefore, many one-dimensional methods are extended to two dimensional versions. Yang *et al.* [11] propose the 2DPCA which can be more accurate to evaluate the covariance matrix and gets better results. Reference [12] propose 2DLDA to compact the discriminant information into a small size matrix by imposing a sequentially optimal image compression mechanism. Chen *et al.* [13] propose 2DLPP that needs less training time and has a higher recognition rate than LPP. Zhang *et al.* [14] extend the NPP to 2DNPP by using the same neighborhood weighting procedure. These 2-D methods have a better performance than their 1-D versions, but they often need much more coefficients than their 1-D versions since they are unilateral projections. In order to alleviate this drawback, bilateral projections schemes of 2DPCA (B2DPCA) are proposed in [15–17], respectively. In [20], Zhang *et al.* further develop B2DNPE which projects both in the column and the row direction. B2DLPP as a bilateral extension of 2DLPP are also proposed in [21] and [22]. These bilateral methods project the two-dimensional data via two projection directions and represent the two-dimensional data effectively with fewer coefficients.

Recently, nuclear norm based criterion arises wide interests in image representation [23–25] and pattern recognition [26–30]. Lu [31] *et al.* propose HVNN-2DLDA which computes the between-class scatter matrix and the within-class scatter matrix by using the nuclear norm and maximizing the ratio of them. Lu [32] *et al.* proposed NN-2DLPP which utilizes the nuclear norm as a regularization term to recover the noisy data. Zhang [26] *et al.* show that nuclear norm is more robust than Frobenius norm and L_1-norm as a basic metric. It is more effective to characterize the similarity and dissimilarity between the data by leveraging nuclear norm. Thus they propose a new model called nuclear norm-based 2-DPCA (N-2-DPCA) and extend N-2-DPCA into a bilateral version N-B2-DPCA. In this paper, inspired by [13, 26], we propose a new model called nuclear-norm-based jointly sparse regression (NJSR) which uses nuclear norm as a distance metric for regression learning based on the image matrix. Since the $L_{2,1}$ regularization term can select jointly sparse features and make the model more interpretable [18, 19], we add a $L_{2,1}$ regularization term to learn a sparse transformation matrix. Furthermore, NJSR is a unilateral method which means that NJSR often needs more coefficients to represent a picture. Thus, NJSR is extended to bilinear case, i.e. BNJSR. The main contributions of this paper are as follows:

1. We propose a novel model called NJSR which is a $L_{2,1}$ norm based jointly sparse learning method using the nuclear norm as a basic metric to characterize the reconstruction error. An iterative algorithm via computing a set of eigen-decomposition is proposed to solve the optimization problem.

2. We extend NJSR to the bilateral scheme, i.e. BNJSR. BNJSR can represent the data more effectively than NJSR. And it can be solved by an iterative algorithm containing two eigenfunctions.

3. Two famous face databases are used to measure the performances of the proposed NJSR and BNJSR. And experimental results show the good performance of the proposed methods comparing with several classical two-dimensional feature extraction methods.

The rest of this paper is organized as follows. In Sect. 2, we review 2DLPP. NJSR and its solution are proposed in Sect. 3. Section 4 extends BNJSR. Section 5 shows the experiments on the face databases. The conclusion is given in Sect. 6.

2 Related Work

2.1 Notation and Definition

Assume that capital letters represent matrices (e.g., S), lower-case letters denote column vectors (e.g., s). $S(i,:)$ is the i-th row of matrix S. S_{ij} denotes the entry of the i-th row and the j-th column in the matrix S. I is the identity matrix with the appropriate size. Furthermore, $||\cdot||_2$, $||\cdot||_F$, $||\cdot||_*$ denote L_2 norm, Frobenius norm and nuclear norm, respectively. And $\text{tr}(\cdot)$ denotes the trace operator.

2.2 Two-Dimensional Locality Preserving Projections (2DLPP)

LPP is a simple and effective vector-based representation feature extraction method. However, when the data is two-dimensional, i.e. in matrix form, it needs to be transformed into vectors which may lead to the fact that the space structures of the images are destroyed. Moreover, LPP may meet some problems such as small sample size problem and the curse of dimensionality dilemma. In order to solve these problems, the two-dimensional extension of LPP, i.e. 2DLPP, is proposed. Given a training data set $X = [X_1, X_2, \ldots, X_s] \in R^{m \times ns}, X_i (i = 1, 2, \ldots, s)$ represents a two-dimensional image matrix, and the s is the number of the samples. The objective function of 2DLPP can be defined as follows:

$$\min \sum_{ij} ||Y_i - Y_j||_F^2 S_{ij} \tag{1}$$

where $Y_i = W^T X_i \in R^{d \times n} (d \ll m)$, and $W \in R^{m \times d}$ is the projection matrix. The definition of S can be defined as follows:

$$S_{ij} = \begin{cases} \exp\left(||X_i - X_j||^2/t\right), & \begin{array}{l} if\ X_j \in N_k(X_i) \\ or\ X_i \in N_k(X_j) \end{array} \\ 0, & otherwise \end{cases} \tag{2}$$

or

$$S_{ij} = \begin{cases} \exp\left(||X_i - X_j||^2/t\right), & ||X_i - X_j||^2 < \varepsilon \\ 0 & otherwise \end{cases} \tag{3}$$

where $X_j \in N_k(X_i)$ represents X_j is one of the k nearest neighbors of X_i. To avoid the trivial solutions, we add the constraint $W^T X (D \otimes I) X^T W = I$. Therefore, the problem (1) can be rewritten as follows:

$$\min_W \ tr\left(W^T X (L \otimes I) X^T W\right) s.t. W^T X (D \otimes I) X^T W = I \tag{4}$$

where $\otimes$ is the Kronecker product of the matrices. The problem (4) can be solved by the following generalized eigen-decomposition problem:

$$X(L \otimes I) X^T W = X(D \otimes I) X^T W \Lambda \tag{5}$$

where Λ is the eigenvalue matrix. And W is the composition of the d eigenvectors corresponding to the d smallest eigenvalues of $\left(X (D \otimes I) X^T\right)^{-1} X (L \otimes I) X^T$.

3   Nuclear-Norm-Based Jointly Sparse Regression

3.1   The Objective Function of NJSR

Recently, it is proved that the nuclear norm is more robust than the Frobenius norm and L_1-norm to characterize the reconstruction error. Inspired by N-2-DPCA, we propose a new model based on 2DLPP called NJSR to achieve the robustness feature extraction. Different from the NN-2DLPP [32] which utilize the nuclear norm as a regularization term, NJSR chooses the nuclear norm as the basic metric. At the same time, a $L_{2,1}$ regularization term is added to the objective function. The capability of $L_{2,1}$ regularization term is to select the more discriminative sparse features jointly. Thus, it is expected to obtain a more robust sparse projective matric for feature extraction. Assume that $X_1, X_2, \ldots, X_s \in R^{m \times n}$ are the s training samples, NJSR can be defined as follows:

$$\min_W \sum_{ij} ||X_i W - X_j W||_* S_{ij} + \alpha ||W||_{2,1} \quad s.t. W^T W = I \tag{6}$$

where $Y_i = X_i W \in R^{m \times d}$ (d $\ll$ n) and α is the parameter. $W \in R^{n \times d}$ is the projection matrix and S is the symmetric similarity matrix. Matrix S is defined as follows:

$$S_{ij} = \begin{cases} 1, \ if \ X_i \in N_k(X_j) \\ \quad or \ X_j \in N_k(X_i) \\ 0, \ otherwise \end{cases} \tag{7}$$

where $X_i \in N_k(X_j)$ means that X_i is one of the k nearest neighbors of X_j. S_{ij} describes the relationship between X_i and X_j. If X_i and X_j are close to each other in the high-dimensional space, Y_i and Y_j will be as close as possible in the low-dimensional space by minimizing (6).

3.2 The Optimal Solution

We first define the following reweighted matrix:

$$G_{ii} = \begin{cases} \frac{1}{2\|W(i,:)\|_2}, & \text{for any } i \\ 0, & \text{otherwise} \end{cases} \tag{8}$$

where G is a diagonal matrix. The relationship between the nuclear norm and Frobenius norm is uncovered in [33]. By using the $\|X\|_* = \left\|\left(XX^T\right)^{-\frac{1}{4}}X\right\|_F^2$, the problem (6) can be rewritten as:

$$\min_W \sum_{ij} \left\|\left((X_i - X_j)WW^T(X_i - X_j)^T\right)^{-\frac{1}{4}}(X_i - X_j)W\right\|_F^2 S_{ij}$$
$$+ \alpha tr\left(W^T GW\right) \quad s.t. \quad W^T W = I \tag{9}$$

As $\|X\|_F^2 = tr(X^T X)$, problem (9) can be rewritten as:

$$\min_W \sum_{ij} tr\left(\left((X_i - X_j)WW^T(X_i - X_j)^T\right)^{\frac{1}{2}}\right)S_{ij}$$
$$+ \alpha tr\left(W^T GW\right) s.t. W^T W = I \tag{10}$$

The problem (10) is hard to solve, so we use an iterative method to get the optimal solution. The problem (10) can be rewritten as:

$$\min_W \sum_{ij} tr\left((X_i - X_j)W_{k+1}W_{k+1}^T(X_i - X_j)^T \tilde{S}_k\right)$$
$$+ \alpha tr\left(W_{k+1}^T G_k W_{k+1}\right) s.t. W^T W = I \tag{11}$$

where W_{k+1} is the optimal solution of the k + 1-th iterative process, G_k is computed based on W_k. And matrix $\tilde{S}_k$ is defined as follows:

$$\tilde{S}_k = S_{ij}\left((X_i - X_j)W_k W_k^T(X_i - X_j)^T\right)^{-\frac{1}{2}} \tag{12}$$

where W_k is the optimal solution of the k-th iteration. The first half part of the problem (11) can be converted as follow:

$$\sum_{ij} tr\left((X_i - X_j)W_{k+1}W_{k+1}^T(X_i - X_j)^T \tilde{S}_k\right)$$
$$= \sum_{ij} tr\left(W_{k+1}^T(X_i - X_j)^T \tilde{S}_k(X_i - X_j)W_{k+1}\right)$$
$$= tr\left(W_{k+1}^T(\sum_{ij}(X_i - X_j)^T \tilde{S}_k(X_i - X_j))W_{k+1}\right)$$
$$= tr\left(W_{k+1}^T P_k W_{k+1}\right) \tag{13}$$

where matrix P_k is defined as:

$$P_k = \sum_{ij} (X_i - X_j)^T \tilde{S}_k (X_i - X_j) \tag{14}$$

Through the analysis of (12), (13) and (14), the problem (11) can be rewritten as:

$$\min_{W^T W = I} tr\left(W_{k+1}^T P_k W_{k+1}\right) + \alpha tr\left(W_{k+1}^T G_k W_{k+1}\right) \tag{15}$$

Using the Lagrange multiplier method, and then letting the deviation respect to W_{k+1} be zero, the following eigenfunction can be derived from (15):

$$(P_k + \alpha G_k) W_{k+1} = W_{k+1} \Lambda \tag{16}$$

where Λ is the eigenvalue matrix of $P_k + \alpha G_k$. And the optimal solution W_{k+1} consists of the d eigenvectors corresponding to the d smallest eigenvalues of $P_k + \alpha G_k$. Algorithm 1 shows the algorithm details of NJSR.

4 Bilateral NJSR

4.1 The Objective Function of BNJSR

NJSR is unilateral projection which means that NJSR often needs more coefficients than LPP or similar methods to represent an image. In order to compress the image matrix to be smaller size, BNJSR, as a bilateral extension of NJSR, will be developed to learn two projection matrices to project the image data from both left and right side at the same time. In order to select the sparse discriminant feature from the image matrix, $L_{2,1}$ regularization terms are also added to the objective function to learn the sparse projection matrices. The objective function of BNJSR can be formulated as follows:

$$\min_{U,V} \sum_{ij} \left\| U^T X_i V - U^T X_j V \right\|_* S_{ij} + \alpha \|U\|_{2,1} + \beta \|V\|_{2,1}$$
$$\text{s.t.} UU^T = I, VV^T = I \tag{17}$$

where $Y_i = U^T X_i V \in R^{l \times d} (l \ll m, d \ll n)$. $U \in R^{m \times l}$ and $V \in R^{n \times d}$ are the left and right projection matrices, respectively. And α and β are the regularization parameters. Matrix S is defined as the same one in (7).

4.2 The Optimal Solution

Since there is no closed-form solution for the problem (17) to obtain the optimal U and V, so we propose an iterative algorithm to alternatively update variables U and V. The problem (17) can be divided into two sub-problems including U-step and V-step. U-step fixes the matrix V to solve the sub-problem (18), while V-step fixes the matrix U to solve the sub-problem (19).

ALGORITHM 1. NJSR ALGORITHM

Input: Assume that $X_1, X_2, \ldots, X_s \in R^{m \times n}$ are the s training samples,
the numbers of iterations T, dimensions d
Output: Low-dimensional representations $Y_i \in R^{m \times d}$ $(i = 1,2,3, \ldots, s)$
Step 1: Initialize $W_1 \in R^{n \times d}$ as a random orthogonal matrix
Step 2: For $i = 1:T$
- Compute the matrix G_i using (8)
- Compute the matrix P_i using (14) while $\tilde{S}_i$ is computed by using (12)
- Compute the optimal solution W_{i+1} using (16)
- if converge, then break
End
Step 3: Using $Y_i = X_i W$ to project the samples into the subspace.

$$\min_{W^T W = I} \sum_{ij} \left\| U^T X_i V - U^T X_j V \right\|_* S_{ij} + \alpha \|U\|_{2,1} \tag{18}$$

$$\min_{W^T W = I} \sum_{ij} \left\| U^T X_i V - U^T X_j V \right\|_* S_{ij} + \beta \|V\|_{2,1} \tag{19}$$

1) U-step. As $\|X\|_* = \|X^T\|_*$, the sub-problem (18) can be rewritten as:

$$\min_{W^T W = I} \sum_{ij} \left\| V^T X_i^T U - V^T X_j^T U \right\|_* S_{ij} + \alpha \|U\|_{2,1} \tag{20}$$

Using $\|X\|_* = \left\| (XX^T)^{-\frac{1}{4}} X \right\|_F^2$ and $\|X\|_F^2 = tr(X^T X)$, the problem (20) can be converted as:

$$\min_{W^T W = I} \sum_{ij} tr\left(\left(V^T (X_i - X_j)^T U U^T (X_i - X_j) V \right)^{\frac{1}{2}} \right) S_{ij} + \alpha tr\left(U^T H U \right) \tag{21}$$

where H is a diagonal matrix and defined by (22):

$$H_{ij} = \begin{cases} \frac{1}{2\|U(i,:)\|_2} & i = j \\ 0 & otherwise \end{cases} \tag{22}$$

However the problem (21) is hard to solve. We use an iterative method to acquire the optimal U. The problem (21) can be rewritten as follows:

$$\min_{W^T W = I} \sum_{ij} tr\left(V_k^T (X_i - X_j)^T U_{k+1} U_{k+1}^T (X_i - X_j) V_k \tilde{D}_k \right)$$
$$+ \alpha tr\left(U_{k+1}^T H_k U_{k+1} \right) \tag{23}$$

where V_k, U_{k+1} are the optimal V and U in the k-th and k + 1-th iteration, respectively. Matrix H_k is computed by U_k. And $\tilde{D}_k$ is defined as:

$$\tilde{D}_k = S_{ij} \left(V_k^T (X_i - X_j)^T U U_k^T (X_i - X_j) V_k \right)^{-\frac{1}{2}} \tag{24}$$

The first half part of the problem (23) can be converted as follow:

$$\sum_{ij} tr\left(V_k^T (X_i - X_j)^T U_{k+1} U_{k+1}^T (X_i - X_j) V_k \tilde{D}_k\right)$$
$$= \sum_{ij} tr\left(U_{k+1}^T (X_i - X_j) V_k \tilde{D}_k V_k^T (X_i - X_j)^T U_{k+1}\right)$$
$$= tr\left(U_{k+1}^T \left(\sum_{ij} (X_i - X_j) V_k \tilde{D}_k V_k^T (X_i - X_j)^T\right) U_{k+1}\right)$$
$$= tr\left(U_{k+1}^T N_k U_{k+1}\right) \tag{25}$$

where N_k is defined as:

$$N_k = \sum_{ij} (X_i - X_j) V_k \tilde{D}_k V_k^T (X_i - X_j)^T \tag{26}$$

Through the analysis of (24), (25) and (26), the problem (23) can be rewritten as:

$$\min_{W^T W = I} tr\left(U_{k+1}^T N_k U_{k+1}\right) + \alpha tr\left(U_{k+1}^T H_k U_{k+1}\right) \tag{27}$$

Leveraging the Lagrange multiplier method, and then letting the deviation respect to U_{k+1} be zero, the following eigenfunction can be derived from (27):

$$(N_k + \alpha H_k) U_{k+1} = U_{k+1} \Lambda \tag{28}$$

where Λ is the eigenvalue matrix. And the optimal solution U_{k+1} consists of the l eigenvectors corresponding to the l smallest eigenvalues of $N_k + \alpha H_k$.

2) V-step. The solutions of the problems (18) and (19) are similar. Since $\|X\|_* = $

$$\left\| \left(XX^T\right)^{-\frac{1}{4}} X \right\|_F^2 \text{ and } \|X\|_F^2 = tr\left(X^T X\right),\text{the problem (19) can be rewritten as:}$$

$$\min_{W^T W = I} \sum_{ij} tr\left(\left(U^T (X_i - X_j) V V^T (X_i - X_j)^T U\right)^{\frac{1}{2}}\right) S_{ij} + \beta tr\left(V^T Q V\right) \tag{29}$$

where Q is a diagonal matrix and defined by (30).

$$Q_{ij} = \begin{cases} \frac{1}{2\|V(i,:)\|_2} & i = j \\ 0 & otherwise \end{cases} \tag{30}$$

The problem (29) is also hard to solve. An iterative algorithm is used to solve it. The problem (29) can be rewritten as follows:

$$\min_{W^T W = I} \sum_{ij} tr\left(U_{k+1}^T (X_i - X_j) V_{k+1} V_{k+1}^T (X_i - X_j)^T U_{k+1} \tilde{E}_k\right)$$
$$+ \beta tr\left(V_{k+1}^T Q_k V_{k+1}\right) \tag{31}$$

where U_{k+1} is the optimal solution in k + 1-th iterative process and V_{k+1} is the optimal solution in k + 1-th iterative process. Matrix Q_k is computed by V_k. And $\tilde{E}_k$ is defined as follows:

$$\tilde{E}_k = S_{ij}\left(U_{k+1}^T(X_i - X_j)V_kV_k^T(X_i - X_j)^TU_{k+1}\right)^{-\frac{1}{2}} \tag{32}$$

The first half part of the problem (31) can be computed as follow:

$$\sum_{ij} tr\left(U_{k+1}^T(X_i - X_j)V_{k+1}V_{k+1}^T(X_i - X_j)^TU_{k+1}\tilde{E}_k\right)$$
$$= \sum_{ij} tr\left(V_{k+1}^T(X_i - X_j)^TU_{k+1}\tilde{E}_kU_{k+1}^T(X_i - X_j)V_{k+1}\right)$$
$$= tr\left(V_{k+1}^T\left(\sum_{ij}(X_i - X_j)^TU_{k+1}\tilde{E}_kU_{k+1}^T(X_i - X_j)\right)V_{k+1}\right)$$
$$= tr\left(V_{k+1}^TM_kV_{k+1}\right) \tag{33}$$

where M_k is defined as:

$$M_k = \sum_{ij}(X_i - X_j)^TU_{k+1}\tilde{E}_kU_{k+1}^T(X_i - X_j) \tag{34}$$

Through the analysis of (32), (33) and (34), the problem (31) can be rewritten as:

$$\min_{W^TW=I} tr\left(V_{k+1}^TM_kV_{k+1}\right) + \beta tr\left(V_{k+1}^TQ_kV_{k+1}\right) \tag{35}$$

Leveraging the Lagrange multiplier method, and then letting the deviation respect to U_{k+1} be zero, the following eigenfunction can be derived from (35):

$$(M_k + \beta Q_k)V_{k+1} = V_{k+1}\Lambda \tag{36}$$

where Λ is the eigenvalue matrix of $M_k + \beta Q_k$. And the optimal solution V_{k+1} consists of the d eigenvectors corresponding to the d smallest eigenvalues of $M_k + \beta Q_k$. Algorithm 2 shows the algorithm details of BNJSR.

ALGORITHM 2. BNJSR ALGORITHM

Input: Assume that $X_1, X_2, ..., X_s \in R^{m \times n}$ are the s training samples,
      the numbers of iterations T, dimensions d, l

Output: Low-dimensional representations $Y_i \in R^{l \times d}$ $(i = 1,2,3,...,s)$

    Step 1: Initialize $U_1 \in R^{m \times l}$ and $V_1 \in R^{n \times d}$ as random orthogonal matrices
    Step 2: For $i = 1:T$
        U-step:
            - Compute the matrix H_i using (22)
                - Compute the matrix N_i using (26) while $\tilde{D}_i$ is computed by using (24)
                - Compute the optimal solution U_{i+1} using (28)
        V-step:
                - Compute the matrix Q_i using (30)
                - Compute the matrix M_i using (34) while $\tilde{E}_i$ is computed by using (32)
                - Compute the optimal solution V_{i+1} using (36)
            - if converge, then break
    End
    Step 3: Using $Y_i = U^TX_iV$ to project the samples into the subspace.

---

5 Experiments

5.1 Details of the Databases

AR face database, which consists of different facial expressions, illumination and occlusions, is used to explore the robustness of the proposed methods. The sample images of one individual are shown in Fig. 1. CMU PIE database can be divided into 13 different subsets according to the poses. In this paper, Pose C27 is chosen for experiments. The sample images of one individual Pose C27 are shown in Fig. 2. Notice that Fig. 2(b) shows the result of randomly adding a 5×5 noise block on the original images.

Fig. 1. Sample images of one person on AR face database

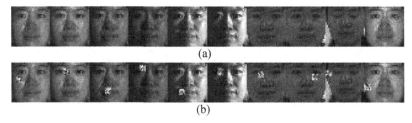

Fig. 2. (a) Sample images of one person on Pose C27 of CMU PIE face database. (b) Sample images with block noise of one person on Pose C27 of CMU PIE face database

5.2 Experimental Setting

In the experiments, the pictures in CMU PIE database are resized to 32×32 pixels while the pictures in AR face database are processed to 40×40 pixels. For each database, ten pictures of each individual are chosen to make up the subset. And l pictures are chosen to be the training set while the rest of the pictures are used to test. We set $l = 4, 5, 6$ for Pose C27 and set $l = 2, 3$ for AR database. We also use Pose C29 to show the effect of regularization parameters.

In the experiments, the compared methods include the unilateral two-dimensional dimensionality reduction methods i.e. two-dimensional Principal Component Analysis (2DPCA) [11] and two-dimensional Locality Preserving Projections (2DLPP) [13], the bilateral two-dimensional dimensionality reduction methods i.e. Bilateral projection-based 2DPCA (B2DPCA) [15] and Bilateral two-dimensional Locality Preserving Projections (B2DLPP) [21].

The initialization of variables in B2DPCA, B2DLPP, NJSR and BNJSR has a small impact on their performance, so the variables are initialized at random. Besides, the value of the regularization parameter α of the NJSR, the regularization parameter α and β of the NJSR are selected from 10^{-5} to 10^5. The similarity matrices of the aforementioned methods are the unsupervised graphs and defined as the (7). The value of the neighborhood parameter K is set to be the same with the number of training images of one individual. The nearest neighbor (NN) classifier is used to classify.

Table 1 and Table 2 show the average recognition rates, standard deviations and the corresponding dimensions of different methods. Figure 3(a) shows the average recognition rates when α changes from 10^{-5} to 10^5. Figure 3(b) shows the average recognition rates when the parameters α and β change from 10^{-5} to 10^5.

Table 1. Comparison of the performance (Recognition accuracy (%), standard deviation, dimension) of different algorithms on AR database

L	2DPCA	2DLPP	B2DPCA	B2DLPP	NJSR	BNJSR
2	84.83 ± 0.70	90.39 ± 0.44	84.92 ± 0.70	88.02 ± 0.48	89.12 ± 0.68	91.23 ± 0.31
	(33)	(12)	(36, 35)	(23, 24)	(35)	(39, 39)
3	92.71 ± 0.44	92.73 ± 0.24	92.79 ± 0.44	96.16 ± 0.49	92.61 ± 0.51	95.96 ± 0.33
	(34)	(14)	(33, 39)	(34, 21)	(35)	(39, 39)

Table 2. Comparsion of the performance (Recognition accuracy (%), Standard deviation, Dimension) of different algorithms on pose C27 of CMU PIE database

L	2DPCA	2DLPP	B2DPCA	B2DLPP	NJSR	BNJSR
4	44.53 ± 0.63	43.33 ± 1.02	44.53 ± 0.63	40.12 ± 1.53	44.29 ± 0.68	50.78 ± 0.78
	(28)	(16)	(32, 28)	(32, 30)	(31)	(27, 31)
5	46.09 ± 1.96	47.97 ± 1.95	46.21 ± 1.98	44.32 ± 1.98	46.18 ± 1.96	54.50 ± 1.97
	(30)	(14)	(30, 30)	(30, 31)	(31)	(27, 31)
6	55.18 ± 0.88	55.86 ± 0.51	55.33 ± 0.91	49.08 ± 1.06	55.12 ± 0.93	61.65 ± 0.98
	(30)	(14)	(31, 31)	(29, 32)	(31)	(31, 31)

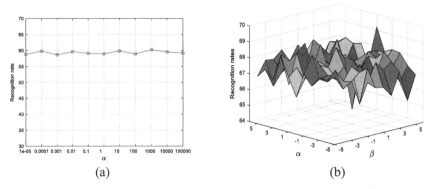

Fig. 3. (a) The recognition rates vs. the parameter α of NJSR on the on Pose C29 of CMU PIE face database. (b) The recognition rates vs. the parameters α and β of BNJSR on the on Pose C29 of CMU PIE face database.

5.3 Experimental Result and Analysis

From the Table 1, Table 2 and Fig. 3, we obtain the following conclusions.

1. In most cases, the average recognition rates of NJSR may be not the highest but BNJSR outperforms the other methods. Compared with BNJSR, NJSR only extracts the information of columns. This may be the reason that it performs worse than BNJSR.
2. The dimension d of NJSR, the dimension l and d of BNJSR are often close to size of the pictures. However, the dimension d of BNJSR is often smaller than the size of the pictures, which means BNJSR needs less coefficients to represent a picture.
3. Despite of comparing with the classical methods, the proposed NJSR may not perform best but its performance is not the worst. The proposed BNJSR perform better than others in the most cases. It is because BNJSR uses the nuclear norm as basic metric and utilizes $L_{2,1}$ norms to select features jointly.
4. For NJSR, the recognition rates have no significant variations when the parameter α is varying. For BNJSR, the recognition rates are different with the different values of the parameters α and β.

6   Conclusion

In this paper, a novel two-dimensional model NJSR is presented. The key idea of NJSR is to measure the reconstruction error by using the nuclear norm instead of Frobenius-norm. The model can be solved by an iterative algorithm via eigen-decomposition. Moreover, NJSR is extended to the bilateral case, i.e. BNJSR. The optimization problem of BNJSR can be solved by iterating two eigenfunctions. Since the BNJSR can extract the row and column information at the same time while NJSR can only extract the information from one direction. BNJSR often has a better performance than NJSR. Experimental results show that BNJSR outperforms other classic methods.

Acknowledgement. This work was supported in part by the Natural Science Foundation of China under Grant 61976145, Grant 61802267 and Grant 61732011, and in part by the Shenzhen Municipal Science and Technology Innovation Council under Grants JCYJ20180305124834854 and JCYJ20190813100801664, and in part by the Natural Science Foundation of Guangdong Province (Grant No. 2019A1515111121).

References

1. Jain, A.K., Duin, R.P.W., Mao, J.: Statistical pattern recognition: a review. IEEE Trans. Pattern Anal. Mach. Intell. **22**(1), 4–37 (2000)
2. Joliffe, I.: Principal Component Analysis. Springer-Verlag, London (1986)
3. Fukunnaga, K.: Introduction to Statistical Pattern Recognition, 2nd edn. Academic, New York (1991)
4. Martinez, A.M., Kak, A.C.: Principal components analysis versus linear discriminant analysis. IEEE Trans. Pattern Anal. Mach. Intell. **23**(2), 228–233 (2001)
5. Roweis, S.T., Saul, L.K.: Nonlinear dimensionality reduction by locally linear embedding. Science **290**(5500), 2323–2326 (2000)
6. Tenenbaum, J.B., de Silva, V., Langford, J.C.: A global geometric framework for nonlinear dimensionality reduction. Science **290**(5500), 2319–2323 (2000)
7. Xu, Y., Song, F., Ge, F., Zhao, Y.: A novel local preserving projection scheme for use with face recognition. Expert Syst. Appl. **37**(9), 6718–6721 (2011)
8. He, X., Niyogi, P.: Locality preserving projections. In: Advances in Neural Information Processing Systems, vol. 16. MIT Press, Cambridge (2003)
9. He, X., Yan, S., Hu, Y., Niyogi, P., Zhang, H.J.: Face recognition using Laplacian faces. IEEE Trans. Pattern Anal. Mach. Intell. **27**(3), 328–340 (2005)
10. Kokiopoulou, E., Saad, Y.: Orthogonal neighborhood preserving projections: a projection-based dimensionality reduction technique. IEEE Trans. Pattern Anal. Mach. Intell. **29**(12), 2143–2156 (2007)
11. Yang, J., Zhang, D., Frangi, A.F., Yang, J.Y.: Two-dimensional PCA: a new approach to appearance based face representation and recognition. IEEE Trans. Pattern Anal. Mach. Intell. **26**(4), 131–137 (2004)
12. Yang, J., Zhang, D., Xu, Y., Yang, J.Y.: Two-dimensional discriminant transform for face recognition. Pattern Recogn. **38**(7), 1125–1129 (2005)
13. Chen, S.B., Zhao, H.F., Kong, M., Luo, B.: 2D-LPP: a two-dimensional extension of locality preserving projections. Neurocomputing **70**, 912–921 (2007)
14. Zhang, H., Wu, Q.J., Chow, T.W., Zhao, M.: A two-dimensional Neighborhood Preserving Projection for appearance-based face recognition. Pattern Recogn. **45**(5), 1866–1876 (2012)
15. Kong, H., Wang, L., Teoh, E.K., Li, X., Wang, J.G., Venkateswarlu, R.: Generalized 2D principal component analysis for face image representation and recognition. Neural Netw. **18**(5–6), 585–594 (2005)
16. Zhang, D.Q., Zhou, Z.H.: $(2D)^2$PCA: Two-directional two-dimensional PCA for efficient face representation and recognition. Neurocomputing **69**(1–3), 224–231 (2005)
17. Mashhoori, A., Jahromi, M.Z.: Block-wise two-directional 2DPCA with ensemble learning for face recognition. Neurocomputing **108**(2), 111–117 (2013)
18. Hou, C., Nie, F., Li, X., Yi, D., Wu, Y.: Joint embedding learning and sparse regression: a framework for unsupervised feature selection. IEEE Trans. Cybern. **44**(6), 793–804 (2014)
19. Gu, Q., Li, Z., Han, J.: Joint feature selection and subspace learning. Proc. Int. Joint Conf. Artif. Intell. (IJCAI) **22**(1), 1294–1299 (2011)

20. Zhang, D., Liu, H., Lu, L., Luo, B.: Image recognition with extension of neighborhood preserving embedding on matrices. J. Inf. Comput. Sci. **9**, 1511–1520 (2012)
21. Song, J., Li, X., Zhong, J., Xu, P., Zhou, M.: A novel face recognition method: bilateral two dimensional locality preserving projections (B2DLPP). In: 2010 Chinese Conference on Pattern Recognition (CCPR), pp. 1–5. IEEE (2010)
22. Chen, S.B., Luo, B., Hu, G.P., Wang, R.H.: Bilateral two-dimensional locality preserving projections. In: IEEE International Conference on Acoustics, Speech and Signal Processing, 2007, ICASSP 2007, vol. 2, pp. II–601. IEEE (2007)
23. Yang, J., Luo, L., Qian, J., Tai, Y., Zhang, F., Xu, Y.: Nuclear norm based matrix regression with applications to face recognition with occlusion and illumination changes. IEEE Trans. Pattern Anal. Mach. Intell. **39**(1), 156–171 (2017)
24. Qian, J., Luo, L., Yang, J., Zhang, F., Lin, Z.: Robust nuclear norm regularized regression for face recognition. Pattern Recogn. **48**, 3145–3159 (2015)
25. Zhang, Z., Yan, S., Zhao, M., Li, F.Z.: Bilinear low-rank coding framework and extension for robust image recovery and feature representation. Knowl.-Based Syst. **86**, 143–157 (2015)
26. Zhang, F., Yang, J., Qian, J., Xu, Y.: Nuclear norm-based 2-DPCA for extracting features from images. IEEE Trans. Neural Netw. Learn. Syst. **26**(10), 2247–2260 (2015)
27. Zhang, Z., Li, F., Zhao, M., Zhang, L., Yan, S.: Robust neighborhood preserving projection by nuclear/L2, 1-norm regularization for image feature extraction. IEEE Trans. Image Process. **26**(4), 1607–1622 (2017)
28. E. J. Candès, X. Li, Y. Ma, and J. Wright, "Robust principal component analysis," *J. ACM*, vol. 58, no. 3, 2009, Art. no. 11
29. Bao, B.K., Liu, G., Xu, C., Yan, S.: Inductive robust principal component analysis. IEEE Trans. Image Process. **21**(8), 3794–3800 (2012)
30. Zhang, Z., Li, F., Zhao, M., Zhang, L., Yan, S.: Joint low-rank and sparse principal feature coding for enhanced robust representation and visual classification. IEEE Trans. Image Process. **25**(6), 2429–2443 (2016)
31. Lu, Y., Yuan, C., Lai, Z., Li, X., Zhang, D., Wong, W.K.: Horizontal and vertical nuclear norm-based 2DLDA for image representation. IEEE Trans. Circ. Syst. Video Technol. **29**(4), 941–955 (2018)
32. Lu, Y., Yuan, C., Lai, Z., Li, X., Wong, W.K., Zhang, D.: Nuclear norm-based 2DLPP for image classification. IEEE Trans. Multimed. **19**(11), 2391–2403 (2017)
33. Fornasier, M., Rauhut, H., Ward, R.: Low-rank matrix recovery via iteratively reweighted least squares minimization. SIAM J. Optim. **21**(4), 1614–1640 (2011)

Dynamically-Passed Contextual Information Network for Saliency Detection

Abdelhafid Dakhia, Tiantian Wang, and Huchuan Lu[(⊠)]

Dalian University of Technology, Dalian, China
dakhia-hafid@hotmail.fr, tiantianwang.ice@gmail.com, lhchuan@dlut.edu.cn

Abstract. Nowadays, deep convolutional neural networks (CNNs) have made significant improvement in detecting salient objects by integrating multi-level convolutional features or exploiting the advantage of dilated convolution. However, how to construct finer structure to produce effective features for saliency detection is still a challenging task. In this paper, we propose a novel deep learning based network by dynamically incorporating multi-level feature maps. The proposed Dynamically-passed Contextual Information Network (DCI-Net) can effectively control the information passage process, incorporate multi-scale context information and alleviate the distraction of background noise to improve the performance of saliency detection. Specifically, we first integrate an effective Passage Unit (PU) that progressively incorporates the low-level information with the high-level cues, in order to preserve the boundary details of salient objects. Second, a Spatial Pyramid Dilation (SPD) module is used to enhance the multi-scale feature representation by using multiple convolution dilations to handle the varied size of salient objects. Finally, we apply a Residual Attention module (RA) to further reinforce the saliency detection. Quantitative and qualitative experiments demonstrate the effectiveness of the proposed framework. Our method can significantly improve the performance based on five popular benchmark datasets.

Keywords: Saliency detection · Dynamically-passed Contextual Information · Spatial pyramid dilation · Residual attention

1 Introduction

Salient object detection aims to localize objects that attract human attention in an image, which has received a lot of interest in a wide range of computer vision applications such as visual tracking [7], scene classification [21,29], person re-identification [2] and image captioning [26]. Many saliency detection methods have been proposed in the literature [19,25]. However, it is still a challenging topic due to the difficulty of locating salient objects in real world scenarios.

A. Dakhia—The author is a Ph.D. student in Dalian University of Technology.

Y. Peng et al. (Eds.): PRCV 2020, LNCS 12307, pp. 369–381, 2020.
https://doi.org/10.1007/978-3-030-60636-7_31

In recent years, CNNs-based methods have shown tremendous performance in classification and recognition tasks. Due to the use of multiple convolution and pooling layers, these models have limitations when employed to dense prediction tasks, such as semantic segmentation, scene parsing, pose estimation and so forth.

Several recent deep learning based methods used for saliency detection focus on exploiting how to integrate multiple features to solve the above limitation, such as MSRNet [12], Amulet [30] and SRM [24]. The key contribution of these methods is based on the multi-level feature integration, which incorporates the features of the lower layers with higher ones to reinforce the saliency detection. However, the simple combination of multi-level features can produce inaccurate features representation, since some complex images with low-contrast or containing multiple objects make this combination unsuitable for locating the salient objects. Figure 1 shows the visual explanation of this limitation.

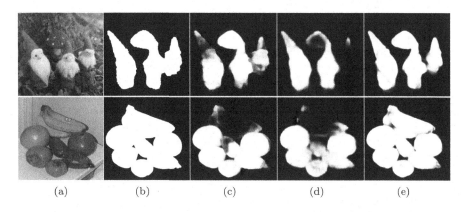

(a)   (b)   (c)   (d)   (e)

Fig. 1. Visual comparison of multi-level feature incorporation based methods. (a) Input images. (b) Ground truth. (c) Amulet [30], (d) SRM [24] and Ours (e).

Inspired by the above analysis, we propose a novel Dynamically-passed Contextual Information Network (DCI-Net) by applying the passage unit to effectively share information among different layers of CNNs. More specifically, DCI-Net incorporates multi-level feature maps to reinforce and control contextual characteristics through the passage units. The aim of this module is to combine detailed information with coarse feature representation. Furthermore, we introduce a spatial pyramid dilation module, which can aggregate the contextual information by consecutively merging multi-scale context representations. Finally, we utilize a residual attention module to remove the cluttered background noise. These three components can improve the saliency detection and produce finer saliency maps.

The key contributions of this paper are three-fold:

- We propose a novel CNN-based encoder-decoder network, which exploits multi-level convolutional features to dynamically control the information passage, which helps to generate more accurate deep feature maps.
- We propose a spatial pyramid dilation module to aggregate the contextual information representation, then we introduce a residual attention module for producing more accurate location of salient objects.
- Compared with 13 state-of-the-art saliency detection methods, our approach achieves the best performance on five benchmark datasets.

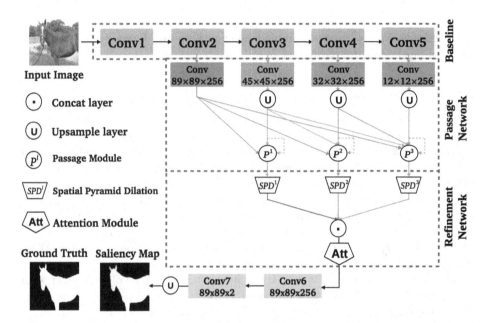

Fig. 2. The architecture of the proposed network. DCI-Net integrates multi-scale feature maps from the second convolution block to the last block. A Passage Unit (PU) is employed to control the passed information. The Spatial Pyramid Dilation module (SPD) is applied to gather contextual information. Then a Residual Attention module (RA) is applied to generate better feature representation. Finally, two convolutional layers are added to produce the final saliency map.

2   The Proposed Method

In this section, we give an overview of the proposed DCI-Net. Figure 2 illustrates the whole architecture. We start from the baseline model in Sect. 2.1, then describe the passage unit in Sect. 2.2. In Sect. 2.3 we show the detailed structure of the spatial pyramid dilation. The final residual attention model is given in Sect. 2.4.

2.1   Baseline Network

We use ResNet-50 [6] as our baseline model and modify it to fit the salient object detection task due to its superior performance in classification task. Specifically, we first remove the average pooling layer, the fully connected layer and the classification layer. In addition, behind the last convolutional layer of ResNet-50, we apply two convolutional layers, one 3×3 convolutional layer with 256 channels and another 1×1 convolutional layer with 2 channels, to produce a coarse saliency map $\mathbf{S}$. Finally, we use the bilinear interpolation to upsample $\mathbf{S}$ in order to obtain the prediction map with the same size as the input image, which is defined by

$$\mathbf{S}' = \mathbf{I}(\mathbf{S}; \alpha), \tag{1}$$

where $\mathbf{S}'$ denotes the final upsampled saliency map and $\mathbf{I}$ represents the interpolation layer with the parameter α.

2.2   Passage Network

In this paper, we address the limitation of the CNNs for salient object detection by controlling the information passage from the encoder network to the decoder one. Motivated by the advantages of multi-scale features and the gated structure [9], we propose a Dynamically-passed Contextual Information Network (DCI-Net), which provides an effective mechanism to control the incorporated information and reduce the unwanted features that damage the saliency prediction. Different from the gated unit model [9] that merges two consecutive features based on the encoder network, the proposed model is built on multiple consecutive layers with a dynamic incorporation of the convolutional features. With this novel structure, we reinforce the deeper layers by transmitting more detailed information from the early layers. We first apply a 3×3 convolution layer with 256 channels behind each convolutional block ($Conv2, ..., Conv5$) to produce four feature maps ($\mathbf{F}^2, ..., \mathbf{F}^5$), respectively. Each feature map $\mathbf{F}^i$ ($i = \{3,4,5\}$) has different resolution due to the progressive decrease of the spatial dimension of the input image. Here, we upsample multi-scale feature maps into the same resolution as $\mathbf{F}^2$ using bilinear interpolation. This helps to produce same spatial size, which can further assist in simultaneously incorporating semantic cues and fine details, which is formulated by

$$\widehat{\mathbf{F}}^i = \mathbf{I}(\mathbf{F}^i; \beta), \tag{2}$$

where $\widehat{\mathbf{F}}^i$ is the upsampled feature maps of the corresponding feature maps $\mathbf{F}^i$ with the factor β. Then, one Passage Unit (PU^j) is connected behind each $\widehat{\mathbf{F}}^i$ to generate three new representations $\mathbf{P}^j$ for $j \in \{1,2,3\}$. This unit controls the information that dynamically passes it, which is formulated by the following,

$$\mathbf{P}^j = \mathbf{W}^j * (\mathbf{F}^2 \times \prod_{i=3}^{j+2} \widehat{\mathbf{F}}^i) + \mathbf{b}^j, \tag{3}$$

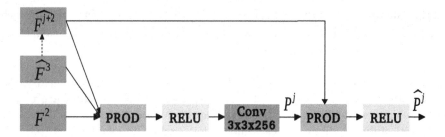

Fig. 3. The detailed structure of the Passage Unit (PU^j). Here 'PROD' means the element-wise multiplication operation.

where $\mathbf{P}^j$ represents the output of each PU^j. $\mathbf{W}^j$ and $\mathbf{b}^j$ denote the weight and bias of the convolutional layers. Finally $\widehat{\mathbf{F}}^{j+2}$ and $\mathbf{P}^j$ are combined by an element-wise multiplication operation, which is defined as follows

$$\widehat{\mathbf{P}}^j = \mathbf{P}^j \times \widehat{\mathbf{F}}^{j+2}, \tag{4}$$

where $\widehat{\mathbf{P}}^j$ is the output of the passage unit that represents a finer feature representation of $\widehat{\mathbf{F}}^i$. The detailed structure of the passage unit PU^j is shown in Fig. 3.

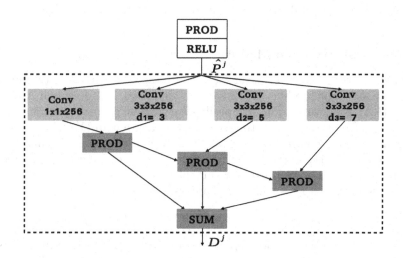

Fig. 4. The detailed structure of the Spatial Pyramid Dilation module (SPD^j).

2.3 Spatial Pyramid Dilation Module

To further generate more precise prediction maps, we propose a Spatial Pyramid Dilation module, which is inspired by the Pyramid Pooling Module (PPM) [33] and the Efficient Spatial Pyramid (ESP) [18]. Each SPD is connected behind each passage unit output $\widehat{\mathbf{P}}^j$ to generate the output $\mathbf{D}^j$ used for handling segmenting objects at multiple scales. As shown in Fig. 4, our SPD architecture consists of one 1×1 convolutional layer and three 3×3 convolutional layers with three different dilated rates d_t, where $d_t = 2 \times t + 1$, $t \in \{1, 2, 3\}$. Specifically, the first convolutional layer with 1×1 kernel is used to generate the feature map with the smallest field of view. Then, we sequentially apply three convolutional layers with different dilated rates, which is followed by an element-wise product operation used to incorporate multi-scale context information. Finally, we apply one element-wise summation operation to merge the three feature maps and better capture the scale variation among different objects.

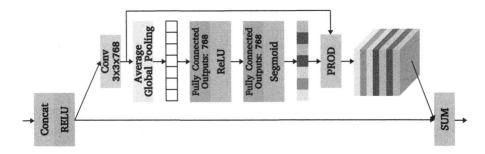

Fig. 5. The detailed structure of the Residual Attention module (RA).

2.4 Residual Attention Module

Motivated by the attention mechanism in filtering background distractors, we exploit the attention module [8] for saliency detection. The Residual Attention module (RA) is shown in Fig. 5. Specifically, we first concatenate the outputs $\{\mathbf{D}^j\}_{j=1,2,3}$ of multi-level SPD to generate the feature map $\mathbf{D}^*$. Then we add a convolutional layer with 3×3 kernel and use the global average pooling layer to obtain a channel-wise statistic, which can generate the weight of each channel of the feature map $\mathbf{D}^*$. Our attention module is constructed by connecting two fully connected layers FCs with 768 channels, which is described as

$$\mathbf{A}_{tt} = \mathbf{D}^* \times \Psi(FC(\sigma(FC(\mathbf{D}^* * \mathbf{W}^* + \mathbf{b}^*)))), \tag{5}$$

where $\mathbf{A}_{tt}$ denotes the attention representation, $\mathbf{W}^*$ and $\mathbf{b}^*$ represent the kernel and bias parameters of the convolutional layer, respectively. Symbol σ denotes the non-linear activation. Ψ and $\times$ represents the sigmoid layer and the multiplication layer, respectively. Furthermore, we adopt the identity mapping by applying an element-wise summarization layer to construct the residual attention module, which is given by

$$\mathbf{A}_{tt}^* = \mathbf{D}^* + \mathbf{A}_{tt}, \tag{6}$$

where $\mathbf{A}_{tt}^*$ represents the output of the attention module with a residual connection.

Figure 6 provides the visual examples of different variants of DCI-Net without PU, SPD or RA. Our final results are shown in the last column. Compared to the other variants, the proposed method can generate more accurate saliency maps with precise boundaries and less background distractors.

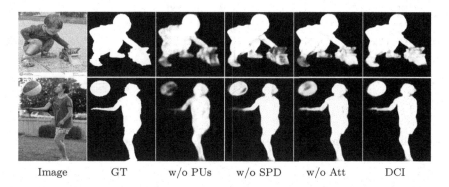

| Image | GT | w/o PUs | w/o SPD | w/o Att | DCI |

Fig. 6. Comparison of DCI-Network with and without PUs, SPD or Att. It can be seen that without the connection of PUs, SPD or Att, the model can miss the detection of the ball or the leg of the kid.

2.5 Implementation Details

We utilize the cross entropy loss function and the DUTS [22] dataset for training our model. Our proposed method is implemented based on the Caffe [10] framework. We initialize the parameters of the baseline network by ResNet-50 model pretrained on ImageNet. For finetuning the proposed model, we resize the input images to the size of 353×353 pixels for training. We set the learning rate to $1e^{-10}$ and the weight decay to 0.0005.

3 Experimental Results

3.1 Datasets

We evaluate the proposed method on five widely-used benchmark datasets: ECSSD [27], DUT-OMRON [28], PASCAL-S [16], HKU-IS [13] and DUTS [22]. **ECSSD** includes 1,000 complex images with various sizes of salient objects. **DUT-OMRON** has high quality variety with 5,168 images, which includes relatively complex background. **PASCAL-S** contains 850 images with multiple objects. **HKU-IS** has 4,447 images and each image has multiple objects or has low contrast against the background. **DUTS** is the latest released dataset with more images, which contains 10,553 training images and 5,019 testing images with more challenging scenarios.

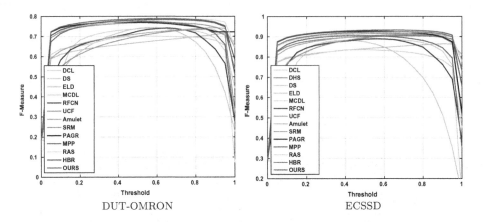

Fig. 7. The comparison of precision-recall curves of the proposed method with existing saliency detection methods on two datasets.

3.2   Evaluation Metrics

To evaluate the performance of the proposed model, we adopt three metrics, including the precision-recall (PR) curve, F-measure and mean absolute error (MAE) score. The precision-recall curve represents the comparison of binarized saliency map with the ground truth. F-measure score is the weighted combination of precision and recall:

$$F_\beta = \frac{(1 + \beta^2) \cdot Precision \cdot Recall}{\beta^2 \cdot Precision + Recall}, \tag{7}$$

where β^2 is set to 0.3 to emphasize on the precision more than the recall [1]. Moreover, we also calculate the mean absolute error (MAE) to measure the averaged per-pixel difference between the estimated saliency map S and the ground truth G suggested by [20].

$$MAE = \frac{1}{W \times H} \sum_{x=1}^{W} \sum_{y=1}^{H} |S(x,y) - G(x,y)|, \tag{8}$$

where W and H are the width and height of the saliency map S and G is the ground truth.

3.3   Performance Comparison

We compare the proposed method with 13 state-of-the-art deep learning-based saliency detection methods, including MCDL [34], DS [15], ELD [11], DCL [14], DHS [17], RFCN [23] UCF [31], Amulet [30], SRM [24], PARG [32],MPP [5], RAS [3] and HBR [4].

Table 1. Comparision of F-measure and MAE scores. The best two results are shown in **bold** and *italic*, respectively.

	ECSSD		DUT-OMRON		PASCAL-S		HKU-IS		DUTS	
	F-measure	MAE	F-measure	MAE	F-measure	MAE	F-measure	MAE	F-measure	MAE
Ours	**0.905**	**0.047**	**0.729**	*0.063*	**0.816**	**0.074**	**0.896**	**0.039**	**0.789**	**0.048**
HBR	*0.896*	*0.050*	*0.720*	0.065	0.803	0.087	0.882	*0.042*	0.767	*0.055*
RAS	0.889	0.056	0.713	**0.062**	-	-	0.871	0.045	0.755	0.060
MPPNet	0.873	0.079	0.695	0.071	0.769	0.120	0.860	0.064	0.722	0.076
PARG	0.894	0.064	0.711	0.072	*0.807*	0.092	*0.886*	0.048	*0.788*	*0.055*
SRM	0.892	0.056	0.707	0.069	0.796	*0.085*	0.874	0.046	0.757	0.059
Amulet	0.869	0.061	0.647	0.098	0.763	0.098	0.839	0.052	0.676	0.085
UCF	0.841	0.080	0.613	0.132	0.702	0.126	0.808	0.074	0.629	0.117
RFCN	0.834	0.109	0.627	0.111	0.747	0.118	0.835	0.089	0.712	0.090
ELD	0.810	0.082	0.611	0.092	0.718	0.123	0.769	0.074	0.628	0.093
DS	0.821	0.124	0.603	0.120	0.659	0.176	0.785	0.078	0.632	0.091
DHS	0.871	0.063	-	-	0.773	0.095	0.852	0.054	0.724	0.067
MCDL	0.796	0.102	0.625	0.089	0.691	0.145	0.757	0.092	0.594	0.105
DCL	0.827	0.151	0.684	0.157	0.714	0.125	0.853	0.136	0.714	0.149

Quantitative Results. Table 1 and Figure 7 indicate that our proposed method outperforms the other state-of-the-art methods and achieves the best performance across all datasets.

We also provide the run-time comparison in Table 2. All the experiments were conducted on a computer with i7-4790 CPU and a single TITAN-X GPU. As it can be seen, our method shows a competitive time compared with other methods with the speed of 20 FPS.

Table 2. Run time comparison with other methods.

	Ours	DCL	MCDL	RFCN	Amulet	UCF	HBR	RAS
Time (s)	0.05	0.41	2.27	4.72	0.10	0.19	0.08	0.05

Qualitative Results. In Figure 8, we present visual comparison of the proposed method with the state-of-the-art methods. We include multiple salient objects (first two rows), objects of low contrast with the background (3th row) and images with cluttered background (5th row). From these examples, we can see that our proposed method generates more accurate saliency maps which are much closer to the ground truth.

3.4 Ablation Analysis

Results of Spatial Pyramid Dilation. To evaluate the efficiency of the spatial pyramid dilation module, we provide F-measure and MAE scores on PASCAL-S and ECSSD datasets. We use ResNet-50 as our baseline model, as

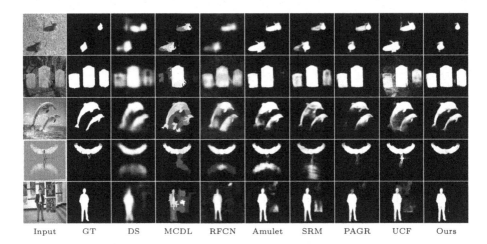

| Input | GT | DS | MCDL | RFCN | Amulet | SRM | PAGR | UCF | Ours |

Fig. 8. Visual comparison of the proposed method compared with state-of-the-arts. Compared to the other methods, our method can localize the objects accurately and generate finer boundaries for the objects.

Table 3. Comparison of F-measure and MAE scores. '+' denotes that 'MPP', 'ESP' and 'SPD' modules are added to the baseline model, respectively.

	PASCAL-S		ECSSD	
	F-measure	MAE	F-measure	MAE
Baseline	0.773	0.094	0.861	0.069
+PPM	0.779	0.090	0.863	0.065
+ESP	0.776	0.093	0.862	0.069
+SPD	**0.784**	**0.084**	**0.870**	**0.060**
w/o PU	0.791	0.082	0.881	0.081
w/o SPD	0.798	0.082	0.891	0.054
w/o Att*	0.808	0.083	0.901	0.057
DCI-Net	**0.816**	**0.074**	**0.905**	**0.047**

described in Sect. 2.1. From Table 3, it can be seen that the proposed module SPD can improve the performance compared to the baseline network, PPM [33] or ESP [18]. The better performance derives from the combination of multi-scale context information.

Effects of Different Variants. We also provide the results to further verify the effectiveness of the proposed three modules, which are shown in Table 3.

We first show the importance of applying PUs to rectify the missed local contextual information. Then, through SPD, the mistakes of localizing the saliency map can be corrected by distinguishing the meaningful semantic features. Finally, the prediction map generated by SPD also benefits from the role that Att plays in refining the boundaries of the saliency map. It can be observed that our DCI-Net achieves the best performance. Furthermore, it can be noted that removing any component will decrease the performance, which demonstrates the comprehensiveness of our proposed saliency detection model.

4   Conclusion

In this paper, we propose a novel dynamically-passed information network (DCI-Net) for salient object detection. To better combine the multi-scale features, we first use multiple passage units that help to control the passed information. Then, we propose a novel spatial pyramid dilation module with multi-scale dilated convolution. In addition, we apply a residual attention module to filter out the background distractors. Experimental evaluation on five benchmark datasets show that our proposed method performs favorably against the 13 state-of-the-art methods.

References

1. Achanta, R., Hemami, S., Estrada, F., Susstrunk., S.: Frequency-tuned salient region detection. In: Proceedings of the IEEE Conference on Computer Vision and Pattern Recognition, pp. 1597–1604 (2009)
2. Bi, S., Li, G., Yu, Y.: Person re-identification using multiple experts with random subspaces. J. Image Graph. **2**(2), 381–392 (2014)
3. Chen, S., Tan, X., Wang, B., Hu, X.: Reverse attention for salient object detection. In: Proceedings of the European Conference on Computer Vision, pp. 234–250 (2018)
4. Dakhia, A., Wang, T., Lu, H.: A hybrid-backward refinement model for salient object detection. Neurocomputing **358**, 72–80 (2019)
5. Dakhia, A., Wang, T., Lu, H.: Multi-scale pyramid pooling network for salient object detection. Neurocomputing **333**, 211–220 (2019)
6. He, K., Zhang, X., Ren, S., Sun, J.: Deep residual learning for image recognition. In: Proceedings of the IEEE Conference on Computer Vision and Pattern Recognition, pp. 770–778 (2016)
7. Hong, S., You, T., Kwak, S., Han, B.: Online tracking by learning discriminative saliency map with convolutional neural network. In: International Conference on Machine Learning, pp. 597–606 (2015)
8. Hu, J., Shen, L., Sun, G.: Squeeze-and-excitation networks. In: Proceedings of the IEEE Conference on Computer Vision and Pattern Recognition, pp. 7132–7141 (2018)
9. Islam, M.A., Rochan, M., Bruce, N.D., Wang, Y.: Gated feedback refinement network for dense image labeling. In: Proceedings of the IEEE Conference on Computer Vision and Pattern Recognition, pp. 4877–4885 (2017)
10. Jia, Y., et al.: Caffe: convolutional architecture for fast feature embedding. In: Proceedings of the 22nd ACM International Conference on Multimedia, pp. 675–678 (2014)
11. Lee, G., Tai, Y.W., Kim, J.: Deep saliency with encoded low level distance map and high level features. In: Proceedings of the IEEE Conference on Computer Vision and Pattern Recognition, pp. 660–668 (2016)

12. Li, G., Xie, Y., Lin, L., Yu, Y.: Instance-level salient object segmentation. In: Proceedings of the IEEE Conference on Computer Vision and Pattern Recognition, pp. 2386–2395 (2017)
13. Li, G., Yu, Y.: Visual saliency based on multiscale deep features. In: Proceedings of the IEEE Conference on Computer Vision and Pattern Recognition, pp. 5455–5463 (2015)
14. Li, G., Yu, Y.: Deep contrast learning for salient object detection. In: Proceedings of the IEEE Conference on Computer Vision and Pattern Recognition, pp. 478–487 (2016)
15. Li, X., et al.: DeepSaliency: multi-task deep neural network model for salient object detection. IEEE Trans. Image Process. **25**(8), 3919–3930 (2016)
16. Li, Y., Hou, X., Koch, C., Rehg, J.M., Yuille, A.L.: The secrets of salient object segmentation. In: Proceedings of the IEEE Conference on Computer Vision and Pattern Recognition, pp. 280–287 (2014)
17. Liu, N., Han, J.: DHSNet: deep hierarchical saliency network for salient object detection. In: Proceedings of the IEEE Conference on Computer Vision and Pattern Recognition, pp. 678–686 (2016)
18. Mehta, S., Rastegari, M., Caspi, A., Shapiro, L., Hajishirzi, H.: ESPNet: efficient spatial pyramid of dilated convolutions for semantic segmentation. In: Proceedings of the European Conference on Computer Vision, pp. 552–568 (2018)
19. Murray, N., Vanrell, M., Otazu, X., Parraga, C.A.: Saliency estimation using a non-parametric low-level vision model. In: IEEE Conference on Computer Vision and Pattern Recognition, pp. 433–440 (2011)
20. Perazzi, F., Krahenbuhl, P., Pritch, Y., Hornung., A.: Saliency filters: contrast based filtering for salient region detection. In: Proceedings of the IEEE Conference on Computer Vision and Pattern Recognition, pp. 733–740 (2012)
21. Van Gemert, J.C.: Exploiting photographic style for category-level image classification by generalizing the spatial pyramid. In: Proceedings of the 1st ACM International Conference on Multimedia Retrieval, p. 14. ACM (2011)
22. Wang, L., et al.: Learning to detect salient objects with image-level supervision. In: Proceedings of the IEEE Conference on Computer Vision and Pattern Recognition, pp. 136–145 (2017)
23. Wang, L., Wang, L., Lu, H., Zhang, P., Ruan, X.: Saliency detection with recurrent fully convolutional networks. In: Leibe, B., Matas, J., Sebe, N., Welling, M. (eds.) ECCV 2016. LNCS, vol. 9908, pp. 825–841. Springer, Cham (2016). https://doi.org/10.1007/978-3-319-46493-0_50
24. Wang, T., Borji, A., Zhang, L., Zhang, P., Lu, H.: A stagewise refinement model for detecting salient objects in images. In: Proceedings of the IEEE Conference on Computer Vision and Pattern Recognition, pp. 4019–4028 (2017)
25. Welleck, S., Mao, J., Cho, K., Zhang, Z.: Saliency-based sequential image attention with multiset prediction. In: Advances in Neural Information Processing Systems, pp. 5173–5183 (2017)
26. Xu, K., et al.: Show, attend and tell: neural image caption generation with visual attention. In: International Conference on Machine Learning, pp. 2048–2057 (2015)
27. Yan, Q., Xu, L., Shi, J., Jia, J.: Hierarchical saliency detection. In: Proceedings of the IEEE Conference on Computer Vision and Pattern Recognition, pp. 1155–1162 (2013)
28. Yang, C., Zhang, L., Lu, H., Ruan, X., Yang, M.H.: Saliency detection via graph-based manifold ranking. In: Proceedings of the IEEE Conference on Computer Vision and Pattern Recognition, pp. 3166–3173 (2013)

29. Zhang, F., Du, B., Zhang, L.: Saliency-guided unsupervised feature learning for scene classification. IEEE Trans. Geosci. Remote Sens. **53**(4), 2175–2184 (2015)
30. Zhang, P., Wang, D., Lu, H., Wang, H., Ruan, X.: Amulet: aggregating multi-level convolutional features for salient object detection. In: Proceedings of the IEEE International Conference on Computer Vision (2017)
31. Zhang, P., Wang, D., Lu, H., Wang, H., Yin, B.: Learning uncertain convolutional features for accurate saliency detection. In: Proceedings of the IEEE International Conference on Computer Vision, pp. 212–221 (2017)
32. Zhang, X., Wang, T., Qi, J., Lu, H., Wang, G.: Progressive attention guided recurrent network for salient object detection. In: Proceedings of the IEEE Conference on Computer Vision and Pattern Recognition, pp. 714–722 (2018)
33. Zhao, H., Shi, J., Qi, X., Wang, X., Jia, J.: Pyramid scene parsing network. In: Proceedings of the IEEE Conference on Computer Vision and Pattern Recognition, pp. 2881–2890 (2017)
34. Zhao, R., Ouyang, W., Li, H., Wang, X.: Saliency detection by multi-context deep learning. In: Proceedings of the IEEE Conference on Computer Vision and Pattern Recognition, pp. 1265–1274 (2015)

MS-DRDNet: Optimization-Inspired Deep Compressive Sensing Network for MRI

Huihui Yue, Jichang Guo, and Xiangjun Yin[✉]

School of Electrical and Information Engineering, Tianjin University, Tianjin, China
{yuehuihui,jcguo,yinxiangjun}@tju.edu.cn

Abstract. Compressive Sensing (CS) is an effective technique for Magnetic Resonance Imaging (MRI) from a small amount of sampled data. With the aim of developing the current CS system to improve the accuracy of MRI, in this paper, we propose a novel deep CS network—Multi-scale Deep Residual Dense Network (MS-DRDNet), by combining the traditional model-based CS methods and data-driven deep learning methods. The MS-DRDNet consists of four components, *i.e.*, multi-scale convolutional difference network, sampling network, initial reconstruction network, and deep reconstruction network, which are optimized jointly. Specifically, the multi-scale convolutional difference network is exploited to capture sparse high-dimensional information of MRI. Then, these information is sent to the sampling network for compression with less measurements. Finally, the initial reconstruction network and the deep reconstruction network are employed to reconstruct MRI image accurately. Extensive CS experiments demonstrate that the proposed MS-DRDNet outperforms state-of-the-art iterative-based and deep learning-based CS methods in MRI image reconstruction accuracy.

Keywords: Multi-scale · Residual dense network · Compressive sensing · MRI

1 Introduction

MRI has become one of the popular techniques in clinical diagnosis and greatly promoted the progress of medicine, neurophysiology and cognitive neuroscience [1]. However, ensuring or even improving the accuracy of MRI is a serious challenge while reducing sampling data. CS is an effective method to meet this challenge [2]. CS first sample a small amount of data in sparse space (K-space), and then reconstruct the image by CS technology, which can fast yet accurate to reconstruct high-quality MRI images. Therefore, many researchers are devoted to CS reconstruction methods. For example, classical greedy methods (OMP [3], CoSaMP [4], SP [5], GOMP [6], etc), reconstruction methods based on ℓ_0-norm (SL0 [7], L2-SL0 [8], NSL0 [9], etc), and reconstruction methods based on ℓ_1-norm (ISTA [10], FISTA [11], ADMM [12], etc). These methods have achieved

© Springer Nature Switzerland AG 2020
Y. Peng et al. (Eds.): PRCV 2020, LNCS 12307, pp. 382–394, 2020.
https://doi.org/10.1007/978-3-030-60636-7_32

effective image reconstruction effect and can be applied well in MRI. However, the common problem of these methods is that they are not trivial to determine the optimal parameters and calculate the iterative optimization.

Based on this, CS-based neural networks began to emerge. For example, in DR^2-Net [13], a neural network is designed for linear mapping and reconstruction of images. Reference [14] proposed a deep ADMM-Net benefited from the ADMM iterative procedures for optimizing a general CS-MRI model. All these methods avoid to hand-adjusted parameters compare with traditional CS-MRI approaches, and achieve promising reconstruction effects. Therefore, the deep neural network indicates an important breakthrough in CS-MRI.

Inspired by these works, we propose a novel deep CS architecture, dubbed MS-DRDNet, to improve the accuracy of MRI. The main contributions are as follows:

- A multi-scale convolutional difference network is designed to realize K-space mapping and capture sparse high-dimensional information of MRI by employing the idea of multi-scale deep learning.
- Considering the Convolutional Neural Networks (CNN), a sampling network is built to obtain under-sampled measurements from K-space data by learning the measurement matrix. This sampling network can improve the flexibility of optimizing measurements while retaining more MRI image structure information.
- Motivated by ResNets [15] and DenseNet [16], an initial reconstruction network and a deep reconstruction network are designed for MRI implementation. The initial reconstruction network firstly helps to generate coarse MRI image as input of the deep reconstruction network, and then the deep reconstruction network contributes to furnishing finer image details. Therefore, this process can well improve the accuracy of MRI image reconstruction and obtain high-quality MRI images.

The rest of this paper is organized as follows. The related works, such as CS, multi-scale deep learning, ResNet, and DenseNet, are reviewed in Sect. 2. Section 3 introduces the proposed MS-DRDNet framework and its details (the multi-scale convolutional difference network, the sampling network, the initial reconstruction network, and the deep reconstruction network). In Sect. 4, the training of the proposed MS-DRDNet are illustrated. The performance of the MS-DRDNet in MRI image reconstruction is verified through simulation experiments in Sect. 5. Section 6 concludes this paper.

2   Related Work

This work involves CS, multi-scale deep learning, and ResNets and DenseNet. In what follows, we give a brief review of these three aspects.

CS. The key of CS is to reconstruct original sparse signal x by the given undersampled measurements y, that is, to solve $y = \Phi x$ with supposed $\{y, \Phi\}$, where

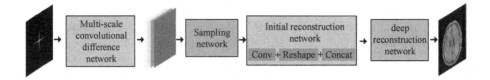

Fig. 1. The framework of the MS-DRDNet.

$y \in \mathbb{R}^M$ is the measurements, $x \in \mathbb{R}^N$ is the original signal in sparse space, and $\Phi \in \mathbb{R}^{M \times N}$ is the measurement matrix, $M \ll N$. References [3–12] show classical CS methods. Although these methods can achieve the goal of reconstructing x, they all have the problems of high calculation cost and difficult parameter optimization. [17,18] introduces deep learning into CS to avoid the above problems while ensuring the reconstruction effect.

Multi-scale Deep Learning. Deep learning has been widely used in the fields of computer vision, image super-resolution, etc. In recent years, deep learning has also been gradually applied to CS. For example, in [19], a deep learning-based network is proposed inspired by the idea of CS. The same deep architecture is also employed in references [20], and [20] shows that the low-frequency components can be captured more than the high-frequency ones by enforcing the multi-scale scheme, thus the reconstruction quality may be improved. Therefore, references [20] adopts multi-scale strategy to decompose the original image in its deep network, and obtains effective recovery performance. Moreover, the multi-scale scheme also employed in [21] to promote the performance of deep learning network.

ResNets and DenseNet. The key of the deep ResNets [15] is to introduce identity shortcut connections in CNN to directly pass the data of one layer to the next, thus effectively avoiding the difficulty of CNN training. Therefore, the ResNets can be used to promote the quality as well as speed of deep network learning. Based on this, the DenseNet [16], which connects each layer to every other layer in a feed-forward fashion, further strengthens feature propagation than ResNets.

3   Proposed MS-DRDNet for MRI

Based on the related work, we propose a novel MS-DRDNet for MRI, as shown in Fig. 1. It contains four tasks: the multi-scale convolutional difference network, the sampling network, the initial reconstruction network, and the deep reconstruction network.

3.1   Multi-scale Convolutional Difference Network

Multi-scale network is first committed to smoothing an original MRI image to different degrees by multi-scale Gaussian filters, and then Different of Gaussian

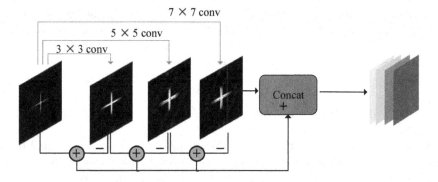

Fig. 2. Multi-scale convolutional difference network.

(DoG) between different layers is calculated [20]. Given original image x, the DoG results can be expressed as:

$$x_i = \begin{cases} x - x \otimes K_1 & if\ i = 1 \\ x \otimes K_{i-1} - x \otimes K_i & if\ i = 2, \dots m-1 \\ x \otimes K_i & if\ i = m \end{cases} \quad (1)$$

where x_i is the DoG image of decomposition level i, $i = 1, \cdots m$, $\otimes$ represents a convolution operator, K_i denotes filter (Gaussian convolution kernel) at the scale i.

In this Multi-scale network, the multi-scale Gaussian filters are implemented by different convolution kernel of sizes 3×3, 5×5, and 7×7, and then the DoG are calculated between two nearby layers. In particular, the last scale of DoG is the smoothed layers with the highest level of Gaussian filtering. The multi-scale convolutional difference network is shown in Fig. 2.

3.2 Sampling Network

The sampling network is designed to obtain under-sampled measurements as in CS. In the sampling network, the input is first divided into non-overlapping blocks with a size of $B \times B \times k$ [19], and then each of these blocks is convolved with n_f filters of size $B \times B \times k$. In fact, this process is consistent with linear mapping data in CS. Specifically, consider each block as a vector x of size kB^2, and then filter each block with $\Phi_f \in \mathbb{R}^{n_f \times kB^2}$ to obtain a compressed vector y of size n_f, that is, $y = \Phi_f x$, where $n_f = \frac{M}{N} \times kB^2$. Therefore, task of obtaining under-sampled data in CS can be realized by the sampling network, and the n_f filters used in this network also can be learned during the training process.

3.3 Initial Reconstruction Network

The initial reconstruction network aims to obtain original MRI image from compressed one. Specifically, given the compressed block y, the initial reconstruction network aims to approximate the original block x by solving the inverse process of $y = \Phi_f x$, that is, $\hat{x} = \Phi_f^\dagger y$, where $\Phi_f^\dagger \in \mathbb{R}^{kB^2 \times n_f}$, $\hat{x}$ is the initial reconstruction results of x. Therefore, each block x can be reconstructed by convolving y with kB^2 filters of size n_f. This operation can be expressed as

$$\hat{x} = P(y) \tag{2}$$

where $P(\cdot)$ denotes filtering for reconstruction in the initial reconstruction network.

It should be noted that there are still some errors between the original block x and the $\hat{x}$ obtained by the initial reconstruction network, so we further use the deep reconstruction network to improve the accuracy of image recovery.

3.4 Deep Reconstruction Network

To further promote the performance of image reconstruction, the idea of ResNets and DenseNet are employed to the deep reconstruction network. This deep reconstruction network can be expressed as an operator $R(\hat{x})$, and we can get the final result

$$\tilde{x} = R(\hat{x}) = \hat{x} + Q(\hat{x}) \tag{3}$$

where the $Q(\hat{x})$ denotes the deep reconstruction network without shortcut connections. Specifically, this network can be briefly described as three operations: dense block, transition layer, and shortcut connection. The dense block benefits from DenseNet, that is, the input of each layer is the feature-maps (*i.e.*, output) of all preceding layers, and the feature-maps of each layer is also the input of all subsequent layers. Therefore, each layer in the dense block has directly connection with all subsequent layers, which greatly improves the information flow. Specifically, for l-th layer we can get:

$$x_l = H_l([x_0, x_1, \cdots, x_{l-1}]) \tag{4}$$

where x_l is the feature-maps of the l-th layer, $[x_0, x_1, \cdots, x_{l-1}]$ is the concatenation of the feature-maps of layers $0, 1, l-1$ (x_0 is obtained from the $\hat{x}$ output by the initial reconstruction network), and $H_l(\cdot)$ is the operator of l-th layer, which is defined as batch normalization (BN)-rectified linear unit (ReLU)-convolution (Conv, 1×1)-BN-ReLU-Conv (3×3).

The transition layer is connected by several convolution operators. The goal of the transition layer is to change the number of feature-maps output by the dense block so as to facilitate the following shortcut connection, that is, the number of feature-maps of the transition layer is the same as the dimensions of the followed dense block input. In fact, the operations of the dense block and the transition layer correspond to $Q(\hat{x})$.

The shortcut connection is employed to promote the training of the deep reconstruction network by turning this network into its counterpart residual version [15]. In fact, the shortcut connection concatenate the input and output of $Q(\hat{x})$ directly. Based on these, the framework of the deep reconstruction network is shown in Fig. 3.

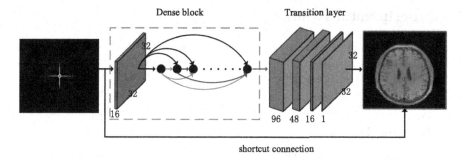

Fig. 3. Deep reconstruction network.

4   MS-DRDNet Training

As introduced above, the proposed MS-DRDNet for MRI includes four operators: the multi-scale convolutional difference network, the sampling network, the initial reconstruction network, and the deep reconstruction network. Given the input MRI image x, it is first mapped to sparse space through the multi-scale convolutional difference network, then the sparse image is transferred to the sampling network to obtain the CS measurements y, and then the x can be accurately reconstructed from y by using the initial reconstruction network and deep reconstruction network. It should be noted that since the output of each operator is the input of the next operator, the MS-DRDNet can be trained end-to-end. Therefore, the input and label of the MS-DRDNet are both MRI image x.

The MS-DRDNet is trained with adaptive moment estimation (Adam) [21] according to the loss function in Eqs. (5) and (6), where the former loss function is used to minimize the initial reconstructed error and the latter is used to minimize the final reconstructed error over all training samples.

$$L1 = \frac{1}{n} \sum_{i=1}^{n} \|x_i - P\left(\Phi_f x_i\right)\|_2^2 \tag{5}$$

$$L2 = \frac{1}{n} \sum_{i=1}^{n} \|x_i - \tilde{x}_i\|_2^2$$
$$= \frac{1}{n} \sum_{i=1}^{n} \|x_i - R\left(P\left(\Phi_f x_i\right)\right)\|_2^2 \tag{6}$$

where n is the number of training samples, and x_i represent the i-th training sample. By optimizing the above two loss functions, the MS-DRDNet is trained to reconstruct MRI images more and more accurately. What's more, it should be noted that although the four operators in the MS-DRDNet are jointly optimized, they can all be used independently.

5   Experimental Results

In this section, we demonstrate the effectiveness of MS-DRDNet in MRI image reconstruction via a series of experiments, and compare it with the state-of-the-art methods. The numerical simulation platform is MATLAB 2017a, the operation system is Windows 7.

5.1   Training Details

Our experiments uses the BSDS500 dataset to generate training data, which is the same as the dataset in [19]. The size of the input training image is 32×32, and then it is decomposed into 4 layers with different smoothness through multi-scale convolutional difference network to connect, that is, $B = 32$, $k = 4$. Then, there are $n_f = \frac{M}{N} \times kB^2$ fliters with $M/N = [0.2, 0.4, 0.6]$ to obtain the measurements. After that, the initial reconstruction network uses B^2 filters to reconstruct the original image. Finally, in the deep reconstruction network for improving image performance, we set the parameter as $L = 16$, $h = 12$, where L is the layers of dense block, h is the number of feature-maps in each layer, and other parameters are shown in Fig. 3. The proposed MS-DRDNet is trained 80 times end-to-end.

After training, we test the performance of the MS-DRDNet in MRI image recovery. Specifically, we show PSNR and SSIM of MRI images reconstructed by the MS-DRDNet, and compare with the reconstruction results of other state-of-the-art approaches.

5.2   Comparison in MRI

We compare the performance of the MS-DRDNet with other traditional iterative-based CS approaches (OMP, ISTA, FISTA, AMP) and advanced deep learning-based approach (CSNet$^+$ [19]) in MRI image reconstruction. The results of these methods on MRI image reconstruction at different M/N ($M/N = [0.2, 0.4, 0.6]$) is as follows.

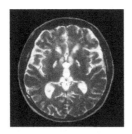 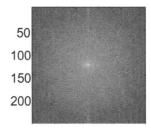

Fig. 4. Original MRI image, left is in time domain, right is in frequency domain.

Figure 4 shows the original MRI image, Figs. 5, 6, and 7 show the vivid reconstruction results at $M/N = [0.2, 0.4, 0.6]$, respectively. From these figures, it

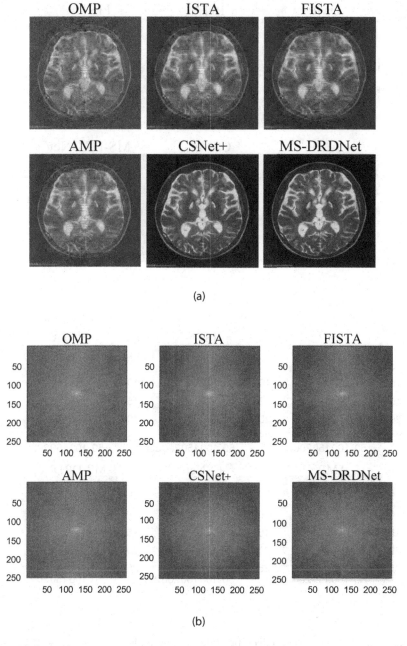

Fig. 5. MRI image recovery effect by different methods in the case of $M/N = 0.2$ (a) Time domain (b) Frequency domain.

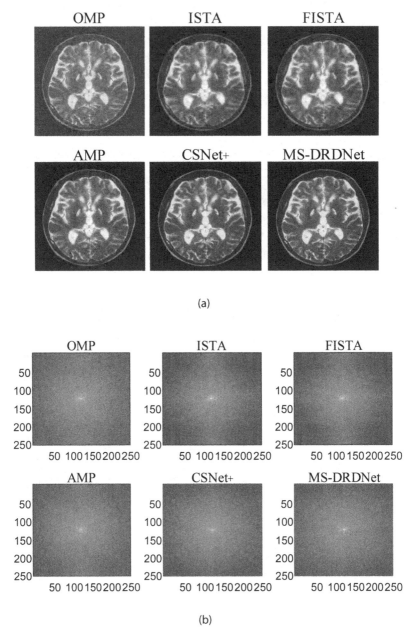

Fig. 6. MRI image recovery effect by different methods in the case of $M/N = 0.4$ (a) Time domain (b) Frequency domain.

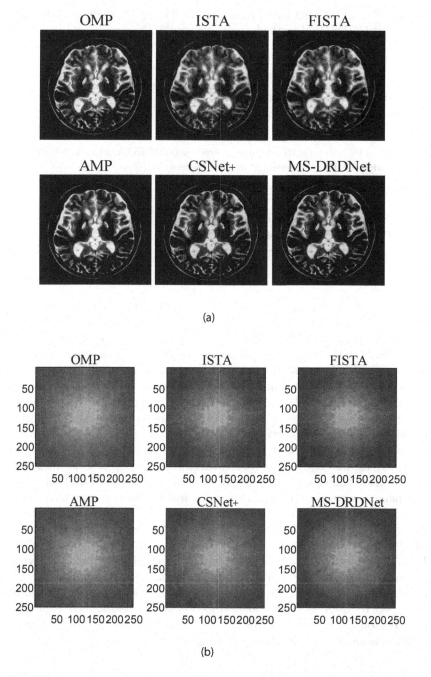

Fig. 7. MRI image recovery effect by different methods in the case of $M/N = 0.6$ (a) Time domain (b) Frequency domain.

Table 1. PSNR of the MRI image recovered by OMP, ISTA, FISTA, AMP, CSNet$^+$, and proposed MS-DRDNet methods under different M/N.

M/N	OMP	ISTA	FISTA	AMP	CSNet$^+$	MS-DRDNet (ours)
0.2	20.67	22.18	22.18	22.77	33.27	**34.22**
0.4	28.48	26.27	26.27	30.67	39.78	**40.70**
0.6	34.18	27.23	27.23	37.31	42.14	**43.49**

Table 2. SSIM (%) of the MRI image recovered by OMP, ISTA, FISTA, AMP, CSNet$^+$, and proposed MS-DRDNet methods under different M/N.

M/N	OMP	ISTA	FISTA	AMP	CSNet$^+$	MS-DRDNet (ours)
0.2	50.71	57.84	57.84	59.77	95.28	**96.97**
0.4	78.89	74.91	74.91	86.43	98.72	**99.19**
0.6	90.66	77.67	77.67	95.45	99.08	**99.31**

can be seen that under any same M/N, the proposed MS-DRDNet can restore MRI image more clearly and with more obvious details than the traditional iterative-based OMP, ISTA, FISTA, AMP methods or advanced deep learning-based CSNet$^+$. Meanwhile, the proposed MS-DRDNet can gather more high-dimensional information and display more low-dimensional information in the corresponding frequency domain. Moreover, the image quality recovered by these algorithms is improved with the increase of M/N, but the MS-DRDNet proposed in this paper always performs best. Therefore, the proposed MS-DRDNet outperforms the traditional iterative-based OMP, ISTA, FISTA, AMP methods and advanced deep learning-based CSNet$^+$.

Further, Tables 1 and 2 show the details of MRI image reconstruction by these methods. From these two tables, it can be seen that the MS-DRDNet proposed in this paper performs better than the other five methods at any M/N, which is consistent with the results shown in Figs. 5, 6, and 7. Compared with the best iterative-based method, i.e. AMP, the MS-DRDNet can improve approximately 11.45 dB, 10.03 dB, and 6.18 dB on PSNR and 0.3720, 0.1276, and 0.0386 on SSIM with respect to $M/N = [0.2, 0.4, 0.6]$, respectively. Compared with the deep learning-based CSNet$^+$, the MS-DRDNet can improve approximately 0.95 dB, 0.92 dB, and 1.35 dB on PSNR and 0.0169, 0.0047, and 0.0023 on SSIM with respect to $M/N = [0.2, 0.4, 0.6]$, respectively. Therefore, these experimental results demonstrate that the MS-DRDNet can reconstruct MRI image more accurately than other state-of-the-art approaches.

6 Conclusions

In this paper, we propose a novel MS-DRDNet for MRI images reconstruction. The MS-DRDNet is connected by four operators: the multi-scale convolutional difference network, the sampling network, the initial reconstruction network, and the deep reconstruction network. Inspired by the idea of CS, the MS-DRDNet composed of these four operators can adaptively map MRI images to sparse space and accurately reconstruct MRI images with fewer measurements. The experimental results show that the MS-DRDNet performs better in MRI image reconstruction accuracy than either the traditional iterative-based or deep learning-based methods. In the future, this MS-DRDNet can also be tried out for other applications.

References

1. Chen, Z., Fu, Y., Xiang, Y., Rong, R.: A novel iterative shrinkage algorithm for CS-MRI via adaptive regularization. IEEE Signal Process. Lett. **PP**(99), 1 (2017)
2. Rajani, S.-R., Reddy, M.-R.: An iterative hard thresholding algorithm for CS MRI. In: Proceedings of SPIE-The International Society for Optical Engineering, vol. 8314, p. 132 (2012)
3. Tropp, J.-A., Gilbert, A.-C.: Signal recovery from random measurements via orthogonal matching pursuit. IEEE Trans. Inf. Theory **53**(12), 4655–4666 (2007)
4. Needell, D., Tropp, J.-A.: CoSaMP: iterative signal recovery from incomplete and inaccurate samples. Appl. Comput. Harmonic Anal. **26**(3), 301–321 (2009)
5. Dai, W., Milenkovic, O.: Subspace pursuit for compressive sensing signal reconstruction. IEEE Trans. Inf. Theory **55**(5), 2230–2249 (2009)
6. Jian, W., Seokbeop, K., Byonghyo, S.: Generalized orthogonal matching pursuit. IEEE Trans. Signal Process. **60**(12), 6202–6216 (2012)
7. Xiao, J., Del-Blanco, C.-R., Cuevas, C., García, N.: Fast image decoding for block compressed sensing based encoding by using a modified smooth ℓ_0-norm. In: IEEE International Conference on Consumer Electronics, pp. 234–236 (2016)
8. Soussen, C., Idier, J., Duan, J., Brie, D.: Homotopy based algorithms for ℓ_0-regularized least squares. IEEE Trans. Signal Process. **63**(13), 3301–3316 (2015)
9. Zhao, R., Lin, W., Hao, L., Shaohai, A.-H.: Reconstruction algorithm for compressive sensing based on smoothed ℓ_0-norm and revised newton method. J. Comput. Aided Des. Comput. Graph. **24**(4), 478–484 (2012)
10. Daubechies, I., Defrise, M., Mol, C.-D.: Sparsity-enforcing regularisation and ISTA revisited. Inverse Prob. **32**(10), 104001 (2016)
11. Zibetti, M.-V.-W., Helou, E.-S., Regatte, R.-R., Herman, G.-T.: Monotone FISTA with variable acceleration for compressed sensing magnetic resonance imaging. Comput. Imaging IEEE Trans. **5**(1), 109–119 (2019)
12. Zha, Z., Zhang, X., Wu, Y., Wang, Q., Liu, X., Tang, L.: Non-convex weighted ℓp nuclear norm based ADMM framework for image restoration. Neurocomputing **311**(15), 209–224 (2018)
13. Yao, H., Dai, F., Zhang, S., Zhang, Y., Tian, Q., Xu, C.: DR^2-Net: deep residual reconstruction network for image compressive sensing. Neurocomputing **359**, 483–493 (2019)
14. Yan, Y., Huibin, L., Zongben, X., Jian, S.: Deep ADMM-Net for compressive sensing MRI. In: Advances in Neural Information Processing Systems (2016)
15. He, K., Zhang, X., Ren, S., Sun, J.: Deep residual learning for image recognition. In: IEEE Conference on Computer Vision and Pattern Recognition (CVPR) (2016)

16. Huang, G., Liu, Z., Maaten, L.-V.-D., Weinberger, K.-Q.: Densely connected convolutional networks. In: IEEE Conference on Computer Vision and Pattern Recognition (CVPR), pp. 2261–2269, Honolulu (2017)
17. Pokala, P.-K., Mahurkar, A.-G., Seelamantula, C.-S.: FirmNet: a sparsity amplified deep network for solving linear inverse problems. In: IEEE International Conference on Acoustics, Speech and Signal Processing (ICASSP), pp. 2982–2986 (2019)
18. Wei, Y., Zhao, M.-M., Zhao, M., Lei, M., Yu, Q.: An AMP-based Network with Deep Residual Learning for mmWave beamspace channel estimation. IEEE Wirel. Commun. Lett. **8**(4), 1289–1292 (2019)
19. Shi, W., Jiang, F., Liu, S., Zhao, D.: Image compressed sensing using convolutional neural network. IEEE Trans. Image Process. **29**, 375–388 (2019)
20. Canh, T.-N., Jeon, B.: Difference of convolution for deep compressive sensing. In: IEEE International Conference on Image Processing (ICIP), pp. 2105–2109 (2019)
21. Canh, T.-N., Jeon, B.: Multi-scale deep compressive sensing network. In: Proceedings IEEE International Conference Visual Communications and Image Process (VCIP) (2018)

Canonical Correlation Cross-Domain Alignment for Unsupervised Domain Adaptation

Desheng Li[1], Wenjing Wang[1], and Yuwu Lu[1,2,3(✉)]

[1] College of Computer Science and Software Engineering, Shenzhen University,
Shenzhen, China
`luyuwu2018@szu.edu.cn`
[2] Laboratory of Intelligent Information Processing, Shenzhen, China
[3] Guangdong Laboratory of Artificial Intelligence and Digital Economy,
Shenzhen, China

Abstract. Domain adaptation has been widely used in the field of computer vision. Current methods of domain adaptation mainly aim to reduce the difference of the marginal and conditional distributions of the source and target domains in a centralized manner. However, most of the existing domain adaptation methods ignore the correlation information of the two domains, or doesn't take it very seriously. That making it difficult to learn related features from the source domain for the target task. A new method, canonical correlation cross-domain alignment (CCCA), is proposed to effectively reduce the cross-domain distribution difference by combining the least squares formula of CCA with domain adaptation. In CCCA, a common latent subspace with the maximum correlation is learned to ensure that the learned features are from the two domains with maximum correlation. A Laplace graph is learned to maintain the structural consistency of CCCA. To verify the performance of our method, we conduct experiments on several benchmark visual databases. The experimental results illustrate its superiority to several other methods.

Keywords: Domain adaptation · Cross-domain · Subspace learning · Canonical correlation analysis

1 Introduction

Most conventional algorithms [2,9] for image processing and classification demand that the training and testing data are independent and identically distributed, a demand that goes unfulfilled in real applications. Test data and training data are often generated under different conditions, hence they have different distributions. For example, in facial recognition, the training samples are infrared images, but the test samples may be images from a real camera. Thus some traditional classifiers have difficulty performing such tasks. Many

© Springer Nature Switzerland AG 2020
Y. Peng et al. (Eds.): PRCV 2020, LNCS 12307, pp. 395–406, 2020.
https://doi.org/10.1007/978-3-030-60636-7_33

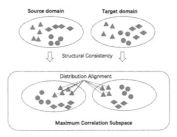

Fig. 1. The idea of canonical correlation cross-domain alignment for unsupervised domain adaptation

domain adaptive methods [11,15,22] have been proposed overcome such problems. Such methods use the source domain data with label information to help the classifier obtain more useful information for the target task.

Based on whether the target domain label is available. Domain adaptation methods mainly can be divided into semi-supervised domain adaptation (SDA) and unsupervised domain adaptation (UDA). In this paper, we focus on UDA. Many UDA methods have been proposed [3,12,15]. Transfer component analysis (TCA) [15] minimizes the maximum mean discrepancy (MMD) distance between the source and target domains based on data mapping theory. Transfer joint matching (TJM) [12] uses the idea of feature selection to enhance robustness. Subspace alignment (SA) [3] through subspace alignment and geodesic flow kernel (GFK) [6] based on manifold learning for UDA. These methods reduce the distribution difference between data domains, but they do not consider the correlations between them.

In this paper, we propose a novel unsupervised domain adaptation method. We are committed to studying how to effectively use the common featrues of cross-domain data. We hope to narrow the data distribution distance between them by maximizing correlation. Inspired by the least squares equation of canonical correlation analysis (CCA) [19], we hope that the data of the source and target domains are projected to a common latent subspace with maximum correlation. To enhance the correlation between the learned features from the source and target domains, we propose a simple and effective unsupervised domain adaptation method, canonical correlation cross-domain alignment (CCCA), for unsupervised domain adaptation. In CCCA, we obtain the maximum correlation by projecting data from the source and target domains into a common feature space. We use the Laplacian matrix of the data to keep the manifold structure. We learn a knowledge matrix to perform the transfer learning task. Our ideas are intuitively reflected in Fig. 1. Our contributions in this paper can be summarized as follows:

- We propose a novel unsupervised domain adaptation method named CCCA, which performs domain adaptation by learning a public latent space with maximum correlation between the source and target domains.

- By introducing two regular matrices, our method solves the imbalance problem of the number of samples in the least squares equation of CCA.
- Proved by expensive experiments that CCCA provides a simple and efficient way to overcome domain shift between cross-domain data.

2   Related Work

2.1   Unsupervised Domain Adaptation

The most idea of UDA [16] is to get a new map to align the distribution of domains. Therefore, UDA methods can effectively use the source domain with labeled information to help analyze the data of the unlabeled target domain. For example, when we use k-nearest neighbor (KNN) or support vector machine (SVM) classifiers to classify unlabeled data, we find that differences in data distributions hinder classifiers in learning category information corresponding to feature distributions. As a result, the classifier cannot attain good accuracy. To solve this problem, domain adaptation methods are proposed to map data from the source and target domains to the same feature space, and then we use various metrics to quantify the distance between the source and target domains [5]. By minimizing the distribution distance to make source and target domains closest in the feature space, TCA [15] uses MMD to measure the difference distribution between the two domains, and it achieves good results by minimizing the MMD distance. MMD has since been widely used in the construction of UDA models, e.g., [1,7]. Joint distribution analysis (JDA) [11] adds conditional distribution matching on the basis of a TCA marginal distribution to achieve joint matching of data distribution. JDA makes the domain adaptation method more stable, and is a classic method in domain adaptation. Balanced distribution adaptation (BDA) [20] adjusts weighting of the conditional and marginal distributions of data to further optimize the distribution. JGSA [23] encodes geometric embedding to reduce data distribution matching, so that the geometric structure information of the data can be retained. Other UDA methods, e.g. manifold learning in UDA is a hot research topic. There are also many excellent methods, such as [6,22]. Some methods to domain adaptation, such as coral [18], align the second-order statistics of the data for domain adaptation. Our approach differs from this in that our approach directly learns a data space with the maximum correlation via mapping. So our method is more easily combined with other subspace learning domain adaptation methods.

2.2   Canonical Correlation Analysis

CCA is widely used in machine learning for correlation analysis of multiple datasets. By finding a pair of projection matrices w_x and w_y, the maximum correlation coefficient of the data can be obtained in a low-dimensional space. CCA can obtain relevant feature information in two datasets, X and Y, and can be formulated as:

$$max_{w_x,w_y} \ w_x^\top \mathbf{X}\mathbf{Y}^\top w_y$$

$$s.t. \ w_x^\top \mathbf{X}\mathbf{X}^\top w_x = 1.$$
$$w_y^\top \mathbf{Y}\mathbf{Y}^\top w_y = 1. \tag{1}$$

3   Canonical Correlation Cross-Domain Alignment

3.1   Notations

Frequently used notation is displayed in Table 1.

Table 1. Frequently used notation.

Notation	Description	Notation	Description
D_s/D_t	Source/target domains	$\mathbf{X}_s/\mathbf{X}_t$	Source/target domain data
n_s/n_t	Source/targetexamples	$\mathbf{X}$	Original data matrix
m	Original features	$\mathbf{P}$	Projected matrix
d	Projected features	$\mathbf{Z}$	Knowledge matrix
$\mathbf{K}_1/\mathbf{K}_2$	Expansion matrix	$\mathbf{L}$	Laplacian matrix
μ	Regularization parameter	β	Regularization parameter

We have the labeled source domain $D_s = \{(x_s, y_s)\}_{i=1}^{n_s} = \{\mathbf{X}_s, y_x\}$ and unlabeled target domain $D_t = \{x_t\}_{j=1}^{n_t} = \{\mathbf{X}_t\}$, where y_s is the label of the source domain data, and n_s and n_t are respective the numbers of source and target domain samples. We assume that $P(\mathbf{X}_s) \neq P(\mathbf{X}_t)$ and $Q(y_s|\mathbf{X}_s) \neq Q(y_t|\mathbf{X}_t)$. That is, the marginal and conditional distributions of the source and target domains are different.

3.2   Proposed Method

CCA can effectively extract the most relevant features between two sets of data. Based on this idea, we introduce CCA to the domain adaptation problem to maximize the correlations between the source and target domains, thereby reducing the differences between them. In order to make CCA more suitable to process domain adaptive tasks, our method is different from the CCA of the least square equation. Based on homogeneous domain adaptation, we simplify the two projection matrices of CCA into one projection matrix to learn the common features of the source and target domains, and we find a common subspace with the greatest correlation between the source and target domains. In CCCA, we utilize CCA regularization to maximize the correlations between the source and target domains, which can be expressed as:

$$\left\| \mathbf{P}^\top \mathbf{X}_s - \mathbf{P}^\top \mathbf{X}_t \right\|_F^2 \tag{2}$$

where $\mathbf{X}_s \in \mathbb{R}^{m \times n_s}$ and $\mathbf{X}_t \in \mathbb{R}^{m \times n_t}$. However, the number of training samples in CCA regularization must be equal, i.e., $n_s = n_t$. The severe imbalance of the number of samples in the source and target domains is a key issue requiring solution in domain adaptation. To alleviate this problem, we extend the alignment of the mapping data by introducing matrices $\mathbf{K}_1$ and $\mathbf{K}_2$, where $\mathbf{K}_1 \in \mathbb{R}^{n_s \times (n_s + n_t)}$ and $\mathbf{K}_2 \in \mathbb{R}^{n_t \times (n_s + n_t)}$. For clarity, we define $\mathbf{I}_n$ as an $n \times n$ identity matrix, and $\mathbf{0}_{m \times n}$ as an $m \times n$ matrix of all zeros. Then we can express $\mathbf{K}_1$ and $\mathbf{K}_2$ as :

$$\mathbf{K}_1 = [\mathbf{I}_{n_s}, \mathbf{0}_{n_s \times n_t}] \tag{3}$$

$$\mathbf{K}_2 = [\mathbf{I}_{n_t}, \mathbf{0}_{n_t \times n_s}], \tag{4}$$

and Eq. (2) can be rewritten as:

$$\left\| \mathbf{P}^\top \mathbf{X}_s \mathbf{K}_1 - \mathbf{P}^\top \mathbf{X}_t \mathbf{K}_2 \right\|_F^2 . \tag{5}$$

By introducing $\mathbf{K}_1$ and $\mathbf{K}_2$, we overcome the limitation of the number of training samples between two domains while preserving the structure of the original data as much as possible. We also introduce the perspective of structural consistency in manifold learning to preserve the local consistency of the original features, so samples of the same category are closer to each other in terms of data distribution. That is, there is structural consistency between labels and data distributions in the same sample. To preserve the structural consistency, we minimize:

$$\sum_{ij} \left\| z_i - z_j \right\|^2 \mathbf{W}_{ij} = \sum_{ij} \left\| \mathbf{P}^\top x_i - \mathbf{P}^\top x_j \right\|^2 \mathbf{W}_{ij}$$
$$= tr(\mathbf{P}^\top \mathbf{X} \mathbf{L} \mathbf{X}^\top \mathbf{P}), \tag{6}$$

where $\mathbf{X} = [\mathbf{X_s}, \mathbf{X}_t]$ is the original data matrix, z_i is the feature representation of x_i in the new latent subspace, and $\mathbf{L} = \mathbf{D} - \mathbf{W}$ is a Laplacian matrix. We use the symmetric adjacency matrix $\mathbf{W}$ to represent the distance relationship between samples. We compute

$$\mathbf{W}_{ij} = \begin{cases} cosine(x_i, x_j), & if \ x_i \in N_k(x_j) \\ 0, & otherwise \end{cases}, \tag{7}$$

where $N_k(x_j)$ is the k nearest neighbors of x_j. $\mathbf{D}$ is a diagonal matrix and $\mathbf{D}_{ii} = \sum_j \mathbf{W}_{ij}$. Therefore, by minimizing (6), the projected data maintain the local structure of the original data as much as possible.

3.3 Problem Optimization

In CCCA, we first use the regular term of CCA to maximize the correlation between the source and target domains. We hope to introduce the idea of structural consistency to protect the local information of the data. It can also prove

---

Algorithm 1. CCCA

Input: Data: $\mathbf{X}_s$, $\mathbf{X}_t$; Parameters: μ, β ; Dimension d.
Output: Project matrix $\mathbf{P}$, knowledge matrix $\mathbf{Z}$.
1: Compute Laplacian matrix $\mathbf{L}$.
2: Compute the smallest eigenvectors by equation (10).
3: Compute the knowledge matrix $\mathbf{Z} = \mathbf{P}^\top \mathbf{X}$.

---

the usability of our method. We combine Eqs. (5) and (6) to difine the objective function of CCCA as:

$$\min_{\mathbf{P}} \left\| \mathbf{P}^\top \mathbf{X}_s \mathbf{K_1} - \mathbf{P}^\top \mathbf{X}_t \mathbf{K_2} \right\|_F^2 + \beta tr(\mathbf{P}^\top \mathbf{XLX}^\top \mathbf{P}) + \mu \left\| \mathbf{P} \right\|_F^2$$
$$s.t. \ \mathbf{P}^\top \mathbf{X}_s \mathbf{X}_s^\top \mathbf{P} = \mathbf{I}, \ \mathbf{P}^\top \mathbf{X}_t \mathbf{X}_t^\top \mathbf{P} = \mathbf{I},$$

(8)

where β and μ are positive parameters. The constraints $\mathbf{P}^\top \mathbf{X}_t \mathbf{X}_t^\top \mathbf{P} = \mathbf{I}$ and $\mathbf{P}^\top \mathbf{X}_s \mathbf{X}_s^\top \mathbf{P} = \mathbf{I}$ is retained to avoid trivial solutions from the least squares formula of CCA. It is notable that Eq. (8) are a nonlinear optimization problem. Hence we use the Lagrangian multiplier method to solve it, as follows:

$$L(\mathbf{P}, \boldsymbol{\Theta}) = tr(\mathbf{P}^\top (\mathbf{X}_s \mathbf{K_1} \mathbf{K_1}^\top \mathbf{X}_s^\top - \mathbf{X}_s \mathbf{K_1} \mathbf{K_2}^\top \mathbf{X}_t^\top$$
$$- \mathbf{X}_t \mathbf{K_2} \mathbf{K_1}^\top \mathbf{X}_s^\top + \mathbf{X}_t \mathbf{K_2} \mathbf{K_2}^\top \mathbf{X}_t^\top + \beta \mathbf{XLX}^\top + \mu \mathbf{I}_m) \mathbf{P})$$
$$+ tr((\mathbf{I} - \mathbf{P}^\top \mathbf{X}_s \mathbf{X}_s^\top \mathbf{P} + \mathbf{I} - \mathbf{P}^\top \mathbf{X}_t \mathbf{X}_t^\top \mathbf{P}) \boldsymbol{\Theta}),$$

(9)

where $\boldsymbol{\Theta} = \text{diag}(\theta_1, \theta_2, \cdots, \theta_d\} \in \mathbb{R}^{m \times m}$ is the Lagrange multiplier. We set $\frac{\partial L(\mathbf{P}, \boldsymbol{\Theta})}{\partial \mathbf{P}} = 0$ to obtain:

$$(\mathbf{X}_s \mathbf{K_1} \mathbf{K_1}^\top \mathbf{X}_s^\top - \mathbf{X}_s \mathbf{K_1} \mathbf{K_2}^\top \mathbf{X}_t^\top - \mathbf{X}_t \mathbf{K_2} \mathbf{K_1}^\top \mathbf{X}_s^\top$$
$$+ \mathbf{X}_t \mathbf{K_2} \mathbf{K_2}^\top \mathbf{X}_t^\top + \beta \mathbf{XLX}^\top + \mu \mathbf{I}_m) \mathbf{P} = (\mathbf{X}_s \mathbf{X}_s^\top + \mathbf{X}_t \mathbf{X}_t^\top) \mathbf{P} \boldsymbol{\Theta}.$$

(10)

We can easily obtain P by computing the d-smallest eigenvectors of Eq. (10). The calculation can be performed as in Algorithm 1.

4   Experimental Results

We performed extensive experiments to verify the performance of CCCA. We chose some advanced methods for comparison, including nearest neighbor (NN), TCA [15], SA [3], GFK [6], JDA [11], TJM [12], BDA [20], ResNet50, JGSA [23], domain adversarial neural network (DANN) [4], domain invariant and class discriminative feature learning (DICD) [10], and joint adaptation network (JAN) [13]. For CCCA, we set μ in the range of 0.1–1000 to control the weight of CCA regular terms, and set β in the range of 1–1000 to control the weight of structure consistency. The parameters of other methods were set as reported in their original papers. It is worth noting that all of the experiments were unsupervised domain adaptation experiments, i.e., the target domain was unlabeled data.

Table 2. Accuracy (%) on CMU pie dataset.

Source	Target	TCA	SA	GFK	JDA	TJM	BDA	JGSA	CCCA
C05	C07	40.76	35.54	26.15	**58.81**	34.81	54.70	52.73	57.21
	C09	41.79	46.38	27.27	54.23	44.36	57.41	51.84	**58.46**
	C27	59.63	63.62	31.15	84.50	60.74	82.82	73.72	**98.85**
	C29	29.35	39.58	17.59	49.75	34.93	40.13	52.39	46.59
C07	C05	41.81	44.24	25.24	57.62	38.75	57.56	**64.26**	49.37
	C09	51.47	44.06	47.37	62.93	49.82	54.60	58.88	**99.82**
	C27	64.73	66.45	54.25	75.82	63.41	76.15	70.71	**76.62**
	C29	33.70	35.48	27.08	39.89	35.23	34.38	49.02	**99.82**
C09	C05	34.69	51.80	21.82	50.96	43.04	44.72	**64.89**	54.59
	C07	47.70	46.41	43.16	57.95	38.74	55.25	59.91	**96.13**
	C27	56.23	68.76	46.41	68.45	65.33	74.98	72.63	**75.04**
	C29	33.15	45.22	26.78	39.95	41.12	40.56	57.72	**100.00**
C27	C05	55.64	69.57	34.24	80.58	63.39	81.81	74.73	**99.01**
	C07	67.83	64.03	62.92	82.63	60.59	84.28	76.24	**84.78**
	C07	75.86	72.06	73.35	87.25	74.39	**87.25**	67.89	83.46
	C29	40.26	55.94	37.38	54.66	50.61	56.56	63.05	**69.98**
C29	C05	26.98	48.50	20.35	46.46	37.18	43.55	**63.99**	40.07
	C07	29.90	35.30	24.62	42.05	29.28	39.47	54.02	**94.9**
	C09	29.90	49.39	28.49	53.31	42.77	36.70	59.87	**100.00**
	C27	33.64	59.51	31.33	57.01	46.77	49.68	**66.39**	59.27
Avg.		44.75	52.09	35.35	60.24	47.77	57.63	62.74	**77.19**

4.1 Databases and Experimental Settings

To comprehensively test the performance of CCCA, we selected several distinctive datasets, which are **CMU PIE, COIL20** [14], **Office-31** [17], and **Office-Home** [21]. **CMU PIE** contains more than 40,000 images of 68 people in different pose, illumination, and expression conditions. All of the images were converted to grayscale and resized to 32×32 pixels. In our experiments, based on previous work [10], we constructed a sub-database from five poses (C05, C07, C09, C27, and C29) that are widely used in transfer learning. We selected two subsets as source and target domains in every transfer learning task. e.g., C05 VS C07, C05 VS C09, and C29 VS C27, as source vs target.

COIL20 has 1440 color images, taken from different angles, of 20 objects. One image is taken every 5° of rotation, so each object has 72 images. In our experiments, we divided the dataset into two parts, COIL1 and COIL2, each with 720 images, and used them as the respective source and target domains for experimental tasks (COIL1 VS COIL2 and COIL2 VS COIL1).

Table 3. Accuracy (%) on Office-31 DECAF7 features and COIL20 dataset.

Source	Target	KNN	TCA	GFK	JDA	TJM	CORAL	BDA	DICD	CCCA
COIL1	COIL2	83.61	88.47	72.5	89.31	91.53	83.61	97.22	95.69	**100.00**
COIL2	COIL1	82.78	85.83	74.17	88.47	91.81	82.92	96.81	93.33	**100.00**
AMAZON	DSLR	50.60	61.85	54.02	61.45	62.05	52.21	59.04	64.26	**64.26**
	WEBCAM	52.33	57.61	45.53	60.13	57.61	53.21	53.96	60.88	**61.89**
DSLR	AMAZON	14.41	46.25	40.68	49.27	47.11	16.05	44.52	52.72	**53.67**
	WEBCAM	85.66	93.84	86.04	94.97	93.20	87.04	90.19	96.23	**96.73**
WEBCAM	AMAZON	26.20	43.27	40.22	46.22	46.33	27.19	45.37	50.16	**50.23**
	DSLR	97.90	98.59	96.18	98.59	96.79	97.79	97.19	**99.20**	96.59
Avg.		61.69	71.96	63.67	73.55	73.30	62.50	73.04	76.56	**77.92**

Office-31 is a widely used standard benchmark dataset for transfer learning. It includes more than 4,000 pictures in 31 categories, collected from three domains: Amazon (A), Webcam (W), and DSLR (D). A is downloaded from amazon.com, and W and D contain images taken by web camera and digital SLR camera, respectively, under different conditions. We selected one domain as the source domain and the another as the target domain. For example, we let A be the source domain, and D or W the target domain. In this way, we could carry out six transfer learning tasks on Office-31.

Office-Home has 15,500 pictures from 65 target categories, and consist of four subsets: Art (AR), Product (PR), Real world (RW), and Clipart (CL). Each subset can be used as a domain. Images in the Art domain are paintings, sketches, and other artistic depictions. Product domain images are collected without backgrounds. Real-world images were taken by an ordinary camera. As in previous work, we used the pre-trained deep features on ResNet. We chose different domains for cross-domain recognition tasks. For example, AR and CL could be used for a task. We performed 12 experiments on this dataset.

4.2 Results

The classification accuracy results on the CMU PIE dataset for unsupervised domain adaptation are shown in Table 2, from which we can see the accuracy performance of various methods. CCCA has outstanding performance in terms of average accuracy, which, at 77.19%, is 14.45% higher than the best comparison method, JGSA. It is a long way from other classic methods. Overall, CCCA obtained the highest accuracy in most cases, and close to 100% on some subsets. To get the best performance from CCCA, we look for the optimal μ and β in the range [1, ..., 1000]. We can also find that CCCA does not need to iterate. It only needs to solve for the eigenvalues once, so it takes the least time. We also find that CCCA has little advantage on a few subsets of PIE, e.g., C05. Maybe this is caused by the between classes distance and the distance with-classes closely. This also shows that our method is highly scalable. CCCA without

Table 4. Accuracy (%) on office-home dataset using resnet features.

Source	Target	Resnet	1NN	TCA	GFK	BDA	CORAL	TJM	DANN	JAN	CCCA
AR	CL	34.9	45.3	38.3	38.9	38.9	42.2	47.5	45.6	45.9	**47.7**
AR	PR	50.0	60.1	58.7	57.1	54.8	59.1	65.6	59.3	61.2	**69.6**
AR	RW	58.0	65.8	61.7	60.1	58.2	64.9	68.8	70.1	68.9	**75.1**
CL	AR	37.4	45.7	39.3	38.7	36.2	46.4	47.1	47.0	50.4	**52.5**
CL	PR	41.9	57.0	52.4	53.1	53.1	56.3	63.1	58.5	59.7	**66.5**
CL	RW	46.2	58.7	56.0	55.5	50.2	58.3	63.2	60.9	61.0	**68.5**
PR	AR	38.5	48.1	42.6	42.2	42.1	45.4	51.9	46.1	45.8	**54.1**
PR	CL	31.2	42.9	37.5	37.6	38.2	41.2	**46.0**	43.7	43.4	44.4
PR	RW	60.4	68.9	64.1	64.6	63.1	68.5	71.7	68.5	70.3	**73.8**
RW	AR	53.9	60.8	52.6	53.8	50.2	60.1	60.3	63.2	63.9	**65.0**
RW	CL	41.2	48.3	41.7	42.3	44.0	48.2	51.5	51.8	52.4	**52.6**
RW	PR	59.9	74.7	70.5	70.6	68.2	73.1	76.4	76.8	76.8	**78.8**
Avg.		46.1	56.4	51.3	51.2	49.8	55.3	59.4	57.6	58.3	**62.4**

adding discriminate information does not appear to have an advantage over other methods in this situation. However, from the experimental results, we can conclude that when there is a large similarity between the source and target domains, CCCA is more effective than other distribution alignment methods in reducing the distance between the domains. In addition, CCCA can overcome the impact on accuracy of databases like PIE with a large number of cases.

The experimental results on the COIL20 and the Office-31 datasets are shown in Table 3. For a more intuitive comparison, we put the accuracy statistics of COIL20 and Office-31 in the same table. For the Office-31 dataset, we used the homogeneous domain adaptation dataset with DECAF7 features. From the experimental results in Table 3, the average accuracy of CCCA is 77.92%, the highest of all compared methods. In addition, because there is a high degree of similarity in the COIL1 and COIL2 datasets, CCCA has a huge advantage on COIL20, reaching 100% accuracy. This means that for CCCA, the higher the similarity of the source and target domains, the better the effect. From Table 3, over the whole experiment, CCCA achieved the highest accuracy of the compared methods in almost all of the recognition tasks.

To evaluate the effectiveness of CCCA on large-scale datasets, we performed experiments on the Office-Home dataset with 2048-dimensional ResNet50 features. We also chose two excellent deep domain adaptation methods, JAN [13] and DANN [4], for comparison. Specific experimental operations can refer to the previous work [21] and some experimental results in Table 4. also come from [21]. Office-Home is generally more challenging than other datasets. However, from the experimental results in Table 3, ours is the most accurate of the compared methods, including JAN and DANN.

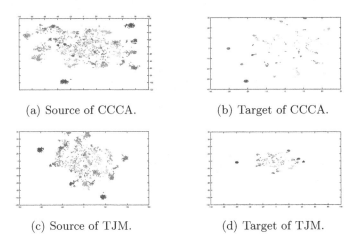

(a) Source of CCCA.   (b) Target of CCCA.

(c) Source of TJM.   (d) Target of TJM.

Fig. 2. t-SNE of CCDA features on source (D) and target (W); t-SNE of TJM features on source (D) and target (W).

4.3   Empirical Analysis

To intuitively reflect the domain adaptability of CCCA learned features, we follow the method of previous work [8] and plot the t-SNE embeddings of the images in task D vs W with CCCA projection feature representations and TJM projection feature representations, respectively. We can see from the visualization chart that the data is transferred from D to W. Compared with Tjm, CCCA pays more attention to the acquaintanceship of the whole data distribution. For the tasks with high similarity of cross-domain data, CCCA has relatively good performance in theory.

Parameter Sensitivity. The influence of each part of the model can be controlled by parameters μ and β. To clearly reflect the impact of parameter changes on the classification effect, Fig. 3 shows the parameter curves of some experiments. Figure 3 (a) shows the variation of transfer classification performance with $\beta = 10$ and $\mu \in [0,...,200]$. Figure 3 (b) shows the impact on classification accuracy when $\mu = 100$, $\beta \in [10,..., 100]$. We can observe that when we fix one of the parameters, another parameter will get the best effect at a certain point. This shows that under different data characteristics and data scales, we need to adjust the weights of CCA regular terms and Laplace graphs to obtain the best classification results, i.e., our method can learn together on the correlation learning and the graph Laplace matrix. By combining with Laplace graphs, we can generalize our proposed CCA regular term to other methods by adjusting the weights.

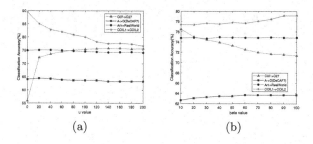

Fig. 3. Impact on classification accuracy of parameter changes on four datasets

5   Conclusions

In this paper, we reduce the distribution distance between the source and target domains by maximizing the correlations between them. Based on this idea, we propose an unsurpevised domain adaptation method, CCCA, for transfer learning. CCCA incorporates CCA into domain adaptation and overcomes the disadvantage that the number of samples must be equal and seeks the direction that the correlations between source and target domains are maximum, and then we learn a knowledge matrix which have the information of cross-domain. Therefore, we can extract the most relevant features of two domains in the latent subspace. By combining CCA regular terms with graph embedding methods, we found that CCA regular terms can be well embedded in other transfer learning models.

References

1. Baktashmotlagh, M., Harandi, M.T., Lovell, B.C., Salzmann, M.: Unsupervised domain adaptation by domain invariant projection. In: Proceedings of the IEEE International Conference on Computer Vision, pp. 769–776 (2013)
2. Ding, C., He, X.: K-means clustering via principal component analysis. In: Proceedings of the Twenty-First International Conference on Machine Learning, p. 29 (2004)
3. Fernando, B., Habrard, A., Sebban, M., Tuytelaars, T.: Unsupervised visual domain adaptation using subspace alignment. In: Proceedings of the IEEE International Conference on Computer Vision, pp. 2960–2967 (2013)
4. Ganin, Y., Lempitsky, V.: Unsupervised domain adaptation by backpropagation. arXiv preprint arXiv:1409.7495 (2014)
5. Geng, B., Tao, D., Xu, C.: DAML: domain adaptation metric learning. IEEE Trans. Image Process. **20**(10), 2980–2989 (2011)
6. Gong, B., Shi, Y., Sha, F., Grauman, K.: Geodesic flow kernel for unsupervised domain adaptation. In: 2012 IEEE Conference on Computer Vision and Pattern Recognition, pp. 2066–2073. IEEE (2012)
7. Hou, C.A., Tsai, Y.H.H., Yeh, Y.R., Wang, Y.C.F.: Unsupervised domain adaptation with label and structural consistency. IEEE Trans. Image Process. **25**(12), 5552–5562 (2016)

8. Li, J., Jing, M., Lu, K., Zhu, L., Shen, H.T.: Locality preserving joint transfer for domain adaptation. IEEE Trans. Image Process. **28**(12), 6103–6115 (2019)
9. Li, M., Yuan, B.: 2D-LDA: a statistical linear discriminant analysis for image matrix. Pattern Recogn. Lett. **26**(5), 527–532 (2005)
10. Li, S., Song, S., Huang, G., Ding, Z., Wu, C.: Domain invariant and class discriminative feature learning for visual domain adaptation. IEEE Trans. Image Process. **27**(9), 4260–4273 (2018)
11. Long, M., Wang, J., Ding, G., Sun, J., Yu, P.S.: Transfer feature learning with joint distribution adaptation. In: Proceedings of the IEEE International Conference on Computer Vision, pp. 2200–2207 (2013)
12. Long, M., Wang, J., Ding, G., Sun, J., Yu, P.S.: Transfer joint matching for unsupervised domain adaptation. In: Proceedings of the IEEE Conference on Computer Vision and Pattern Recognition, pp. 1410–1417 (2014)
13. Long, M., Zhu, H., Wang, J., Jordan, M.I.: Deep transfer learning with joint adaptation networks. In: Proceedings of the 34th International Conference on Machine Learning, vol. 70, pp. 2208–2217. JMLR.org (2017)
14. Nene, S.A., Nayar, S.K., Murase, H., et al.: Columbia object image library (coil-20) (1996)
15. Pan, S.J., Tsang, I.W., Kwok, J.T., Yang, Q.: Domain adaptation via transfer component analysis. IEEE Trans. Neural Netw. **22**(2), 199–210 (2010)
16. Pan, S.J., Yang, Q.: A survey on transfer learning. IEEE Trans. Knowl. Data Eng. **22**(10), 1345–1359 (2009)
17. Saenko, K., Kulis, B., Fritz, M., Darrell, T.: Adapting visual category models to new domains. In: Daniilidis, K., Maragos, P., Paragios, N. (eds.) ECCV 2010. LNCS, vol. 6314, pp. 213–226. Springer, Heidelberg (2010). https://doi.org/10.1007/978-3-642-15561-1_16
18. Sun, B., Feng, J., Saenko, K.: Return of frustratingly easy domain adaptation (2015)
19. Sun, L., Ji, S., Ye, J.: Canonical correlation analysis for multilabel classification: a least-squares formulation, extensions, and analysis. IEEE Trans. Pattern Anal. Mach. Intell. **33**(1), 194–200 (2010)
20. Wang, J., Chen, Y., Hao, S., Feng, W., Shen, Z.: Balanced distribution adaptation for transfer learning. In: 2017 IEEE International Conference on Data Mining (ICDM), pp. 1129–1134. IEEE (2017)
21. Wang, J., Chen, Y., Yu, H., Huang, M., Yang, Q.: Easy transfer learning by exploiting intra-domain structures. arXiv preprint arXiv:1904.01376 (2019)
22. Wang, J., Feng, W., Chen, Y., Yu, H., Huang, M., Yu, P.S.: Visual domain adaptation with manifold embedded distribution alignment. In: 2018 ACM Multimedia Conference on Multimedia Conference, pp. 402–410. ACM (2018)
23. Zhang, J., Li, W., Ogunbona, P.: Joint geometrical and statistical alignment for visual domain adaptation. In: Proceedings of the IEEE Conference on Computer Vision and Pattern Recognition, pp. 1859–1867 (2017)

LSAM: Local Spatial Attention Module

Miao-Miao Lv, Si-Bao Chen[✉], and Bin Luo

Anhui Provincial Key Lab of Multimodal Cognitive Computation,
MOE Key Lab of ICSP, School of Computer Science and Technology,
Anhui University, Hefei, China
sbchen@ahu.edu.cn

Abstract. We focus on spatial attention weighting to improve feature representation power of convolutional neural networks (CNNs) and propose a concise and efficient spatial attention unit based on local similarity, which is termed Local Spatial Attention Module (LSAM). Spatial neighbor points likely share similar attention. A hyper-parameter is adopted to select appropriate size of spatial neighborhood for local similarity. LSAM can be easily embedded in existing CNNs for joint end-to-end training and the cost of consumed resources is negligible. Extensive classification experiments with various backbone networks demonstrate the effectiveness of the proposed LSAM.

Keywords: Convolutional neural networks · Attention mechanism · Spatial weighting · Local similarity

1 Introduction

Nowadays, convolutional neural networks (CNNs) play a pivotal role in computer vision tasks by virtue of their powerful feature extraction and expression capabilities. Since the advent of AlexNet [7], various deep network architectures have sprung up, such as VGGNet [14], ResNet [3], GoogLeNet [16] and DenseNet [6]. Increasing the depth or width of the network architecture to extract richer and more abstract feature information is a philosophy that CNNs share. Although these backbone networks have their own sparkles and exhibit powerful performance in computer vision tasks, the cost of performance improvement, however, requires sacrificing substantial resources (computing and storage) to match the surge of parameters in neural networks.

In recent years, attention mechanism has gradually become one of research hotspots. The works including [1,5,11,19] are all cases of successful application of attention mechanism on CNNs. Distinguish from the previous works, we shed some novel insights on the utility of attention in CNNs. In computer vision tasks,

---

The first author is a student. Thanks to NSFC Key Project of International (Regional) Cooperation and Exchanges (No. 61860206004), National Natural Science Foundation of China (No. 61976004) and Collegiate Natural Science Fund of Anhui Province (No. KJ2017A014) for funding.

© Springer Nature Switzerland AG 2020
Y. Peng et al. (Eds.): PRCV 2020, LNCS 12307, pp. 407–418, 2020.
https://doi.org/10.1007/978-3-030-60636-7_34

the semantics expressed by elements within a certain spatial neighborhood of an image or feature map are similar. In other words, there is little difference (high similarity/correlation) in the significance of features within a certain spatial neighborhood.

It is our intention to learn that "where" on an image or feature map needs emphasis or suppression via attention mechanism. To this end, we propose a concise and efficient spatial attention unit based on local similarity/correlation to improve feature representation power of CNNs, which is named Local Spatial Attention Module (LSAM). Given a convolutional feature map, LSAM divides it into multiple spatial blocks according to hyper-parameter neighborhood size ε, and generates weighting operators for all blocks to alternatively emphasize or suppress the semantics of features within each block (as shown in Fig. 1 and Fig. 2). Therefore, LSAM can assist important/informative features propagate efficiently along CNNs. Furthermore, there is no multi-channel convolution operation in LSAM, the parameters and computational overheads are negligible. Moreover, LSAM contains merely one hyper-parameter and can be easily integrated into existing CNNs to achieve "plug and play" for enhancement of feature representation power of CNNs.

2   Related Works

Network Architecture. With the introduction of AlexNet [7], CNNs have grown into one of the indispensable carriers for computer vision research. Ingeniously designed network architecture can dramatically improve the performance of various visual tasks. Increasing the depth of network by stacking convolutional layers is the intuitive consideration. VGGNet [14] is the masterpiece of this concept. The subsequent Inception series of networks [15–17] promote incorporating multi-scale operations into CNNs. Although deeper networks can theoretically extract more meaningful features, the reality that gradients are difficult to propagate back disillusions this ambition. ResNets [3] introduce the identity-based skip-connection operation to reinforce the extraction crafts of the networks. Based on this, many scholars have developed advanced versions of ResNets [3] from the perspective of extending width, including WideResNet [21]. Another kind of works pursue network "slimming", such as MobileNets [4,13] and ShuffleNets [9,22]. In order to satisfy the need of mobile terminal deployment, they reduce the network capacity by decomposing neural network calculations (including depthwise separable convolution, shuffling channels, etc.). Our work focuses another novel yet nonnegligible aspect: attention, and proposes a new architectural unit.

Attention Module. The neural structure of the primate visual system can selectively perceive and then rapidly direct their gaze towards objects of interest in visual environment. This owes to the favourable utilization of the attention mechanism in the visual system, which is also illustrated in [2,12]. Attention mechanism not only can tell "what" and "where" to focus on but also

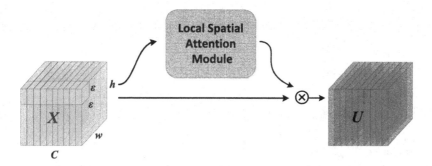

Fig. 1. The overview of Local Spatial Attention Module (LSAM)

can improve the feature representation power of interests. In computer vision tasks, attention weighting is adopted to increase feature representation power by stressing on important features and restraining insignificant ones. Attention can be interpreted as an approach that distribute the finite computational force to more informative parts [8,10,18]. SE [5] introduces the "Squeeze-and-Excitation" module to model channel-wise correlation of the convolutional features, without taking into account the utilizability of spatial information. The work of Woo et al. [11,19] is analogous to ours. CBAM [19] empirically demonstrates that both max and average pooling operations contribute to the attention mechanism. It generates attention maps of feature maps in the order of first channel and then spatial branches. However, spatial branch in CBAM [19] tends to exploit the global pooling operation to infer attention of the spatial point on the feature map. It fails to stress on the phenomena that elements within a certain spatial neighborhood of feature map have similar semantics. Based on the above, we propose LSAM, a network module that focuses on local spatial-wise attention with different neighborhoods in the feature maps.

3   Local Spatial Attention Module

3.1   The Formulation

We focus on spatial attention mechanism (spatial weighting) to improve the feature representation power. Spatial neighbor points most likely share similar attention importance degree. We utilize local similarity (spatial local pooling) to implement spatial attention and term it Local Spatial Attention Module (LSAM). The overall process of LSAM is shown in Fig. 2. The specific details of LSAM are as follows. For a given image or feature map X, LSAM generates a spatial attention weight map to enhance the representation power of X. Firstly, we apply local spatial max-pooling and average-pooling (kernel and stride equal to ε) in parallel to all channels of X, which generates two compressed spatial attention descriptors X^{LM} and X^{LA} by aggregating features within all ε-neighborhoods of X. Subsequently, conventional max-pooling and

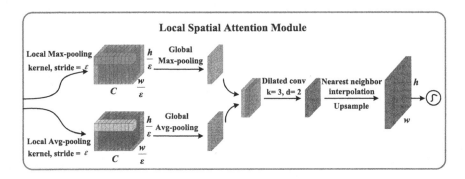

Fig. 2. Detailed structure diagram of Local Spatial Attention Module (LSAM)

average-pooling further tighten X^{LM} and X^{LA} along channel direction to generate descriptors X^{CM} and X^{CA}. X^{CM} and X^{CA} are then concatenated to reduce computational cost. In order to alleviate feature loss caused by multistep pooling operations, a 3×3 dilated convolution [20] is added as follow-up. The dilated convolution can also enhance the non-linear representation power of spatial attention descriptors. Finally, the nearest neighbor interpolation as up-sampling descriptor is applied to the final spatial attention weight operator. In summary, the formulae of LSAM are as the following:

$$X^{LM} = LocalMaxPool_{k,s=\varepsilon}(X), \tag{1}$$

$$X^{LA} = LocalAvgPool_{k,s=\varepsilon}(X), \tag{2}$$

$$X^{CM} = ChannelMaxPool(X^{LM}), \tag{3}$$

$$X^{CA} = ChannelAvgPool(X^{LA}), \tag{4}$$

$$F_{LSAM}(X) = \sigma(I(D([X^{CM}; X^{CA}]))), \tag{5}$$

where $LocalMaxPool(*)$ and $LocalAvgPool(*)$ denote local max/average pooling operations in the spatial domain with ε kernel and stride size, $Channel-MaxPool(*)$ and $ChannelAvgPool(*)$ are max/average pooling operations along channel direction, $D(*)$ denotes a 3×3 dilated convolution, $I(*)$ is the nearest neighbor interpolation up-sampling operator and $\sigma(*)$ is the sigmoid activation function.

The LSAM module infers a local spatial attention weight map $F_{LSAM}(X)$. The function of $F_{LSAM}(X)$ is to generate feature responses of elements in different spatial neighborhoods of X, thereby allowing features with similar semantics in spatial neighborhood to receive similar attention values. Spatial attention weighting will be similar in local neighborhood. That is, spatial attention weighting with higher values will be continuous and change slowly in local neighborhood. This will help important/informative features propagate more effectively along the network. Then, the operator $F_{LSAM}(X)$ is applied to all channels of X through the element-wise multiplication to obtain the refined output U. The overall calculation process can be summarized as:

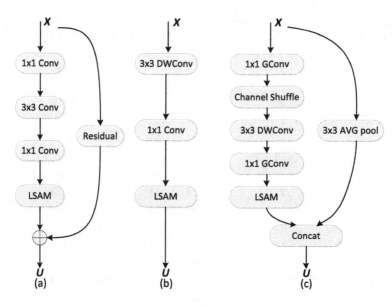

Fig. 3. The schema of LSAM-integrated CNNs units. (a) LSAM-integrated ResNet bottleneck; (b) LSAM-integrated MobileV1 unit; (c) LSAM-integrated ShuffleV1 unit.

$$U = X \otimes F_{LSAM}(X), \tag{6}$$

where feature response tensor X and $U \in R^{C \times H \times W}$. Spatial attention weighting map $F_{LSAM}(X) \in R^{1 \times H \times W}$. Operator $\otimes$ represents element-wise multiplication. During the multiplication, the spatial attention weighting values are duplicated across all the channel dimension.

3.2   Integrating with CNN Architectures

The proposed LSAM module can be integrated seamlessly into a great quantity of existing CNN networks, such as classical ResNet [3], MobileNet [4,13] and ShuffleNet [9,22]. For the ResNet series architectures [3], LSAM module can be placed behind the convolution operation before the shortcut connection in each residual unit. In MobileNet [4,13], the LSAM module can be inserted after every depthwise separable convolution. Similarly, the LSAM module can be plugged in each shuffle unit of ShuffleNet [9,22], which follows a 1×1 group convolution operation before concatenation (as shown in Fig. 3).

LSAM-integrated CNN networks can be trained as those corresponding original CNN networks. Since there is no multi-channel convolution operations in the proposed LSAM module, the parameters and computational cost introduced by LSAM are negligible. Therefore, the training and testing time and cost of LSAM-integrated CNN networks are almost the same as those corresponding original CNN networks. Although the convolution operation can achieve similar function by the spatial attention module in [11], the computational cost of pooling in LSAM is much smaller.

Table 1. Ablation studies on different local neighborhood parameter ε of the proposed LSAM on CIFAR-100 dataset, where '-' denotes raw baselines.

Architecture	Value of ε	Params	GFLOPs	Top1%	Top5%
ResNet34 [3]	-	21.33M	1.162	23.45	7.03
	2	21.33M	1.163	**22.07**	**6.46**
	4	21.33M	1.163	22.20	6.59
	8	21.33M	1.163	22.32	6.53
	16	21.33M	1.163	22.29	6.65
ResNet50 [3]	-	23.71M	1.308	22.66	6.37
	2	23.71M	1.311	**20.51**	**5.39**
	4	23.71M	1.311	20.90	5.56
	8	23.71M	1.311	20.59	5.40
	16	23.71M	1.311	21.28	5.66
ShuffleV1 [22]	-	0.96M	0.042	29.34	9.25
	2	0.96M	0.042	**27.84**	**8.29**
	4	0.96M	0.042	27.88	8.44
	8	0.96M	0.042	28.45	8.35
	16	0.96M	0.042	28.34	8.59

3.3 Relation with Closely Related Works

The proposed LSAM module assumes that the semantics expressed by elements in a certain spatial neighborhood of the feature map are similar. It tends to focus on local similarity/correlation of spatial elements, which is intended to allow the network to more fully absorb and digest important/informative features. LSAM approximates that the features in a certain spatial neighborhood possess similar importance degree. Hereby, LSAM introduces hyper-parameter ε in local spatial pooling operators to adjust the size of neighborhood. The presence of ε enables LSAM to dynamically and flexibly process feature maps with different neighborhood sizes to utilize different local similarity/correlation.

Closely related work SE [5] models inter-channel correlation by exploiting average pooling. No spatial attention is considered in SE and there is no max pooling in SE. CBAM [19] adopted both max pooling and average pooling in spatial and channel attention modules since they found max pooling is also useful. The spatial attention module of CBAM (CBAM_S, for short) [19] directly exploits the global pooling operation to infer the attention weight operator of the corresponding spatial point on the feature map along channel direction. There is no consideration of local similarity/correlation in CBAM_S. In a sense, the proposed LSAM can be regarded as an extension of CBAM_S and CBAM_S can be regarded as a special case of LSAM when ε equals to 1.

Table 2. Effectiveness of LSAM plugged in different layers of ResNet34 [3] on CIFAR-100 dataset.

Architecture	conv2_x	conv3_x	conv4_x	conv5_x	Params	GFLOPs	Top 1%	Top 5%
ResNet34 [3]					21.33M	1.162	23.45	7.03
	√				21.33M	1.163	22.80	6.86
	√	√			21.33M	1.163	22.28	6.61
	√	√	√	√	21.33M	1.163	**22.07**	**6.46**

Table 3. Effectiveness of LSAM plugged in different layers of ShuffleV1 [22] on CIFAR-100 dataset.

Architecture	Stage 2	Stage 3	Stage 4	Params	GFLOPs	Top 1%	Top 5%
ShuffleV1 [22]				0.96M	0.042	29.34	9.25
	√			0.96M	0.042	28.88	8.87
	√	√		0.96M	0.042	28.41	8.64
	√	√	√	0.96M	0.042	**27.84**	**8.29**

4   Experiments

In order to evaluate the proposed LSAM module, we implement classification experiments on CIFAR-10 and CIFAR-100 benchmarks[1]. The proposed LSAM module is integrated with classical network architectures including ResNet [3], MobileNet [4,13] and ShuffleNet [9,22]. Based on the PyTorch framework, we reproduce the results of those baseline networks for fair comparisons. The location of LSAM on those baseline networks is described in Subsect. 3.2. All LSAM-integrated CNN networks are trained the same as those corresponding original CNN networks.

4.1   Ablation Studies

We evaluate the effect of local neighborhood size ε of the proposed LSAM on CIFAR-100 dataset. The CIFAR-100 dataset consists of 60,000 images in a total of 100 classes, each with 500 training images and 100 test images. The learning rate is initially set as 0.1. We iteratively train 200 epochs using the cosine attenuation strategy. Top 1 and top 5 classification error rates on test set are recorded.

Value of Local Neighborhood Size ε. As described in Sect. 3, LSAM focuses on the similarity/correlation of local spatial neighborhoods of images and feature maps. It approximates that the features in a certain spatial neighborhood possess similar importance and introduces hyper-parameter ε to pick the suitable size of the neighborhoods to process feature maps of various sizes. The image size of

---

[1] http://www.cs.toronto.edu/~kriz/cifar.html.

the CIFAR dataset is 32×32. We set ε to the power of two (the form of 2^n). In this way, the result of spatial up-sampling operator in LSAM is easy to match the size of the original feature map.

The comparison results of four different ε values with three backbone networks on CIFAR-100 dataset are shown in Table 1. The value of ε corresponds to the size of the local spatial neighborhood. Notice that all settings can significantly improve the classification performance of the baseline. In comparison, as we expected, the improvements when ε is set to 2 in Table 1 present consistent minimum errors. We consider the semantics of spatial features, that is, the semantics of features in smaller spatial neighborhood are more similar, which is also the philosophy respected by the proposed LSAM. To fully verify this, we carry out experiments by setting ε to 8 and 16 as well, and their improvements on baseline are indeed fall behind smaller values. According to Table 1, we set ε as 2 in the following experiments.

The effectiveness of LSAM. In order to observe the efficiency of the proposed method clearly and thoroughly, we focused on two representative backbone networks, ResNet34 [3] and ShuffleV1 [22], to embed LSAM layer by layer in the network layer to verify its promotion function for CNN performance.

To ensure the fairness and credibility of the experimental results, we place our modules layer by layer in strict accordance with the network architecture constructed in the original works [3,22]. The elaborate comparison experiments are shown in Table 2 and Table 3. We can clearly observe that as the number of LSAM embedded in the network layer gradually increases, the classification error of the backbone network also decreases accordingly. When LSAM is implanted in the entire network layers, the baseline classification performance is obviously the best. At the same time, the amount of parameters and computational overhead introduced by placing LSAM is negligible. It can be seen that the excellent performance exhibited by LSAM.

4.2   Comparison of Classification Results on CIFAR Benchmark

Constrained by limited computational resources, it is difficult to conduct experiments on large classification benchmarks. Therefore, the CIFAR benchmarks (CIFAR-100 and CIFAR-10 datasets), which are also fair and convincing, are selected to verify the effectiveness of our module. Tables 4 and 5 show the experimental results of classification on CIFAR-100 and CIFAR-10 dataset, respectively. Obviously, plugging LSAM significantly reduces the classification error of the baseline. It can be seen that raw ResNet50 achieves 22.66% error on the CIFAR-100, while the ResNet34 integrated with LSAM has reached a comparable performance with 22.07% error. It is also worth noting that the ResNe50 with LSAM (20.51% error) in Table 4 outperforms raw ResNet101 (21.46% error) with only half of the parameters.

Meanwhile, thanks to no multi-channel convolution operation in our module, the parameters and computational cost introduced by LSAM are negligible. In order to further verify the versatility and effectiveness of LSAM, we accomplish experiments by placing LSAM on lightweight network including MobileNet

Table 4. Comparison results of various LSAM-integrated architectures on CIFAR-100 dataset.

Architecture	Params	GFLOPs	Top 1%	Top 5%
ResNet18 [3]	11.22M	0.558	23.52	7.11
ResNet18+LSAM	11.22M	0.558	**23.29**	**7.04**
ResNet34 [3]	21.33M	1.162	23.45	7.03
ResNet34+LSAM	21.33M	1.163	**22.07**	**6.46**
ResNet50 [3]	23.71M	1.308	22.66	6.37
ResNet50+LSAM	23.71M	1.311	**20.51**	**5.39**
ResNet101 [3]	42.69M	2.525	21.46	5.78
ResNet101+LSAM	42.69M	2.531	**20.45**	**5.31**
MobileV1 [4]	3.31M	0.047	31.84	10.74
MobileV1+LSAM	3.31M	0.048	**30.84**	**10.19**
MobileV2 [13]	2.41M	0.095	24.76	6.40
MobileV2+LSAM	2.41M	0.096	**24.11**	**6.17**
ShuffleV1 [22]	0.96M	0.042	29.34	9.25
ShuffleV1+LSAM	0.96M	0.042	**27.84**	**8.29**
ShuffleV2 [9]	1.36M	0.047	27.35	8.05
ShuffleV2+LSAM	1.36M	0.047	**26.91**	**7.74**

Table 5. Comparison results of various LSAM-integrated architectures on CIFAR-10 dataset.

Architecture	Params	GFLOPs	Top 1%	Top 5%
ResNet34 [3]	21.282M	1.162	4.64	0.20
ResNet34+LSAM	21.282M	1.163	**4.54**	**0.16**
ResNet50 [3]	23.521M	1.308	4.37	0.16
ResNet50+LSAM	23.521M	1.311	**4.30**	**0.14**
ResNet101 [3]	42.513M	2.525	4.55	0.18
ResNet101+LSAM	42.513M	2.531	**4.19**	**0.11**
MobileV1 [4]	3.217M	0.047	8.20	0.35
MobileV1+LSAM	3.217M	0.048	**8.05**	**0.33**
ShuffleV1 [22]	0.887M	0.042	8.04	0.29
ShuffleV1+LSAM	0.888M	0.042	**7.27**	**0.27**

[4,13] and ShuffleNet [9,22]. Experimental results in Table 4 and Table 5 show that, although these networks have limited capacity, LSAM also promotes their classification performance with little cost, which manifests that LSAM can effectively improve the utilization of informative features along CNNs with negligible overhead.

4.3   Comparison with Closely Related Methods

We also compare the proposed LSAM with its closely related state-of-the-arts SE [5] and CBAM_S [19]. We implement two experimental schemes to demonstrate the efficiency and powerful generalization ability of LSAM.

Scheme 1: We plug the SE module [5] and CBAM_S module [19] into the raw baselines independently to compare with LSAM.

Scheme 2: Due to both SE and the channel attention module of CBAM (CBAM_C, for short) [19] place emphasis on the channel attention mechanism. Therefore, we consider combining LSAM with the two modules separately to generate two new attention modules that concentrate on both the channel and the space, which are similar to the raw CBAM [19]. Regarding the order of the two, we follow the order of channel-first and spatial-second (SE-first, LSAM-second and CBAM_C-first, LSAM-second) which are agreed in CBAM [19] to construct two new "enhanced" attention modules, and embed them into the raw baseline separately for experimental comparison.

Table 6 summarizes the experimental comparison results of the two schemes, where the first four rows in each architecture column represent the comparison results of the single module of scheme 1, and the next three rows are the comparison results of the combined modules of scheme 2.

Comparison result of scheme 1: It is easy to note that LSAM outperforms state-of-the-art SE [5] with fewer parameters and computational cost in most cases. This indicates that our module is powerful, and it also reflects the researchability and practicality of spatial attention. And although the cost of LSAM and CBAM_S [19] is almost equivalent, however the performance of LSAM is consistently superior to the CBAM_S method in all cases. This empirically confirms that the concept followed by LSAM is practical. That is, semantics of features in a certain spatial neighborhood are similar.

Comparison result of scheme 2: It can be seen from the Table 6 that the performance of the two combined "enhanced" modules precede independent placement without bells and whistles in most cases. The combined effect with the SE module [5] is particularly noteworthy. Compared with the situation where the SE [5] is embedded alone, the combined module has reached a maximum increase of 1.39% points (in ResNet50 column). This shows that the proposed LSAM can be well coupled with the existing attention channel preference module to achieve positive performance improvement, which is worthy of celebration. Moreover, two combined "enhanced" attention modules surpass the raw CBAM [19]by virtue of excellent performance, which can be described as a "strong combination". This also implies empirically that our proposed LSAM has good generalization ability and portability.

Table 6. Comparison results with state-of-the-arts on CIFAR-100 dataset. (Black bold denotes the best, blue bold denotes second-best.)

Architecture	Attention-module	Params	GFLOPs	Top 1%	Top 5%
ResNet34 [3]	-	21.33M	1.162	23.45	7.03
	SE [5]	21.49M	1.163	**21.89**	**6.45**
	CBAM_S [19]	21.33M	1.163	22.68	6.87
	LSAM	21.33M	1.163	**22.07**	**6.46**
	CBAM[19]	21.49M	1.163	23.04	6.83
	CBAM_C [19]+LSAM	21.48M	1.163	**21.85**	**6.35**
	SE [5]+LSAM	21.49M	1.163	**21.56**	**6.31**
ResNet50 [3]	-	23.71M	1.308	22.66	6.37
	SE [5]	26.24M	1.312	21.36	5.75
	CBAM_S [19]	23.71M	1.311	**21.12**	**5.64**
	LSAM	23.71M	1.311	**20.51**	**5.39**
	CBAM[19]	26.24M	1.313	20.66	5.52
	CBAM_C [19]+LSAM	26.24M	1.313	**20.61**	**5.46**
	SE [5]+LSAM	26.24M	1.313	**19.97**	**5.02**
ShuffleV1 [22]	-	0.96M	0.042	29.34	9.25
	SE [5]	1.39M	0.042	**27.98**	**8.55**
	CBAM_S [19]	0.96M	0.042	28.05	8.43
	LSAM	0.96M	0.042	**27.84**	**8.29**
	CBAM[19]	1.39M	0.043	27.70	8.20
	CBAM_C [19]+LSAM	1.39M	0.043	**27.45**	**8.28**
	SE [5]+LSAM	1.39M	0.042	**27.19**	**7.87**

5   Conclusion and Future Work

In this work, we focus on spatial attention weighting to improve feature representation power and propose Local Spatial Attention Module (LSAM). Spatial neighbor points most likely share similar attention importance degree. LSAM can be easily embedded into existing CNNs with negligible cost to achieve "plug and play" and promote substantial performance improvements. The hyper-parameter ε is used to pick the suitable size of the spatial neighborhood. Extensive classification experiments with various backbone networks on CIFAR-10 and CIFAR-100 datasets demonstrate the effectiveness of the proposed LSAM.

The proposed LSAM is spatial weighting which focuses on "where" is meaningful given an input image or feature map. Since each channel of a feature map is considered as a feature detector, channel attention focuses on "what" is important, which is complementary to the spatial attention. Therefore, in the future we will extend the proposed LSAM by combining it with channel weighting and investigate the combination of spatial attention with channel attention. Furthermore, more application areas besides of image classification, such as object detection and adversarial learning, will be considered to evaluate the fusion of attention weighting.

References

1. Cao, Y., Xu, J., Lin, S., Wei, F., Hu, H.: GCNet: non-local networks meet squeeze-excitation networks and beyond (2019). http://arxiv.org/abs/1904.11492
2. Corbetta, M., Shulman, G.L.: Control of goal-directed and stimulus-driven attention in the brain. Nat. Rev. Neurosci. **3**(3), 201–215 (2002)
3. He, K., Zhang, X., Ren, S., Sun, J.: Deep residual learning for image recognition. In: CVPR, pp. 770–778 (2016)
4. Howard, A.G., et al.: MobileNets: efficient convolutional neural networks for mobile vision applications (2017). http://arxiv.org/abs/1704.04861
5. Hu, J., Shen, L., Sun, G.: Squeeze-and-excitation networks. In: CVPR, pp. 7132–7141 (2018)
6. Huang, G., Liu, Z., van der Maaten, L., Weinberger, K.Q.: Densely connected convolutional networks. In: CVPR, pp. 2261–2269 (2017)
7. Krizhevsky, A., Sutskever, I., Hinton, G.E.: ImageNet classification with deep convolutional neural networks. In: Neural Information Processing Systems, pp. 1106–1114 (2012)
8. Larochelle, H., Hinton, G.E.: Learning to combine foveal glimpses with a third-order Boltzmann machine. In: NIPS, pp. 1243–1251 (2010)
9. Ma, N., Zhang, X., Zheng, H., Sun, J.: ShuffleNet V2: practical guidelines for efficient CNN architecture design. In: ECCV, pp. 122–138 (2018)
10. Mnih, V., Heess, N., Graves, A., Kavukcuoglu, K.: Recurrent models of visual attention. In: NIPS, pp. 2204–2212 (2014)
11. Park, J., Woo, S., Lee, J., Kweon, I.S.: BAM: bottleneck attention module. In: BMCV, p. 147 (2018)
12. Rensink, R.: The dynamic representation of scenes. Vis. Cogn. **7**(1–3), 17–42 (2000)
13. Sandler, M., Howard, A.G., Zhu, M., Zhmoginov, A., Chen, L.C.: MobileNet V2: inverted residuals and linear bottlenecks. In: CVPR, pp. 4510–4520 (2018)
14. Simonyan, K., Zisserman, A.: Very deep convolutional networks for large-scale image recognition. In: International Conference on Learning Representations (2015)
15. Szegedy, C., Ioffe, S., Vanhoucke, V., Alemi, A.A.: Inception-v4, inception-ResNet and the impact of residual connections on learning. In: AAAI, pp. 4278–4284 (2017)
16. Szegedy, C., et al.: Going deeper with convolutions. In: CVPR, pp. 1–9 (2015)
17. Szegedy, C., Vanhoucke, V., Ioffe, S., Shlens, J., Wojna, Z.: Rethinking the inception architecture for computer vision. In: CVPR, pp. 2818–2826 (2016)
18. Vaswani, A., et al.: Attention is all you need. In: NIPS, pp. 5998–6008 (2017)
19. Woo, S., Park, J., Lee, J., Kweon, I.S.: CBAM: Convolutional block attention module. In: ECCV, pp. 3–19 (2018)
20. Yu, F., Koltun, V.: Multi-scale context aggregation by dilated convolutions. In: ICLR (2016)
21. Zagoruyko, S., Komodakis, N.: Wide residual networks. In: BMCV (2016)
22. Zhang, X., Zhou, X., Lin, M., Sun, J.: ShuffleNet: an extremely efficient convolutional neural network for mobile devices. In: CVPR, pp. 6848–6856 (2018)

Pruning Deep Convolutional Neural Networks via Gradient Support Pursuit

Jue Wang$^{(\boxtimes)}$, Fanfan Ji, and Xiao-Tong Yuan

Jiangsu Key Laboratory of Big Data Analysis Technology, School of Automation,
Nanjing University of Information Science and Technology, Nanjing 210044, China
20181223068@nuist.edu.cn

Abstract. In this paper, we propose a filter pruning method, namely,
Filter Pruning via Gradient Support Pursuit (FPGraSP), which can
accelerate and compress very deep Convolutional Neural Networks effectively in an iterative way. Previous work reports that Gradient Support
Pursuit (GraSP) is well employed for sparsity-constrained optimization
in Machine Learning. We seek to develop a modification that GraSP can
be applied to structured pruning in deep CNNs. Specifically, we select
the filters with the maximum gradient values and merge their indices
with the indices of the filters with the largest weights. We then update
parameters over the above union. Finally, we utilize filter selection in
a dynamic way to get the filters with the largest magnitude. Different from some previous methods which remove filters of smaller weights
but neglect the influence of gradients, we exploit gradient information.
Our experimental results on MNIST, CIFAR-10 and CIFAR-100 clearly
demonstrate the efficiency of our FPGraSP algorithm. As an example,
for pruning ResNet-56 on CIFAR-10, our FPGraSP without fine-tuning
obtains 0.04% accuracy drop, achieving 52.63% FLOPs reduction.

Keywords: Filter pruning · Gradient support pursuit algorithm ·
Deep convolutional neural network

1 Introduction

Contemporarily, we have witnessed the tremendous success of excessively large
Convolutional Neural Networks (CNNs) [14, 22], which are substantially boosting
their superior performances in various fields such as computer vision and natural
language processing. Generally, the deeper and wider the network architectures
are, the better the models perform. The outstanding performance of deep CNNs
can be attributed to their considerable learnable parameters, which brings the
strong expressivity of CNNs.

However, in spite of the impressive success of deep CNNs, they suffer from
over-parameterization. It is impractical for deep CNNs to deploy on resource-
constrained platforms, e.g., embedded sensors, drones and mobile devices. Three

Jue Wang is currently working toward the Master degree in the School of Automation,
Nanjing University of Information Science and Technology.

ⓒ Springer Nature Switzerland AG 2020
Y. Peng et al. (Eds.): PRCV 2020, LNCS 12307, pp. 419–432, 2020.
https://doi.org/10.1007/978-3-030-60636-7_35

crucial problems are included as follows: much run-time memory, a tremendous number of trainable parameters and huge computational costs. For example, ResNet-152 [7] consumes more than 200MB storage space and requires 23 Giga floating-point operations (FLOPs) when classifying an image with resolution 224×224, which leads to heavy computation burden [8].

For alleviating the problems discussed above, practitioners have proposed several novel achievements to improve acceleration and compression of over-parameterized deep CNNs, namely, low-rank decomposition [25], quantization [1,26], knowledge distillation [11] and network pruning [6,8,17]. They seek to achieve a good trade-off between pursuing high accuracy and reducing computational costs as well as storage requirements.

We now focus on filter pruning due to its notable advantages. Firstly, it can be applied to any CNNs task, e.g., object detection, face recognition and semantic segmentation. Secondly, filter pruning can decrease FLOPs dramatically without damaging network structure and speed up inference. Consequently, we can compress the pruned models further by other techniques such as quantization [1,26]. Additionally, filter pruning can be supported by existing efficient deep learning libraries instead of specialized hardware or software.

Some representative works [8,17] measure the importance of filters by calculating ℓ_p-norm values in a particular layer and sort them. Accordingly, they discard the unimportant filters of small ℓ_p-norm and achieve the narrower convolutional layers. However, these criteria only focus on the magnitude of parameters but ignore the gradient information.

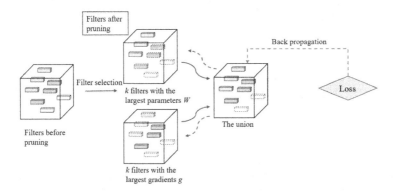

Fig. 1. Verview of our FPGraSP procedure for deep CNNs. k means the number of the remaining filters in an individual layer after pruning. The large box means the filter space in an individual layer. In the filter space, the yellow boxes are denoted as the filters with the k-largest weights., the green boxes are denoted as the filters of the k-largest gradients, the white boxes are the rest of filters, and the dashed boxes indicate the filters which are set to zero. W means a matrix of weights, and g means a matrix of gradients in an individual layer. (Color figure online)

In this paper, we develop a novel filter-level pruning method, Filter Pruning via Gradient Support Pursuit (FPGraSP), to address the above drawbacks. As explained in Fig. 1, we make use of gradient information and prune filters at every iteration based on the theory of Gradient Support Pursuit (GraSP) [2]. We intend to implement FPGraSP as an optimizer, and prune filters simultaneously in all layers. Concretely, we compute ℓ_1-norm of gradients, sort them and get the largest ones, which are called the largest gradients. We choose the indices of the filters that have the k largest gradients. Subsequently, we combine them with the indices of the filters with the largest ℓ_1-norm achieved in the previous iteration, and produce a union set, which contains the gradient information and the parameter information. Then, we update parameters over the union mentioned above through Stochastic Gradient Descent with Momentum (SGDM) [21]. At the end of each iteration, we compute the sums of the filters' absolute weights (i.e., ℓ_1-norm), sort them, select the k filters corresponding to the largest ones, and set the remaining filters to zero. We allow the filters which have been zeroized to be updated in the next iteration. FPGraSP iterates until convergence. We reconstruct the network and finally obtain a slimmer network.

Contributions. Our major contributions are highlighted as follows: (1) We investigate FPGraSP for accelerating deep CNNs with the additional gradient support. What's more, we take into comprehensive consideration the gradient information and the parameter information. (2) Compared with the hard filter pruning algorithms [10,17,19], our FPGraSP algorithm trains from scratch, and doesn't require a pre-trained model. Besides, there is no need for a fine-tuning procedure. (3) Extensive experiments on three benchmark datasets indicate that FPGraSP can provide exceptional performance.

2   Related Work

Network pruning becomes one of the significant compression techniques, which can obviously reduce model size, storage space and computational requirements (such as FLOPs) of over-parameterized networks with negligible loss in accuracy. These algorithms can be grouped into two categories, namely, unstructured pruning and structured pruning.

Unstructured Pruning. LeCun et al. [16] first introduced Optimal Brain Damage (OBD), a pioneer work to remove unimportant neurons. However, it could not be applied to deep CNNs. Han et al. [5,6] explore a pruning method to delete the connections whose weights are lower than a predefined threshold in the pre-trained network and then fine-tune the compact model to retrieve its accuracy. Therefore, the model scale can be decreased in Deep Neural Networks (DNNs), but connections can't be recovered if weights are incorrectly pruned. To tackle this problem, Guo et al. [4] propose a dynamic network surgery that can restore the important connections through the operations of pruning and splicing, thus reducing the number of training iterations significantly. Jin et al. [12] add an ℓ_0-norm constraint to the objective function and make the model sparse.

It updates the parameters with larger weights, and reactivates all the connections. Nevertheless, unstructured pruning can prune DNNs but can't make full use of existing BLAS libraries. Its acceleration at inference time is not obvious in real-world applications, so we require special libraries (e.g., cuSPARSE) and hardware platforms.

Structured Pruning. To the best of our knowledge, structured pruning delete filters directly in order to reduce FLOPs, memory space and power consumption significantly. Wen et al. [24] propose an early work called Structured Sparsity Learning (SSL). It introduces a group Lasso regularization in the loss function to zero out some filters gradually. Liu et al. [18] introduce the scaling parameters γ in the batch normalization (BN) layers to the objective function, leverage ℓ_1-norm of γ as a penalty term, and prune the corresponding channel with a small γ. There are some pruning methods based on evaluating the importance of filters: Li et al. [17] calculate the sum of absolute values of the convolution kernel weights for each filter on a pre-trained model and prune insignificant filters directly. This method is based on ℓ_1-norm and can speed up its inference procedure. Nevertheless, the pruned filters can't be updated during the training process, limiting the expressive capacity of the model. In response to this problem, He et al. [8] propose a Soft Filter Pruning (SFP) method, which prunes the filters with smaller ℓ_2-norm and trains from scratch. The pruned filters can be updated dynamically in a soft manner, saving the time of the fine-tuning procedure. However, when we use the norm-based pruning criterion, we should meet two requirements: the norm deviation is large; the minimum norm is close to zero. But these two conditions do not always hold. He et al. [9] propose the Filter Pruning via Geometric Median (FPGM) method with the criterion of the geometric median of filters. The filters whose smallest sum of the Euclidean distances with other filters in the same layer are discarded so that the filters with redundancy can be pruned. Wang et al. [23] propose a correlation-based pruning (COP) method and calculate the Pearson correlation coefficient to measure the redundancy between the two filters. COP uses the global max normalization technology to compare the importance of filters within different layers. Here are some pruning methods based on the reconstruction: Luo et al. [19] propose a ThiNet framework, which reformulates the channel selection into an optimization problem and calculates statistics information from its next layer in the pre-trained model. It minimizes the reconstruction error on the output feature maps between the pre-trained model and the pruned one. He et al. [10] transform channel selection into a LASSO regression problem (ℓ_1-norm) with linear least squares. Zhuang et al. [27] propose a discrimination-aware channel pruning (DCP) algorithm, which introduces additional discrimination-aware losses into the loss function of the reconstruction error to improve the classification accuracy.

Discussion. Hence it should be noted that the above algorithms can't exploit the gradient information. Our FPGraSP scheme focuses on structured pruning and has realistic acceleration, which selects the filters with large gradients in the current optimizer step and merges their indices with the support of the sparse result obtained in the previous iteration. We update the parameters over the union set and select the larger filters. Compared with off-the-shelf pruning methods that use parameter information, FPGraSP utilizes gradient learning.

3   The Proposed Method

In this section, we introduce a Filter Pruning via Gradient Support Pursuit (FPGraSP) algorithm. We first introduce the theory of the GraSP algorithm for sparsity-constrained optimization, which is applied to machine learning. Then we outline how to extend GraSP to filter-level pruning and propose the algorithm description of FPGraSP for accelerating deep CNNs.

3.1   Gradient Support Pursuit

The FPGraSP we propose is inspired by Gradient Support Pursuit (GraSP) [2]. GraSP is proposed as an approximate solution to the sparsity-constrained optimization in the field of machine learning. It is an iterative greedy algorithm that approximates the sparse optimum of loss. The notation in this section are introduced in Table 1.

Table 1. Notation used in Sect. 3.1.

Symbol	Description
$x \in \mathbb{R}^d$	A vector
$\hat{x}$	The sparse estimate of x
$\|x\|_0$	The ℓ_0-norm of vector x that merely counts the number of nonzero of vector x
$supp(x)$	The support set of vector x (i.e., indices of the non-zero entries of x)
$A \cup B$	The union of set A and set B
$\mathbb{T}^C$	Complement of set $\mathbb{T}$
b_k	The largest k-term (in modulus) approximation of vector b

Formally, people consider the following sparsity-constrained optimization problem:

$$\min_x f(x) \quad s.t. \|x\|_0 \leqslant k, \tag{1}$$

where x is the model parameter vector. $f(x) = n^{-1} \sum_{i=1}^{n} f_i(x)$ is a loss function. k constrains the number of nonzero elements in x, which controls the sparsity of the vector x.

First, GraSP calculates the current gradient z of loss function as follows:

$$z = \nabla f(\hat{x}), \tag{2}$$

where $\hat{x}$ is the sparse estimate.

It chooses $2k$ maximum entries (in absolute values) of vector z. Its index set $\mathbb{Z}$ is shown in Eq. (3).

$$\mathbb{Z} = supp(z_{2k}). \tag{3}$$

Then, GraSP merges the above indices $\mathbb{Z}$ with the support set of the current estimate $\hat{x}$, so it can obtain a union set $\mathbb{T}$. Thus, we can get:

$$\mathbb{T} = \mathbb{Z} \cup supp(\hat{x}), \tag{4}$$

where $supp(\hat{x})$ is the support set of $\hat{x} = b_k$ in Eq. (6) (i.e., indices of the non-zero entries of $\hat{x}$), which is updated to select the k-largest entries in absolute at the previous iteration.

Subsequently, GraSP minimizes the loss function $f(x)$ over the restricted support $\mathbb{T}$, that is, the intermediate estimate b. Let the indices of vector b be the universal set, and $x|_{\mathbb{T}^c}$ is set to zero. It minimizes the objective function $f(x)$ according to the following formula:

$$b = \arg\min f(x) \quad s.t. \ x|_{\mathbb{T}^c} = 0. \tag{5}$$

Finally, the estimate $\hat{x}$ is updated to select the k-largest entries of the intermediate estimate b by computing their absolute values. The update rule is shown in Eq. (6):

$$\hat{x} = b_k. \tag{6}$$

In the training process, it iterates until convergence.

GraSP combines the k non-zero entries of $\hat{x}$ obtained at the previous iteration with the top $2k$ entries of gradients, and it obtains a union set of size $3k$ at most. GraSP minimizes the loss over this union set, and finally generates the best k-term approximation. In [2], we can see the efficiency of GraSP when utilizing GraSP for sparse logistic regression. Thus, for the purpose of model compression, we make a modification and generalize GraSP innovatively to prune filters.

3.2 Filter Pruning via Gradient Support Pursuit

Notation. In CNNs, let i be the layer index. The parameters are $\{W_i \in \mathbb{R}^{N_{i+1} \times N_i \times K \times K}, 1 \leq i \leq L\}$, where W_i denotes a matrix of parameters in the i-th convolutional layer. N_i represents the number of input channels of the i-th layer, and N_{i+1} represents the number of output channels of the i-th layer. $K \times K$ denotes the size of a convolutional kernel. L denotes the number of convolutional layers. The pruning rate P_i represents the proportion of pruned filters in an individual convolutional layer. $W_{i,j} \in \mathbb{R}^{N_i \times K \times K}$ is the j-th filters in the i-th convolutional layer. $nonzero(x)$ denotes the location (indices) of nonzero elements in x. $topk(x)$ denotes the indices of the k largest entries of x.

Filter pruning is a promising approach to accelerate networks without damaging network architecture. Compared with the recent pruning approaches which are dependent on parameter information [8,17], our scheme compresses deep CNNs on the basis of gradient learning. The gradient provides the significant information about whether we eliminate the filters. Thus we take advantage of such information through FPGraSP.

In practice, we define ℓ_p-norm as follows:

$$\|W_{i,j}\|_p = \sqrt[p]{\sum_{n=1}^{N_i}\sum_{k_1=1}^{K}\sum_{k_2=1}^{K}|W_{i,j}(n,k_1,k_2)|^p}, \tag{7}$$

where N_i is the number of input channels in the i-th layer. We calculate ℓ_1-norm to evaluate the importance of the filter. Specifically, we compute ℓ_1-norms, sort them and choose the largest ones, which is called as ℓ_1-norm criterion. In this paper, k can be computed by $N_{i+1}(1 - P_i)$. N_{i+1} represents the number of output channels of the i-th layer. We utilize the same pruning rate P_i within all convolutional layers.

In FPGraSP, we select the filters of k-largest gradients by ℓ_1-norm criterion in the current step and combine their indices with the support of parameters in the pruned models at the previous iteration. Then we update parameters over this restricted union set. At the end of each iteration, we choose the largest filters by ℓ_1-norm criterion and prune the smallest ones.

We summarize illustratively the overall FPGraSP algorithm in Algorithm 1. Our proposed method applies the theory of GraSP to structured pruning in CNNs and makes the following adjustments and improvements. It prunes all layers simultaneously and trains CNNs from scratch.

Firstly, we conduct the pruning procedure iteratively in the optimizer and randomly initialize parameters.

Algorithm 1: Filter Pruning via Gradient Support Pursuit.

Input: Pruning rate P_i, learning rate η, model parameters
$\quad\quad W = \{W_i, 1 \leq i \leq L\}$, the number of convolutional layer L.
Output: The compact model and its parameters W.

1 Initialize randomly network parameters
2 **for** $epoch = 1; epoch \leq epoch_{max}; epoch + +$ **do**
3 $\quad$ **for** $step = 1; step \leq step_{max}; step + +$ **do**
4 $\quad\quad$ Calculate the current gradient: $g = \nabla f(W^{step})$;
5 $\quad\quad$ **for** $i = 1; i \leq L; i + +$ **do**
6 $\quad\quad\quad$ Compute the ℓ_1-norm for each gradient $g_{i,j}$ in g_i, sort them and
$\quad\quad\quad$ select the filter index: $\mathbb{Z} = topk(g_i)$;
7 $\quad\quad\quad$ Let $\mathbb{T} = \mathbb{Z} \cup nonzero(W_i^{step})$;
8 $\quad\quad\quad$ Update parameters W_i^{step+1} over the support set $\mathbb{T}$:
$\quad\quad\quad W_i^{step+1}|_{\mathbb{T}} = W_i^{step}|_{\mathbb{T}} - \eta\nabla f(W_i^{step})|_{\mathbb{T}}$ and $W_i^{step+1}|_{\mathbb{T}^{\complement}} = 0$;
9 $\quad\quad\quad$ Compute the ℓ_1-norm for each filter $\|W_{i,j}\|_1, 1 \leq j \leq N_{i+1}$;
10 $\quad\quad\quad$ Zero the lowest $N_{i+1}P_i$ filters based on ℓ_1-norm criterion.
11 $\quad\quad$ **end**
12 $\quad$ **end**
13 **end**
14 Reconstruct the model and obtain a slimmer network.

At the *step*-th iteration, $f(W^{step})$ is the current loss function. We compute the current gradient g via back propagation:

$$g = \nabla f(W^{step}), \tag{8}$$

Then, the entries of g_i with the k-largest ℓ_1-norm are selected. We can get:

$$\mathbb{Z} = topk(g_i), \tag{9}$$

where g_i denotes a matrix of the gradients corresponding to the filters in the i-th layer. $topk(g_i)$ denotes the indices of the k largest gradients g_i in the i-th layer. We require to calculate the ℓ_1-norm of $g_{i,j}$, sort them and choose the largest ones. $g_{i,j}$ means the gradient corresponding to the j-th filter in the i-th layer. $\mathbb{Z}$ is the support set of the k coordinates of g_i that have the largest ℓ_1-norm.

Additionally, we can achieve a union $\mathbb{T}$ by combining the indices $\mathbb{Z}$ shown in Eq. (9) with the support set of the current parameter weights W_i^{step} so that we get a combined set $\mathbb{T}$, which is shown as follows:

$$\mathbb{T} = \mathbb{Z} \cup nonzero(W_i^{step}), \tag{10}$$

where $nonzero(W_i^{step})$ is used to get the location (indices) of nonzero entries in W_i^{step}, which is acquired to choose the filters with the largest ℓ_1-norm obtained in the previous iteration. Concretely, $\mathbb{T}$ is the union of both the indices of the k maximum entries of the gradient g_i and the indices of nonzero entries of W_i^{step}. In this way, we can get the k maximum entries of parameters by ℓ_1-norm and the filters with important gradient information in the current iteration. The filters with larger gradients may be recovered. We take into comprehensive consideration the first-order and the zero-order information.

We update parameters W_i^{step} over the fixed supporting set $\mathbb{T}$. We achieve the intermediate estimate W_i^{step+1} in the *step*-th iteration according to the following formula:

$$W_i^{step+1}|_{\mathbb{T}} = W_i^{step}|_{\mathbb{T}} - \eta \nabla f(W_i^{step})|_{\mathbb{T}}, \tag{11}$$

where η is a learning rate. Let the indices of vector W_i be the universal set, and we set $W_i^{step+1}|_{\mathbb{T}^{\complement}} = 0$. The filters whose indices are contained in the subset $\mathbb{T}$ can be reserved.

Finally, the parameter W_i is then updated with selecting the k-largest entries of the intermediate estimate W_i^{step+1} by ℓ_1-norm criterion. For evaluating the importance of filters, we calculate $\|W_{i,j}\|_1$ of filters, sort them and select the largest ones. We use filter selection dynamically to choose the lowest $N_{i+1}P_i$ filters and set them to zero in a soft manner. We prune the filters by ℓ_1-norm, which can be updated in subsequent iterations during the whole training process. $W_{i,j} \in \mathbb{R}^{N_i \times K \times K}$ is the j-th filters in the i-th convolutional layer.

FPGraSP iterates until convergence during the whole training procedure. So we reconstruct the network, and our proposed approach can generate a compact model. In conclusion, FPGraSP leverages gradient learning and takes into consideration the gradient and the parameter information.

4   Experiments

We carry out FPGraSP to prune several common network architectures on three benchmark datasets (i.e., MNIST [15], CIFAR-10 [13] and CIFAR-100 [13]), and contrast our pruning algorithm against the state of the arts. We implement the proposed method to prune LeNet-5 [15] on MNIST and accelerate ResNet [7] on CIFAR-10 and CIFAR-100. Moreover, we utilize Pytorch [20] to conduct experiments for confirming the capabilities of FPGraSP. The GPU we use is NVIDIA GeForce GTX 1080Ti. For each trial, we adopt the standard data argumentation techniques as utilized in Pytorch's official examples. Additionally, we conduct the pruning procedure iteratively in the optimizer step and apply FPGraSP on all the layers simultaneously. For comparison, we focus on the pruning rate and the accuracy change. In this paper, we use Top-1 accuracy to measure the performance of both baseline and the pruned model.

4.1   Datasets and Experimental Settings

Datasets. MNIST dataset [15] is a widely-used dataset with handwritten digits which contains a training set of 60,000 examples and a test set of 10,000 examples. CIFAR-10 [13], a small dataset for identifying universal objects, comprises 60,000 color images with resolution 32×32 in 10 categories, containing 50K training images and 10K test images. CIFAR-100 [13] is similar to CIFAR-10 with 100 categories and 600 pictures in each category.

Baseline Training. Firstly, we perform experiments on MNIST with LeNet-5. LeNet-5 [15] is a conventional CNN which consists of two convolutional layers and two fully connected layers, including 431K learnable parameters. For MNIST experiments, we use SGDM [21] with a momentum coefficient $\beta = 0.9$ and a weight decay of 0.0005. We train from scratch for 200 epochs with a batch size of 64. We use the initial learning rate of 0.01 and multiply it by 0.2 at the epoch 60, 120 and 160. Secondly, for CIFAR-10 and CIFAR-100 experiments, we prune the ResNet-20, 32, 56 and 110. We use a momentum coefficient of 0.9 and a weight decay of 0.0005. We train all models from scratch by 250 epochs with a batch size of 128. The learning rate schedule is $\eta = 0.1, 0.02, 0.004, 0.0008, 0.0002$ at the epoch 1, 40, 120, 160 and 200, respectively.

Specifically, for CIFAR-10 experiments, we make quantitative comparisons with the following competing methods: Pruning Filters (L1-pruning-A, L1-pruning-B) [17], Channel-pruning [10], More is Less (LCCL) [3], Soft Filter Pruning (SFP) [8], Filter Pruning via Geometric Median (FPGM) [9].

4.2   LeNet on MNIST

We prune the two convolutional layers in LeNet-5 based on MNIST dataset through FPGraSP algorithm and use specified pruning rates drawn from $\{10\%, 20\%, 30\%, 40\%, 50\%, 60\%, 70\%, 80\%\}$. Table 2 shows the pruning results of LeNet-5 on MNIST. We can successfully prune 50% of the filters from the two

Table 2. Results of Pruning LeNet-5 on MNIST with higher pruning rates of filters (only pruning filters in the two convolutional layers). In the "Method" column, the percentage shown in brackets represents the pruning rate P_i. The "Drop Acc" means the top-1 of the uncompressed model minus that of the compact model.

Model	Method	Baseline Acc(%)	Pruned Acc(%)	Drop Acc(%)
LeNet-5	FPGraSP(10%)	99.34	99.22	0.12
	FPGraSP(20%)		99.28	0.06
	FPGraSP(30%)		**99.29**	0.05
	FPGraSP(40%)		99.20	0.14
	FPGraSP(50%)		99.22	0.12
	FPGraSP(60%)		98.93	0.41
	FPGraSP(70%)		98.95	0.39
	FPGraSP(80%)		98.61	0.73

convolutional layers, and it only degrades the top-1 accuracy by 0.12%. Moreover, we prune 80% with maintaining the classification accuracy. Therefore, we preliminarily testify the practicality and efficiency of our algorithm and demonstrate that GraSP can be applied on CNNs. In the subsections described as follows, we can further implement FPGraSP on significantly deeper models such as ResNets and compare our method with other pruning approaches.

4.3   ResNet on CIFAR-10

For CIFAR-10 experiments, we employ FPGraSP to prune the ResNet-20, 32, 56 and 110 model with five different pruning rates.

Moreover, FPGraSP algorithm we propose selects and zeroizes unimportant filters based on the criterion discussed above in the optimizer at each training iteration.

Table 3 illustrates the results on CIFAR-10, comparing FPGraSP we adopt with baseline methods listed above. For instance, for compressing ResNet-56, FPGM-mix [9] with fine-tuning achieves 52.63% FLOPs reduction with 0.33% accuracy drop, while FPGraSP without finetuning obtains 0.04% accuracy drop. When reducing 40.78% FLOPs at a comparable pruning rate of 30% on ResNet-110, FPGraSP obtains 94.18% accuracy with 0.01% performance improvement. There is no need for a fine-tuning procedure, so FPGraSP can save training time.

Accordingly, these satisfying results demonstrate that FPGraSP can use both gradient-based criterion and parameter-based criterion, which results in its outstanding performance consistently and shows a satisfactory balance between pursuing high accuracy and compressing model.

4.4   ResNet on CIFAR-100

We apply FPGraSP on CIFAR-100 dataset to compress ResNet-20, 32, 56 and 110. For example, as depicted in Table 4, FPGraSP delivers 73.08% Top-1 accu-

Table 3. Comparison of pruning ResNet on CIFAR-10. The "Pruned FLOPs" means the FLOPs reduction in the pruned model.

Depth	Method	Baseline Acc(%)	Pruned Acc(%)	Fine-tune	Pruned FLOPs(%)
20	SFP [8](10%)	92.20	92.24	No	15.24
	FPGraSP(10%)	92.39	**92.44**	No	15.24
	LCCL [3]	91.53	91.43	No	20.3
	SFP [8](20%)	92.20	91.20	No	29.31
	FPGraSP(20%)	92.39	**91.79**	No	29.31
	SFP [8](30%)	92.20	90.83	No	42.22
	FPGM-only [9](30%)	92.20	91.09	No	42.22
	FPGraSP(30%)	92.39	**91.51**	No	42.22
	FPGM-only [9](40%)	92.20	90.44	No	54.00
	FPGraSP(40%)	92.39	**90.65**	No	54.00
32	SFP [8](10%)	92.63	93.22	No	14.93
	FPGraSP(10%)	92.63	**93.42**	No	14.93
	SFP [8](20%)	92.63	92.63	No	28.77
	FPGraSP(20%)	92.63	**92.83**	No	28.77
	SFP [8](30%)	92.63	92.08	No	41.51
	FPGM-only [9](30%)	92.63	92.31	No	41.51
	FPGraSP(30%)	92.63	**92.32**	No	41.51
	FPGM-mix [9](40%)	92.63	91.91	No	53.20
	FPGraSP(40%)	92.63	**92.22**	No	53.20
56	L1-pruning-A [17]	93.04	93.10	Yes	10.40
	SFP [8](10%)	93.59	93.89	No	14.74
	FPGraSP(10%)	93.43	**94.03**	No	14.74
	SFP [8](20%)	93.59	93.47	No	28.42
	FPGraSP(20%)	93.43	**93.87**	No	28.42
	LCCL [3]	92.33	90.74	No	31.2
	SFP [8](30%)	93.59	93.10	No	41.06
	FPGraSP(30%)	93.43	**93.73**	No	41.06
	SFP [8](40%)	93.59	92.26	No	52.63
	FPGM-mix [9](40%)	93.59	93.26	Yes	52.63
	FPGraSP(40%)	93.43	**93.39**	No	52.63
	Channel-pruning [10]	92.63	91.80	Yes	50.00
	FPGraSP(50%)	93.43	**92.28**	No	63.16
110	L1-pruning-A [17]	93.53	93.55	Yes	15.90
	SFP [8](10%)	93.68	93.83	No	14.62
	FPGraSP(10%)	94.17	**94.59**	No	14.62
	SFP [8](20%)	93.68	93.93	No	28.21
	FPGraSP(20%)	94.17	**94.31**	No	28.21
	L1-pruning-B [17]	93.53	93.30	Yes	38.60
	LCCL [3]	93.63	93.44	No	34.20
	SFP [8](30%)	93.68	93.86	Yes	40.78
	FPGraSP(30%)	94.17	**94.18**	No	40.78
	FPGM-mix [9](40%)	93.68	93.85	No	52.30
	FPGraSP(40%)	94.17	**93.97**	No	52.30

Table 4. Pruning filters in ResNet based on CIFAR-100 with different pruning rates. The "Drop Acc" represents the dropped accuracy percentage after pruning.

Depth	Method	Baseline Acc(%)	Pruned Acc(%)	Drop Acc(%)	Pruned FLOPs(%)
20	FPGraSP(10%)	68.95	67.80	1.15	15.24
	FPGraSP(20%)		67.51	1.44	29.31
	FPGraSP(30%)		66.10	2.85	42.22
32	FPGraSP(10%)	70.08	69.58	0.50	14.93
	FPGraSP(20%)		69.38	0.70	28.77
	FPGraSP(30%)		68.10	1.98	41.51
56	FPGraSP(10%)	72.01	72.45	−0.44	14.74
	FPGraSP(20%)		71.04	0.97	28.42
	FPGraSP(30%)		70.46	1.55	41.06
110	FPGraSP(10%)	73.91	73.93	−0.02	14.62
	FPGraSP(20%)		73.08	0.83	28.21
	FPGraSP(30%)		73.08	0.83	40.78

racy by pruning 40.78% FLOPs on ResNet-110 while the baseline accuracy is 73.91%. In summary, we now discover empirically that exploiting the gradient information is conducive to determining which filters should be preserved in an individual layer.

5 Conclusion

In this paper, we propose a novel Filter Pruning via Gradient Support Pursuit (FPGraSP). We apply GraSP to filter pruning in deep CNNs. We take into account both the current gradients and the parameters of filters retained at the previous iteration. Extensive experiments on several benchmarks show our method can facilitate CNNs acceleration at a high pruning rate without observing obvious performance loss. For pruning ResNet-56 on CIFAR-10, our FPGraSP without fine-tuning obtains 0.04% accuracy drop with 40% parameters reduction, achieving 52.63% FLOPs reduction.

Acknowledgements. This work was supported in part by National Major Project of China for New Generation of AI under Grant No. 2018AAA0100400 and in part by Natural Science Foundation of China (NSFC) under Grant No. 61876090 and No. 61936005.

References

1. Alizadeh, M., Fernández-Marqués, J., Lane, N.D., Gal, Y.: An empirical study of binary neural networks' optimisation (2018)
2. Bahmani, S., Raj, B., Boufounos, P.T.: Greedy sparsity-constrained optimization. J. Mach. Learn. Res. **14**(Mar), 807–841 (2013)
3. Dong, X., Huang, J., Yang, Y., Yan, S.: More is less: a more complicated network with less inference complexity. In: Proceedings of the IEEE Conference on Computer Vision and Pattern Recognition, pp. 5840–5848 (2017)

4. Guo, Y., Yao, A., Chen, Y.: Dynamic network surgery for efficient dnns. In: Advances In Neural Information Processing Systems, pp. 1379–1387 (2016)
5. Han, S., Mao, H., Dally, W.J.: Deep compression: compressing deep neural networks with pruning, trained quantization and huffman coding. arXiv preprint arXiv:1510.00149 (2015)
6. Han, S., Pool, J., Tran, J., Dally, W.: Learning both weights and connections for efficient neural network. In: Advances in Neural Information Processing Systems, pp. 1135–1143 (2015)
7. He, K., Zhang, X., Ren, S., Sun, J.: Deep residual learning for image recognition. In: Proceedings of the IEEE Conference on Computer Vision and Pattern Recognition, pp. 770–778 (2016)
8. He, Y., Kang, G., Dong, X., Fu, Y., Yang, Y.: Soft filter pruning for accelerating deep convolutional neural networks. arXiv preprint arXiv:1808.06866 (2018)
9. He, Y., Liu, P., Wang, Z., Hu, Z., Yang, Y.: Filter pruning via geometric median for deep convolutional neural networks acceleration. In: Proceedings of the IEEE Conference on Computer Vision and Pattern Recognition, pp. 4340–4349 (2019)
10. He, Y., Zhang, X., Sun, J.: Channel pruning for accelerating very deep neural networks. In: Proceedings of the IEEE International Conference on Computer Vision, pp. 1389–1397 (2017)
11. Hinton, G., Vinyals, O., Dean, J.: Distilling the knowledge in a neural network. arXiv preprint arXiv:1503.02531 (2015)
12. Jin, X., Yuan, X., Feng, J., Yan, S.: Training skinny deep neural networks with iterative hard thresholding methods. arXiv preprint arXiv:1607.05423 (2016)
13. Krizhevsky, A., Hinton, G., et al.: Learning multiple layers of features from tiny images. Technical repor, Citeseer (2009)
14. Krizhevsky, A., Sutskever, I., Hinton, G.E.: Imagenet classification with deep convolutional neural networks. In: Advances in Neural Information Processing Systems, pp. 1097–1105 (2012)
15. LeCun, Y., et al.: Gradient-based learning applied to document recognition. Proc. IEEE **86**(11), 2278–2324 (1998)
16. LeCun, Y., Denker, J.S., Solla, S.A.: Optimal brain damage. In: Advances in Neural Information Processing Systems, pp. 598–605 (1990)
17. Li, H., Kadav, A., Durdanovic, I., Samet, H., Graf, H.P.: Pruning filters for efficient convnets. arXiv preprint arXiv:1608.08710 (2016)
18. Liu, Z., Li, J., Shen, Z., Huang, G., Yan, S., Zhang, C.: Learning efficient convolutional networks through network slimming. In: Proceedings of the IEEE International Conference on Computer Vision, pp. 2736–2744 (2017)
19. Luo, J.H., Wu, J., Lin, W.: Thinet: a filter level pruning method for deep neural network compression. In: Proceedings of the IEEE International Conference on Computer Vision, pp. 5058–5066 (2017)
20. Paszke, A., et al: Automatic differentiation in pytorch (2017)
21. Qian, N.: On the momentum term in gradient descent learning algorithms. Neural Netw. **12**(1), 145–151 (1999)
22. Singh, B., Najibi, M., Davis, L.S.: Sniper: efficient multi-scale training. In: Advances in Neural Information Processing Systems, pp. 9310–9320 (2018)
23. Wang, W., Fu, C., Guo, J., Cai, D., He, X.: Cop: customized deep model compression via regularized correlation-based filter-level pruning. arXiv preprint arXiv:1906.10337 (2019)
24. Wen, W., Wu, C., Wang, Y., Chen, Y., Li, H.: Learning structured sparsity in deep neural networks. In: Advances in Neural Information Processing Systems, pp. 2074–2082 (2016)

25. Ye, J., et al.: Learning compact recurrent neural networks with block-term tensor decomposition. In: Proceedings of the IEEE Conference on Computer Vision and Pattern Recognition, pp. 9378–9387 (2018)
26. Zhuang, B., Shen, C., Tan, M., Liu, L., Reid, I.: Towards effective low-bitwidth convolutional neural networks. In: Proceedings of the IEEE Conference on Computer Vision and Pattern Recognition, pp. 7920–7928 (2018)
27. Zhuang, Z., et al.: Discrimination-aware channel pruning for deep neural networks. In: Advances in Neural Information Processing Systems, pp. 875–886 (2018)

Synthesizing Large-Scale Datasets for License Plate Detection and Recognition in the Wild

Chaochen Wang, Wenzhong Wang[(✉)], Chenglong Li, and Jin Tang

School of Computer Science and Technology, Anhui University, Hefei, China
chaochen.wang@foxmail.com, lcl1314@foxmail.com,
{wenzhong,tj}@ahu.edu.cn

Abstract. License Plate Detection and Recognition (LPDR) plays a key role in modern intelligent transportation systems. Recent state-of-the-art methods of LPDR are based on deep convolutional neural networks (DCNN), which require learning a huge number of parameters from a sufficient amount of labeled training images. However, collecting and manually annotating a large collection of diverse license plate images is tedious and challenging. In this paper, we propose to use a virtual world simulator to automatically generate realistic images with precise annotations, effectively avoiding the need for laborious image acquisition and labeling. Our method can generate any type of license plates, and simulate different scene backgrounds, illumination conditions, and viewpoints. In order to validate the effectiveness of synthesized images, we have generated a large collection of images with three types of annotations, including bounding box, corner points and plate numbers. In many real scenarios, the image regions of plates are rarely axis-aligned, and thus the axis-aligned bounding box is inappropriate for describing plate positions. Motivated by this observation, we propose to detect the four corners of the plate, and present a DCNN based method for plate corner detection. We conduct experiments on three tasks, including bounding box detection, corner detection and plate recognition, using the synthesized dataset combined with a real dataset. Experimental results show that our simulated image datasets can improve the performance clearly on all of the three tasks.

Keywords: Synthetic dataset · License plate detection and recognition · Convolutional neural network · Corner detection

1 Introduction

As an important part of intelligent transportation, automatic license plate detection and recognition (LPDR) has a high practical value. Its main purpose is to detect and identify vehicle license plate (LP) information in traffic scenes, which is widely used in road monitoring, regional vehicle access control, etc. Although

© Springer Nature Switzerland AG 2020
Y. Peng et al. (Eds.): PRCV 2020, LNCS 12307, pp. 433–445, 2020.
https://doi.org/10.1007/978-3-030-60636-7_36

the task of LPDR has been studied for many years, due to the complex scenes in reality and the differences of LPs in various regions, there is still a lot of room for the research and landing of LPDR algorithm.

Since the widely adoption of deep convolutional neural networks in computer vision community, the latest dominant approaches for LPDR [1–4] are DCNN based methods. DCNNs are over-parameterized, highly nonlinear models which imply the learning of millions of parameters, and accordingly, they require a large amount of accurately labelled training images. However, the LP images are different from other images such as those in the ImageNet [5] dataset in many aspects. Firstly, the specifications and appearances of LPs are regional, they vary a lot from region to region, and country to country. This characteristic makes any LP images collected from one region are less useful in other regions. For example, the LP images from the USA are almost useless for LPDR in Japan. Secondly, the distributions of LP images are locally clustered, and one has to collect LP images in different areas in order to vendor LPDR services in those areas. Thirdly, the LP specifications might evolve, leading to the emergence of new LPs. For example, the LP specification for the so called new-energy vehicle in China is different from others. Therefore, effort must be made to collect and annotate new images for emerging LPs. These factors make the collection and labeling of a widely applicable dataset for LPDR highly difficult.

There are some public LP image datasets [1,3,6–9], these datasets are collected in different countries. Most of them are ad-hoc small sets aiming for specific applications such as access control, road patrol, etc. The largest one among those is the CCPD dataset, containing over 250k images, taken with handheld cameras. However, the viewpoints of these images are limited, and not appropriate for other scenarios such as surveillance.

To address the above problems, and following the recent successful practice of synthesizing virtual images for computer vision tasks [10,11], we propose to generate synthetic LP images using a virtual world. Our LP image synthesizing method is developed on the Unity3D (U3D) platform[1]. We generate virtual LP models according to the official LP specifications, and then automatically assemble the LP models onto variate 3D vehicle models in a variety of realistic background scenes. The virtual scenes are then rendered with many different randomly chosen camera settings and lighting conditions, creating realistic LP images. We process these images by randomly changing their contrasts and brightness, and add different random noises to better mimic imaging conditions in real world. Since our images are rendered from 3D models in which we know the 3D coordinates and numbers of the LPs, we can automatically generate annotations using this information. In our method, we generate three types of labels, e.g., the 2D bounding box, the image coordinates of the four corner points of LP, and the number of LP. The first two labels can be used in LP detection, and the third one is aiming at LP recognition. Our LP image dataset generation tool can efficiently generate millions of different LP images with precise annotations, effectively avoiding tedious and costly dataset collection and labeling process.

---

[1] unity.com.

In our experiments, we show that our synthesized dataset is effective in training DCNN based detection and recognition models.

In addition, inspired by the success of DCNN based object detection, many researchers have adopted general object detection models such as YOLO [12] to LP detection. However, in the general models, the objects are represented by axis-aligned bounding boxes (AABBs). Such a representation is inappropriate for LPs. The LP is a rectangle shaped plate in real world, when projected onto the image plane, the shape of its boundary in the image is changed by the projective transformation, and may not aligned with image axes. The AABBs enclosing LPs may contain much background, as shown in Fig. 1(a). When recognizing such LP images, the LP regions must be rectified to horizontally oriented regions containing only plate numbers (Fig. 1(b)). In comprehension of this point, we propose to directly detect the four corners of the LPs. Our newly designed LP detection model is modified from FSSD [13] by adding new branch to regress corner coordinate. Our experiments show that the performance of our corner regression model surpasses the original SSD [14] model.

We've made three contributions in this paper. The first one is our new tool for automatically generating realistic LP images with precise annotations. The second is a new DCNN model for LP detection, in which we directly regress the four corner points of LPs. The third one is a large-scale synthesized LP image dataset, and the experimental validation of the effectiveness of our synthesized dataset.

(a)   (b)

Fig. 1. (a) The license plate inclines, where the green boxes are the detection results of axis-aligned bounding boxes, and the red ones are the corner detection results. (b) The front view of LP images aligned by homography transformation with corner detection. (Color figure online)

2   Related Work

2.1   License Plate Detection and Recognition Datasets

UFPR [3] and SSIG [6] datasets are all built in Brazil, UFPR includes 4500 images collected from cars and motorcycles, where every image has the vehicle's position and type as well as the AABB of the LP. SSIG contains 2000 Brazilian LPs consisting of 14000 alphanumeric symbols and their corresponding AABB.

AOLP [7] and AOLPE [1] datasets contain three scenarios: access control, traffic law enforcement, road patrol, with the total of 4200 images. They include different weathers, times, distances and tilt labels, and are collected from Taiwan, China. ReID [8] dataset is a large dataset, including 1.4k surveillance video sequences, collected in Europe, without the change of perspective. CCPD [9] is the largest and complex open dataset, contains over 250k unique images, taken by parking toll collectors with a hand-held camera in China in complex environments. The annotations include LP text, AABB, corner position, angle, etc. However, due to the large number of images, there are some errors and incomplete annotations.

2.2   License Plate Detection

With the development of DCNNs, it has brought effective solutions to tasks in many fields, and researchers have also applied it to the field of LPDR. The most advanced CNN based object detection models can be roughly divided into two categories: two-stage R-CNN series [15–17] and one-stage YOLO series [12,18, 19], SSD series [13,14]. The speed of two-stage model is slow but its accuracy is high. The speed of one-stage model is fast, but its accuracy is slightly lower than that of the two-stage model. Generally, LPDR needs a real-time system, therefore most researchers adopt the method of one-stage models, [1–3] detects the LP by modifying the YOLO, and Montazzolli et al. [2] also considers LP in the unrestricted scene. They propose a WPOD net, which transforms the distorted LP into a rectangular shape in the front view through the coefficient of regression affine transformation. Meng et al. [4] skip LP detection and detect the corners of the detected LP image.

2.3   License Plate Recognition

The task of LP character recognition is similar to optical character recognition (OCR). This task is usually divided into segmentation-based method and segmentation-free method, The former usually does character segmentation before character recognition, such as [20,21]. All the characters are segmented and recognized by image processing methods such as binarization and morphology. Meng et al. [4] uses the method based on CNN, using the model to predict the segmentation position of LP text in the picture, and then recognize the segmented text. In the method of segmentation-free method, the better one is CRNN [22], which comes from the natural scene character recognition, for the detection of indefinite length text. They use CNN to extract features, and then use the combination of Bilstm and CTC loss to identify characters, but this method can't recognize multiple lines of text.

3   Synthetic Dataset Generation Method

In this paper, we propose a method for LP dataset synthesis, which can synthesize any type of LP dataset, to deal with the difficulty in collecting and labeling

Fig. 2. Illustration of the whole generation process of our synthetic dataset. First, we randomly select the appropriate vehicle model, LP and background (left). Second, we combine them in the virtual scene established by U3D (middle). Finally, we render the corresponding image and generate the corresponding label from the script (right).

LP images. We use U3D and built-in C# script as our rendering tool, and the main rendering process is shown in Fig. 2. We use the random combination of LP, 3D vehicle model, background, road and light to render and automatically calculate the label information. In the near future, we will release the generated LP dataset and the generator with codes.

3.1   License Plate Generator

LP synthesis is an independent step. It is necessary to obtain materials and rules of LPs from official documents of various countries, including background, text, layout, etc. For example, different types of Chinese LPs have different background colors, characters, sizes and layout. By using OpenCV, we combine materials according to LP generation rules, and finally synthesize various types of compliant LPs. Figure 3 shows different kinds of LP images generated automatically. At the same time, we can get the text of the LP, and these images and text are provided for subsequent steps.

Fig. 3. Different types of license plates in China are generated according to the rules.

3.2   Scene Settings

We decompose the scene in the real world into a vehicle with LP, background, light, etc. To increase the diversity of background and reduce the amount of computation during rendering, we collect high-resolution panoramic images of various scenes in Google Street View instead of building a solid scene through models. In the rendering phase, we change the background by changing the panoramic image. In order to correct the perspective relationship, we also build a road model, and give the road map, as the initialization plane of the vehicles.

For vehicles, we collect more than ten kinds of 3D models of cars, buses, SUVs, pickups, etc. Aiming to increase the diversity, we randomly change the vehicle color during the generation process. Through the C# script, the LP generated in Sect. 3.1 is fitted to the corresponding mesh in the vehicle model as a texture map.

In order to simulate real sunlight, we use a built-in component named Directional Light. The light rendered by Directional Light is parallel, similar to the sun. By setting the color, intensity and rotation of Directional Light to simulate sunlight at different times of the day, such as soft orange sunlight at morning and evening and strong white light at noon, shown in Fig. 4, After adjusting the light parameters, U3D will automatically calculate the reflection effect of the object surface and the shadow relationship between objects.

Fig. 4. Different rendering effects by changing the sunlight.

3.3   Camera Settings

As mentioned in Sect. 2.1, most of the datasets do not consider the complex angle of view. They mostly collect from the front or rear of the vehicle. In U3D, the field of view (FOV) can be changed by adjusting the focal length and the sensor size of the camera, and the perspective deformation and scale of the LP in the rendered image can be changed by changing the camera position and rotation.

After the vehicle position is determined, the front or rear LP is randomly selected as the initialization center point of the camera position. The pose of the object in U3D is determined by six parameters, including position (x, y, z) and rotation (r, θ, φ). For example, we set the parameters of camera position as $x \in [0.5, 5]$, $y \in [0, 2]$, $z \in [-2, 2]$ in meters relative to the center of LP. In this way, the camera will be randomly positioned in a cube in front or behind the vehicle. We set the camera location relative to the LP, then adjust the rotation of the camera by randomly choosing $r \in [-15, 15]$, $\theta \in [-5, 5]$, $\varphi \in [-15, 15]$ in degrees. Some of the rendered images are shown in Fig. 5.

3.4   Post Processing

We also consider the problem of data degradation under real conditions. We use OnRenderImage API in U3D which is called after all rendering is completed to

Fig. 5. Some samples are generated by random settings of camera position and rotation.

render the post-processing effects of images. We mainly modify the rendering texture of objects to change the brightness, contrast and saturation of the final rendering. The changed effect is shown in Fig. 6. For camera shake or motion blur and other degradation effects, in order not to slow the generator, we added noise and motion blur to some images randomly after the image generation.

Fig. 6. Adjustment with different rendering effects through post-processing.

3.5 Automatic Annotation

Based on the random scene generation above, the LP may not be included in the camera's FOV, thus we set four sub-objects of the LP positions of all vehicle models as anchor points. Through the calculation of the projection matrix to the position of anchor points in the pixel coordinate, the LP rendering image beyond the canvas scope is discarded.

Through getting the corner positions of the LP, we infer the AABB and write all this into the label file, and the imported LP number can also be saved at the same time. All label files are created in PASCAL VOC [23] format, and each corresponding image is saved in PNG format. In this way, there will be no error or missing annotation caused by manual annotation.

4 The FSSD-Corner Net

4.1 Base Network

Inspired by FPN [24], Li et al. [13] propose feature fusion single shot multibox detector (FSSD) by modifying the SSD [14] to use feature fusion to improve the detection accuracy of small targets. We use this as our base network for LP detection. As shown in Fig. 7, FSSD reduces the channel of conv4_3, fc7 and conv7_2 to 256 by ConvNet of 1×1, and interpolates fc7 and conv7_2 to 38×38 of the same size as conv4, and finally concatenates the three layers of feature map and generates feature pyramid from this fusion feature.

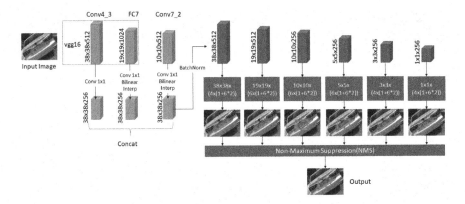

Fig. 7. The overall network architecture of our method. When the feature of the image is extracted through the network, additional parameters are added to regress the corresponding corner points.

4.2 Corner Detection

After getting fusion feature, we modify the detector, shown in Fig. 7, each extra feature layer is convolved with two different ConvNet of 3 * 3, one of which is for plate classification and the other one is for corner regression. In regression step, the original FSSD only regresses (x, y, h, w), and we add additional neurons to output $(x_i, y_i)_{i \in (0,3)}$, the corner points of the LP. The convolutional results of the position of the prior box matching the ground truth(GT) box in training is used as the positive sample to calculate the loss. The total loss consists of three parts $L_{conf}, L_{loc}, L_{cor}$:

$$L = \frac{1}{N}(L_{conf} + L_{loc} + L_{cor}) \tag{1}$$

where N is the number of prior box matched with the GT box on the feature map, L_{conf} is the Softmax loss to calculate whether it is a LP, L_{loc} is the smooth L1 loss for plate bounding box regression and L_{cor} is the smooth L1 loss for plate corner regression.

We refer the strategy of Textboxes++ [25], calculate the relative offset between the corner points in GT and the corner points of the rectangle in prior box in clockwise order from top left to bottom left, and regress the corner points by the following formula:

$$L_{cor} = \sum_{i \in PB}^{N} \sum_{m \in \{x_k, y_k\}} x_{ij} smooth_{L1}(p_i^m - \hat{g}_j^m),$$

$$
\begin{aligned}
\hat{g}_j^{x_0} &= (g_j^{x_0} - (d_i^x - d_i^w/2))/d_i^w, \hat{g}_j^{y_0} = (g_j^{y_0} - (d_i^y - d_i^h/2))/d_i^h \\
\hat{g}_j^{x_1} &= (g_j^{x_1} - (d_i^x + d_i^w/2))/d_i^w, \hat{g}_j^{y_1} = (g_j^{y_1} - (d_i^y - d_i^h/2))/d_i^h \\
\hat{g}_j^{x_2} &= (g_j^{x_2} - (d_i^x + d_i^w/2))/d_i^w, \hat{g}_j^{y_2} = (g_j^{y_2} - (d_i^y + d_i^h/2))/d_i^h \\
\hat{g}_j^{x_3} &= (g_j^{x_3} - (d_i^x - d_i^w/2))/d_i^w, \hat{g}_j^{y_3} = (g_j^{y_3} - (d_i^y + d_i^h/2))/d_i^h
\end{aligned}
\tag{2}
$$

where $x_{ij} = \{0, 1\}$ represents whether the i-th prior box matches the j-th GT box, p and g represent the predicted and GT values, respectively. Each corner point is calculated with the corresponding corner point of the rectangular box in prior box relative to its width(w) and height(h), and the offset value is used for regression.

5   Experiments

In general, different datasets have different data distribution, and the model trained on a dataset can only perform well on the data with similar distribution, which is called domain shift [26]. Synthetic data and real data have different image styles. To solve this problem, we use Balanced Gradient Contribution (BGC) method introduced in [27]. In the training phase, the proportion of real data and synthetic data is fixed in each batch of training data, which makes the real data in the dominant position. BGC method does not need much real data, and in the experiment, it can effectively improve the performance of the model with a small amount real data.

5.1   Comparison with Real Dataset in Detection

In order to verify the effectiveness of synthetic dataset in LP detection, we have conducted two experiments. In both experiments, we use SSD as our LP detection model. To evaluate the detection results, we use the metric of average precision (AP) at the intersection over union (IoU) threshold of 0.5.

Table 1. Comparison between synthetic dataset and real dataset for LP detection.

Model	Train set	Test set	AP
SSD	CCPD(20k)	Surveillance Scene(7k)	84.10%
	SLP(20k)		84.24%
	CCPD(500)	CCPD(7k)	90.26%
	SLP(20k)		80.15%
	CCPD(20k)		90.65%
	CCPD(500)+SLP(20k)(BGC)		90.49%

In the first experiment, we randomly select 20K images from the CCPD dataset [9] as training set, and 7K as test set(CCPD7K). We'v also synthesized 20K images as synthetic training set (SLP20K), and collected and labeled another test set consisting of 7K images from surveillance videos. We trained two SSD model using these two training sets and tested them on the the surveillance dataset. Note that there are domain shifts in between the training sets and test set. The test APs are shown in Table 1. SSD trained with pure synthetic dataset slightly outperforms SSD trained with real dataset. Since both training sets are of the same volumn, this result indicates that synthesized dataset is comparable with real datasets in terms of detection accuracy, while significantly reduce the cost of image collection and annotation.

In the second experiment, we are trying to figure out whether synthetic dataset can be used to boost the detection performance when there are only a small amount of real training images. We trained four SSD models using four different training sets and then tested them on the CCPD7K test set. The four training sets are CCPD500 (which is a small subset randomly select from CCPD2K), SLP20K, CCPD20K, and CCPD500 combined with SLP20K. We use the BGC method when training with the combined dataset. The test results are shown in Table 1. The model trained with CCPD20K is significantly superior to the model trained using SLP20K, we believe this discrepancy in performance is due to the domain shift between the SLP dataset and the CCPD dataset. When trained with limited dataset (CCPD500), the detection precision is 90.26%. It can be improved to 90.65% (0.39%↑) by using the remaining 19.5K CCPD data. By combining the limited CCPD500 and SLP20k, we've achieved the AP of 90.49% (0.23%↑), which is comparable to the improvement made by the 19.5K real data. This means that synthetic dataset, combined with a small amount of real data, can achieve state-of-the-art detection results.

Furthermore, unlike CCPD dataset, which only has a single type of LP, our synthetic dataset contains many types of LPs in China, as shown in Fig. 8, and the detector trained with the synthetic dataset can detect many types of LPs.

Fig. 8. Detectors trained with synthetic data can detect various types of license plates.

5.2   Comparison with Real Dataset in Recognition

For recognition, we also use AP as the evaluation metric, when the predicted LP numbers are exactly the same as GT, it is recorded as correct. We use CRNN [22] as recognition model, and use the same dataset as detection, where the difference is that the images that make up the dataset are intercepted from the LP area and transformed by homography. The test results are shown in Table 2. Compared with the prediction results of the model with only a small amount of real data in training, the model with combined data and trained by BGC method has a great improvement, and it has the similar results as the model trained with a large amount of real data, and some example are shown in Fig. 9.

Table 2. Comparison between synthetic dataset and real dataset for LP recognition.

Model	Train set	Test set	AP
CRNN	CCPD(500)	CCPD(7k)	93.26%
	SLP(20k)		92.67%
	CCPD(20k)		96.95%
	CCPD(500)+SLP(20k)(BGC)		96.44%

Table 3. Comparison between our method and SSD

Model	Train set	Test set	AP
SSD	SLP(20k)	CCPD(7k)	80.15%
FSSD-corner			81.56%

5.3 FSSD-corner Detection

Since there is no good evaluation method for corner detection, we only use the AABB predicted by FSSD-corner as the result to compare the IoU overlap with the GT. Table 3 shows the performance of our method against SSD. Compared with SSD, our method shows improved detection accuracy. In addition to bounding box detection, our method can also estimate the four corners of the LP, which can be used for LP rectification to improve the subsequent recognition task. In Fig. 9, we show some test results of our method and SSD.

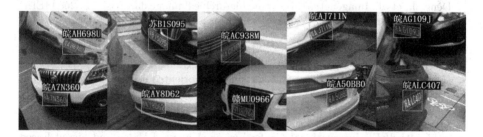

Fig. 9. Example of detection and recognition results. All models are trained with synthetic data, where the green boxes are SSD results, the red ones are our results of FSSD corner and the white texts represent the recognition results predicted by CRNN. (Color figure online)

6   Conclusions

We propose a method for LP dataset synthesis, which can synthesize any type of LP in any region, and automatically generate accurate annotations. The synthesized dataset is diverse enough in terms of background, light, perspective, scale and so on. In the experiment, we verify that synthetic data is comparable to the real data for model training when real data is scarce. We proposed FSSD-Corner, a DCNN based detection model for license plate corner detection. FSSD-Corner outputs the four corners of a plate, which could be used to rectify the plate area. Our method effectively solved the problem of traditional detection method in which the plates are depicted using unrealistic axis-aligned bounding box.

In the future, We plan to synthesize annotation data for more intelligent transportation tasks, such as data with vehicle speed and real location, for vehicle speed detection and 3D vehicle detection, etc. The development of algorithms in the field of intelligent transportation can be achieved with orders of magnitude reduction in annotation cost.

References

1. Hsu, G.S., Ambikapathi, A., Chung, S.L., Su, C.P.: Robust license plate detection in the wild. In: 2017 14th IEEE International Conference on Advanced Video and Signal Based Surveillance (AVSS), pp. 1–6. IEEE (2017)
2. Montazzolli Silva, S., Rosito Jung, C.: License plate detection and recognition in unconstrained scenarios. In: Proceedings of the European Conference on Computer Vision (ECCV), pp. 580–596 (2018)
3. Laroca, R., et al.: A robust real-time automatic license plate recognition based on the yolo detector. In: 2018 International Joint Conference on Neural Networks (IJCNN), pp. 1–10. IEEE (2018)
4. Meng, A., Yang, W., Xu, Z., Huang, H., Huang, L., Ying, C.: A robust and efficient method for license plate recognition. In: 2018 24th International Conference on Pattern Recognition (ICPR), pp. 1713–1718. IEEE (2018)
5. Deng, J., et al.: Imagenet: a large-scale hierarchical image database. In: 2009 IEEE Conference on Computer Vision and Pattern Recognition, pp. 248–255. IEEE (2009)
6. Gonçalves, G.R., da Silva, S.P.G., Menotti, D., Schwartz, W.R.: Benchmark for license plate character segmentation. J. Electron. Imaging **25**(5), 053034 (2016)
7. Hsu, G.S., Chen, J.C., Chung, Y.Z.: Application-oriented license plate recognition. IEEE Trans. Veh. Technol. **62**(2), 552–561 (2012)
8. Špaňhel, J., Sochor, J., Juránek, R., Herout, A., Maršík, L., Zemčík, P.: Holistic recognition of low quality license plates by CNN using track annotated data. In: 2017 14th IEEE International Conference on Advanced Video and Signal Based Surveillance (AVSS), pp. 1–6. IEEE (2017)
9. Xu, Z., et al.: Towards end-to-end license plate detection and recognition: a large dataset and baseline. In: Proceedings of the European Conference on Computer Vision (ECCV), pp. 255–271 (2018)
10. Ros, G., Sellart, L., Materzynska, J., Vazquez, D., Lopez, A.M.: The synthia dataset: a large collection of synthetic images for semantic segmentation of urban scenes. In: Proceedings of the IEEE Conference on Computer Vision and Pattern Recognition, pp. 3234–3243 (2016)
11. Šlosár, P., Juránek, R., Herout, A.: Cheap rendering vs. costly annotation: rendered omnidirectional dataset of vehicles. In: Proceedings of the 30th Spring Conference on Computer Graphics, pp. 71–78 (2014)

12. Redmon, J., Divvala, S., Girshick, R., Farhadi, A.: You only look once: unified, real-time object detection. In: Proceedings of the IEEE Conference on Computer Vision and Pattern Recognition, pp. 779–788 (2016)
13. Li, Z., Zhou, F.: Fssd: feature fusion single shot multibox detector. arXiv preprint arXiv:1712.00960 (2017)
14. Liu, W., et al.: SSD: single shot multibox detector. In: Leibe, B., Matas, J., Sebe, N., Welling, M. (eds.) ECCV 2016. LNCS, vol. 9905, pp. 21–37. Springer, Cham (2016). https://doi.org/10.1007/978-3-319-46448-0_2
15. Girshick, R., Donahue, J., Darrell, T., Malik, J.: Rich feature hierarchies for accurate object detection and semantic segmentation. In: Proceedings of the IEEE Conference on Computer Vision and Pattern Recognition, pp. 580–587 (2014)
16. Ren, S., He, K., Girshick, R., Sun, J.: Faster r-cnn: towards real-time object detection with region proposal networks. In: Advances in Neural Information Processing Systems, pp. 91–99 (2015)
17. Girshick, R.: Fast r-cnn. In: Proceedings of the IEEE International Conference on Computer Vision, pp. 1440–1448 (2015)
18. Redmon, J., Farhadi, A.: Yolo9000: better, faster, stronger. In: Proceedings of the IEEE Conference on Computer Vision and Pattern Recognition, pp. 7263–7271 (2017)
19. Redmon, J., Farhadi, A.: Yolov3: an incremental improvement. arXiv preprint arXiv:1804.02767 (2018)
20. Guo, J.M., Liu, Y.F.: License plate localization and character segmentation with feedback self-learning and hybrid binarization techniques. IEEE Trans. Veh. Technol. **57**(3), 1417–1424 (2008)
21. Chang, S.L., Chen, L.S., Chung, Y.C., Chen, S.W.: Automatic license plate recognition. IEEE Trans. Intell. Transp. Syst. **5**(1), 42–53 (2004)
22. Shi, B., Bai, X., Yao, C.: An end-to-end trainable neural network for image-based sequence recognition and its application to scene text recognition. IEEE Trans. Pattern Anal. Mach. Intell. **39**(11), 2298–2304 (2016)
23. Everingham, M., Eslami, S.A., Van Gool, L., Williams, C.K., Winn, J., Zisserman, A.: The pascal visual object classes challenge: a retrospective. Int. J. Comput. Vis. **111**(1), 98–136 (2015)
24. Lin, T.Y., Dollár, P., Girshick, R., He, K., Hariharan, B., Belongie, S.: Feature pyramid networks for object detection. In: Proceedings of the IEEE Conference on Computer Vision and Pattern Recognition, pp. 2117–2125 (2017)
25. Liao, M., Shi, B., Bai, X.: Textboxes++: a single-shot oriented scene text detector. IEEE Trans. Image Process. **27**(8), 3676–3690 (2018)
26. Saenko, K., Kulis, B., Fritz, M., Darrell, T.: Adapting visual category models to new domains. In: Daniilidis, K., Maragos, P., Paragios, N. (eds.) ECCV 2010. LNCS, vol. 6314, pp. 213–226. Springer, Heidelberg (2010). https://doi.org/10.1007/978-3-642-15561-1_16
27. Ros, G., Stent, S., Alcantarilla, P.F., Watanabe, T.: Training constrained deconvolutional networks for road scene semantic segmentation. arXiv preprint arXiv:1604.01545 (2016)

Large-Scale Network Representation Learning Based on Improved Louvain Algorithm and Deep Autoencoder

Shou-Jiu Xiong[1], Si-Bao Chen[1(✉)], Chris H. Q. Ding[2], and Bin Luo[1]

[1] Anhui Provincial Key Lab of Multimodal Cognitive Computation,
MOE Key Lab of ICSP, School of Computer Science and Technology,
Anhui University, Hefei 230601, China
`sbchen@ahu.edu.cn`
[2] Department of CSE, University of Texas at Arlington, Arlington, TX 76019, USA

Abstract. In recent years, feature learning of nodes in network has become a research hot spot. However, with the growth of the network scale, network structure has become more and more complicated, which makes it extremely difficult for network representation learning in large and complex networks. This paper proposes a fast large-scale network representation learning method based on improved Louvain algorithm and deep autoencoder. First, it quickly folds large and complex network into corresponding small network kernel through effective improved Louvain strategy. Then based on network kernel, a deep autoencoder method is conducted to represent nodes in kernel. Finally, the representations of the original network nodes are obtained by a coarse-to-refining procedure. Extensive experiments show that the proposed method perform well on large and complex real networks and its performance is better than most network representation learning methods.

Keywords: Network representation learning · Graph folding · Louvain algorithm · Autoencoder · Graph embedding

1 Introduction

In recent years, there is an important research direction for researchers in network representation learning. It is to study how to properly represent network information. The study of network representation learning aims to explore the ability to study better, analyze the relationships between nodes in complex information networks, and find universal methods to solve different practical problems in the context of information networks, in order to act on various practical tasks, such as link prediction, community detection, and visualization problems [5,6].

The first author is a student. Thanks to NSFC Key Project of International (Regional) Cooperation and Exchanges (No. 61860206004), National NSFC (No. 61976004) and Collegiate Natural Science Fund of Anhui Province (No. KJ2017A014) for funding.

© Springer Nature Switzerland AG 2020
Y. Peng et al. (Eds.): PRCV 2020, LNCS 12307, pp. 446–459, 2020.
https://doi.org/10.1007/978-3-030-60636-7_37

Traditional network representation methods usually use high-dimensional sparse vectors for representation. These methods generally need much computation and storage consumption. To learn network representation better, there are two challenges: (1) Data sparsity in preserving the integrity of large and complex network structure. In order to learn representations of network nodes better, we need to fully preserve the integrity of overall structure of the network. However, the network infrastructure is very complex [18]. (2) The efficiency of the network represents learning. At present, some classical network embedding methods, such as DeepWalk [16] and LINE [20], consume a lot of runtime. Based on this, a method NetMF [17] was proposed to display the decomposition of matrix, which learns the representation of nodes through matrix decomposition methods. However, this type of method requires a lot of computing space. There are millions and even billions of nodes in the real world. As far as we know, there is no universal method that can be applied to large and complex networks in reality and has achieved good results. Based on numerous studies, we try to explore a method to solve the challenges brought by large and complex networks.

We propose a new network embedding framework. The framework is mainly composed of three parts: the graph fast folding layer, base embedding on folding layer and coarse-to-refining layer. The graph fast folding layer is mainly to repeatedly fold the nodes in the input original graph into super-nodes through some folding strategy, and finally form the rough graph kernel. Base embedding on folded layer is the representation learning for the nodes of the thickest layer graph. Therefore, we can get the low-dimensional vector feature representation of each node in the network by this method. The node representation of the coarsest layer graph can be learned at a lower cost and we can capture the global structure of the entire network. Coarse-to-refining layer is mainly refined from the rough graph kernel to the original graph. Here we propose a refined framework of graph, that is the process coarsening from the original graph to the rough graph and the process of restoring from the rough graph to the original graph, which ensures the integrity of the entire graph structure.

The proposed method of the network learning has the following characteristics:

1. Our method is efficient. Classical network representation methods have good performance on small networks, but the performance on large networks are not good. In particular, it consumes a lot of running time and is inefficient. However, our method makes up for this shortcoming, which performs extremely well in time performance.
2. Our method is extensible. Under the framework we proposed, we can not only use all network embedding methods to learn low-dimensional feature vectors of each nodes in the network, but also we can combine deep learning based on this to propose different network representation learning methods for learning.

2 Related Work

2.1 Louvain Algorithm

In recent years, community detection has become a research focus and has an important role in studying the characteristics of complex networks. Many scholars have proposed community detection algorithms by observing and analyzing the community structure in complex networks. The hierarchical clustering algorithm of graphs is the classic representative of community detection algorithms, including FN (Fast Newman) algorithm [14] and Louvain algorithm [3], of which Louvain algorithm is considered to be one of the best performing community detection algorithms [25].

Louvain algorithm [3] is a greedy algorithm based on modularity [13]. Its main idea is described in two parts. First, by continuously removing the node from the current community into a separate node, and then reassigning this node to one of the adjacent communities, the merger with the community has the largest modularity increment. Second, each community is folded after the stable point into a super node, and all super nodes reconstruct a new graph. Finally, it turns to other levels of folding and division.

2.2 Network Embedding

Network Representation Learning technologies have been successively proposed in the recent years. Since 2014, two representative deep learning models based on word2vec [10–12] have appeared: Deepwalk [16] and LINE [20]. DeepWalk treats nodes as a form of artificial language word, and obtains a random walk path by performing a random walk in the network. Therefore, the data representation obtained by this method can be directly used in word2vec algorithm as a vector representation of training nodes. LINE algorithm defines the first-order and second-order similar empirical probabilities. SDNE [22] adopts the idea of deep automatic encoder as a whole. There are methods such as GraRep [4] and NetMF [17] based on matrix factorization.

2.3 Graph Reduction

At present, in order to overcome the challenge of large and complex graphics embedding, some researchers try to combine multi-level structures to capture more comprehensive network information. On the one hand, it focuses on the scalability [2, 24] of network embedding, but the embedding strategy is not universal. On the other hand, many methods are proposed to reduce the size of graphics. However, changing the size of graphics does not mean losing much information.

In the process of network embedding, the coarsening of the graph is mainly divided into two categories. One is mixed type coarsening, for example: Louvain algorithm [3] and k-clique [15]. The other is structural roughening, such as:

hybrid matching [9], random selecting mismatched neighbors [7], and selecting the node with the highest weight to merge [8].

3   Problem Formulation

Given a large and complex network G, our goal is to effectively learn low-dimensional representations. Not only the global structure information of the network should be considered, but also the integrity of the local information of the network should be preserved. The low-dimensional representation can be further used for subsequent network reality tasks. This section gives the notations and definitions throughout this paper.

3.1   Network

A network is denoted as $G(V, E)$, where V is a set of vertex of the network, and E is a set of edges betweens vertex. A is an adjacency matrix. $A_{i,j} = 1$ if there is an edge between node V_i and node V_j in an unweighted network G. Otherwise, $A_{i,j} = 0$. In a weighted network G, $W_{i,j}$ is weight of edge from node V_i to V_j, then $A_{i,j} = W_{i,j}$.

3.2   Modularity

Modularity is used to measure whether the division of a community is better or no [13]. A relatively good result has a high degree of similarity within the community and a low degree of similarity outside the community. The degree of modularity is defined as the proportion of the total number of edges inside the community to the total number of edges in the network minus an expected value. The expected value is the proportion of the sum of edges within the community to the sum of edges in the network, and the proportion is formed by the same community allocation when the network is set to a random network. It is defined as follows:

$$Q = \frac{1}{2m} \sum_{vw} (A_{vw} - \frac{k_v k_w}{2m}) \delta(c_v, c_w),$$

$$A_{vw} = \begin{cases} 1, & \text{if vertices } v \text{ and } w \text{ are connected,} \\ 0, & \text{otherwise.} \end{cases}$$

(1)

Here A_{vw} is an element of the adjacency matrix of the network. k_v is the degree of vertex v, and $k_v = \sum_w A_{vw}$. c_v represents the community of vertex v, and if v and w in the same community, $\delta(c_v, c_w) = 1$, otherwise $\delta(c_v, c_w) = 0$. m represents the total number of connected edges between nodes in the network.

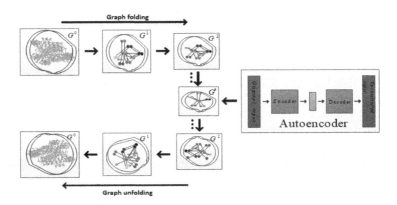

Fig. 1. An overview of the network representation learning framework.

3.3 Gain of Modularity

Gain of modularity is the increase in modularity caused by merging an isolated node V into its adjacent community C [3]. Its calculation formula is:

$$\Delta Q = [\frac{\sum_{in} + 2k_{v,in}}{2m} - (\frac{\sum_{tot} + \lambda_v}{2m})^2] - [\frac{\sum_{in}}{2m} - (\frac{\sum_{tot}}{2m})^2 - (\frac{\lambda_v}{2m})^2]$$
$$= \frac{k_{v,in}}{m} - \frac{\sum_{tot} \times \lambda_v}{2m^2}. \qquad (2)$$

Here $\sum_{in}$ is the sum of the weights in the community C before the merger, and $\sum_{tot}$ is the sum of the weights of the points and edges in the community C before the merger. $k_{v,in}$ is the sum of the weights of nodes v to nodes in community C. λ_v is the sum of the weights of the edges connected to node v. m is the number of edges.

4 The Proposed Framework

In this section, we mainly introduce a network representation learning framework. The framework is mainly composed of three parts: the graph fast folding layer, base embedding on folded layer, and coarse-to-refining layer. Generally speaking, the whole process is shown in Fig. 1. First of all, the nodes in the input graph are continuously folded and merged into a super node based on improved Louvain algorithm. The merged super nodes reconstruct a new graph and have $G^0 > G^1 > ... > G^t$. Secondly, on the coarse graph kernel, the low-dimensional feature vectors of the nodes are learned by deep autoencoder network embedding method, which is based on similar matrix transformation. Finally, the coarse-to-refining layer first performs graph convolution, and then gradually refines the rough graph to restore the original graph structure.

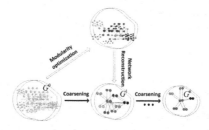

Fig. 2. Two parts of the roughening of the graph. First, we combine the nodes in the large network into coarse nodes through a modular optimization strategy, and then reconstruct these coarse nodes into a new small network. Through iteration, we obtain a series of smaller graphs, $G^0 > G^1 > ... > G^t$.

4.1 Graph Fast Folding Layer

In this section, we describe fast graph folding in detail. Large and complex graph is continuously roughened as in Fig. 2 into a series of smaller graphs, $G^0 > G^1 > ... > G^t$. Multiple nodes are folded to form super nodes through a coarsening strategy. Figure 3 also give an example to help understand. In this paper, we use Louvain algorithmic strategy based on improved modularity, which is summarized in Algorithm 1.

Generally, in the iteration process of Louvain algorithm, if the community attribution of the same node changes, other vertices will be removed from its original community, and then reincorporated into an adjacent community. It also requires calculations even though there is community division changes, and the resulting double calculations will cause a lot of overhead.

However, in the improved algorithm proposed in this paper, we only consider the merge of random neighborhood set nodes at each interaction, which greatly saves the merge time. Folding and merging nodes, this strategy performs well in terms of efficiency and effectiveness, especially in execution speed. Furthermore, it can discover the hierarchical network structure, which has good scalability.

4.2 Base Embedding on Folded Layer

After each folding, the number of the super nodes in each layer of the network will increase rapidly. Ideally, the number of nodes in each layer of the network is halved each time. After several folding and merging, we get the coarse graph kernel G^t. Finally, we use the graph embedding method $f(.)$ to learn the coarsest graph G^t.

All graph embedding algorithms can be used for basic embedding on the folded graph. In this paper, we adopt classic basic graph embedding methods, including DeepWalk [16], GraRep [4] and NetMF [17]. Based on this, we propose a deep autoencoder method (DAM) for fast network representation learning, which includes similarity matrix transformation and deep autoencoder. Our method has more advantages in data represetation than several other methods, such as: DeepWalk [16], NetMF [17], GraRep [4] and Node2ver [6].

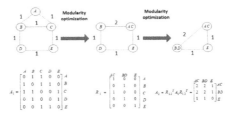

Fig. 3. Example of graph fast folding strategy. In the original graph, we first consider the nodes A, B, C, D, E as independent communities. Second, reassign these nodes to an adjacent community. If the increase in modularity brought about by the merger with the community is maximized, the merger is performed. Otherwise, the original number of community nodes does not change. In this figure, we assume that the modularity gain brought about by the allocation of node A to community C is the largest, so we combine nodes A and C, and so on.

In general, we can describe a graph by an adjacency matrix. However, we can only simply express the relationship between directly connected nodes in the graph through the adjacency matrix, but we cannot get the relationship between unconnected nodes [23]. There are some relationships between directly connected nodes in the graph, and there are also similar relationships between different degrees of unconnected nodes. Therefore, this module uses a matrix transformation method to obtain a new similarity matrix X, which not only retains the similar relationship information between multiple vertex pairs, but also reflects local and global information between vertices.

Inspired by the modularity function Q, it is defined to be on all vertex pairs. That is, the difference between the number of edges of the super node and the expected number of edges. Formally, the modularity matrix $B = [x_{ij}] \in R^{N \times N}$ is used to describe two nodes with similar relationship, which can be written as follows:

$$x_{i,j} = a_{i,j} - \frac{k_i k_j}{2m}. \tag{3}$$

Here $a_{i,j}$ is an element of the adjacency matrix of the network. $\frac{k_i k_j}{2m}$ is the expected number of edges between nodes i and j if edges are placed randomly, k_i is the degree of vertex i and $m = \frac{1}{2} \sum_i k_i$ is the total number of edges in the network.

We use a deep autoencoder framework to extract the low-dimensional feature representation of the coarsest network node data by reconstructing the original data. A simple autoencoder consists of two key components: an encoder and a decoder. The deep autoencoder built in this module is a deep network constructed by multiple simple autoencoders. The purpose of this network is to reconstruct its input so that the hidden layer learning can effectively extract the low-dimensional features of the complex network, thereby helping improve the detection capability of complex networks [23]. Its structure is shown in Fig. 4. The similarity matrix $X = [x_{ij}] \in R^{p \times N}$ is used as the input matrix of the

---

Algorithm 1. Graph Fast Folding based on Improved Louvain Algorithm (GFL)

Input: network $G = (V, E)$ and total number of folding t.
Output: folded network $G^k = (V_k, E_k)$ and relational correspondence matrix $R_{k,k+1}$ between neighboring layers, $(k = 0, 2, ..., t - 1)$.

1: $k = 0$, $G^0 = G$;
2: **for** $k = 0, 1, 2, ..., t - 1$ **do**
3:     make a simple clustering C^k of G^k such that $C_i^k = i$;
4:     **for** node $i \in G^k$ **do**
5:         remove the node i from its community C_i^k ;
6:         C_N = random set of neighbour communities of node i ;
7:         $C_j^k = argmax_{C_{j'}^k \in C_N} \Delta Q(i, C_{j'}^k)$;

8:         **if** $\Delta Q(i, C_j^k) > 0$ **then**
9:             add the node i to the community C_j^k;
10:        **else**
11:            leave the node i to the community C_i^k;
12:     Until the node division cannot be further improved or reach the maximum number of iterations;
13:     Build a new graph G^{k+1} whose nodes are the communities of C^k;
14:     Update node weights and edge weights;
15:     Computer relational correspondence matrix $R_{k,k+1}$ and the adjacency matrix A_k for graph G^k using $A_{k+1} = R_{k,k+1}^T A_k R_{k,k+1}$.

---

autoencoder. The encoder maps the data B to the low-dimensional embedding $Z = [h_{ij}] \in R^{d \times N}$, where $d < p$.

$$h_i^{(1)} = f(\hat{x}_i) = s_f(W_1 x_i + b_1). \tag{4}$$

Here x_i and $\hat{x}_i$ are the input data and reconstructed data. $h_i^{(k)}$ is the k-th layer hidden representations. $s_f(\cdot)$ is an activation function of autoencoder. Here we use sigmoid function $s_f(x) = \frac{1}{1+e^{-x}}$, which is often used as activation function for neural networks. It maps variables between 0 and 1. The autoencoder encodes the input original data B to obtain a new low-dimensional feature Z, and reconstructs the original data through the low-dimensional feature Z, The process of encoder and decoder are as follows:

$$\begin{aligned} h_i^{(k)} &= f(h_i^{(k-1)}) = s_f(W_1 h_i^{(k-1)} + b_1), \\ h_j^{(k)} &= f(h_j^{(k+1)}) = s_f(W_2 h_j^{(k+1)} + b_2). \end{aligned} \tag{5}$$

Here $W_1 \in R^{d \times k}$ and $b_1 \in R^{d \times 1}$ are the weight and bias terms, respectively, to be learned by the encoder. $W_2 \in R^{k \times d}$ and $b_2 \in R^{k \times 1}$ are the weight and bias terms, respectively, to be learned by the decoder. The autoencoder is dedicated to learn a low-dimensional feature representation Z that can better reconstruct the original data B, that is, to minimize the difference between the original data B and the reconstructed data $\hat{B}$ under parameter $\theta = \{W_1, W_2, b_1, b_2\}$. The objective function is as follows:

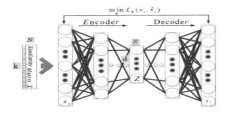

Fig. 4. Deep autoencoder embedding on the folded graph. It includes a similarity matrix and an autoencoder. The similarity matrix not only retains the relationship between directly connected nodes in the network, but also reflects the similarity relationship between unconnected nodes. We obtain the low-dimensional feature vectors of the network nodes by inputting the transformed similarity matrix M and learning in the autoencoder.

$$
\begin{aligned}
J_1 = \min_\theta \sum_{i-1}^{N} L_\theta(x_i, \hat{x}_i) &= \min_\theta \sum_{i}^{N} \|x_i - \hat{x}_i\|_2^2 \\
&= \min_\theta \sum_{i}^{N} \|s_f(W_2 s_f(W_1 h_i^{(k)} + b_1) + b_2) - x_i\|_2^2.
\end{aligned}
\tag{6}
$$

It is not only the global structure of the network must be considered, but also indispensable for capturing the local structure of the network. Therefore, the loss function is defined as follows:

$$
J_2 = \min_\theta \sum_{i,j=1}^{N} (h_i^{(k)}, h_j^{(k)}) = \min_\theta \sum_{i,j=1}^{N} \|h_i^{(k)} - h_j^{(k)}\|_2^2.
\tag{7}
$$

In general, in order to avoid overfitting of the model and improve its generalization ability, we introduce regularization terms of the parameters, which can be written as follows:

$$
J_3 = \|W_1\|_2^2 + \|W_2\|_2^2 + \|b_1\|_2^2 + \|b_2\|_2^2.
\tag{8}
$$

Therefore, the overall loss function can be defined as follows:

$$
J(\theta) = J_1 + J_2 + \beta J_3.
\tag{9}
$$

We can use the stochastic gradient descent propagation algorithm (SGD) to continuously update the parameter θ of the loss function $J(\theta)$. The update rules are as follows:

$$
W_\xi^{(k)} = W_\xi^{(k)} - \alpha \frac{\partial}{\partial W_\xi^{(k)}} J(\theta),
\tag{10}
$$

$$
b_\xi^{(k)} = b_\xi^{(k)} - \alpha \frac{\partial}{\partial b_\xi^{(k)}} J(\theta),
\tag{11}
$$

where $\xi \in \{1, 2\}$ represents the encoding and decoding process respectively.

Algorithm 2. Algorithm of Coarse-to-Refined Graph Unfolding

Input: the features $f(G^t)$ of the last folded graph layer G^t, and the correspondence matrix $R_{k-1,k}$ between neighboring layers ($k = 1, 2, ..., t$).
Output: the refined features $f(G) = f(G^0)$ of the original graph layer.
1: **for** $k = t, t-1, ..., 1$ **do**
2:     Compute the initial embedding: $f'(G^{k-1}) \leftarrow project\ (f(G^k), R_{k-1,k})$;
3:     Compute the refined embedding: $f(G^{k-1}) \leftarrow refined\ (G^{k-1}, f'(G^{k-1}))$;

Table 1. Statistics of datasets used in experiments

Datasets	# of Nodes	# of Edges	# of Classes
PPI	3,852	37,841	50
BlogCatalog	10,312	333,983	39
Flicker	80,513	5,899,882	195

4.3 Coarse-to-Refining Layer

The last part of the framework is coarse-to-refining layer. We will seek a framework to restore graph G^t to graph $G^{t-1}, G^{t-2}, ..., G^0$ by a series of relational correspondence matrix $R_{0,1}, R_{1,2}, ..., R_{t-1,t}$. Finally, we give the framework as in Algorithm 2.

First, we map the representation of the coarse node of the G^t layer to the G^{t-1} layer through $project(\cdot)$, and serve as the initial representation of the G^{k-1} layer node. Note that V_k and E_k are vertex set and edge set of G^k, respectively. $project(\cdot)$ is used to make the representation of the coarse node of the previous layer as an initial representation of the corresponding child node of the next refining layer. Then, the initial representation of the node of this layer and the relational correspondence matrix $R_{k,k+1}$ are used to further obtain the final representation vector through $refined(\cdot)$. Finally, according to the above method, we can obtain the original representation of the nodes of G^{t-2}, G^{t-3}, ..., G^1 and G^0.

5 Experiments

In this section, we evaluate the proposed method in real-world multi-label vertex classification tasks. Our experiments are mainly composed of two parts. In the first part, we quickly fold the original input network to get the coarse network, then use the classical network embedding method on the coarse layer network, and finally refine the network embedding. The vertex classification performance and speed of the proposed method are compared with classical network embedding methods, which are based on the original network directly. In the second part, we introduce the deep self-coding network embedding method based on the first part. We find a slight improvement in performance on several data sets.

5.1 Datasets

We conduct comparative experiments on three public network datasets: Protein-protein Interactions (PPI) [19], BlogCatalog [1,21] and Flicker [21]. PPI is a subgraph of the PPI network for Homo Sapiens, which consists of $3,852$ proteins classified into 50 classes. BlogCatalog is a network of social relationships of online bloggers. Flicker is a social network for users to share pictures and videos. A brief statistics of these datasets can be found in Table 1.

5.2 Baseline Methods

DeepWalk (DW) [16]: DeepWalk is a simple neural network algorithm that uses the information of random walk sequences in the network structure to learn the low-dimensional vectors of network nodes.

Node2vec (NV) [6]: node2vec is an extension method of DeepWalk. By combining BFS and DFS search to improve the random walk strategy of the Deep-Walk model, it can generate higher quality node sequences.

NetMF (NM) [17]: NetMF is a method to implement network representation learning through matrix factorization. It provides a theoretical connection to skip network embedding algorithms between graphs.

GraRep (GR) [4]: GraRep is an algorithm based on the relation matrix. It reduces the dimension of the relationship matrix through SVD decomposition to obtain the representation of the nodes in the network.

5.3 Evaluation Metrics

In multi-label classification tasks, $micro\_F1$ and $macro\_F1$ are usually adopted as evaluation metrics, which are defined as: $micro\_F1 = \frac{2*Precision*Recall}{Precision+Recall}$, $macro\_F1 = \frac{2 \times macro\_P \times macro\_R}{macro\_P + macro\_R}$. Here $Recall = \frac{TP}{TP+FN}$ and $Precision = \frac{TP}{TP+FP}$ are recall and precision respectively. TP, FP and FN are true positive, false positive and false negative. $macro\_P = \frac{1}{n}\sum_{i=1}^{n} Precision_i$ and $macro\_R = \frac{1}{n}\sum_{i=1}^{n} Recall_i$.

5.4 Experimental Results

In this section, we evaluate the performance of different network representation learning methods on multi-label classification tasks. The theory shows that a good network representation learning method performs better on multi-label classification tasks. For each data set, we use three evaluation indicators $Micro\_F1$, $Macro\_F1$ and time. We come to the following conclusions:

1. Our method is efficient. Classical network learning representations have good performances in small networks, but in larger networks, the performances are not good, especially they consume a lot of running time and inefficient. Table 2, 3 and 4 show that the proposed method combining the fast folding and merging nodes with classic network representation learning methods is more efficient in running speed, and its running time can be increased by about 35%.

Table 2. Comparative performance of the proposed method combined with classical network representation learning methods on PPI dataset.

Method	Micro_F1	Macro_F1	Time (min)
DeepWalk [16]	22.8	18.2	2.31
GFL+DW	**24.3**	**19.8**	**1.81**
Node2ver [6]	24.2	19.4	3.84
GFL+NV	**24.7**	**19.6**	**1.87**
NetMF [17]	24.5	19.8	0.62
GFL+NM	**25.4**	**20.1**	**0.39**
GraRep [4]	25.2	19.8	3.01
GFL+GR	**25.3**	**18.6**	**1.46**
DAM	**25.8**	**19.6**	**4.30**
GFL+DAM	**26.7**	**20.1**	**2.52**

Table 3. Comparative performance of the proposed method combined with classical network representation learning methods on BlogCatalog dataset.

Method	Micro_F1	Macro_F1	Time (min)
DeepWalk [16]	36.2	20.4	7.87
GFL+DW	**41.0**	**25.3**	**4.30**
Node2ver [6]	38.2	22.7	12.71
GFL+NV	**39.0**	**23.1**	**6.89**
NetMF [17]	41.0	24.6	2.87
GFL+NM	**42.1**	**25.3**	**1.49**
GraRep [4]	39.5	23.2	28.56
GFL+GR	**40.2**	**24.5**	**13.55**
DAM	**41.2**	**25.1**	**32.4**
GFL+DAM	**41.8**	**25.4**	**18.73**

2. Our method is extensible. Under our proposed framework, we can not only use network representation learning method to learn low-dimensional feature vectors of nodes, but also we can combine deep learning to propose different network representation learning methods for learning. Table 2, 3 and 4 show that our method performs better than four classical methods on different data sets, about 1% to 2%.

Table 4. Comparative performance of the proposed method combined with classical network representation learning methods on Flicker dataset. (— indicates that the corresponding algorithm is unable to handle the computation due to excessive space and memory consumption.)

Method	Micro_F1	Macro_F1	Time (min)
DeepWalk [16]	38.2	25.7	49.20
GFL+DW	**38.4**	**26.0**	**37.32**
Node2ver [6]	38.5	26.2	80.60
GFL+NV	**38.6**	**27.1**	**56.80**
NetMF [17]	30.9	13.7	67.72
GFL+NM	**32.2**	**15.3**	**32.51**
GraRep [4]	—	—	—
GFL+GR	**35.6**	**17.5**	**731.20**
DAM	**35.8**	**17.9**	**927.64**
GFL+DAM	**36.7**	**18.6**	**741.73**

6   Conclusion and Future Work

In this work, we propose a new framework for large and complex network representation learning, which is based on improved Louvain algorithm and deep autoencoder. First, it folds large and complex network into corresponding small coarse network kernel by improved Louvain algorithm. Then a deep autoencoder method is conducted to represent nodes in kernel. Finally, the representations of the original network nodes are obtained by a coarse-to-refining procedure. Extensive experiments show that the proposed method perform well on large and complex real networks and its performance is better than most network representation learning methods.

This framework is not only efficient but also extensible. It's known that network representation learning and community detection are both effective representations of node learning, and there is a certain correlation and similarity between them. In future, we will migrate the proposed network representation learning framework to community detection, and hope to get better results on large and complex networks. In addition, we can also use the method to solve the problem of link prediction and visualization.

References

1. Agarwal, N., Liu, H., Murthy, S., Sen, A., Wang, X.: A social identity approach to identify familiar strangers in a social network. In: Third International AAAI Conference on Weblogs and Social Media (2009)
2. Ahmed, N.K., et al.: A framework for generalizing graph-based representation learning methods. arXiv preprint arXiv:1709.04596 (2017)
3. Blondel, V.D., et al.: Fast unfolding of communities in large networks. J. Stat. Mech.: Theory Exp. **2008**(10), P10008 (2008)

4. Cao, S., Lu, W., Xu, Q.: Grarep: learning graph representations with global structural information. In: International Conference on Information and Knowledge Management, pp. 891–900. ACM (2015)

5. Dong, Y., Chawla, N.V., Swami, A.: metapath2vec: scalable representation learning for heterogeneous networks. In: Proceedings of the 23rd ACM SIGKDD International Conference on Knowledge Discovery and Data Mining, pp. 135–144. ACM (2017)

6. Grover, A., Leskovec, J.: node2vec: scalable feature learning for networks. In: Proceedings of the 22nd ACM SIGKDD, pp. 855–864. ACM (2016)

7. Hendrickson, B.: A multi-level algorithm for partitioning graphs. SC **95**(28), 1–14 (1995)

8. Karypis, G., Kumar, V.: A fast and high quality multilevel scheme for partitioning irregular graphs. SIAM J. Sci. Comput. **20**(1), 359–392 (1998)

9. Liang, J., Gurukar, S., Parthasarathy, S. Mile: A multi-level framework for scalable graph embedding. arXiv preprint arXiv:1802.09612 (2018)

10. Mikolov, T., Chen, K., Corrado, G., Dean, J.: Efficient estimation of word representations in vector space. arXiv preprint arXiv:1301.3781 (2013)

11. Mikolov, T., Sutskever, I., Chen, K., Corrado, G.S., Dean, J.: Distributed representations of words and phrases and their compositionality. In: Advances in Neural Information Processing Systems, pp. 3111–3119 (2013)

12. Mikolov, T., et al.: Linguistic regularities in continuous space word representations. In: Proceedings of the 2013 Conference of the North American Chapter of the Association for Computational Linguistics: Human Language Technologies, pp. 746–751 (2013)

13. Newman, M.E., Girvan, M.: Finding and evaluating community structure in networks. Phys. Rev. E **69**(2), 026113 (2004)

14. Newman, M.E.J.: Fast algorithm for detecting community structure in networks. Phys. Rev. E **69**(6), 066133 (2004)

15. Palla, G., et al.: Uncovering the overlapping community structure of complex networks in nature and society. Nature **435**(7043), 814 (2005)

16. Perozzi, B., Al-Rfou, R., Skiena, S.: Deepwalk: online learning of social representations. In: Proceedings of the 20th ACM SIGKDD, pp. 701–710. ACM (2014)

17. Qiu, J., et al.: Network embedding as matrix factorization: unifying deepwalk, line, pte, and node2vec. In Proceedings of the Eleventh ACM International Conference on Web Search and Data Mining, pp. 459–467. ACM (2018)

18. Shaw B, Jebara T.: Structure preserving embedding. In Proceedings of the 26th Annual International Conference on Machine Learning, pp. 937–944. ACM (2009)

19. Stark, C., et al.: The biogrid interaction database: 2011 update. Nucleic Acids Res. **39**(suppl-1), D698–D704 (2010)

20. Tang, J., et al.: Line: large-scale information network embedding. In: Proceedings of the 24th International Conference on World Wide Web, International World Wide Web Conferences Steering Committee, pp. 1067–1077 (2015)

21. Tang, L., Liu, H.: Relational learning via latent social dimensions. In: Proceedings of the 15th ACM SIGKDD, pp. 817–826. ACM (2009)

22. Wang, D., Cui, P., Zhu, W.: Structural deep network embedding. In: Proceedings of the 22nd ACM SIGKDD, pp. 1225–1234. ACM (2016)

23. Xie, Y., Wang, X., Jiang, D., et al.: High-performance community detection in social networks using a deep transitive autoencoder. Inf. Sci. **493**, 75–90 (2019)

24. Yang, C., Sun, M., Liu, Z., Tu, C.: Fast network embedding enhancement via high order proximity approximation. In: IJCAI, pp. 3894–3900 (2017)

25. You, X., Yin, B.: Community discovery research based on Louvain algorithm. In: 2017 4th International Conference on Machinery, Materials and Computer (MACMC 2017). Atlantis Press (2018)

Clinical Pathway Optimal Scheduling Based on Hybrid Intelligent Optimization Algorithm

Xin Sun[1]([⊠]), Xiaohao Xie[1], Yingjie Zhang[2], and Jiaming Cui[3]

[1] School of Computer Science and Technology,
Beijing Institute of Technology, Beijing 100081, China
{sunxin,3120191060}@bit.edu.cn
[2] Beijing Institute of Radio Metrology and Measurement, Beijing 100854, China
619289852@qq.com
[3] School of Information Science and Technology, Fudan University, Shanghai 200433, China
2992555093@qq.com

Abstract. Clinical pathways are management plans that display goals for patients and the sequence and timing of actions necessary to achieve those goals with optimal efficiency. Given the resource competition between multiple clinical pathways, clinical pathway scheduling is an urgent and meaningful question to be solved, which is a typical resource constrained multi-project scheduling problem (RCMPSP). Intelligent optimization algorithms are widely used to solve RCMPSP problems. In this paper, considering the shortcomings of the existing optimal scheduling algorithms, which is insufficient in search and easy to fall into local optimum, we construct a model for clinical pathway scheduling and propose a hybrid intelligent optimization algorithm. We also design the encoding and decoding rules and fitness function of the optimization. Experiment results on renal calculi clinical pathway show that the proposed algorithm has a better search capabilities in clinical pathway scheduling and preforms better performance when the number of patients increases.

Keywords: Clinical pathway · Optimal scheduling · Intelligent optimization · PSO · GWO

1 Introduction

Clinical pathway is the popular health care management tools which can give professional standards in healthcare to avoid overtreatment and improve medical quality [1]. Medical institutions in China have widely applied clinical pathways to their processes and obtained great benefits. Given the limited medical resources of hospitals and the large number of patients, there is a resource competition between multiple clinical pathways. Therefore, how to properly coordinate the treatment sequence of clinical pathway subtasks and solve the optimal scheduling scheme under the condition of limited resources is significant for improving the utilization of medical resources and medical efficiency of patients.

© Springer Nature Switzerland AG 2020
Y. Peng et al. (Eds.): PRCV 2020, LNCS 12307, pp. 460–472, 2020.
https://doi.org/10.1007/978-3-030-60636-7_38

There are two points worthy of attention in the clinical pathway scheduling. Firstly, medical resources in hospitals are limited, which could lead to a shortage of resources. Secondly, the clinical pathways of multiple patients are running in parallel in different departments of the hospital, so that there is medical resources competition among these clinical pathways. Thus, clinical pathway scheduling can be regarded as resource constrained multi-project scheduling problem (RCMPSP).

RCMPSP is a kind of generalized optimization problem, aiming at maximizing the benefits under the conditions of resource constraints, such as the shortest period, minimum cost, maximum profit, etc. In recent years, with the development of artificial intelligence technology, many researchers try to solve RCMPSP by intelligent optimization algorithm, including simulated annealing (SA) [2], genetic algorithm (GA) [3], ant colony optimization (ACO) [4], particle swarm optimization (PSO) [5], etc., instead of branch and bound algorithm and heuristic algorithms [6]. Intelligent optimization algorithms have made great contributions to the RCMPSP. However, due to the problems of vulnerable into local optimum, insufficient precision and parameter constraints, these algorithms are facing many difficulties. Besides, according to our research, few studies have attempted to combine RCMPSP problem with the clinical pathway scheduling problem.

In this paper, we propose the hybrid particle swarm optimization and grey wolf optimizer algorithm (HPSOGWO), which combined the advantages of individual information in PSO and group information in grey wolf optimizer (GWO) [7]. The model we design based on the HPSOGWO first encodes the particles through clinical pathways and then searches for the optimal solution in the solution space. The final clinical pathway scheduling scheme is obtained by decoding the optimal solution. The objective of the model is minimizing clinical pathways total hospitalization day under the condition of meeting the medical resource constraints and the precedence relation constraints of some medical orders.

The remainder of this paper is organized as follows. Section 2 provides some background information on medical resource optimization scheduling and RCMPSP, along with the related work. Thereafter, in Sect. 3, we describe the proposed hybrid intelligent optimization algorithm and clinical pathway scheduling model. Experimental settings and results are summarized in Sect. 4. Section 5 concludes this paper.

2 Related Work

2.1 Medical Resource Optimization Scheduling

The problem of optimal allocation of medical resources has received much attention. Al-Refaie et al. [8] designed three optimization models for emergency patients to frequently disrupt the scheduled timing of hospital operating rooms to optimize operating room scheduling during accidents. Gartner et al. [9] hypothesized that multiple selective patients could be classified according to the diagnostic related group (DRG) and clinical pathways, trying to solve hospital patient flow problems to maximize hospital profit margins.

Whereas, the above studies generally focused on the optimal scheduling of individual medical activities or medical resources. As for the optimal scheduling of clinical pathways, Zeng al. [10] studied clinical scheduling problem with overbooking for patients with heterogeneous no-show probabilities, and developed a guided local search algorithm based on the properties of an optimal schedule. G Du al. [11] combined a genetic algorithm with PSO and used the relative patient waiting time and relative time efficiency as measure indexes. Since the limitations of the medical background, there are few studies on clinical pathway optimal scheduling.

2.2 Resource Constrained Multi-project Scheduling Problem

Resource Constrained Multi-Project Scheduling Problem (RCMPSP) assumes that there are parallel projects that compete for a limited amount of updatable resources, which can be used by multiple projects and reused after being released, except for resource competition these projects are generally independent of each other. The original method to solve RCMPSP is a purely mathematical method. In order to overcome the limitations of mathematical methods that are sensitive to parameters and difficult to accurately express complex scheduling problems, researchers have begun to try the application of branch and bound algorithm on RCMPSP. Speranza et al. [12] proposed an integer programming model based on branch and bound algorithm to help planners understand resource allocation and solve non-preemptive multi-project management problems. Davari et al. [13] proposed an improved branch and bound algorithm, introducing two different branching schemes and eight different finite rules to solve resource-constrained and opportunity-constrained project scheduling problems.

Recently, more scholars have tried to use heuristic algorithms to solve multi-project scheduling problems. The heuristic algorithm is an intuitive or empirically constructed algorithm that gives an approximate optimal solution to a scheduling problem at an acceptable computational cost. But the priority rules on which the heuristic algorithm is based usually applies to a particular type of problem, and it is difficult to guarantee an optimal solution. With the advancement of artificial intelligence technology, researchers turned their attention to the intelligent optimization algorithm. Dalfard [14] proposed a hybrid algorithm based on SA and GA to solve the problem of combined flow shop scheduling problem with time-order dependence, with the optimization goal of minimizing the construction period. Zhou et al. [15] proposed a new 2-opt constraint for ant colony algorithm to solve resource-constrained project scheduling problems under the premise of ensuring priority among tasks.

These work confirms the validity of swarm intelligence algorithm in RCMPSP problem. But because they only use one of the intelligent optimization algorithms, or combine with randomization algorithm, it is difficult to achieve better search performance, and easy to fall into local optimum.

3 Methods

In order to obtain the optimal clinical pathway scheduling scheme, we combine two kinds of intelligent optimization algorithms, the PSO and GWO, which can make full use of individual and population information, and has a certain improvement in search performance.

3.1 Problem Statement

We state our assumptions and put forward the necessary symbols at first.

- The study focus on the clinical pathway of single disease.
- The clinical pathways are independent of each other, and multiple clinical pathways are in parallel.
- The shared medical resources are all renewable resources, and the types and quantities of each resource are determined.
- There may be precedence relation constraints between subtasks of clinical pathways.

Table 1 defines the symbolic representation of the clinical pathway optimization scheduling model.

Table 1. The symbolic representation of the clinical pathway optimization scheduling model.

Symbol	Meaning
n	Number of clinical pathways
m	Number of subtasks per clinical pathway
J_{ij}	Subtask j in clinical pathway i
S_{ij}	Start time of J_{ij}
f_{ij}	End time of J_{ij}
d_{ij}	Duration of J_{ij}
P_{ij}	All precedence task sets for J_{ij}
R_k	The total number of medical resources K
r_k	The remaining amount of medical resources K
r_{ijk}	The number of resources K is required when J_{ij} executes

To simplify problem solving, we add virtual tasks (do not take up time, and do not consume resources) J_0 before all tasks start, and J_{mn+1} after all tasks, then the objective of the clinical pathway optimization scheduling problem is shown below.

$$min(f_{m \cdot n+1} - S_0)$$

$$f_{ij} - f_h \geq d_{ij}, \forall h \in P_{ij} \tag{1}$$

$$\sum_{i=1}^{n}\sum_{j=1}^{m} r_{ijk} \leq R_k$$

where f_{mn+1} refers to the end time of the task $J_{m\,n+1}$, and s_0 refers to the start time of the task J_0. At the same time, the task must also meet the resource constraints and the precedence relation constraints.

3.2 HPSOGWO Algorithm

Particle swarm optimization (PSO) is a kind of swarm intelligence algorithm. Its basic idea is to find the optimal solution through the cooperation and information sharing among individuals in the group. The PSO algorithm abstracts birds into particles without mass and volume, each of which represents a feasible solution for the N-dimensional search space. In the search process, each particle has its velocity vector V (the next flight direction and velocity) and the position vector X (the position of the particle in the solution space). The fitness function is used to judge the quality of each position, which will be explained later. In each iteration, the best experience of particle $Pbest$ and the best experience of particle group $Gbest$ are obtained, and the velocity vector is updated according to the following formula:

$$V_i(t+1) = V_i(t) + c_1 r_1 (Pbest_i - X_i) + c_2 r_2 (Gbest - X_i) \qquad (2)$$

where $V_i = (v_{i1}, v_{i2}, ..., v_{in})$ is the velocity vector of particle i, $X_i = (x_{i1}, x_{i2}, ..., x_{in})$ is the position vector, $Pbest_i$ is the best historical location of particle i, $Gbest$ is the best historical location of the particle swarm, t is the current number of iterations, c_1, c_2 are learning factors and r_1, r_2 are random numbers between [0, 1].

Then the position vector is updated as follows:

$$X_i(t+1) = X_i(t) + V_i(t+1) \qquad (3)$$

Each iteration of the particle is described in Fig. 1.

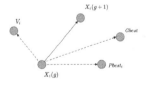

Fig. 1. Iteration of the particle.

In each iteration of the particle in PSO algorithm, only one group optimal value is used, that will result in local optimality without accurate optimal solution. Similar to the particle swarm optimization algorithm, GWO is inspired by the hunting behavior of the gray wolf population. As shown in Fig. 2, the grey wolf optimization algorithm sets four types of wolves, α, β, δ, and ω, to simulate the leadership of the gray wolf.

During the hunt, GWO assumes that α, β, and δ wolves have a better understanding of the potential location of the prey. Select the three historically optimal values α, β, and δ, and use them to approximate the position of the prey. Then update positions of other wolves (including ω) based on these three positions.

$$D_\alpha = |C_1 X_\alpha - X|$$
$$D_\beta = |C_2 X_\beta - X|$$
$$D_\delta = |C_3 X_\delta - X| \tag{4}$$

$$X_1 = |X_\alpha - A_1 D_\alpha|$$
$$X_2 = |X_\beta - A_2 D_\beta|$$
$$X_3 = |X_\delta - A_3 D_\delta| \tag{5}$$

Fig. 2. Gray wolf leadership division map.

$$X(t+1) = \frac{X_1 + X_2 + X_3}{3} \tag{6}$$

where t represents the current number of iterations, A and C are coefficient vectors and calculated by (7) and (8), X_α, X_β, X_δ are the simulated prey position vectors, X is the position vector of the gray wolf. D represents the distance between the wolf and the prey.

$$A = 2_{ar_1} - a \tag{7}$$

$$C = 2_{r_2} \tag{8}$$

note that a is linearly iterated from 2 to 0 during the iteration, and r_1 and r_2 are random vectors over the interval [0, 1].

Combining the advantages of both PSO and GWO algorithms, HPSOGWO introduces the wolf individual position update result in the GWO algorithm into the PSO algorithm, replacing *Gbest* in the speed update formula of PSO algorithm:

$$V_i(t+1) = \omega V_i(t) + c_1 r_1 (Pbest_i - X_i) + c_2 r_2 (X_{GWO} - X_i) \tag{9}$$

where X_{GWO} is the result of the (6). In this way, the particles use more group information in each iteration, which helps to avoid the algorithm falling into the local optimal solution to some extent.

Referring to Shi and Eberhart [16], the inertia weight ω introduced by the speed update formula of the HPSOGWO algorithm. The value of ω is in the range [0, 1] and linearly decreases as the number of iterations increases. The linear decrement formula is shown in (10).

$$\omega = (\omega_s - \omega_e)\frac{(g_{max} - t)}{g_{max}} + \omega_e \tag{10}$$

in which g_{max} is the maximum number of iterations and t is the current iteration. ω_s is the initial inertia weight of the algorithm, and ω_e is the ending inertia weight. The HPSOGWO algorithm follows the suggested setting of $\omega_s = 0.9$; $\omega_e = 0.4$ by Shi and Eberhart [16].

The specific process of HPSOGWO is shown in Algorithm 1.

Algorithm 1 HPSOGWO algorithm

1: Initialization the particle swarm position $X_i(i = 1,2,...,m)$, ω, a, A, C, and maximum number of iterations g_{max}
2: Calculate the fitness of each particle. Get $Pbest_i$ and X_α, X_β, X_δ
3: while $t < g_{max}$ do
4:    for $i < m$ do
5:        Calculate the GWO position X_{GWO} according to (4), (5) and (6)
6:        Speed update: update particle speed according to (9)
7:        Location Update: Update particle location according to (3)
8:    end for
9:    Update ω, a, A, C
10:   Calculate the fitness of each particle
11:   Update X_α, X_β, X_δ
12:       $t = t + 1$
13: end while
14: return X_α

3.3 Clinical Pathway Scheduling Model

When applying the HPSOGWO algorithm to solve the clinical pathway scheduling problem, we first need to encode the particle. Here, we encode the particle into the starting order of multiple clinical pathway subtasks, that is to say, different codes of task starting order correspond to different scheduling schemes. In the solution space of HPSOGWO, the particle $X_i = (x_{i1}, x_{i2}, ..., x_{in})$ is a point in space, and the fitness of each particle corresponds to the score of the scheduling scheme. Each dimension x_{ij} of the particle corresponds to the execution order of the tasks in the scheduling, and the value represents the priority of the task in the scheduling process. The larger the value, the higher the priority. Therefore, each dimension of the particle x_{ij} belongs to the [0, 1] interval, and each dimension of the particle velocity vector V_i belongs to the [−1, 1] interval. The particle is initialized to a random number in the interval [−1, 1], and if the interval is exceeded, the boundary value is taken.

The fitness function of HPSOGWO, which is the objective function of RCMPSP, is the minimum total hospitalization day for all clinical pathways in the model, as shown in (1). However, our particle coding method cannot guarantee that the scheduling scheme obtained meets the precedence relation constraints between clinical pathway subtasks. We use the penalty function to solve the problem of generating infeasible solutions. The precedence relation constraints between clinical pathway subtasks is shown in (1), and we construct a penalty function for cases that do not satisfy this constraint, as shown by (11).

$$f_{punish} = \alpha \sum_{i=1}^{n} \sum_{j=1}^{m} limit(s_{ij} - f_h), \forall h \in P_{ij} \tag{11}$$

where α is the penalty factor that determines the extent of the penalty. $limit()$ is the limiter function, as shown below, ensuring that the penalty value for the immediate constraint subtask is 0.

$$limit(x) = \begin{cases} x, x > 0 \\ 0, x < 0 \end{cases} \tag{12}$$

Therefore, the fitness function with the penalty term we used is

$$minf = (f_{mn+1} - s_0) + f_{punish} \tag{13}$$

In order to generate the scheduling scheme corresponding to each particle, we need decode the solution obtained by HPSOGWO algorithm, and then calculate the objective function value according to (13).

Considering that multiple clinical pathways are independent of each other, there are only resource constraints between clinical pathways, and no precedence relation constraints, which can be performed in parallel. During the generation process, there are three sets are maintained, that is: completed task sets, ongoing task sets, and feasible task sets. Under the premise of satisfying the resource constraint and the precedence relation constraints, a task is selected from the feasible task set to the ongoing task set according to the task starting order obtained by the particle decoding, and automatically enter the completed task sets after finished. At last, the final optimal scheduling scheme can also be generated through this strategy.

The complete flow of the clinical pathway scheduling model is shown in Fig. 3.

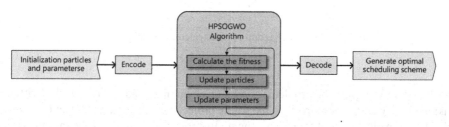

Fig. 3. Clinical pathway scheduling model.

4   Experiment

In this section, we select the clinical pathway of renal calculi as the research object. The problem we solve is the clinical pathway optimization scheduling problem of renal calculi under resource constraints, with the goal of solving the minimum total hospital stay for multiple patients.

4.1 Experimental Settings and Parameters

Firstly, the following assumptions were made:

1) In the experiment, the length of stay is calculated according to the 8 h working day of the hospital, that is, 480 min for each hospital stay.
2) All doctors involved in the treatment of renal calculi are set as residents. The examination equipment is bound to the inspector, the operating room and the clinician and can be combined into one medical resource. Therefore, the inspection equipment and the operating room are used to represent the corresponding medical resources.
3) Renal calculi surgery (percutaneous nephrolithotomy) is the bottleneck task of the clinical pathway, and the rehabilitation phase after the surgery has little effect on the scheduling problem. Therefore, the post operation stage scheduling is not considered in the experiment.
4) The clinical pathway for renal calculi requires a single day for operation, but one operating room (clinician) can perform multiple renal calculi in one day. So we set the operation time to 480 min (one day) and the number of operating rooms to the number of renal calculi that could have been done in one day.
5) Based on the relevant research, we list the key medical tasks in the clinical pathway of renal calculi, the resources used and the maximum time spent performing the tasks. There is a precedence relationship between tasks. As shown in Table 2, according to the task label in the table and the precedence relationship between the tasks, the task network diagram of the clinical pathway of the renal calculi is shown in Fig. 4.

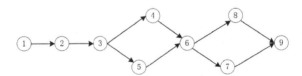

Fig. 4. Network diagram of renal calculi clinical pathway.

In order to simplify the problem solving, this experiment adds virtual tasks (without taking up time and no resources) to the whole project at the beginning and end of multiple clinical pathways, and transforms the multi-project scheduling problem into single project scheduling, without affecting the original resources and the precedence relation constraints of the original clinical pathway subtasks. As shown in Fig. 5, it is the corresponding clinical pathway merged network map for eight patients. The multi-project scheduling is converted into single-project scheduling through the virtual task 1 and the virtual task 74. Eight different colors represent the clinical pathway of renal calculi for eight patients. This algorithm is constrained by the precedence relation constraints of the network diagram, as well as the time consumption and resource constraints of Table 2,

Table 2. Clinical pathway list of renal calculi.

No.	Medical order	Resources	Maximum use time (min)	Pre task
1	Preliminary diagnosis/creation of medical records/release checklist	Resident	50	–
2	Routine inspection/medical examination	Inspection equipment	90	1
3	Diagnosis/hospitalization/issued orders	Resident	45	2
4	Admission education/ask about medical history/physical examination	Nurse	40	3
5	Urology care routine/tertiary care	Nurse	30	3
6	Superior doctor rounds	Resident	10	4,5
7	Preoperative diagnosis	Resident	90	6
8	Preoperative care/signed informed consent form	Nurse	60	6
9	Percutaneous nephrolithotomy (PCNL)	Operating room	480	7,8
*	Postoperative care/postoperative examination/rehabilitation	–	–	–

and search solution space to get the minimum total hospitalization day and the specific clinical pathway scheduling scheme.

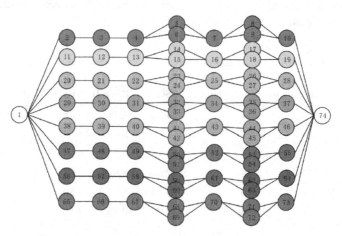

Fig. 5. Clinical pathway merge network diagram: taking 8 patients as an example.

The medical resources of this experiment are set as 6 residents, 7 nurses, 1 inspection equipment, and 2 operating rooms (equivalent to setting up one operating room to complete 2 renal calculi one day). Assuming that patients with renal calculi arrive at the hospital at the same time, 7 cases of 6 to 18 patients with renal calculi were tested. In addition to HPSOGWO algorithm, PSO and GWO algorithm are used as contrast. The relevant parameters are set as follows: the number of particle populations is 15, the learning factor is $c_1 = c_2 = 2$, and the fitness function penalty factor $\alpha = 100$, the algorithm iteration number is $t = 200$. The experimental results converted the units of the total cycle of multiple clinical pathways into days by 480 min per day, retaining two decimal places. Other parameters are set according to the experimental design and algorithm description above.

4.2 Experimental Results

The experimental results are shown in Table 3. It can be concluded that as the number of patients' increases, the solutions obtained by the PSO algorithm and the GWO algorithm are greater than or equal to the HPSOGWO algorithm, that is, the latter obtains a relative optimal solution. The HPSOGWO algorithm has a better search capabilities in solving the clinical pathway scheduling problem and is not easy to fall into the local optimal solution.

Then the optimal scheduling scheme can be generated. Figure 6 is the Gantt diagram of the clinical pathway scheduling scheme for eight patients generated by the algorithm. The number of each sub-task corresponds to that of the network in Fig. 5. Medical Source 1 to 4 correspond to four medical resources for residents, nurses, inspection equipment, and operating room. The Gantt chart gives the execution start time of each subtask in each clinical pathway in detail. According to the arrangement of the diagnosis and treatment process, the patient's hospitalization time can be shortened as much as possible, and the economic burden of the patient can be reduced. At the same time, the hospital's patient reception capacity can be improved, and patients with treatment needs can immediately enter the clinical pathway and get discharged soon.

Table 3. Experimental results of clinical pathway scheduling of renal calculi.

No. of patients	No. of subtasks	PSO(d)	GWO(d)	HPSOGWO(d)
8	74	4.88	4.88	4.88
10	92	5.99	5.83	5.83
12	110	6.65	6.65	6.65
14	128	7.84	8.01	7.84
16	146	9.05	8.99	8.80
18	164	10.05	10.05	9.86

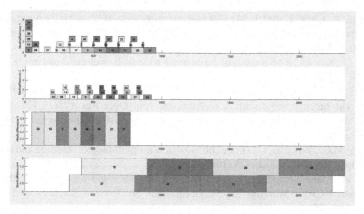

Fig. 6. Gantt chart of clinical pathway scheduling: taking 8 patients as an example.

5 Conclusion

In this paper, we convert the clinical pathway optimization scheduling problem into the RCMPSP problem and propose a model based on HPSOGWO algorithm. Considering the inadequate utilization of particle swarm information in each iteration of PSO, the idea of GWO algorithm is integrated into the algorithm. The model encode scheduling schemes as particles and search for optimal solution in the space using HPSOGWO algorithm. Then the optimal scheduling scheme can be generated according to the optimal solution. The experimental results of the clinical pathway optimization of renal calculi show that the HPSOGWO algorithm has a better optimal solution search ability in the clinical pathway optimization problem, and the effect is better when the number of patients increases, which indicates the potential and effectiveness of the proposed model.

References

1. Yan, H., Gorp, P.V., Kaymak, U., Lu, X., Ji, L., Chiau, C.C., et al.: Aligning event logs to task-time matrix clinical pathways in BPMN for variance analysis. J. Biomed. Health Inform. **99**, 1 (2018)
2. Kirkpatrick, S., Vecchi, M.P.: Optimization by simulated annealing. In: Spin Glass Theory and Beyond: An Introduction to the Replica Method and Its Applications, pp. 339–348 (1987)
3. Goldberg, D.E.: Genetic Algorithm in Search Optimization and Machine Learning, vol. xiii, pp. 2104–2116. Addison Wesley, Boston (1989). 7
4. Dorigo, M., Marco, V., Colorni, A.: Ant system: optimization by a colony of cooperating agents. IEEE Trans. Syst. Man Cybern. Part B Cybern. **26**(1), 29 (1996). A Publication of the IEEE Systems Man & Cybernetics Society
5. Kennedy, J., Eberhart, R.: Particle swarm optimization. In: ICNN 1995 - International Conference on Neural Networks IEEE, pp. 1942–1948 (2002)
6. Blazewicz, J., Lenstra, J.K., Kan, A.H.G.R.: Scheduling subject to resource constraints: classification and complexity. Discrete Appl. Math. **5**(1), 11–24 (1983)
7. Mirjalili, S., Mirjalili, S.M., Lewis, A.: GreyWolf optimizer. Adv. Eng. Softw. **69**(3), 46–61 (2014)

8. Al-Refaie, A., Chen, T., Judeh, M.: Optimal operating room scheduling for normal and unexpected events in a smart hospital. Oper. Res. **18**(3), 579–602 (2016). https://doi.org/10.1007/s12351-016-0244-y

9. Gartner, D., Kolisch, R.: Scheduling the hospital-wide flow of elective patients. Eur. J. Oper. Res. **233**(3), 689–699 (2014)

10. Zeng, B., Turkcan, A., Lin, J., Lawley, M.: Clinic scheduling models with overbooking for patients with heterogeneous noshow probabilities. Ann. Oper. Res. **178**(1), 121–144 (2010)

11. Du, G., Yao, Y., Diao, X.: Clinical pathways scheduling using hybrid genetic algorithm. J. Med. Syst. **37**(3), 1–17 (2013)

12. Speranza, M.G., Vercellis, C.: Hierarchical models for multiproject planning and scheduling. Eur. J. Oper. Res. **64**(2), 312–325 (1993)

13. Davari, M., Demeulemeester, E.: A novel branch-and-bound algorithm for the chance-constrained RCPSP. Working Papers Department of Decision Sciences & Information Management (2016)

14. Dalfard, V.M., Ranjbar, V.: Multi-projects scheduling with resource constraints & priority rules by the use of simulated annealing algorithm. Tehnicki Vjesnik **19**(3), 493–499 (2012)

15. Zhou, Y., Guo, Q., Gan, R.: Improved ACO algorithm for resource-constrained project scheduling problem. In: International Conference on Artificial Intelligence and Computational Intelligence, pp. 358–365 (2010)

16. Shi, Y., Eberhart, R.: Modified particle swarm optimizer. In: Proceedings of IEEE ICEC Conference, pp. 69–73. Anchorage (1999)

Gradient Analysis of Loss Function Based on System Balance

Suman Xia$^{(\boxtimes)}$, Cheng Cheng, Haoyuan Wang, and Xuguang Wang

Suzhou Institute of Nano-Tech and Nano-Bionics (SINANO),
Chinese Academy of Sciences, Suzhou, China
smxia2018@sinano.ac.cn

Abstract. In recent years, deep learning has been widely used in various fields of social life. The theoretical understanding on how it works also makes people curious.

In this paper we treat features of sample as points in multi-dimensional space and gradients as stress between these points. In this system we can prove that the property "strong convexity" we defined is a sufficient condition for softmax loss function to converge to a good model. We also showed an example to estimate the capacity of features of fixed dimensions.

During the proof we can see that the convergence process could be divided into two stages. In the first stage the strong convexity is formed. In the second stage this property stably guide the features to the ideal place.

Keywords: Loss function · Deep learning theory

1 Introduction

Deep learning models have powerful representation and modeling capabilities. Through supervised or unsupervised training methods, they can automatically learn the feature representation of the target layer by layer, and realize the abstraction and description of object hierarchies. But how does deep learning works? That is an interesting question.

Theoretical research on deep learning algorithms can be traced back to 1989. Haxwell [1] proved that as long as the number of nodes is sufficient, a two-layer neural network can fit any continuous function. This was a major breakthrough in the basic theory of deep learning at the time, but in fact this theory could not judge how many nodes were enough. On this basis, Cybenko [2], Barron [3], etc. have theoretically proved that deep learning neural networks have sufficient performance capabilities.

In terms of the convergence of the algorithm, Safran [4] proved that under high probability, there is a continuous decreasing path from the random starting point to the global minimum, but in fact the SGD descending algorithm may not follow this path. The results of Zhong [5] show that after initialization using

© Springer Nature Switzerland AG 2020
Y. Peng et al. (Eds.): PRCV 2020, LNCS 12307, pp. 473–484, 2020.
https://doi.org/10.1007/978-3-030-60636-7_39

tensor decomposition, gradient descent can find the global optimal value of a neural network with a hidden layer. Li [6] introduced additional potential energy parameters to prove the convergence of SGD on a two-layer neural network. In addition, for some models that meet certain assumptions, Alexandr [7], Arora [8], etc., Du [9], etc. can prove the algorithm's convergence.

2   Preliminaries

Deep neural network turns a sample into a feature vector point in a multi-dimensional space through a trainable neural network. The purpose of training is to make feature be able to represent sample more accurately. Certainly similar samples, such as samples from the same class, should have similar features and vice versa. Then construct a loss function based on this thought and use its gradients to update all the parameters.

In multi-dimensional space, the gradient of the loss function for each vector point can be decomposed into the attraction or repulsion stress received from other vector points, and the motion path of the vector point under the stress is analyzed on this basis. If we use the cosine distance to calculate the similarity between vector points, then consider the polar coordinate stress between the vector points that is, each vector point forms a stress field determined by its own direction.

The following uses the traditional softmax loss function [10] as an example to analyze how loss function works on all feature vectors and which property will affect a lot all along this process.

The softmax loss function introduces class vector points. It classifies samples by calculating the similarity between the feature of the sample and the class vector points. The softmax loss function generates a N group of binary relations (attraction or repulsion) for each iteration of a sample. Iterating through all samples can generate all the required binary relations, and then iterating the model to converge. The specific calculation process is as follows.

For the sample vector x (the feature of a sample a_x), its length is denoted by F. Introduce N class vectors $W = (W_1, W_2, ..., W_N)$ and form a matrix of $F \times N$. Here N is the number of classes among all samples. First calculate the similarities between the sample and all the class vector by cosine distance as $y_k = xW$. Then use the softmax function to calculate the probability of outputting the sample vector x to class k as $p_k = \frac{e^{y_k}}{\sum_j e^{y_j}}$. $(p_1, p_2, \cdots, p_N)$ is called the **probability vector** of the sample vector x. If the label of sample x is i, that is sample x belongs to class i, the loss of sample x in this system is $-\ln p_i$. This loss is the softmax loss

$$Loss = -\ln \frac{e^{xW_i}}{\sum_j e^{xW_j}}.$$

The gradient of the loss function to the sample vector x is

$$\sum_{j\neq i} p_j(-W_j) + (1-p_i)W_i = (1-p_i)\overrightarrow{OW_i} + \sum_{j\neq i} p_j\overrightarrow{W_jO},$$

Here $\overrightarrow{OW_i}$ represent that sample vector point x is positively effected in the stress field formed by the class vector point W_i in the direction of $\overrightarrow{OW_i}$, which can be regarded as the attraction stress of W_i to x. Similarly, $\overrightarrow{W_jO}$ can be regarded as the repulsive stress of W_j to x. The magnitude of these stresses is determined by the product of the coefficient and the length of each class vector.

During the training process, various descending algorithms such as NAG [11], Momentum [12], Adam [13] can be selected, and how much the parameters update is determined by the gradient. The parameter update is consistent in the general direction, so only consider the effect of gradients on parameters. It can be known from the definition of the gradient that when the learning rate is sufficiently small, after the parameter update every vector point approximately advanced in the direction of the gradient vector, and the distance is positively related to the learning rate and the size of the gradient. The selectable range of the learning rate is related to the smoothness of the parameter space and the selected descending algorithm, ultimately up to the specific network structure.

2.1   Convexity Parameter

Definition 2.1. *For a set of vectors $a_1, a_2, \cdots, a_n$, the vector a_i is called **convex** in the vector set. For any $1 \leqslant j \leqslant n$, there is $a_i \cdot a_j \leqslant |a_i|^2$. If each vector in a vector set is convex, the vector set is called to have strong convexity.*

The value $\min_{j\neq i}\{a_i^2 - a_i \cdot a_j\}$ is the convexity parameter of vector a_i in vector set $A = \{a_1, a_2, \cdots, a_n\}$, denoted by $Conv_A(a_i)$. The value $Conv(A) = \min_i\{Conv_A(a_i)\}$ is the convexity parameter of vector set A. Obviously if $Conv(A) > 0$, then vector set A has strong convexity.

Intuitively speaking, a convex vector in a vector set is the most "protruding" point of the vector set in the direction of the vector, as shown in Fig. 1. Let the vector a_i be convex in the vector set $a_1, a_2, \cdots, a_n$, then the vector a_i has the following properties:

1. Draw the plane perpendicular to vector a_i passing through the end point of a_i, then all other vectors are on the same side of the plane;
2. The component length of all vectors in the direction of the vector a_i does not exceed the length of vector a_i;
3. For any vector a_j in the vector set, the angle between the vector $a_i - a_j$ and the vector a_i is not an obtuse angle.

The strong convexity of the fully connected layer W has a clear physical meaning in this loss function. That is, the class vector W_i itself will be most probably classified to class i in this model. And the most important thing is the

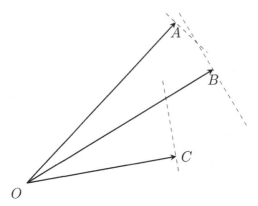

Fig. 1. In a vector set consisting of three vectors, the vector OA and the vector OB are convex, but the vector OC is not.

strong convexity of W could ensure that all the sample vectors will move towards the positive direction if the corresponding W_i during the training process. Then the full connected layer W will guide sample vectors to direct place like a heart pumping blood to different organs.

2.2   Equilibrium

If we treat all the features and class vectors as vector points in multi-dimensional space, together with the attraction and repulsion between them they form a physical system. When the stress of all vector points became balanced, this state is called as **equilibrium**.

Suppose the label of sample x is i. The gradient of the loss function to the class vector W_i is $(1 - p_i)\overrightarrow{Ox}$, and the gradient to the class vector W_j $(j \neq i)$ is $p_j\overrightarrow{xO}$. Since $(1 - p_i) = \sum\limits_{j \neq i} p_j$, when the number of classes is large, the effect of the sample to W_j $(j \neq i)$ is negligible. So we only consider the attraction stress $\overrightarrow{Ox}$ of sample vector x to W_i in equilibrium.

For the equilibrium of class vector W we mainly consider the attraction effect of the sample vector x of the corresponding class on W and the origin of W generated by the regularization of W on the attraction of W. The attraction of the origin to W is $R|W|$, and the direction points to origin O. The attractiveness of the sample vector x to the label direction W_i is $(1 - p_i)|x|$, and the direction is the same as the direction of the sample vector x. When the model reaches equilibrium $\overrightarrow{OW} = \frac{1-p_i}{R}\overrightarrow{Ox_i}$.

Since there are too many parameters for calculating the sample vector x, the impact of regularization is small. So the equilibrium of sample vector x can be defined as followed: for sample vector x belongs to class i, the similarity between x and W_i is greater than the similarity between x and W_i by a fixed constant D.

Under this definition, we have the following theorem.

Theorem 2.1. *If the fully connected layer W has strong convexity, then the sample vector points x of the same class in the equilibrium are distributed in a radial single connected region, and the distance between the samples from differ-ent class i and class j is greater than $\frac{2D}{|W_i - W_j|}$.*

That is, if the fully connected layer W has strong convexity, the equilibrium is a state in which sample vectors from the same class converge with each other, and sample vectors from different classes are far away from each other, as shown in Fig. 2.

Fig. 2. Common sample vector distribution in deep learning models.

2.3   Analysis and Discussion

As shown in Fig. 3, according to the definition, the strong convexity of the vector set is directly affected by the two factors: the angle between vectors and the length of vectors.

The first one is the angle between vectors. If the two vectors W_i, W_j satisfy $|W_i|^2 \geqslant W_i \cdot W_j = |W_i| \cdot |W_j| \cdot \cos\langle W_i, W_j\rangle$, then the inequality $|W_i| \geqslant |W_j| \cdot \cos\langle W_i, W_j\rangle$ is true. Here $\langle W_i, W_j\rangle$ represents the angle between the two vectors W_i and W_j. If the angle is greater than $\frac{\pi}{2}$, the inequality must be true. Therefore, the greater the angle between the vectors in the class feature vector set, the easier it is to hold strong convexity. At the same time, the larger the angle between the vectors in the class feature vector set can ensure that the sample vectors of the corresponding class are scattered as much as possible, which helps increase the generalization accuracy of the model. However, when the feature vector dimension is fixed, the more the   number of classes of the training data, the smaller the angle between the vectors in the class feature vector set. According to this, we can give a rough estimate of the capacity of the program.

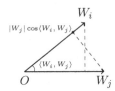

Fig. 3. Factors that effect convexity

Theorem 2.2. *For* $n \geqslant 1$, *in the* 2^n *dimensional space, if the number of extracted vectors does not exceed* $f(n) = n \cdot 2^{2n+1} + 2^{2n} + 4$, *then there is a way to make the angle between the vectors not less than* $\frac{\pi}{3}$.

Proof. When $n = 2$, each component in the four-dimensional space takes $\pm\frac{1}{2}$, and you can take out $2^4 = 16$ vectors with a modulus of 1, and the inner product of each pair is no more than $\frac{1}{2}$, so the angle between these 16 vectors is not less than $\frac{\pi}{3}$.

Suppose in the set $\{1, 2, \cdots, 2^n\}$, we can extract a_n quaternion subsets, so that the intersection of any two subsets does not exceed two elements, treat then as the position of a 2^n-dimensional vector. Fill in $\pm\frac{1}{2}$ in the position to get $16a_n$ vectors whose inner product does not exceed $\frac{1}{2}$. So the angle between any two vectors is not less than $\frac{\pi}{3}$. The following proves $a_n \geqslant C_{2^{n-1}}^2 + 4a_{n-1}$.

In 2^{n-1} binary sets $\{2k - 1, 2k\}, 1 \leqslant k \leq 2^{n-1}$, any two of them form a quaternary set.

For a_{n-1} quaternions with no more than two elements in the pairwise intersection $\{k_1, k_2, k_3, k_4\} \subseteq \{1, 2, \cdots, 2^{n-1}\}$, you can take $4a_{n-1}$ quaternary sets $\{2k_1 - 1, 2k_2 - 1, 2k_3 - 1, 2k_4 - 1\}, \{2k_1 - 1, 2k_2 - 1, 2k_3, 2k_4\}, \{2k_1, 2k_2, 2k_3 - 1, 2k_4 - 1\}, \{2k_1, 2k_2, 2k_3, 2k_4\}$.

The $C_{2^{n-1}}^2 + 4a_{n-1}$ quaternary sets extracted in this way do not exceed two elements in the intersection of two pairs, so $a_n \geqslant C_{2^{n-1}}^2 + 4a_{n-1}$.

It can be calculated from $a_2 = 1$,

$$a_n \geqslant 2^{2n-3} - 2^{n-2} + 4a_{n-1}$$

$$\frac{a_n}{2^{2n}} - \frac{a_{n-1}}{2^{2(n-1)}} \geqslant \frac{1}{8} - \frac{1}{2^{n+2}}$$

$$16a_n \geqslant n \cdot 2^{2n+1} + 2^{2n} + 4.$$

In summary, the proposition is true.

That is, if the minimum angle between class vectors should be larger than $\frac{\pi}{3}$, n-dimensional feature could allow at least $f(n)$ classes of samples be used in training. Besides we can not make the minimum angle between class vectors be greater than $\frac{\pi}{2}$.

Proposition 2.2. *At most* $n + 1$ *vectors in a* n-*dimensional space can satisfy that angle between any two vectors is greater than* $\frac{\pi}{2}$.

The second factor is the length of the vector. As long as the angle $\langle W_i W_j \rangle$ between two vectors W_i, W_j satisfies $\cos\langle W_i W_j \rangle \leqslant \min\{\frac{|W_i|}{|W_j|}, \frac{|W_j|}{|W_i|}\}$, then $W_i \cdot W_j \leqslant |W_i|^2$ and $W_i \cdot W_j \leqslant |W_j|^2$ are true. Therefore, the closer the length of the vectors in the vector set is, the smaller the angle requirement between the vectors is.

The influence of these two factors on the algorithm has been partially verified in Liu's article [14] and Wu's article [15]. Liu et al. proposed an auxiliary loss function in [14] called Minimum Hyperspherical Energy. The basic expression of this auxiliary function is

$$Loss_{MHE} = \frac{1}{m(N-1)} \sum_{i=1}^{m} \sum_{j=1, j \neq i}^{N} f_s(|\hat{W}_{y_i} - \hat{W}_j|),$$

Here m is the number of samples entered at one time, N is the total number of samples in the sample, and y_i is the label of the first i sample entered, $\hat{W}_i = \frac{W_i}{|W_i|}$ is the unit vector in the direction of W_i, and $f_s(x)$ can take functions such as $\frac{1}{x}$ or $-\ln x$ which are convex in the interval $(0,1)$ and take positive infinity at 0. The purpose is to evenly distribute the spherical distance of the class vector. Its impact on the degree of dispersion of class vectors is shown in Fig. 4 and 5. After using auxiliary loss, the distribution of class vectors is more uniformly dispersed, and the resulting model also has improved accuracy.

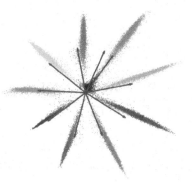

Fig. 4. Without auxiliary loss function

Fig. 5. After using auxiliary loss function

And Wu et al. proposed the auxiliary function Center Invariant Loss in [15]. The expression of this loss function is

$$Loss_{CIL} = (\|W_{y_i}\|^2 - \frac{\sum_{k=1}^{m} \|W_{y_k}\|^2}{m})^2,$$

Here m is the number of samples entered at one time, and y_i is the label of the i sample entered. This auxiliary loss function calculates the variance of the length of the class vector in the direction of the input sample label. Training this auxiliary loss function with basic loss functions such as softmax can also improve the accuracy of the model after training.

3   Theorem and Proof

3.1   Core Theorem

Theorem 3.1. *If the fully connected layer W has strong convexity, the model can reach equilibrium.*

This theorem will be proved in the next section. Here we first analyze the sample distribution of the equilibrium state under strong convexity. Decompose all sample vectors into $x = k_x \frac{W_i}{|W_i|} + a_x$, where $k \in R, a_x \perp W_i$.

Theorem 3.2. *If the fully connected layer W has strong convexity, then the sample vector points x of the same class in the equilibrium state are distributed in a radial single connected region that satisfies $k_x > f_{\frac{a_x}{|a_x|}}(|a_x|)$, here $f_{\frac{a_x}{|a_x|}}(\cdot)$ is a linear function related to the direction of the vector a_x and the fully connected layer W.*

Proof. As W satisfies strong convexity, inequality $\frac{W_i}{|W_i|}(W_i - W_j) > 0$ holds. For the sample vector $x \in C_i$,

$$xW_i - xW_j > D$$
$$\Leftrightarrow (k\frac{W_i}{|W_i|} + a_x)(W_i - W_j) > D$$
$$\Leftrightarrow k > \frac{D}{\frac{W_i}{|W_i|}(W_i - W_j)} - |a_x| \cdot \frac{\frac{a_x}{|a_x|}(W_i - W_j)}{\frac{W_i}{|W_i|}(W_i - W_j)},$$

The proposition is proven.

Theorem 3.3. *In the equilibrium state, the distance between the samples belongs to different class i and class j is greater than $\frac{2D}{|W_i - W_j|}$.*

Proof. Take $x_1 \in C_i, x_2 \in C_j$. As $x_iW_i - x_iW_j > D$ and $x_jW_j - x_jW_i > D$, inequality $2D < (x_i - x_j)(W_i - W_j) \leqslant |x_i - x_j||W_i - W_j|$ holds, so $|x_i - x_j| > \frac{2D}{|W_i - W_j|}$.

The proposition is proven.

3.2   Proof of Theorem 3.1

Theorem 3.4. *During the parameter update process, W_i can reach equilibrium.*

Proof. The direction of motion of W_i is controlled by the attractiveness from the sample and the origin. Passing W_i draw the vertical line of Ox, the vertical point is H, then the direction of movement of W_i can be decomposed into

$$a_1\overrightarrow{Ox} + a_2\overrightarrow{W_iO}$$
$$= a_3\overrightarrow{Hx} + a_2(\overrightarrow{W_iH} + \overrightarrow{HO})$$
$$= a_2\overrightarrow{W_iH} + (a_3\overrightarrow{Hx} + a_2\overrightarrow{HO})$$

Therefore, as W_i updates, $|W_iH|$ decreases, and H reaches equilibrium on Ox, so W_i can reach equilibrium.

Theorem 3.5. *If the class vector set W has strong convexity, then x can reach equilibrium during the parameter update process.*

Proof. For any sample vector x, suppose the label of x is i, as

$$xW_i - xW_j = (k\frac{W_i}{|W_i|} + a_x)(W_i - W_j) = k\frac{W_i}{|W_i|}(W_i - W_j) + a_x(W_i - W_j),$$

and $\frac{W_i}{|W_i|}(W_i - W_j) > 0$, Therefore, when the sample vector x is updated in the direction of $\overrightarrow{OW_i}$, $xW_i - xW_j$ continues to increase until it reaches infinity. The class vector set W satisfies strong convexity, so this process has nothing to do with the choice of W_j, and the loss function can approach infinitely zero without considering regularization. At this time, the probability of classifying the sample into the correct class is infinitely close to $1 > \frac{1}{1+e^{-D}}$. Therefore, if the class vector set W satisfies strong convexity, then there is an update curve with a continuously decreasing loss function between the initial position of the sample vector x and the equilibrium state.

On the other hand, the moving direction of the sample x is $a\sum_{j\neq i} p_j\overrightarrow{W_jO} + (1-p_i)\overrightarrow{OW_i} = a\sum_{j\neq i} p_j\overrightarrow{W_jW_i}$, here a is the given learning rate parameter. The update amount of k_x is

$$a\sum_{j\neq i} p_j\overrightarrow{W_jW_i} \cdot \frac{W_i}{|W_i|}$$
$$= a\sum_{j\neq i} p_j\frac{|W_i|^2 - W_j \cdot W_i}{|W_i|}$$
$$> a(\sum_{j\neq i} p_j)\min_{j\neq i}\{\frac{|W_i|^2 - W_j \cdot W_i}{|W_i|}\}$$
$$= a(1 - p_i)Conv_W(W_i),$$

It can be seen from the strong convexity of W, when $p_i < \frac{1}{1+e^{-D}}$, the update amount is greater than a fixed constant which is greater than 0, so before reaching equilibrium, k_x monotonously increases and tends to infinity.

The following proves that during the parameter update process k_x and a_x can reach a state of affairs as $k_x > \max_{j \neq i}\{\frac{D}{\frac{W_i}{|W_i|}(W_i-W_j)} - |a_x| \cdot \frac{\frac{a_x}{|a_x|}(W_i-W_j)}{\frac{W_i}{|W_i|}(W_i-W_j)}\}$. The Theorem 3.2 shows that the sample vector x reaches equilibrium at this time Now consider $\frac{a_x}{|a_x|}$ in all directions perpendicular to W_i.

(1) If for any $j \neq i$ inequality $a_x \cdot (W_i - W_j) \geqslant 0$ holds, it can be known from $W_i \cdot (W_i - W_j) > 0$ that $k_x > \max_{j \neq i}\{\frac{D}{\frac{W_i}{|W_i|}(W_i-W_j)}\}$ can satisfy the condition. The right side is a constant which is unrelated to a_x. As k_x monotonously increases and tends to infinity before reaching equilibrium, x can reach equilibrium.

(2) If the inner product of a_x and the gradient direction of x is less than 0, that is $a_x \cdot \sum_{j \neq i} p_j \overrightarrow{W_j W_i} < 0$, at this time, $|a_x|$ decreases during the update process, so the value range of $|a_x|$ during the update process is limited. So $\max_{j \neq i}\{\frac{D}{\frac{W_i}{|W_i|}(W_i-W_j)} - |a_x| \cdot \frac{\frac{a_x}{|a_x|}(W_i-W_j)}{\frac{W_i}{|W_i|}(W_i-W_j)}\}$ is limited. That is, the condition can be satisfied when k_x is greater than a fixed finite value. As k_x monotonously increases and tends to infinity before reaching equilibrium, x can reach equilibrium.

(3) If $a_x \cdot \sum_{j \neq i} p_j \overrightarrow{W_j W_i} > 0$ and there is a $j \neq i$ which makes $a_x \cdot (W_i - W_j) < 0$.

Consider the moving point $T = x + ta_x, t \in \mathbf{R}$. Denote the probability vector at point T by $(p_{T1}, p_{T2}, \cdots, p_{TN})$, then the gradient to samples from class i sample at point T is $\nabla_T = \sum_{j \neq i} p_{Tj} \overrightarrow{W_j W_i}$. Consider the function $h_{a_x}(t) = \frac{\nabla_T}{p_{Ti}} \overrightarrow{W_j W_i} \cdot a_x$. Easy to know that $h_{a_x}(0) > 0$ and

$$h_{a_x}(t) = \sum_{j \neq i} \frac{p_{Tj}}{p_{Ti}} \overrightarrow{W_j W_i} \cdot a_x$$

$$= \sum_{j \neq i} e^{T \cdot W_j - T \cdot W_i} \overrightarrow{W_j W_i} \cdot a_x$$

$$= \sum_{j \neq i} e^{(x+ta_x) \cdot (W_j - W_i)} \overrightarrow{W_j W_i} \cdot a_x$$

$$= e^{x \cdot (W_j - W_i)} \sum_{j \neq i} e^{t \overrightarrow{W_i W_j} \cdot a_x} \overrightarrow{W_j W_i} \cdot a_x$$

$$= K \sum_{j \neq i} A_j e^{-A_j t}.$$

Here K represents constant unrelated to a_x and t, $A_j = \overrightarrow{W_j W_i} \cdot a_x$. When $A_j \geqslant 0$, the extreme point shows that $A_j e^{-A_j t} \leqslant \frac{1}{te}$. It can be seen from the assumption that $A_j < 0$ exists. Suppose $A_{j_0} < 0$, then $h_{a_x}(t) \leqslant k(\frac{N-2}{te}) +$

$A_{j_0}e^{-A_{j_0}t}$, $h_{a_x}(\frac{N-2}{A_{j_0}e}) < 0$. Then there is a $0 < t_0 < \frac{N-2}{A_{j_0}e}$ which makes $h(t_0) = 0$. Suppose $T_0 = x + t_0 a_x$, then the distance from a_x to T_0 decreases during the parameter update. Therefore, when the sample vector point x' of the i class is in the direction of $\frac{a_x}{|a_x|}$ during the entire update process, $|a_{x'}| \cdot (\frac{a_x}{|a_x|}(W_i - W_j))$ does not exceed $(1+t)|a_x| \cdot (\frac{a_x}{|a_x|}(W_i - W_j))$. This formula has a consistent upper limit when the direction of a_x changes. From (2), we can see that x can reach equilibrium.

According to (1), (2) and (3), if the class vector set W satisfies strong convexity, then x can reach equilibrium.

According to the above proof, the higher the larger $Conv(W)$ is, the faster the loss function converges. We can see that the full-connected layer W is like a heart of the algorithm, and $Conv(W)$ is the power of heart. During each iteration W pushes sample vector x to move towards a direction related to its label i.

4   Conclusion and Future Work

According to the loss function convergence process, it can be preliminarily presumed that the algorithm convergence process is divided into two stages. In the first stage, each class vector W_i is updated from a random initial value to roughly indicate the direction of the sample in the class. In the second stage, all vector points are updating toward an approximately fixed direction when the fully connected layer W remains strongly convex. During the entire algorithm convergence process the updating direction of samples will not change too much. At the same time, the strong convexity of the fully connected layer plays an important role in the entire algorithm convergence process. Adjusting the convexity of the fully connected layer can have a positive impact on the convergence and accuracy of the deep learning algorithm training.

Future work plan mainly includes the following aspects:

1. Research the impact of data imbalance on the convexity of the fully connected layer W under this theoretical framework.
2. The premise of the establishment of this theoretical framework is that the step size of each gradient update is small enough. On this basis, analysis the influence of different network structures such as ResNet on the optional step size.
3. Calculate the influence of the regularization of the convolutional layer on the sample vector x, and try to find a minimum number of nodes necessary in the deep neural network according to the equilibrium condition of x.

Acknowledgements. Thanks to Professor Huang Kaizhu for his guidance on thesis writing. Thanks to Zhou Yiming and Xu Chao for their suggestions and help in building the theoretical framework.

References

1. Hornic, K.: Multilayer feedforward networks are universal approximators. Neural Netw. **2**(5), 359–366 (1989)
2. Cybenko, G.: Approximation by superpositions of a sigmoidal function. Math. Control Sig. Syst. **2**(4), 303–314 (1992)
3. Barron, A.R.: Universal approximation bounds for superpositions of a sigmoidal function. IEEE Trans. Inf. Theory **39**(3), 930–945 (1993)
4. Safran, I., Shamir, O.: On the quality of the initial basin in overspecified neural networks. In: International Conference on Machine Learning, pp. 774–782 (2016)
5. Zhong, K., Song, Z., Jain, P., Bartlett, P.L., Dhillon, I.S.: Recovery guarantees for one-hidden-layer neural networks. In: International Conference on Machine Learning (2017)
6. Li, Y., Yuan, Y.: Convergence analysis of two-layer neural networks with relu activation. In: Neural Information Processing Systems (2017)
7. Andoni, A., Panigrahy, R., Valiant, G., Zhang, L.: Learning polynomials with neural networks, pp. 1908–1916 (2014)
8. Arora, S., Bhaskara, A., Ge, R., Ma, T.: Provable bounds for learning some deep representations. In: International Conference on Machine Learning, pp. 584–592 (2014)
9. Du, S.S., Lee, J.D., Tian, Y., Poczos, B., Singh, A.: Gradient descent learns one-hidden-layer CNN: don't be afraid of spurious local minima. In: International Conference on Machine Learning (2018)
10. Taigman, Y., Yang, M., Ranzato, M., Wolf, L.: Deepface: closing the gap to human-level performance in face verification. In: Computer Vision and Pattern Recognition, pp. 1701–1708 (2014)
11. Nesterov, Y.: A method for solving the convex programming problem with convergence rate $o(1/k^2)$. Dokl.akad.nauk Sssr, pp. 543–547 (1983)
12. Qian, N.: On the momentum term in gradient descent learning algorithms. Neural Netw.: Official J. Int. Neural Netw. Soc. **12**(1), 145–151 (1999)
13. Kingma, D., Jimmy, B.: Adam: a method for stochastic optimization. In: International Conference on Learning Representations, pp. 1–13 (2015)
14. Liu, W., et al.: Learning towards minimum hyperspherical energy (2018)
15. Wu, Y., Liu, H., Li, J., Fu, Y.: Deep face recognition with center invariant loss. In: ACM Multimedia, pp. 408–414 (2017)

TeeRNN: A Three-Way RNN Through Both Time and Feature for Speech Separation

Runze Ma[(⊠)] and Shugong Xu

Shanghai Institute for Advanced Communication and Data Science,
Shanghai University, Shanghai 200444, China
{runzema,shugong}@shu.edu.cn

Abstract. Recurrent neural networks (RNNs) have been widely used in speech signal processing. Because it is powerful to modeling some sequential information. While most of the networks about RNNs are on frame sight, we propose three-way RNN called TeeRNN which both process the input through the time and the features. According to that, TeeRNN is better to explore the relationship between the features in each frame of encoded speech. As an additional contribution, we also generated a mixture dataset based on LibriSpeech where the devices mismatched and different noises contained making the separation task harder.

Keywords: Recurrent neural network · Speech processing · Speech separation

1 Introduction

The cocktail problem is important for audio signal processing. In the real situation, devices will often record more information than we need, for example, environment noise, room reverberant, irrelevant speech, and something else. Automatic speech separation aims at separating individual speaker voices from a recording mixed with more than one speaker.

Since the deep learning algorithms snowballing rapidly, many researchers who focus on speech separation moved their eyesight to build high-performance neural networks. Many powerful algorithms are proposed. Hershey et al. proposed Deep Clustering [1] which uses neural networks to generate the embeddings of each Time-Frequency bin from magnitude spectrogram on speech mixture, then use k-means to cluster those embeddings to decide each bin belongs to which speaker. In [4], Luo et al. proposed a two heads architecture, called chimera: one deep clustering head and one mask-inference head. Later, Wang et al. proposed chimera++ network which achieves a better result by trying alternative loss functions [12]. All above masking methods apply the mask on magnitude

---

R. Ma—Is a student.

spectrogram, and then using the phase information from the original mixture speech. In other words, they separate on the magnitude and generating estimated speech combined with a mismatched phase spectrogram. The mismatched phase information may leads some unwanted distortion. Some experiments extend the separating operation to the phase [9, 11]. They use a waveform-level loss to converge the distance between target speech and the estimated separated speech based on chimera++ network. Experiments show that their architecture achieves a much better performance. After that, TasNet [6] and Conv-TasNet [7] directly do separation on time domain. The difference between them is that TasNet using Long-short term memory (LSTM) [2] architecture while Conv-TasNet changes the LSTM to convolutional networks.

The Recurrent neural network (RNN) including LSTM has been noticed in many tasks based on data sequences. In Speech separation, we split speech into frames then put those frames into RNN as a sequence. As to most RNN architecture, some hidden states will be calculated. Recently, Luo et al. proposed dual-path RNN (DPRNN) [5] to replace convolutional layers in Conv-TasNet and achieved an exceeding performance on monaural speech separation. DPRNN splits the long sequential input mixture speech into smaller chunks and then apply RNN on two paths of those chunks: Intra- and inter-chunks. The advantage of using RNN to replace 1-D convolutional neural networks (1-D CNNs) is that 1-D CNNs have a limitation on the receptive field which is decided by the kernel size of each convolutional layer and it is hard to conclude all information in the sequence. But it is easy to modeling whole utterance into the hidden states of RNN.

In this paper, we propose TeeRNN, a recurrent processing block that can modeling not only through the frame but the segment and feature dimensions. To get over the mismatched phase problem, we use an 1-D convolution layer to encode the mixture audio input. Then we segment the encoded signal. After that, there are three paths inside the segments. The first path, unlikely other applications of RNN, treats the features of each segment as a sequence. The second path is regarding the frames in each segment as a sequence, which is the popular usage about RNN. The last one is to concatenate the same position on frame index in all segments then input to RNN as a sequence, in other words, this part is a dilated RNN that the dilated rate is based on the segment length. Respectively, those last two paths of the RNN are both about time, which can model the local and global frame information inside an utterance. And the feature path can model the connection among the different parts of features in each encoded segment. In TeeRNN, those three paths are processed sequentially. The encoded speech was input into the feature RNN layer, frame RNN layer, and segment RNN layer to extract information from the feature, local time gap, and global utterance. We use LSTM in those three RNN layers and these operations repeated 6 times. After that, we use a shallow convolutional network to generate feature masks of each speaker from the final hidden state output from TeeRNN. To simulate the actual situation of recording, we use LibriSpeech dataset [8] to generate LibriSpeech-2mix-reverb dataset, and further, we also use the Image

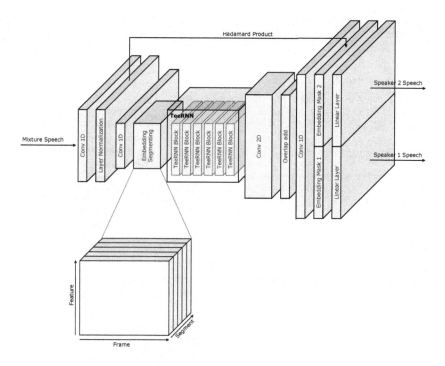

Fig. 1. Proposed system framework

source method to simulate much different room impulse response to add some reverberant in this dataset. All experiments are produced on LibriSpeech-2mix-reverb dataset.

2   Methods

In the speech separation task, our input mixture signal $y(t)$ of T samples can be described as the following equation:

$$y(t) = \sum_{i=1}^{I} s_i(t), \quad t = 0, \dots, T$$

where $s_i(t)$ means speech from the i-th speaker, I means the total number of speakers inside one mixture speech. In our case, $I = 2$, says there are 2 speakers mixed up in the input mixture. It worth mentioning that $s_i(t)$ for each speaker i might be reverberant.

2.1   System Architecture

When we trying to separate each $s_i(t)$ from the mixture signal $y(t)$, there are several general methods to do just like mentioned in the introduction. In our case,

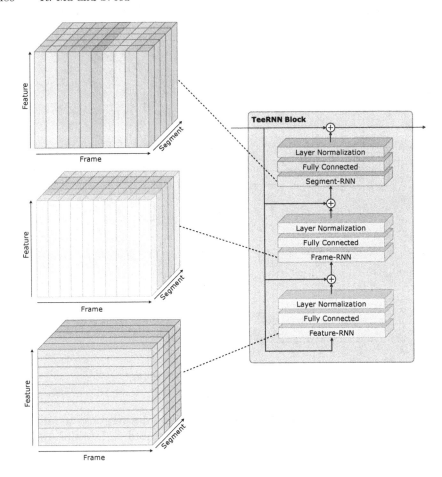

Fig. 2. TeeRNN block details

we firstly input the mixture to an encoder, then we segment the output of the features from encoder into multiple overlapped segments. After that, TeeRNN is used to compute the hidden states of each RNN layers and there are also residual connections between input segments and the output of each layer. A convolution network is applied after the final TeeRNN block, then the convolution network will produce i masks for each speaker i. The separated audio signal is from an overlap-add operation on the mask-applied feature segments after a linear layer.

Encoder. As mentioned before, the phase problem is tricky for frequency domain speech separation. To avoid the mismatch phase problem, we encode the mixture signal in the time domain instead of classical STFT. Our encoder includes an 1-D convolutional layer and a layer normalization (LN) operation. Inorder to match the designed input size of following TeeRNN block, an 1-D convolutional layer is also applied as described below:

$$E = \text{Conv1D}(\text{LN}(\text{Conv1D}(\boldsymbol{y})))$$

where $\boldsymbol{E} \in \mathcal{R}^{N \times L_E}$ is the N dimensional embedding feature of $y(t)$, L_E is the sequence length after convolution, which is the total number of frames. $\text{LN}(\cdot)$ and $\text{Conv1D}(\cdot)$ stands for layer normalization and 1-D convolutional layer respectively. After the encoder, all information in the original mixture signal will be encoded into real domain embedding features unlike the STFT where the output is in complex domain. Further, this encoding operation is learnable, which might be more appropriate for a specific task.

Segmenting. The output from encoder $\boldsymbol{E} \in \mathcal{R}^{N \times L_E}$ is segmented with overlap to better cohesion the information between each as below:

$$\boldsymbol{C}_s = \boldsymbol{E}[(s-1) \times P + 1 : (s-1) \times P + K - 1]_{L_E}, \quad s = 1, \ldots, S$$

where $\boldsymbol{C}_s \in \mathcal{R}^{N \times K}$ is segment $s = 1, \ldots, S$ split from embedding feature $\boldsymbol{E}$ by $\boldsymbol{E}[a : b]$ operation which stands for extracting one segment from $\boldsymbol{E}$ between a to b on L_E dimension, K is the frame number inside each segment, and P in equation above means the hop stride because of overlap. Then every segments $\boldsymbol{C}_s$ are concatenated together to a segmented embedding $\boldsymbol{W} \in \mathcal{R}^{N \times K \times S}$.

TeeRNN Block and Mask Method. Each TeeRNN block contains three parts: Feature RNN part, Frame RNN part and Segment RNN part. Each part is made from one RNN layer, one linear layer and a layer normalization operation.

Firstly, we construct some feature sequences $\boldsymbol{Q}_{\text{feature}}$ from each $\boldsymbol{C}_s$ in segmented embedding $\boldsymbol{W}$ as following operation:

$$\boldsymbol{Q}_{\text{feature}}(n, s) = \boldsymbol{C}_s[n]_N, \quad n = 1, \ldots, N, \quad s = 1, \ldots, S$$

where $\boldsymbol{C}_s[n]_N \in \mathcal{R}^{1 \times K}$ means extract one row n on feature dimension N in $\boldsymbol{C}_s$. Then we input each $\boldsymbol{Q}_{\text{feature}}$ from $\boldsymbol{W}$ to Feature RNN part. Donate this part as a function $F_{\text{feature}}(\cdot)$, an residual connection is applied between the output and the original input segmented embedding $\boldsymbol{W}$ to calculate the next input $\boldsymbol{W}'$ for frame RNN block:

$$\boldsymbol{W}' = \boldsymbol{W} + F_{\text{feature}}(\boldsymbol{W})$$

and each $\boldsymbol{C}_s$ in $\boldsymbol{W}$ becomes $\boldsymbol{C}'_s$ similarly.

For frame RNN block, we will input the embedding feature $\boldsymbol{W}'$ to it as common frame sequences. The sequences $\boldsymbol{Q}_{\text{frame}}$ are defined as below:

$$\boldsymbol{Q}_{\text{frame}}(k, s) = \boldsymbol{C}'_s[k]_K, \quad k = 0, \ldots, K, \quad s = 1, \ldots, S$$

where $\boldsymbol{C}'_s[k]_K \in \mathcal{R}^{N \times 1}$ means extract all feature from frame index k. Then we input each $\boldsymbol{Q}_{\text{frame}}$ from $\boldsymbol{W}$ input the frame RNN part. Also, the residual connection is applied between the output from this part and the original $\boldsymbol{W}$, then calculate $\boldsymbol{W}''$ as the input to segment RNN part. Donate the simplified function about this part as $F_{\text{frame}}(\cdot)$, then $\boldsymbol{W}''$ is defined as following:

$$\boldsymbol{W}'' = \boldsymbol{W} + F_{\text{frame}}(\boldsymbol{W}')$$

and each $\boldsymbol{C}_s$ in $\boldsymbol{W}$ becomes $\boldsymbol{C}_s''$.

If the frame RNN part is able to cohesion the connections in each segment, then segment RNN part can extend the receptive field of RNN from each single segment to all segments. In this part, the frames has same index in each segment are treated as a new sequence which is dilated compared with the origin. The sequence $\boldsymbol{Q}_{\text{segment}}$ which is going to input to segment RNN part is construct from $\boldsymbol{W}''$ as described in the following equation:

$$\boldsymbol{Q}_{\text{segment}}(s, k) = [\boldsymbol{C}_s''[k]]_S, \quad s = 1, \ldots, S, \quad k = 1, \ldots, K$$

A little different from the operations defined in $\boldsymbol{Q}_{\text{feature}}(n, s)$ and $\boldsymbol{Q}_{\text{frame}}(k, s)$, this $[\boldsymbol{C}_s''[k]]_S \in \mathcal{R}^{1 \times K}$ means concatenating one frame index k in all segments s. The output from segment RNN part is also added by the original segmented embedding $\boldsymbol{W}$. Donate the final output as $\hat{\boldsymbol{W}}$ and the segment RNN part simplified function as $F_{\text{segment}}(\cdot)$, so there is the following equation:

$$\hat{\boldsymbol{W}} = \boldsymbol{W} + F_{\text{segment}}(\boldsymbol{W}'')$$

All the above is one procedure of a single TeeRNN block, and this procedure can repeat several times to make the whole network deep. As shown in Fig. 1, we repeated the TeeRNN block 6 times. The output from each block will be the input of the next TeeRNN block. The final output from last TeeRNN block is then overlap-added back to the size of original unsegmented embedding $\boldsymbol{E} \in \mathcal{R}^{N \times L_E}$. Then a shallow convolutional network is applied to generate the mask $\boldsymbol{M}_i \in \mathcal{R}^{N \times L_E}$ for each speaker $i = 1, \ldots, I$ which is able to applied on the mixture embedding $\boldsymbol{E}$ as following:

$$\hat{\boldsymbol{E}}_i = \boldsymbol{E} \odot \boldsymbol{M}_i, \quad i = 1, \ldots, I$$

where $\hat{\boldsymbol{E}}_i \in \mathcal{R}^{N \times L_E}$ is the encoded estimated target speech for speaker i, and $\odot$ means Hadamard product (also known as the element-wise product). After getting the estimated $\hat{\boldsymbol{E}}_i$, a linear layer, and another overlap-add operation is applied to generate the speech signal $\hat{s}_i(t)$ for each speaker i finally. As plotted in Fig. 2, each color group of bars means a sequence, each bar in a sequence means an element which is input to the RNN layer one by one as a recurrent process.

2.2   Permutation Invariant Training

The permutation invariant training (PIT) [13] are proposed to solve the label ambiguity problem of speech separation. The PIT method is able to find the permutation with the minimum loss at frame level. However, finding the right permutation at frame level may trigger some glitch of the permutation even

Table 1. Experimental results on Deep Clustering, Conv-TasNet, DPRNN and TeeRNN with SI-SDRi (SI-SDR improvement), PESQ and STOI score. The ablation experiments are listed as the last two models using Feature + Frame RNN parts or Feature + Segment RNN parts.

Models		SI-SDRi/dB	PESQ	STOI
Deep Clustering		6.863	1.280	0.722
Conv-TasNet		9.534	1.470	0.847
DPRNN	4 samples	10.402	2.384	0.849
	32 samples	7.728	2.023	0.800
TeeRNN	4 samples	14.037	3.039	0.905
	32 samples	8.282	2.108	0.811
Feature + Frame RNN		7.184	1.952	0.787
Feature + Segment RNN		6.295	1.909	0.771

the target speakers not changed. To solve this problem, utterance- level PIT (uPIT) [3] is proposed. With uPIT, we are able to find the right permutation based on whole utterance information. We use uPIT to calculate the minimum loss between estimated speech and the clean target speech. The loss function is defined as following, also known as Scale-invariant Signal-to-distortion ratio:

$$\mathcal{L} = 10 \log_{10} \left(\frac{||e_{\text{target}}||^2}{||e_{\text{res}}||^2} \right) = 10 \log_{10} \left(\frac{||\frac{\hat{s}^T s}{||s||^2} s||^2}{||\frac{\hat{s}^T s}{||s||^2} s - \hat{s}||^2} \right).$$

where $e_{\text{target}} = \alpha s$ is the scaled reference, $e_{\text{res}} = \hat{s} - e_{\text{target}}$ is the residual distortion. α is defined as optimal scaling factor for the target, obtained as $\alpha = \hat{s}^T s / ||s||^2$.

3   Experiments and Results

3.1   Experiment Setup

We prepared a mixture dataset called LibriSpeech-2mix-reverb (LS2r) based on LibriSpeech [8]. The components of this dataset are original from some subsets of LibriSpeech: training set is using *train-clean-100* to mix, development set is using *dev-clean* and test set is using *test-clean* in LibriSpeech. Our dataset has 31375 utterances in the training set, 780 utterances in development set, and also 780 utterances in the test set, all utterances are 8-s wave files with 16 kHz sample rate. Each utterance is mixed by the speeches of two speakers from all possible permutations in the original LibriSpeech subset. Then the mixing SNR is randomly generated from the standard normal Gaussian distribution. Before mixing two speeches to one final utterance, reverberation is added to each speech. The room impulse responses are generated from 10000 different simulated rooms including different room size, speaker positions, and microphone positions.

In the training stage, an online data augmentation method is applied. We randomly select a 4-s segment from the 8-s origin signal as the actual input to avoid over-fitting. We use Adam optimizer to optimize the SI-SDR loss by uPIT. The learning rate is beginning at 0.001 and then times 0.98 every 2 epochs. In our paper, all models are trained using the Pytorch framework on GeForce RTX 2080Ti Graphics Cards. DPRNN, TeeRNN and ablation models are trained for 300 epochs, other models follow the original configurations based on the references.

3.2   Experimental Results

We compared TeeRNN with existing works as Deep Clustering [1], Conv-TasNet [7] and DPRNN [5]. The results are summarized in Table 1, as the SI-SDRi stands for SI-SDR improvements. STOI and PESQ stand for Short-time objective intel-ligibility (STOI) [10] and perceptual evaluation of speech quality (PESQ, accord-ing to ITU-T P.862.2) scores respectively. All matrics higher are better. In TeeRNN and DPRNN, the number of samples means the kernel size of the encoder convolutional layer, and we are using 32-sample kernel size in our abla-tion study. As we can see in Table 1, our proposal TeeRNN outperforms than the baseline system Deep Clustering at least 1.419 dB on SI-SDRi. On 4-sample configuration, the performance improvements are increased to 7.174 dB. Both 4-sample and 32-sample kernel size configuration of TeeRNN are better than DPRNN with the same kernel size. The improvements on SI-SDRi are 3.635 dB with 4-sample and 0.554 dB with 32-sample kernel size. So the narrower convo-lutional kernel can encode more information from original speech to do better inference while separating. On the STOI score, the 4-sample TeeRNN gains the best in our study, which is 0.905, better than 4-sample DPRNN with 0.056 improvements. The Conv-TasNet performs similarly as 4-sample DPRNN on STOI. The result shows that the original Conv-TasNet performs even better than 32-sample DPRNN and 32-sample TeeRNN who both using the long kernel to extract features on the noisy and device mismatched dataset. In this situation, the smaller kernel size is able to extract more features that empower the network more abilities. In our ablation study, using 32-sample kernel size, the model with feature and frame RNN works better than the model with feature and segment RNN, which means the frame RNN part, in other words, frame-level RNN is more important than segment RNN which can be treated as dilated RNN. The experiments about using frame and segment RNN parts network is as same as DPRNN. Similar to the hypothesis mentioned above, if we only use one single part in TeeRNN, the network is not able to converge on the dataset, so the single part ablation experiments are not listed.

4   Conclusion

In our paper, we proposed the TeeRNN network which inputs the encoded embedding of mixture speech to RNN through both the time and the feature dimensions. Different from other networks, TeeRNN has one way to find the information in each point of the features from our segmented speech embedding. To simulate a more real recording situation, we also generated a brand new mixture dataset called LibriSpeech-2mix-reverb dataset which is made up of mismatched devices and artificial reverberation from simulated room impulse response. We compared TeeRNN with Deep Clustering, Conv-TasNet, and DPRNN. The results showing that, in most cases, TeeRNN outperformed than other separation networks on SI-SDRi, PESQ, and STOI, but the configurations with long kernel size to embed mixture is not always better. How to optimize the architecture to improve the performance while using long kernel size is planed in our further work.

References

1. Hershey, J.R., Chen, Z., Le Roux, J., Watanabe, S.: Deep clustering: discriminative embeddings for segmentation and separation. In: 2016 IEEE International Conference on Acoustics, Speech and Signal Processing (ICASSP), pp. 31–35, March 2016. https://doi.org/10.1109/ICASSP.2016.7471631. iSSN: 2379-190X
2. Hochreiter, S., Schmidhuber, J.: Long short-term memory. Neural Comput. **9**(8), 1735–1780 (1997). https://doi.org/10.1162/neco.1997.9.8.1735. https://www.mitpressjournals.org/doi/10.1162/neco.1997.9.8.1735
3. Kolbæk, M., Yu, D., Tan, Z.H., Jensen, J.: Multi-talker speech separation with utterance-level permutation invariant training of deep recurrent neural networks. arXiv:1703.06284, July 2017
4. Luo, Y., Chen, Z., Hershey, J.R., Roux, J.L., Mesgarani, N.: Deep clustering and conventional networks for music separation: stronger together. In: 2017 IEEE International Conference on Acoustics, Speech and Signal Processing (ICASSP), pp. 61–65, March 2017. https://doi.org/10.1109/ICASSP.2017.7952118. arXiv: 1611.06265
5. Luo, Y., Chen, Z., Yoshioka, T.: Dual-path RNN: efficient long sequence modeling for time-domain single-channel speech separation. arXiv:1910.06379, October 2019
6. Luo, Y., Mesgarani, N.: TasNet: time-domain audio separation network for real-time, single-channel speech separation. arXiv:1711.00541, April 2018
7. Luo, Y., Mesgarani, N.: Conv-TasNet: surpassing ideal time-frequency magnitude masking for speech separation. IEEE/ACM Trans. Audio Speech Lang. Process. **27**(8), 1256–1266 (2019). https://doi.org/10.1109/TASLP.2019.2915167. arXiv: 1809.07454
8. Panayotov, V., Chen, G., Povey, D., Khudanpur, S.: Librispeech: an ASR corpus based on public domain audio books. In: 2015 IEEE International Conference on Acoustics, Speech and Signal Processing (ICASSP), pp. 5206–5210. IEEE, South Brisbane, April 2015. https://doi.org/10.1109/ICASSP.2015.7178964. http://ieeexplore.ieee.org/document/7178964/
9. Roux, J.L., Wichern, G., Watanabe, S., Sarroff, A., Hershey, J.R.: Phasebook and friends: leveraging discrete representations for source separation. IEEE J. Sel. Topics Signal Process. **13**(2), 370–382 (2019). https://doi.org/10.1109/JSTSP.2019.2904183. arXiv: 1810.01395
10. Taal, C.H., Hendriks, R.C., Heusdens, R., Jensen, J.: A short-time objective intelligibility measure for time-frequency weighted noisy speech. In: 2010 IEEE International Conference on Acoustics, Speech and Signal Processing, pp. 4214–4217, March 2010. https://doi.org/10.1109/ICASSP.2010.5495701. iSSN: 2379-190X

11. Wang, Z.Q., Roux, J.L., Wang, D., Hershey, J.R.: End-to-end speech separation with unfolded iterative phase reconstruction. arXiv:1804.10204, April 2018

12. Wang, Z.Q., Tan, K., Wang, D.: Deep learning based phase reconstruction for speaker separation: a trigonometric perspective. arXiv:1811.09010, November 2018

13. Yu, D., Kolbæk, M., Tan, Z.H., Jensen, J.: Permutation invariant training of deep models for speaker-independent multi-talker speech separation. arXiv:1607.00325, January 2017

Author Index

Printed in the United States
By Bookmasters